Killer Game Programming

in Java™

Other Java™ resources from O'Reilly

Related titles

Head First Java™
Hardcore Java™
J2ME in a Nutshell
Java™ in a Nutshell
QuickTime for Java™:
  A Developer's Notebook

Physics for Game Developers
Gaming Hacks
AI for Game Developers
Java™ 2D Graphics

Java Books Resource Center

java.oreilly.com is a complete catalog of O'Reilly's books on Java and related technologies, including sample chapters and code examples.

OnJava.com is a one-stop resource for enterprise Java developers, featuring news, code recipes, interviews, weblogs, and more.

Conferences

O'Reilly brings diverse innovators together to nurture the ideas that spark revolutionary industries. We specialize in documenting the latest tools and systems, translating the innovator's knowledge into useful skills for those in the trenches. Visit *conferences.oreilly.com* for our upcoming events.

Safari Bookshelf (*safari.oreilly.com*) is the premier online reference library for programmers and IT professionals. Conduct searches across more than 1,000 books. Subscribers can zero in on answers to time-critical questions in a matter of seconds. Read the books on your Bookshelf from cover to cover or simply flip to the page you need. Try it today with a free trial.

Killer Game Programming
in Java™

Andrew Davison

O'REILLY®

Beijing · Cambridge · Farnham · Köln · Paris · Sebastopol · Taipei · Tokyo

Killer Game Programming in Java™
by Andrew Davison

Published by O'Reilly Media, Inc., 1005 Gravenstein Highway North, Sebastopol, CA 95472.

O'Reilly books may be purchased for educational, business, or sales promotional use. Online editions are also available for most titles (*safari.oreilly.com*). For more information, contact our corporate/institutional sales department: (800) 998-9938 or *corporate@oreilly.com*.

Editor:	Brett McLaughlin
Production Editor:	Matt Hutchinson
Production Services:	GEX, Inc.
Cover Designer:	Emma Colby
Interior Designer:	David Futato

Printing History:

May 2005:	First Edition.

ISBN-10: 0-596-00730-2
ISBN-13: 978-0-596-00730-0
[M]

Table of Contents

Preface

Who Are You?

Yes, you. Sit up straight, and stop slouching. (Don't you just love this assertive writing style?)

You're a programmer who wants to apply your abilities to 2D, 3D, and network games programming, for entertainment or as the first step in becoming a games programming professional. You want to write a game that uses the latest Java technology, not an applet showing a penguin waving its flipper.

You've done an introductory course on Java, so you understand about classes, objects, inheritance, exception handling, threads, and basic graphics. But you need information about more advanced stuff like the APIs for Java 2D, Java Sound, networking, and Java 3D.

You're probably most interested in multiplayer 3D games programming, because they're the coolest. They are hard to code, but this book will get you up to speed on how to build one.

You don't want to reinvent the wheel since Java is about abstraction, information hiding, and reuse. That translates into building games with existing libraries/classes/tools.

What This Book Is About

This book describes modern (i.e., fast and efficient) Java programming techniques for writing a broad range of games, including 2D arcade-style, isometric (2.5D), 3D, and network games, with a strong emphasis on 3D programming using Java 3D.

The 3D topics include loading externally produced 3D models, 3D sprites, first person shooters (FPS), terrain generation, particle systems and flocking, and different approaches to animation.

Several chapters on network games build to an example where users move sprites around a networked 3D arena.

I focus on J2SE 1.4.2, J2SE 5.0 and Java 3D 1.3.1. Under the hood, Java 3D utilizes OpenGL or Direct3D, which means that it'll work on all current versions of Windows, various flavors of Linux and Unix, and the Mac. Java 3D requires no special graphics hardware and is compatible with all modern graphics cards.

J2SE 5.0 (or 1.4.2) and Java 3D 1.3.1 can be downloaded from *http://www.java.com:80/ en/download/manual.jsp* and *http://java.sun.com/products/java-media/3D/*.

Which Software Versions?

My Java code is designed to compile and run in J2SE 5.0 and J2SE 1.4, which means that I avoid using new language features and API introduced in J2SE 5.0. The main reason is to allow my code to be backward compatible with older (and still popular) Java versions. The main areas where I lose out are in the availability of type-safe collections and the nanosecond time method, System.nanoTime( ), introduced in J2SE 5.0.

However, my code uses the J2SE 1.4 collections in type-safe ways, and I utilize the Java 3D nanosecond timer instead of nanoTime( ) to achieve the same timing accuracy. In Chapter 2, I discuss these issues in more detail.

I use Java 3D 1.3.1. although there is a bug release version, 1.3.2, which is regularly updated. I decided to employ Version 1.3.1 since it's stable and well-documented. In Chapter 14, I talk about Java 3D in more detail.

This Book (and More) Is Online

This book has been growing for a long time, with chapters and code appearing regularly at *http://fivedots.coe.psu.ac.th/~ad/jg/*. I've found it a useful way of gaining *lots* of feedback. The site is still worth visiting since a few chapters didn't make it in here along with the source code.

What This Book Is Not About

I'm not going to spend 200 pages explaining classes and objects, inheritance, exception handling, and threads. Many books do that already. A good Java introduction is *Thinking in Java* by Bruce Eckel. It's won awards and can be downloaded at *http:// www.mindview.net/Books/TIJ/*.

You won't find any large games here, such as a complete FPS or a multiplayer fantasy world. Describing one of those in detail would require hundreds of pages. Instead, I focus on the building blocks for games (e.g., reusable elements such as loaders, and algorithms such as A* pathfinding). Shooting in a 3D world is described in Chapters 23 and 24, and Chapter 32 explains a simple multiuser 3D space.

I've reduced the quantity of code listings; you won't find page after page of undocumented code here. The documentation uses modern visual aids, including UML class diagrams, sequence diagrams, state charts, and 3D scene graphs.

The 3D material concentrates on Java 3D, because it's a high-level 3D API using a stable and well-documented scene graph. Java has alternative ways of programming 3D applications, including JOGL, LWJGL, Xith3D, jME OpenMind, and more. I'll discuss them in Chapter 14, at the start of the Java 3D coverage.

I won't be talking about J2ME games programming on mobile devices. It's an exciting subject, especially now that a mobile 3D API is available (for example, in the J2ME Wireless Toolkit v2.2, *http://java.sun.com/products/j2mewtoolkit/*). Unfortunately, this book is groaning at the seams, and something has to be left out. For those interested in J2ME games programming, I suggest *J2ME Games with MIDP2* by Carol Hamer (but, it doesn't cover the 3D API, which is too new). I've written several chapters on the API, which can be downloaded from this book's web site at *http://fivedots.coe.psu.ac.th/~ad/jg/*.

This is not a games design text, a topic deserving its own book or two. Two I like are *Game Architecture and Design: A New Edition* by Andrew Rollings and Dave Morris, and *Chris Crawford on Game Design* by Chris Crawford.

If you prefer online sources, the following sites are full of gaming articles, reviews, and opinions:

- Gamasutra (*http://www.gamasutra.com/*)
- GameDev.net (*http://www.gamedev.net/*)
- flipCode (*http://www.flipcode.com/*)
- IGDA, the International Game Developers forum (*http://www.igda.org/Forums/*)

A Graphical View of This Book

This book has four parts: 2D programming, 3D programming with Java 3D, network programming, and two appendixes on installation. The following figures give more details about each one in a visual way. Each oval is a chapter, and the arrows show the main dependencies between the chapters. Chapters on a common theme are grouped inside dotted, rounded gray squares.

2D Programming

Figure P-1 shows the 2D-programming chapters.

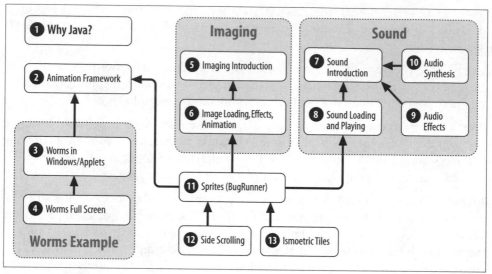

Figure P-1. 2D-programming chapters

Chapter 1 is a defense of Java for gaming, which Java zealots can happily skip. The animation framework used in the 2D examples is explained in Chapter 2, followed by two chapters applying it to a simple *Worms* example, first as a windowed application, then as an applet, then using full screen mode, and almost full screen mode. Chapters 3 and 4 contain timing code for comparing the frame rate speeds of these approaches.

Chapters 5 and 6 are about imaging, mostly concentrating on Java 2D. Chapter 6 has three main topics: classes for loading images, visual effects, and animation.

Chapters 7 through 10 are about Java Sound: Chapter 8 develops classes for loading and playing WAV and MIDI audio, and Chapters 9 and 10 are on sound effects and music synthesis.

A reader who isn't much interested in visual and audio special effects can probably skip the latter half of Chapter 6, and all of Chapters 9 and 10. However, the classes for loading images and audio developed in the first half of Chapter 6 and in Chapter 8 are utilized later.

Chapter 11 develops a 2D Sprite class, and applies it in a BugRunner game. Chapter 12 is about side scrollers (as immortalized by *Super Mario Bros.*), and Chapter 13 is about isometric tile games (*Civilization* is an example of that genre).

3D Programming

The 3D-programming chapters are shown in Figure P-2.

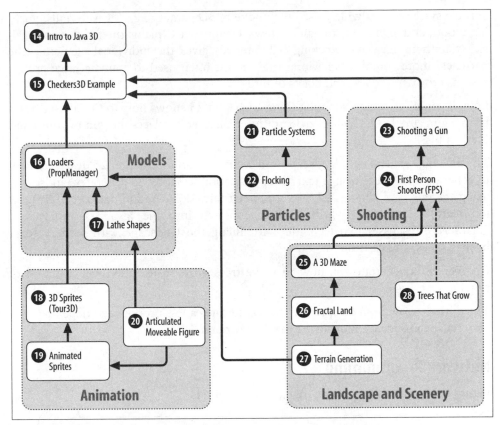

Figure P-2. 3D-programming chapters

Java 3D is introduced in Chapter 14, followed by the Checkers3D example in Chapter 15; its checkerboard floor, lighting, and background appear in several later chapters.

There are five main subtopics covered in the 3D material: models, animation, particle systems, shooting techniques, and landscape and scenery.

Chapter 16 develops two applications, LoaderInfo3D and Loader3D, which show how to load and manipulate externally created 3D models. The PropManager class used in Loader3D is employed in other chapters when an external model is required as part of the scene. Chapter 17 develops a LatheShape class, which allows complex shapes to be generated using surface revolution.

A 3D sprite class is described in Chapter 18, leading to a Tour3D application that allows the user to slide and rotate a robot around a scene. Chapters 19 and 20 examine two approaches for animating the parts of a figure: Chapter 19 uses keyframe sequences, and Chapter 20 develops an articulated figure whose limbs can be moved and rotated.

Particle systems are a widely used technique in 3D games (e.g., for waterfalls, gushing blood, and explosions to name a few). Chapter 21 explains three different particle systems in Java 3D. Flocking (Chapter 22) gives the individual elements (the particles) more complex behavioral rules and is often used to animate large groups such as crowds, soldiers, and flocks of birds.

Lots of games are about shooting things. Chapter 23 shows how to fire a laser beam from a gun situated on a checkerboard floor. Chapter 24 places the gun in your hand (i.e., an FPS).

The 3D chapters end with landscape and scenery creation. Chapter 25 describes how to generate a 3D maze from a text file specification. Chapter 26 generates landscapes using fractals, and Chapter 27 uses a popular terrain generation package, *Terragen*, to create a landscape, which is then imported into the Java 3D application. Chapter 27 discusses two techniques for filling the landscape with scenery (e.g., bushes, trees, and castles).

Chapter 28 concentrates on how to make trees grow realistically over a period of time.

The dotted arrow from Chapters 24 to 28 indicates a less pronounced dependency; I only reuse the code for moving the user's viewpoint.

Network Programming

Figure P-3 shows the network-programming chapters.

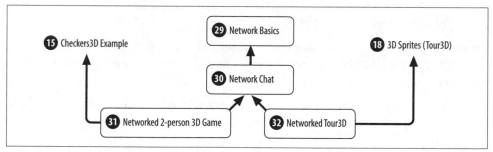

Figure P-3. Network programming chapters

Chapter 29 supplies information on networking fundamentals (e.g., the client/server and peer-to-peer models), and explains basic network programming with sockets, URLs, and servlets. Chapter 30 looks at three chat variants: one using a client/server model, one employing multicasting, and one chatting with servlets.

Chapter 31 describes a networked version of the FourByFour application, a turn-based game demo in the Java 3D distribution. It requires a knowledge of Java 3D. Chapter 32 revisits the Tour3D application of Chapter 18 (the robot moving about a checkerboard) and adds networking to allow multiple users to share the world. I discuss some of the advanced issues concerning networked virtual environments (NVEs), of which NetTour3D is an example.

The Appendixes

The appendixes are shown in Figure P-4.

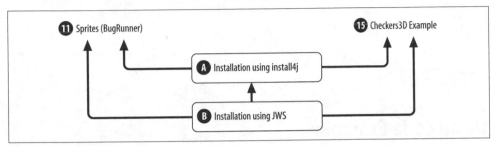

Figure P-4. The appendixes

Appendix A describes install4j, a cross-platform tool for creating native installers for Java applications. Appendix B is about Java Web Start (JWS), a web-enabled installer for Java applications.

Both appendixes use the same two examples. BugRunner (from Chapter 11, which discusses 2D sprites) uses the standard parts of J2SE *and* the J3DTimer class from Java 3D. Checkers3D, from Chapter 15, is my first Java 3D example.

Conventions Used in This Book

The following typographical conventions are used in this book:

Plain text
> Indicates menu titles, menu options, menu buttons, and keyboard accelerators (such as Alt and Ctrl).

Italic
> Indicates new terms, URLs, email addresses, filenames, file extensions, pathnames, directories, and Unix utilities.

Bold
> Emphasizes important text.

Constant width
> Indicates commands, options, switches, variables, attributes, keys, functions, types, classes, namespaces, methods, modules, properties, parameters, values, objects, events, event handlers, XML tags, HTML tags, macros, the contents of files, and the output from commands.

Constant width bold
> Shows commands or other text that should be typed literally by the user.

Constant width italic
> Shows text that should be replaced with user-supplied values.

 This icon signifies a tip, suggestion, or general note.

 This icon indicates a warning or caution.

Using Code Examples

This book is here to help you get your job done. In general, you may use the code in this book in your programs and documentation. You do not need to contact O'Reilly for permission unless you're reproducing a significant portion of the code. For example, writing a program that uses several chunks of code from this book does not require permission. Selling or distributing a CD-ROM of examples from O'Reilly books *does* require permission. Answering a question by citing this book and quoting example code does not require permission. Incorporating a significant amount of example code from this book into your product's documentation *does* require permission.

We appreciate, but do not require, attribution. An attribution usually includes the title, author, publisher, and ISBN. For example: *"Killer Game Programming with Java* by Andrew Davison. Copyright 2005 O'Reilly Media, Inc., 0-596-00730-2."

If you feel your use of code examples falls outside fair use or the permission given above, feel free to contact us at *permissions@oreilly.com*.

All the code examples can be downloaded from the book's web site at *http://fivedots. coe.psu.ac.th/~ad/jg*.

Comments and Questions

Please address comments and questions concerning this book to the publisher:

> O'Reilly Media, Inc.
> 1005 Gravenstein Highway North
> Sebastopol, CA 95472
> (800) 998-9938 (in the United States or Canada)
> (707) 829-0515 (international or local)
> (707) 829-0104 (fax)

O'Reilly maintains a web page for this book that lists errata, examples, and any additional information. You can access this page at:

http://www.oreilly.com/catalog/killergame/

To comment or ask technical questions about this book, send email to:

bookquestions@oreilly.com

You can also contact me at:

ad@fivedots.coe.psu.ac.th

For more information about O'Reilly books, conferences, Resource Centers, and the O'Reilly Network, see O'Reilly's web site at:

http://www.oreilly.com

Safari Enabled

 When you see a Safari® Enabled icon on the cover of your favorite technology book, it means the book is available online through the O'Reilly Network Safari Bookshelf.

Safari offers a solution that's better than e-books. It's a virtual library that lets you easily search thousands of top technology books, cut and paste code samples, download chapters, and find quick answers when you need the most accurate, current information. Try it for free at *http://safari.oreilly.com*.

Acknowledgments

Time to climb up on stage, grab the microphone, and tearfully thank every relative, friend, and acquaintance I've ever known, while the audience gradually slips off to the Land of Nod and viewers worldwide start channel hopping. "Oh my God, I love you all, I really do."

First, I should thank you for buying this book, which will mean that I can buy a *Tivoli* chocolate-like bar when I go for lunch. If you haven't bought this book, then why are reading this bit? Are you desperate or something?

My wife, Supatra, and son, John, have been a constant support, especially when my back is causing problems.

Thanks to my current and past department heads, Ajarns Pichaya, Sinchai, Amnuay, and Weerapant, and many other staff and colleagues, who have let me potter about on this mighty edifice. But why does my office have the word "Broom Cupboard" stenciled on the door? But seriously, Prince of Songkla University is a great place to work.

Greetings to the numerous students who have suffered as guinea pigs for various parts of this book. Your looks of incredulity and boredom were a wondrous spur: "Goodbye Mr. Chips" should be banned.

Special thanks to the hundreds of people who have sent me emails saying how useful the online book has been; their kind words have been a great source of encouragement. I've also received suggestions about how to improve the book and a few bug reports. I credit those people at the relevant places in the text.

Finally, my best regards to O'Reilly and my editor Brett McLaughlin and figures illustrator Chris Reilly, who have knocked this book into better shape. Any remaining rough edges are due to me.

CHAPTER 1

Why Java for Games Programming?

One of my assumptions is that the reader (that's you) has had an introductory knowledge of Java, the sort of stuff gleaned from a semester's course at college. Near the start of that course, you were probably regaled with Java's many advantages: an object-oriented paradigm, cross-platform support, code reuse, ease of development, tool availability, reliability and stability, good documentation, support from Sun Microsystems, low development costs, the ability to use legacy code (e.g., C, C++), and increased programmer productivity.

Rather than explain each of these again, I will take a different approach and discuss Java's suitability for games programming in terms of the typical misconceptions and complaints wheeled out by people who think that games must be implemented in C, C++, assembler, or whatever (just so long as it's not Java).

Here's the list of objections to Java:

- Java is too slow for games programming.
- Java has memory leaks.
- Java is too high-level.
- Java application installation is a nightmare.
- Java isn't supported on games consoles.
- No one uses Java to write real games.
- Sun Microsystems isn't interested in supporting Java gaming.

It's worth saying that I think almost all of these objections are substantially wrong. Java is roughly the same speed as C++. Memory leaks can be avoided with good programming and techniques like profiling. Yes, Java is high-level, but it offers more direct access to graphics hardware and external devices. Installation isn't a nightmare if you use decent installation software. There's a growing number of excellent, fun Java games, and an enormous amount of support available from Sun and Sun-sponsored sites.

If you're keeping count, I haven't disagreed with the lack of a games consoles port, which is a tad embarrassing for a "write once, run anywhere" language. Things may be changing in this category, as I'll explain later.

A general point about these objections is that they had more validity in the late 1990s when the language and its libraries were less sophisticated and slower. Java's user and developer communities are burgeoning and have produced a plethora of useful tools, online help, and code examples. The games forums dedicated to Java barely existed 2 to 3 years ago. Java is a great language for games programming, as I hope this book demonstrates. Now, back to the criticisms.

Java Is Too Slow for Games Programming

This is better rephrased as "Java is slow compared to C and C++, the dominant languages for games programming." This argument was valid when Java first appeared (around 1996) but has become increasingly ridiculous with each new release. Some figures put JDK 1.0, that first version of the language, at 20 to 40 times slower than C++. However, J2SE 5.0, the current release, is typically only 1.1 times slower.

These numbers depend greatly on the coding style used. Java programmers must be good programmers to utilize Java efficiently, but that's true of any language. Jack Shirazi's *Java Performance Tuning* site (*http://www.javaperformancetuning.com/*) is a good source for performance tips, with links to tools and other resources. A recent benchmarking of Java vs. C++ by Keith Lea caused quite a stir (*http://www. theserverside.com/news/thread.tss?thread_id=26634*). He found that Java may sometimes be faster than C++. The response from the C++ crowd was typically vitriolic.

The speed-up in Java is mostly due to improvements in compiler design. The Hotspot technology introduced in J2SE 1.3 enables the runtime system to identify crucial areas of code that are utilized many times, and these are aggressively compiled. Hotspot technology is relatively new, and it's quite likely that future versions of Java will yield further speed-ups. For example, J2SE 5.0 is reportedly 1.2 to 1.5 times faster than its predecessor (Version 1.4).

 Hotspot technology has the unfortunate side effect that program execution is often slow at the beginning until the code has been analyzed and compiled.

Swing Is Slow

Swing often comes under attack for being slow. Swing GUI components are created and controlled from Java, with little OS support; this increases their portability and makes them more controllable from within a Java program. Speed is supposedly compromised because Java imposes an extra layer of processing above the OS. This is one reason why some games applications still utilize the original Abstract Windowing Toolkit (AWT) since it's mostly simple wrapper methods around OS calls.

Even if Swing is slow (and I'm not convinced of that), most games don't require complex GUIs; full-screen game play with mouse and keyboard controls is the norm. GUI elements maintained by Swing, such as menu bars, button, and text fields aren't needed, and mouse and keyboard processing is dealt with by the AWT. The latest versions of Java offer an efficient full-screen mode by suspending the normal windowing environment.

My Program Is Slow Because of Java

A crucial point about speed is knowing what to blame when a program runs slowly. Typically, a large part of the graphics rendering of a game is handled by hardware or software outside of Java. For example, Java 3D passes its rendering tasks down to OpenGL or DirectX, which may emulate hardware capabilities such as bump mapping. Often the performance bottleneck in network games is the network and not the Java language.

Java Has Memory Leaks

When C/C++ programmers refer to memory leaks in Java, they probably don't understand how Java works. Java doesn't offer pointer arithmetic; typical C-style memory leaks, such as out-of-bounds array accesses, are caught by the Java compiler.

However, these programmers may mean that objects that are no longer needed by the program are not being garbage collected. This becomes an issue if the program keeps creating new objects and requiring more memory, and eventually crashes when the maximum memory allocation is exceeded.

This kind of problem is a consequence of bad programming style, since the garbage collector can only do its job when an object is completely *dereferenced*, meaning the program no longer refers to the object. A good profiling tool, such as JProfiler (*http://www.ej-technologies.com/products/jprofiler/overview.html*), can help identify code using excessive amounts of memory.

 JProfiler is a commercial product; many open source profilers are listed at *http://java-source.net/*.

Another memory-related complaint is that the Java garbage collector is executing at poorly timed intervals, causing the application to halt for seconds as the collector sweeps and cleans. The Java Virtual Machine (JVM) comes with several different garbage collectors, which collect in various ways and can be selected and fine-tuned from the command line. Information on the performance of the chosen collector can be gathered and analyzed. A good hands-on explanation of this topic, centered around the JTune visualization tool, can be found at *http://www-106.ibm.com/developerworks/java/library/j-perf06304/*. Another possibility is GC Portal (*http://java.sun.com/developer/technicalArticles/Programming/GCPortal/*).

Java Is Too High-level

This complaint is the age-old one of abstraction versus speed and control. The details of the argument often include the following statements:

1. Java's use of classes, objects, and inheritance add too much overhead without enough coding benefit.
2. Java's machine independence means that low-level, fast operations, e.g., direct Video RAM I/O are impossible.

Statement 1 ignores the obvious benefits of reusing and extending Java's large class library, which includes high-speed I/O, advanced 2D and 3D graphics, and many networking techniques, from lowly sockets to distributed agents. Also forgotten are the advantages of object-oriented design, typified by UML, which makes complex, large, real-world systems more manageable during development, implementation, and maintenance.

Statement 2 impacts gaming when we consider high-speed graphics, but it's been addressed in recent versions of Java. J2SE 1.4 introduced *a full-screen exclusive mode* (FSEM), which suspends the normal windowing environment and allows an application to access the underlying graphics hardware more directly. It permits techniques, e.g., page flipping, and provides control over the screen's resolution and image depth. The principal aim of FSEM is to speed up graphics-intensive applications, such as games.

Statement 2 comes into play for game peripherals, e.g., joysticks and game pads; machine independence seems to suggest that nonstandard I/O devices won't be useable. Java games requiring these types of devices can utilize the Java Native Interface (JNI) to link to C or C++ and, therefore, to the hardware. There's also JInput, a new game controller API.

An interesting historical observation is that the gaming community used to think that C and C++ were too high-level for fast, efficient games programming when compared to assembly language. Opinions started to change only after the obvious success of games written in C, such as *Doom* and *Dungeon Master*, in the mid-1980s. Also important was the appearance of cross-platform development tools that supported C, such as RenderWare.

Java Application Installation Is a Nightmare

The naysayers claim that the user needs to be a Java expert to install and execute a Java application, whereas most game players want to point and click on a few dialog boxes to get a game up and running. More specific comments include the following:

1. Java (specifically, the JRE) has to be on the machine before the application will run.

2. Code bloat since even small programs require a 15 MB JRE. Downloading this can be slow.

3. Frequently changing JVMs make it hard to write code that will work for every possible version of Java.

4. Nonstandard components are often required—e.g., Java 3D, causing even more installation problems.

5. It's impossible to compile the application for a specific platform.

6. The .jar extension is commonly hijacked by other software (e.g., by compression programs) at execution time, meaning that the user can't double-click on a JAR to get it to start.

7. The JRE is slower to start up compared to a native compiled application.

All these problems, aside from perhaps 2 and 7, can be solved by using good installation software. I have two appendixes dedicated to installation: Appendix A is about install4j, a cross-platform tool for creating native installers for Java applications, and Appendix B is about Java Web Start (JWS), a web-enabled installer.

The code bloat comment is increasingly irrelevant, with many games weighing in at over 100 MB and many graphics and sound card drivers being made larger than 15 MB. Network speeds are a problem, especially overseas, but broadband usage is growing rapidly.

Sun Microsystems estimates that more than 50 percent of all new PCs come with a pre-installed JRE, though a game installer must still cater to the other 50 percent.

There's some truth to point 7, but the slow startup time is fairly negligible compared to the total running time of an average game.

I was interested in what other Java games programmers had to say about this criticism, so posted it to the Java Games Forum as thread *http://www.javagaming.org/cgi-bin/JGNetForums/YaBB.cgi?board=announcements;action=display;num=1092970902*. The responses are similar to mine, though often phrased somewhat more stridently.

Java Isn't Supported on Games Consoles

Unfortunately, this criticism has some justification. Video gaming is a multi-billion-dollar industry, with estimates placing revenues at $29 billion by 2007 with the market catering to over 235 million gamers. PCs and game consoles account for almost all the income, but only about 10–20 percent of it is from PCs, the majority coming from three consoles: Sony's PlayStation 2 (PS2), Microsoft's Xbox, and Nintendo's GameCube. Sony is the dominant console maker, having nearly twice as many units in homes compared to Microsoft and Nintendo combined. Microsoft accounts for about 95 percent of the desktop PC market. Arguably, two important games platforms exist, the PS2 and Windows, and Java isn't available on the PlayStation.

This problem has long been recognized by Sun. Back at the JavaOne conference in 2001, Sony and Sun announced their intention to port the JVM to the PS2. Nothing has been released, but there are persistent rumors about a JVM on the PlayStation 3, earmarked to appear in 2006.

In the future, Java may have a better chance of acceptance into the closed world of console makers because of two trends: consoles mutating into home media devices and the meteoric rise of online gaming. Both trends require consoles to offer complex networking and server support, strong areas for Java and Sun.

The Phantom console from Infinium Labs was announced at JavaOne in 2004 (*http://www.phantom.net/index.php*). It's essentially a PC running an embedded Windows XP installation, with an nVidia graphics card, a hard drive, and a broadband connection. Most importantly for Java gaming, the Phantom will come with a complete JRE. It was demoed during Electronic Entertainment Exposition (E3) in 2004, where it was shown running *Law and Order: Dead on the Money* (which uses Java 3D).

Die-hard programmers may point out that it's possible to get Java running on a PS2. One approach is to install Kaffe, an open source, non-Sun JVM, on top of PlayStation Linux. Kaffe can be obtained from *http://www.kaffe.org/*; details on Linux for the PlayStation are at *http://playstation2-linux.com/*. The gallant programmer will need a Java-to-bytecode translator, such as Jikes (*http://www-124.ibm.com/developerworks/oss/jikes/*).

The Linux kit adds a hard disk to the PS2, so this development strategy won't work for ordinary PlayStations. Configuring the software looks to be far beyond the capabilities (or desires) of ordinary console owners, and I couldn't find any documentation about using Jikes or Kaffe on a PS2. The PlayStation only comes with 32 MB of RAM, while a typical JVM and its libraries requires 5 to 10 MB, so how much would be left for a game once Linux was up and running?

The difficulties of this approach should be contrasted to the availability of feature-rich C/C++ tools and engines for consoles, such as RenderWare (*http://www.renderware.com/*) and Gamebryo (*http://www.ndl.com/*). They have a track record of best-selling games and can port games across the PS2, Xbox, GameCube, and PCs.

The lack of Java on consoles is a serious issue, but the remaining PC market is large. Microsoft estimates that there are 600 million Windows PCs, growing to more than 1 billion by 2010. Games on PCs benefit from superior hardware—such as video cards, RAM, and Internet connections—and can offer more exciting game play. There are many more PC games, particularly in the area of multiplayer online games. It's estimated that 40 percent of all gamers will start playing online in 2005. Revenues may reach $1.1 billion by 2008.

Another rapidly expanding market is the one for mobile games, with sales of $530 million in 2003, potentially rising to $1.93 billion in 2006. There are perhaps 200 million Java-enabled phones at the moment.

No One Uses Java to Write Real Games

The word "real" here probably means commercial games. The number of commercial Java games is small compared to ones coded in C or C++, but the number is growing and many have garnered awards and become bestsellers:

Puzzle Pirates by Three Rings (http://www.puzzlepirates.com/)
> This is a multiplayer pirate game that includes Tetris-like or Columns-like puzzles at various points. The client and server are written in Java. It won several awards during 2004, including the Technical Excellence and Audience Choice prizes at the Game Developers Conference.

Chrome by Techland (http://www.chromethegame.com/en/show.php)
> *Chrome* is a futuristic multiplayer FPS (first person shooter) made up of 14 different missions, in an amazing variety of landscapes. It received a Duke's Choice Award from Sun Microsystems in 2004 for the most innovative product using Java technology.

Law and Order II by Legacy Interactive. (http://www.lawandordergame.com/index2.htm)
> This is a detective game written in Java, Java 3D, and QuickTime for Java. The first *Law and Order* sold over 100,000 units.

Kingdom of Wars by Abandoned Castle Studios (http://www.abandonedcastle.com/)
> This is a fantasy game set in the world of Jairon.

Alien Flux by Puppy Games (http://www.puppygames.net/info.php?game=Alien_Flux)
> *Alien Flux* is an exciting arcade shoot-em-up.

War! Age of Imperialism by Eagle Games (http://www.eaglegames.net/products/WAR_AOI/wai.shtml)
> *War!* is a computer version of the award-winning board game from Eagle Games.

Runescape by Jagex (http://www.runescape.com)
> *Runescape* is a massive 3D multiplayer fantasy adventure game. Clients can use a Java applet to play or download a Windows-based client application.

Star Wars Galaxies by LucasArts (http://www.lucasarts.com/products/galaxies/)
> This one has its game logic coded in Java.

IL-2 Sturmovik by Ubi-Soft (http://www.il2sturmovik.com/)
> Award winning WW II aerial combat using Java and C++, this and the new version (*IL2-Forgotten Battles*) are great examples of Java in games.

Pernica by Starfire Research (http://www.starfireresearch.com/pernica/pernica.html)
> *Pernica* is an online fantasy role-playing game first implemented in Java 3D.

Cosm by Navtools, Inc. (http://www.cosm-game.com/)
> *Cosm* is another fun online fantasy-based role-playing game.

C&C Attack Copter by Electronic Arts (http://www.eagames.com/free/home.jsp)
> This is a free online action game based on the *Command & Conquer* series.

Roboforge by Liquid Edge Games (http://www.roboforge.com)
> Train a 3D robot to fight in online tournaments. It was given an "Excellent 87%" by *PC Gamer Magazine*.

Galactic Village by Galactic Village Games (http://www.galactic-village.com)
> *Galactic Village* is a massively multiplayer strategy game, written entirely in Java. Not yet finished though alpha versions have been appearing.

Wurm Online by Mojang Specifications (http://www.wurmonline.com/)
> This is another massively multiplayer fantasy game, written in Java. It's still in the alpha stages of development, but the screenshots look great.

Jellyvision (http://www.jellyvision.com/)
> *Jellyvision* used a mix of Java and C++ in their popular *Who Wants to Be a Millionaire* (2000) and *You Don't Know Jack* (1995) games. They employed Java for the game logic, an approach used in *Majestic* (2001) by Electronic Arts.

Vampire the Masquerade: Redemption (2000) by Nihilistic software (http://www.nihilistic.com/).
> Java was utilized as a scripting language in this highly acclaimed game.

Tom Clancy's Politika (1997) by Red Storm Entertainment (http://www.redstorm.com/)
> This game was written in almost pure Java. *Shadow Watch* (2000) and *Tom Clancy's ruthless.com* (1998) mixed Java and C/C++.

A good source for nontechnical lists of Java games, both commercial and freeware/shareware, can be found on the Java games pages at java.com (*http://www.java.com/en/games/*). The pages divide games into several categories: action, adventure, strategy, puzzle, cards, sports, and so on.

Freeware/Shareware Games

Many Java games are out on the Web, but finding a game that's written well requires a careful search. Many applets date from the late 1990s and were designed using the outdated JDK 1.0 and 1.1 with their feeble media APIs (e.g., graphics, sounds). The initial Java euphoria produced some less than exciting games, more concerned with technical trickery than quality. This large pool of useless applets got Java labeled as a toy language.

Recent versions of Java are different. The speed has improved and APIs crucial to gaming—such as graphics and audio—are of a high quality. There's been a move away from applets towards the downloading of client-side applications using JWS.

Java's backward compatibility allows the applets from 1996 to 1998 to be executed, and they'll often run quicker than the original applets. However, it's probably best to steer clear of these Java dinosaurs and look for more modern code.

Numerous web sites use Java games. The emphasis of the following list is on applications/applets for playing:

Java Games Factory (JGF) (http://grexengine.com/sections/externalgames/)
    There aren't many games at this site (about 50), but they're all high quality. The aim is to show off various modern Java game technologies.

ArcadePod.com (http://www.arcadepod.com/java/)
    Over 750 Java games, nicely categorized.

Java 4 Fun (http://www.java4fun.com/java.html)
    Similar in style to ArcadePod, with a good set of links to other sites.

jars.com (http://www.jars.com)
    A general Java site with a ratings scheme. There are many games, but a lot of them are old applets.

Java Shareware (http://www.javashareware.com/)
    Another general site: look under the categories applications/games and applets/games.

Java Games Central (http://www.mnsi.net/~rkerr/)
    A personal web site that lists games with ratings and links. It was last updated in 2001.

Some of my favorite freeware/shareware games are:

Super Elvis; also known as Hallucinogenesis (http://www.puppygames.net/downloads/hallucinogenesis/hallucinogenesis.jnlp)
    This game won the Sun Microsystems 2004 Technology Game Development Contest. Super Elvis can be downloaded from the puppygames web site using JWS.

FlyingGuns (http://www.flyingguns.com/)
    A 3D multiplayer WWI fighter plane game/simulator. This came second in the contest but is my favorite.

Cosmic Trip (http://www.mycgiserver.com/~movegaga/cosmictrip.html)
    An arcade-style 3D game with striking graphics.

Squareheads (http://home.halden.net/tombr/squareheads/squareheads.html)
    A multiplayer FPS (it came third in the developer contest).

Escape (http://javaisdoomed.sourceforge.net/)
  A *Doom*-like FPS.

CazaPool3D (http://membres.lycos.fr/franckcalzada/Billard3D/Pool.html)
  A pool game that allows online (single/multiplayer) play in an applet or as a standalone application.

Programmers looking for source code should start at one of the following sites:

SourceForge (http://sourceforge.net/search/)
  SourceForge acts as a repository and management tool for software projects, many with source code. A recent search for (java + game) returned over 70 projects that had 40 percent or greater activity. One of the drawbacks of SourceForge is that deciding if a project is vaporware is difficult. Good projects that have been completed will show low activity after a time, dropping down the list of search results.

FreshMeat.com (http://freshmeat.net/)
  FreshMeat maintains thousands of applications, most released under open source licenses. The search facilities are excellent and can be guided by game category terms. The results include rating, vitality, and popularity figures for each piece of software. A recent search for Java in the Games/Entertainment category returned nearly 70 hits. Many applications turn up at *SourceForge* and *FreshMeat*.

The "Your Games Here" Java Games Forum (http://www.javagaming.org/cgi-bin/ JGNetForums/YaBB.cgi?board=Announcements)
  Implementers can post links to their games, and (perhaps more importantly) users can post their opinions as follow-ups.

Code Beach (http://www.codebeach.com)
  CodeBeach has a searchable subsection for Java games that contains nearly 90 examples.

Programmers Heaven (http://www.programmersheaven.com/zone13/)
  It has a "Java zone" containing some games.

Sun Microsystems Isn't Interested in Supporting Java Gaming

The games market isn't a traditional one for Sun, and it'll probably never have the depth of knowledge of a Sony or Nintendo. However, the last few years have demonstrated Sun's increasing commitment to gaming.

J2SE has strengthened its games support through successive versions: Version 1.3 improved its graphics and audio capabilities, and Version 1.4 introduced full-screen mode and page flipping in hardware. Faster I/O, memory mapping, and support for nonblock sockets, which is especially useful in client/server multiplayer games, also appeared first in 1.4. Version 5.0 has a decent nanosecond timer at last. Java extension libraries, such as Java 3D, the Java Media Framework (JMF), the Java Communications API, Jini, and JAXP (Java's peer-to-peer API) offer something to games programmers.

Sun started showing an interest in gaming back in 2001, with its announcement of the Java Game Profile, a collaboration with several other companies, including Sega and Sony, to develop a Java gaming API. The profile was perhaps too ambitious, and was abandoned at the end of 2003. However, it did produce three game-focused technologies: a Java binding for OpenGL called JOGL, a binding for OpenAL (a 3D audio library) called JOAL, and JInput.

Part of the 2001 initiative was the creation of the JavaGaming.org web site (*http://www.javagaming.org*), initially manned by volunteers. In 2003, the Game Technology Group was formed, and JavaGaming.org received a substantial makeover as part of the creation of the new java.net portal (*http://www.java.net*) aimed at the technical promotion of Java. Java.net hosts many discussion forums, user groups, projects, communities, and news. The communities include: Java Desktop, Java Education and Learning, Java Enterprise, and Java Games.

The Java Games community pages can be accessed through *http://www.javagaming.org* or *http://community.java.net/games/*. The site includes Java games forums, projects, news, weblogs, a wiki (*http://wiki.java.net/bin/view/Games/WebHome*), and links to games affiliates.

Numerous Java game forums can be accessed from *http://www.javagaming.org/cgi-bin/JGNetForums/YaBB.cgi*. These are probably the best sources of technical advice on Java gaming on the Web, with over 4,500 opinionated registered users. Discussion topics include Java 3D, Java 2D, Java Sound, J2ME, networking, online games development, performance tuning, JOGL, JOAL, and JInput. There are also sections on projects and code examples.

The project sections (*https://games.dev.java.net/*) mostly concentrate on JOGL, JOAL, and JInput, but the games middleware and games forge sections are wider ranging. The games forge projects include Chinese chess, jbantumi (a strategic game from Africa), and an online fantasy football management system.

The most relevant Java user group for gaming is GameJUG (*https://gamejug.dev.java.net/*). Its sections include online and downloadable Java games, presentations and articles, lists of Java game programming web sites, and a collaborative web page and mailing list for teachers of Java game programming.

 I'm a former GameJUG president, a role that sounds grander than it really was. The real work was done by David Wallace Croft and James Richards.

Sun's substantial presence at *http://community.java.net/games/* is mostly as a host for community forums and open source projects (or projects with licenses very close to open source). The projects include JOGL, JOAL, JInput, and Java 3D. Sun is relying on community involvement to move these projects forward, since the Game Technology Group is quite small.

One in-house product is a server architecture for massively multiplayer online games, the Sun Game Server, first demoed at the Game Developers Conference in 2004. This focus isn't surprising since Sun makes its money from selling server hardware. Online multiplayer gaming is a potential growth area for its servers.

CHAPTER 2

An Animation Framework

A core technology for a good game is an animation algorithm that produces reliably fast game play across various operating systems (e.g., flavors of Windows, Linux, and Macintosh), and in different kinds of Java programs (e.g., applets, windowed, and full-screen applications).

 I distinguish between windowed and full-screen applications because J2SE 1.4 introduced *full-screen exclusive mode* (FSEM). It suspends the normal windowing environment and allows an application to access the underlying graphics hardware more directly. FSEM permits techniques such as page flipping and provides control over the screen's resolution and image depth. The principal aim of FSEM is to accelerate graphics-intensive applications, such as games.

The common ground between windowed and full-screen application is the game's animation algorithm, which is the subject of this chapter.

The algorithm is embedded in a JPanel subclass (called GamePanel), which acts as a canvas for drawing 2D graphics (e.g., lines, circles, text, images). The animation is managed by a thread, which ensures that it progresses at a consistent rate, as independent of the vagaries of the hardware and OS as possible. The rate is measured in terms of *frames per second* (FPS), where a frame corresponds to a single rendering of the application to the canvas.

GamePanel is gradually refined and expanded through the chapter, introducing the following notions:

- The {update, render, sleep} animation loop
- Starting and terminating an animation
- Double buffering
- User interaction
- Active rendering

- Animation control based on a user's requested FPS
- The management of inaccuracies in the timer and sleep operations
- Combining FPS and game state *updates per second* (UPS)
- Game pausing and resumption

Though most of this chapter is about the GamePanel animation loop, I will consider two other popular approaches to implementing animation: using the Swing timer and the utility timer in java.util.timer.

 The example programs used in this chapter can be found in the *Timings/* directory. All the code directories mentioned in the chapters can be downloaded from the book's web site at *http://fivedots.coe.psu.ac.th/ ~ad/jg*.

In Chapters 3 and 4, I develop applet, windowed, and full-screen applications for a WormChase game using the final version of GamePanel (with minor variations). As a side effect of the game play, statistics are gathered, including the average FPS and UPS, to show that GamePanel supports consistently high-speed animation.

Animation as a Threaded Canvas

A JPanel is employed as a drawing surface, and an animation loop is embedded inside a thread local to the panel. The loop consists of three stages: game update, rendering, and a short sleep.

The code in Example 2-1 shows the main elements of GamePanel, including the run( ) method containing the animation loop. As the chapter progresses, additional methods and global variables will be added to GamePanel, and some of the existing methods (especially run( )) will be changed and extended.

Example 2-1. The GamePanel class (initial version)

```
public class GamePanel extends JPanel implements Runnable
{
  private static final int PWIDTH = 500;   // size of panel
  private static final int PHEIGHT = 400;

  private Thread animator;              // for the animation
  private volatile boolean running = false;    // stops the animation

  private volatile boolean gameOver = false;   // for game termination

  // more variables, explained later
  //         :

  public GamePanel()
  {
```

Example 2-1. The GamePanel class (initial version) (continued)

```java
    setBackground(Color.white);      // white background
    setPreferredSize( new Dimension(PWIDTH, PHEIGHT));

    // create game components
    // ...
  }  // end of GamePanel( )


  public void addNotify( )
  /* Wait for the JPanel to be added to the
     JFrame/JApplet before starting. */
  {
    super.addNotify( );   // creates the peer
    startGame( );         // start the thread
  }


  private void startGame( )
  // initialise and start the thread
  {
    if (animator == null || !running) {
      animator = new Thread(this);
      animator.start( );
    }
  } // end of startGame( )


  public void stopGame( )
  // called by the user to stop execution
  {  running = false;     }


  public void run( )
  /* Repeatedly update, render, sleep */
  {
    running = true;
    while(running) {
      gameUpdate( );   // game state is updated
      gameRender( );   // render to a buffer
      repaint( );      // paint with the buffer

      try {
        Thread.sleep(20);  // sleep a bit
      }
      catch(InterruptedException ex){}
    }
    System.exit(0);    // so enclosing JFrame/JApplet exits
  } // end of run( )


  private void gameUpdate( )
  { if (!gameOver)
```

Example 2-1. The GamePanel class (initial version) (continued)

```
    // update game state ...
  }

  // more methods, explained later...

} // end of GamePanel class
```

GamePanel acts as a fixed size white canvas, which will be embedded inside a JFrame in applications and inside JApplet in applets. The embedding will only require minor changes, except when GamePanel is used in applications using full-screen exclusive mode (FSEM). Even in that case, the animation loop will stay essentially the same.

addNotify( ) is called automatically as GamePanel is being added to its enclosing GUI component (e.g., a JFrame or JApplet), so it is a good place to initiate the animation thread (animator). stopGame( ) will be called from the enclosing JFrame/JApplet when the user wants the program to terminate; it sets a global Boolean, running, to false.

Just Stop It

Some authors suggest using Thread's stop( ) method, a technique deprecated by Sun. stop( ) causes a thread to terminate immediately, perhaps while it is changing data structures or manipulating external resources, leaving them in an inconsistent state. The running Boolean is a better solution because it allows the programmer to decide how the animation loop should finish. The drawback is that the code must include tests to detect the termination flag.

Synchronization Concerns

The executing GamePanel object has two main threads: the animator thread for game updates and rendering, and a GUI event processing thread, which responds to such things as key presses and mouse movements. When the user presses a key to stop the game, this *event dispatch thread* will execute stopGame( ). It will set running to false at the same time the animation thread is executing.

Once a program contains two or more threads utilizing a shared variable, data structure, or resource, then thorny synchronization problems may appear. For example, what will happen if a shared item is changed by one thread at the same moment that the other one reads it? The Java Memory Model (JMM) states that accesses and updates to all variables, other than longs or doubles, are atomic, i.e., the JMM supports 32-bit atomicity. For example, an assignment to a Boolean cannot be interleaved with a read. This means that the changing of the running flag by stopGame( ) cannot occur at the same moment that the animation thread is reading it.

The atomicity of read and writes to Booleans is a useful property. However, the possibility of synchronization problems for more complex data structures cannot be ignored, as you'll see in Chapter 3.

Application and Game Termination

A common pitfall is to use a Boolean, such as running, to denote application termination and game termination. The end of a game occurs when the player wins (or loses), but this is typically not the same as stopping the application. For instance, the end of the game may be followed by the user entering details into a high scores table or by the user being given the option to play again. Consequently, I represent game ending by a separate Boolean, gameOver. It can be seen in gameUpdate( ), controlling the game state change.

Why Use Volatile?

The JMM lets each thread have its own local memory (e.g., registers) where it can store copies of variables, thereby improving performance since the variables can be manipulated more quickly. The drawback is that accesses to these variables by other threads see the original versions in main memory and not the local copies.

The running and gameOver variables are candidates for copying to local memory in the GamePanel thread. This will cause problems since other threads use these variables. running is set to false by stopGame( ) called from the GUI thread (gameOver is set to true by the GUI thread as well, as I'll explain later). Since running and gameOver are manipulated by the GUI thread and not the animation thread, the original versions in main memory are altered and the local copies used by the animation thread are unaffected. One consequence is that the animation thread will never stop since its local version of running will never become false!

This problem is avoided by affixing the volatile keyword to running and gameOver. volatile prohibits a variable from being copied to local memory; the variable stays in main memory. Thus, changes to that variable by other threads will be seen by the animation thread.

Why Sleep?

The animation loop includes an arbitrary 20 ms of sleep time:

```
while(running) {
  gameUpdate();    // game state is updated
  gameRender();    // render to a buffer
  repaint();       // paint with the buffer

  try {
    Thread.sleep(20);  // sleep a bit
```

```
        }
        catch(InterruptedException ex){}
    }
```

Why is this necessary? There are three main reasons.

The first is that sleep( ) causes the animation thread to stop executing, which frees up the CPU for other tasks, such as garbage collection by the JVM. Without a period of sleep, the GamePanel thread could hog all the CPU time. However, the 20-ms sleep time is somewhat excessive, especially when the loop is executing 50 or 100 times per second.

The second reason for the sleep( ) call is to give the preceding repaint( ) time to be processed. The call to repaint( ) places a *repaint request* in the JVM's event queue and then returns. Exactly how long the request will be held in the queue before triggering a repaint is beyond my control; the sleep( ) call makes the thread wait before starting the next update/rendering cycle, to give the JVM time to act. The repaint request will be processed, percolating down through the components of the application until GamePanel's paintComponent( ) is called. An obvious question is whether 20 ms is sufficient time for the request to be carried out. Perhaps it's overly generous?

It may seem that I should choose a smaller sleep time, 5 ms perhaps. However, any fixed sleep time may be too long or too short, depending on the current game activity and the speed of the particular machine.

Finally, the sleep( ) call reduces the chance of *event coalescence*: If the JVM is overloaded by repaint requests, it may choose to combine requests. This means that some of the rendering request will be skipped, causing the animation to "jump" as frames are lost.

Double Buffering Drawing

gameRender( ) draws into its own Graphics object (dbg), which represents an image the same size as the screen (dbImage).

```
// global variables for off-screen rendering
private Graphics dbg;
private Image dbImage = null;

private void gameRender()
// draw the current frame to an image buffer
{
  if (dbImage == null){  // create the buffer
    dbImage = createImage(PWIDTH, PHEIGHT);
    if (dbImage == null) {
      System.out.println("dbImage is null");
      return;
    }
    else
```

```
        dbg = dbImage.getGraphics();
    }

    // clear the background
    dbg.setColor(Color.white);
    dbg.fillRect (0, 0, PWIDTH, PHEIGHT);

    // draw game elements
    // ...

    if (gameOver)
      gameOverMessage(dbg);
  }  // end of gameRender( )


  private void gameOverMessage(Graphics g)
  // center the game-over message
  { // code to calculate x and y...
    g.drawString(msg, x, y);
  }  // end of gameOverMessage( )
```

This technique is known as *double buffering* since the (usually complex) drawing operations required for rendering are not applied directly to the screen but to a secondary image.

The dbImage image is placed on screen by paintComponent( ) as a result of the repaint request in the run( ) loop. This call is only made after the rendering step has been completed:

```
public void paintComponent(Graphics g)
{
  super.paintComponent(g);
  if (dbImage != null)
    g.drawImage(dbImage, 0, 0, null);
}
```

The principal advantage of double buffering is to reduce on-screen flicker. If extensive drawing is done directly to the screen, the process may take long enough to become noticeable by the user. The call to drawImage( ) in paintComponent( ) is fast enough that the change from one frame to the next is perceived as instantaneous.

Another reason for keeping paintComponent( ) simple is that it may be called by the JVM independently of the animation thread. For example, this will occur when the application (or applet) window has been obscured by another window and then brought back to the front.

 The placing of game behavior inside paintComponent( ) is a common mistake. This results in the animation being driven forward by its animation loop and by the JVM repainting the window.

Adding User Interaction

In full-screen applications, there will be no additional GUI elements, such as text fields or Swing buttons. Even in applets or windowed applications, the user will probably want to interact directly with the game canvas as much as is possible. This means that GamePanel must monitor key presses and mouse activity.

GamePanel utilizes key presses to set the running Boolean to false, which terminates the animation loop and application. Mouse presses are processed by testPress( ), using the cursor's (x, y) location in various ways (details are given in later chapters).

The GamePanel( ) constructor is modified to set up the key and mouse listeners:

```java
public GamePanel( )
{
  setBackground(Color.white);
  setPreferredSize( new Dimension(PWIDTH, PHEIGHT));

  setFocusable(true);
  requestFocus( );    // JPanel now receives key events
  readyForTermination( );

  // create game components
  // ...

  // listen for mouse presses
  addMouseListener( new MouseAdapter() {
    public void mousePressed(MouseEvent e)
    { testPress(e.getX( ), e.getY( )); }
  });
}  // end of GamePanel( )
```

readyForTermination( ) watches for key presses that signal termination and sets running to false. testPress( ) does something with the cursor's (x, y) coordinate but only if the game hasn't finished yet:

```java
private void readyForTermination( )
{
  addKeyListener( new KeyAdapter() {
  // listen for esc, q, end, ctrl-c
    public void keyPressed(KeyEvent e)
    { int keyCode = e.getKeyCode( );
      if ((keyCode == KeyEvent.VK_ESCAPE) ||
          (keyCode == KeyEvent.VK_Q) ||
          (keyCode == KeyEvent.VK_END) ||
          ((keyCode == KeyEvent.VK_C) && e.isControlDown()) ) {
        running = false;
      }
    }
  });
}  // end of readyForTermination( )
```

```
private void testPress(int x, int y)
// is (x,y) important to the game?
{
  if (!gameOver) {
    // do something
  }
}
```

Converting to Active Rendering

The current painting strategy is to call repaint( ) in run( )'s animation loop:

```
while(running) {
  gameUpdate();   // game state is updated
  gameRender();   // render to a buffer
  repaint();      // paint with the buffer

  try {
    Thread.sleep(20);  // sleep a bit
  }
  catch(InterruptedException ex){}
}
```

Since a call to repaint( ) is only a request, it's difficult to know when the repaint has been completed. This means that the sleep time in the animation loop is little more than a guess; if the specified delay is too long, then the animation speed is impaired for no reason. If the delay is too short, then repaint requests may be queued by the JVM and skipped if the load becomes too large.

In fact, no single sleep time is satisfactory since the time taken to update and render a frame will vary depending on the activity taking place in the game. The sleep time must be calculated afresh each time round the loop after measuring the iteration's update and rendering periods. Unfortunately, the repaint( ) part of the rendering is done by the JVM and cannot be easily measured.

As a first step to dealing with these issues, I switch to *active rendering*, shown below as modifications to run( ):

```
public void run()
/* Repeatedly update, render, sleep */
{
  running = true;
  while(running) {
    gameUpdate();   // game state is updated
    gameRender();   // render to a buffer
    paintScreen();  // draw buffer to screen

    try {
      Thread.sleep(20);  // sleep a bit
    }
    catch(InterruptedException ex){}
  }
}
```

```
    System.exit(0);
  } // end of run( )


  private void paintScreen( )
  // actively render the buffer image to the screen
  {
    Graphics g;
    try {
      g = this.getGraphics( );   // get the panel's graphic context
      if ((g != null) && (dbImage != null))
        g.drawImage(dbImage, 0, 0, null);
      Toolkit.getDefaultToolkit( ).sync( );   // sync the display on some systems
      g.dispose( );
    }
    catch (Exception e)
    { System.out.println("Graphics context error: " + e);  }
  } // end of paintScreen( )
```

The call to repaint( ) is gone, as is the overriding of paintComponent( ); its functionality has been incorporated into paintScreen( ).

Active rendering puts the task of rendering the buffer image to the screen into my hands. This means that the rendering time can be accurately measured, and concerns about repaint requests being delayed or skipped by the JVM disappear.

However, the panel's graphics context may be changed by the JVM, typically when the canvas is resized or when it becomes the front window after being behind others. The context may disappear if the application or applet exits while the animation thread is running. For these reasons, the graphics context must be freshly obtained each time it is needed (by calling getGraphics( )), and its use must be surrounded by a try-catch block to capture any failure due to its disappearance.

In practice, if the program has a fixed window size, then the most likely time for an exception is when a game applet is terminated by the user closing its surrounding web page.

The call to Toolkit.sync( ) after drawImage( ) ensures that the display is promptly updated. This is required for Linux, which doesn't automatically flush its display buffer. Without the sync( ) call, the animation may be only partially updated, creating a "tearing" effect. My thanks to Kyle Husmann for pointing this out.

FPS and Sleeping for Varying Times

A weakness of the animation loop is that its execution speed is unconstrained. On a slow machine, it may loop 20 times per second; the same code on a fast machine may loop 80 times, making the game progress four times faster and perhaps making it unplayable. The loop's execution speed should be about the same on all platforms.

A popular measure of how fast an animation progresses is frames per second (FPS). For GamePanel, a frame corresponds to a single pass through the update-render-sleep loop inside run( ). Therefore, the desired 100 FPS imply that each iteration of the loop should take 1000/100 == 10 ms. This iteration time is stored in the period variable in GamePanel.

The use of active rendering makes it possible to time the update and render stages of each iteration. Subtracting this value from period gives the sleep time required to maintain the desired FPS. For instance, 100 FPS mean a period of 10 ms, and if the update/render steps take 6 ms, then sleep( ) should be called for 4 ms. Of course, this is different on each platform, so must be calculated at runtime.

The following modified run( ) method includes timing code and the sleep time calculation:

```
public void run( )
/* Repeatedly: update, render, sleep so loop takes close
   to period ms */
{
  long beforeTime, timeDiff, sleepTime;

  beforeTime = System.currentTimeMillis( );

  running = true;
  while(running) {
    gameUpdate( );
    gameRender( );
    paintScreen( );

    timeDiff = System.currentTimeMillis( ) - beforeTime;
    sleepTime = period - timeDiff;   // time left in this loop

    if (sleepTime <= 0)  // update/render took longer than period
      sleepTime = 5;     // sleep a bit anyway

    try {
      Thread.sleep(sleepTime);  // in ms
    }
    catch(InterruptedException ex){}

    beforeTime = System.currentTimeMillis( );
  }

  System.exit(0);
} // end of run( )
```

timeDiff holds the execution time for the update and render steps, which becomes part of the sleep time calculation.

One problem with this approach is if the update and drawing take longer than the specified period, then the sleep time becomes negative. The solution to this problem is to set the time to some small value to make the thread sleep a bit. This permits other threads and the JVM to execute if they wish. Obviously, this solution is still problematic: Why use 5 ms and not 2 or 20?

A more subtle issue is the resolution and accuracy of the timer and sleep operations (currentTimeMillis( ) and sleep( )). If they return inaccurate values, then the resulting FPS will be affected. These are such important problems that I'm going to spend the rest of this section looking at ways to ensure the timer has good resolution and the next major section considering sleep accuracy.

Timer Resolution

Timer resolution, or *granularity*, is the amount of time that must separate two timer calls so that different values are returned. For instance, what is the value of diff in the code fragment below?

```
long t1 = System.currentTimeMillis( );
long t2 = System.currentTimeMillis( );
long diff = t2 - t1;  // in ms
```

The value depends on the resolution of currentTimeMillis( ), which unfortunately depends on the OS.

 To be more precise, this depends on the resolution of the standard clock interrupt.

In Windows 95 and 98, the resolution is 55 ms, which means that repeated calls to currentTimeMillis( ) will only return different values roughly every 55 ms.

In the animation loop, the overall effect of poor resolution causes the animation to run slower than intended and reduces the FPS. This is due to the timeDiff value, which will be set to 0 if the game update and rendering time is less than 55 ms. This causes the sleep time to be assigned the iteration period value, rather than a smaller amount, causing each iteration to sleep longer than necessary.

To combat this, the minimum iteration period in GamePanel should be greater than 55 ms, indicating an upper limit of about 18 FPS. This frame rate is widely considered inadequate for games since the slow screen refresh appears as excessive flicker.

On Windows 2000, NT, and XP, currentTimeMillis( ) has a resolution of 10 to 15 ms, making it possible to obtain 67 to 100 FPS. This is considered acceptable to good for games. The Mac OS X and Linux have timer resolutions of 1 ms, which is excellent.

What's a Good FPS?

It's worth taking a brief diversion to consider what FPS values make for a good game.

A lower bound is dictated by the human eye and the *critical flicker frequency* (CFF), which is the rate at which a flickering light appears to be continuous. This occurs somewhere between 10 and 50 Hz, depending on the intensity of the light (translating into 10 to 50 FPS). For larger images, the position of the user relative to the image affects the perceived flicker, as well as the color contrasts and amount of detail in the picture.

Movies are shown at 24 FPS, but this number is somewhat misleading since each frame is projected onto the screen twice (or perhaps three times) by the rapid opening and closing of the projector's shutter. Thus, the viewer is actually receiving 48 (or 72) image flashes per second.

An upper bound for a good FPS values are the monitor refresh rate. This is typically 70 to 90 Hz, i.e., 70 to 90 FPS. A program doesn't need to send more frames per second than the refresh rate to the graphics card as the extra frames will not be displayed. In fact, an excessive FPS rate consumes needless CPU time and stretches the display card.

My monitor refreshes at 85 Hz, making 80 to 85 FPS the goal of the code here. This is the best FPS values since they match the monitor's refresh rate. Games often report higher values of 100 or more, but they're probably really talking about game UPS, which I'll consider a bit later on.

Am I Done Yet? (Nope)

Since the aim is about 85 FPS, then is the current animation loop sufficient for the job? Do I have to complicate it any further? For modern versions of Windows (e.g., NT, 2000, XP), the Mac, and Linux, their average/good timer resolutions mean that the current code is probably adequate.

The main problem is the resolution of the Windows 98 timer (55 ms; 18.2 FPS). Google Zeitgeist, a web site that reports interesting search patterns and trends taken from the Google search engine (*http://www.google.com/press/zeitgeist.html*), lists operating systems used to access Google. Windows 98 usage stood at about 16 percent in June 2004, having dropped from 29 percent the previous September. The winner was XP, gaining ground from 38 percent to 51 percent in the same interval.

If I'm prepared to extrapolate OS popularity from these search engine figures, then Windows 98 is rapidly on its way out. By the time you read this, sometime in 2005, Windows 98's share of the OS market will probably be below 10 percent—it may be acceptable to ignore the slowness of its timer since few people will be using it.

Well, I'm not going to give up on Windows 98 since I'm still using it at home. Also, it's well worth investigating other approaches to see if they can give better timer resolution. This will allow us to improve the frame rate and to correct for errors in the sleep time and updates per second, both discussed in later sections.

Improved J2SE Timers

J2SE 1.4.2 has a microsecond accurate timer hidden in the undocumented class sun.misc.Perf. The diff calculation can be expressed as follows:

```
Perf perf = Perf.getPerf();
long countFreq = perf.highResFrequency();

long count1 = perf.highResCounter();
long count2 = perf.highResCounter();
long diff =  (count2 - count1) * 1000000000L / countFreq ;
                 // in nanoseconds
```

Perf is not a timer but a high-resolution counter, so it is suitable for measuring time *intervals*. highResCounter() returns the current counter value, and highResFrequency(), the number of counts made per second. Perf's typical resolution is a few microseconds (2 to 6 microseconds on different versions of Windows).

My timer problems are solved in J2SE 5.0, with its System.nanoTime() method, which can be used to calculate time intervals in a similar way to the Perf timer. As the name suggests, nanoTime() returns an elapsed time in nanoseconds:

```
long count1 = System.nanoTime();
long count2 = System.nanoTime();
long diff = (count2 - count1);    // in nanoseconds
```

The resolution of nanoTime() on Windows is similar to the Perf timer (1 to 6 microseconds).

Also, J2SE 5.0's new java.util.concurrent package for concurrent programming includes a TimeUnit class that can measure down to the nanosecond level.

Using Non-J2SE Timers

It's possible to employ a high resolution timer from one of Java's extensions. The Java Media Framework (JMF) timer is an option but, since the majority of this book is about Java 3D, I'll use the J3DTimer class.

The diff calculation recoded using the Java 3D timer becomes:

```
long t1 = J3DTimer.getValue();
long t2 = J3DTimer.getValue();
long diff =  t2 - t1 ;    // in nanoseconds
```

getValue() returns a time in nanoseconds (ns). On Windows 98, the Java 3D timer has a resolution of about 900 ns, which improves to under 300 ns on my test XP box.

A drawback of using Java 3D is the need to install it in addition to J2SE, but it's quite straightforward. Sun's top-level web page for Java 3D is at *http://java.sun.com/products/java-media/3D/*. With a little work, the timer can be extracted from the rest of Java 3D, reducing the amount of software that needs to be installed. (See Appendix A for details.)

Another approach is to use a timer from a game engine. My favourite is *Meat Fighter* by Michael Birken (*http://www.meatfighter.com*). The `StopWatchSource` class provides a static method, `getStopWatch()`, which uses the best resolution timer available in your system; it considers `currentTimeMillis()` and the JMF and Java 3D timers, if present. On Windows, *Meat Fighter* includes a 40-KB DLL containing a high-resolution timer. The GAGE timer is a popular choice (*http://java.dnsalias.com/*) and can employ J2SE 5.0's `nanoTime()` if it's available.

The main issue with using a timer that isn't part of Java's standard libraries is how to package it up with a game and ensure it can be easily installed on someone else's machine. The appendixes explain how to write installation routines for games that use the Java 3D timer.

Choosing to use a non-J2SE timer is a good choice for portability reasons. Code using `nanoTime()` is not backward-compatible with earlier versions of J2SE, which means you have to ensure the gamer has J2SE 5.0 installed to play your game.

Measuring Timer Resolution

The `TimerRes` class in Example 2-2 offers a simple way to discover the resolution of the `System`, `Perf`, and Java 3D timers on your machine. `Perf` is only available in J2SE 1.4.2, and Java 3D must be installed for `J3DTimer.getResolution()` to work.

Example 2-2. Testing timer resolution

```
import com.sun.j3d.utils.timer.J3DTimer;

public class TimerRes
{
  public static void main(String args[])
  { j3dTimeResolution();
    sysTimeResolution();
    perfTimeResolution();
  }

  private static void j3dTimeResolution()
  { System.out.println("Java 3D Timer Resolution: " +
                  J3DTimer.getResolution() + " nsecs");
  }
```

Example 2-2. Testing timer resolution (continued)

```
private static void sysTimeResolution()
{
  long total, count1, count2;

  count1 = System.currentTimeMillis();
  count2 = System.currentTimeMillis();
  while(count1 == count2)
    count2 = System.currentTimeMillis();
  total = 1000L * (count2 - count1);

  count1 = System.currentTimeMillis();
  count2 = System.currentTimeMillis();
  while(count1 == count2)
    count2 = System.currentTimeMillis();
  total += 1000L * (count2 - count1);

  count1 = System.currentTimeMillis();
  count2 = System.currentTimeMillis();
  while(count1 == count2)
    count2 = System.currentTimeMillis();
  total += 1000L * (count2 - count1);

  count1 = System.currentTimeMillis();
  count2 = System.currentTimeMillis();
  while(count1 == count2)
    count2 = System.currentTimeMillis();
  total += 1000L * (count2 - count1);

  System.out.println("System Time resolution: " +
                        total/4 + " microsecs");
} // end of sysTimeResolution()


private static void perfTimeResolution()
{
  StopWatch sw = new StopWatch();
  System.out.println("Perf Resolution: " +
                  sw.getResolution() + " nsecs");

  sw.start();
  long time = sw.stop();
  System.out.println("Perf Time " + time  + " nsecs");
}

} // end of TimerRes class
```

The output for TimerRes running on a Windows 98 machine is shown below. The drawback of using currentTimeMillis() is quite apparent.

```
> java TimerRes
Java 3D Timer Resolution: 838 nsecs
System Time resolution: 55000 microsecs
```

```
    Perf Resolution: 5866 nsecs
    Perf Time 19276 nsecs
```

StopWatch is my own class (shown in Example 2-3) and wraps up the Perf counter to make it easier to use as a kind of stopwatch. A getResolution( ) method makes getting results easier.

Example 2-3. A wrapper utility for Perf

```java
import sun.misc.Perf;      // only in J2SE 1.4.2

public class StopWatch
{
  private Perf hiResTimer;
  private long freq;
  private long startTime;

  public StopWatch( )
  { hiResTimer = Perf.getPerf( );
    freq = hiResTimer.highResFrequency( );
  }

  public void start( )
  {   startTime = hiResTimer.highResCounter( ); }


  public long stop( )
  //   return the elapsed time in nanoseconds
  {   return (hiResTimer.highResCounter( ) -
                        startTime)*1000000000L/freq;   }


  public long getResolution( )
  // return counter resolution in nanoseconds
  {
    long diff, count1, count2;

    count1 = hiResTimer.highResCounter( );
    count2 = hiResTimer.highResCounter( );
    while(count1 == count2)
      count2 = hiResTimer.highResCounter( );
    diff = (count2 - count1);

    count1 = hiResTimer.highResCounter( );
    count2 = hiResTimer.highResCounter( );
    while(count1 == count2)
      count2 = hiResTimer.highResCounter( );
    diff += (count2 - count1);

    count1 = hiResTimer.highResCounter( );
    count2 = hiResTimer.highResCounter( );
    while(count1 == count2)
      count2 = hiResTimer.highResCounter( );
    diff += (count2 - count1);
```

Example 2-3. A wrapper utility for Perf (continued)

```
      count1 = hiResTimer.highResCounter();
      count2 = hiResTimer.highResCounter();
    while(count1 == count2)
      count2 = hiResTimer.highResCounter();
    diff += (count2 - count1);

    return (diff*1000000000L)/(4*freq);
  } // end of getResolution()

} // end of StopWatch class
```

The start() and stop() methods add a small overhead to the counter, as illustrated in the perfTimeResolution() method in TimerRes. The smallest time that can be obtained is around 10 to 40 ms, compared to the resolution of around 2 to 6 ms.

The resolution of System.nanoTime() can be measured using a variant of sysTimeResolution().

```
    private static void nanoTimeResolution()
    {
      long total, count1, count2;

      count1 = System.nanoTime();
      count2 = System.nanoTime();
      while(count1 == count2)
        count2 = System.nanoTime();
      total = (count2 - count1);

      count1 = System.nanoTime();
      count2 = System.nanoTime();
      while(count1 == count2)
        count2 = System.nanoTime();
      total += (count2 - count1);

      count1 = System.nanoTime();
      count2 = System.nanoTime();
      while(count1 == count2)
        count2 = System.nanoTime();
      total += (count2 - count1);

      count1 = System.nanoTime();
      count2 = System.nanoTime();
      while(count1 == count2)
        count2 = System.nanoTime();
      total += (count2 - count1);

      System.out.println("Nano Time resolution: " + total/4 + " ns");
    } // end of nanoTimeResolution()
```

The output of the method is in nanoseconds, e.g., 5866 ns for Windows 98 (about 6 ms). Here are values for other operating systems: 440 ns on Mac OS X, 1,000 ns on Linux, and 1,116 ns on Windows 2000 Pro.

Java 3D Timer Bug Alert

There's a rarely occurring bug in the J3DTimer class: J3DTimer.getResolution( ) and J3DTimer.getValue( ) return 0 on some versions of Windows XP and Linux. This can be checked by running the TimerRes application from the last section, or by executing this snippet of code:

```
System.out.println("J3DTimer resolution (ns): " + J3DTimer.getResolution( ));
System.out.println("Current time (ns): " + J3DTimer.getValue( ));
```

If there's a problem, both numbers will be 0.

This bug's history can be found at *https://java3d.dev.java.net/issues/show_bug.cgi?id=13* and has been fixed in the bug release version of Java 3D 1.3.2, which is "experimental" at the moment (December 2004), but will have been finished by the time you read this. It can be downloaded from *https://java3d.dev.java.net/*.

Here are two other solutions:

- Switch back to System.currentTimeMillis( ), which is fast enough on Windows XP.
- If you're using J2SE 5.0, then replace all the calls to J3DTimer.getValue( ) with System.nanoTime( ).

Sleeping Better

The animation loop in run( ) depends on a good timer and the accuracy of the sleep( ) call. The previous major section dealt with alternatives to currentTimeMillis( ). In this section, I consider ways of improving the sleep( ) code in run( ), so the required frame rate is consistently achieved.

The SleepAcc class measures sleep accuracy. Example 2-4 calls sleep( ) with increasingly small values and measures the actual sleep time using the Java 3D timer.

Example 2-4. Measuring sleep() accuracy

```
import java.text.DecimalFormat;
import com.sun.j3d.utils.timer.J3DTimer;

public class SleepAcc
{
  private static DecimalFormat df;

  public static void main(String args[])
  {
    df = new DecimalFormat("0.##");  // 2 dp

    // test various sleep values
    sleepTest(1000);
    sleepTest(500);
    sleepTest(200);
    sleepTest(100);
```

Example 2-4. Measuring sleep( ) accuracy (continued)

```
    sleepTest(50);
    sleepTest(20);
    sleepTest(10);
    sleepTest(5);
    sleepTest(1);
  } // end of main( )


  private static void sleepTest(int delay)
  {
    long timeStart = J3DTimer.getValue( );

    try {
      Thread.sleep(delay);
    }
    catch(InterruptedException e) {}

    double timeDiff =
        ((double)(J3DTimer.getValue( ) - timeStart))/(1000000L);
    double err = ((delay - timeDiff)/timeDiff) * 100;

    System.out.println("Slept: " + delay + " ms  J3D: " +
                        df.format(timeDiff) + " ms  err: " +
                        df.format(err) + " %" );
  }  // end of sleepTest( )

} // end of SleepAcc class
```

The difference between the requested and actual sleep delay is negligible for times of 50 ms or more and gradually increases to a +/–10 to 20 percent error at 1 ms. A typical run is:

```
D>java SleepAcc
Slept: 1000 ms   J3D: 999.81 ms  err: 0.02 %
Slept: 500 ms   J3D: 499.54 ms  err: 0.09 %
Slept: 200 ms   J3D: 199.5 ms  err: 0.25 %
Slept: 100 ms   J3D: 99.56 ms  err: 0.44 %
Slept: 50 ms   J3D: 49.59 ms  err: 0.82 %
Slept: 20 ms   J3D: 20.53 ms  err: -2.59 %
Slept: 10 ms   J3D: 10.52 ms  err: -4.91 %
Slept: 5 ms   J3D: 5.42 ms  err: -7.78 %
Slept: 1 ms   J3D: 1.15 ms  err: -13.34 %
  :  // more lines until ctrl-C is typed
```

The reason for this inaccuracy is probably due to the complexity of the operation, involving the suspension of a thread and context switching with other activities. Even after the sleep time has finished, a thread has to wait to be selected for execution by the thread scheduler. How long it has to wait depends on the overall load of the JVM (and OS) at that moment.

sleep( )'s implementation varies between operating systems and different versions of Java, making analysis difficult. Under Windows 98 and J2SE 1.4.2, sleep( ) utilizes a large native function (located in *jvm.dll*), which employs the Windows kernel sleep( ) function with a reported accuracy of 1 ms.

The conclusion is that I should extend the animation loop to combat sleep( )'s inaccuracies.

Handling Sleep Inaccuracies

This version of run( ) in this section revises the previous one in three main ways:

- It uses the Java 3D timer.
- sleep( )'s execution time is measured, and the error (stored in overSleepTime) adjusts the sleeping period in the next iteration.
- Thread.yield( ) is utilized to give other threads a chance to execute if the animation loop has not slept for a while.

Here's the updated method:

```
private static final int NO_DELAYS_PER_YIELD = 16;
/* Number of frames with a delay of 0 ms before the
   animation thread yields to other running threads. */


public void run()
/* Repeatedly update, render, sleep so loop takes close
   to period nsecs. Sleep inaccuracies are handled.
   The timing calculation use the Java 3D timer.
*/
{
  long beforeTime, afterTime, timeDiff, sleepTime;
  long overSleepTime = 0L;
  int noDelays = 0;

  beforeTime = J3DTimer.getValue();

  running = true;
  while(running) {
    gameUpdate();
    gameRender();
    paintScreen();

    afterTime = J3DTimer.getValue();
    timeDiff = afterTime - beforeTime;
    sleepTime = (period - timeDiff) - overSleepTime;

    if (sleepTime > 0) {   // some time left in this cycle
      try {
        Thread.sleep(sleepTime/1000000L);   // nano -> ms
      }
```

```
            catch(InterruptedException ex){}
            overSleepTime =
                (J3DTimer.getValue( ) - afterTime) - sleepTime;
        }
        else {     // sleepTime <= 0; frame took longer than the period
            overSleepTime = 0L;

            if (++noDelays >= NO_DELAYS_PER_YIELD) {
                Thread.yield( );   // give another thread a chance to run
                noDelays = 0;
            }
        }
        beforeTime = J3DTimer.getValue( );
    }

    System.exit(0);
} // end of run( )
```

If the sleep( ) call sleeps for 12 ms instead of the desired 10 ms, then overSleepTime
will be assigned 2 ms. On the next iteration of the loop, this value will be deducted
from the sleep time, reducing it by 2 ms. In this way, sleep inaccuracies are corrected.

If the game update and rendering steps take longer than the iteration period, then
sleepTime will have a negative value and this iteration will not include a sleep
stage. This causes the noDelays counter to be incremented, and when it reaches
NO_DELAYS_PER_YIELD, yield( ) will be called. This allows other threads to execute
if they need to and avoids the use of an arbitrary sleep period in run( ).

The switch to the Java 3D timer is mostly a matter of changing the calls to System.
currentTimeMillis( ) to J3DTimer.getValue( ). Time values change from milliseconds to nanoseconds, which motivates the change to long variables. Also, the sleep
time must be converted from nanoseconds to milliseconds before calling sleep( ), or
I'll be waiting a long time for the game to wake up.

If you prefer to use System.nanoTime( ) from J2SE 5.0, you can globally search and
replace, changing every J3DTimer.getValue( ) call to System.nanoTime( ). You don't
have to import the Java 3D packages if you choose this approach.

FPS and UPS

Apart from FPS, there is another useful measure of animation speed: UPS. The current animation loop carries out one update and one render in each iteration, but this
correspondence isn't necessary. The loop could carry out two updates per each rendering, as illustrated by the following code fragment:

```
public void run( )
// Repeatedly update, render, sleep
{ ...
  running = true;
  while(running) {
```

```
      gameUpdate();    // game state is updated
      gameUpdate();    // game state is updated again

      gameRender();    // render to a buffer
      paintScreen();   // paint with the buffer

      // sleep a bit
    }
    System.exit(0);
  } // end of run()
```

If the game offers 50 FPS (i.e., 50 iterations of the animation loop per second), then it is doing 100 updates per second.

This coding style causes the game to advance more quickly since the game state is changing twice as fast but at the cost of skipping the rendering of those extra states. However, this may not be noticeable, especially if the FPS value is 20 or higher.

Separating Updates from Rendering

One limitation on high FPS rates is the amount of time that the update and render steps require. Satisfying a period of 5 ms (1000/5 == 200 FPS) is impossible if these steps take more than 5 ms to accomplish. Most of this execution time is usually consumed by the rendering stage.

In this situation, the way to increase game speed is to increase the number of UPS. In programming terms, this translates into calling gameUpdate() more than once during each iteration. However, too many additional calls will cause the game to flicker, as too many successive states are not rendered. Each update adds to the execution time, which will further reduce the maximum achievable FPS value.

The new run() is:

```
    private static int MAX_FRAME_SKIPS = 5;
      // no. of frames that can be skipped in any one animation loop
      // i.e the games state is updated but not rendered


    public void run()
    /* Repeatedly update, render, sleep so loop takes close
       to period nsecs. Sleep inaccuracies are handled.
       The timing calculation use the Java 3D timer.

       Overruns in update/renders will cause extra updates
       to be carried out so UPS ~== requested FPS
    */
    {
      long beforeTime, afterTime, timeDiff, sleepTime;
      long overSleepTime = 0L;
      int noDelays = 0;
      long excess = 0L;

      beforeTime = J3DTimer.getValue();
```

```
    running = true;
    while(running) {
      gameUpdate( );
      gameRender( );
      paintScreen( );

      afterTime = J3DTimer.getValue( );
      timeDiff = afterTime - beforeTime;
      sleepTime = (period - timeDiff) - overSleepTime;

      if (sleepTime > 0) {    // some time left in this cycle
        try {
          Thread.sleep(sleepTime/1000000L);   // nano -> ms
        }
        catch(InterruptedException ex){}
        overSleepTime =
              (J3DTimer.getValue( ) - afterTime) - sleepTime;
      }
      else {     // sleepTime <= 0; frame took longer than the period
        excess -= sleepTime;  // store excess time value
        overSleepTime = 0L;

        if (++noDelays >= NO_DELAYS_PER_YIELD) {
          Thread.yield( );   // give another thread a chance to run
          noDelays = 0;
        }
      }

      beforeTime = J3DTimer.getValue( );

      /* If frame animation is taking too long, update the game state
         without rendering it, to get the updates/sec nearer to
         the required FPS. */
      int skips = 0;
      while((excess > period) && (skips < MAX_FRAME_SKIPS)) {
        excess -= period;
        gameUpdate( );        // update state but don't render
        skips++;
      }
    }

    System.exit(0);
  } // end of run( )
```

If the update/render step takes 12 ms and the required period is 10 ms, then sleepTime will be –2 ms (perhaps even smaller after overSleepTime has been deducted). This excessive execution time is added to the excess variable, which acts as a total of all the overruns by the update-render calls.

When excess exceeds the iteration period, the equivalent of one frame has been lost. A while loop is entered, which updates the game for each period amount lost, up to a maximum of MAX_FRAME_SKIPS (five updates). The remaining time overrun is stored for use in a later iteration. The MAX_FRAME_SKIPS value is arbitrary, but the larger it is, the more sudden the jump forward in the game may be if the maximum number of frames are skipped.

The outcome is that when a game can't update and render fast enough to match the desired FPS, then additional calls will be made to gameUpdate( ). This changes the state without rendering it, which the user sees as the game moving "faster," even though the number of rendered frames remains the same.

Pausing and Resuming

Even with the most exciting game, there comes a time when the user wants to pause it (and resume later).

One largely discredited coding approach is to use Thread.suspend( ) and resume( ). These methods are deprecated for a similar reason to Thread.stop( ); suspend( ) can cause an applet/application to suspend at any point in its execution. This can easily lead to deadlock if the thread is holding a resource since it will not be released until the thread resumes.

Instead, the Java documentation for the Thread class recommends using wait( ) and notify( ) to implement pause and resume functionality. The idea is to suspend the animation thread, but the event dispatcher thread will still respond to GUI activity. To implement this approach, I introduce an isPaused Boolean, which is set to true via pauseGame( ):

```
// global variable
private volatile boolean isPaused = false;

public void pauseGame()
{ isPaused = true;    }


public void run()
// Repeatedly (possibly pause) update, render, sleep
// This is not a good approach, and is shown for illustration only.
{ ...
  running = true;
  while(running) {
    try {
      if (isPaused) {
        synchronized(this) {
          while (isPaused && running)
            wait();
        }
      }
    } // of try block
    catch (InterruptedException e){}

    gameUpdate();   // game state is updated
    gameRender();   // render to a buffer
    paintScreen();  // paint with the buffer
```

```
     // sleep a bit
   }
   System.exit(0);
} // end of run()
```

The isPaused flag is detected in run( ) and triggers a wait( ) call to suspend the animation thread. The flag must be volatile so run( ) is sure to see the change made by pauseGame( ) (otherwise the variable may be cached locally).

The thread is resumed by resumeGame( ) or stopGame( ), both of which call notify( ). These methods must be synchronized so the animation thread doesn't miss the notification and remain suspended indefinitely:

```
public synchronized void resumeGame( )
{  isPaused = false;    // I do not do this
   notify( );
}

public synchronized void stopGame( )
{  running = false;     // I do not do this
   notify( );
}
```

This coding style can be criticized for combining two notions: game pausing/resuming and program pausing/resuming. This is the main reason why I do not use it.

Though the elements of the game seen by the user can pause, it is often useful for the other parts to continue executing. For example, in a network game, it may be necessary to monitor sockets for messages coming from other players.

The drawback of keeping the application running is the cost of executing the animation thread when the user is not playing.

My approach uses an isPaused Boolean, which is set with pauseGame( ):

```
// this is my approach
private volatile boolean isPaused = false;

public void pauseGame( )
{ isPaused = true;    }
```

However, isPaused is not monitored in run( ) since the animation thread doesn't suspend. isPaused is used to switch off testPress( ) and gameUpdate( ):

```
private void testPress(int x, int y)
// is (x,y) important to the game?
{
   if (!isPaused && !gameOver) {
     // do something
   }
}
```

```
    private void gameUpdate( )
    { if (!isPaused && !gameOver)
        // update game state ...
    }
```

Key presses are still handled by the KeyListener method since it must be possible to quit even in the paused state.

isPaused is set to false with resumeGame( ):

```
    public void resumeGame( )
    {  isPaused = false;  }
```

The animation loop isn't suspended when isPaused is set true, so rendering will continue. This is important if the game screen is iconified and expanded or is momentarily obscured by another window. The game will only be redrawn if the animation loop is still operating. By contrast, a game loop using paint( ) or paintComponent( ) can be suspended since the JVM will automatically call these methods when the game window is redisplayed.

When to Pause

The situations that trigger pausing and resuming vary between the different types of Java programs.

In an applet, the animation should pause when the applet is stopped and should resume when the applet is restarted by the browser. A stop occurs when the user leaves the page, for example, to go to another page. When the user returns to the page, the applet starts again. The same sequence should be triggered when the user minimizes the applet's page and reopens it later.

In an application, pausing should be initiated when the window is minimized or deactivated, and execution should resume when the window is enlarged or activated. A window is deactivated when it is obscured and activated when brought back to the front.

In a full-screen application, pausing and resumption will be controlled by buttons on the canvas since the user interface lacks a title bar and the OS taskbar is hidden.

Examples of these approaches can be found in Chapters 3 and 4.

Other Animation Approaches

This chapter has been concerned with developing a threaded animation loop inside a JPanel. But other ways of implementing animation in Java exist, and I'll briefly consider two of them:

* Using the Swing timer
* Using the utility timer from java.util.timer

Both of them use a timer to trigger method calls at regular intervals. However, I'll present timing figures that show that the Swing timer doesn't have the necessary accuracy for my needs, while the utility timer is a possible alternative.

Swing Timer Animation

The Swing timer (in `javax.swing.Timer`) is used as the basis of animation examples in many Java textbooks.

The essential coding technique is to set a `Timer` object to "tick" every few milliseconds. Each tick sends an event to a specified `ActionEvent` listener, triggering a call to `actionPerformed()`. `actionPerformed()` calls `repaint()` to send a repaint request to the JVM. Eventually, repainting reaches the `paintComponent()` method for the `JPanel`, which redraws the animation canvas. These stages are shown in Figure 2-1, which represents the test code in *SwingTimerTest.java*.

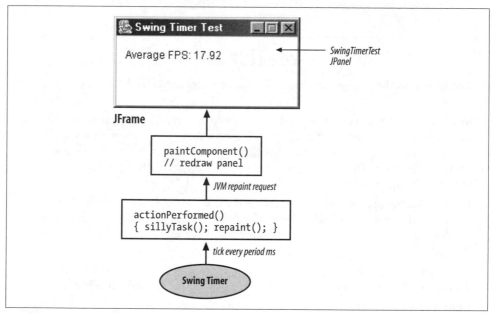

Figure 2-1. Swing timer animation

The `SwingTimerTest` class uses the Swing timer to draw the current average FPS values repeatedly into a `JPanel`. The period for the timer is obtained from the requested FPS given on the command line. The average FPS are calculated every second, based on FPS values collected over the previous 10 seconds.

`main()` reads in the user's required FPS and converts them to a period. It creates a `JFrame` and puts the `SwingTimerPanel` inside it.

The `SwingTimerTest()` constructor creates the timer and sends its "ticks" to itself:

```
new Timer(period, this).start();
```

`actionPerformed( )` wastes some time by calling a `sillyTask( )` method that does a lot of looping and then requests a repaint:

```
public void actionPerformed(ActionEvent e)
{ sillyTask( );
  repaint( );
}
```

`paintComponent( )` updates the JPanel and records statistics:

```
public void paintComponent(Graphics g)
{
  super.paintComponent(g);

  // clear the background
  g.setColor(Color.white);
  g.fillRect (0, 0, PWIDTH, PHEIGHT);

  // report average FPS
  g.setColor(Color.black);
  g.drawString("Average FPS: " + df.format(averageFPS), 10, 25);

  reportStats( );   // record/report statistics
} // end of paintComponent( )
```

The most complicated part of this example is the statistics gathering done by `reportStats( )`. It's worth looking at the code since it appears again in Chapters 3 and 4.

`reportStats( )` prints a line of statistics every second:

```
D>java SwingTimerTest 50
fps: 50; period: 20 ms
1 3.0099s 200.99% 50c 16.61 16.61 afps
1 2.7573s 175.73% 100c 17.34 16.98 afps
1 2.7344s 173.44% 150c 17.64 17.2 afps
1 2.746s 174.6% 200c 17.78 17.34 afps
1 2.7545s 175.45% 250c 17.85 17.45 afps
1 2.7522s 175.22% 300c 17.91 17.52 afps
1 2.7299s 172.99% 350c 17.96 17.59 afps
1 2.7581s 175.81% 400c 17.98 17.64 afps
  :  // more lines until ctrl-C is typed
```

The first line of the output lists the requested FPS and the corresponding period used by the timer. It's followed by multiple statistic lines, with a new line generated when the accumulated timer period reaches 1 second since the last line was printed.

Each statistics line presents six numbers. The first three relate to the execution time. The first number is the accumulated timer period since the last output, which will be close to one second. The second number is the actual elapsed time, measured with the Java 3D timer, and the third value is the percentage error between the two numbers.

The fourth number is the total number of calls to `paintComponent( )` since the program began, which should increase by the requested FPS value each second.

The fifth number is the current FPS, calculated by dividing the total number of calls by the total elapsed time since the program began. The sixth number is an average of the last 10 FPS numbers (or fewer, if 10 numbers haven't been calculated yet).

The reportStats( ) method, and its associated global variables, are shown here:

```
private static long MAX_STATS_INTERVAL = 1000L;
  // record stats every 1 second (roughly)

private static int NUM_FPS = 10;
   // number of FPS values stored to get an average

// used for gathering statistics
private long statsInterval = 0L;     // in ms
private long prevStatsTime;
private long totalElapsedTime = 0L;

private long frameCount = 0;
private double fpsStore[];
private long statsCount = 0;
private double averageFPS = 0.0;

private DecimalFormat df = new DecimalFormat("0.##");  // 2 dp
private DecimalFormat timedf = new DecimalFormat("0.####");  //4 dp

private int period;        // period between drawing in ms

private void reportStats( )
{
  frameCount++;
  statsInterval += period;

  if (statsInterval >= MAX_STATS_INTERVAL) {
    long timeNow = J3DTimer.getValue( );

    long realElapsedTime = timeNow - prevStatsTime;
           // time since last stats collection
    totalElapsedTime += realElapsedTime;

    long sInterval = (long)statsInterval*1000000L;   // ms --> ns
    double timingError =
       ((double)(realElapsedTime - sInterval)) / sInterval * 100.0;

    double actualFPS = 0;     // calculate the latest FPS
    if (totalElapsedTime > 0)
      actualFPS = (((double)frameCount / totalElapsedTime) * 1000000000L);
    // store the latest FPS
    fpsStore[ (int)statsCount%NUM_FPS ] = actualFPS;
    statsCount = statsCount+1;

    double totalFPS = 0.0;      // total the stored FPSs
    for (int i=0; i < NUM_FPS; i++)
      totalFPS += fpsStore[i];
```

```
            if (statsCount < NUM_FPS)   // obtain the average FPS
                averageFPS = totalFPS/statsCount;
            else
                averageFPS = totalFPS/NUM_FPS;

            System.out.println(
                timedf.format( (double) statsInterval/1000) + " " +
                timedf.format((double) realElapsedTime/1000000000L) + "s " +
                df.format(timingError) + "% " +
                frameCount + "c " +
                df.format(actualFPS) + " " +
                df.format(averageFPS) + " afps"   );

            prevStatsTime = timeNow;
            statsInterval = 0L;   // reset
        }
    }  // end of reportStats()
```

reportStats( ) is called in paintComponent( ) after the timer has "ticked." This is recognized by incrementing frameCount and adding the period amount to statsInterval.

The FPS values are stored in the fpsStore[] array. When the array is full, new values overwrite the old ones by cycling around the array. The average FPS smooth over variations in the application's execution time.

Table 2-1 shows the reported average FPS on different versions of Windows when the requested FPSs were 20, 50, 80, and 100.

Table 2-1. Reported average FPS for SwingTimerTest

Requested FPS	20	50	80	100
Windows 98	18	18	18	18
Windows 2000	19	49	49	98
Windows XP	16	32	64	64

Each test was run three times on a lightly loaded machine, running for a few minutes. The results show a wide variation in the accuracy of the timer, but the results for the 80 FPS request are poor to downright awful in all cases. The Swing timer can't be recommended for high frame rate games.

The timer is designed for repeatedly triggering actions after a fixed period. However, the actual action frequency can drift because of extra delays introduced by the garbage collector or long-running game updates and rendering. It may be possible to code round this by dynamically adjusting the timer's period using setDelay( ).

The timer uses currentTimeMillis( ) internally, with its attendant resolution problems.

The official Java tutorial contains more information about the Swing timer and animation, located in the Swing trail in "Performing Animations" (*http://java.sun.com/docs/books/tutorial/uiswing/painting/animation.html*).

The Utility Timer

A timer is available in the java.util.Timer class. Instead of scheduling calls to actionPerformed( ), the run( ) method of a TimerTask object is invoked.

The utility timer provides more flexibility over scheduling than the Swing timer: Tasks can run at a fixed rate or a fixed period after a previous task. The latter approach is similar to the Swing timer and means that the timing of the calls can drift. In fixed-rate scheduling, each task is scheduled relative to the scheduled execution time of the initial task. If a task is delayed for any reason (such as garbage collection), two or more tasks will occur in rapid succession to catch up.

The most important difference between javax.Swing.Timer and java.util.Timer is that the latter does not run its tasks in the event dispatching thread. Consequently, the test code employs three classes: one for the timer, consisting of little more than a main( ) function, a subclass of TimerTask for the repeated task, and a subclass of JPanel as a canvas.

These components are shown in Figure 2-2, which represents the test code in *UtilTimerTest.java.*

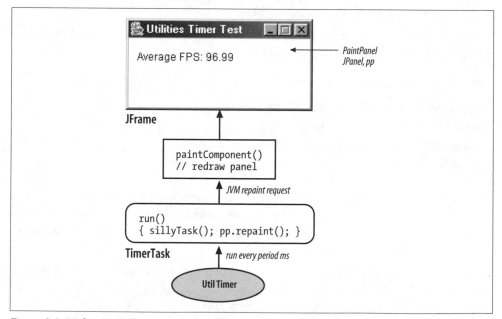

Figure 2-2. Utility timer animation

The timer schedules the TimerTask at a fixed rate:

```
MyTimerTask task = new MyTimerTask(...);
Timer t = new Timer( );
t.scheduleAtFixedRate(task, 0, period);
```

The `TimerTask` `run( )` method wastes some time looping in `sillyTask( )` and then repaints its JPanel:

```
class MyTimerTask extends TimerTask
{
  // global variables and other methods

  public void run( )
  { sillyTask( );
    pp.repaint( );
  }

  private void sillyTask( )
  {...}

} // end of MyTimerTask
```

The `JPanel` is subclassed to paint the current average FPS values onto the canvas, and to call `reportStats( )` to record timing information. Its `paintComponent( )` and `reportStats( )` are the same as in `SwingTimerTest`.

Table 2-2 shows the reported average FPS on different versions of Windows, when the requested FPSs are 20, 50, 80, and 100.

Table 2-2. Reported average FPSs for UtilTimerTest

Requested FPS	20	50	80	100
Windows 98	20	47	81	94
Windows 2000	20	50	83	99
Windows XP	20	50	83	95

The average FPS are excellent, which is somewhat surprising since `currentTimeMillis( )` is employed in the timer's scheduler. The average hides that it takes 1 to 2 minutes for the frame rate to rise towards the average. Also, JVM garbage collection reduces the FPS for a few seconds each time it occurs.

The average FPS for a requested 80 FPS are often near 83 due to a quirk of my coding. The frame rate is converted to an integer period using (int) 1000/80 == 12 ms. Later, this is converted back to a frame rate of 1000/12, which is 83.333.

The drawback of the utility timer is that the details of the timer and sleeping operations are mostly out of reach of the programmer and so, are not easily modified, unlike the threaded animation loop.

The Java tutorial contains information about the utility timer and `TimerTasks` in the threads trail under the heading "Using the Timer and TimerTask Classes" (*http:// java.sun.com/docs/books/tutorial/essential/threads/timer.html*).

CHAPTER 3

Worms in Windows and Applets

In this chapter, I test the threaded animation loop of Chapter 2 inside a windowed application and an applet. To simplify comparisons between the approaches, the programs are all variants of the same WormChase game. In Chapter 4, I will continue the comparisons, concentrating on several kinds of full-screen applications.

Figure 3-1 shows the windowed WormChase application on the left and the applet version on the right.

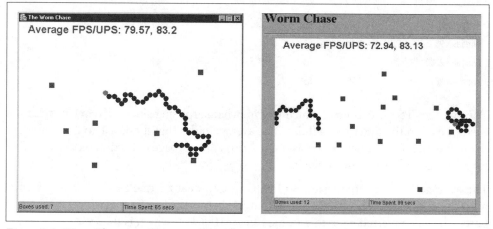

Figure 3-1. WormChase in a JFrame and JApplet

The aim of the game is to click the cursor on the red head of the rapidly moving worm. If the player misses the worm's head, then a blue box is added to the canvas (unless the worm's black body was clicked upon).

The worm must go around the boxes in its path, so the boxes may make the worm easier to catch. When the worm moves off the top edge of the window it appears at the bottom, and vice versa. When it travels past the left or right edge, it appears at the opposite side. The worm gradually gets longer until it reaches a maximum length, which it maintains for the rest of the game.

When the game finishes, a score is displayed in the center of the window, calculated from the number of boxes used and the time taken to catch the worm. Fewer boxes and less time will produce a higher score. The current time and the number of boxes are displayed below the game canvas in two text fields.

Preliminary Considerations

This chapter and the next are concerned with several variants of WormChase, and a few issues apply to all the versions which need to be considered before we begin.

The Choice of Timer

The main drawback of the animation loop in Chapter 2 is the need to install Java 3D so its timer is available. Consequently, two versions of the windowed WormChase application are investigated here: one using the Java 3D timer and the other using the System timer. A comparison of the two will show when the Java 3D timer is beneficial.

 As mentioned in the last chapter, programmers using J2SE 5.0 may choose to do a global search and replace on the Java 3D timer version of WormChase, changing every J3DTimer.getValue( ) call to System.nanoTime( ).

Class Reuse

All the WormChase versions in this chapter and the next use the same game-specific classes (i.e., Worm and Obstacles, shown throughout this chapter). They employ a similar WormPanel class, which corresponds to the GamePanel animation class in Chapter 2.

The main differences between the programs lie in their top-level classes. For example, in this chapter, the windowed application uses a subclass of JFrame while the applet utilizes JApplet. This requires changes to how game pausing and resumption are triggered, and the way of specifying the required FPS.

Testing for Speed

Testing is done via the gathering of statistics using a version of the reportStats( ) method detailed in the section "Swing Timer Animation" in Chapter 2. The main change to that method is that the average UPS are calculated alongside the average FPS. The overall aim of the testing is to see if the animation loop can deliver 80 to 85 FPS. Failing this, the programs should produce 80 to 85 updates per second without an excessive number of frames being skipped.

Class Diagrams for the WormChase Application

Figure 3-2 shows the class diagrams for the WormChase application. The class names and public methods are shown.

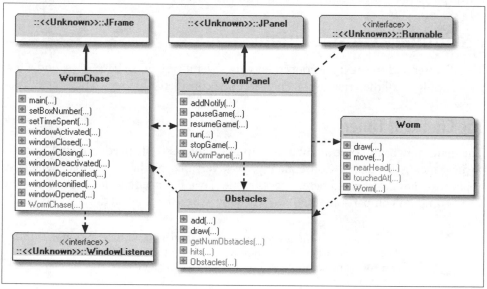

Figure 3-2. Class diagrams for the WormChase application

 The code for this version of WormChase is in the directory *Worm/WormP/*.

WormChase is the top-level JFrame, managing the GUI, and processing window events. WormPanel is the game panel holding the threaded animation loop.

The Worm class maintains the data structures and methods for the on-screen worm. The Obstacles class handles the blue boxes. Worm and Obstacles have their own draw() method, which is called by WormPanel to render the worm and boxes.

The Worm-Chasing Application

Figure 3-3 shows a class diagram for WormChase, including all its variables and methods.

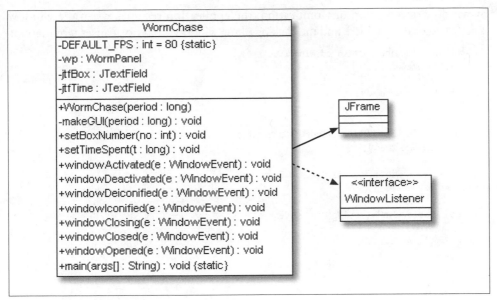

Figure 3-3. WormChase in detail

The main( ) function in WormChase reads the requested FPS from the command line, converting it to a delay in *nanoseconds*, which is passed to the WormChase( ) constructor:

```
public static void main(String args[])
{
  int fps = DEFAULT_FPS;
  if (args.length != 0)
    fps = Integer.parseInt(args[0]);

  long period = (long) 1000.0/fps;
  System.out.println("fps: " + fps + "; period: " +period+ " ms");

  new WormChase(period*1000000L);     // ms --> nanosecs
}
```

The WormChase constructor creates the WormPanel canvas, as well as two text fields for displaying the number of boxes added to the scene (jtfBox) and the current time (jtfTime). These text fields can be updated via two public methods:

```
public void setBoxNumber(int no)
{  jtfBox.setText("Boxes used: " + no);  }

public void setTimeSpent(long t)
{  jtfTime.setText("Time Spent: " + t + " secs");  }
```

setBoxNumber( ) is called from the Obstacles object when a new box (obstacle) is created. setTimeSpent( ) is called from WormPanel.

The pausing, resumption, and termination of the game are managed through window listener methods (WormChase implements WindowListener). Pausing is triggered by window deactivation or iconification; the application resumes when the window is activated or de-iconified, and the clicking of the window close box causes termination:

```
public void windowActivated(WindowEvent e)
{ wp.resumeGame( );  }

public void windowDeactivated(WindowEvent e)
{  wp.pauseGame( );  }

public void windowDeiconified(WindowEvent e)
{  wp.resumeGame( );  }

public void windowIconified(WindowEvent e)
{  wp.pauseGame( ); }

public void windowClosing(WindowEvent e)
{  wp.stopGame( );  }
```

wp refers to the WormPanel object.

The Game Panel

The WormPanel class is similar to the GamePanel class developed in Chapter 2, with some additional methods for drawing the game scene. WormPanel contains an extended version of the reportStats( ) method used for timing the Swing and utility timers in Chapter 2, called printStats( ). Its principal extension is to report the average UPS (updates per second) in addition to the average FPS.

A class diagram showing all the WormPanel methods is given in Figure 3-4.

The WormPanel constructor sets up the game components and initializes timing elements:

```
public WormPanel(WormChase wc, long period)
{
  wcTop = wc;
  this.period = period;

  setBackground(Color.white);
  setPreferredSize( new Dimension(PWIDTH, PHEIGHT));

  setFocusable(true);
  requestFocus( );    // now has focus, so receives key events
  readyForTermination( );

  // create game components
  obs = new Obstacles(wcTop);
  fred = new Worm(PWIDTH, PHEIGHT, obs);

  addMouseListener( new MouseAdapter() {
    public void mousePressed(MouseEvent e)
```

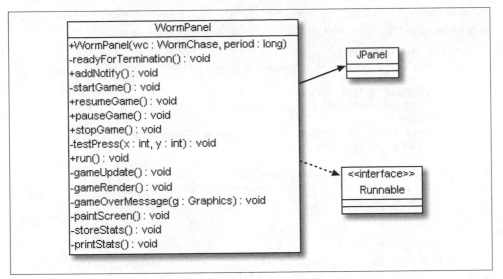

Figure 3-4. WormPanel methods in detail

```
    { testPress(e.getX( ), e.getY( )); }
  });

  // set up message font
  font = new Font("SansSerif", Font.BOLD, 24);
  metrics = this.getFontMetrics(font);

  // initialise timing elements
  fpsStore = new double[NUM_FPS];
  upsStore = new double[NUM_FPS];
  for (int i=0; i < NUM_FPS; i++) {
    fpsStore[i] = 0.0;
    upsStore[i] = 0.0;
  }
}  // end of WormPanel( )
```

The time period intended for each frame (in nanoseconds) is passed to WormPanel from WormChase and stored in a global variable. readyForTermination( ) is the same as in Chapter 2: a KeyListener monitors the input for termination characters (e.g., Ctrl-C), then sets the running Boolean to false.

The message font is used to report the score when the game ends. fpsStore[] and upsStore[] are global arrays holding the previous ten FPS and UPS values calculated by the statistics code.

User Input

The testPress( ) method handles mouse presses on the canvas, which will be aimed at the worm's red head. If the press is sufficiently near to the head, then the game is won. If the press touches the worm's body (the black circles), then nothing occurs; otherwise, an obstacle is added to the scene at that (x, y) location:

```
private void testPress(int x, int y)
// is (x,y) near the head or should an obstacle be added?
{
  if (!isPaused && !gameOver) {
    if (fred.nearHead(x,y)) {    // was mouse press near the head?
      gameOver = true;
      score = (40 - timeSpentInGame) + 40 - obs.getNumObstacles());
          // hack together a score
    }
    else {    // add an obstacle if possible
      if (!fred.touchedAt(x,y))    // was worm's body not touched?
        obs.add(x,y);
    }
  }
} // end of testPress()
```

testPress( ) starts by testing isPaused and gameOver. If isPaused is true then the game is paused, and mouse presses should be ignored. Similarly, if the game is over (gameOver == true), then the input is disregarded.

WormChase's WindowListener methods respond to window events by calling the following methods in WormPanel to affect the isPaused and running flags:

```
public void resumeGame()
// called when the JFrame is activated / deiconified
{  isPaused = false;  }

public void pauseGame()
// called when the JFrame is deactivated / iconified
{  isPaused = true;   }

public void stopGame()
// called when the JFrame is closing
{  running = false;   }
```

As discussed in Chapter 2, pausing and resumption don't utilize the Thread wait( ) and notify( ) methods to affect the animation thread.

The Animation Loop

For the sake of completeness, I include the run( ) method from WormPanel. The parts of it which differ from the animation loop in the section "Separating Updates from Rendering" in Chapter 2 are marked in bold:

```
public void run()
/* The frames of the animation are drawn inside the while loop. */
{
  long beforeTime, afterTime, timeDiff, sleepTime;
  long overSleepTime = 0L;
  int noDelays = 0;
  long excess = 0L;
```

```
    gameStartTime = J3DTimer.getValue();
    prevStatsTime = gameStartTime;
    beforeTime = gameStartTime;

    running = true;
    while(running) {
      gameUpdate();
      gameRender();
      paintScreen();

      afterTime = J3DTimer.getValue();
      timeDiff = afterTime - beforeTime;
      sleepTime = (period - timeDiff) - overSleepTime;

      if (sleepTime > 0) {    // some time left in this cycle
        try {
          Thread.sleep(sleepTime/1000000L);  // nano -> ms
        }
        catch(InterruptedException ex){}
        overSleepTime = (J3DTimer.getValue() - afterTime) - sleepTime;
      }
      else {     // sleepTime <= 0; frame took longer than the period
        excess -= sleepTime;   // store excess time value
        overSleepTime = 0L;

        if (++noDelays >= NO_DELAYS_PER_YIELD) {
          Thread.yield();    // give another thread a chance to run
          noDelays = 0;
        }
      }

      beforeTime = J3DTimer.getValue();

      /* If frame animation is taking too long, update the game state
         without rendering it, to get the updates/sec nearer to
         the required FPS. */
      int skips = 0;
      while((excess > period) && (skips < MAX_FRAME_SKIPS)) {
        excess -= period;
        gameUpdate();     // update state but don't render
        skips++;
      }
      framesSkipped += skips;

      storeStats();
    }

    printStats();
    System.exit(0);    // so window disappears
  } // end of run()
```

The global variables, gameStartTime and prevStatsTime, are utilized in the statistics calculations, as is the frameSkipped variable. frameSkipped holds the total number of skipped frames since the last UPS calculation in storeStats(). printStats() reports selected numbers and statistics at program termination time.

Statistics Gathering

storeStats() is a close relative of the reportStats() method of the section "Swing Timer Animation" in Chapter 2. Again for completeness, I list the method here, as well as the new global variables which it manipulates in addition to the ones described in Chapter 2. The parts of reportStats(), which are new (or changed), are marked in bold:

```
// used for gathering statistics
    : // many, see "Swing Timer Animation" section, chapter 2
private long gameStartTime;
private int timeSpentInGame = 0;    // in seconds

private long framesSkipped = 0L;
private long totalFramesSkipped = 0L;
private double upsStore[];
private double averageUPS = 0.0;


private void storeStats()
{
  frameCount++;
  statsInterval += period;

  if (statsInterval >= MAX_STATS_INTERVAL) {
    long timeNow = J3DTimer.getValue();
    timeSpentInGame =
      (int) ((timeNow - gameStartTime)/1000000000L);   // ns-->secs
    wcTop.setTimeSpent( timeSpentInGame );

    long realElapsedTime = timeNow - prevStatsTime;
        // time since last stats collection
    totalElapsedTime += realElapsedTime;

    double timingError = (double)
        (realElapsedTime-statsInterval) / statsInterval)*100.0;

    totalFramesSkipped += framesSkipped;

    double actualFPS = 0;     // calculate the latest FPS and UPS
    double actualUPS = 0;
    if (totalElapsedTime > 0) {
      actualFPS = (((double)frameCount / totalElapsedTime) *
                                        1000000000L);
      actualUPS = (((double)(frameCount + totalFramesSkipped) /
                    totalElapsedTime) * 1000000000L);
    }

    // store the latest FPS and UPS
    fpsStore[ (int)statsCount%NUM_FPS ] = actualFPS;
```

```
        upsStore[ (int)statsCount%NUM_FPS ] = actualUPS;
        statsCount = statsCount+1;

        double totalFPS = 0.0;      // total the stored FPSs and UPSs
        double totalUPS = 0.0;
        for (int i=0; i < NUM_FPS; i++) {
          totalFPS += fpsStore[i];
          totalUPS += upsStore[i];
        }

        if (statsCount < NUM_FPS) { // obtain the average FPS and UPS
          averageFPS = totalFPS/statsCount;
          averageUPS = totalUPS/statsCount;
        }
        else {
          averageFPS = totalFPS/NUM_FPS;
          averageUPS = totalUPS/NUM_FPS;
        }
/*
    System.out.println(
        timedf.format( (double) statsInterval/1000000000L) + " " +
        timedf.format((double) realElapsedTime/1000000000L)+"s "+
        df.format(timingError) + "% " +
        frameCount + "c " +
        framesSkipped + "/" + totalFramesSkipped + " skip; " +
        df.format(actualFPS) + " " + df.format(averageFPS)+" afps; " +
        df.format(actualUPS) + " " + df.format(averageUPS)+" aups" );
*/
        framesSkipped = 0;
        prevStatsTime = timeNow;
        statsInterval = 0L;    // reset
      }
    }  // end of storeStats()
```

gameStartTime is used to calculate timeSpentInGame, which WormPanel reports to the player by writing to the time text field in the top-level window. As in Chapter 2, the statsInterval value is a sum of the requested periods adding up to MAX_STATS_INTERVAL. The difference is that the period is measured in nanoseconds here (due to the use of the Java 3D timer). This means that the timingError calculation doesn't need to translate the statsInterval value from milliseconds to nanoseconds before using it.

The main additions to storeStats() are the calculation of UPS values, the storage in the upsStore[] array, and the use of that array to calculate an average UPS. The UPS value comes from these statements:

```
totalFramesSkipped += framesSkipped;

actualUPS = (((double)(frameCount + totalFramesSkipped) /
                  totalElapsedTime) * 1000000000L);
```

frameCount is the total number of rendered frames in the game so far, which is added to the total number of skipped frames.

A skipped frame is a game state update which wasn't rendered.

The total is equivalent to the total number of game updates. The division by the total elapsed time and multiplication by 1,000,000,000 gives the UPS.

The large `println( )` call in `storeStats( )` produces a line of statistics. It is commented out since it is intended for debugging purposes. Here is the typical output:

```
>java WormChase 80
fps: 80; period: 12 ms
1.008 1.2805s 27.03% 84c 22/22 skip; 65.6 65.6 afps; 82.78 82.78 aups
1.008 1.0247s 1.66% 168c 2/24 skip; 72.88 69.24 afps; 83.29 83.04 aups
1.008 1.0287s 2.06% 252c 1/25 skip; 75.59 71.36 afps; 83.08 83.05 aups
1.008 1.0107s 0.27% 336c 0/25 skip; 77.34 72.85 afps; 83.09 83.06 aups
1.008 1.0087s 0.07% 420c 0/25 skip; 78.46 73.97 afps; 83.13 83.07 aups
1.008 1.0087s 0.07% 504c 0/25 skip; 79.22 74.85 afps; 83.15 83.09 aups
1.008 1.0087s 0.07% 588c 0/25 skip; 79.77 75.55 afps; 83.17 83.1 aups
1.008 1.0088s 0.08% 672c 0/25 skip; 80.19 76.13 afps; 83.18 83.11 aups
Frame Count/Loss: 707 / 25
Average FPS: 76.13
Average UPS: 83.11
Time Spent: 8 secs
Boxes used: 0
```

Each statistics line presents ten numbers. The first three relate to the execution time. The first number is the accumulated timer period since the last output, which will be close to one second. The second number is the actual elapsed time, measured with the Java 3D timer, and the third value is the percentage error between the two numbers.

The fourth number is the total number of calls to `run( )` since the program began, which should increase by the FPS value each second. The fifth and sixth numbers (separated by a /) are the frames skipped in this interval and the total number of frames skipped since the game began. A frame skip is a game update without a corresponding render. The seventh and eighth numbers are the current UPS and average. The ninth and tenth numbers are the current FPS and the average.

The output after the statistics lines comes from `printStats( )`, which is called as `run( )` is finishing. It gives a briefer summary of the game characteristics:

```
private void printStats()
{
  System.out.println("Frame Count/Loss: " + frameCount +
                     " / " + totalFramesSkipped);
  System.out.println("Average FPS: " + df.format(averageFPS));
  System.out.println("Average UPS: " + df.format(averageUPS));
  System.out.println("Time Spent: " + timeSpentInGame + " secs");
  System.out.println("Boxes used: " + obs.getNumObstacles());
} // end of printStats()
```

Drawing the Canvas

The behavior specific to the WormChase game originates in two method calls at the start of the animation loop:

```
while(running) {
  gameUpdate();      // game state is updated
  gameRender();      // render to a buffer
  paintScreen();     // paint with the buffer

  // sleep a bit
  // perhaps call gameUpdate()
  // gather statistics
}
```

gameUpdate() changes the game state every frame. For WormChase, this consists of requesting that the worm (called fred) moves:

```
private void gameUpdate()
{ if (!isPaused && !gameOver)
    fred.move();
}
```

The details of the move are left to fred in the usual object-oriented style. No move will be requested if the game is paused or has finished.

gameRender() draws the game elements (e.g., the worm and obstacles) to an image acting as a buffer:

```
private void gameRender()
{
  if (dbImage == null){
    dbImage = createImage(PWIDTH, PHEIGHT);
    if (dbImage == null) {
      System.out.println("dbImage is null");
      return;
    }
    else
      dbg = dbImage.getGraphics();
  }

  // clear the background
  dbg.setColor(Color.white);
  dbg.fillRect (0, 0, PWIDTH, PHEIGHT);

  dbg.setColor(Color.blue);
  dbg.setFont(font);

  // report average FPS and UPS at top left
  dbg.drawString("Average FPS/UPS: " + df.format(averageFPS) +
          ", " + df.format(averageUPS), 20, 25);

  dbg.setColor(Color.black);
```

```
    // draw game elements: the obstacles and the worm
    obs.draw(dbg);
    fred.draw(dbg);

    if (gameOver)
      gameOverMessage(dbg);
  } // end of gameRender( )
```

gameRender( ) begins in the manner described in Chapter 2: the first call to the method causes the image and its graphics context to be created, and the following lines draw the background, game elements, and finally the "game over" message. The ordering is important: things further back in the game are drawn first.

 A useful debugging addition to gameRender( ) is to draw the average FPS and UPS values on the canvas; these operations would normally be commented out when the coding is completed.

The actual game elements are drawn by passing draw requests onto the worm and the obstacles objects:

```
    obs.draw(dbg);
    fred.draw(dbg);
```

This approach relieves the game panel of drawing work and moves the drawing activity to the object responsible for the game component's behavior.

The gameOverMessage( ) method uses font metrics and the length of the message to place it in the center of the drawing area. Typical output is shown in Figure 3-5.

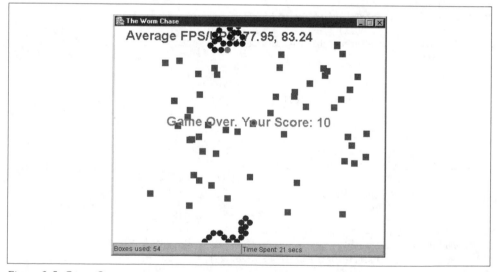

Figure 3-5. Game Over message

As the number of obstacles indicates, a frame rate of 80 FPS makes it very difficult for the player to hit the worm.

paintScreen() actively renders the buffer image to the JPanel canvas and is unchanged from the section "Converting to Active Rendering" in Chapter 2:

```
private void paintScreen()
// use active rendering to put the buffered image on-screen
{
  Graphics g;
  try {
    g = this.getGraphics();
    if ((g != null) && (dbImage != null))
      g.drawImage(dbImage, 0, 0, null);
    Toolkit.getDefaultToolkit().sync();  // sync the display on some systems
    g.dispose();
  }
  catch (Exception e)
  { System.out.println("Graphics context error: " + e);  }
} // end of paintScreen()
```

Storing Worm Information

The Worm class stores coordinate information about the worm in a circular buffer. It includes testing methods for checking if the player has clicked near the worm's head or body and includes methods for moving and drawing the worm.

The issues which make things more complicated include:

- Having the worm grow in length up to a maximum size
- Regulating the worm's movements to be semi-random so that it mostly moves in a forward direction
- Getting the worm to go around obstacles in its path

Growing a Worm

The worm is grown by storing a series of Point objects in a cells[] array. Each point represents the location of one of the black circles of the worm's body (and the red circle for its head). As the worm grows, more points are added to the array until it is full; the worm's maximum extent is equivalent to the array's size.

Movement of the full-size worm is achieved by creating a new head circle at its front and removing the tail circle (if necessary). This removal frees up a space in the cells[] array where the point for the new head can be stored.

The growing and movement phases are illustrated by Figure 3-6, which shows how the cells[] array is gradually filled and then reused. The two indices, headPosn and tailPosn, make it simple to modify the head and tail of the worm, and nPoints records the length of the worm.

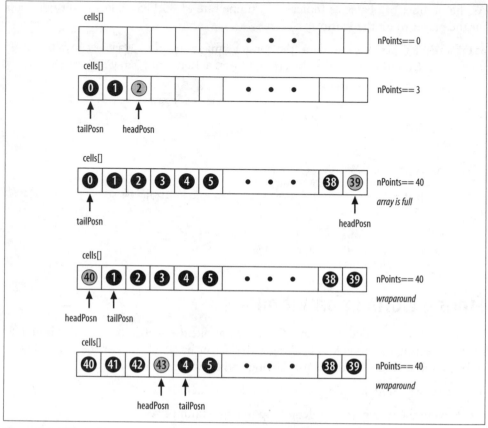

Figure 3-6. Worm data structures during growth and movement

The numbered black dots (and red dot) represent the Point objects which store the
(x, y) coordinates of the worm's parts. The numbers are included in the figure to
indicate the order in which the array is filled and over-written; they are not part of
the actual data structure, which is defined like so:

```
private static final int MAXPOINTS = 40;

private Point cells[];
private int nPoints;
private int tailPosn, headPosn;    // tail and head of buffer
// additional variables already defined

cells = new Point[MAXPOINTS];    // initialise buffer
nPoints = 0;
headPosn = -1;  tailPosn = -1;
```

The other important Worm data structure is its current bearing, which can be in one of eight predefined compass directions: N = north, NE = northeast, and so on, around to NW = northwest. The choices are shown in Figure 3-7.

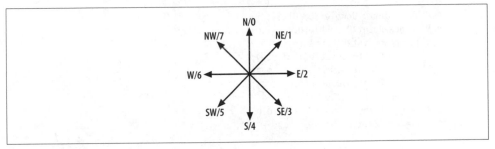

Figure 3-7. Compass directions and corresponding integers

Each compass direction is represented by an integer, which labels the bearings in clockwise order. The relevant constants and variable are shown here:

```
// compass direction/bearing constants
private static final int NUM_DIRS = 8;
private static final int N = 0;  // north, etc going clockwise
private static final int NE = 1;
private static final int E = 2;
private static final int SE = 3;
private static final int S = 4;
private static final int SW = 5;
private static final int W = 6;
private static final int NW = 7;

private int currCompass;  // the current compass dir/bearing
```

Limiting the possible directions that a worm can move allows the movement steps to be predefined. This reduces the computation at run time, speeding up the worm.

When a new head is made for the worm, it is positioned in one of the eight compass directions, offset by one "unit" from the current head. This is illustrated in Figure 3-8.

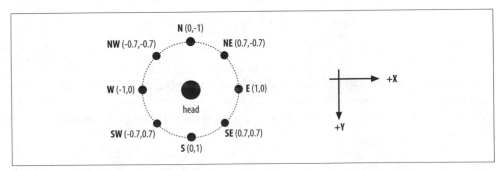

Figure 3-8. Offsets from the current head position

The offsets are defined as Point2D.Double objects (a kind of Point class that can hold doubles). They are stored in an incrs[] array, created at Worm construction time:

```
Point2D.Double incrs[];

incrs = new Point2D.Double[NUM_DIRS];
incrs[N] = new Point2D.Double(0.0, -1.0);
incrs[NE] = new Point2D.Double(0.7, -0.7);
incrs[E] = new Point2D.Double(1.0, 0.0);
incrs[SE] = new Point2D.Double(0.7, 0.7);
incrs[S] = new Point2D.Double(0.0, 1.0);
incrs[SW] = new Point2D.Double(-0.7, 0.7);
incrs[W] = new Point2D.Double(-1.0, 0.0);
incrs[NW] = new Point2D.Double(-0.7, -0.7);
```

Calculating a New Head Point

nextPoint() employs the index position in cells[] of the current head (called prevPosn) and the chosen bearing (e.g., N, SE) to calculate a Point for the new head.

The method is complicated by the need to deal with wraparound positioning top to bottom and left to right. For example, if the new head is placed off the top of the canvas, it should be repositioned to just above the bottom.

```
private Point nextPoint(int prevPosn, int bearing)
{
  // get the increment for the compass bearing
  Point2D.Double incr = incrs[bearing];

  int newX = cells[prevPosn].x + (int)(DOTSIZE * incr.x);
  int newY = cells[prevPosn].y + (int)(DOTSIZE * incr.y);

  // modify newX/newY if < 0, or > pWidth/pHeight; use wraparound
  if (newX+DOTSIZE < 0)      // is circle off left edge of canvas?
    newX = newX + pWidth;
  else if (newX > pWidth)  // is circle off right edge of canvas?
    newX = newX - pWidth;

  if (newY+DOTSIZE < 0)      // is circle off top of canvas?
    newY = newY + pHeight;
  else if (newY > pHeight) // is circle off bottom of canvas?
    newY = newY - pHeight;
  return new Point(newX,newY);
} // end of nextPoint()
```

The code uses the constant DOTSIZE (12), which is the pixel length and height of the circle representing a part of the worm. The new coordinate (newX, newY) is obtained by looking up the offset in incr[] for the given bearing and adding it to the current head position.

Each circle is defined by its (x, y) coordinate and its DOTSIZE length. The (x, y) value is not the center of the circle but is its top-left corner, as used in drawing operations such as fillOval( ) (see Figure 3-9).

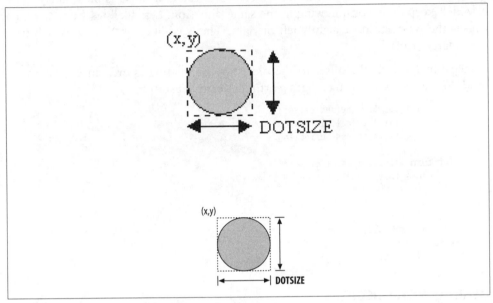

Figure 3-9. The coordinates of a worm circle

This explains the wraparound calculations which check if the circle is positioned off the left, right, top or bottom edges of the canvas. The panel dimensions, pWidth and pHeight, are passed to the Worm object by WormPanel at construction time.

Choosing a Bearing

The compass bearing used in nextPoint( ) comes from varyBearing( ):

```
int newBearing = varyBearing( );
Point newPt = nextPoint(prevPosn, newBearing);
```

varyBearing( ) is defined as:

```
private int varyBearing( )
// vary the compass bearing semi-randomly
{ int newOffset =
      probsForOffset[ (int)( Math.random( )*NUM_PROBS )];
  return calcBearing(newOffset);
}
```

The probsForOffset[] array is randomly accessed and returns a new offset:

```
int[] probsForOffset = new int[NUM_PROBS];
probsForOffset[0] = 0;  probsForOffset[1] = 0;
probsForOffset[2] = 0;  probsForOffset[3] = 1;
```

```
probsForOffset[4] = 1;   probsForOffset[5] = 2;
probsForOffset[6] = -1;  probsForOffset[7] = -1;
probsForOffset[8] = -2;
```

The distribution of values in the array means that the new offset is most likely to be 0, which keeps the worm moving in the same direction. Less likely is 1 or –1, which causes the worm to turn slightly left or right. The least likely is 2 or –2, which triggers a larger turn.

calcBearing( ) adds the offset to the old compass bearing (stored in currCompass), modulo the compass setting ranges North to North West (0 to 7):

```
private int calcBearing(int offset)
// Use the offset to calculate a new compass bearing based
// on the current compass direction.
{
  int turn = currCompass + offset;
  // ensure that turn is between N to NW (0 to 7)
  if (turn >= NUM_DIRS)
    turn = turn - NUM_DIRS;
  else if (turn < 0)
    turn = NUM_DIRS + turn;
  return turn;
}  // end of calcBearing( )
```

Dealing with Obstacles

newHead( ) generates a new head using varyBearing( ) and nextPoint( ), and it updates the cell[] array and compass setting:

```
private void newHead(int prevPosn)  // not finished yet
{
  int newBearing = varyBearing( );
  Point newPt = nextPoint(prevPosn, newBearing );

  // what about obstacles?
  // code to deal with obstacles

  cells[headPosn] = newPt;      // new head position
  currCompass = newBearing;     // new compass direction
}
```

Unfortunately, this code is insufficient for dealing with obstacles: what will happen when the new head is placed at the same spot as an obstacle?

The new point must be tested against the obstacles to ensure it isn't touching any of them. If it is touching, then a new compass bearing and point must be generated. I try three possible moves: turn left by 90 degrees, turn right by 90 degrees and, failing those, turn around and have the worm go back the way it came.

These moves are defined as offsets in the fixedOffs[] array in newHead():

```
private void newHead(int prevPosn)
{
  int fixedOffs[] = {-2, 2, -4};   // offsets to avoid an obstacle

  int newBearing = varyBearing();
  Point newPt = nextPoint(prevPosn, newBearing );

  if (obs.hits(newPt, DOTSIZE)) {
    for (int i=0; i < fixedOffs.length; i++) {
      newBearing = calcBearing(fixedOffs[i]);
      newPt = nextPoint(prevPosn, newBearing);
      if (!obs.hits(newPt, DOTSIZE))
        break;      // one of the fixed offsets will work
    }
  }
  cells[headPosn] = newPt;        // new head position
  currCompass = newBearing;       // new compass direction
} // end of newHead()
```

Key to this strategy is the assumption that the worm can always turn around. This is possible since the player cannot easily add obstacles behind the worm because the worm's body prevents the user from placing a box on the floor.

Moving the Worm

The public method move() initiates the worm's movement, utilizing newHead() to obtain a new head position and compass bearing.

The cells[] array, tailPosn and headPosn indices, and the number of points in cells[] are updated in slightly different ways depending on the current stage in the worm's development. These are the three stages:

1. When the worm is first created

2. When the worm is growing, but the cells[] array is not full

3. When the cells[] array is full, so the addition of a new head must be balanced by the removal of a tail circle:

```
public void move()
{
  int prevPosn = headPosn;
               // save old head posn while creating new one
  headPosn = (headPosn + 1) % MAXPOINTS;

  if (nPoints == 0) {   // empty array at start
    tailPosn = headPosn;
    currCompass = (int)( Math.random()*NUM_DIRS );   // random dir.
    cells[headPosn] = new Point(pWidth/2, pHeight/2); //center pt
    nPoints++;
```

```
      }
      else if (nPoints == MAXPOINTS) {      // array is full
        tailPosn = (tailPosn + 1) % MAXPOINTS;     // forget last tail
        newHead(prevPosn);
      }
      else {      // still room in cells[]
        newHead(prevPosn);
        nPoints++;
      }
    }  // end of move( )
```

Drawing the Worm

WormPanel calls Worm's draw( ) method to render the worm into the graphics context g.
The rendering starts with the point in cell[tailPosn] and moves through the array
until cell[headPosn] is reached. The iteration from the tailPosn position to headPosn
may involve jumping from the end of the array back to the start:

```
public void draw(Graphics g)
// draw a black worm with a red head
{
  if (nPoints > 0) {
    g.setColor(Color.black);
    int i = tailPosn;
    while (i != headPosn) {
      g.fillOval(cells[i].x, cells[i].y, DOTSIZE, DOTSIZE);
      i = (i+1) % MAXPOINTS;
    }
    g.setColor(Color.red);
    g.fillOval( cells[headPosn].x, cells[headPosn].y, DOTSIZE, DOTSIZE);
  }
}  // end of draw( )
```

Testing the Worm

nearHead( ) and touchedAt( ) are Boolean methods used by WormPanel. nearHead( )
decides if a given (x, y) coordinate is near the worm's head, and touchedAt( ) examines its body:

```
public boolean nearHead(int x, int y)
// is (x,y) near the worm's head?
{ if (nPoints > 0) {
    if( (Math.abs( cells[headPosn].x + RADIUS - x) <= DOTSIZE) &&
        (Math.abs( cells[headPosn].y + RADIUS - y) <= DOTSIZE) )
      return true;
  }
  return false;
} // end of nearHead( )


public boolean touchedAt(int x, int y)
// is (x,y) near any part of the worm's body?
```

```
{
  int i = tailPosn;
  while (i != headPosn) {
    if( (Math.abs( cells[i].x + RADIUS - x) <= RADIUS) &&
        (Math.abs( cells[i].y + RADIUS - y) <= RADIUS) )
      return true;
    i = (i+1) % MAXPOINTS;
  }
  return false;
} // end of touchedAt()
```

The RADIUS constant is half the DOTSIZE value. The test in nearHead( ) allows the (x, y) coordinate to be within two radii of the center of the worm's head; any less makes hitting the head almost impossible at 80+ FPS. touchedAt( ) only checks for an intersection within a single radius of the center.

The addition of RADIUS to the (x, y) coordinate in cells[] offsets it from the top-left corner of the circle (see Figure 3-9) to its center.

Worm Obstacles

The Obstacles object maintains an array of Rectangle objects called boxes. Each object contains the top-left hand coordinate of a box and the length of its square sides.

The public methods in the Obstacles class are synchronized since the event thread of the game could add a box to the obstacles list (via a call to add( )) while the animation thread is examining or drawing the list.

add( ) is defined as

```
synchronized public void add(int x, int y)
{
  boxes.add( new Rectangle(x,y, BOX_LENGTH, BOX_LENGTH));
  wcTop.setBoxNumber( boxes.size() );   // report new no. of boxes
}
```

The method updates the boxes text field at the top-level of the game by calling setBoxNumber( ).

WormPanel delegates the task of drawing the obstacles to the Obstacles object, by calling draw( ):

```
synchronized public void draw(Graphics g)
// draw a series of blue boxes
{
  Rectangle box;
  g.setColor(Color.blue);
  for(int i=0; i < boxes.size(); i++) {
    box = (Rectangle) boxes.get(i);
    g.fillRect( box.x, box.y, box.width, box.height);
  }
} // end of draw()
```

Worm communicates with Obstacles to determine if its new head (a Point object, p) intersects with any of the boxes:

```
synchronized public boolean hits(Point p, int size)
{
  Rectangle r = new Rectangle(p.x, p.y, size, size);
  Rectangle box;
  for(int i=0; i < boxes.size( ); i++) {
    box = (Rectangle) boxes.get(i);
    if (box.intersects(r))
      return true;
  }
  return false;
} // end of hits()
```

Application Timing Results

This version of WormChase is a windowed application, with an animation loop driven by the Java 3D timer. Can it support frame rates of 80 to 85 FPS?

I consider the average UPS, which gives an indication of the speed of the game. Table 3-1 shows the FPS and UPS figures for different requested FPS amounts, on different versions of Windows.

Table 3-1. Average FPS/UPSs for the windowed WormChase using the Java 3D timer

Requested FPS	20	50	80	100
Windows 98	20/20	48/50	81/83	96/100
Windows 2000	20/20	43/50	59/83	58/100
Windows XP	20/20	50/50	83/83	100/100

Each test was run three times on a lightly loaded machine, executing for a few minutes.

The numbers are for the machines hosting Windows 98 and XP, but the frame rates on the Windows 2000 machine plateaus at about 60. This behavior is probably due to the extreme age of the machine: a Pentium 2 with a paltry 64 MB of RAM. On a more modern CPU, the frame rates are similar to the XP row of Table 3-1.

A requested frame rate of 80 is changed to 83.333 inside the program, explaining why the 80's column shows numbers close to 83 in most cases. The frame rate is divided into 1,000 using integer division, so that 1000/80 becomes 12. Later, this period value is converted back to a frame rate using doubles, so 1000.0/12 becomes 83.3333.

The Windows 2000 figures show that slow hardware is an issue. The processing power of the machine may not deliver the requested frame rate due to excessive time spent in modifying the game state and rendering. Fortunately, the game play on the

Windows 2000 machine does not appear to be slow, since the UPS stay near to the request FPS.

Close to 41 percent of the frames are skipped ([83–59]/83), meaning that almost every second game update is not rendered. Surprisingly, this is not apparent when playing the game. This shows the great benefit of decoupling game updates from rendering, so the update rate can out perform a poor frame rate.

Timing Results Using currentTimeMillis( )

It is interesting to examine the performance of a version of WormChase using System.currentTimeMillis( ) rather than the Java 3D timer.

The WormChase class and its associated main( ) function must be modified to represent the period value in milliseconds rather than nanoseconds. In WormPanel, the calls to J3DTimer.getValue( ) in run( ) and storeStats( ) must be replaced by System.currentTimeMillis( ). The sleep( ) call in run( ) no longer needs to change sleepTime to milliseconds:

```
Thread.sleep(sleepTime);  // already in ms
```

storeStats( ) must be edited to take account of the millisecond units.

The code for this version of WormChase is in *Worm/WormPMillis/*. The timing results are given in Table 3-2.

Table 3-2. Average FPS/UPSs for the windowed WormChase using the System timer

Requested FPS	20	50	80	100
Windows 98	19/20	43/50	54/83	57/100
Windows 2000	20/20	50/50	57/83	58/100
Windows XP	20/20	50/50	83/83	100/100

The Windows 98 row shows the effect of the System timer's poor resolution: it causes the animation loop to sleep too much at the end of each update and render, leading to a reduction in the realized frame rate. However, the UPS are unaffected, making the game advance quickly.

The Windows 2000 row illustrates the slowness of the host machine. The figures are comparable to the version of WormChase using the Java 3D timer. The Windows XP row shows that the System timer's performance is essentially equivalent to the Java 3D timer. The System timer's resolution on Windows 2000 and XP is 10 to 15 ms (67 to 100 FPS).

WormChase as an Applet

Figure 3-1 shows the WormChase game as an applet and as an application. It has the same GUI interface as the windowed version: a large canvas with two text fields at the bottom used to report the number of boxes added to the scene, and the time.

Class diagrams showing the public methods are given in Figure 3-10. A comparison with the diagrams for the windowed version in Figure 3-2 show the classes stay mainly the same. The only substantial change is to replace JFrame by JApplet at the top level.

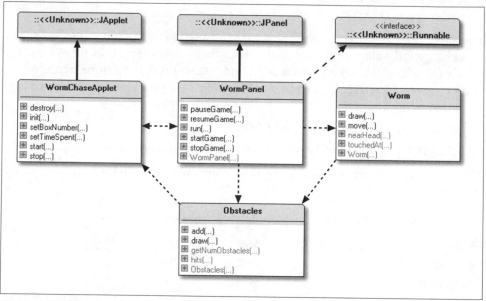

Figure 3-10. Class diagrams for the WormChase applet

 The code for this version of WormChase is in the directory *Worm/ WormApplet/*.

The Worm class is unchanged from the windowed version. The Obstacles class now calls setBoxNumber( ) in WormChaseApplet rather than WormChase.

WormPanel reports its termination statistics in a different way, but the animation loop and statistics gathering are unchanged. WormChaseApplet handles pausing, resumption, and termination by tying them to events in the applet life cycle. By comparison, WormChase utilizes Window events.

The applet's web page passes the requested frame rate to it as a parameter:

```
<applet code="WormChaseApplet.class" width="500" height="415">
    <param name="fps" value="80">
</applet>
```

The WormChaseApplet Class

Figure 3-11 shows the class diagram for WormChaseApplet with all its variables and methods.

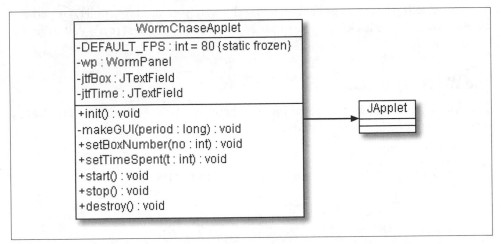

Figure 3-11. WormChaseApplet in detail

The applet's init( ) method reads the FPS value from the web page, sets up the GUI, and starts the game:

```
public void init( )
{
  String str = getParameter("fps");
  int fps = (str != null) ? Integer.parseInt(str) : DEFAULT_FPS;

  long period = (long) 1000.0/fps;
  System.out.println("fps: " + fps + "; period: "+period+" ms");

  makeGUI(period);
  wp.startGame( );
}
```

makeGUI( ) is the same as the one in the JFrame version. The call to startGame( ) replaces the use of addNotify( ) in the JPanel.

The applet life-cycle methods—start( ), stop( ), and destroy( )—contain calls to WormPanel to resume, pause, and terminate the game:

```
public void start()
{ wp.resumeGame(); }

public void stop()
{ wp.pauseGame(); }

public void destroy()
{ wp.stopGame(); }
```

A browser calls destroy( ) prior to deleting the web page (and its applet) or perhaps as the browser itself is closed. The browser will wait for the destroy( ) call to return before exiting.

The WormPanel Class

The only major change to WormPanel is how printStats( ) is called. The stopGame( ) method is modified to call finishOff( ), which calls printStats( ):

```
public void stopGame()
{ running = false;
  finishOff();  // new bit, different from the application
}

private void finishOff()
{ if (!finishedOff) {
    finishedOff = true;
    printStats();
  }
} // end of finishedOff()
```

finishOff( ) checks a global finishedOff Boolean to decide whether to report the statistics. finishedOff starts with the value false.

finishOff( ) is called at the end of run( ) as the animation loop finishes. The first call to finishOff( ) will pass the if test, set the finishedOff flag to true, and print the data. The flag will then prevent a second call from repeating the output.

 A *race condition* could occur, with two simultaneous calls to finishOff( ) getting past the if test at the same time, but it's not serious or likely, so I ignore it.

In the windowed application, stopGame( ) only sets running to false before returning, with no call to finishOff( ). The threaded animation loop may then execute for a short time before checking the flag, stopping, and calling printStats( ).

This approach is fine in an application where the animation thread will be allowed to finish before the application terminates. Unfortunately, as soon as an applet's destroy( )

method returns, then the applet or the browser can exit. In this case, the animation thread may not have time to reach its printStats( ) call.

To ensure the statistics are printed, finishOff( ) is called in the applet's stopGame( ) method. The other call to finishOff( ) at the end of run( ) is a catch-all in case I modify the game so it can terminate the animation loop without passing through stopGame( ).

Timing Results

The timing results are given in Table 3-3.

Table 3-3. Average FPS/UPS for the applet version of WormChase

Requested FPS	20	50	80	100
Windows 98	20/20	50/50	82/83	97/100
Windows 2000	20/20	46/50	63/83	61/100
Windows XP	20/20	50/50	83/83	100/100

The poor showing for the frame rate on the Windows 2000 machine is expected, but the applet performs well on more modern hardware.

Compilation in J2SE 5.0

One of my aims is to make the examples portable, which means that they should compile and execute in J2SE 5.0 and J2SE 1.4. At the moment, May 2005, many Java users haven't upgraded to the latest version, and many PCs come with JRE 1.4 preinstalled.

As mentioned in the Preface, the main areas where I lose out because of this portability are in type-safe collections and the nanosecond time method, System.nanoTime( ). The Java 3D nanosecond timer is a good replacement for nanoTime( ). But what about type-safe collections?

What Is a Type-Safe Collection?

A type-safe collection is a *generified* collection declared with a type argument for its generic component. For example, this J2SE 1.4 code doesn't use generics:

```
ArrayList al = new ArrayList();
al.add(0, new Integer(42));
int num = ((Integer) al.get(0)).intValue();
```

Collections without generic arguments are called raw types.

The following J2SE 5.0 code uses a generified `ArrayList` with an `Integer` type:

```
ArrayList<Integer> al = new ArrayList<Integer>();
al.add(0, new Integer(42));
int num = ((Integer) al.get(0)).intValue();
```

Type safety means that the compiler can detect if the programmer tries to add a non-Integer object to the `ArrayList`. Poor coding like that would only be caught at runtime in J2SE 1.4, as a `ClassCastException`.

Generified collections can make use of J2SE 5.0's enhanced for loop, enumerations, and autoboxing. For example, the code snippet above can be revised to employ autoboxing and autounboxing:

```
ArrayList<Integer> al = new ArrayList<Integer>();
al.add(0, 42);
int num = al.get(0);
```

This is less verbose, and much easier to understand, debug, and maintain.

Dealing with Raw Types in J2SE 5.0

The J2SE 5.0 compiler will accept raw types (such as the `ArrayList` in the first code fragment in the previous section) but will issue warnings. This can be seen when the WormChase application is compiled with J2SE 5.0:

```
>javac *.java
Note: Obstacles.java uses unchecked or unsafe operations.
Note: Recompile with -Xlint:unchecked for details.
```

The code has been compiled, but the unchecked warning indicates a raw type may be in Obstacles. Recompiling with the −Xlint argument leads to the following:

```
>javac -Xlint:unchecked *.java
Obstacles.java:27: warning: [unchecked] unchecked call to add(E) as a member of
the raw type java.util.ArrayList
   { boxes.add( new Rectangle(x,y, BOX_LENGTH, BOX_LENGTH));
           ^
1 warning
```

The problem is the boxes collection in the Obstacles class, specifically when a Rectangle object is added to it.

I've two options at this point: ignore the warning or fix it. Fixing it is straightforward, so I'll work through the stages here. Here is the original declaration of boxes in the Obstacles class:

```
private ArrayList boxes;    // arraylist of Rectangle objects
```

This should be generified:

```
private ArrayList<Rectangle> boxes;    // arraylist of Rectangle objects
```

The line that creates the boxes object must be changed from:

```
boxes = new ArrayList();
```

to:

```
boxes = new ArrayList<Rectangle>();
```

The program now compiles without any warnings.

A brisk introduction to the new features in J2SE 5.0 can be found in *Java 1.5 Tiger: A Developer's Notebook* by David Flanagan and Brett McLaughlin (O'Reilly). The issues involved with making type-safe collections are explored in more detail in: "Case Study: Converting to Java 1.5 Type-Safe Collections" by Wes Munsil in the *Journal of Object Technology*, September 2004 (*http://www.jot.fm/issues/issue_2004_09/column1*).

CHAPTER 4

Full-Screen Worms

A popular aim for games is to be an immersive experience, where the player becomes so enthralled with the game that he or she forgets everyday trivia such as eating and visiting the bathroom. One simple way of encouraging immersion is to make the game window the size of the desktop; a full-screen display hides tiresome text editors, spreadsheets, or database applications requiring urgent attention.

I'll look at three approaches to creating full-screen games:

- An almost full-screen JFrame (I'll call this AFS)
- An undecorated full-screen JFrame (UFS)
- Full-screen exclusive mode (FSEM)

FSEM is getting a lot of attention since its introduction in J2SE 1.4 because it has increased frame rates over traditional gaming approaches using repaint events and paintComponent( ). However, comparisons between AFS, UFS, and FSEM show their maximum frame rates to be similar. This is due to my use of the animation loop developed in Chapter 2, with its active rendering and high-resolution Java 3D timer. You should read Chapter 2 before continuing.

The examples in this chapter will continue using the WormChase game, first introduced in Chapter 3, so you'd better read that chapter as well. By sticking to a single game throughout this chapter, the timing comparisons more accurately reflect differences in the animation code rather than in the game-specific parts.

The objective is to produce 80 to 85 FPS, which is near the limit of a typical graphics card's rendering capacity. If the game's frame rate falls short of this, then the updates per second (UPS) should still stay close to 80 to 85, causing the game to run quickly but without every update being rendered.

An Almost Full-Screen (AFS) Worm

Figure 4-1 shows the WormChase application running inside a JFrame that almost covers the entire screen. The JFrame's titlebar, including its close box and iconification/de-iconfication buttons are visible, and a border is around the window. The OS desktop controls are visible (in this case, Windows's task bar at the bottom of the screen).

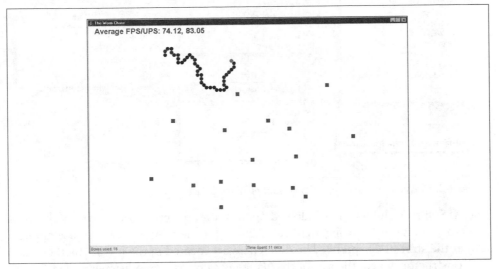

Figure 4-1. An AFS WormChase

These JFrame and OS components allow the player to control the game (e.g., pause it by iconification) and to switch to other applications in the usual way, without the need for GUI controls inside the game. Also, little code has to be modified to change a windowed game into an AFS version, aside from resizing the canvas.

Though the window can be iconified and switched to the background, it can't be moved. To be more precise, it can be selected and dragged, but as soon as the mouse button is released, the window snaps back to its original position.

 This is a fun effect, as if the window is attached by a rubber band to the top lefthand corner of the screen.

Figure 4-2 gives the class diagrams for the AFS version of WormChase, including the public methods.

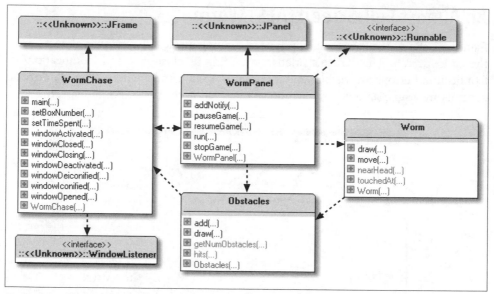

Figure 4-2. Class diagrams for the AFS version of WormChase

The AFS approach and the windowed application are similar as shown by the class diagrams in Figure 4-2 being identical to those for the windowed WormChase application at the start of Chapter 3. The differences are located in the private methods and the constructor, where the size of the JFrame is calculated and listener code is put in place to keep the window from moving.

WormPanel is almost the same as before, except that WormChase passes it a calculated width and height (in earlier version these were constants in the class). The Worm and Obstacles classes are unaltered from Chapter 3.

 The code for the AFS WormChase can be found in the directory *Worm/ WormAFS/*.

The AFS WormChase Class

Figure 4-3 gives a class diagram for WormChase showing all its variables and methods.

The constructor has to work hard to obtain correct dimensions for the JPanel. The problem is that the sizes of three distinct kinds of elements must be calculated:

- The JFrame's insets (e.g., the titlebar and borders)
- The desktop's insets (e.g., the taskbar)
- The other Swing components in the window (e.g., two text fields)

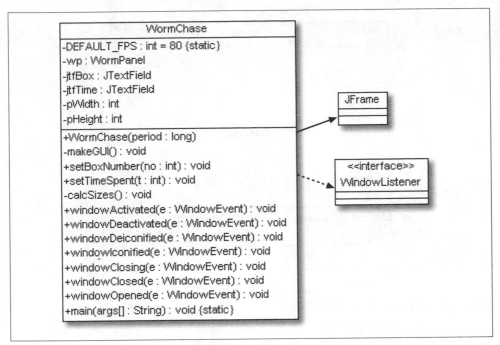

Figure 4-3. WormChase in detail

The *insets* of a container are the unused areas around its edges (at the top, bottom, left, and right). Typical insets are the container's border lines and its titlebar. The widths and heights of these elements must be subtracted from the screen's dimensions to get WormPanel's width and height. Figure 4-4 shows the insets and GUI elements for WormChase.

The subtraction of the desktop and JFrame inset dimensions from the screen size is standard, but the calculation involving the on-screen positions of the GUI elements depends on the game design. For WormChase, only the heights of the text fields affect WormPanel's size.

A subtle problem is that the dimensions of the JFrame insets and GUI elements will be unavailable until the game window has been constructed. In that case, how can the panel's dimensions be calculated if the application has to be created first?

The answer is that the application must be constructed in stages. First, the JFrame and other pieces needed for the size calculations are put together. This fixes their sizes, so the drawing panel's area can be determined. The sized JPanel is then added to the window to complete it, and the window is made visible. The WormChase constructor utilizes these stages:

```
public WormChase(long period)
{ super("The Worm Chase");

  makeGUI();
```

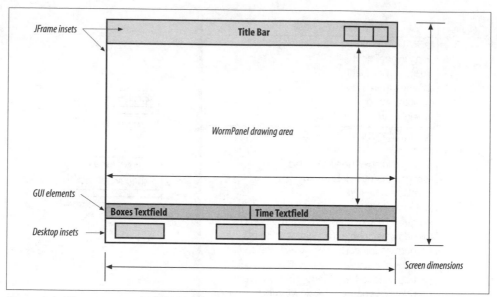

Figure 4-4. Dimensions in the AFS WormChase

```
    pack( );      // first pack (the GUI doesn't include the JPanel yet)
    setResizable(false);  //so sizes are for nonresizable GUI elems
    calcSizes( );
    setResizable(true);     // so panel can be added

    Container c = getContentPane( );
    wp = new WormPanel(this, period, pWidth, pHeight);
    c.add(wp, "Center");
    pack( );        // second pack, after JPanel added

    addWindowListener( this );

    addComponentListener( new ComponentAdapter( ) {
      public void componentMoved(ComponentEvent e)
      {  setLocation(0,0);  }
    });

    setResizable(false);
    setVisible(true);
  }  // end of WormChase( ) constructor
```

makeGUI( ) builds the GUI without a drawing area, and the call to pack( ) makes the JFrame displayable and calculates the component's sizes. Resizing is turned off since some platforms render insets differently (i.e., with different sizes) when their enclosing window can't be resized.

calcSizes( ) initializes two globals, pWidth and pHeight, which are later passed to the WormPanel constructor as the panel's width and height:

```
    private void calcSizes( )
    {
```

```
GraphicsConfiguration gc = getGraphicsConfiguration( );
Rectangle screenRect = gc.getBounds( );  // screen dimensions

Toolkit tk = Toolkit.getDefaultToolkit( );
Insets desktopInsets = tk.getScreenInsets(gc);

Insets frameInsets = getInsets( );     // only works after pack( )

Dimension tfDim = jtfBox.getPreferredSize( );  // textfield size

pWidth = screenRect.width
            - (desktopInsets.left + desktopInsets.right)
            - (frameInsets.left + frameInsets.right);

pHeight = screenRect.height
            - (desktopInsets.top + desktopInsets.bottom)
            - (frameInsets.top + frameInsets.bottom)
            - tfDim.height;
}
```

 If the JFrame's insets (stored in frameInsets) are requested before a call to pack( ), then they will have zero size.

An Insets object has four public variables—top, bottom, left, and right—that hold the thickness of its container's edges. Only the dimensions for the box's text field (jtfBox) is retrieved since its height will be the same as the time-used text field. Back in WormChase( ), resizing is switched back on so the correctly sized JPanel can be added to the JFrame. Finally, resizing is switched off permanently, and the application is made visible with a call to show( ).

Stopping Window Movement

Unfortunately, there is no simple way of preventing an application's window from being dragged around the screen. The best you can do is move it back to its starting position as soon as the user releases the mouse.

The WormChase constructor sets up a component listener with a componentMoved( ) handler. This method is called whenever a move is completed:

```
addComponentListener( new ComponentAdapter( ) {
  public void componentMoved(ComponentEvent e)
  {  setLocation(0,0);  }
});
```

setLocation( ) positions the JFrame so its top-left corner is at the top left of the screen.

Timings for AFS

Timing results for the AFS WormChase are given in Table 4-1.

Table 4-1. Average FPS/UPS rates for the AFS WormChase

Requested FPS	20	50	80	100
Windows 98	20/20	49/50	75/83	86/100
Windows 2000	20/20	20/50	20/83	20/100
Windows XP (1)	20/20	50/50	82/83	87/100
Windows XP (2)	20/20	50/50	75/83	75/100

WormChase on the slow Windows 2000 machine is the worst performer again, as seen in Chapter 3, though its slowness is barely noticeable due to the update rate remaining high.

The Windows 98 and XP boxes produce good frame rates when 80 FPS is requested, which is close to or inside my desired range (80 to 85 FPS). The numbers start to flatten as the FPS request goes higher, indicating that the frames can't be rendered any faster.

 The timing tests for Windows XP were run on two machines to highlight the variation in WormChase's performance at higher requested FPSs.

An Undecorated Full-Screen (UFS) Worm

Figure 4-5 shows the UFS version of WormChase, a full-screen JFrame without a titlebar or borders.

The absence of a titlebar means I have to rethink how to pause and resume the application (previously achieved by minimizing/maximizing the window) and how to terminate the game. The solution is to draw Pause and Quit buttons on the canvas at the bottom-right corner. Aside from using the Quit button, ending the game is possible by typing the Esc key, Ctrl-C, the q key, or the End key. Data that were previously displayed in text fields are written to the canvas at the lower-left corner.

Figure 4-6 gives the class diagrams for the UFS version of WormChase, including the public methods.

A comparison with the AFS class diagrams in Figure 4-2 shows a considerable simplification of WormChase and fewer methods in WormPanel.

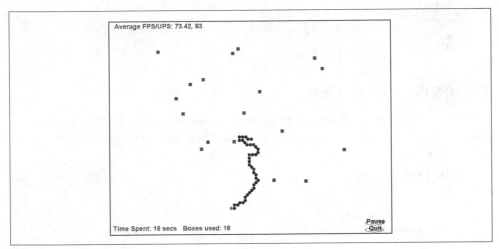

Figure 4-5. The UFS worm

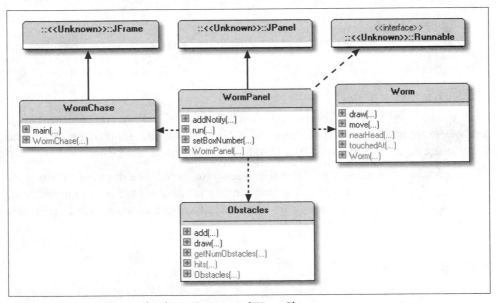

Figure 4-6. Class diagrams for the UFS version of WormChase

The WormChase class no longer has to be a WindowListener and, therefore, doesn't contain window handler methods, such as windowClosing(). The pauseGame(), resumeGame(), and stopGame() methods in WormPanel are no longer required. The Worm class is unchanged, and the Obstacles class is altered only so it can call setBoxNumber() in WormPanel; this method was formerly in WormChase and wrote to a text field.

The code for the UFS WormChase can be found in the *Worm/WormUFS/* directory.

The UFS WormChase Class

With the removal of the WindowListener methods, WormChase hardly does anything. It reads the requested FPS value from the command line, and its constructor creates the WormPanel object:

```
public WormChase(long period)
{ super("The Worm Chase");

  Container c = getContentPane();
  c.setLayout( new BorderLayout() );

  WormPanel wp = new WormPanel(this, period);
  c.add(wp, "Center");

  setUndecorated(true);    // no borders or titlebar
  setIgnoreRepaint(true);  // turn off paint events since doing active rendering
  pack();
  setResizable(false);
  setVisible(true);
} // end of WormChase() constructor
```

The titlebars and other insets are switched off by calling setUndecorated(). setIgnoreRepaint() is utilized since no GUI components require paint events; WormPanel uses active rendering and, therefore, doesn't need paint events.

The simplicity of WormChase indicates that a separate JPanel as a drawing canvas is no longer needed. Moving WormPanel's functionality into WormChase is straightforward, and I'll explore that approach as part of the FSEM version of WormChase later in this chapter.

The Game Panel

WormPanel's constructor sets its size to that of the screen and stores the dimensions in the global variables pWidth and pHeight:

```
Toolkit tk = Toolkit.getDefaultToolkit();
Dimension scrDim = tk.getScreenSize();
setPreferredSize(scrDim);   // set JPanel size

pWidth = scrDim.width;      // store dimensions for later
pHeight = scrDim.height;
```

The constructor creates two rectangles, pauseArea and quitArea, which represent the screen areas for the Pause and Quit buttons:

```
private Rectangle pauseArea, quitArea;  // globals

// in WormPanel()
// specify screen areas for the buttons
pauseArea = new Rectangle(pWidth-100, pHeight-45, 70, 15);
quitArea  = new Rectangle(pWidth-100, pHeight-20, 70, 15);
```

The drawing of these buttons is left to gameRender( ), which is described in the next section.

Button Behavior

As is common with many games, the Pause and Quit buttons are highlighted when the mouse moves over them. This transition is shown in Figure 4-7 when the mouse passes over the Pause button.

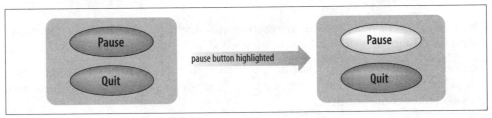

Figure 4-7. Highlighting the Pause button

Another useful kind of feedback is to indicate that the game is paused by changing the wording of the Pause button to "Paused," as in Figure 4-8.

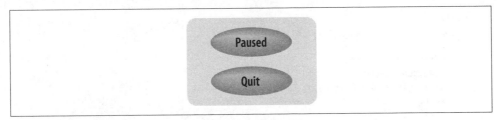

Figure 4-8. The Pause button when the game is paused

 When the mouse moves over the Paused button, the text turns green.

The first step to implementing these behaviors is to record when the cursor is inside the pause or quit screen area. This is done by monitoring mouse movements, started in the constructor for WormPanel:

```
addMouseMotionListener( new MouseMotionAdapter() {
  public void mouseMoved(MouseEvent e)
  { testMove(e.getX(), e.getY()); }
});
```

testMove( ) sets two global Booleans (isOverPauseButton and isOverQuitButton) depending on whether the cursor is inside the pause or quit area:

```
private void testMove(int x, int y)
// is (x,y) over the Pause or Quit button?
{
  if (running) {    // stops problems with a rapid move
                    // after pressing Quit
    isOverPauseButton = pauseArea.contains(x,y) ? true : false;
    isOverQuitButton = quitArea.contains(x,y) ? true : false;
  }
}
```

The test of the running Boolean prevents button highlight changes after the player has pressed Quit but before the application exits.

The other aspect of button behavior is to deal with a mouse press on top of a button. This is handled by extending testPress( ), which previously only dealt with clicks on or near the worm:

```
// in the WormPanel constructor
addMouseListener( new MouseAdapter() {
  public void mousePressed(MouseEvent e)
  { testPress(e.getX(), e.getY()); }
});


private void testPress(int x, int y)
{
  if (isOverPauseButton)
    isPaused = !isPaused;       // toggle pausing
  else if (isOverQuitButton)
    running = false;
  else {
    if (!isPaused && !gameOver) {
      // was mouse pressed on or near the worm?
      . . .
    }
  }
}
```

The highlighted lines in testPress( ) replace the functionality supported by resumeGame( ), pauseGame( ), and stopGame( ) in the earlier windowed versions of WormChase.

Drawing the Game Canvas

The WormPanel canvas contains two elements absent in previous examples:

- The time used and boxes information, drawn in the bottom-left corner
- The Pause and Quit buttons, drawn in the bottom-right corner

The buttons are drawn in a different way if the cursor is over them, and the wording on the Pause button changes depending on whether the game is paused.

These new features are implemented in gameRender( ):

```
private void gameRender( )
{
  // as before: create the image buffer initially
  // set the background to white
  ...

  // report average FPS and UPS at top left
  dbg.drawString("Average FPS/UPS: " + df.format(averageFPS) +
                  ", " + df.format(averageUPS), 20, 25);

  // report time used and boxes used at bottom left
  dbg.drawString("Time Spent: " + timeSpentInGame + " secs", 10, pHeight-15);
  dbg.drawString("Boxes used: " + boxesUsed, 260, pHeight-15);

  // draw the Pause and Quit "buttons"
  drawButtons(dbg);

  dbg.setColor(Color.black);

  // as before: draw game elements: the obstacles and the worm
  obs.draw(dbg);
  fred.draw(dbg);

  if (gameOver)
    gameOverMessage(dbg);
}  // end of gameRender( )


private void drawButtons(Graphics g)
{
  g.setColor(Color.black);

  // draw the Pause "button"
  if (isOverPauseButton)
    g.setColor(Color.green);

  g.drawOval( pauseArea.x, pauseArea.y, pauseArea.width, pauseArea.height);
  if (isPaused)
    g.drawString("Paused", pauseArea.x, pauseArea.y+10);
  else
    g.drawString("Pause", pauseArea.x+5, pauseArea.y+10);
```

```
      if (isOverPauseButton)
        g.setColor(Color.black);

      // draw the Quit "button"
      if (isOverQuitButton)
        g.setColor(Color.green);

      g.drawOval(quitArea.x, quitArea.y, quitArea.width, quitArea.height);
      g.drawString("Quit", quitArea.x+15, quitArea.y+10);

      if (isOverQuitButton)
        g.setColor(Color.black);
  }  // drawButtons()
```

Each button is an oval with a string over it. Highlighting triggers a change in the foreground color, using `setColor()`. Depending on the value of the `isPaused` Boolean, "Paused" or "Pause" is drawn.

Exiting the Game

The primary means for terminating the game remains the same as in previous examples: When the running Boolean is true, the animation loop will terminate. Before `run()` returns, the `finishOff()` method is called:

```
private void finishOff()
{ if (!finishedOff) {
    finishedOff = true;
    printStats();
    System.exit(0);
  }
}
```

The `finishedOff` Boolean is employed to stop a second call to `finishOff()` from printing the statistics information again.

The other way of calling `finishOff()` is from a shutdown hook (handler) set up when the JPanel is created:

```
Runtime.getRuntime().addShutdownHook(new Thread() {
  public void run()
  { running = false;
    System.out.println("Shutdown hook executed");
    finishOff();
  }
});
```

This code is normally called just before the application exits and is superfluous since `finishOff()` will have been executed. Its real benefit comes if the program terminates unexpectedly. The shutdown hook ensures that the statistics details are still reported in an abnormal exit situation.

This kind of defensive programming is often useful. For example, if the game state must be saved to an external file before the program terminates or if critical resources, such as files or sockets, must be properly closed.

Timings for UFS

Timing results for the UFS WormChase are given in Table 4-2.

Table 4-2. Average FPS/UPS rates for the UFS WormChase

Requested FPS	20	50	80	100
Windows 98	20/20	48/50	70/83	70/100
Windows 2000	18/20	19/50	18/83	18/100
Windows XP (1)	20/20	50/50	77/83	73/100
Windows XP (2)	20/20	50/50	68/83	69/100

WormChase on the Windows 2000 machine is the slowest, as usual, with marginally slower FPS values than the AFS version (it produces about 20 FPS). However, the poor performance is hidden by the high UPS number.

The Windows 98 and XP boxes produce reasonable to good frame rates when the requested FPS are 80 but are unable to go much faster. UFS frame rates are about 10 FPS slower than the AFS values at 80 FPS, which may be due to the larger rendering area. The UPS figures are unaffected.

A Full-Screen Exclusive Mode (FSEM) Worm

Full-screen exclusive mode (FSEM) suspends most of Java's windowing environment, bypassing the Swing and AWT graphics layers to offer almost direct access to the screen. It allows graphics card features, such as page flipping and stereo buffering, to be exploited and permits the screen's resolution and bit depth to be adjusted.

The graphics hardware acceleration used by FSEM has a disadvantage: it utilizes video memory (VRAM), which may be grabbed back by the OS when, for example, it needs to draw another window, display a screensaver, or change the screen's resolution. The application's image buffer, which is stored in the VRAM, will have to be reconstructed from scratch. A related issue is that VRAM is a finite resource, and placing too many images there may cause the OS to start swapping them in and out of memory, causing a slowdown in the rendering.

Aside from FSEM, J2SE 1.4 includes a VolatileImage class to allow images to take advantage of VRAM. Only opaque images and those with transparent areas are accelerated; translucent images can be accelerated as well but only in J2SE 5.0. Many forms of image manipulation can cause the acceleration to be lost.

In practice, direct use of VolatileImage is often not required since most graphical applications, such as those written with Swing, attempt to employ hardware acceleration implicitly. For instance, Swing uses VolatileImage for its double buffering and visuals loaded with getImage() are accelerated if possible, as are images used by the Java 2D API (e.g., those built using createImage()). However, more complex rendering features, such as diagonal lines, curved shapes, and anti-aliasing utilize software rendering at the JVM level.

Another issue with hardware acceleration is that it is principally a Windows feature since DirectDraw is employed by the JVM to access the VRAM. Neither Solaris nor Linux provide a way to directly contact the VRAM.

 A Sun tutorial for FSEM is at *http://java.sun.com/docs/books/tutorial/ extra/fullscreen/*, and the rationale behind the VolatileImage class is described at *http://java.sun.com/j2se/1.4/pdf/VolatileImage.pdf*.

Figure 4-9 shows a screenshot of the FSEM version of WormChase, which is identical to the UFS interface in Figure 4-5.

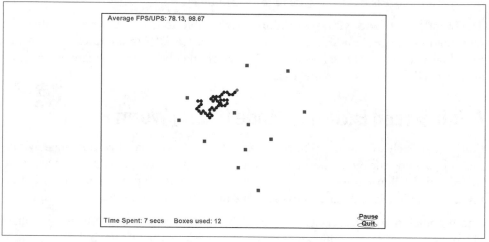

Figure 4-9. The FSEM WormChase

Class diagrams showing the public methods for this version of WormChase are shown in Figure 4-10.

The WormChase and WormPanel classes have been combined into a single WormChase class; it now contains the animation loop, which explains its use of the Runnable interface. This approach could be employed in the UFS version of WormChase. The Worm and Obstacles classes are unchanged.

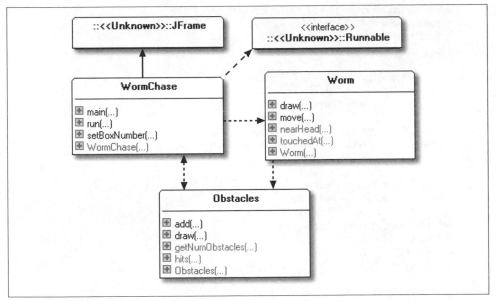

Figure 4-10. Class diagrams for the FSEM version of WormChase

The code for the FSEM WormChase can be found in the *Worm/Worm-FSEM/* directory.

The FSEM WormChase Class

The constructor for WormChase is similar to the constructors for the WormPanel classes of previous sections:

```
public WormChase(long period)
{
  super("Worm Chase");

  this.period = period;
  initFullScreen( );   // switch to FSEM

  readyForTermination( );

  // create game components
  obs = new Obstacles(this);
  fred = new Worm(pWidth, pHeight, obs);

  addMouseListener( new MouseAdapter() {
    public void mousePressed(MouseEvent e)
    { testPress(e.getX( ), e.getY( )); }
  });
```

```
    addMouseMotionListener( new MouseMotionAdapter() {
      public void mouseMoved(MouseEvent e)
      { testMove(e.getX( ), e.getY( )); }
    });

    // set up message font
    font = new Font("SansSerif", Font.BOLD, 24);
    metrics = this.getFontMetrics(font);

    // specify screen areas for the buttons
    pauseArea = new Rectangle(pWidth-100, pHeight-45, 70, 15);
    quitArea = new Rectangle(pWidth-100, pHeight-20, 70, 15);

    // initialise timing elements
    fpsStore = new double[NUM_FPS];
    upsStore = new double[NUM_FPS];
    for (int i=0; i < NUM_FPS; i++) {
      fpsStore[i] = 0.0;
      upsStore[i] = 0.0;
    }

    gameStart( );  // replaces addNotify( )
  }  // end of WormChase( )
```

WormChase( ) ends with a call to gameStart( ), which contains the code formerly in the
addNotify( ) method. As you may recall, addNotify( ) is called automatically as its
component (e.g., a JPanel) and is added to its container (e.g., a JFrame). Since I'm no
longer using a JPanel, the game is started directly from WormChase's constructor.

Setting Up Full-Screen Exclusive Mode

The steps necessary to switch the JFrame to FSEM are contained in initFullScreen( ):

```
    // globals used for FSEM tasks
    private GraphicsDevice gd;
    private Graphics gScr;
    private BufferStrategy bufferStrategy;

    private void initFullScreen()
    {
      GraphicsEnvironment ge =
        GraphicsEnvironment.getLocalGraphicsEnvironment( );
      gd = ge.getDefaultScreenDevice( );

      setUndecorated(true);    // no menu bar, borders, etc.
      setIgnoreRepaint(true);
            // turn off paint events since doing active rendering
      setResizable(false);

      if (!gd.isFullScreenSupported()) {
        System.out.println("Full-screen exclusive mode not supported");
        System.exit(0);
      }
      gd.setFullScreenWindow(this); // switch on FSEM
```

```
    // I can now adjust the display modes, if I wish
    showCurrentMode( );    // show the current display mode

    // setDisplayMode(800, 600, 8);    // or try 8 bits
    // setDisplayMode(1280, 1024, 32);

    pWidth = getBounds( ).width;
    pHeight = getBounds( ).height;

    setBufferStrategy( );
  } // end of initFullScreen( )
```

The graphics card is accessible via a `GraphicsDevice` object, gd. It's tested with `GraphicsDevice.isFullScreenSupported( )` to see if FSEM is available. Ideally, if the method returns `false`, the code should switch to using AFS or UFS, but I give up and keep things as simple as possible.

Once FSEM has been turned on by calling `GraphicsDevice.setFullScreenWindow( )`, modifying display parameters, such as screen resolution and bit depth, is possible. Details on how this can be done are explained below. In the current version of the program, `WormChase` only reports the current settings by calling my `showCurrentMode( )`; the call to my `setDisplayMode( )` is commented out.

`initFullScreen( )` switches off window decoration and resizing, which otherwise tend to interact badly with FSEM. Paint events are not required since I'm continuing to use active rendering, albeit a FSEM version (which I explain in the section "Rendering the Game").

After setting the display characteristics, the width and height of the drawing area are stored in `pWidth` and `pHeight`. Once in FSEM, a buffer strategy for updating the screen is specified by calling `setBufferStrategy( )`:

```
    private void setBufferStrategy( )
    { try {
        EventQueue.invokeAndWait( new Runnable( ) {
          public void run( )
          { createBufferStrategy(NUM_BUFFERS);  }
        });
      }
      catch (Exception e) {
        System.out.println("Error while creating buffer strategy");
        System.exit(0);
      }

      try {  // sleep to give time for buffer strategy to be done
        Thread.sleep(500);  // 0.5 sec
      }
      catch(InterruptedException ex){}

      bufferStrategy = getBufferStrategy( );  // store for later
    }
```

`Window.createBufferStrategy()` is called with a value of 2 (the `NUM_BUFFERS` value), so *page flipping* with a primary surface and one back buffer is utilized.

 Page flipping is explained in detail in the next section.

`EventQueue.invokeAndWait()` is employed to avoid a possible deadlock between the `createBufferStrategy()` call and the event dispatcher thread, an issue that's been fixed in J2SE 5.0. The thread holding the `createBufferStrategy()` call is added to the dispatcher queue, and executed when earlier pending events have been processed. When `createBufferStrategy()` returns, so will `invokeAndWait()`.

However, `createBufferStrategy()` is an asynchronous operation, so the `sleep()` call delays execution for a short time so the `getBufferStrategy()` call will get the correct details.

The asynchronous nature of many of the FSEM methods is a weakness of the API making it difficult to know when operations have been completed. Adding arbitrary `sleep()` calls is inelegant and may slow down execution unnecessarily.

 Other asynchronous methods in `GraphicsDevice` include `setDisplayMode()` and `setFullScreenWindow()`.

Double Buffering, Page Flipping, and More

All of my earlier versions of `WormChase` have drawn to an off-screen buffer (sometimes called a back buffer), which is copied to the screen by a call to `drawImage()`. The idea is illustrated in Figure 4-11.

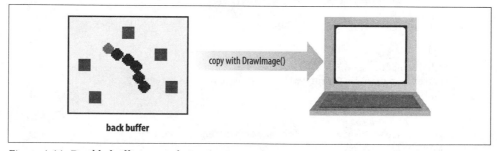

Figure 4-11. Double buffering rendering

The problem with this approach is that the amount of copying required to display one frame is substantial. For example, a display of 1,024×768 pixels, with 32-bit depth, will need a 3-MB copy (1024×768×4 bytes), occurring as often as 80 times per second. This is the principal reason for modifying the display mode: switching to 800×600 pixels and 16 bits reduces the copy size to about 940 KB ($800 \times 600 \times 2$).

Page flipping avoids these overheads by using a video pointer if one is available since a pointer may not be offered by older graphics hardware. The video pointer tells the graphics card where to look in VRAM for the image to be displayed during the next refresh. Page flipping involves two buffers, which are used alternatively as the primary surface for the screen. While the video pointer is pointing at one buffer, the other is updated. When the next refresh cycle comes around, the pointer is changed to refer to the second buffer and the first buffer is updated.

This approach is illustrated by Figures 4-12 and 4-13.

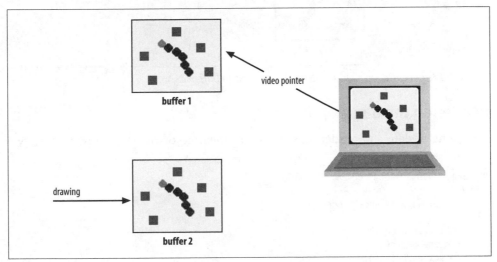

Figure 4-12. Page flipping (1); point to buffer 1; update buffer 2

The great advantage of this technique is that only pointer manipulation is required, with no need for copying.

 I'll be using two buffers in my code, but it's possible to use more, creating a *flip chain*. The video pointer cycles through the buffers while rendering is carried out to the other buffers in the chain.

In `initFullScreen()`, `Window.createBufferStrategy()` sets up the buffering for the window, based on the number specified (which should be two or more). The method tries a page flipping strategy with a video pointer first and then copies using hardware acceleration is used as a fallback. If both of these are unavailable, an unaccelerated copying strategy is used.

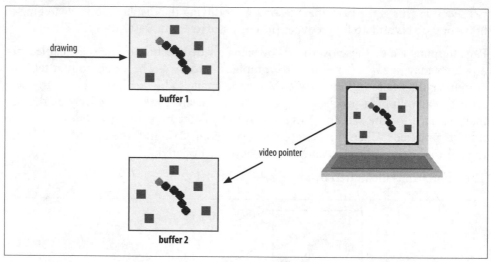

Figure 4-13. Page flipping (2); update buffer 1; point to buffer 2

Rendering the Game

The game update and rendering steps are at the core of run( ), represented by two method calls:

```
public void run( )
{
  // previously shown code

  while(running) {
    gameUpdate( );
    screenUpdate( );
    // sleep a while
    // maybe do extra gameUpdate( )'s
  }

  // previously shown code
}
```

gameUpdate( ) is unchanged from before; it updates the worm's state. screenUpdate( ) still performs active rendering but with the FSEM buffer strategy created in initFullScreen( ):

```
private void screenUpdate( )
{ try {
    gScr = bufferStrategy.getDrawGraphics( );
    gameRender(gScr);
    gScr.dispose( );
    if (!bufferStrategy.contentsLost( ))
```

```
      bufferStrategy.show( );
    else
      System.out.println("Contents Lost");
    Toolkit.getDefaultToolkit( ).sync( );    // sync the display on some systems
  }
  catch (Exception e)
  { e.printStackTrace( );
    running = false;
  }
} // end of screenUpdate( )
```

screenUpdate( ) utilizes the bufferStrategy reference to get a graphics context (gScr) for drawing. The try-catch block around the rendering operations means their failure causes the running Boolean to be set to false, which will terminate the animation loop.

gameRender( ) writes to the graphic context in the same way that the gameRender( ) methods in earlier versions of WormChase write to their off-screen buffer:

```
private void gameRender(Graphics gScr)
{
  // clear the background
  gScr.setColor(Color.white);
  gScr.fillRect (0, 0, pWidth, pHeight);

  gScr.setColor(Color.blue);
  gScr.setFont(font);

  // report frame count & average FPS and UPS at top left
  // report time used and boxes used at bottom left

  // draw the Pause and Quit buttons
  // draw game elements: the obstacles and the worm
  // game over stuff
} // end of gameRender( )
```

The only change is at the start of gameRender( ); there's no longer any need to create an off-screen buffer because initFullScreen( ) does it by calling createBufferStrategy( ).

Back in screenUpdate( ), BufferStrategy.contentsLost( ) returns true or false, depending on if the VRAM used by the buffer has been lost since the call to getDrawGraphics( ); buffer loss is caused by the OS taking back the memory.

Normally, the result will be false, and BufferStrategy.show( ) will then make the buffer visible on screen. This is achieved by changing the video pointer (*flipping*) or by copying (*blitting*).

If contentsLost( ) returns true, it means the entire image in the off-screen buffer must be redrawn. In my code, redrawing will happen anyway, during the next iteration of the animation loop, when screenUpdate( ) is called again.

Finishing Off

The finishOff( ) method is called in the same way as in the UFS version of WormChase: either at the end of run( ) as the animation loop is finishing or in response to a shutdown event:

```
private void finishOff()
{
  if (!finishedOff) {
    finishedOff = true;
    printStats();
    restoreScreen();
    System.exit(0):
  }
}

private void restoreScreen()
{ Window w = gd.getFullScreenWindow();
  if (w != null)
    w.dispose();
  gd.setFullScreenWindow(null);
}
```

The call to restoreScreen( ) is the only addition to finishOff( ). It switches off FSEM by executing GraphicsDevice.setFullScreenWindow(null). This method also restores the display mode to its original state if it was previously changed with setDisplayMode( ).

Displaying the Display Mode

initFullScreen( ) calls methods for reading and changing the display mode (though the call to setDisplayMode( ) is commented out). The display mode can only be changed after the application is in full-screen exclusive mode:

```
public void initFullScreen()
{
  // existing code

  gd.setFullScreenWindow(this); // switch on FSEM

  // I can now adjust the display modes, if I wish
  showCurrentMode();

  // setDisplayMode(800, 600, 8);      // 800 by 600, 8 bits, or
  // setDisplayMode(1280, 1024, 32);  // 1280 by 1024, 32 bits

  // more previously existing code

}  // end of initFullScreen()
```

showCurrentMode( ) prints the display mode details for the graphic card:

```
private void showCurrentMode()
{
  DisplayMode dm = gd.getDisplayMode();
  System.out.println("Current Display Mode: (" +
          dm.getWidth() + "," + dm.getHeight() + "," +
          dm.getBitDepth() + "," + dm.getRefreshRate() + ")  " );
}
```

A display mode is composed of the width and height of the monitor (in pixels), bit depth (the number of bits per pixel), and refresh rate. DisplayMode.getBitDepth( ) returns the integer BIT_DEPTH_MULTI (–1) if multiple bit depths are allowed in this mode (unlikely on most monitors). DisplayMode.getRefreshRate( ) returns REFRESH_RATE_UNKNOWN (0) if no information is available on the refresh rate and this means the refresh rate cannot be changed.

The output from showCurrentMode( ) is shown below, with a screen resolution of 1,024×768, 32-bit depth and an unknown (unchangeable) refresh rate:

```
>java WormChase 100
fps: 100; period: 10 ms
Current Display Mode: (1024,768,32,0)
```

Changing the Display Mode

A basic question is, "Why bother changing the display mode since the current setting is probably the most suitable one for the hardware?"

The answer is to increase performance. A smaller screen resolution and bit depth reduces the amount of data transferred when the back buffer is copied to the screen. However, this advantage is irrelevant if the rendering is carried out by page flipping with video pointer manipulation.

A game can run more quickly if its images share the same bit depth as the screen. This is easier to do if I fix the bit depth inside the application. A known screen size may make drawing operations simpler, especially for images that would normally have to be scaled to fit different display sizes.

My setDisplayMode( ) method is supplied with a width, height, and bit depth, and attempts to set the display mode accordingly:

```
private void setDisplayMode(int width, int height, int bitDepth)
{
  if (!gd.isDisplayChangeSupported()) {
    System.out.println("Display mode changing not supported");
    return;
  }
```

```
    if (!isDisplayModeAvailable(width, height, bitDepth)) {
      System.out.println("Display mode (" + width + "," +
                    height + "," + bitDepth + ") not available");
      return;
    }

    DisplayMode dm = new DisplayMode(width, height, bitDepth,
            DisplayMode.REFRESH_RATE_UNKNOWN);    // any refresh rate
    try {
      gd.setDisplayMode(dm);
      System.out.println("Display mode set to: (" +
              width + "," + height + "," + bitDepth + ")");
    }
    catch (IllegalArgumentException e)
    {  System.out.println("Error setting Display mode (" +
              width + "," + height + "," + bitDepth + ")");  }

    try {  // sleep to give time for the display to be changed
      Thread.sleep(1000);  // 1 sec
    }
    catch(InterruptedException ex){}
  }  // end of setDisplayMode()
```

The method checks if display mode changing is supported (the application must be in FSEM for changes to go ahead) and if the given mode is available for this graphics device, via a call to my isDisplayModeAvailable( ) method.

isDisplayModeAvailable( ) retrieves an array of display modes usable by this device, and cycles through them to see if one matches the requested parameters:

```
  private boolean isDisplayModeAvailable(int width, int height, int bitDepth)
  /* Check that a displayMode with this width, height, and
     bit depth is available.
     I don't care about the refresh rate, which is probably
     REFRESH_RATE_UNKNOWN anyway.
  */
  { DisplayMode[] modes = gd.getDisplayModes(); // modes list
    showModes(modes);

    for(int i = 0; i < modes.length; i++) {
      if ( width == modes[i].getWidth() &&
           height == modes[i].getHeight() &&
           bitDepth == modes[i].getBitDepth() )
        return true;
    }
    return false;
  }  // end of isDisplayModeAvailable()
```

showModes( ) is a pretty printer for the array of DisplayMode objects:

```
  private void showModes(DisplayMode[] modes)
  {
    System.out.println("Modes");
    for(int i = 0; i < modes.length; i++) {
      System.out.print("(" + modes[i].getWidth() + "," +
```

```
                    modes[i].getHeight() + "," +
                    modes[i].getBitDepth() + "," +
                    modes[i].getRefreshRate() + ")   ");
      if ((i+1)%4 == 0)
        System.out.println();
    }
    System.out.println();
  }
```

Back in my setDisplayMode( ), a new display mode object is created and set with
GraphicDevice's setDisplayMode( ), which may raise an exception if any of its arguments are incorrect. GraphicDevice.setDisplayMode( ) is asynchronous, so the subsequent sleep( ) call delays execution a short time in the hope that the display will be
changed before the method returns. Some programmers suggest a delay of two
seconds.

The GraphicsDevice.setDisplayMode( ) method (different from my setDisplayMode( ))
is known to have bugs. However, it has improved in recent versions of J2SE 1.4, and
in J2SE 5.0. My tests across several versions of Windows, using J2SE 1.4.2, sometimes resulted in a JVM crash, occurring after the program had been run successfully
a few times. This is one reason why the call to my setDisplayMode( ) is commented
out in initFullScreen( ).

My setDisplayMode( ) can be employed to set the screen size to 800x600 with an
8-bit depth:

```
setDisplayMode(800, 600, 8);
```

The resulting on-screen appearance is shown in Figure 4-14. The reduced screen resolution means that the various graphical elements (e.g., the text, circles, and boxes)
are bigger. The reduced bit depth causes a reduction in the number of available colors, but the basic colors used here (blue, black, red, and green) are still present.

The output from WormChase lists the initial display mode, the range of possible
modes, and the new mode:

```
D>java WormChase 100
fps: 100; period: 10 ms
Current Display Mode: (1024,768,32,0)
Modes
(400,300,8,0)  (400,300,16,0)  (400,300,32,0)  (512,384,8,0)
(512,384,16,0)  (512,384,32,0)  (640,400,8,0)  (640,400,16,0)
(640,400,32,0)  (640,480,8,0)  (640,480,16,0)  (640,480,32,0)
(800,600,8,0)  (800,600,16,0)  (800,600,32,0)  (848,480,8,0)
(848,480,16,0)  (848,480,32,0)  (1024,768,8,0)  (1024,768,16,0)
(1024,768,32,0)  (1152,864,8,0)  (1152,864,16,0)  (1152,864,32,0)
(1280,768,8,0)  (1280,768,16,0)  (1280,768,32,0)  (1280,960,8,0)
(1280,960,16,0)  (1280,960,32,0)  (1280,1024,8,0)  (1280,1024,16,0)
(1280,1024,32,0)
Display mode set to: (800,600,8)
```

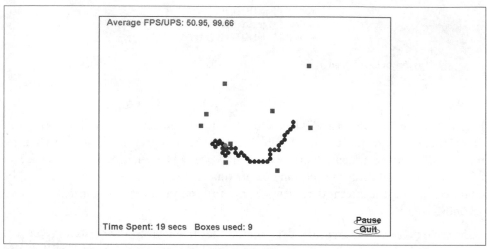

Figure 4-14. WormChase with a modified display mode

An essential task if the display mode is changed is to change it back to its original setting at the end of the application. `WormChase` does this by calling `gd.setFullScreenWindow(null)` in `restoreScreen( )`.

Timings for FSEM

Timing results for the FSEM `WormChase` are given in Table 4-3.

Table 4-3. Average FPS/UPS rates for the FSEM WormChase

Requested FPS	20	50	80	100
Windows 98	20/20	50/50	81/83	84/100
Windows 2000	20/20	50/50	60/83	60/100
Windows XP (1)	20/20	50/50	74/83	76/100
Windows XP (2)	20/20	50/50	83/83	85/100

`WormChase` on the Windows 2000 machine is the worst performer as usual, but its UPS values are fine. FSEM produces a drastic increase in the frame rate; it produces 60 FPS when 80 is requested compared to the UFS version of `WormChase`, which only manages 18 FPS.

The Windows 98 and XP boxes produce good to excellent frame rates at 80 FPS, but can't go any faster. FSEM improves the frame rates by around 20 percent compared to UFS, except in the case of the first XP machine.

One reason for flattening out the frame rate values may be that BufferStrategy's show( ) method—used in my screenUpdate( ) to render to the screen—is tied to the frequency of the vertical synchronization (often abbreviated to *vsync*) of the monitor. In FSEM, show( ) blocks until the next vsync signal.

Frame rates for Windows-based FSEM applications can be collected using the FRAPS utility (*http://www.fraps.com*). Figure 4-15 shows WormChase with a FRAPS-generated FPS value in the top righthand corner.

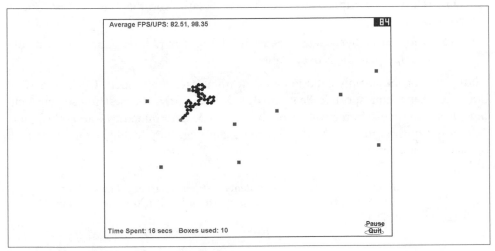

Figure 4-15. FSEM WormChase with FRAPS output

Timings at 80 to 85 FPS

Table 4-4 shows the UFS, AFS, and FSEM results for different versions of Windows when 80 FPS are requested.

Table 4-4. Average FPS/UPS rates for the AFS, UFS, and FSEM versions of WormChase when 80 FPS are requested

Requested 80 FPS	AFS	UFS	FSEM
Windows 98	75/83	70/83	81/83
Windows 2000	20/83	18/83	60/83
Windows XP (1)	82/83	77/83	74/83
Windows XP (2)	75/83	68/83	83/83

The numbers send mixed signals and, in any case, the sample size is too small for strong conclusions. Nevertheless, I'll make a few observations:

- The use of additional state updates to keep the UPS close to the requested FPS is an important technique for giving the appearance of speed even when the rendering rate is sluggish.

- FSEM offers better frame rates than UFS, sometimes dramatically better. However, FSEM's benefits rely on MS Window's access to the graphics device via DirectDraw. The improvements on Linux, Solaris, and the Mac OS may not be so striking.

- AFS produces higher frame rates than UFS and may be a good choice if full-screen exclusive mode is unavailable.

All the approaches supply good to excellent frame rates on modern CPUs (the Windows 2000 machine sports a Pentium II). Consequently, the best full-screen technique for a particular game will probably have to be determined by timing the game. Additional optimization techniques, such as clipping, may highlight the benefits of one technique over another.

 I'd like to thank two of my students, Patipol Kulasi and Thana Konglikhit, who helped gather the timing data used in this chapter and Chapter 3.

CHAPTER 5

An Introduction to Java Imaging

This chapter presents an overview of image loading and processing in Java, areas that have seen major changes in recent releases of the SDK, mainly driven by the wish for speed. It's principally about introducing concepts that are illustrated in more detail in Chapter 6.

I begin by reviewing the (rather outmoded) AWT imaging model, which is being superseded by the `BufferedImage` and `VolatileImage` classes, `ImageIO`, and the wide range of `BufferedImageOp` image operations offered by Java 2D. If these aren't enough, then Java Advanced Imaging (JAI) has even more capabilities.

Many of the topics discussed here are utilized in Chapter 6, where I develop a `ImagesLoader` class. It loads images from a Java ARchive (JAR) file using `ImageIO`'s `read( )` and holds them as `BufferedImage` objects.

Chapter 6 utilizes `ImagesLoader` in an `ImagesTests` application, which demonstrates 11 different visual effects, including zapping, teleportation, reddening, blurring, and flipping. The effects are derived from Java 2D operations, such as convolution and affine transformation.

Image Formats

A game will typically use a mix of the GIF, JPEG, and PNG images, popular graphics formats that have advantages and disadvantages.

A Graphics Interchange Format (GIF) image is best for cartoon-style graphics using few colors, since only a maximum of 256 colors can be represented in a file. This is due to GIF's use of a 256-element color table to store information.

One of these color table entries can represent a "transparent" color, which Java honors by not drawing.

GIF offers rudimentary animation by permitting a file to contain several images. These are drawn consecutively when the file is displayed (e.g., with `drawImage( )` in Java). This feature isn't of much use since there's no simple way of controlling the animation from within Java.

A Joint Photographic Experts Group (JPEG) file employs 3 bytes (24 bits) per pixel (1 byte for each of the red, green, and blue [RGB] components), but a lossy compression scheme reduces the space quite considerably. This may cause large areas using a single color to appear blotchy, and sharp changes in contrast can become blurred (e.g., at the edges of black text on a white background). JPEG files are best for large photographic images, such as game backgrounds. JPEG files do not offer transparency.

The Portable Network Graphics (PNG) format is intended as a replacement for GIF. It includes an alpha channel along with the usual RGB components, which permits an image to include translucent areas. Translucency is particularly useful for gaming effects like laser beams, smoke, and ghosts (of course). Other advantages over GIF are gamma correction, which enables image brightness to be controlled across platforms, as well as 2D interlacing and (slightly) better lossless compression. This last feature makes PNG a good storage choice while a photographic image is being edited, but JPEG is probably better for the finished image since its lossy compression achieves greater size reductions.

 Some developers prefer PNG since it's an open source standard (see *http://www.libpng.org/pub/png/*), with no patents involved; the GIF format is owned by CompuServe.

The AWT Imaging Model

JDK 1.0 introduced the AWT imaging model for downloading and drawing images. Back then, it was thought that the most common use of imaging would involve applets pulling graphics from the Web. A standard '90s example (with the exception of using JApplet) is shown in Example 5-1.

Example 5-1. ShowImage applet (Version 1) using Image

```
import javax.swing.*;
import java.awt.*;

public class ShowImage extends JApplet
{
  private Image im;

  public void init()
  {  im = getImage( getDocumentBase( ), "ball.gif");  }

  public void paint(Graphics g)
  {  g.drawImage(im, 0, 0, this);  }
}
```

The getDocumentBase( ) method returns the URL of the directory holding the original web document, and this is prepended to the image's filename to get a URL suitable for getImage( ).

The central problem with networked image retrieval is speed. Consequently, the Java designers considered it a bad idea to have an applet stop while an image crawled over from the server side. As a result, we have confusing behavior for getImage( ) and drawImage( ). Neither of these do what their name implies. The getImage( ) method is poorly named since it doesn't get (or download) the image at all; instead it prepares an empty Image object (im) for holding the image, returning immediately after that. The downloading is triggered by drawImage( ) in paint( ), which is called as the applet is loaded into the browser after init( ) has finished.

The fourth argument supplied to drawImage( ) is an ImageObserver (usually the applet or JFrame in an application), which will monitor the gradual downloading of the image. As data arrives, the Component's imageUpdate( ) is repeatedly called. imageUpdate( )'s default behavior is to call repaint( ), to redraw the image since more data are available, and return true. However, if an error has occurred with the image retrieval then imageUpdate( ) will return false. imageUpdate( ) can be overridden and modified by the programmer.

The overall effect is that paint( ) will be called repeatedly as the image is downloaded, causing the image to appear gradually on-screen. This effect is only noticeable if the image is coming over the network; if the file is stored locally, then it will be drawn in full almost instantaneously.

The result of this coding style means that the Image (im) contains no data until paint( ) is called and even then may not contain complete information for several seconds or minutes. This makes programming difficult: for instance, a GUI cannot easily allocate an on-screen space to the image since it has no known width or height until painting has started.

Since the introduction of JDK 1.0, experience has shown that most programs do not want graphics to be drawn incrementally during execution. For example, game sprites should be fully realized from the start.

The getImage( ) method is only for applets; there is a separate getImage( ) method for applications, accessible from Toolkit. For example:

```
Image im = Toolkit.getDefaultToolkit( ).getImage("http://....");
```

As with the getImage( ) method for applets, it doesn't download anything. That task is done by paint( ).

The MediaTracker Class

Most programs (and most games) want to preload images before drawing them. In other words, we do not want to tie downloading to painting.

One solution is the java.awt.MediaTracker class: a MediaTracker object can start the download of an image and suspend execution until it has fully arrived or an error occurs. The init( ) method in the ShowImage class can be modified to do this:

```
public void init( )
{
   im = getImage( getDocumentBase( ), "ball.gif");

   MediaTracker tracker = new MediaTracker(this);
   tracker.addImage(im, 0);
   try {
      tracker.waitForID(0);
   }
   catch (InterruptedException e)
   {  System.out.println("Download Error"); }
}
```

waitForID( ) starts the separate download thread, and suspends until it finishes. The ID used in the MediaTracker object can be any positive integer.

 This approach means that the applet will be slower to start since init( )'s execution will be suspended while the image is retrieved.

In paint( ), drawImage( ) will only draw the image since a download is unnecessary. Consequently, drawImage( ) can be supplied with a null (empty) ImageObserver:

```
drawImage(im, 0, 0, null);
```

A common way of accelerating the downloading of multiple images is to spawn a pool of threads, each one assigned to the retrieval of a single image. Only when every thread has completed will init( ) return.

ImageIcon

Writing MediaTracker code in every applet/application can be boring, so an ImageIcon class was introduced, which sets up a MediaTracker by itself. The ImageIcon name is a bit misleading: any size of image can be downloaded, not just an icon.

Using ImageIcon, the init( ) method becomes:

```
public void init( )
{ im = new ImageIcon( getDocumentBase( )+"ball.gif").getImage( );  }
```

The ImageIcon object can be converted to an Image (as here) or can be painted with ImageIcon's paintIcon( ) method.

The Rise of JARs

A JAR file is a way of packaging code and resources together into a single, compressed file. Resources can be almost anything, including images and sounds.

If an applet (or application) is going to utilize a lot of images, repeated network connections to download them will severely reduce execution speed. It's better to create a single JAR file containing the applet (or application) and all the images and to have the browser (or user) download it. Then, when an image comes to be loaded, it's a fast, local load from the JAR file. From a user's point of view, the download of the code takes a little longer, but it executes without any annoying delays caused by image loading.

At the end of Chapter 6, I'll explain how to package the ImagesTests code, and the large number of images it uses, as a JAR file. The only coding change occurs in specifying the location of an image file. Going back to a simpler example, the ImageIcon example from above would need to be rewritten this way:

```
im = new ImageIcon( getClass( ).getResource("ball.gif") ).getImage( );
```

getClass( ) gets the Class reference for the object (e.g., ShowImage), and getResource( ) specifies the resource is stored in the same place as that class.

AWT Image Processing

It can be difficult to access the various elements of an Image object, such as pixel data or the color model. For instance, the image manipulation features in AWT are primarily aimed at modifying individual pixels as they pass through a filter. A stream of pixel data is sent out by a ImageProducer, passes through an ImageFilter, and on to an ImageConsumer (see Figure 5-1). This is known as the *push model* since stream data are "pushed" out by the producer.

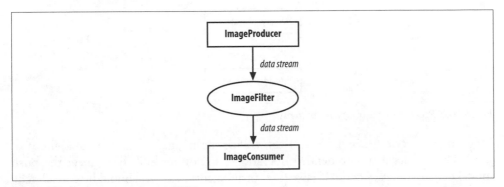

Figure 5-1. Image processing in AWT

The two predefined `ImageFilter` subclasses are `CropImageFilter` for cropping regions of pixels and `RGBImageFilter` for processing individual pixels.

 Chaining filters together is possible by making a consumer of one filter the producer for another.

This stream-view of filtering makes it difficult to process groups of pixels, especially ones that are noncontiguous. For example, a convolution operation for image smoothing would require a new subclass of `ImageFilter` and a new `ImageConsumer` to deal with the disruption to the pixels stream.

An alternative approach is to use the `PixelGrabber` class to collect all the pixel data from an image into an array, where it can then be conveniently processed in its entirety. The `MemoryImageSource` class is necessary to output the changed array's data as a stream to a specified `ImageConsumer`. The additional steps in the push model are shown in Figure 5-2.

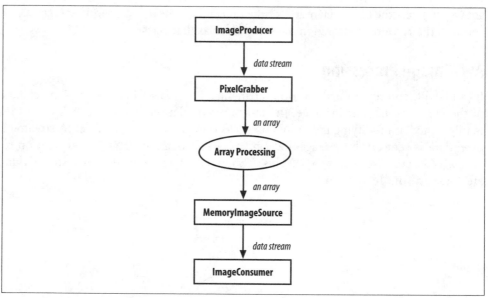

Figure 5-2. Processing the image as an array

Modern Java code (since J2SE 1.2) can utilize the image processing capabilities of Java 2D, with its many predefined operations, so you're unlikely to meet the push model except in legacy code. If Java 2D is insufficient, then JAI should be considered.

An Overview of Java 2D

Java 2D offers a set of graphics features that address the inadequacies in the older AWT graphics classes. Weaknesses in AWT include only supporting single pixel thickness lines, limited fonts, poor shape manipulation (e.g., no rotation), and no special fills, gradients, or patterns inside shapes.

Java 2D replaces most of the shape primitives in AWT (e.g., rectangles, arcs, lines, ellipses, polygons) with versions that can take double or floating pointing coordinates, though many people still use the old `drawLine()`, `drawRect()`, and `fillRect()` methods. Of more interest is the ability to create arbitrary geometric shapes by using set operations on other shapes with union, intersection, subtraction, and exclusive-or. A `GeneralPath` class permits a shape to be built from a series of connected lines and curves, and curves can be defined using splines. (A spline's curviness is specified using a series of control point.)

Java 2D distinguishes between shape stroking and filling. *Stroking* is the drawing of lines and shape outlines, which may employ various patterns and thicknesses. Shape *filling* can use a solid color (as in AWT), and patterns, color gradients, and images acting as textures.

Affine transformations can be applied to shapes and images, including translation, rotation, scaling, and shearing, and groups of transformations can be composed together. `drawImage()` can be supplied with such a transformation, which is applied before the image is rendered. Shapes and images can be drawn together using eight different compositing rules, optionally combined with varying transparency values. Clipping can be applied, based on an arbitrary shape (not just a rectangle, as in AWT).

Rendering hints include the anti-aliasing of shapes and text (i.e., the smoothing of their jagged edges), image interpolation, and whether to use high-speed or high-quality rendering.

 As a bonus, Java-based printing became relatively easy to control with Java 2D.

Java's top-level web page for Java 2D is *http://java.sun.com/products/java-media/2D/*, with extensive documentation and a tutorial trail in J2SE.

The Graphics2D Class

The central Java 2D class is `Graphics2D`, a subclass of AWT's `Graphics`. `paint()` or `paintComponent()` must cast the graphics context to become a `Graphics2D` object before Java 2D operations can be employed, as shown in the paintComponent( ) method:

```
public void paintComponent(Graphics g)
// draw a blue square
{
  super.paintComponent(g);
  Graphics2D g2d = (Graphics2D) g;  // cast the graphics context

  g2d.setPaint(Color.blue);
  Rectangle2D.Double square = new Rectangle2D.Double(10,10,350,350);
  g2d.fill(square);
}
```

The shape can be drawn in outline with draw( ) or filled using the current pen settings by calling fill( ).

Java 2D and Active Rendering

Java 2D operations can be easily utilized in the active rendering approach described in Chapters 2 through 4. As you may recall, a Graphics object for the off-screen buffer is obtained by calling getGraphics( ) inside gameRender( ). This can be cast to a Graphics2D object:

```
// global variables for off-screen rendering
private Graphics2D dbg2D;      // was a Graphics object, dbg
private Image dbImage = null;


private void gameRender( )
// draw the current frame to an image buffer
{
  if (dbImage == null){  // create the buffer
    dbImage = createImage(PWIDTH, PHEIGHT);
    if (dbImage == null) {
      System.out.println("dbImage is null");
      return;
    }
    else
      dbg2D = (Graphics2D) dbImage.getGraphics();
  }

  // clear the background using Java 2D
  // draw game elements using Java 2D
  // existing logic

  if (gameOver)
    gameOverMessage(dbg2D);
} // end of gameRender( )
```

Methods called from gameRender( ), such as gameOverMessage( ), can utilize the Graphics2D object, dbg2D.

In FSEM, the Graphics object is obtained by calling getDrawGraphics( ), and its result can be cast:

```
private Graphics2D gScr2d;      // global, was Graphics gScr


private void screenUpdate( )
{ try {
    gScr2d = (Graphics2D) bufferStrategy.getDrawGraphics( );
    gameRender(gScr2d);
    gScr2d.dispose( );
    // previously shown logic
  }
```

gameRender( ) receives a Graphics2D object, so it has the full range of Java 2D operations at its disposal.

Buffering an Image

The BufferedImage class is a subclass of Image, so it can be employed instead of Image in methods such as drawImage( ). BufferedImage has two main advantages: the data required for image manipulation are easily accessible through its methods, and BufferedImage objects are automatically converted to *managed images* by the JVM (when possible). A managed image may allow hardware acceleration to be employed when the image is being rendered.

The code in Example 5-2 is the ShowImage applet, recoded to use a BufferedImage.

Example 5-2. ShowImage applet (Version 2) using BufferedImage

```
import javax.swing.*;
import java.awt.*;
import java.io.*;
import java.awt.image.*;
import javax.imageio.ImageIO;


public class ShowImage extends JApplet
{
  private BufferedImage im;

  public void init( )
  { try {
      im = ImageIO.read( getClass( ).getResource("ball.gif") );
    }
    catch(IOException e) {
      System.out.println("Load Image error:");
    }
  } // end of init( )

  public void paint(Graphics g)
  { g.drawImage(im, 0, 0, this);  }
}
```

The simplest, and perhaps fastest, way of loading a BufferedImage object is with read( ) from the ImageIO class. Some tests suggest that it may be 10 percent faster than using ImageIcon, which can be significant when the image is large. InputStream, and ImageInputStream are different versions of read( ) for reading from a URL.

Optimizing the BufferedImage is possible so it has the same internal data format and color model as the underlying graphics device. This requires us to make a copy of the input image using GraphicsConfiguration's createCompatibleImage( ). The various steps are packaged together inside a loadImage( ) method; the complete (modified) class is given in Example 5-3.

Example 5-3. ShowImage applet (Version 3) using an optimized BufferedImage

```java
import javax.swing.*;
import java.awt.*;
import java.io.*;
import java.awt.image.*;
import javax.imageio.ImageIO;


public class ShowImage extends JApplet
{
  private GraphicsConfiguration gc;
  private BufferedImage im;

  public void init( )
  {
    // get this device's graphics configuration
    GraphicsEnvironment ge =
        GraphicsEnvironment.getLocalGraphicsEnvironment( );
    gc = ge.getDefaultScreenDevice( ).getDefaultConfiguration( );

    im = loadImage("ball.gif");
  } // end of init( )


  public BufferedImage loadImage(String fnm)
  /* Load the image from <fnm>, returning it as a BufferedImage
     which is compatible with the graphics device being used.
     Uses ImageIO. */
  {
    try {
      BufferedImage im = ImageIO.read(getClass( ).getResource(fnm));

      int transparency = im.getColorModel( ).getTransparency( );
      BufferedImage copy =  gc.createCompatibleImage(
                             im.getWidth( ),im.getHeight( ),transparency );

      // create a graphics context
      Graphics2D g2d = copy.createGraphics( );
```

```
    // copy image
    g2d.drawImage(im,0,0,null);
    g2d.dispose( );
    return copy;
  }
  catch(IOException e) {
    System.out.println("Load Image error for " + fnm + ":\n" + e);
    return null;
  }
} // end of loadImage( )


public void paint(Graphics g)
{  g.drawImage(im, 0, 0, this);  }

} // end of ShowImage class
```

The three-argument version of createCompatibleImage( ) is utilized, which requires the BufferedImage's width, height, and transparency value. The possible transparency values are Transparency.OPAQUE, Transparency.BITMASK, and Transparency.TRANSLUCENT. The BITMASK setting is applicable to GIFs that have a transparent area, and TRANSLUCENT can be employed by translucent PNG images.

There's a two-argument version of createCompatibleImage( ), which only requires the image's width and height, but if the source image has a transparent or translucent component, then it (most probably) will be copied incorrectly. For instance, the transparent areas in the source may be drawn as solid black.

Fortunately, it's quite simple to access the transparency information in the source BufferedImage, by querying its ColorModel (explained later):

```
int transparency = im.getColorModel( ).getTransparency( );
```

The BufferedImage object copy is initialized by drawing the source image into its graphics context.

Another reason for the use of createCompatibleImage( ) is that it permits J2SE 1.4.2 to mark the resulting BufferedImage as a managed image, which may later be drawn to the screen using hardware acceleration. In J2SE 5.0, the JVM knows that anything read in by ImageIO's read( ) can become a managed image, so the call to createCompatibleImage( ) is no longer necessary for that reason. The call should still be made though since it optimizes the BufferedImage's internals for the graphics device.

From Image to BufferedImage

Legacy code usually employs Image, and it may not be feasible to rewrite the entire code base to utilize BufferedImage. Instead, is there a way to convert an Image object to a BufferedImage object? makeBIM( ) makes a gallant effort:

```
private BufferedImage makeBIM(Image im, int width, int height)
// make a BufferedImage copy of im, assuming an alpha channel
{
  BufferedImage copy = new BufferedImage(width, height,
                                 BufferedImage.TYPE_INT_ARGB);
  // create a graphics context
  Graphics2D g2d = copy.createGraphics( );

  // copy image
  g2d.drawImage(im,0,0,null);
  g2d.dispose( );
  return copy;
}
```

This method can be used in ShowImage:

```
public void init( )
// load an imageIcon, convert to BufferedImage
{
  ImageIcon imIcon = new ImageIcon( getClass( ).getResource("ball.gif") );
  im = makeBIM(imIcon.getImage( ), imIcon.getIconWidth( ),
                         imIcon.getIconHeight( ));
}
```

I load an ImageIcon (to save on MediaTracker coding) and pass its Image, width, and height into makeBIM( ), getting back a suitable BufferedImage object.

A thorny issue with makeBIM( ) is located in the BufferedImage( ) constructor. The constructor must be supplied with a type, and there's a lot to choose from (look at the Java documentation for BufferedImage for a complete list). A partial list appears in Table 5-1.

Table 5-1. Some BufferedImage types

BufferedImage type	Description
TYPE_INT_ARGB	8-bit alpha, red, green, and blue samples packed into a 32-bit integer
TYPE_INT_RGB	8-bit red, green, and blue samples packed into a 32-bit integer
TYPE_BYTE_GRAY	An unsigned byte grayscale image (1 pixel/byte)
TYPE_BYTE_BINARY	A byte-packed binary image (8 pixels/byte)
TYPE_INT_BGR	8-bit blue, green, and red samples packed into a 32-bit integer
TYPE_3BYTE_RGB	8-bit blue, green, and red samples packed into 1 byte each

An image is made up of pixels (of course), and each pixel is composed from (perhaps) several samples. *Samples* hold the color component data that combine to make the pixel's overall color.

A standard set of color components are red, green, and blue (RGB for short). The pixels in a transparent or translucent color image will include an alpha (A) component to specify the degree of transparency for the pixels. A grayscale image only utilizes a single sample per pixel.

BufferedImage types specify how the samples that make up a pixel's data are packed together. For example, TYPE_INT_ARGB packs its four samples into 8 bits each so that a single pixel can be stored in a single 32-bit integer. This is shown graphically in Figure 5-3.

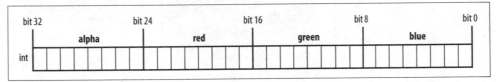

Figure 5-3. A TYPE_INT_ARGB pixel

This format is used for the BufferedImage object in makeBIM( ) since it's the most general. The RGB and alpha components can have 256 different values (2^8), with 255 being full-on. For the alpha part, 0 means fully transparent, ranging up to 255 for fully opaque.

Is such flexibility always needed, for instance, when the image is opaque or a grayscale? It may not be possible to accurately map an image stored using a drastically different color model to the range of colors here. An example would be an image using 16-bit color components. Nevertheless, makeBIM( ) deals with the normal range of image formats, e.g., GIF, JPEG, and PNG, and so is satisfactory for our needs.

A more rigorous solution is to use AWT's imaging processing capabilities to analyze the source Image object and construct a BufferedImage accordingly. A PixelGrabber can access the pixel data inside the Image and determine if an alpha component exists and if the image is grayscale or RGB.

A third answer is to go back to basics and ask why the image is being converted to a BufferedImage object at all? A common reason is to make use of BufferedImageOp operations, but they're available without the image being converted. It's possible to wrap a BufferedImageOp object in a BufferedImageFilter to make it behave like an AWT ImageFilter.

The Internals of BufferedImage

The data maintained by a BufferedImage object are represented by Figure 5-4.

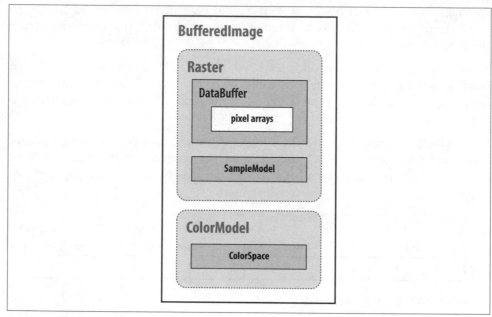

Figure 5-4. BufferedImage internals

A BufferedImage instance is made up of a Raster object that stores the pixel data and a ColorModel, which contains methods for converting those data into colors. DataBuffer holds a rectangular array of numbers that make up the data, and SampleModel explains how those numbers are grouped into the samples for each pixel.

One way of viewing the image is as a collection of bands or channels: a *band* is a collection of the same samples from all the pixels. For instance, an ARGB file contains four bands for alpha, red, green, and blue.

The ColorModel object defines how the samples in a pixel are mapped to color components, and ColorSpace specifies how the components are combined to form a renderable color.

Java 2D supports many color spaces, including the standardized RGB (sRGB) color space, which corresponds to the TYPE_INT_ARGB format in Figure 5-3. The BufferedImage method getRGB(x,y) utilizes this format: (x, y) is the pixel coordinate, and a single integer is returned which, with the help of bit manipulation, can expose its 8-bit alpha, red, green, and blue components.

setRGB( ) updates an image pixel, and there are get and set methods to manipulate all the pixels as an array of integers. Two of the ImagesTests visual effects in Chapter 6 use these methods.

BufferedImageOp Operations

Java 2D's image processing operations are (for the most part) subclasses of the `BufferedImageOp` interface, which supports an immediate imaging model. *Image processing* is a filtering operation that takes a source `BufferedImage` as input and produces a new `BufferedImage` as output. The idea is captured by Figure 5-5.

Figure 5-5. *The BufferedImageOp imaging model*

This doesn't appear to be much different from the `ImageFilter` idea in Figure 5-1. The differences are in the expressibility of the operations that can, for instance, manipulate groups of pixels and affect the color space. This is due to the data model offered by `BufferedImage`.

The code fragment below shows the creation of a new `BufferedImage`, by manipulating a source `BufferedImage` using `RescaleOp`; `RescaleOp` implements the `BufferedImageOp` interface:

```
RescaleOp negOp = new RescaleOp(-1.0f, 255f, null);
BufferedImage destination = negOp.filter(source, null);
```

The `filter()` method does the work, taking the `source` image as input and returning the resulting image as `destination`.

Certain image processing operations can be carried out *in place*, which means that the destination `BufferedImage` can be the source; there's no need to create a new `BufferedImage` object.

Another common way of using a `BufferedImageOp` is as an argument to `drawImage()`; the image will be processed, and the result drawn straight to the screen:

```
g2d.drawImage(source, negOp, x, y);
```

The predefined `BufferedImageOp` image processing classes are listed in Table 5-2.

Table 5-2. *Image processing classes*

Class name	Description	Some possible effects	In place?
AffineTransformOp	Apply a geometric transformation to the image's coordinates.	Scaling, rotating, shearing.	No
BandCombineOp	Combine bands in the image's Raster.	Change the mix of colors.	Yes
ColorConvertOp	ColorSpace conversion.	Convert RGB to grayscale.	Yes

Table 5-2. Image processing classes (continued)

Class name	Description	Some possible effects	In place?
ConvolveOp	Combine groups of pixel values to obtain a new pixel value.	Blurring, sharpening, edge detection.	No
LookupOp	Modify pixel values based on a table lookup.	Color inversion, reddening, brightening, darkening.	Yes
RescaleOp	Modify pixel values based on a linear equation.	Mostly the same as LookupOp.	Yes

Various examples of these, together with more detailed explanations of the operations, will be given in Chapter 6 when I discuss ImagesTests.

Managed Images

A managed image is automatically cached in video memory (VRAM) by the JVM. When drawImage( ) is applied to its original version located in system memory (RAM), the JVM uses the VRAM cache instead, and employs a hardware copy (*blit*) to draw it to the screen. The payoff is speed since a hardware blit will be faster than a software-based copy from RAM to the screen. This idea is illustrated by Figure 5-6.

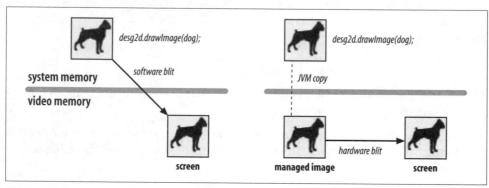

Figure 5-6. Drawing images and managed images

A managed image is not explicitly created by the programmer because there's no ManagedImage class that can be used to instantiate suitable objects. Managed images are created at the whim of the JVM, though the programmer can "encourage" the JVM to make them.

Image, ImageIcon, and BufferedImage objects qualify to become managed images if they have been created with createImage( ), createCompatibleImage( ), read in with getImage( ) or ImageIO's read( ), or created with the BufferedImage( ) constructor. Opaque images and images with BITMASK transparency (e.g., GIF files) can be managed. Translucent images can be managed but require property flags to be set, which vary between Windows and Linux/Solaris.

The JVM will copy an image to VRAM when it detects that the image has not been changed or edited for a significant amount of time; typically, this means when two consecutive drawImage( ) calls have used the same image. The VRAM copy will be scrapped if the original image is manipulated by an operation that is not hardware accelerated, and the next drawImage( ) will switch back to the RAM version.

Exactly which operations are hardware accelerated depends on the OS. Virtually nothing aside from image translation is accelerated in Windows; this is not due to inadequacies in DirectDraw but rather to the Java interface. The situation is a lot better on Linux/Solaris where all affine transformations, composites, and clips will be accelerated. However, these features depend on underlying OS support for a version of OpenGL that offers pbuffers. A *pbuffer* is a kind of off-screen rendering area, somewhat like a pixmap but with support for accelerated rendering.

Bearing in mind how the JVM deals with managed images, it is inadvisable to modify them excessively at run time since their hardware acceleration will probably be lost, at least for a short time.

 In some older documentation, managed images are known as *automated images*.

VolatileImage

Whereas managed images are created by the JVM, the VolatileImage class allow programmers to create and manage their own hardware-accelerated images. In fact, a VolatileImage object exists only in VRAM; it has no system memory copy at all (see Figure 5-7).

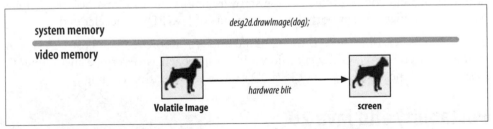

Figure 5-7. A VolatileImage object

VolatileImage objects stay in VRAM, so they get the benefits of hardware blitting all the time. Well, that's sort of true, but it depends on the underlying OS. In Windows, VolatileImage is implemented using DirectDraw, which manages the image in video memory, and may decide to grab the memory back to give to another task, such as a screensaver or new foreground process. This means that the programmer must keep checking his VolatileImage objects to see if they're still around. If a

VolatileImage's memory is lost, then the programmer has to re-create the object. The situation is better on Linux/Solaris since VolatileImage is implemented with OpenGL pbuffers, which can't be deallocated by the OS.

Another drawback with VolatileImages is that any processing of an image must be done in VRAM, which is generally slower to do as a software operation than similar calculations in RAM. Of course, if the manipulation (e.g., applying an affine transform such as a rotation) can be done by the VRAM hardware, then it will be faster than in system memory. Unfortunately, the mix of software/hardware-based operations depends on the OS.

Bearing in mind the issues surrounding VolatileImage, when is it useful? Its key benefit over managed images is that the programmer is in charge rather than the JVM. The programmer can decide when to create, update, and delete an image.

However, managed image support is becoming so good in the JVM that most programs probably do not need the complexity that VolatileImage adds to the code. ImagesTests in Chapter 6 uses only managed images, which it encourages by creating only BufferedImages.

Java 2D Speed

The issues over the speed of Java 2D operations mirror my discussion about the use of managed images and VolatileImages, since speed depends on which operations are hardware accelerated, and the hardware accelerated options depends on the OS.

On Windows, hardware acceleration is mostly restricted to the basic 2D operations such as filling, copying rectangular areas, line drawing (vertical and horizontal only), and basic text rendering. Unfortunately, the fun parts of Java 2D—such as curves, anti-aliasing, and compositing—all use software rendering. In Linux/Solaris, so long as OpenGL buffers are supported, most elements of Java 2D are accelerated.

The situation described here is for J2SE 5.0 and will improve. The best check is to profile your code. A Java 2D-specific profiling approach is described in Chapter 6, based around the switching on of Java 2D's low-level operation logging.

Portability and Java 2D

The current situation with Java 2D's hardware acceleration exposes a rather nasty portability problem with Java. Graphics, especially gaming graphics, require speed, and the Java implementers have taken a two-track approach. The Windows-based version of Java utilizes DirectX and other Windows features, yet on other platforms, the software underlying Java 2D relies on OpenGL.

This approach seems like an unnecessary duplication of effort and a source of confusion to programmers. The same situation exists for Java 3D, as described in Chapter 14 and beyond.

In my opinion, Java graphics should restrict itself to OpenGL, an open standard that is under active development by many talented people around the world. In fact, this view may already be prevailing inside Sun, indicated by its promotion of a Java/OpenGL (JOGL) (*https://jogl.dev.java.net/*) binding.

JAI

Java Advanced Imaging (JAI) offers extended image processing capabilities beyond those found in Java 2D. For example, geometric operations include translation, rotation, scaling, shearing, transposition, and warping. Pixel-based operations utilize lookup tables and rescaling equations but can be applied to multiple sources, then combined to get a single outcome. Modifications can be restricted to regions in the source, statistical operations are available (e.g., mean and median), and frequency domains can be employed.

An intended application domain for JAI is the manipulation of images too large to be loaded into memory in their entirety. A TiledImage class supports pixel editing based on tiles, which can be processed and displayed independently of their overall image.

Image processing can be distributed over a network by using RMI to farm out areas of the image to servers, with the results returned to the client for displaying.

JAI employs a *pull imaging model*, where an image is constructed from a series of source images, arranged into a graph. When a particular pixel (or tile) is required, only then will the image request data from the necessary sources. These kinds of extended features aren't usually required for gaming and aren't used in this book.

More information on JAI can be found at its home page: *http://java.sun.com/products/java-media/jai/*.

CHAPTER 6

Image Loading, Visual Effects, and Animation

Images are a central part of every game, and this chapter examines how we can (efficiently) load and display them, apply visual effects such as blurring, fading, and rotation, and animate them.

The ImagesTests application is shown in Figure 6-1. The screenshot includes the name of the images for ease of reference later.

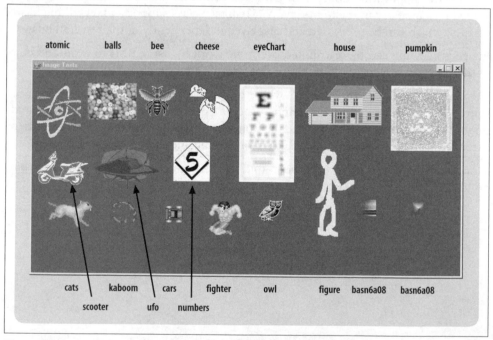

Figure 6-1. ImagesTests and image names

An *image name* is the filename of the image, minus its extension.

The images (in GIF, JPEG, or PNG format) are loaded by my own `ImagesLoader` class from a JAR file containing the application and the images. The images are loaded using `ImageIO`'s `read( )`, and stored as `BufferedImage` objects, to take advantage of the JVM's "managed image" features.

`ImagesLoader` can load individual images, image strips, and multiple image files that represent an animation sequence.

The animation effects utilized by `ImagesTests` fall into two categories:

- Those defined by repeatedly applying a visual effect, such as blurring, to the same image but by an increasing amount
- Those where the animation is represented by a series of different images displayed one after another

Table 6-1 lists the image names against the visual effect they demonstrate.

Table 6-1. Images names and their visual effects

Image name	Visual effect
atomic	Rotation
balls	Mixed colors
basn6a08	
bee	Teleportation (uneven fading)
cheese	Horizontal/vertical flipping
eyeChart	Progressive blurring
house	Reddening
pumpkin	Zapping (red/yellow pixels)
scooter	Brightening
ufo	Fading
owl	Negation
basn6a16	Resizing
cars	Numbered animation
kaboom	
cats	
figure	
fighter	Named animation
numbers	Callback animation

The effects are mostly implemented with Java 2D operations, such as convolution or affine transformation. Occasionally, I make use of capabilities in drawImage( ), e.g., for resizing and flipping an image.

The majority of the images are GIFs with a transparent background; *balls.jpg* is the only JPEG. The PNG files are: *owl.png*, *pumpkin.png*, *basn6a08.png*, and *basn6a16.png*. The latter two use translucency, and come from the PNG suite maintained by Willem van Schaik at *http://www.schaik.com/pngsuite/pngsuite.html*.

I've utilized several images from the excellent SpriteLib sprite library by Ari Feldman, available at *http://www.arifeldman.com/games/spritelib.html*, notably for the cats, kaboom, cars, and fighter animations.

 The application code for this chapter can be found in the *ImagesTests/* directory.

Class Diagrams for the Application

Figure 6-2 shows the class diagrams for the ImagesTests application. The class names, public methods, and constants are shown.

ImagesTests creates a JFrame and the JPanel where the images are drawn, and it starts a Swing timer to update its images every 0.1 second.

ImagesTests employs an ImagesLoader object to load the images named in a configuration file (*imsInfo.txt* in the *Images/* subdirectory). ImagesLoader will be used in several subsequent chapters to load images and animations into my games.

The visual effects methods, such as blurring, are grouped together in ImagesSFXs. Animations represented by sequences of images (e.g., numbers, cars, kaboom, cats, and figure) are controlled by ImagesPlayer objects. A sequence may be shown repeatedly, stopped, and restarted.

A completed animation sequence can call sequenceEnded( ) in an object implementing the ImagesPlayerWatcher interface. ImagesTests implements ImagesPlayerWatcher and is used as a callback by the numbers sequence.

Loading Images

The ImagesLoader class can load four different formats of images, which I call o, n, s, and g images. The images are assumed to be in a local JAR file in a subdirectory *Images/* below ImagesLoader. They are loaded as BufferedImages using ImageIO's read( ), so they can become managed images.

The typical way of using an ImagesLoader object is to supply it with a configuration file containing the filenames of the images that should be loaded before game play

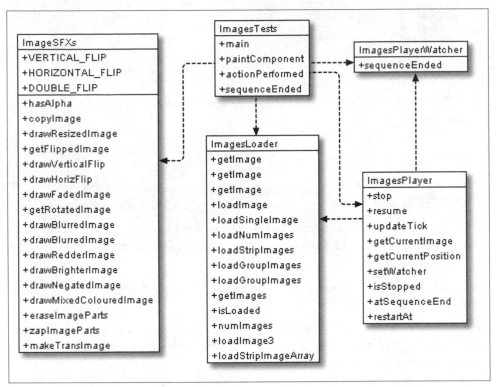

Figure 6-2. Class diagrams for ImagesTests

begins. However, it is possible to call ImagesLoader's load methods at any time during execution.

Here is the *imsInfo.txt* configuration file used in ImagesTests:

```
// imsInfo.txt images

o atomic.gif
o balls.jpg
o bee.gif
o cheese.gif
o eyeChart.gif
o house.gif
o pumpkin.png
o scooter.gif
o ufo.gif
o owl.png

n numbers*.gif  6
n figure*.gif 9

g fighter  left.gif right.gif still.gif up.gif
```

```
s cars.gif 8
s cats.gif 6
s kaboom.gif 6

o basn6a08.png
o basn6a16.png
```

Blank lines, and lines beginning with //, are ignored by the loader. The syntax for the four image formats is:

```
o <fnm>
n <fnm*.ext> <number>
s <fnm> <number>
g <name> <fnm> [ <fnm> ]*
```

An o line causes a single filename, called <fnm>, to be loaded from *Images/*.

A n line loads a series of numbered image files, whose filenames use the numbers 0–<number>-1 in place of the * character in the filename. For example:

```
n numbers*.gif  6
```

This indicates that the files *numbers0.gif*, *numbers1.gif*, and so forth, up to *numbers5.gif*, should be loaded.

An s line loads a *strip file* (called fnm) containing a single row of <number> images. After the file's graphic has been loaded, it's automatically divided up into the component images. For instance:

```
s kaboom.gif 6
```

This refers to the strip file *kaboom.gif* containing a row of six images, as shown in Figure 6-3.

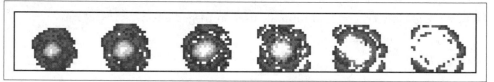

Figure 6-3. The kaboom.gif strip file

A g line specifies a group of files with different names. After being loaded, the images can be accessible using a positional notation or by means of their filenames (minus the extension). For example, the fighter g images are defined this way:

```
g fighter  left.gif right.gif still.gif up.gif
```

Subsequently, the image in *right.gif* can be accessed using the number 1 or the string "right".

Internal Data Structures

The ImagesLoader object creates two main data structures as it loads the images, both of them HashMaps:

```
private HashMap imagesMap, gNamesMap;
```

The imagesMap key is the image's name, and its value is an ArrayList of BufferedImage objects associated with that name. The exact meaning of the name depends on the type of image loaded:

- For an o image (e.g., "o atomic.gif"), the name is the filename minus its extension (i.e., *atomic*), and the ArrayList holds just a single image.
- For an n image (e.g., "n numbers*.gif 6"), the name is the part of the filename before the * (i.e., *numbers*), and the ArrayList holds several images (six in this case).
- For an s image (e.g., "s cars.gif 8"), the name is the filename minus the extension (i.e., *cars*), and the ArrayList holds the images pulled from the strip graphic (eight in this example).
- For a g image (e.g., "g fighter left.gif right.gif still.gif up.gif"), the name is the string after the g character (i.e., *fighter*), and the ArrayList is as large as the sequence of filenames given (four).

The loading of g images also causes updates to the gNamesMap HashMap. Its key is the g name (e.g., *fighter*), but its value is an ArrayList of filename strings (minus their extensions). For instance, the *fighter* name has an ArrayList associated with it holding the strings "left", "right", "still", and "up".

Getting an Image

The image accessing interface is uniform and independent of whether o, n, s, or g images are being accessed.

Three public getImage() methods are in ImagesLoader and getImages(). Their prototypes are shown here:

```
BufferedImage getImage(String name);
BufferedImage getImage(String name, int posn);
BufferedImage getImage(String name, String fnmPrefix);
ArrayList getImages(String name);
```

The single argument version of getImage() returns the image associated with name and is intended primarily for accessing o images, which only have a single image. If an n, s, or g image is accessed, then the first image in the ArrayList will be returned.

The two-argument version of getImage( ), which takes an integer position argument, is more useful for accessing n, s, and g names with multiple images in their ArrayLists. If the supplied number is negative, then the first image will be returned. If the number is too large, then it will be reduced modulo the ArrayList size.

The third getImage( ) method takes a String argument and is aimed at g images. The String should be a filename, which is used to index into the g name's ArrayList.

The getImages( ) method returns the entire ArrayList for the given name.

Using ImagesLoader

ImagesTests employs ImagesLoader by supplying it with an images configuration file:

```
ImagesLoader imsLoader = new ImagesLoader("imsInfo.txt");
```

The ImagesLoader constructor assumes the file (and all the images) is in the *Images/* subdirectory below the current directory, and everything is packed inside a JAR.

  Details about creating the JAR are given at the end of this chapter.

Loading o images is straightforward:

```
BufferedImage atomic = imsLoader.getImage("atomic");
```

Loading n, s, and g images usually requires a numerical value:

```
BufferedImage cats1 = imsLoader.getImage("cats", 1);
```

A related method is numImages( ), which returns the number of images associated with a given name:

```
int numCats = imsLoader.numImage("cats");
```

g images can be accessed using a filename prefix:

```
BufferedImage leftFighter = imsLoader.getImage("fighter", "left");
```

If a requested image cannot be found, then null will be returned by the loader.

An alternative way of using ImagesLoader is to create an empty loader (in other words, no configuration file is supplied to the constructor). Then public methods for loading o, n, s, and g images can then be called by the application, rather than being handled when a configuration file is loaded:

```
ImagesLoader imsLoader = new ImagesLoader();  // empty loader

imsLoader.loadSingleImage("atomic.gif");  // load images at run-rime
imsLoader.loadNumImages("numbers*.gif", 6);
imsLoader.loadStripImages("kaboom.gif", 6);

String[] fnms = {"left.gif", "right.gif", "still.gif", "up.gif"};
imsLoader.loadGroupImages("fighter", fnms );
```

Implementation Details

A large part of ImagesLoader is given over to parsing and error checking. The top-level method for parsing the configuration file is loadImagesFile():

```
private void loadImagesFile(String fnm)
{
  String imsFNm = IMAGE_DIR + fnm;
  System.out.println("Reading file: " + imsFNm);
  try {
    InputStream in = this.getClass().getResourceAsStream(imsFNm);
    BufferedReader br = new BufferedReader(
                          new InputStreamReader(in));
    String line;
    char ch;
    while((line = br.readLine()) != null) {
      if (line.length() == 0)  // blank line
        continue;
      if (line.startsWith("//"))    // comment
        continue;
      ch = Character.toLowerCase( line.charAt(0) );
      if (ch == 'o')  // a single image
        getFileNameImage(line);
      else if (ch == 'n')  // a numbered sequence of images
        getNumberedImages(line);
      else if (ch == 's')  // an images strip
        getStripImages(line);
      else if (ch == 'g')  // a group of images
        getGroupImages(line);
      else
        System.out.println("Do not recognize line: " + line);
    }
    br.close();
  }
  catch (IOException e)
  { System.out.println("Error reading file: " + imsFNm);
    System.exit(1);
  }
}  // end of loadImagesFile()
```

One line of the file is read at a time, and a multiway branch decides which syntactic form should be processed, depending on the first character on the input line. The input stream coming from the configuration file is created using Class. getResourceAsStream(), which is needed when the application and all the resources all wrapped up inside a JAR.

getFileNameImage() is typical in that it extracts the tokens from the line and processes them by calling loadSingleImage():

```
private void getFileNameImage(String line)
// format is   o <fnm>
{ StringTokenizer tokens = new StringTokenizer(line);
```

```
      if (tokens.countTokens( ) != 2)
        System.out.println("Wrong no. of arguments for " + line);
      else {
        tokens.nextToken( );    // skip command label
        System.out.print("o Line: ");
        loadSingleImage( tokens.nextToken( ) );
      }
    }
```

loadSingleImage( ) is the public method for loading an o image. If an entry for the image's name doesn't exist, then imagesMap will be extended with a new key (holding name) and an ArrayList containing a single BufferedImage:

```
public boolean loadSingleImage(String fnm)
{
  String name = getPrefix(fnm);

  if (imagesMap.containsKey(name)) {
    System.out.println( "Error: " + name + "already used");
    return false;
  }

  BufferedImage bi = loadImage(fnm);
  if (bi != null) {
    ArrayList imsList = new ArrayList();
    imsList.add(bi);
    imagesMap.put(name, imsList);
    System.out.println("  Stored " + name + "/" + fnm);
    return true;
  }
  else
    return false;
}
```

Image Loading

We arrive at the image-loading method, loadImage( ), which is at the heart of the processing of n and g lines. Its implementation is almost identical to the loadImage( ) method described in the section "The Internals of BufferedImage" in Chapter 5:

```
public BufferedImage loadImage(String fnm)
{
  try {
    BufferedImage im =  ImageIO.read(
                getClass( ).getResource(IMAGE_DIR + fnm) );

    int transparency = im.getColorModel( ).getTransparency( );
    BufferedImage copy =  gc.createCompatibleImage(
                            im.getWidth( ), im.getHeight( ),
                            transparency );

    // create a graphics context
    Graphics2D g2d = copy.createGraphics( );
```

```
        // reportTransparency(IMAGE_DIR + fnm, transparency);

        // copy image
        g2d.drawImage(im,0,0,null);
        g2d.dispose();
        return copy;
    }
    catch(IOException e) {
        System.out.println("Load Image error for " +
                    IMAGE_DIR + "/" + fnm + ":\n" + e);
        return null;
    }
} // end of loadImage() using ImageIO
```

reportTransparency( ) is a debugging utility for printing out the transparency value of the loaded image. It's useful for checking if the transparency/translucency of the image has been detected.

 As this is the version of code ready to use, reportTransparency( ) is commented out. For debugging purposes, you may want to uncomment this method's invocation.

ImagesLoader contains two other versions of loadImages( ), called loadImages2( ) and loadImages3( ). They play no part in the functioning of the class and are only included to show how BufferedImages can be loaded using ImageIcon or Image's getImage( ). The ImageIcon code in loadImages2( ) uses this code:

```
ImageIcon imIcon = new ImageIcon( getClass().getResource(IMAGE_DIR + fnm) );
```

Then, it calls makeBIM( ) to convert its Image into a BufferedImage. makeBIM( ) is described in the section "From Image to BufferedImage" in Chapter 5.

The Image code in loadImage3( ) uses a MediaTracker to delay execution until the image is fully loaded and then calls makeBIM( ) to obtain a BufferedImage.

Loading Strip File Images

The images from a strip file are obtained in steps: First, the entire graphic is loaded from the file, cut into pieces, and each resulting image is placed in an array. This array is subsequently stored as an ArrayList in imagesMap under the s name:

```
public BufferedImage[] loadStripImageArray(String fnm, int number)
{
  if (number <= 0) {
    System.out.println("number <= 0; returning null");
    return null;
  }

  BufferedImage stripIm;
  if ((stripIm = loadImage(fnm)) == null) {
```

```
        System.out.println("Returning null");
        return null;
    }

    int imWidth = (int) stripIm.getWidth() / number;
    int height = stripIm.getHeight();
    int transparency = stripIm.getColorModel().getTransparency();

    BufferedImage[] strip = new BufferedImage[number];
    Graphics2D stripGC;

    // each BufferedImage from the strip file is stored in strip[]
    for (int i=0; i < number; i++) {
      strip[i]=gc.createCompatibleImage(imWidth,height,transparency);

      // create a graphics context
      stripGC = strip[i].createGraphics();

      // copy image
      stripGC.drawImage(stripIm,
                0,0, imWidth,height,
                i*imWidth,0, (i*imWidth)+imWidth,height, null);
      stripGC.dispose();
    }
    return strip;
  } // end of loadStripImageArray()
```

drawImage( ) is used to clip the images out of the strip.

> An alternative approach would be to use a CropImageFilter combined
> with a FilteredImageSource. However, this is too much work for
> images that are positioned so simply in their source graphic.

Applying Image Effects

ImagesTests uses a Swing timer to animate its image effects rather than the active
rendering approach developed in early chapters. This is purely a matter of preventing the code from becoming overly complicated since the high accuracy offered by
active rendering isn't required. The visual effects employed here are generally composed from 5 to 10 distinct frames, displayed over the course of one or two seconds;
this implies a need for a maximum of 10 FPS, which is within the capabilities of the
Swing timer.

> If necessary, the effects techniques can be easily translated to an active
> rendering setting.

The timer-driven framework is illustrated by Figure 6-4. The details of
actionPerformed( ) and paintComponent( ) are explained below.

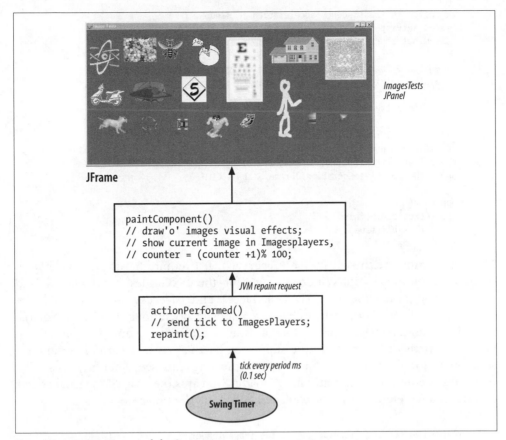

ImagesTests JPanel

JFrame

```
paintComponent()
// draw'o' images visual effects;
// show current image in Imagesplayers,
// counter = (counter +1)% 100;
```

JVM repaint request

```
actionPerformed()
// send tick to ImagesPlayers;
repaint();
```

*tick every period ms
(0.1 sec)*

Swing Timer

Figure 6-4. ImagesTests and the Swing timer

ImagesTests maintains a global variable (counter) that starts at 0 and is incremented at the end of each paintComponent( ) call, modulo 100.

> The modulo operation isn't significant but is used to keep the counter value from becoming excessively large.

counter is used in many places in the code, often to generate input arguments to the visual effects.

Starting ImagesTests

The main( ) method for ImagesTests creates a JFrame and adds the ImagesTests JPanel to it:

```
public static void main(String args[])
{
```

```
        // switch on translucency acceleration in Windows
        System.setProperty("sun.java2d.translaccel", "true");
        System.setProperty("sun.java2d.ddforcevram", "true");

        // switch on hardware acceleration if using OpenGL with pbuffers
        // System.setProperty("sun.java2d.opengl", "true");

        ImagesTests ttPanel = new ImagesTests();

        // create a JFrame to hold the test JPanel
        JFrame app = new JFrame("Image Tests");
        app.getContentPane().add(ttPanel, BorderLayout.CENTER);
        app.setDefaultCloseOperation(JFrame.EXIT_ON_CLOSE);

        app.pack();
        app.setResizable(false);
        app.setVisible(true);
    } // end of main()
```

More interesting are the calls to setProperty( ). If I require hardware acceleration of translucent images in Windows (e.g., for the PNG files *basn6a08.png* and *basn6a16.png*), then the Java 2D translaccel and ddforcevram flags should be switched on. They also accelerate alpha composite operations. On Linux/Solaris, only the opengl flag is required for hardware acceleration, but pbuffers are an OpenGL extension, so may not be supported by the graphics card. The simplest solution is to try code with and without the flag and see what happens. The ImagesTests constructor initiates image loading, creates the ImageSFXs visual effects object, obtains references to the o images, and starts the timer:

```
// globals
private ImagesLoader imsLoader;   // the image loader
private int counter;
private boolean justStarted;
private ImageSFXs imageSfx;       // the visual effects class

private GraphicsDevice gd;        // for reporting accl. memory usage
private int accelMemory;
private DecimalFormat df;


public ImagesTests()
{
  df = new DecimalFormat("0.0");  // 1 dp

  GraphicsEnvironment ge =
        GraphicsEnvironment.getLocalGraphicsEnvironment();
  gd = ge.getDefaultScreenDevice();

  accelMemory = gd.getAvailableAcceleratedMemory();  // in bytes
  System.out.println("Initial Acc. Mem.: " +
        df.format( ((double)accelMemory)/(1024*1024) ) + " MB" );
```

```
        setBackground(Color.white);
        setPreferredSize( new Dimension(PWIDTH, PHEIGHT) );

        // load and initialise the images
        imsLoader = new ImagesLoader(IMS_FILE);   // "imsInfo.txt"
        imageSfx = new ImageSFXs();
        initImages();

        counter = 0;
        justStarted = true;

        new Timer(PERIOD, this).start();    // PERIOD = 0.1 sec
    } // end of ImagesTests()
```

The `GraphicsDevice.getAvailableAcceleratedMemory()` call returns the current amount of available hardware-accelerated memory. The application continues to report this value as it changes to give an indication of when `BufferedImage` objects become managed images. This is explained more fully later in this chapter.

Initializing Images

`initImages()` does three tasks: It stores references to the o images as global variables, creates ImagesPlayers objects for the n and s images and references the first g fighter image, its left image:

```
    // global variables
    // hold the single 'o' images
    private BufferedImage atomic, balls, bee, cheese, eyeChart,
                          house, pumpkin, scooter,
                          fighter, ufo, owl, basn8, basn16;

    // for manipulating the 'n' and 's' images
    private ImagesPlayer numbersPlayer, figurePlayer, carsPlayer,
                         catsPlayer, kaboomPlayer;


    private void initImages()
    {
        // initialize the 'o' image variables
        atomic = imsLoader.getImage("atomic");
        balls = imsLoader.getImage("balls");
        bee = imsLoader.getImage("bee");
        cheese = imsLoader.getImage("cheese");
        eyeChart = imsLoader.getImage("eyeChart");
        house = imsLoader.getImage("house");
        pumpkin = imsLoader.getImage("pumpkin");
        scooter = imsLoader.getImage("scooter");
        ufo = imsLoader.getImage("ufo");
        owl = imsLoader.getImage("owl");
        basn8 = imsLoader.getImage("basn6a08");
        basn16 = imsLoader.getImage("basn6a16");
```

```
        /* Initialize ImagesPlayers for the 'n' and 's' images.
           The 'numbers' sequence is not cycled, the other are.
        */
        numbersPlayer = new ImagesPlayer("numbers", PERIOD, 1, false, imsLoader);
        numbersPlayer.setWatcher(this);
                // report the sequence's finish back to ImagesTests

        figurePlayer =  new ImagesPlayer("figure", PERIOD, 2, true, imsLoader);
        carsPlayer = new ImagesPlayer("cars", PERIOD, 1, true, imsLoader);
        catsPlayer = new ImagesPlayer("cats", PERIOD, 0.5, true, imsLoader);
        kaboomPlayer = new ImagesPlayer("kaboom", PERIOD, 1.5, true, imsLoader);

        // the 1st 'g' image for 'fighter' is set using a filename prefix
        fighter = imsLoader.getImage("fighter", "left");
    } // end of initImages()
```

The ImagesPlayer class wraps up code for playing a sequence of images. ImagesTests
uses ImagesPlayer objects for animating the n and s figure, cars, kaboom, and cats
images. Each sequence is shown repeatedly.

numbers is also an n type, made up of several images, but its ImagesPlayer is set up a
little differently. The player will call sequenceEnded( ) in ImagesTests when the end of
the sequence is reached, and it doesn't play the images again. The callback requires
that ImagesTests implements the ImagesPlayerWatcher interface:

```
public class ImagesTests extends JPanel
            implements ActionListener, ImagesPlayerWatcher
{  // other methods

  public void sequenceEnded(String imageName)
  // called by ImagesPlayer when its images sequence has finished
  {  System.out.println( imageName + " sequence has ended");  }


}
```

The name of the sequence (i.e., numbers) is passed as an argument to sequenceEnded( )
by its player. The implementation in ImagesTests only prints out a message, but it
could do something more useful. For example, the end of an animation sequence
could trigger the start of the next stage in a game.

Updating the Images

Image updating is carried out by imagesUpdate( ) when actionPerformed( ) is called
(i.e., every 0.1 second):

```
public void actionPerformed(ActionEvent e)
// triggered by the timer: update, repaint
{
  if (justStarted)   // don't do updates the first time through
    justStarted = false;
  else
    imagesUpdate( );
```

```
    repaint();
  } // end of actionPerformed()


  private void imagesUpdate()
  {
    // numbered images ('n' images); using ImagesPlayer
    numbersPlayer.updateTick();
    if (counter%30 == 0)      // restart image sequence periodically
      numbersPlayer.restartAt(2);

    figurePlayer.updateTick();

    // strip images ('s' images); using ImagesPlayer
    carsPlayer.updateTick();
    catsPlayer.updateTick();
    kaboomPlayer.updateTick();

    // grouped images ('g' images)
    // The 'fighter' images are the only 'g' images in this example.
    updateFighter();
  } // end of imagesUpdate()
```

imagesUpdate() does nothing to the o images, since they are processed by paintComponent(); instead, it concentrates on the n, s, and g images.

updateTick() is called in all of the ImagesPlayers (i.e., for numbers, figure, cars, cats, and kaboom). This informs the players that another animation period has passed in ImagesTests. This is used to calculate timings and determine which of the images in a sequence is the current one.

The n numbers images are utilized differently: When the counter value reaches a multiple of 30, the sequence is restarted at image number 2:

```
    if (counter%30 == 0)
      numbersPlayer.restartAt(2);
```

The on-screen behavior of numbers is to step through its six images (pictures numbered 0 to 5) and stop after calling sequenceEnded() in ImagesTests. Later, when ImagesTests's counter reaches a multiple of 30, the sequence will restart at picture 2, step through to picture 5 and stop again (after calling sequenceEnded() again). This behavior will repeat whenever the counter reaches another multiple of 30.

With a little more work, behaviors such as this can be quite useful. For example, a repeating animation may skip its first few frames since they contain startup images. This is the case for a seated figure that stands up and starts dancing. The numbers behavior illustrates that ImagesPlayer can do more than endlessly cycle through image sequences.

updateFighter() deals with the g fighter images, defined in *imsInfo.txt*:

```
    g fighter  left.gif right.gif still.gif up.gif
```

Back in initImages( ), the global BufferedImage variable, fighter, was set to refer to the "left" image. updateFighter( ) cycles through the other images using the counter value modulo 4:

```
private void updateFighter()
/* The images are shown using their filename prefixes (although a
   positional approach could be used, which would allow an
   ImagesPlayer to be used.
*/
{ int posn = counter % 4;  // number of fighter images;
         // could use  imsLoader.numImages("fighter")
  switch(posn) {
    case 0:
      fighter = imsLoader.getImage("fighter", "left");
      break;
    case 1:
      fighter = imsLoader.getImage("fighter", "right");
      break;
    case 2:
      fighter = imsLoader.getImage("fighter", "still");
      break;
    case 3:
      fighter = imsLoader.getImage("fighter", "up");
      break;
    default:
      System.out.println("Unknown fighter group name");
      fighter = imsLoader.getImage("fighter", "left");
      break;
  }
}  // end of updateFighter()
```

This code only updates the fighter reference; the image is not displayed until paintComponent( ) is called.

Painting the Images

paintComponent( ) has four jobs:

- Applies a visual effect to each o image and displays the result
- Requests the current image from each ImagesPlayer and displays it
- Displays any change in the amount of hardware accelerated memory (VRAM)
- Increments the counter (modulo 100)

Here's the implementation:

```
public void paintComponent(Graphics g)
{
  super.paintComponent(g);
  Graphics2D g2d = (Graphics2D)g;

  //antialiasing
  g2d.setRenderingHint(RenderingHints.KEY_ANTIALIASING,
                       RenderingHints.VALUE_ANTIALIAS_ON);
```

```
      // smoother (and slower) image transforms  (e.g., for resizing)
      g2d.setRenderingHint(RenderingHints.KEY_INTERPOLATION,
                           RenderingHints.VALUE_INTERPOLATION_BILINEAR);

      // clear the background
      g2d.setColor(Color.blue);
      g2d.fillRect(0, 0, PWIDTH, PHEIGHT);

      // ----------------- 'o' images --------------------
      /* The programmer must manually edit the code here in order to
         draw the 'o' images with different visual effects. */

      // drawImage(g2d, atomic, 10, 25);    // only draw the image

      rotatingImage(g2d, atomic, 10, 25);
      mixedImage(g2d, balls, 110, 25);
      teleImage = teleportImage(g2d, bee, teleImage, 210, 25);
      flippingImage(g2d, cheese, 310, 25);
      blurringImage(g2d, eyeChart, 410, 25);
      reddenImage(g2d, house, 540, 25);
      zapImage = zapImage(g2d, pumpkin, zapImage, 710, 25);
      brighteningImage(g2d, scooter, 10, 160);
      fadingImage(g2d, ufo, 110, 140);
      negatingImage(g2d, owl, 450, 250);
      mixedImage(g2d, basn8, 650, 250);
      resizingImage(g2d, basn16, 750, 250);

      // --------------- numbered images -------------------
      drawImage(g2d, numbersPlayer.getCurrentImage( ), 280, 140);
      drawImage(g2d, figurePlayer.getCurrentImage( ), 550, 140);

      // --------------- strip images ----------------------
      drawImage(g2d, catsPlayer.getCurrentImage( ), 10, 235);
      drawImage(g2d, kaboomPlayer.getCurrentImage( ), 150, 250);
      drawImage(g2d, carsPlayer.getCurrentImage( ), 250, 250);

      // --------------- grouped images --------------------
      drawImage(g2d, fighter, 350, 250);

      reportAccelMemory( );
      counter = (counter + 1)% 100;    // 0-99 is a large enough range
    } // end of paintComponent( )
```

The calls to Graphics2D.setRenderingHint( ) show how Java 2D can make rendering
requests, based around a key and value scheme.

The anti-aliasing rendering hint has no appreciable effect in this example since no
lines, shapes, or text are drawn in the JPanel. Consequently, it might be better not to
bother with it, thereby gaining a little extra speed. The interpolation hint is more
useful though, especially for the resizing operation. For instance, there is a noticeable improvement in the resized smoothness of *basn6a16* with the hint compared to
when the hint is absent.

The 11 visual effects applied to the o images are explained below. However, all the methods have a similar interface, requiring a reference to the graphics context, the name of the image, and the (x, y) coordinate where the modified image will be drawn.

The n and s images are managed by ImagesPlayer objects, so the current image is obtained by calling the objects' getCurrentImage( ) method. The returned image reference is passed to drawImage( ), which wraps a little extra error processing around Graphics' drawImage( ) method:

```
private void drawImage(Graphics2D g2d, BufferedImage im, int x, int y)
/* Draw the image, or a yellow box with ?? in it if
   there is no image. */
{
  if (im == null) {
    // System.out.println("Null image supplied");
    g2d.setColor(Color.yellow);
    g2d.fillRect(x, y, 20, 20);
    g2d.setColor(Color.black);
    g2d.drawString("??", x+10, y+10);
  }
  else
    g2d.drawImage(im, x, y, this);
}
```

Information on Accelerated Memory

reportAccelMemory( ) prints the total amount of VRAM left and the size of the change since the last report. This method is called at the end of every animation loop but only writes output if the VRAM quantity has changed:

```
private void reportAccelMemory( )
// report any change in the amount of accelerated memory
{
  int mem = gd.getAvailableAcceleratedMemory( );   // in bytes
  int memChange = mem - accelMemory;

  if (memChange != 0)
    System.out.println(counter + ". Acc. Mem: " +
            df.format( ((double)accelMemory)/(1024*1024) ) +
                    " MB; Change: " +
            df.format( ((double)memChange)/1024 ) + " K");
  accelMemory = mem;
}
```

A typical run of ImagesTests produces the following stream of messages edited to emphasize the memory related prints:

```
DirectDraw surfaces constrained to use vram
Initial Acc. Mem.: 179.6 MB
Reading file: Images/imsInfo.txt
    // many information lines printed by the loader
```

```
 0. Acc. Mem: 179.6 MB; Change: -1464.8 K
 1. Acc. Mem: 178.1 MB; Change: -115.5 K
 3. Acc. Mem: 178.0 MB; Change: -113.2 K
 4. Acc. Mem: 177.9 MB; Change: -16.3 K
 5. Acc. Mem: 177.9 MB; Change: -176.8 K
numbers sequence has ended
 6. Acc. Mem: 177.7 MB; Change: -339.0 K
 7. Acc. Mem: 177.4 MB; Change: -99.0 K
     // 9 similar accelerated memory lines edited out

18. Acc. Mem: 176.6 MB; Change: -16.2 K
19. Acc. Mem: 176.6 MB; Change: -93.9 K
21. Acc. Mem: 176.5 MB; Change: -48.8 K
25. Acc. Mem: 176.4 MB; Change: -60.0 K
numbers sequence has ended
numbers sequence has ended
numbers sequence has ended
numbers sequence has ended
     // etc.
```

The images use about 120 K in total and appear to be moved into VRAM at load time, together with space for other rendering tasks (see line number 0). The large additional allocation is probably caused by Swing, which uses VolatileImage for its double buffering.

The later VRAM allocations are due to the rendering carried out by the visual effect operations, and they stop occurring after the counter reaches 25 (or thereabouts). Since each loop takes about 0.1 seconds, this means that new VRAM allocations cease after about 2.5 seconds. VRAM isn't claimed in every animation loop; for instance, no VRAM change is reported when the counter is 20, 22, and 24.

This behavior can be understood by considering how the visual effects methods behave. Typically, about every few animation frames, they generate new images based on the original o images. The operations are cyclic, i.e., after a certain number of frames they start over. The longest running cyclic is the fade method, which completes one cycle after 25 frames (2.5 seconds). Some of the operations write directly to the screen, and so will not require additional VRAM; others use temporary BufferedImage variables. These will probably trigger the VRAM allocations. Once these claims have been granted, the space can be reused by the JVM when the methods restart their image processing cycle.

Consider if the ddforcevram flag is commented out from main( ) in ImagesTests:

```
// System.setProperty("sun.java2d.ddforcevram", "true");
```

Only the first reduction to VRAM occurs (of about 1.4 MB), and the subsequent requests are never made. In this case, the benefits of using the flag are fairly minimal, but its utility depends on the mix of graphics operations used in the application.

More information can be obtained about the low-level workings of Java 2D by turning on logging:

```
java -Dsun.java2d.trace=log,count,out:log.txt ImagesTests
```

This will record all the internal calls made by Java 2D, together with a count of the calls, to the text file *log.txt*. Unfortunately, the sheer volume of data can be overwhelming. However, if only the call counts are recorded, then the data will be more manageable:

```
java -Dsun.java2d.trace=count,out:log.txt ImagesTests
```

The vast majority of the calls, about 92 percent, are software rendering operations for drawing filled blocks of color (the MaskFill( ) function). The percentage of hardware-assisted copies (blits) is greater when the ddforcevram flag is switched on. These operations have "Win32," "DD," or "D3D" in their names. Nevertheless, the percentage increases from a paltry 0.5 percent to 2.3 percent.

The comparatively few hardware-based operations in the log is a reflection of Java's lack of support for image processing operations in Windows. Undoubtedly, this will improve in future versions of the JVM and depends on the mix of operations that an application utilizes. It may be worth moving the application to FSEM since VolatileImages are automatically utilized for page flipping in FSEM.

Displaying Image Sequences

ImagesPlayer is aimed at displaying the sequence of images making up an n, s, or g set of images.

The ImagesPlayer constructor takes the image's name, an animPeriod value, a seqDuration value, a Boolean indicating if the sequence should repeat, and a reference to the ImagesLoader:

```
ImagesPlayer player = new ImagesPlayer(imagesName, animPeriod, seqDuration,
                                       isRepeating, imsLoader);
```

seqDuration is the total time required to show the entire sequence. Internally, this is used to calculate showPeriod, the amount of time each image will be the current one before the next image takes its place. animPeriod states how often ImagesPlayer's updateTick( ) method will be called (the animation period). updateTick( ) will be called periodically by the update( ) method in the top-level animation framework.

The current time is calculated when updateTick( ) is called and used to calculate imPosition, which specifies which image should be returned when getCurrentImage( ) is called. This process is illustrated in Figure 6-5.

This approach relies on the animation loop calling updateTick( ) regularly at a fixed time interval, which is true for ImagesTests. Another implicit assumption is that the showPeriod time duration will be larger than animPeriod. For example, showPeriod might be in tenths of seconds even though animPeriod may be in milliseconds. If showPeriod is less than animPeriod, then rendering progresses too slowly to display all

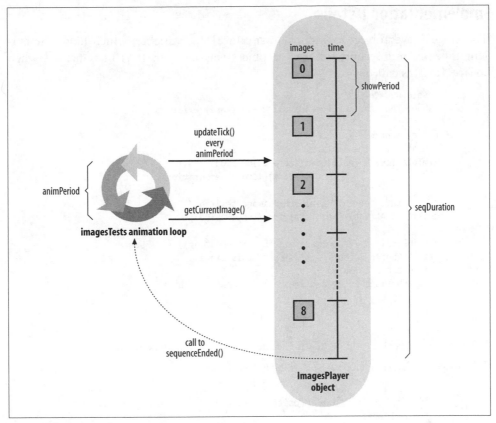

Figure 6-5. ImagesPlayer in use

the images within the required seqDuration time, and images (frames) will be skipped.

When the sequence finishes, a callback, sequenceEnded( ), can be invoked on a specified object implementing the ImagesPlayerWatcher interface. This is done for the n numbers images:

```
numbersPlayer = new ImagesPlayer("numbers", PERIOD, 1, false, imsLoader);
numbersPlayer.setWatcher(this);
    // report sequence's finish to ImagesTests
```

In the case of numbers, animPeriod is PERIOD (0.1 seconds), seqDuration is one second, and the sequence will not repeat. Since there are six numbers files, showPeriod will be about 0.17 seconds and, therefore, (just) greater than the animPeriod.

Though ImagesPlayer is principally aimed at supporting regularly repeating animations, it also includes public methods for stopping, resuming, and restarting an animation at a given image position.

Implementation Details

The `ImagesPlayer` object maintains an `animTotalTime` variable, which holds the current time (in milliseconds) since the object was created. It is incremented when `updateTick()` is called:

```
public void updateTick()
// I assume that this method is called every animPeriod ms
{
  if (!ticksIgnored) {
    // update total animation time, modulo seq duration
    animTotalTime = (animTotalTime + animPeriod) %
                              (long)(1000 * seqDuration);

    // calculate current displayable image position
    imPosition = (int) (animTotalTime / showPeriod);

    if ((imPosition == numImages-1) && (!isRepeating)) {  //seq end
      ticksIgnored = true;    // stop at this image
      if (watcher != null)
        watcher.sequenceEnded(imName);   // call callback
    }
  }
}
```

`imPosition` holds the index into the sequence of images. `showPeriod` is defined as:

```
showPeriod = (int) (1000 * seqDuration / numImages);
```

 This means that `imPosition` can only be a value between 0 and `numImages-1`.

`getCurrentImage()` uses `imPosition` to access the relevant image in the loader:

```
public BufferedImage getCurrentImage()
{ if (numImages != 0)
    return imsLoader.getImage(imName, imPosition);
  else
    return null;
}
```

`getCurrentImage()`'s test of `numImages` is used to detect problems which may have arisen when the `ImagesPlayer` was created, for example, when the image name (`imName`) is unknown to the loader.

The `ticksIgnored` Boolean is employed to stop the progression of a sequence. In `updateTick()`, if `ticksIgnored` is true, then the internal time counter, `animTotalTime`, will not be incremented. It is controlled by the `stop()`, `resume()`, and `restartAt()` methods. `stop()` sets the `ticksIgnored` Boolean:

```
public void stop()
{ ticksIgnored = true;  }
```

Visual Effects for 'o' Images

A quick look at Table 6-1 shows that ImagesTests utilizes a large number of visuals effects. These can be classified into two groups:

- Animations of image sequences, carried out by ImagesPlayer objects
- Image-processing operations applied to o images

I've already described the first group, which leaves a total of 11 effects. These are applied to the o images inside paintComponent( ) of ImagesTests. The relevant code fragment is:

```
// ----------------- 'o' images ---------------------
/* The programmer must manually edit the code here in order to
   draw the 'o' images with different visual effects. */

// drawImage(g2d, atomic, 10, 25); // only draw the image

rotatingImage(g2d, atomic, 10, 25);
mixedImage(g2d, balls, 110, 25);
teleImage = teleportImage(g2d, bee, teleImage, 210, 25);
flippingImage(g2d, cheese, 310, 25);
blurringImage(g2d, eyeChart, 410, 25);
reddenImage(g2d, house, 540, 25);
zapImage = zapImage(g2d, pumpkin, zapImage, 710, 25);
brighteningImage(g2d, scooter, 10, 160);
fadingImage(g2d, ufo, 110, 140);
negatingImage(g2d, owl, 450, 250);
mixedImage(g2d, basn8, 650, 250);
resizingImage(g2d, basn16, 750, 250);
```

All the methods have a similar interface, requiring a reference to the graphics context (g2d), the name of the image, and the (x, y) coordinate where the modified image will be drawn.

The operations can be grouped into eight categories, shown in Table 6-2.

Table 6-2. Visual-effect operations by category

Category	Example methods	Description
drawImage( )-based	resizingImage( )	Make the image grow.
	flippingImage( )	Keep flipping the image horizontally and vertically.
Alpha compositing	fadingImage( )	Smoothly fade the image away to nothing.
Affine transforms	rotatingImage( )	Spin the image in a clockwise direction.
ConvolveOp	blurringImage( )	Make the image increasingly more blurred.
LookupOp	reddenImage( )	Turn the image ever more red, using LookupOp.
RescaleOp	reddenImage( )	Turn the image ever more red , this time using RescaleOp.
	brighteningImage( )	Keep turning up the image's brightness.
	negatingImage( )	Keep switching between the image and its negative.

Table 6-2. Visual-effect operations by category (continued)

Category	Example methods	Description
BandCombineOp	mixedImage( )	Keep mixing up the colors of the image.
Pixel effects	teleportImage( )	Make the image fade, groups of pixels at a time.
	zapImage( )	Change the image to a mass of red and yellow pixels.

The following subsections are organized according to the eight categories, with the operations explained in their relevant category. However, some general comments can be made about them here.

The methods in ImagesTest do not do image processing. Their main task is to use the current counter value, modulo some constant, to generate suitable arguments to the image processing methods located in ImageSFXs. The use of the modulo operator means that the effects will repeat as the counter progresses. For example, resizingImage( ) makes the image grow for six frames, at which point the image is redrawn at its starting size and growth begins again.

The image processing methods in ImagesSFXs do not change the original o images. Some of the methods write directly to the screen, by calling drawImage( ) with an image processing operator. Other methods generate a temporary BufferedImage object, which is subsequently drawn to the screen. The object exists only until the end of the method.

teleportImage( ) and zapImage( ) are different in that their images are stored globally in ImagesTests, in the variables teleImage and zapImage. This means that method processing can be cumulative since earlier changes will be stored and remembered in the global variables. These operations don't modify the original o images; they only modify the teleImage and zapImage variables. The main reason for not changing the original images is to allow them to be reused as the effects cycles repeat. Another reason is that any changes to the images will cause the JVM to drop them from VRAM. This would make their future rendering slower for a short time.

Where possible, image operations should be applied through drawImage( ) directly to the screen, as this will make hardware acceleration more likely to occur. If a temporary variable is necessary, then apply the image operation to a copy of the graphic in a VolatileImage object, forcing processing to be carried out in VRAM. There is a chance that this will allow the operation to be accelerated, but it may slow things down.

On Windows, the ddforcevram flag appears to force the creation of managed images for temporary BufferedImage variables, so the VolatileImage approach is unnecessary.

Precalculation Is Faster

The main drawback with image processing operations is their potentially adverse effect on speed. On Windows, none of the operations, except perhaps for those using `drawImage( )` resizing and flipping, will be hardware accelerated.

 The situation should be considerably better on Solaris/Linux.

In general, visual effects based around image processing operations should be used sparingly due to their poor performance. In many cases, alternatives using image sequences can be employed; rotation is an example. The s cars images display an animated series of rotated car images, which may all be in VRAM since the images are never modified. By comparison, the `rotatingImage( )` method applied to the atomic o image makes it rotate, but this is achieved by generating new images at runtime using affine transformations. On Windows, none of these images would be hardware-accelerated.

One way of viewing this suggestion is that graphical effects should be precalculated outside of the application and stored as ready-to-use images. The cost/complexity of image processing is, therefore, separated from the executing game.

drawImage( )-Based Processing

Several variants of `drawImage( )`, useful for visual effects such as scaling and flipping, are faster than the corresponding `BufferedImageOp` operations.

The version of `drawImage( )` relevant for resizing is:

```
boolean drawImage(Image im, int x, int y,
                  int width, int height, ImageObserver imOb)
```

The `width` and `height` arguments scale the image so it has the required dimensions. By default, scaling uses a nearest neighbor algorithm; the color of an on-screen pixel is based on the scaled image pixel that is nearest to the on-screen one. This tends to make an image look blocky if it is enlarged excessively. A smoother appearance, though slower to calculate, can be achieved with bilinear interpolation. The color of an on-screen pixel is derived from a combination of all the scaled image pixels that overlap the on-screen one. Bilinear interpolation can be requested at the start of `paintComponent( )`:

```
g2d.setRenderingHint(RenderingHints.KEY_INTERPOLATION,
                     RenderingHints.VALUE_INTERPOLATION_BILINEAR);
```

Here's the `resizingImage( )` method in `ImagesTests`:

```
private void resizingImage(Graphics2D g2d, BufferedImage im,
                                           int x, int y)
```

```
{ double sizeChange = (counter%6)/2.0 + 0.5;     // gives 0.5 -- 3
  imageSfx.drawResizedImage(g2d, im, x, y, sizeChange, sizeChange);
}
```

The sizeChange value is calculated from the counter value so it increases from 0.5 to 3.0, in steps of 0.5, and then restarts. This causes the image (basn6a16) to start at half-size and grow to three times its actual dimensions.

The two copies of sizeChange passed into drawResizedImage( ) in ImageSFXs become widthChange and heightChange. After some error-checking, this is the method's resizing code:

```
int destWidth = (int) (im.getWidth( ) * widthChange);
int destHeight = (int) (im.getHeight( ) * heightChange);

// adjust top-left (x,y) coord of resized image so remains centered
int destX = x + im.getWidth( )/2 - destWidth/2;
int destY = y + im.getHeight( )/2 - destHeight/2;

g2d.drawImage(im, destX, destY, destWidth, destHeight, null);
```

The drawing coordinate (destX, destY) is adjusted so the image's center point doesn't move on-screen when the image is resized.

Here is the version of drawImage( ) suitable for image flipping:

```
boolean drawImage(Image im, int dx1, int dy1, int dx2, int dy2,
                            int sx1, int sy1, int sx2, int sy2,
                  ImageObserver imOb)
```

The eight integers represent four coordinates: (sx1, sy1) and (sx2, sy2) are the top-left and bottom-right corners of the image, and (dx1, dy1) and (dx2, dy2) are the top-left and bottom-right corners of a rectangle somewhere on-screen where those points will be drawn. This idea is illustrated by Figure 6-6.

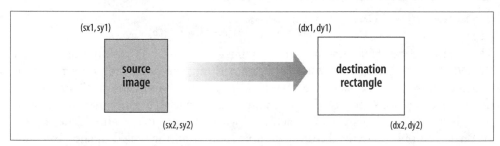

Figure 6-6. Drawing an image into an on-screen rectangle

Usually, the image coordinates are (0, 0) and (width, height) so the entire image is drawn. The versatility comes in the range of possibilities for the on-screen rectangle; it can be used to scale, stretch, and flip.

flippingImage( ) in ImagesTests calls getFlippedImage( ) in ImageSFXs with an ImageSFXs flipping constant:

```
private void flippingImage(Graphics2D g2d, BufferedImage im,
                                        int x, int y)
{ BufferedImage flipIm = null;
  if (counter%4 == 0)
    flipIm = im;     // no flipping
  else if (counter%4 == 1)
    flipIm = imageSfx.getFlippedImage(im, ImageSFXs.HORIZONTAL_FLIP);
  else if (counter%4 == 2)
    flipIm = imageSfx.getFlippedImage(im, ImageSFXs.VERTICAL_FLIP);
  else
    flipIm = imageSfx.getFlippedImage(im, ImageSFXs.DOUBLE_FLIP);

  drawImage(g2d, flipIm, x, y);
}
```

The counter value is manipulated so the image (cheese) will be repeatedly drawn normally, flipped horizontally, vertically, then flipped both ways. The image returned from getFlippedImage( ) is drawn by drawImage( ). This code does not make further use of flipIm, but it might be useful to store flipped copies of images for use later.

getFlippedImage( ) creates an empty copy of the source BufferedImage and then writes a flipped version of the image into it by calling renderFlip( ):

```
public BufferedImage getFlippedImage(BufferedImage im,int flipKind)
{
  if (im == null) {
    System.out.println("getFlippedImage: input image is null");
    return null;
  }

  int imWidth = im.getWidth( );
  int imHeight = im.getHeight( );
  int transparency = im.getColorModel( ).getTransparency( );

  BufferedImage copy =
        gc.createCompatibleImage(imWidth, imHeight, transparency);
  Graphics2D g2d = copy.createGraphics( );

  // draw in the flipped image
  renderFlip(g2d, im, imWidth, imHeight, flipKind);
  g2d.dispose( );

  return copy;
} // end of getFlippedImage( )
```

renderFlip( ) is a multiway branch based on the flipping constant supplied in the top-level call:

```
private void renderFlip(Graphics2D g2d, BufferedImage im,
                    int imWidth, int imHeight, int flipKind)
{
```

```
    if (flipKind == VERTICAL_FLIP)
      g2d.drawImage(im, imWidth, 0,  0, imHeight,
                        0, 0,  imWidth, imHeight, null);
    else if (flipKind == HORIZONTAL_FLIP)
      g2d.drawImage(im, 0, imHeight,  imWidth, 0,
                        0, 0,  imWidth, imHeight, null);
    else    // assume DOUBLE_FLIP
      g2d.drawImage(im, imWidth, imHeight,  0, 0,
                        0, 0,  imWidth, imHeight, null);
  }
```

To illustrate how the flipping works, consider the vertical flip shown in Figure 6-7.

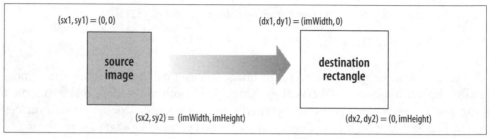

Figure 6-7. A vertical flip

ImageSFXs contains two flipping methods that draw directly to the screen:
drawVerticalFlip( ) and drawHorizFlip( ) are not used by ImagesTests.

Alpha Compositing

Compositing is the process of combining two images. The existing image (often the screen's drawing surface) is called the *destination*, and the image being rendered onto it is the *source*. Java 2D offers eight compositing rules which specify various ways that the source can be combined with the destination. The most useful is probably SRC_OVER (source over destination); the others include DST_OVER (destination over source), and SRC_IN, which clips the source to be visible only inside the boundaries of the destination.

Java 2D's AlphaComposite class adds another element to the compositing rules: the alpha values for the source and destination. This can be somewhat confusing, especially when both images have alpha channels. However, for the SRC_OVER case, when the destination image is opaque (e.g., the on-screen background), the alpha applies only to the source image. An alpha value of 0.0f makes the source disappear, and 1.0f makes it completely opaque; various degrees of translucency exist between.

Figure 6-8 shows the result of applying three different alpha values to a rectangle.

fadingImage( ) in ImagesTests hacks together an alpha value based on counter, such that as the counter increases toward 25, the alpha value goes to 0. The result is that

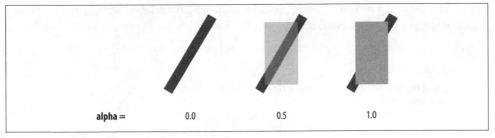

| alpha = | 0.0 | 0.5 | 1.0 |

Figure 6-8. Alpha values applied to a rectangle

the image (ufo in ImagesTests) will fade in 2.5 seconds (25 frames, each of 0.1 second) and then spring back into view as the process starts again:

```
private void fadingImage(Graphics2D g2d, BufferedImage im,
                                              int x, int y)
{ float alpha = 1.0f - (((counter*4)%100)/100.0f);
  imageSfx.drawFadedImage(g2d, ufo, x, y, alpha);
}
```

drawFadedImage( ) in ImageSFXs does various forms of error checking, and then creates an AlphaComposite object using SRC_OVER and the alpha value:

```
Composite c = g2d.getComposite( );  // backup the old composite

g2d.setComposite( AlphaComposite.getInstance(
                      AlphaComposite.SRC_OVER, alpha) );
g2d.drawImage(im, x, y, null);

g2d.setComposite(c);
  // restore old composite so it doesn't mess up future rendering
```

g2d is the screen's graphics context, and its composite is modified prior to calling drawImage( ). Care must be taken to back up the existing composite so it can be restored after the draw.

Affine Transforms

rotatingImage( ) in ImagesTests rotates the image (atomic) in steps of 10 degrees in a clockwise direction, using the image's center as the center of rotation.

The ImageSFXs method getRotatedImage( ) utilizes an AffineTransform operation to rotate a copy of the image, which is returned to rotatingImage( ) and drawn:

```
private void rotatingImage(Graphics2D g2d, BufferedImage im, int x, int y)
{ int angle = (counter * 10) % 360;
  BufferedImage rotIm = imageSfx.getRotatedImage(im, angle);
  drawImage(g2d, rotIm, x, y);
}
```

getRotatedImage( ) makes a new BufferedImage, called dest. An AffineTransform object is created, which rotates dest's coordinate space by angle degrees counterclockwise around its center. The source image is copied in, which makes it appear to be rotated by angle degrees clockwise around the center of dest:

```
public BufferedImage getRotatedImage(BufferedImage src, int angle)
{
  if (src == null) {
    System.out.println("getRotatedImage: input image is null");
    return null;
  }

  int transparency = src.getColorModel().getTransparency();
  BufferedImage dest = gc.createCompatibleImage(
                      src.getWidth(), src.getHeight(), transparency );
  Graphics2D g2d = dest.createGraphics();

  AffineTransform origAT = g2d.getTransform();  // save original

  // rotate the coord. system of the dest. image around its center
  AffineTransform rot = new AffineTransform();
  rot.rotate( Math.toRadians(angle), src.getWidth()/2, src.getHeight()/2);
  g2d.transform(rot);

  g2d.drawImage(src, 0, 0, null);   // copy in the image

  g2d.setTransform(origAT);    // restore original transform
  g2d.dispose();

  return dest;
}
```

The AffineTransform object (rot) could be composed from multiple transforms—such as translations, scaling, and shearing—by applying more operations to it. For instance, translate( ), scale( ), and shear( ) applied to rot will be cumulative in effect. Ordering is important since a translation followed by a rotation is not the same as a rotation followed by a translation.

The main problem with this approach is the image is transformed within the image space of dest, which acts as a clipping rectangle. Thus, if the image is translated/rotated/sheared outside dest's boundaries, for example, beyond the bottom-right corner. Then, the image will be clipped or perhaps disappear completely This problem can occur even with rotations around dest's center; a look at the rotating atomic image highlights the problem.

The simplest solution is a careful design of the graphic to ensure that its opaque areas all fall within a rotation circle placed at the center of the image file, with a radius constrained by the file's dimensions. For example, image (a) in Figure 6-9 is safe to rotate around the file's center point, and image (b) is not.

When an image is rotated, areas in the destination image may not correspond to pixels in the source. For instance, in image (b) in Figure 6-9, strips on the left and right of the rotated image don't correspond to pixels in the original. They are drawn transparently if

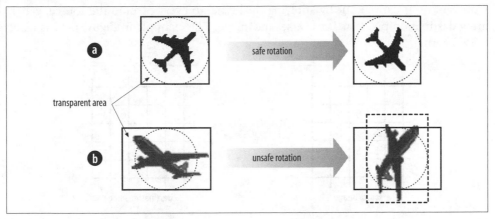

Figure 6-9. Safe and unsafe rotations

the original image has an alpha channel. However, if the original image is opaque (e.g., a JPEG), then the pixels will be colored black.

For example, the *balls.jpg* image can be rotated with:

```
rotatingImage(g2d, balls, 110, 25);
```

Figure 6-10 shows the image after being rotated clockwise; black strips are visible on the left and right.

Figure 6-10. Rotation of an opaque image

ConvolveOp Processing

A convolution operator calculates the color of each pixel in a destination image in terms of a combination of the colors of the corresponding pixel in the source image, and its neighbors. A matrix (called a *kernel*) specifies the neighbors and gives weights for how their colors should be combined with the source pixel to give the destination pixel value. The kernel must have an odd number of rows and columns (e.g., 3 × 3) so the central cell can represent the source pixel (e.g., cell [1, 1]) and the surrounding cells its neighbors.

Convolution is carried out by applying the kernel to every pixel in the source, generating destination pixels as it traverses the image. The example in Figure 6-11 is using a 3×3 kernel.

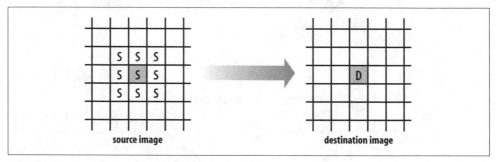

Figure 6-11. Convolution from source to destination

Figure 6-12 is a typical 3×3 kernel.

$$\begin{pmatrix} \frac{1}{9} & \frac{1}{9} & \frac{1}{9} \\ \frac{1}{9} & \frac{1}{9} & \frac{1}{9} \\ \frac{1}{9} & \frac{1}{9} & \frac{1}{9} \end{pmatrix}$$

Figure 6-12. A kernel for blurring an image

The 1/9 values are the weights. This kernel combines the source pixel and its eight neighbors using equal weights, which causes the destination pixel to be a combination of all those pixel's colors, resulting in an overall blurry image.

The weights should add up to 1 in order to maintain the brightness of the destination image. A total weight of more than 1 will make the image brighter, and less than 1 will darken it. The resulting pixel color values are constrained to be between 0 and 255; values higher than 255 are converted to 255.

One tricky aspect is what to do at the edges of the image. For example, what happens with the source pixel at (0, 0), which has no left and top neighbors? In most image processing packages, the solution is to treat the graphic as a wraparound so the pixels at the bottom of the image are used as the top neighbors, and the pixels at the right edge as left neighbors. Unfortunately, Java 2D is a little lacking in this area since its edge behaviors are simplistic. Either the destination pixel (e.g., [0, 0]) is automatically filled with black or set to contain the source pixel value unchanged. These possibilities are denoted by the ConvolveOp constants EDGE_ZERO_FILL and EDGE_NO_OP.

Aside from blurring, convolution is utilized for edge detection and sharpening. Examples of both are given in Figure 6-13.

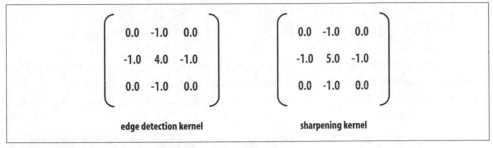

Figure 6-13. Edge detection and sharpening kernels

The edge detection kernel highlights the places where the colors in the image change sharply (usually at the boundaries between parts of the images), drawing them in white or gray. Meanwhile, large blocks of similar color will be cast into gloom. The result is a destination image showing only the edges between areas in the original picture.

The sharpening kernel is a variant of the edge detection matrix, with more weight applied to the source pixel, making the overall weight 1.0 so the destination image's brightness is maintained. The result is that the original image will remain visible, but the edges will be thicker and brighter.

ImageSFXs contains a drawBluredImage( ) method, which applies a precalculated blurring kernel:

```
private ConvolveOp blurOp;      // global for image blurring


private void initEffects( )
// Create pre-defined ops for image negation and blurring.
{ // image negative, explained later...

    // blur by convolving the image with a matrix
    float ninth = 1.0f / 9.0f;

    float[] blurKernel = {      // the 'hello world' of Image Ops :)
        ninth, ninth, ninth,
        ninth, ninth, ninth,
        ninth, ninth, ninth
    };
    blurOp = new ConvolveOp(
            new Kernel(3, 3, blurKernel), ConvolveOp.EDGE_NO_OP, null);
}


public void drawBlurredImage(Graphics2D g2d,
                    BufferedImage im, int x, int y)
```

```
     // blurring with a fixed convolution kernel
  { if (im == null) {
      System.out.println("getBlurredImage: input image is null");
      return;
    }
    g2d.drawImage(im, blurOp, x, y);   // use predefined ConvolveOp
  }
```

When the ImageSFXs object is created, initEffects( ) is called to initialize the blurOp ConvolveOp object. A 3×3 array of floats is used to create the kernel. The EDGE_NO_OP argument states that pixels at the edges of the image will be unaffected by the convolution.

drawBlurredImage( ) uses the version of drawImage( ) which takes a BufferedImageOp argument, so the modified image is written directly to the screen.

This coding is satisfactory, but I require an image to become increasingly blurry over a period of several frames (see "eyeChart" in Figure 6-1). One solution would be to store the destination image at the end of the convolution and apply blurring to it again during the next frame. Unfortunately, ConvolveOps cannot be applied in place, so a new destination image must be created each time. Instead, my approach is to generate increasingly blurry ConvolveOps in each frame and apply this to the original image via drawImage( ).

Increasingly blurry kernels are larger matrices that generate a destination pixel based on more neighbors. I begin with a 3×3 matrix, then a 5×5, and so on, increasing to 15×15. The matrices must have odd length dimensions so there's a center point. The weights in the matrix must add up to 1 so, for instance, the 5×5 matrix will be filled with 1/25s.

The top-level method in ImagesTests is blurringImage( ):

```
  private void blurringImage(Graphics2D g2d, BufferedImage im, int x, int y)
  {
    int fadeSize = (counter%8)*2 + 1;    // gives 1,3,5,7,9,11,13,15
    if (fadeSize == 1)
      drawImage(g2d, im, x, y);    // start again with original image
    else
      imageSfx.drawBlurredImage(g2d, im, x, y, fadeSize);
  }
```

drawBlurredImage( ) in ImageSFXs takes a fadeSize argument, which becomes the row and column lengths of the kernel. The method is complicated by ensuring the kernel dimensions are odd, not too small, and not bigger than the image:

```
  public void drawBlurredImage(Graphics2D g2d,
                          BufferedImage im, int x, int y, int size)
  /* The size argument is used to specify a size*size blur kernel,
     filled with 1/(size*size) values. */
  {
    if (im == null) {
      System.out.println("getBlurredImage: input image is null");
```

```
    return;
  }
  int imWidth = im.getWidth( );
  int imHeight = im.getHeight( );
  int maxSize = (imWidth > imHeight) ? imWidth : imHeight;

  if ((maxSize%2) == 0)  // if even
    maxSize--;  // make it odd

  if ((size%2) == 0) {  // if even
    size++;   // make it odd
    System.out.println(
      "Blur size must be odd; adding 1 to make size = " + size);
  }

  if (size < 3) {
    System.out.println("Minimum blur size is 3");
    size = 3;
  }
  else if (size > maxSize) {
    System.out.println("Maximum blur size is " + maxSize);
    size = maxSize;
  }

  // create the blur kernel
  int numCoords = size * size;
  float blurFactor = 1.0f / (float) numCoords;

  float[] blurKernel = new float[numCoords];
  for (int i=0; i < numCoords; i++)
    blurKernel[i] = blurFactor;

  ConvolveOp blurringOp = new ConvolveOp(
      new Kernel(size, size, blurKernel),
      ConvolveOp.EDGE_NO_OP, null);    // leaves edges unaffected
    // ConvolveOp.EDGE_ZERO_FILL, null); //edges filled with black

  g2d.drawImage(im, blurringOp, x, y);
} // end of drawBlurredImage( ) with size argument
```

A drawback with larger kernels is that more of the pixels at the edges of the source image will be affected by the edge behavior constants. With EDGE_NO_OP, an increasingly thick band of pixels around the edges will be unaffected. With EDGE_ZERO_FILL, the band will be pitch black. Figure 6-14 shows both effects when blurring is applied to the balls image with:

```
blurringImage(g2d, balls, 110, 25);
```

The black-edged image was generated after the ConvolveOp.EDGE_NO_OP constant was replaced by ConvolveOp.EDGE_ZERO_FILL in the call to ConvolveOp's constructor in drawBlurredImage( ).

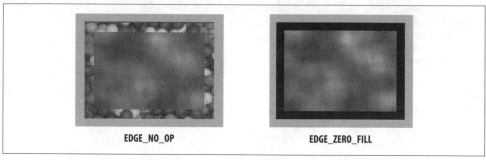

| EDGE_NO_OP | EDGE_ZERO_FILL |

Figure 6-14. Edge behaviors with ConvolveOp

There's a need for more edge behavior options in future versions of the ConvolveOp class.

LookupOp Processing

At the heart of LookupOp is the representation of a pixel using the sRGB color space, which stores the red, green, blue, and alpha channels in 8 bits (1 byte) each, snugly fitting them all into a single 32-bit integer. This is shown in Figure 6-15.

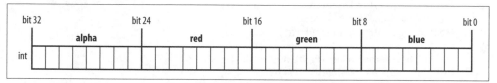

Figure 6-15. The sRGB color space format

The red, green, blue, and alpha components can each have 256 different values (2^8), with 255 being full on. For the alpha part, 0 means fully transparent, and 255 means fully opaque.

A LookupOp operation utilizes a lookup table with 256 entries. Each entry contains a color value (i.e., an integer between 0 and 255), so the table defines a mapping from the image's existing color values to new values.

The simplest form of LookupOp is one that uses one lookup table. The example below converts a color component value i to (255-i) and is applied to all the channels in the image. For example, a red color component of 0 (no red) is mapped to 255 (full on red). In this way, the table inverts the color scheme:

```
short[] invert = new short[256];
for (int i = 0; i < 256; i++)
  invert[i] = (short)(255 - i);
```

```
LookupTable table = new ShortLookupTable(0, invert);
LookupOp invertOp = new LookupOp(table, null);

g2d.drawImage(im, invertOp, x, y);    // draw the image
```

The ShortLookupTable constructor is supplied with an array to initialize the table mapping. A ByteLookupTable is built with an array of bytes.

A visual way of understanding the mapping defined by invert[] is shown in Figure 6-16.

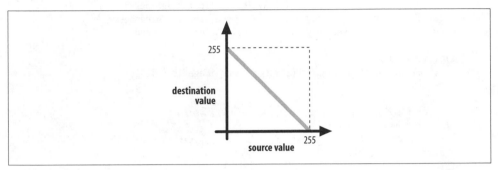

Figure 6-16. The invert[] lookup table

The table defines a straight line in this case, but a table can hold any mapping from source color component values to destination values. It's more common to utilize several lookup tables, using different ones for different channels. Also, no mapping is generally applied to an alpha channel of a transparent or translucent image.

reddenImage( ) in ImagesTests draws its source image with increasing amounts of red over a period of 20 frames and then starts again (e.g., see the *house* image). The original image is unaffected since the LookupOp writes directly to the screen via drawImage( ). To increase the effect, as the redness increases, the amount of green and blue decreases, necessitating two lookup tables: one for red and one for green and blue. Any alpha component in the image is left unaffected:

```
private void reddenImage(Graphics2D g2d, BufferedImage im,
                                              int x, int y)
{
  float brightness = 1.0f + (((float) counter%21)/10.0f);
          // gives values in the range 1.0-3.0, in steps of 0.1
  if (brightness == 1.0f)
    drawImage(g2d, im, x, y);    // start again with original image
  else
    imageSfx.drawRedderImage(g2d, im, x, y, (float) brightness);
}
```

A minor hassle, illustrated by drawRedderImage( ), is dealing with opaque versus nonopaque images. An opaque image requires two lookup tables (one for red, one for green and blue), and a nonopaque image requires a third lookup table for the alpha channel. This separation occurs in all LookupOp methods that are passed both types of image. The same issue arises with RescaleOp and BandCombineOp operations. drawRedderImage( ) in ImageSFXs changes the colors, based on a brightness value that ranges from 1.0 to 3.0:

```
public void drawRedderImage(Graphics2D g2d, BufferedImage im,
                            int x, int y, float brightness)
/* Draw the image with its redness is increased, and its greenness
   and blueness decreased. Any alpha channel is left unchanged.
*/
{ if (im == null) {
    System.out.println("drawRedderImage: input image is null");
    return;
  }

  if (brightness < 0.0f) {
    System.out.println("Brightness must be >= 0.0f;set to 0.0f");
    brightness = 0.0f;
  }
  // brightness may be less than 1.0 to make the image less red

  short[] brighten = new short[256];    // for red channel
  short[] lessen = new short[256];   // for green and blue channels
  short[] noChange = new short[256];    // for the alpha channel

  for(int i=0; i < 256; i++) {
    float brightVal = 64.0f + (brightness * i);
    if (brightVal > 255.0f)
      brightVal = 255.0f;
    brighten[i] = (short) brightVal;
    lessen[i] = (short) ((float)i / brightness);
    noChange[i] = (short) i;
  }

  short[][] brightenRed;
  if (hasAlpha(im)) {
    brightenRed = new short[4][];
    brightenRed[0] = brighten;  // for the red channel
    brightenRed[1] = lessen;    // for the green channel
    brightenRed[2] = lessen;    // for the blue channel
    brightenRed[3] = noChange;  // for the alpha channel
      // without this the LookupOp fails; a bug (?)
  }
  else {  // not transparent
    brightenRed = new short[3][];
    brightenRed[0] = brighten;    // red
    brightenRed[1] = lessen;      // green
    brightenRed[2] = lessen;      // blue
  }
```

```
    LookupTable table = new ShortLookupTable(0, brightenRed);
    LookupOp brightenRedOp = new LookupOp(table, null);

    g2d.drawImage(im, brightenRedOp, x, y);
  } // end of drawRedderImage()
```

The three lookup tables—brighten[], lessen[], and noChange[]—are shown in Figure 6-17 when brightness has the value 2.0. As the value increases, more of the red color components will be mapped to full on and the blue and green color values will be lowered further.

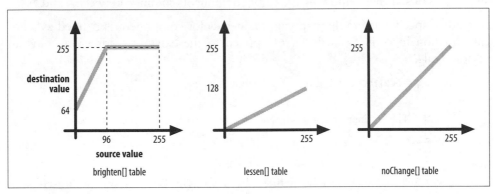

Figure 6-17. Lookup tables used in drawReddenImage()

A 2D array, brightenRed[][], is declared and filled with three or four tables depending on if the image is opaque (i.e., only has RGB components) or also has an alpha channel. This array is used to create a LookupOp table called table, and then the operation proceeds.

A LookupOp operation will raise an exception if the source image has an alpha channel and the operation only contains three tables. Therefore, check for the presence of an alpha band in the image, which is achieved with hasAlpha():

```
public boolean hasAlpha(BufferedImage im)
// does im have an alpha channel?
{
  if (im == null)
    return false;

  int transparency = im.getColorModel().getTransparency();

  if ((transparency == Transparency.BITMASK) ||
      (transparency == Transparency.TRANSLUCENT))
    return true;
  else
    return false;
}
```

A color model may use BITMASK transparency (found in GIFs), TRANSULENT (as in translucent PNGs), or OPAQUE (as in JPEGs).

RescaleOp Processing

The rescaling operation is a specialized form of LookupOp. As with a lookup, a pixel is considered to be in sRGB form; the red, green, blue (and alpha) channels are each stored in 8 bits (1 byte), allowing the color components to range between 0 and 255.

Instead of specifying a table mapping, the new color component is defined as a linear equation involving a scale factor applied to the existing color value, plus an optional offset:

$$color_{dest} = scaleFactor^*color_{source} + offset$$

The destination color is bounded to be between 0 and 255.

Any LookupOp table that can be defined by a straight line can be rephrased as a RescaleOp operation. Conversely, any RescaleOp can be written as a LookupOp. LookupOp is more general since the table mapping permits nonlinear relationships between the source and destination color components.

Since LookupOp is functionally a superset of RescaleOp and probably more efficient to execute, why Java 2D offers RescaleOp at all is unclear.

drawReddenImage( ), which was defined as a LookupOp using three (or four) tables, can be rephrased as a RescaleOp consisting of three (or four) rescaling equations. Each equation has two parts, which are a scale factor and an offset:

```
RescaleOp brigherOp;
if (hasAlpha(im)) {
  float[] scaleFactors = {brightness, 1.0f/brightness, 1.0f/brightness, 1.0f};
      // don't change alpha
      // without the 1.0f the RescaleOp fails; a bug (?)
  float[] offsets = {64.0f, 0.0f, 0.0f, 0.0f};
  brigherOp = new RescaleOp(scaleFactors, offsets, null);
}
else {  // not transparent
  float[] scaleFactors = {brightness, 1.0f/brightness, 1.0f/brightness};
  float[] offsets = {64.0f, 0.0f, 0.0f};
  brigherOp = new RescaleOp(scaleFactors, offsets, null);
}
g2d.drawImage(im, brigherOp, x, y);
```

The `RescaleOp` constructor takes an array of scale factors, an array of offsets, and optional rendering hints as its arguments.

The three equations are employed in the code fragment:

- $red\_color_{dest} = brightness*red\_color_{source} + 64$
- $green/blue\_color_{dest} = (1/brightness)*green/blue\_color_{source} + 0$
- $alpha\_color_{dest} = 1*alpha\_color_{source} + 0$

The new red color component is bounded at 255 even if the equation returns a larger value. The green/blue_color equation is used for the green and blue channels.

 These equations are the same as the `LookupOp` tables in the first version of `drawReddenImage( )`.

As with `LookupOp`, the right number of scale factors and offsets must be supplied according to the number of channels in the image. For instance, if only three equations are defined for an image with an alpha channel, then an exception will be raised at runtime when the operation is applied.

Brightening the image

`ImagesTests`'s `brighteningImage( )` increases the brightness of its image over a period of nine frames and starts again with the original colors. (Take a look at the scooter image in ImageTests for an example.) The original image is unaffected since the operation writes to the screen. The brightness only affects the RGB channels; the alpha component remains unchanged:

```
private void brighteningImage(Graphics2D g2d, BufferedImage im,
                                              int x, int y)
{ int brightness = counter%9;     // gives 0-8
  if (brightness == 0)
    drawImage(g2d, im, x, y);     // start again with original image
  else
    imageSfx.drawBrighterImage(g2d, im, x, y, (float) brightness);
}
```

The ImageSFXs method, `drawBrighterImage( )`, uses a `RescaleOp` based around the following equations:

- $RGB\_color_{dest} = brightness*RGB\_color_{source} + 0$
- $alpha\_color_{dest} = 1*alpha\_color_{source} + 0$

The RGB_color equation is used for the red, green, and blue channels. When the source image has no alpha, I can utilize a `RescaleOp` constructor that takes a single scale factor and offset. It will automatically apply the equation to all the RGB channels:

```
public void drawBrighterImage(Graphics2D g2d, BufferedImage im,
                              int x, int y, float brightness)
```

```
{ if (im == null) {
    System.out.println("drawBrighterImage: input image is null");
    return;
  }
  if (brightness < 0.0f) {
    System.out.println("Brightness must be >= 0.0f; set to 0.5f");
    brightness = 0.5f;
  }
  RescaleOp brigherOp;
  if (hasAlpha(im)) {
    float[] scaleFactors = {brightness, brightness, brightness, 1.0f};
    float[] offsets = {0.0f, 0.0f, 0.0f, 0.0f};
    brigherOp = new RescaleOp(scaleFactors, offsets, null);
  }
  else    // not transparent
    brigherOp = new RescaleOp(brightness, 0, null);

  g2d.drawImage(im, brigherOp, x, y);
}  // end of drawBrighterImage( )
```

Negating the image

ImagesTests's negatingImage( ) keeps switching between the original image and its negative depending on the counter value. (See the owl image in ImageTests to see this in action—e.g., as shown in Figure 6-1.) A color component value, i, is converted to (255-i) in the RGB channels, but the alpha is untouched:

```
private void negatingImage(Graphics2D g2d, BufferedImage im, int x, int y)
{
  if (counter%10 < 5)    // show the negative
    imageSfx.drawNegatedImage(g2d, im, x, y);
  else  // show the original
    drawImage(g2d, im, x, y);
}
```

When the ImageSFXs object is first created, the negative rescaling operations, negOp and negOpTrans, are predefined. negOpTrans is used when the image has an alpha channel, and contains these equations:

- $RGB\_color_{dest} = -1 * RGB\_color_{source} + 255$
- $alpha\_color_{dest} = 1 * alpha\_color_{source} + 0$

The RGB_color equation is applied to the red, green, and blue channels.

negOp is for opaque images, so only requires the RGB equation:

```
// global rescaling ops for image negation
private RescaleOp negOp, negOpTrans;


private void initEffects( )
{
  // image negative.
  // Multiply each color value by -1.0 and add 255
  negOp = new RescaleOp(-1.0f, 255f, null);
```

```
    // image negative for images with transparency
    float[] negFactors = {-1.0f, -1.0f, -1.0f, 1.0f};
                            // don't change the alpha
    float[] offsets = {255f, 255f, 255f, 0.0f};
    negOpTrans = new RescaleOp(negFactors, offsets, null);

    // other initialization code
}


public void drawNegatedImage(Graphics2D g2d, BufferedImage im, int x, int y)
{
  if (im == null) {
    System.out.println("drawNegatedImage: input image is null");
    return;
  }
  if (hasAlpha(im))
    g2d.drawImage(im, negOpTrans, x, y);   // predefined RescaleOp
  else
    g2d.drawImage(im, negOp, x, y);
}  // end of drawNegatedImage( )
```

BandCombineOp Processing

LookupOp and RescaleOp specify transformations that take a single color component in a pixel (e.g., the red color) and maps it to a new value. A BandCombineOp generalizes this idea to allow a new color component to be potentially defined in terms of a combination of *all* the color components in the source pixel.

The destination pixel {redN, greenN, blueN, alphaN} is created from some combination of the source pixel {red, green, blue, alpha}, where the combination is defined using matrix multiplication, as in Figure 6-18.

$$\begin{pmatrix} m11 & m12 & m13 & m14 \\ m21 & m22 & m23 & m24 \\ m31 & m32 & m33 & m34 \\ m41 & m42 & m43 & m44 \end{pmatrix} * \begin{pmatrix} red_{sample} \\ green_{sample} \\ blue_{sample} \\ alpha_{sample} \end{pmatrix} = \begin{pmatrix} redN_{sample} \\ greenN_{sample} \\ blueN_{sample} \\ alphaN_{sample} \end{pmatrix}$$

source pixel   destination pixel

Figure 6-18. BandCombineOp as a matrix operation

Here's an example equation:

$$redN_{sample} = m11^{*}red_{sample} + m12^{*}green_{sample} + m13^{*}blue_{sample} + m14^{*}alpha_{sample}$$

If the source image has no alpha channel, then a 3×3 matrix is used.

BandCombineOp is different from the other operations I've discussed since it implements the RasterOp interface and not BufferedImageOp. This means that a little extra work is required to access the Raster object inside the source BufferedImage, and that the resulting changed Raster must be built up into a destination BufferedImage.

ImagesTests's mixedImage( ) draws an image with its green and blue bands modified in random ways, while keeping the red band and any alpha band unchanged. See the balls and basn6a08 images for examples:

```
private void mixedImage(Graphics2D g2d, BufferedImage im, int x, int y)
{ if (counter%10 < 5)    // mix it up
    imageSfx.drawMixedColouredImage(g2d, im, x, y);
  else  // show the original
    drawImage(g2d, im, x, y);
}
```

drawMixedColouredImage( ) distinguishes if the source has an alpha channel and creates a 4×4 or 3×3 matrix accordingly. The source Raster is accessed, the operation applied using filter( ), and the result is packaged as a new BufferedImage that is then drawn:

```
public void drawMixedColouredImage(Graphics2D g2d,
                                BufferedImage im, int x, int y)
{
  // Mix up the colors in the green and blue bands
  { if (im == null) {
    System.out.println("drawMixedColouredImage: input is null");
    return;
  }
  BandCombineOp changecolorsOp;
  Random r = new Random( );
  if (hasAlpha(im)) {
    float[][] colorMatrix = {    // 4 by 4
      { 1.0f, 0.0f, 0.0f, 0.0f },    // new red band, unchanged
      { r.nextFloat( ), r.nextFloat( ), r.nextFloat( ), 0.0f }, // new green band
      { r.nextFloat( ), r.nextFloat( ), r.nextFloat( ), 0.0f }, // new blue band
      { 0.0f, 0.0f, 0.0f, 1.0f} };   // unchanged alpha

    changecolorsOp = new BandCombineOp(colorMatrix, null);
  }
  else {     // not transparent
    float[][] colorMatrix = {  // 3 by 3
      { 1.0f, 0.0f, 0.0f },            // new red band, unchanged
      { r.nextFloat( ), r.nextFloat( ), r.nextFloat( ) },    // new green band
      { r.nextFloat( ), r.nextFloat( ), r.nextFloat( ) }};  // new blue band

    changecolorsOp = new BandCombineOp(colorMatrix, null);
  }
```

```
    Raster sourceRaster = im.getRaster();  // access source Raster
    WritableRaster destRaster = changecolorsOp.filter(sourceRaster, null);

    // make the destination Raster into a BufferedImage
    BufferedImage newIm = new BufferedImage(im.getColorModel(),
                                        destRaster, false, null);

    g2d.drawImage(newIm, x, y, null);   // draw it
  } // end of drawMixedColouredImage()
```

The matrices are filled with random numbers in the rows applied to the green and blue components of the source pixel.

The matrix row for the red component is {1, 0, 0, 0}, which will send the red source unchanged into the destination pixel. Similarly, the alpha component is {0, 0, 0, 1}, which leaves the alpha part unchanged.

It's possible to treat a pixel as containing an additional unit element, which allows the BandCombineOp matrix to contain an extra column. This permits a wider range of equations to be defined. Figure 6-19 shows the resulting multiplication using a 4×5 matrix.

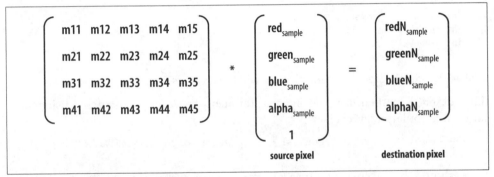

Figure 6-19. BandCombineOp with an additional pixel element

Here's an example:

$$redN_{sample} = m11^*red_{sample} + m12^*green_{sample} + m13^*blue_{sample} + m14^*alpha_{sample} + \mathbf{m15}$$

The additional m15 element can be used to define equations that do not have to pass through the origin. This means that a zero input sample doesn't need to produce a zero output.

 If the source image has no alpha channel, then a 3×4 matrix is used.

Pixel Effects

The great advantage of BufferedImage is the ease with which its elements can be accessed (e.g., pixel data, sample model, color space). However, a lot can be done using only the BufferedImage methods, getRGB( ) and setRGB( ), to manipulate a given pixel (or array of pixels).

Here are the single pixel versions:

```
int getRGB(int x, int y);

void setRGB(int x, int y, int newValue);
```

The getRGB( ) method returns an integer representing the pixel at location (x, y), formatted using sRGB. The red, green, blue, and alpha channels use 8 bits (1 byte) each, so they can fit into a 32-bit integer result. The sRGB format is shown in Figure 6-15.

The color components can be extracted from the integer using bit manipulation:

```
BufferedImage im = ...;  // load the image
int pixel = im.getRGB(x,y);

int alphaVal = (pixel >> 24) & 255;
int redVal = (pixel >> 16) & 255;
int greenVal = (pixel >> 8) & 255;
int blueVal = pixel & 255;
```

alphaVal, redVal, greenVal, and blueVal will have values between 0 and 255.

The setRGB( ) method takes an integer argument, newValue, constructed using similar bit manipulation in reverse:

```
int newValue = blueVal | (greenVal << 8) | (redVal << 16) | (alphaVal << 24);
im.setRGB(x, y, newVal);
```

Care should be taken that alphaVal, redVal, greenVal, and blueVal have values between 0 and 255, or the resulting integer will be incorrect. Error checking at runtime may be a solution but will have an impact on performance.

Of more use are the versions of getRGB( ) and setRGB( ) that work with an array of pixels. getRGB( ) is general enough to extract an arbitrary rectangle of data from the image, returning it as a one-dimensional array. However, its most common use is to extract all the pixel data. Then a loop can be employed to traverse over the data:

```
int imWidth = im.getWidth( );
int imHeight = im.getHeight( );

// make an array to hold the data
int[] pixels = new int[imWidth * imHeight];

// extract the data from the image into pixels[]
im.getRGB(0, 0, imWidth, imHeight, pixels, 0, imWidth);
```

```
for(int i=0; i < pixels.length; i++) {
  // do something to pixels[i]
}
// update the image with pixels[]
im.setRGB(0, 0, imWidth, imHeight, pixels, 0, imWidth);
```

At the end of the loop, the updated pixels[] array can be placed back inside the BufferedImage via a call to setRGB( ).

The prototypes for the array versions of getRGB( ) and setRGB( ) are:

```
int[] getRGB(int startX, int startY, int w, int h,
                int[] RGBArray, int offset, int scansize);
void setRGB(int startX, int startY, int w, int h,
                int[] RGBArray, int offset, int scansize);
```

The extraction rectangle is defined by startX, startY, w, and h. offset states where in the pixel array the extracted data should start being written. scansize specifies the number of elements in a row of the returned data and is normally the width of the image.

Teleporting an image

The teleport effect causes an image to disappear, multiple pixels at a time, over the course of seven frames (after which the effect repeats). Individual pixels are assigned the value 0, which results in their becoming transparent. The bee image has this effect applied to it.

This pixilated visual should be compared with the smoother fading offered by fadingImage( ), described in the section "Alpha Compositing."

The changes are applied to a copy of the image (stored in the global teleImage). The copy is assigned an alpha channel, if the original doesn't have one, to ensure the image becomes transparent (rather than black). A global is used so pixel erasing can be repeatedly applied to the same image and be cumulative.

The relevant ImageSFXs method is eraseImageParts( ). Its second argument specifies that the affected pixels are located in the image's pixel array at positions, which are a multiple of the supplied number:

```
private BufferedImage teleportImage(Graphics2D g2d,
            BufferedImage im, BufferedImage teleIm, int x, int y)
{
  if (teleIm == null) {    // start the effect
    if (imageSfx.hasAlpha(im))
      teleIm = imageSfx.copyImage(im);
    else   // no alpha channel
      teleIm = imageSfx.makeTransImage(im);  // give the copy an alpha channel
  }
```

```
    int eraseSteps = counter%7;     // range is 0 to 6
    switch(eraseSteps) {
      case 0:        // restart the effect
        if (imageSfx.hasAlpha(im))
          teleIm = imageSfx.copyImage(im);
        else  // not transparent
          teleIm = imageSfx.makeTransImage(im);
        break;
      case 1:
        imageSfx.eraseImageParts(teleIm, 11); break; // every 11th pixel goes
      case 2:
        imageSfx.eraseImageParts(teleIm, 7); break;  // every 7th pixel
      case 3:
        imageSfx.eraseImageParts(teleIm, 5); break;  // 5th
      case 4:
        imageSfx.eraseImageParts(teleIm, 3); break;  // 3rd
      case 5:
        imageSfx.eraseImageParts(teleIm, 2); break;  // every 2nd pixel
      case 6:
        imageSfx.eraseImageParts(teleIm, 1); break;
                              // every pixel goes, i.e., fully erased
      default:
        System.out.println("Unknown count for teleport");
        break;
    } // end switch

    drawImage(g2d, teleIm, x, y);
    return teleIm;
  } // end of teleportImage()
```

The ImageSFXs support methods, copyImage() and makeTransImage(), make copies of a BufferedImage, and are similar. copyImage() utilizes GraphicsConfiguration's createCompatibleImage() to make a BufferedImage object, and then the source image is drawn into it. makeTransImage() creates a new BufferedImage object of type TYPE_INT_ARGB to ensure it has an alpha channel. Then the source image is drawn into it:

```
public BufferedImage makeTransImage(BufferedImage src)
{
  if (src == null) {
    System.out.println("makeTransImage: input image is null");
    return null;
  }
  BufferedImage dest = new BufferedImage(
              src.getWidth(), src.getHeight(),
              BufferedImage.TYPE_INT_ARGB);  // alpha channel
  Graphics2D g2d = dest.createGraphics();

  // copy image
  g2d.drawImage(src, 0, 0, null);
  g2d.dispose();
  return dest;
}
```

ImageSFXs's eraseImageParts( ) has the same structure as the array-based getRGB( ) and setRGB( ) code outlined above:

```
public void eraseImageParts(BufferedImage im, int spacing)
{
  if (im == null) {
    System.out.println("eraseImageParts: input image is null");
    return;
  }
  int imWidth = im.getWidth( );
  int imHeight = im.getHeight( );
  int [] pixels = new int[imWidth * imHeight];
  im.getRGB(0, 0, imWidth, imHeight, pixels, 0, imWidth);

  int i = 0;
  while (i < pixels.length) {
    pixels[i] = 0;      // make transparent (or black if no alpha)
    i = i + spacing;
  }
  im.setRGB(0, 0, imWidth, imHeight, pixels, 0, imWidth);
}
```

The loop jumps over the array, setting every ith pixel to have the value 0. This causes the red, green, blue, and alpha channels to be filled with 0 bits. Due to the alpha channel, this causes the pixel to become transparent. If no alpha existed, then the 0 bits would signify that red, green, and blue are switched off, and the pixel would be drawn in black.

Zapping an image

Zapping means the gradual changing of the image's visible parts to a random mix of red and yellow pixels. The number of changed pixels increases over the course of the effect (11 frames). See pumpkin for an example of the effect in action. The changes are applied to a copy of the image (stored in the global zapImage). After 11 frames, the image is restored and the effect begins again.

 View the pumpkin image to sample this effect.

As with the teleportation effect, a global is used so the color changes can be repeatedly applied to the same image and be cumulative. The amount of zapping is controlled by the likelihood value which increases from 0 to 1.

The method used in ImageSFXs is zapImageParts( ):

```
private BufferedImage zapImage(Graphics2D g2d, BufferedImage im,
                               BufferedImage zapIm, int x, int y)
{ if ((zapIm == null) || (counter%11 == 0))
    zapIm = imageSfx.copyImage(im);    // restart the effect
  else {
```

```
      double likelihood = (counter%11)/10.0;   // produces range 0 to 1
      imageSfx.zapImageParts(zapIm, likelihood);
    }
    drawImage(g2d, zapIm, x, y);
    return zapIm;
  }
```

zapImageParts() uses the same approach as previously shown: the pixel array is
extracted, modified in a loop, and then written back into the BufferedImage object:

```
public void zapImageParts(BufferedImage im, double likelihood)
{
  if (im == null) {
    System.out.println("zapImageParts: input image is null");
    return;
  }
  if ((likelihood < 0) || (likelihood > 1)) {
    System.out.println("likelihood must be in the range 0 to 1");
    likelihood = 0.5;
  }

  int redCol = 0xf90000;     // nearly full-on red
  int yellowCol = 0xf9fd00;  // a mix of red and green

  int imWidth = im.getWidth();
  int imHeight = im.getHeight();
  int [] pixels = new int[imWidth * imHeight];
  im.getRGB(0, 0, imWidth, imHeight, pixels, 0, imWidth);

  double rnd;
  for(int i=0; i < pixels.length; i++) {
    rnd = Math.random();
    if (rnd <= likelihood) {
      if (rnd <=  15*likelihood/16 )    // red more likely
        pixels[i] = pixels[i] | redCol;
      else
        pixels[i] = pixels[i] | yellowCol;
    }
  }

  im.setRGB(0, 0, imWidth, imHeight, pixels, 0, imWidth);
} // end of eraseImageParts()
```

The random effect of changing pixels to red or yellow is achieved by the use of
Math.random().

The red color (redCol) is defined as the octal 0xf90000 and yellow (yellowCol) as
0xf9fd00. To understand these, remember that the sRGB format stores color components in the order alpha, red, green, and blue, each in 8 bits. Eight bits can be represented by the octals 0x00 to 0xFF, as in Figure 6-20.

Consequently, the red field in the sRGB format will be the fifth and sixth octal digits
from the right, and the green field will be the third and fourth.

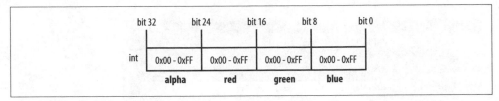

Figure 6-20. The sRGB format in octal

The octals are bitwise-ORed with a pixel, which causes the relevant color components to be overwritten. `redCol` overwrites the red color component only, and `yellowCol` replaces the red and yellow parts, which is a more drastic change. This is balanced in the code by having the red change done more often.

Packaging the Application as a JAR

I'm converting the `ImagesTests` application into a JAR so all the resources (images, in this case) are packaged with the code in a single file. This makes the application easier to transport, and I get the additional benefit of compression.

 I won't consider how to use applets and JAR together or advanced topics, like signing and manipulating JARs from inside Java code. The Java tutorial (trail) on JARs should be consulted on these matters.

Before JARing begins, it's important to organize the resources in relation to the application. The `ImagesTests` code is located in the directory *ImagesTests/* (see Figure 6-21), which acts as the top-level directory for the JAR. The images are placed in an *Images/* subdirectory within *ImagesTests/*. This makes their inclusion into the JAR easy.

One issue with using Windows is that it displays filenames in a user-friendly lowercase format. Unfortunately, Java is less forgiving, and will be unable to find a file such as *BASN6A08.PNG* if told to load *basn6a08.png*. The application developer should open a DOS window and check the filenames in *Images/* directly.

The next step is to create a text file, which will become the basis of the manifest inside the JAR file. The *manifest* holds a range of meta-information about the JAR, related to matters like authentication, extensions, and sealing. However, I'll only add the name of the top-level class, `ImagesTests`, which contains the `main( )` method. This permits the application to be started by double-clicking.

The text file, *mainClass.txt* (any name will do), contains a single line:

```
Main-Class: ImagesTests
```

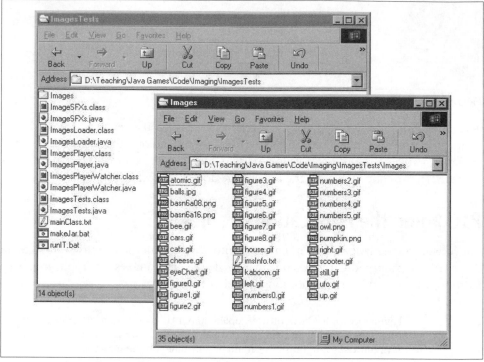

Figure 6-21. The ImagesTests/ directory and Images/ subdirectory

The file should be stored in the same directory as the application. The JAR file can be made using the command:

```
jar cvmf mainClass.txt ImagesTests.jar *.class Images
```

This command should be executed in the application directory. It has the following format:

```
jar <options> <manifest info file> <name of JAR file>
                <list of input files/directories>
```

The options, cvmf, specify the following:

c   Create a JAR file.

v   Verbose output goes to stdout during the creation process, including a list of everything added to the JAR.

m   A manifest information file is included on the command line, and its information should be incorporated into the JAR's manifest.

f   A filename for the resulting JAR is given on the command line.

The list of input files can use the wildcard symbol (*). All the *.class* files in the current directory are added to the JAR (e.g., *ImageSFXs.class*, *ImagesLoader.class*,

ImagesPlayer.class, *ImagesPlayerWatcher.class*, and *ImagesTests.class*). Also, the sub-directory *Images/* is added together with all its contents.

The *ImagesTests.jar* file will appear in *ImagesTests/* and can be started by double-clicking its icon. The JAR file's size is about 130 KB, compressed by 13 percent from the original collection of files.

The application can be started from the command line as well, by typing:

```
java -jar ImagesTests.jar
```

The advantage of this approach is that the output from the application will appear in the DOS window, whereas it is lost if the program is started via its icon.

 A simple way of checking the contents of the JAR file is to open it with a zip utility, such as WinZip (*http://www.winzip.com*). Alternatively, type this:

```
jar tf ImagesTests.jar
```

CHAPTER 7

Introducing Java Sound

This chapter talks about three different approaches to sound in Java: the basic `Applet` `play()` method, the more sophisticated `AudioClip` class, and the Java Sound API, which supports the recording, playback, and synthesis of sampled audio and Musical Instrument Digital Interface (MIDI) sequences.

Due to its great flexibility (and complexity), most of this chapter and the next three focus on the Java Sound API. Its overview in this chapter is illustrated with small examples showing the playback of clips, streamed audio, and MIDI sequences. I'll compare the Sound API with the Java Media Framework (JMF) and Java OpenAL (JOAL), a Java binding to OpenGL's audio API.

 One large topic missing from my coverage is audio capture, which seems less important for games. Good web resources on this topic (and others related to the Java Sound API) are listed at the end of this chapter.

Chapter 8 considers a single large application, `LoadersTests`, which demonstrates my Java Sound API-based `ClipsLoader` and `MidisLoader` classes for loading, playing, pausing, resuming, stopping, and looping clips and sequences. These loader classes will be used in later chapters when audio is required.

Chapters 9 and 10 examine less commonly needed Sound API capabilities for producing audio effects (e.g., echoes, dynamic volume changes) and runtime audio synthesis/generation.

Applet Playing

The `Applet` `play()` method loads a sound (perhaps from across the network) and plays it once. `play()` causes the applet's drawing and event handling to freeze while the audio data are retrieved and does nothing if the audio can't be found (i.e., no exception is raised). The sound is marked for garbage collection after being played, so it may need to be downloaded again when play( ) is called again. Example 7-1 is a typical 1990s example:

Example 7-1. Simple applet that uses the play() method

```
import java.applet.Applet;
import java.awt.*;

public class OldMcDonald extends Applet
{
  public void init( )
  {  play( getCodeBase( ), "McDonald.mid");  }

  public void paint(Graphics g)
  {  g.drawString("Older McDonald", 25, 25);  }

} // end of OldMcDonald class
```

The MIDI file (containing the tune "Old McDonald") is loaded and played as the applet is loaded. getCodeBase( ) indicates that the file can be found in the same place as the applet's *.class* file. An alternative is getDocumentBase( ), which specifies a location relative to the enclosing web page.

 The code for the OldMcDonald applet can be found in the *SoundExamps/McDonalds/* directory.

Early versions of Java only supported 8-bit mono Windows Wave files, but the various formats were extended in JDK 1.2 to include Sun Audio (AU files), Mac AIFF files, Musical Instrument Digital Interface (MIDI) files (type 0 and type 1), and Rich Media Format (RMF). Data can be 8-bit or 16-bit, mono or stereo, with sample rates between 8,000 and 48,000 Hz.

The AudioClip Class

Many of the shortcomings of Applet's play( ) method are remedied by the AudioClip class. AudioClip separates loading from playing and allows looping and termination via the loop( ) and stop( ) methods. Example 7-2 is an updated McDonald applet using AudioClip.

Example 7-2. Applet using the AudioClip class

```
import java.awt.*;
import javax.swing.*;
import java.applet.AudioClip;
```

Example 7-2. Applet using the AudioClip class (continued)

```java
public class McDonald extends JApplet
{
  private AudioClip mcdClip;

  public void init()
  { mcdClip = getAudioClip(getCodeBase(), "mcdonald.mid");  }

  public void paint(Graphics g)
  { g.drawString("Old McDonald", 25, 25);  }

  public void stop()
  { mcdClip.stop(); }

  public void start()
  /* A looping play (and a call to play()) always starts at
     the beginning of the clip. */
  { mcdClip.loop();  }

} // end of McDonald class
```

The clip is loaded with getAudioClip( ) in init( ), causing the applet to suspend until the download is completed. The sound is played repeatedly due to the loop( ) call in start( ), continuing until the applet is removed from the browser (triggering a call to stop( )). If the page is displayed again, start( )'s call to loop( ) will play the music from the beginning.

An application employs AudioClips in just about the same way, except that the clip is loaded with newAudioClip( ) from the Applet class, as shown in the PlaySound application (see Example 7-3).

Example 7-3. Using newAudioClip() from an applet

```java
import java.applet.Applet;
import java.applet.AudioClip;

public class PlaySound
{
  public PlaySound(String fnm)
  { try {
      AudioClip clip = Applet.newAudioClip(
                             getClass().getResource(fnm) );
      clip.play();  // play the sound once
    }
    catch (Exception e) {
      System.out.println("Problem with " + fnm);
    }
  }

  public static void main(String[] args)
  { if (args.length != 1) {
      System.out.println("Usage: java PlaySound <sound file>");
```

Example 7-3. Using newAudioClip( ) from an applet (continued)

```
    System.exit(0);
  }
  new PlaySound(args[0]);
  }
} // end of PlaySound class
```

Despite `AudioClip`'s simplicity, useful applications and applets can be written with it. One of its great strengths is the large number of file formats that it supports. Another is that multiple `AudioClips` can be played at the same time.

A drawback of this approach is the suspension caused by calls to `getAudioClip( )` and `newAudioClip( )`. Sun's Java Sound tutorial suggests threads as a solution: the tutorial's `SoundApplet` and `SoundApplication` examples fire off a separate thread to load the audio, allowing the main program to continue. Another answer is to download the sound resources with the code, wrapped together in a JAR file, making the subsequent loading a local, fast operation.

A stubborn problem with `AudioClip` is the lack of information about when a piece of audio finishes. This knowledge can be useful in games since linking events to the end of an audio commentary or music clip is common. A hacky workaround is to call `sleep( )` for a period based on the audio file's byte size (which can be obtained via a `File` object).

A third issue is the lack of low-level access to the sound data (or the audio device it is playing on) to permit runtime effects like volume changing, panning between speakers, and echoing. Related to this is the inability to generate new sounds during execution (i.e., sound and music synthesis) though many early Java texts proudly included variants of the class shown in Example 7-4.

Example 7-4. Using the beep( ) method

```
public class Bells
{
  public static void main(String[] args)
  {
    // \u0007 is the ASCII bell
    System.out.println("BELL 1 \u0007");

    try {
      Thread.sleep(1000);    // separate the bells
    }
    catch(InterruptedException e) {}

    // ring the bell again, using the Toolkit this time
    java.awt.Toolkit.getDefaultToolkit().beep();
    System.out.println("BELL 2");
    System.out.flush();
  } // end of main()

} // end of Bells class
```

The ASCII character bell works on many platforms, but only Java applications can employ the Toolkit beep( ) method.

What Bells illustrates is the poor low-level access offered by Java. The introduction of the Java Sound API in J2SE 1.3 fixed this weakness.

The examples from this section (McDonald.java, PlaySound.java, and Bells.java) can be found in the *SoundExamps/McDonalds/* directory.

The Sound Player

SoundPlayer.java (located in *SoundExamps/SoundPlayer/*) shows off the capabilities of the AudioClip class (see Figure 7-1) in a longer example.

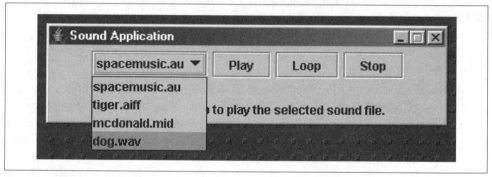

Figure 7-1. The SoundPlayer application

A selection of sound files in different formats (all located in the *Sounds/* subdirectory below *SoundPlayer/*) are offered up. They can be played once, looped, or stopped. It's possible to have multiple clips playing and looping simultaneously, and the stop button terminates all the currently playing clips. This example is somewhat similar to the Java Sound tutorial example, SoundApplication.

Figure 7-2 gives the class diagram for SoundPlayer, showing all the public and private methods and variables in the class.

Two important data structures are in play here:

```
private HashMap soundsMap;
private ArrayList playingClips;
```

soundsMap holds the loaded AudioClips, indexed by their filenames. playingClips maintains a list of currently playing AudioClips (or, to be more precise, what I think is playing).

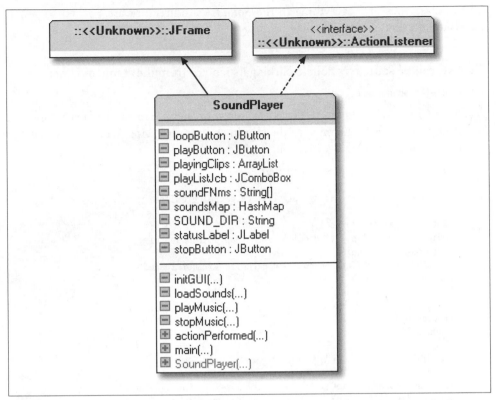

Figure 7-2. Class diagram for SoundPlayer

`loadSounds()` loads the `AudioClips` and stores them in `soundsMap` for later use:

```
private void loadSounds()
{
  soundsMap = new HashMap();
  for (int i=0; i < soundFNms.length; i++) {
    AudioClip clip = Applet.newAudioClip(
                getClass().getResource(SOUND_DIR + soundFNms[i]) );
    if (clip == null)
      System.out.println("Problem loading "+SOUND_DIR+soundFNms[i]);
    else
      soundsMap.put(soundFNms[i], clip);
  }
}
```

`newAudioClip()` is employed since `SoundPlayer` is an application, and the URL is specified using the assumption that the files are locally stored in the `SOUND_DIR` subdirectory (*Sounds/*). The final version of `SoundPlayer` is a JAR file, created in this way:

```
jar cvmf mainClass.txt SoundPlayer.jar SoundPlayer.class Sounds
```

All the class files and everything in the *Sounds/* subdirectory are packed together. *mainClass.txt* contains a single line:

```
Main-Class: SoundPlayer
```

The JAR can be started by double-clicking its icon or from the command line:

```
java -jar SoundPlayer.jar
```

playMusic() in SoundPlayer retrieves the relevant AudioClip, and plays it once or repeatedly. It stores a reference to the clip in the playingClips ArrayList to register that the clip is playing:

```
private void playMusic(boolean toLoop)
{
  String chosenFile = (String) playListJcb.getSelectedItem();

  // try to get the AudioClip.
  AudioClip audioClip = (AudioClip) soundsMap.get(chosenFile);
  if (audioClip == null) {
    statusLabel.setText("Sound " + chosenFile + " not loaded");
    return;
  }

  if (toLoop)
    audioClip.loop();
  else
    audioClip.play();       // play it once

  playingClips.add(audioClip);    // store a ref to the playing clip
  String times = (toLoop) ? " repeatedly" : " once";
  statusLabel.setText("Playing sound " + chosenFile + times);
}  // end of playMusic()
```

playMusic() is called from actionPerformed() when the user presses the Play or Loop button and is passed a toLoop argument to distinguish between the two.

stopMusic() stops all the playing music by calling AudioClip.stop() on all the references in playingClips. An issue is that some of the clips may have finished but there's no way to detect them. This isn't really a problem since calling stop() on a stopped AudioClip has no effect:

```
private void stopMusic()
{
  if (playingClips.isEmpty())
    statusLabel.setText("Nothing to stop");
  else {
    AudioClip audioClip;
    for(int i=0; i < playingClips.size(); i++) {
      audioClip = (AudioClip) playingClips.get(i);
      audioClip.stop();    // may already have stopped, but calling
                           // stop() again does no harm
    }
```

```
        playingClips.clear();
        statusLabel.setText("Stopped all music");
    }
}
```

The Java Sound API

So far, I've considered the Applet play() method and the more useful AudioClip class. AudioClip is probably sufficient for the straightforward playing and looping of audio, as illustrated by the SoundPlayer application of the last section.

The Java Sound API has more extensive playback capabilities than AudioClip because it offers low-level access to, and manipulation of, audio data and the underlying machine's audio hardware and software. The API also supports audio capture and synthesis, features not found in AudioClip.

The Sound API's power makes it complex to use, so the rest of this chapter will be given over to introducing its basic playback features for sampled audio (e.g., WAV files) and MIDI sequences. Chapter 8 will develop Sound API-based classes for loading and playing audio, which I'll use frequently in later chapters to play music and sound clips in my games. Chapter 9 is about applying audio effects to existing sampled audio and sequences using the Sound API. Chapter 10 describes various ways of synthesizing samples and sequences with the API.

The Java Sound API has two main parts: a javax.sound.sampled package for manipulating sampled audio and javax.sound.midi for MIDI sequences. The rest of this chapter will first discuss sampled audio, followed by MIDI.

The API has two service provider packages, javax.sound.sampled.spi and javax.sound.midi.spi, to encourage extensibility. They can be utilized to add new audio devices (e.g., new mixers, synthesizers) and formats (e.g., MP3). I won't be looking at them—this book is long enough without going off on tangents.

Sampled Audio

Sampled audio is a series of digital samples extracted from analog signals, as illustrated by Figure 7-3. Each sample represents the amplitude (loudness) of the signal at a given moment.

The quality of the digital result depends on two factors: time resolution (the *sampling rate*), measured in Hertz (Hz), and amplitude resolution (*quantization*), the number of bits representing each sample. For example, a CD track is typically sampled at 44.1 kHz (44,100 samples per second), and each sample uses 16 bits to encode a possible 65,536 amplitudes.

Descriptions of sampled audio often talk about frames (e.g., frame size, frame rate). For most audio formats, a *frame* is the number of bytes required to represent a single

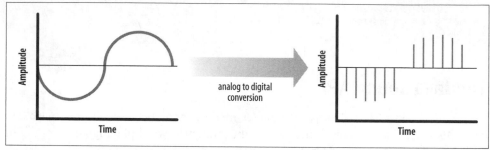

Figure 7-3. From analog to digital audio

sample. For example, a sample in 8-bit mono pulse code modulation (PCM) format requires one frame (one byte) per sample. 16-bit mono PCM samples require two frames, and 16-bit stereo PCM needs four frames: 2 bytes each for the left and right 16-bit samples in the stereo.

As the sample rate and quantization increase, so do the memory requirements. For instance, a three-second stereo CD track, using 16-bit PCM, requires $44,100 \times 4 \times 3$ bytes of space, or 517 KB. The "4" in the calculation reflects the need for four frames to store each stereo 16-bit sample.

The higher the sample rate and quantization, the better the sound quality when the digital stream is converted back to an analog signal suitable for speakers or headphones. Figure 7-4 shows that the smoothness and detail of the signal depends on the number of samples and their amplitude accuracy.

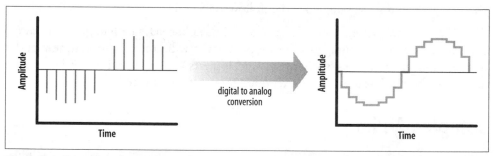

Figure 7-4. From digital to analog audio

Figure 7-5 shows the conversion of a digital stream for the same sine wave but encoded at a higher sample rate. The resulting audio is closer to the original than the one shown in Figure 7-4.

Sampled audio can be encoded with the Clip or SourceDataLine classes.

A Clip object holds sampled audio small enough to be loaded completely into memory during execution; therefore, a Clip is similar to AudioClip.

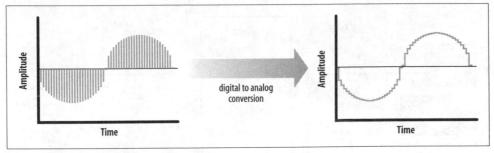

Figure 7-5. Conversion of a digital stream with a higher sample rate

 "Small enough" usually means less than 2 MB.

A SourceDataLine is a buffered stream that permits chunks of the audio to be delivered to the mixer in stages over time without requiring the entire thing to be in memory at once. The buffered streaming in SourceDataLine shouldn't be confused with the video and audio streaming offered by JMF. The difference is that JMF supports time-based protocols, such as RTP, which permits the audio software and hardware to manage the network latency and bandwidth issues when data chunks are transferred to it over a network. I'll say a little more about JMF at the end of this chapter.

Streaming in Java Sound does not have timing capabilities, making it difficult to maintain a constant flow of data through a SourceDataLine if the data are coming from the network; clicks and hisses can be heard as the system plays the sound. However, if SourceDataLine obtains its data from a local file, such problems are unlikely to occur.

The Mixer

Clip and SourceDataLine are subclasses of the Line class; *lines* are the piping that allows digital audio to be moved around the audio system, for instance, from a microphone to the mixer and from the mixer to the speakers (see Figure 7-6).

Figure 7-6 is a stylized view of a mixer, intended to help explain the various classes and coding techniques for sampled audio.

Inputs to a mixer may include data read as a Clip object or streamed in from a device or the network, or generated by a program. Output can include audio written to a file, sent to a device, transmitted over the network, or sent as streamed output to a program.

The mixer, represented by the Mixer class, may be a hardware audio device (e.g., the sound card) or software interfaced to the sound card. A mixer can accept audio

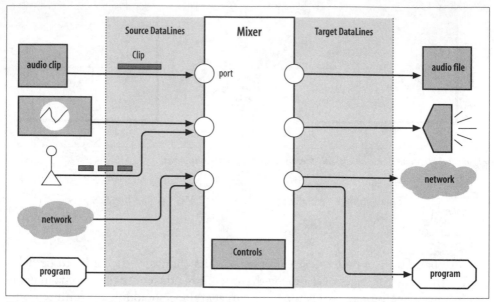

Figure 7-6. Audio I/O to/from the mixer

streams coming from several source lines and pass them onto target lines, perhaps mixing the audio streams together in the process and applying audio effects like volume adjustment or panning.

The capabilities of Java Sound's default mixer have changed in the transition from J2SE 1.4.2 to J2SE 5.0. In J2SE 1.4.2 or earlier, the default mixer was the Java Sound Audio Engine, which had playback capabilities but could not capture sound; that was handled by another mixer. In J2SE 5.0, the Direct Audio Device is the default and supports playback and recording.

Clip, SourceDataLine, and TargetDataLine are part of the Line class hierarchy shown in Figure 7-7.

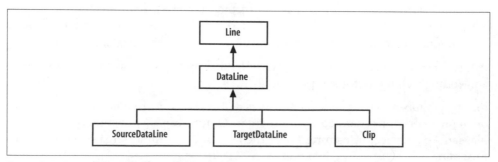

Figure 7-7. Part of the Line hierarchy

DataLine adds media features to Line, including the ability to determine the current read/write position, to start/stop/pause/resume the sound, and to retrieve status details.

The SourceDataLine adds methods for buffering data for playback by the mixer. The name of the class is a little confusing: "source" refers to a source of data for the mixer. From the programmer's point of view, data is written out to a SourceDataLine to send it a mixer.

The TargetDataLine is a streaming line in the same way as SourceDataLine. "Target" refers to the destination of the data sent out by the mixer. For instance, an application might use a TargetDataLine to receive captured data gathered by the mixer from a microphone or CD drive. A TargetDataLine is a source of audio for the application.

A Clip is preloaded rather than streamed, so its duration is known before playback. This permits it to offer methods for adjusting the starting position and looping.

A LineListener can be attached to any line to monitor LineEvents, which are issued when the audio is opened, closed, started, or stopped. The "stopped" event can be utilized by application code to react to a sound's termination.

Figure 7-6 shows that lines are linked to the mixer through ports. A Port object typically allows access to sound card features dealing with I/O. For example, an input port may be able to access the analog-to-digital converter. An output port may permit access to the digital-to-analog converter used by the speakers or headphones. A change to a port will affect all the lines connected to it. The Port class was not implemented prior to J2SE 5.0.

The box marked "Controls" inside the mixer in Figure 7-6 allows audio effects to be applied to incoming clips or SourceDataLines. The effects may include volume control, panning between speakers, muting, and sample rate control, though the exact selection depends on the mixer. Chapter 9 has an example where mixer controls are applied to a clip.

Another form of audio manipulation is to modify the sample data before it is passed through a SourceDataLine to the mixer. For example, volume control is a matter of amplitude adjustment, coded by bit manipulation. Chapter 9 has a volume control example.

Playing a Clip

PlayClip.java (in *SoundExamps/SoundPlayer/*) loads an audio file specified on the command line as a clip and plays it once:

The main( ) method creates a PlayClip object and exits afterward.

```
public static void main(String[] args)
{ if (args.length != 1) {
    System.out.println("Usage: java PlayClip <clip file>");
```

```
      System.exit(0);
    }
    new PlayClip(args[0]);
    System.exit(0);      // required in J2SE 1.4.2. or earlier
  }
```

The call to exit( ) must be present in J2SE 1.4.2 or earlier (it's unnecessary if you're using J2SE 5.0). The problem is that the sound engine doesn't terminate all of its threads when it finishes, which prevents the JVM from terminating without an exit( ) call.

The PlayClip class implements the LineListener interface to detect when the clip has finished. The LineListener update( ) method is described below.

```
public class PlayClip implements LineListener
{ ... }   // PlayClip must implement update()
```

The PlayClip( ) constructor loads and plays the clip.

```
public PlayClip(String fnm)
{
  df = new DecimalFormat("0.#");  // 1 dp
  loadClip(SOUND_DIR + fnm);
  play();

  // wait for the sound to finish playing; guess at 10 mins!
  System.out.println("Waiting");
  try {
    Thread.sleep(600000);    // 10 mins in ms
  }
  catch(InterruptedException e)
  { System.out.println("Sleep Interrupted"); }
}
```

The PlayClip constructor has a problem: it shouldn't return until the sound has finished playing. However, play( ) starts the sound playing and returns immediately, so the code must wait in some way. I make it sleep for 10 minutes. This doesn't mean PlayClip hangs around for 10 minutes after it has finished playing a one-second clip. The LineListener update( ) method will allow PlayClip to exit as soon as the clip has ended.

loadClip( ) is the heart of PlayClip and illustrates the low-level nature of Java Sound. The length of its code is due to AudioSystem's lack of direct support for ULAW and ALAW formatted data. ULAW and ALAW are compression-based codings that affect the meaning of the bits in a sample. By default, only linear encodings (such as PCM) are understood.

The playing of a ULAW or ALAW file is dealt with by converting its data into PCM format as it's read into the Clip object. If I ignore this conversion code and other error-handling, then loadClip( ) carries out six tasks:

```
// 1. Access the audio file as a stream
AudioInputStream stream = AudioSystem.getAudioInputStream(
                              getClass().getResource(fnm) );
```

```
// 2. Get the audio format for the data in the stream
AudioFormat format = stream.getFormat();

// 3. Gather information for line creation
DataLine.Info info = new DataLine.Info(Clip.class, format);

// 4. Create an empty clip using that line information
Clip clip = (Clip) AudioSystem.getLine(info);

// 5. Start monitoring the clip's line events
clip.addLineListener(this);

// 6. Open the audio stream as a clip; now it's ready to play
clip.open(stream);
stream.close();  // I've done with the input stream
```

The monitoring of the clip's line events, which include when it is opened, started, stopped, and closed, is usually necessary to react to the end of a clip.

In task 1, AudioInputStream can take its input from a file, input stream, or URL, so it is a versatile way of obtaining audio input. The complete method is shown here:

```
private void loadClip(String fnm)
{
  try {
    AudioInputStream stream = AudioSystem.getAudioInputStream(
                      getClass().getResource(fnm) );

    AudioFormat format = stream.getFormat();

    // convert ULAW/ALAW formats to PCM format
    if ( (format.getEncoding() == AudioFormat.Encoding.ULAW) ||
         (format.getEncoding() == AudioFormat.Encoding.ALAW) ) {
      AudioFormat newFormat =
        new AudioFormat(AudioFormat.Encoding.PCM_SIGNED,
                    format.getSampleRate(),
                    format.getSampleSizeInBits()*2,
                    format.getChannels(),
                    format.getFrameSize()*2,
                    format.getFrameRate(), true);  // big endian
      // update stream and format details
      stream = AudioSystem.getAudioInputStream(newFormat, stream);
      System.out.println("Converted Audio format: " + newFormat);
      format = newFormat;
    }

    DataLine.Info info = new DataLine.Info(Clip.class, format);

    // make sure the sound system supports this data line
    if (!AudioSystem.isLineSupported(info)) {
      System.out.println("Unsupported Clip File: " + fnm);
      System.exit(0);
    }
```

```
    clip = (Clip) AudioSystem.getLine(info);
    clip.addLineListener(this);
    clip.open(stream);
    stream.close(); // I've done with the input stream

    // duration (in secs) of the clip
    double duration = clip.getMicrosecondLength( )/1000000.0;
    System.out.println("Duration: " + df.format(duration)+" secs");
  } // end of try block

  catch (UnsupportedAudioFileException audioException) {
    System.out.println("Unsupported audio file: " + fnm);
    System.exit(0);
  }
  catch (LineUnavailableException noLineException) {
    System.out.println("No audio line available for : " + fnm);
    System.exit(0);
  }
  catch (IOException ioException) {
    System.out.println("Could not read: " + fnm);
    System.exit(0);
  }
  catch (Exception e) {
    System.out.println("Problem with " + fnm);
    System.exit(0);
  }
} // end of loadClip( )
```

PCM creation uses the AudioFormat constructor:

```
public AudioFormat(AudioFormat.Encoding encoding,
        float sampleRate, int sampleSizeInBits,
        int channels, int frameSize,
        float frameRate, boolean bigEndian);
```

loadClip( ) uses the constructor:

```
AudioFormat newFormat =
  new AudioFormat(AudioFormat.Encoding.PCM_SIGNED,
        format.getSampleRate( ), format.getSampleSizeInBits( )*2,
        format.getChannels( ), format.getFrameSize( )*2,
        format.getFrameRate( ), true);  // big endian
```

ALAW and ULAW use an 8-bit byte to represent each sample, but after this has been decompressed the data requires 14 bits. Consequently, the PCM encoding must use 16 bits (2 bytes) per sample. This explains why the sampleSizeInBits and frameSize arguments are double the values obtained from the file's original audio format details.

Once the sample size goes beyond a single byte, the ordering of the multiple bytes must be considered. *Big endian* specifies a high-to-low byte ordering, while *little endian* is low-to-high. This is relevant if later I want to extract the sample's amplitude as a short or integer since the multiple bytes must be combined together correctly. The channels arguments refer to the use of mono (one channel) or stereo (two channels).

The audio encoding is PCM_SIGNED, which allows a range of amplitudes that include negatives. For 16-bit data, the range will be -2^{15} to $2^{15} - 1$ (–32768 to 32767). The alternative is PCM_UNSIGNED, which only offers positive values, 0 to 2^{16} (65536).

PlayClip's play( ) method is trivial:

```
private void play( )
{ if (clip != null)
    clip.start( );   // start playing
}
```

This starts the clip playing without waiting. PlayClip sleeps, for as much as 10 minutes, while the clip plays. However, most clips will finish after a few seconds. Due to the LineListener interface, this will trigger a call to update( ):

```
public void update(LineEvent lineEvent)
// called when the clip's line detects open,close,start,stop events
{
  // has the clip reached its end?
  if (lineEvent.getType( ) == LineEvent.Type.STOP) {
    System.out.println("Exiting...");
    clip.stop( );
    lineEvent.getLine( ).close( );
    System.exit(0);
  }
}
```

 The calls to stop( ) and close( ) aren't unnecessary but they ensure that the audio system resources are in the correct state before termination.

Short Sound Bug in J2SE 5.0

PlayClip.java works perfectly in J2SE 1.4.2 but fails when given short sound files in J2SE 5.0. For example, *dog.wav* is 0.5 seconds long, and PlayClip is silent for 0.5 seconds when asked to play it:

```
java PlayClip dog.wav
```

However, if the requested sound clip is longer than 1 second, PlayClip will work as expected.

 I have registered this bug with Sun at *http://bugs.sun.com/bugdatabase/ view_bug.do?bug_id=5085008*. I encourage you to vote for its fixing.

There's a similar bug reported at *http://bugs.sun.com/bugdatabase/ view_bug.do?bug_id=5070730*. Vote for that one, too.

A rather hacky solution is to force the sound to loop several times until its total playing time exceeds one second. An outline of that solution can be found on the previous bug report web page and is implemented in *PlayClipBF.java* in *SoundExamps/*

SoundPlayer/ (BF for "bug fix"), which is almost identical to *PlayClip.java*, except in two places.

A loop counter is calculated, based on the clip's duration:

```
double duration = clip.getMicrosecondLength( )/1000000.0;
loopCount = (int) (1.0 / duration);
```

This code is added to loadClip( ), and loopCount is defined as a global integer. In play( ), the clip is not started with a call to start( ) but made to loop loopCount times:

```
// clip.start( );    // start looping not playing (in play( ))
clip.loop(loopCount);
```

In my future code, I'll assume that any sound files are longer than one second in length, so it won't fix things through looping. However, I will add a duration test and a warning message. For example, loadClip( ) in PlayClip is modified to call checkDuration( ):

```
void checkDuration( )
{
  double duration = clip.getMicrosecondLength( )/1000000.0;
  if (duration <= 1.0) {
 System.out.println("WARNING. Duration <= 1 sec : " + df.format(duration) + " secs");
 System.out.println("       The clip may not play in J2SE 1.5 -- make it longer");
  }
  else
     System.out.println("Duration: " + df.format(duration) + " secs");
}
```

Playing a Buffered Sample

As Figure 7-5 suggests, a program can pass audio data to the mixer by sending discrete packets (stored in byte arrays) along the SourceDataLine. The main reason for using this approach is to handle large audio files that cannot be loaded into a Clip.

BufferedPlayer.java does the same task as *PlayClip.java*, which is to play an audio file supplied on the command line. The differences are only apparent inside the code. One cosmetic change is that the program is written as a series of static methods called from main( ). This is just a matter of taste; the code could be "objectified" to look similar to *PlayClip.java*; it's shown using the static approach here:

```
// globals
private static AudioInputStream stream;
private static AudioFormat format = null;
private static SourceDataLine line = null;


public static void main(String[] args)
{ if (args.length != 1) {
    System.out.println("Usage: java BufferedPlayer <clip file>");
    System.exit(0);
  }
```

```
  createInput("Sounds/" + args[0]);
  createOutput();

  int numBytes = (int)(stream.getFrameLength() *
                            format.getFrameSize());
      // use getFrameLength() from the stream, since the format
      // version may return -1 (WAV file formats always return -1)
  System.out.println("Size in bytes: " + numBytes);

  checkDuration();
  play();
  System.exit(0);     // necessary in J2SE 1.4.2 and earlier
}
```

 BufferedPlayer.java can be found in the *SoundExamps/SoundPlayer/* directory.

createInput( ) is similar to PlayClip's loadClip( ) method but a little simpler. If I ignore the PCM conversion code for ULAW and ALAW formatted data, and other error handling, it does two tasks:

```
// access the audio file as a stream
stream = AudioSystem.getAudioInputStream( new File(fnm) );

// get the audio format for the data in the stream
format = stream.getFormat();
```

createOutput( ) creates the SourceDataLine going to the mixer:

```
private static void createOutput()
{
  try {
    // gather information for line creation
    DataLine.Info info =
          new DataLine.Info(SourceDataLine.class, format);
    if (!AudioSystem.isLineSupported(info)) {
      System.out.println("Line does not support: " + format);
      System.exit(0);
    }
    // get a line of the required format
    line = (SourceDataLine) AudioSystem.getLine(info);
    line.open(format);
  }
  catch (Exception e)
  {  System.out.println( e.getMessage());
     System.exit(0);
  }
}  // end of createOutput()
```

createOutput( ) collects line information and then creates a SourceDataLine based on that information.

checkDuration( ) calculates a duration using the audio stream's attributes and prints a warning if the sound file is one second long or less. This warning is the same as the one issued by checkDuration( ) in PlayClip. However, PlayClip's code obtains the duration using:

```
double duration = clip.getMicrosecondLength( )/1000000.0;
```

getMicrosecondLength( ) isn't available to an AudioInputStream object, so the time in BufferedPlayer is calculated with:

```
double duration = ((stream.getFrameLength( )*1000)/
                        stream.getFormat( ).getFrameRate( ))/1000.0;
```

play( ) repeatedly reads a chunk of bytes from the AudioInputStream and writes them to the SourceDataLine until the stream is empty. As a result, BufferedPlayer only requires memory large enough for the byte array buffer, not the entire audio file:

```
private static void play( )
{
  int numRead = 0;
  byte[] buffer = new byte[line.getBufferSize( )];

  line.start( );
  // read and play chunks of the audio
  try {
    int offset;
    while ((numRead = stream.read(buffer,0,buffer.length)) >= 0) {
      offset = 0;
      while (offset < numRead)
        offset += line.write(buffer, offset, numRead-offset);
    }
  }
  catch (IOException e)
  {  System.out.println( e.getMessage( )); }

  // wait until all data is played, then close the line
  line.drain( );
  line.stop( );
  line.close( );
}
```

The size of the buffer is determined by asking the SourceDataLine via getBufferSize( ). Alternatively, I could calculate a size myself.

After the loop finishes, drain( ) causes the program to wait until all the data in the line has been passed to the mixer. Then it's safe for the line to be stopped and closed and for the program to terminate.

MIDI

The previous section looked at the basic support in the Java Sound API for playing sampled audio. Now, I'll consider the other major part of the API, which is its support for playing MIDI sequences.

A key benefit of the MIDI is that it represents musical data in an efficient way, leading to drastic reductions in file sizes compared to sampled audio. For instance, files containing high-quality stereo sampled audio require about 10 MB per minute of sound, while a typical MIDI sequence may need less than 10 KB.

The secret to this phenomenal size reduction is that a MIDI sequence stores "instructions" for playing the music rather than the music itself. A simple analogy is that a sequence is the written score for a piece of music rather than a recording of it.

The drawback is that the sequence must be converted to audio output at runtime. This is achieved using a sequencer and synthesizer. Their configuration is shown in greatly simplified form in Figure 7-8.

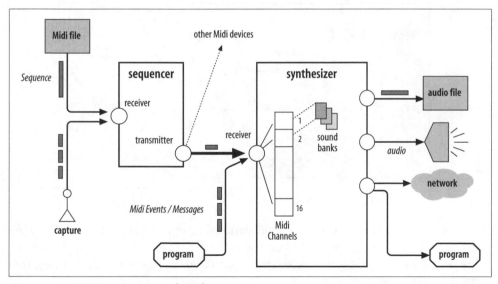

Figure 7-8. A MIDI sequencer and synthesizer

A MIDI sequencer allows MIDI data sequences to be captured, stored, edited, combined, and performed, while the MIDI data's transformation into audio is being carried out by the synthesizer.

Continuing my analogy, the sequencer is the orchestral conductor who receives the score to play, perhaps making changes to it in the process. The synthesizer is the orchestra, made up of musicians playing different parts of the score. The musicians correspond to the MidiChannel objects in the synthesizer. They are allocated instruments from the sound banks, and play concurrently. Usually, a complete sequence (a complete score) is passed to the sequencer, but it's possible to send it a stream of MIDI events.

In J2SE 1.4.2 and earlier, the sequencer and synthesizer were represented by a single Sequencer object. This has changed in J2SE 5.0, and it's now necessary to obtain distinct Sequencer and Synthesizer objects and link them together using Receiver and Transmitter objects.

A MIDI Sequence

A Sequence object represents a multitrack data structure, each track containing time-ordered MIDIEvent objects. These events are time-ordered, based on an internal "tick" value (a timestamp). Each event contains musical data in a MidiMessage object. The sequence structure is illustrated in Figure 7-9.

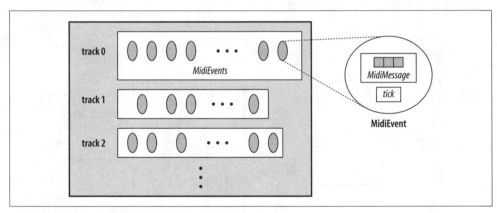

Figure 7-9. The internals of a MIDI sequence

Tracks are employed as an optional organizational layer to place "related" MIDI data together, and the synthesizer makes no use of the information. Java Sound supports Type 0 and Type 1 MIDI sequences, the main difference between them being that Type 0 files only have a single track.

MIDI messages are encoded using three subclasses of MidiMessage: ShortMessage, SysexMessage, and MetaMessage. SysexMessage deals with system-exclusive messages, such as patch parameters or sample data sent between MIDI devices, which are usually specific to the MIDI device. MetaMessages are used to transmit meta-information about the sequence, such as tempo settings, and instrument information.

ShortMessage is the most important class since it includes the NOTE_ON and NOTE_OFF messages for starting and terminating note playing on a given MidiChannel. Typically, one MidiEvent contains a NOTE_ON for beginning the playing, and a later

MidiEvent holds a NOTE_OFF for switching it off. The duration of the note corresponds to the time difference between the tick values in the two events.

As shown in Figure 7-8, a program can directly communicate with the synthesizer, sending it a stream of MidiEvents or MidiMessages. The difference between the approaches is the timing mechanism; a stream of MidiEvents contains tick values, which the synthesizer can use to space out note playing and other activities. A stream of MidiMessages contains no timing data, so it's up to the program to send the messages at the required time intervals.

 Examples of these techniques are given in the "MIDI Synthesis" section in Chapter 10.

The internal format of a MidiMessage is simple: there's an 8-bit status byte, which identifies the message type followed by two data bytes. Depending on the message, one or both of these bytes may be utilized. The byte size means that values usually range between 0 and 127.

One source of confusion for a programmer familiar with MIDI is that the MidiMessage class and its subclasses do not correspond to the names used in the MIDI specification (online at *http://www.midi.org*). ShortMessage includes the MIDI channel voice, channel mode, system common, and system real-time messages—in other words, everything except system exclusive and meta-events. In the rest of this chapter, I'll use the Java Sound MIDI class names as opposed to those names used in the specification.

Playing a MIDI Sequence

PlayMidi.java (stored in *SoundExamps/SoundPlayer/*) loads a MIDI sequence and plays it once:

```
public static void main(String[] args)
{ if (args.length != 1) {
    System.out.println("Usage: java PlayMidi <midi file>");
    System.exit(0);
  }
  new PlayMidi(args[0]);
  System.exit(0);     // required in J2SE 1.4.2. or earlier
}
```

 As with PlayClip, the call to exit( ) must be present in J2SE 1.4.2 or earlier, but is unnecessary in J2SE 5.0.

The PlayMidi class implements the MetaEventListener interface to detect when the sequence has reached the end of its tracks:

```
public class PlayMidi implements MetaEventListener
{
  // midi meta-event constant used to signal the end of a track
  private static final int END_OF_TRACK = 47;

  private final static String SOUND_DIR = "Sounds/";

  private Sequencer sequencer;   // globals
  private Synthesizer synthesizer;
  private Sequence seq = null;
  private String filename;

  private DecimalFormat df;
        :  // the rest of the class
}
```

The PlayMidi constructor initializes the sequencer and synthesizer, loads the sequence, and starts it playing:

```
public PlayMidi(String fnm)
{
  df = new DecimalFormat("0.#");  // 1 dp

  filename = SOUND_DIR + fnm;
  initSequencer();
  loadMidi(filename);
  play();

  // wait for the sound to finish playing; guess at 10 mins!
  System.out.println("Waiting");
  try {
    Thread.sleep(600000);   // 10 mins in ms
  }
  catch(InterruptedException e)
  { System.out.println("Sleep Interrupted"); }
}
```

As with PlayClip, PlayMidi waits to give the sequence time to play. When the sequence finishes, the call to meta( ) allows PlayMidi to exit from its slumbers ahead of time.

initSequence( ) obtains a sequencer and synthesizer from the MIDI system and links them together. It also sets up the meta-event listener:

```
private void initSequencer()
{
  try {
    sequencer = MidiSystem.getSequencer();

    if (sequencer == null) {
      System.out.println("Cannot get a sequencer");
```

```
        System.exit(0);
      }

      sequencer.open();
      sequencer.addMetaEventListener(this);

      // maybe the sequencer is not the same as the synthesizer
      // so link sequencer --> synth (this is required in J2SE 5.0)
      if (!(sequencer instanceof Synthesizer)) {
        System.out.println("Linking the sequencer to a synthesizer");
        synthesizer = MidiSystem.getSynthesizer();
        synthesizer.open();
        Receiver synthReceiver = synthesizer.getReceiver();
        Transmitter seqTransmitter = sequencer.getTransmitter();
        seqTransmitter.setReceiver(synthReceiver);
      }
      else
        synthesizer = (Synthesizer) sequencer;
          // I don't use the synthesizer in this simple code,
          // so storing it as a global isn't really necessary
    }
    catch (MidiUnavailableException e){
      System.out.println("No sequencer available");
      System.exit(0);
    }
  } // end of initSequencer()
```

loadMidi() loads the sequence by calling MidiSystem.getSequence() inside a large
try-catch block to catch the many possible kinds of errors that can occur:

```
  private void loadMidi(String fnm)
  {
    try {
      seq = MidiSystem.getSequence( getClass().getResource(fnm) );
      double duration = ((double) seq.getMicrosecondLength()) / 1000000;
      System.out.println("Duration: " + df.format(duration)+" secs");
    }
     // several catch blocks go here; see the code for details
  }
```

play() loads the sequence into the sequencer and starts it playing:

```
  private void play()
  { if ((sequencer != null) && (seq != null)) {
      try {
        sequencer.setSequence(seq);  // load MIDI into sequencer
        sequencer.start();    // start playing it
      }
      catch (InvalidMidiDataException e) {
        System.out.println("Corrupted/invalid midi file: " + filename);
        System.exit(0);
      }
    }
  }
```

start( ) will return immediately, and PlayMidi will go to sleep back in the constructor.

meta( ) is called frequently as the sequence begins playing, but I'm only interested in responding to the end-of-track event:

```
public void meta(MetaMessage event)
{ if (event.getType( ) == END_OF_TRACK) {
    System.out.println("Exiting...");
    close( );
    System.exit(0);
  }
}
```

Java Sound API Compared with JMF and JOAL

The Java Media Framework, or JMF, (*http://java.sun.com/products/java-media/jmf/*) supports streaming multimedia, such as video and audio, with an emphasis on streaming over a network where bandwidth and latency are issues. This means support for time-based protocols, such as RTP, and services such as compression and media streams synchronization.

The Performance Pack versions of JMF (for Windows, Solaris, and Linux) use the Java Sound API to play and capture sound data, so Sound API techniques can be utilized. However, the Cross Platform version of JMF uses sun.audio classes to play sound rather than the API (and audio capture isn't available).

JMF supports more sound formats than the Sound API, including MPEG-1 (see *http://java.sun.com/products/java-media/jmf/2.1.1/formats.html* for an extensive list). Even better, it's possible to plug additional codecs into Java Sound via the service provider interface. For example, MP3 (MPEG 1/2/2.5 Layer 1/2/3) and Ogg Vorbis formatted files can be read through an AudioInputStream by utilizing plug-ins from JavaZoom (*http://www.javazoom.net/projects.html*).

JMF can be used with JDK 1.1 or later, so is suitable for applets running inside JVMs on older browsers; the Java Sound API requires J2RE 1.3 or higher.

JOAL (*https://joal.dev.java.net/*) is a set of Java bindings for OpenAL, a 3D sound API for OpenGL. JOAL's area of strength is 3D positional audio and offers little support for audio mixing or synthesis; consequently, it doesn't "compete" with Java Sound. A combination of JOAL and Java Sound may replace the buggy audio elements of Java 3D in its next major release (the latter half of 2005).

Java Sound API Resources

The lengthy Java Sound API programmer's guide comes with the J2SE documentation, and can be found at *http://java.sun.com/j2se/1.5.0/docs/guide/sound/programmer_guide/*.

It's a little bit old now (it dates from October 2001) but still informative. The best place for examples, links, and a great FAQ is the Java Sound resources site (*http://www.jsresources.org/*).

Lots of specialized information can be extracted from the javasound-interest mailing list at *http://archives.java.sun.com/archives/javasound-interest.html*. The Java Games Forum on Java Sound help searchable; visit *http://www.javagaming.org/cgi-bin/JGNetForums/YaBB.cgi?board=Sound*.

Sun's Java Sound site at *http://java.sun.com/products/java-media/sound/* contains links to articles, a FAQ, a large demo, instruments soundbanks, and service provider plug-ins for nonstandard audio formats. The Java Almanac offers code fragments illustrating various techniques (*http://javaalmanac.com/egs/?*). Look under the javax.sound.sampled and javax.sound.midi package headings.

An excellent set of Java Sound examples can be found in *Java Examples in a Nutshell* by David Flanagan (O'Reilly). He includes a MIDI synthesizer based around the processing of musical notes, covering similar ground to my SeqSynth application in Chapter 10, but with additional features. All the examples can be downloaded from O'Reilly's web site at *http://www.oreilly.com/catalog/jenut3/index.html?CMP=ILC-0PY480989785*, and two excerpts from the Java Sound chapter (Chapter 17) are at *http://www.onjava.com/pub/a/onjava/excerpt/jenut3_ch17/index.html* and *http://www.onjava.com/pub/a/onjava/excerpt/jenut3_ch17/index1.html*.

Extended coverage of Java Sound appears in Chapter 22 of *Java: How to Program, Fourth Edition* by Harvey and Paul Deitel (Deitel Int.). The MIDI example combines synthesis, playback, recording, and saving. The code can be downloaded from *http://www.deitel.com/books/downloads.html*.

 Unfortunately, the Java Sound material has been cut from later editions of this book.

Sing Li has written an article using some of the new J2SE 5.0 features in Java Sound (e.g., the Direct Audio Device and the Port class implementation), called "Making Sense of Java Sound with JDK 1.5" (*http://www.vsj.co.uk/articles/display.asp?id=370*). It cumulates in a karaoke recording application. Dick Baldwin has written several Java Sound tutorials, found at *http://dickbaldwin.com/tocadv.htm*; topics include "Capturing microphone data into an audio file" and "Creating, playing, and saving synthetic sounds."

A good starting point for Java Sound software, including tools and libraries, is the Google directory: *http://directory.google.com/Top/Computers/Multimedia/Music_and_Audio/Software/Java/?il=1*.

Audio Resources

Two Windows-based audio editing tools that I've used are WavePad (*http://nch.com.au/ wavepad/*) and Anvil Studio (*http://www.anvilstudio.com/*).

The source for all things MIDI is *http://www.midi.com*, with articles, the official spec-ification, a search engine, and links to other sites. Harmony Central has a good MIDI resource section, including a useful tutorial:, *http://www.harmony-central.com/MIDI/*.

FindSounds (*http://www.findSounds.com*) offers a versatile search engine for sampled audio (AIFF, AU, WAV). MusicRobot (*http://www.musicrobot.com*) has a MIDI search engine and a WAV search engine (*http://www.musicrobot.com/cgi-bin/windex.pl*). Audio clip web sites with plenty of sound effects, such as gunshots, sirens, and explo-sions, include *http://www.freeaudioclips.com*, *http://www.wavsource.com*, and *http:// www.a1freesoundeffects.com/*.

Loading and Playing Sounds

Chapter 7 introduced the Java Sound API, with small examples showing the play-back of clips, streamed audio, and MIDI sequences. This chapter is given over to a single application, LoadersTests, which demonstrates my ClipsLoader and MidisLoader classes for loading, playing, pausing, resuming, stopping, and looping clips and sequences. These loader classes will be used in later chapters for games requiring sounds or music. Figure 8-1 shows the LoadersTests GUI.

Figure 8-1. The LoadersTests application

The left side of the control panel offers a choice between four MIDI sequences (all with a farming theme). The selection can be played once or repeatedly. Once play-ing, the Pause and Stop buttons are enabled. If the Pause button is pressed, the music pauses until resumed with the Resume button (which is the Pause button renamed). Only a single sequence can be played at a time.

The right side of the control panel is a series of check boxes for turning looping on and off for the "dog," "cat," "sheep," and "chicken" clips. A clip is started by the user clicking on the relevant image in the top half of the GUI. Multiple clips can be played at once, complementing an already playing MIDI sequence. My personal favorite is a looping "Old McDonald" with all the clips playing repeatedly. The joys of silence soon become apparent.

 The LoadersTests application is located in *SoundExamps/LoadersTests/*.

Figure 8-2 shows the class diagrams for LoadersTests, with only the public methods visible.

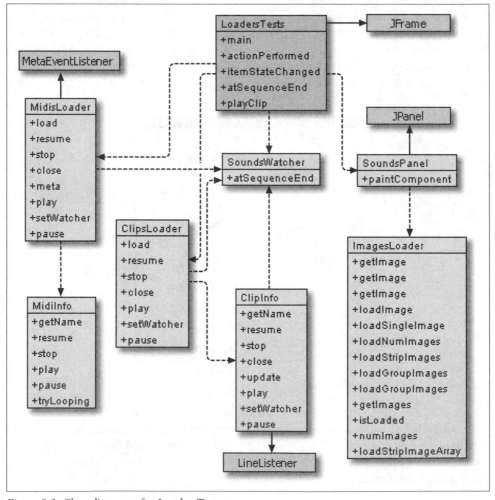

Figure 8-2. Class diagrams for LoadersTests

LoadersTests creates the GUI, initializes the loaders, and deals with user input. The images panel is coded in the SoundsPanel class.

The largest class is ImagesLoaders, previously described in Chapter 6. It's used here to load the four animal GIFs, arguably an example of coding overkill for such simple tasks. MidisLoader loads and manages multiple MIDI sequences, with each sequence stored in its own MidiInfo object. ClipsLoader does the same for clips, which are stored in ClipInfo objects.

The MIDI sequence and clips can be configured to call atSequenceEnd( ) in SoundsWatcher when they finish playing. In this example, LoadersTests implements the SoundsWatcher interface.

Loader Design and Implementation Issues

Before embarking on a detailed examination of LoadersTests, I'd like to explain some of the design and implementation decisions that underpin ClipsLoader, MidisLoader, and their support classes, ClipsInfo and MidisInfo:

Background music

I'm assuming that a MIDI sequence will be utilized for background music (an action-packed, adrenaline-fueled technobeat or, perhaps, "I'm just a little black rain cloud"). The use of a sequence makes sense because MIDI files are considerably smaller than sampled audio recordings of the same music. As I mentioned in the previous chapter, high-quality stereo sampled audio may require about 10 MB per minute of sound, but a typical MIDI sequence may need less than 10 KB. A long piece of music should be encoded as a MIDI sequence to save disk space and load time. Since a game needs one background tune at a time, I've restricted MidisLoader to play only one sequence at a time. As a consequence, only one Sequencer object needs to be created at runtime, which reduces the loader's processing overheads.

Audio effects

Sound clips will be employed for audio effects, such as explosions, laser swooshes, and anguished cries—short-lived sounds for the most part. Several sound effects may need to be played at the same time, or overlap in time, so ClipsLoader supports concurrent playing of several clips. However, a proviso is built into the Java Sound API: one instance of a Clip object can be executing at a time. This means that an explosion clip, for example, cannot be played three times at once (you might want to do this to create an overlapping effect of multiple blasts). The solution is to load the explosion three times into ClipsLoader, with different names, creating three distinct Clip objects that can be played together.

This coding strategy is used for the fireball sounds in the JumpingJack example in Chapter 12.

Though I've assumed that clips will be short pieces of audio, longer sounds can be loaded and played; ClipsLoader's pause and resume features are useful for these longer files.

Preloading

Multiple clips and sequences can be loaded at startup based on filename lists supplied in text files or loaded via method calls during execution.

Most programmers will want to preload their audio so the sounds are ready to play during the game. I haven't included any methods for unloading clips or sequences, but they would be easy to add.

Sound formats

ClipsLoader supports more sound formats than WAV. The playing of ULAW or ALAW files is dealt with by converting them into PCM format as they're read in. This is achieved using the conversion code I wrote for the PlayClip class in Chapter 7.

The WAV bug

I've chosen not to code around the WAV file bug in Java Sound in J2SE 5.0, described in the last chapter. Instead, ClipsLoader issues a warning message if a clip is one second long or less. It's up to the programmer to lengthen short sounds, perhaps with a quiet hiss, to get their length up to at least 1.1 seconds.

Callbacks

Java Sound's Clip and Sequencer classes support looping, but they're inadequate for my purposes. I want the program to be notified when a loop iteration finishes, so the program has the option of carrying out some activity, such as stopping the sound or changing a visual element in the game. Therefore, when iteration ends in ClipsLoader and MidisLoader, a callback method named atSequenceEnd( ) will automatically be invoked.

The callback reports when a clip or sequence has finished. This occurs during the end of a loop iteration and the end of the audio and is distinguished by constants passed to the atSequenceEnd( ) call.

Similar APIs

Some effort has been made to make the APIs offered by ClipsLoader and MidisLoader as similar as possible, which is why, for example, they offer the atSequenceEnd( ) callback.

Copyright

One serious issue to consider before releasing a game with numerous sounds is copyright.

In Windows, a sound's copyright can be viewed as a side effect of playing it in the Windows Media Player: the details appear in the GUI. For example, the "Bach Sheep" and "Farmer in the Dell" sequences used in LoadersTests are copyrighted by David E Lovell and Diversified Software, respectively.

In general, I advise a do-it-yourself (DIY) policy on audio elements. Many sound effects can be generated by recording noises through a PC's microphone, then distorting them in a package such as WavePad. MIDI sequences should be created from scratch, perhaps with the help of a musician.

Testing the Loaders

The constructor for LoadersTests creates the images canvas (a SoundsPanel object) and the rest of the GUI, and it initializes the loaders:

```
// the clip and midi sound information files, located in Sounds/
private final static String SNDS_FILE = "clipsInfo.txt";
private final static String MIDIS_FILE = "midisInfo.txt";

// global variables
private ClipsLoader clipsLoader;
private MidisLoader midisLoader;

public LoadersTests( )
{ super( "Sounds Tests" );
  Container c = getContentPane( );
  c.setLayout( new BorderLayout( ) );

  SoundsPanel sp = new SoundsPanel(this);    // the images canvas
  c.add( sp, BorderLayout.CENTER);
  initGUI(c);                         // the rest of the controls

  // initialise the loaders
  clipsLoader = new ClipsLoader(SNDS_FILE);
  clipsLoader.setWatcher("dog", this);     // watch the dog clip

  midisLoader = new MidisLoader(MIDIS_FILE);
  midisLoader.setWatcher(this);         // watch the midi sequence

  addWindowListener(new WindowAdapter( ) {
    public void windowClosing(WindowEvent ev) {
      midisLoader.close( );   // shut down the sequencer
      System.exit(0);
    }
  });
```

```
        pack();
        setResizable(false);  // fixed size display
        centerFrame();         // placed in the center of the screen
        setVisible(true);
    }
```

Watching the Loaders

As part of the loaders setup, setWatcher() is called in the ClipsLoader and
MidisLoader objects:

```
    clipsLoader.setWatcher("dog", this);    // watch the dog clip

    midisLoader.setWatcher(this);           // watch midi playing
```

A call to setWatcher() tells the loader that this object (LoadersTest) should be notified whenever the specified sound reaches the end of an iteration when looping or
when finished.

This notification is achieved by having the loader call atSequenceEnd() in the object,
which requires that LoadersTest implements the SoundsWatcher interface. LoadersTest
has, therefore, become a watcher.

 A watcher can be assigned to multiple clips and to the currently playing MIDI sequence. MidisLoader can play one sequence at a time, so
there's no need to specify the sequence's name when setWatcher() is
called.

atSequenceEnd() is defined by LoadersTests this way:

```
    public void atSequenceEnd(String name, int status)
    // can be called by the ClipsLoader or MidisLoader
    {
      if (status == SoundsWatcher.STOPPED)
        System.out.println(name + " stopped");
      else if (status == SoundsWatcher.REPLAYED)
        System.out.println(name + " replayed");
      else
        System.out.println(name + " status code: " + status);
    }
```

The two possible meanings of "sequence end" are represented by the SoundsWatcher
constants STOPPED and REPLAYED. The name argument of atSequenceEnd() is a string
assigned to the clip or sequence by the loader.

Termination

When LoadersTests is terminated, windowClosing() calls close() in the MidisLoader
to terminate its sequencer. This is preferable to relying on the audio system to release

---

the resources. windowClosing( ) calls exit( ) to force the JVM to terminate even though some audio threads are still running.

 This call to exit( ) isn't necessary in J2SE 5.0.

The Listener Methods

In initGUI( ), ActionListeners are attached to the buttons and ItemListeners to the check boxes.

A simplified version of actionPerformed( ) is shown below, with the many calls to Component.setEnable( ) edited out. setEnable( ) manages the user's behavior by restricting the available buttons, which is a useful GUI trick. When nothing is playing, Play and Loop are enabled. When a sequence is executing, only Pause and Stop are available. When a piece of music is paused, only the Resume button is active (this is the renamed Pause button):

```
public void actionPerformed(ActionEvent e)
/* Triggered by a "Play", "Loop", "Pause/Resume", "Stop" button
   press. The relevant method in MidisLoader is called.

   A lot of effort is spent on disabling/enabling buttons,
   which I've edited out from the code here.
*/
{ // which song is currently selected?
  String songName = shortSongNames[ namesJcb.getSelectedIndex( ) ];

  if (e.getSource( ) == playJbut)         // "Play" pressed
    midisLoader.play(songName, false); // play sequence, no looping
  else if (e.getSource( ) == loopJbut)  // "Loop" pressed
    midisLoader.play(songName, true);   // play with looping
  else if (e.getSource( ) == pauseJbut) {  // "Pause/Resume" pressed
    if (isPauseButton) {
      midisLoader.pause( );     // pause the sequence
      pauseJbut.setText("Resume");        // Pause --> Resume
    }
    else {
      midisLoader.resume( );  // resume the sequence
      pauseJbut.setText("Pause");        // Resume --> Pause
    }
    isPauseButton = !isPauseButton;
  }
  else if (e.getSource( ) == stopJbut)    // "Stop" pressed
    midisLoader.stop( );    // stop the sequence
  else
    System.out.println("Action unknown");
} // end of actionPerformed( )
```

The correspondence between button presses and calls to the MidisLoader is fairly clear. A once-only play, as well as repeated playing of a clip, are handled by play( ) with a Boolean argument to distinguish the two modes.

itemStateChanged( ) handles the four checkboxes on the right side of the GUI, which specifies if clips should be looped when played. However, a clip only starts to play when the user clicks on its image in the SoundsPanel.

The looping settings for all the clips are maintained in an array of Booleans called clipLoops[]. The relevant Boolean passes to ClipsLoader's play( ) method when the clip is played:

```
// global clip image names (used to label the checkboxes)
private final static String[] names =
                     {"dog", "cat", "sheep", "chicken"};

// global clip loop flags, stored in names[] order
private boolean[] clipLoops = {false, false, false, false};


public void itemStateChanged(ItemEvent e)
// Triggered by selecting/deselecting a clip looping checkbox
{
  // get the name of the selected checkbox
  String name = ((JCheckBox)e.getItem( )).getText( );
  boolean isSelected =  (e.getStateChange( ) == e.SELECTED) ? true : false;

  boolean switched = false;
  for (int i=0; i < names.length; i++)
    if (names[i].equals(name)) {
      clipLoops[i] = !clipLoops[i];    // update the clip loop flags
      switched = true;
      break;
    }
  if (!switched)
    System.out.println("Item unknown");
  else {
    if (!isSelected)   // user just switched off looping for name
      clipsLoader.stop(name);    // so stop playing name's clip
  }
}
```

The checkbox's name is found in the names[] array, and the corresponding index is used to choose the Boolean in clipsLoops[] to be modified.

A quirk of LoadersTests's GUI is the lack of a button to stop a repeating clip. Instead, the deselection of its looping checkbox causes it to stop. This is perhaps counter-intuitive. Design decisions such as this one should be tested on users who are not involved in the application's design or implementation.

LoadersTests has no interface for allowing a clip to be paused and resumed, although this functionality is present in ClipsLoader.

The Sounds Panel

SoundsPanel implements a JPanel that draws a white background and four images. The interesting part of the code is the setting up and use of the images' hot spots (rectangular areas the same size as each image). If a mouse press is inside one of the hot spots, then LoadersTests' playClip( ) plays the associated clip.

The SoundsPanel constructor stores a reference to LoadersTests, calls initImages( ), and sets up the MouseListener to call selectImage( ):

```
// globals
private static final int PWIDTH = 350;      // size of this panel
private static final int PHEIGHT = 350;

private LoadersTests topLevel;


public SoundsPanel(LoadersTests sts)
{ topLevel = sts;
  setPreferredSize( new Dimension(PWIDTH, PHEIGHT) );
  initImages( );
  addMouseListener( new MouseAdapter() {
    public void mousePressed( MouseEvent e)
    { selectImage( e.getX( ), e.getY( )); }
  } );
}
```

initImages( ) uses ImagesLoader to load the four GIFs, whose names are hard-wired into the code in the names[] array. The width and height of each image is used to build the array of Rectangle objects that represent the hot spots:

```
// globals
// clip image names
private final static String[] names = {"dog", "cat", "sheep", "chicken"};

// on-screen top-left coords for the images
private final static int[] xCoords = {20, 210, 20, 210};
private final static int[] yCoords = {25, 25, 170, 170};

// location of image and sound info
private final static String IMS_FILE = "imagesInfo.txt";

private int numImages;
private BufferedImage[] images;
private Rectangle[] hotSpots;
// a click inside these triggers the playing of a clip
```

```
  private void initImages()
  // load and initialise the images, and build their "hot spots"
  {
    numImages = names.length;
    hotSpots = new Rectangle[numImages];
    images = new BufferedImage[numImages];

    ImagesLoader imsLoader = new ImagesLoader(IMS_FILE);

    for (int i=0; i < numImages; i++) {
      images[i] = imsLoader.getImage(names[i]);
      hotSpots[i] = new Rectangle( xCoords[i], yCoords[i],
                    mages[i].getWidth(), images[i].getHeight());
        // use images' dimensions for the size of the rectangles
    }
  }
```

Each hot-spot rectangle is defined by a top-left coordinate, taken from the xCoords[] and yCoords[] arrays and from a width and height obtained from the loaded image. paintComponent() draws the images in the panel using the same xCoords[] and yCoords[] data as the hot-spot rectangles, thereby ensuring that they occupy the same spaces.

selectImage() tries to find the hot spot containing the mouse press coordinates. A matching hot spot's index position in hotSpots[] is used to retrieve a clip name from names[]. playClip() is passed the name and the index:

```
  private void selectImage(int x, int y)
  /* Work out which image was clicked on (perhaps none),
     and request that its corresponding clip be played. */
  {
    for (int i=0; i < numImages; i++)
      if (hotSpots[i].contains(x,y)) {     // (x,y) inside hot spot?
        topLevel.playClip(names[i], i);    // play that name's clip
        break;
      }
  }
```

Back in LoadersTests, playClip() is defined as:

```
  public void playClip(String name, int i)
  // called from SoundsPanel to play a given clip (looping or not)
  { clipsLoader.play(name, clipLoops[i]); }
```

The index parameter is employed to look inside clipLoops[] to get the playing mode. This coding approach works because I've ensured that the clipLoops[] array refers to the clips in the same order as the arrays in SoundsPanel.

The Clips Loader

ClipsLoader stores a collection of ClipInfo objects in a HashMap, keyed by their names. The name and filename for a clip are obtained from a sounds information file, which is loaded when ClipsLoader is created. The information file is assumed to be in the subdirectory *Sounds/*.

ClipsLoader allows a specified clip to be played, paused, resumed, looped, and stopped. A SoundsWatcher can be attached to a clip. All this functionality is handled in the ClipInfo object for the clip.

 It's possible for many clips to play simultaneously, since each ClipInfo object is responsible for playing its own clip.

The first ClipsLoader constructor loads a sounds information file, and the second initializes the HashMap of clips:

```
// globals
private HashMap clipsMap;
    /* The key is the clip 'name', the object (value)
        is a ClipInfo object /


public ClipsLoader(String soundsFnm)
{ this();
  loadSoundsFile(soundsFnm);
}

public ClipsLoader()
{  clipsMap = new HashMap();  }
```

loadSoundsFile( ) parses the information file, assuming each line contains a name and filename. For example, *clipsInfo.txt* used by LoadersTests is:

```
// sounds
cat cat.wav
chicken chicken.wav
dog dog.wav
sheep sheep.wav
```

 The name can be any string. The file may contain blank lines and comment lines beginning with //.

After a line's name and filename have been extracted, load( ) is called:

```
public void load(String name, String fnm)
// create a ClipInfo object for name and store it
{
  if (clipsMap.containsKey(name))
    System.out.println( "Error: " + name + "already stored");
  else {
```

```
        clipsMap.put(name, new ClipInfo(name, fnm) );
        System.out.println("-- " + name + "/" + fnm);
    }
}
```

A `ClipInfo` object is created, and added to the `HashMap`.

 load( ) is public so a user can directly add clips to the loader.

Playing Clips

play( ) illustrates the coding style used by the other public methods in `ClipsLoader`. In each method (play( ), close( ), stop( ), pause( ), resume( ), and setWatcher( )), the name of the clip is provided, along with if it should be looped. The `ClipInfo` object is retrieved using that name, errors are handled, and then the requested operation is delegated to the object:

```
public void play(String name, boolean toLoop)
// play (perhaps loop) the specified clip
{   ClipInfo ci = (ClipInfo) clipsMap.get(name);
    if (ci == null)
        System.out.println( "Error: " + name + "not stored");
    else
        ci.play(toLoop);    // delegate operation to ClipInfo obj
}
```

Audio manipulation is delegated to the `ClipInfo` object associated with the specified clip name.

Storing Clip Information

A `ClipInfo` object is responsible for loading a clip and plays, pauses, resumes, stops, and loops that clip when requested by `ClipsLoader`. Additionally, an object implementing the `SoundsWatcher` interface (a watcher) can be notified when the clip loops or stops.

Much of the manipulation carried out by `ClipInfo`, such as clip loading, is almost identical to that found in *PlayClip.java* in Chapter 7. Perhaps the largest difference is that `PlayClip` exits when it encounters a problem, and `ClipInfo` prints an error message and soldiers on.

loadClip( ) is similar to `PlayClip`'s loadClip( ), so certain parts have been commented away in the code below to simplify matters:

```
// global
private Clip clip = null;
```

```
    private void loadClip(String fnm)
    {
      try {
        // 1. access the audio file as a stream
        AudioInputStream stream = AudioSystem.getAudioInputStream(
                          getClass().getResource(fnm) );

        // 2. Get the audio format for the data in the stream
        AudioFormat format = stream.getFormat();

        // convert ULAW/ALAW formats to PCM format...
        // several lines, which update stream and format

        // 3. Gather information for line creation
        DataLine.Info info = new DataLine.Info(Clip.class, format);

        // make sure the sound system supports the data line
        if (!AudioSystem.isLineSupported(info)) {
          System.out.println("Unsupported Clip File: " + fnm);
          return;
        }

        // 4. create an empty clip using the line information
        clip = (Clip) AudioSystem.getLine(info);

        // 5. Start monitoring the clip's line events
        clip.addLineListener(this);

        // 6. Open the audio stream as a clip; now it's ready to play
        clip.open(stream);
        stream.close(); // I'm done with the input stream

        checkDuration();
      } // end of try block

      // several catch blocks go here ...
    } // end of loadClip()
```

checkDuration( ) checks the length of this clip and issues a warning if it's one second or less. This warning is due to the WAV file bug in Java Sound in J2SE 5.0, first mentioned in Chapter 7 when I coded *PlayClip.java*.

 If a clip is too short, it'll fail to play and often affects the playing of other clips in LoadersTests, even those longer than one second.

play( ) starts the loop playing:

```
    public void play(boolean toLoop)
    { if (clip != null) {
```

```
    isLooping = toLoop;    // store playing mode
    clip.start(); // start playing from where stopped
  }
}
```

The Clip class has a loop( ) method, which is not used by my play( ) method when toLoop is true. Instead, the looping mode is stored in the isLooping global and is utilized later in update( ). This allows the loader to execute a callback method in a watcher at the end of each iteration.

Clip's start( ) method is asynchronous, so the play( ) method will not suspend. This makes it possible for a user to start multiple clips playing at the same time.

 If play( ) is called again for a playing clip, start( ) will have no effect.

Stopping Clips

The stop( ) method stops the clip and resets it to the beginning, ready for future playing:

```
public void stop( )
{ if (clip != null) {
    isLooping = false;
    clip.stop( );
    clip.setFramePosition(0);
  }
}
```

Clip.setFramePosition( ) can set the playing position anywhere inside the clip.

Pausing and Resuming Clips

The pause( ) and resume( ) methods are similar to stop( ) and play( ):

```
public void pause( )
// stop the clip at its current playing position
{ if (clip != null)
    clip.stop( );
}

public void resume( )
{ if (clip != null)
    clip.start( );
}
```

The big difference between pause( ) and stop( ) is that pause( ) doesn't reset the clip's playing position. Consequently, resume( ) will start playing the clip from the point where the sound was suspended.

Handing Line Events

ClipInfo implements the LineListener interface, so it is notified when the clip generates line events. Audio lines, such as clips, fire events when they're opened, started, stopped, or closed. update( ) only deals with STOP line events:

```
public void update(LineEvent lineEvent)
{
  // when clip is stopped / reaches its end
  if (lineEvent.getType() == LineEvent.Type.STOP) {
    clip.stop();
    clip.setFramePosition(0);
    if (!isLooping) {  // it isn't looping
      if (watcher != null)
        watcher.atSequenceEnd(name, SoundsWatcher.STOPPED);
    }
    else {        // else play it again
      clip.start();
      if (watcher != null)
        watcher.atSequenceEnd(name, SoundsWatcher.REPLAYED);
    }
  }
}
```

A STOP event is triggered in two different situations: when the clip reaches its end and when the clip is stopped with Clip.stop( ).

When the clip reaches its end, it may have been set to loop. This isn't implemented by using Clip's loop( ) method but by examining the value of the global isLooping Boolean. If isLooping is false, then the watcher (if one exists) is told the clip has stopped. If isLooping is true then the clip will start again, and the watcher is told that the clip is playing again. This explicit restarting of a looping clip, instead of calling loop( ), allows me to insert additional processing (e.g., watcher notification) between the clip's finishing and restarting.

The Midi Sequences Loader

MidisLoader stores sequences as a collection of MidiInfo objects in a HashMap, keyed by their names. The name and filename for a sequence are obtained from an information file loaded when MidisLoader is created. The file is assumed to be in the subdirectory *Sounds/*.

MidisLoader allows a specified sequence to be played, stopped, resumed, and looped. A SoundsWatcher can be attached to the sequencer and not to a sequence. MidisLoader deliberately offers almost the same interface as ClipsLoader (see Figure 8-2), though it has some internal differences.

MidisLoader was designed to have one Sequencer object for playing all the sequences, which avoids the overhead of supporting multiple sequencers. Consequently, one sequence will play at a time. This contrasts with ClipsLoader, where multiple clips can be playing concurrently since multiple Clip objects are created by ClipsLoader. A reference to the sequencer is passed to each MidiInfo object, thereby giving them the responsibility for playing, stopping, resuming and looping their sequences.

The MidisLoader initializes the sequencer using initSequencer() and loads the information file:

```
// globals
private Sequencer sequencer;
private HashMap midisMap;
private MidiInfo currentMidi = null;
      // reference to currently playing MidiInfo object


public MidisLoader()
{ midisMap = new HashMap();
  initSequencer();
}

public MidisLoader(String soundsFnm)
{ midisMap = new HashMap();
  initSequencer();
  loadSoundsFile(soundsFnm);
}
```

 The simpler versions of the constructor allow the loader to be created without an information file.

initSequencer() is similar to the version in *PlayMidi.java* in Chapter 7. loadSoundsFile() is similar to the same named method in ClipsLoader since it parses the information file, assuming each line contains a name and filename. For example, *midisInfo.txt* used by LoadersTests is

```
// midis
baa bsheep.mid
farmer farmerinthedell.mid
mary maryhadalittlelamb.mid
mcdonald mcdonald.mid
```

 The name can be any string. The file may contain blank lines and comment lines beginning with //.

After a line's name and filename have been extracted, load() is called:

```
public void load(String name, String fnm)
// create a MidiInfo object, and store it under name
{
```

```
    if (midisMap.containsKey(name))
      System.out.println( "Error: " + name + "already stored");
    else if (sequencer == null)
      System.out.println( "No sequencer for: " + name);
    else {
      midisMap.put(name, new MidiInfo(name, fnm, sequencer) );
      System.out.println("-- " + name + "/" + fnm);
    }
  }
```

This creates a MidiInfo object for the sequence and stores it in the midisMap HashMap.
The last MidiInfo constructor argument is the sequencer.

Playing Sequences

Playing a sequence is a matter of looking up the specified name in midisMap and calling its play( ) method. A slight complication is that one sequence will play at a time,
a restriction included in the loader design to reduce processing overheads. play( )
only plays the requested tune if no sequence is playing; a reference to that sequence
is stored in the currentMidi global:

```
public void play(String name, boolean toLoop)
// play (perhaps loop) the sequence
{
  MidiInfo mi = (MidiInfo) midisMap.get(name);
  if (mi == null)
    System.out.println( "Error: " + name + "not stored");
  else {
    if (currentMidi != null)
      System.out.println("Sorry, " + currentMidi.getName( ) + " already playing");
    else {
    currentMidi = mi;   // store a reference to playing midi
    mi.play(toLoop);    // pass play request to MidiInfo object
    }
  }
}
```

Playing is prohibited if currentMidi is not null, which means that a sequence is
playing.

Pausing and Resuming Sequences

Pausing and resuming is handled by passing the tasks to the playing MidiInfo object:

```
public void pause( )
{ if (currentMidi != null)
    currentMidi.pause( );
  else
    System.out.println( "No music to pause");
}
```

```
public void resume( )
{ if (currentMidi != null)
    currentMidi.resume( );
  else
    System.out.println("No music to resume");
}
```

Stopping Sequences

Stopping a sequence uses the same delegation strategy as pausing and resuming. The stop( ) method in MidisInfo will trigger an end-of-track metaevent in the sequencer, which is handled by MidisLoader's meta( ) method:

```
public void stop( )
{ if (currentMidi != null)
    currentMidi.stop( );  // this will cause an end-of-track event
  System.out.println("No music playing");
}


public void meta(MetaMessage meta)
{
  if (meta.getType( ) == END_OF_TRACK) {
    String name = currentMidi.getName( );
    boolean hasLooped = currentMidi.tryLooping( );  // music still looping?
    if (!hasLooped)    // no it's finished
      currentMidi = null;

    if (watcher != null) {    // tell the watcher
      if (hasLooped)          // the music is playing again
        watcher.atSequenceEnd(name, SoundsWatcher.REPLAYED);
      else                    // the music has finished
        watcher.atSequenceEnd(name, SoundsWatcher.STOPPED);
    }
  }
} // end of meta( )
```

The code in meta( ) only deals with an end-of-track metaevent. These end-of-track events are triggered by a MidiInfo object when its sequence reaches its end or is stopped. However, a sequence at its end may be looping, which is checked by calling tryLooping( ) in MidiInfo. If there is a watcher, that watcher is notified of the status of the sequence.

Closing Sequences

As LoadersTests terminates, it calls close( ) in MidisLoader to release the sequencer:

```
public void close( )
{
  stop( );    // stop the playing sequence
  if (sequencer != null) {
```

```
       if (sequencer.isRunning())
         sequencer.stop();

       sequencer.removeMetaEventListener(this);
       sequencer.close();
       sequencer = null;
    }
  }
```

Storing Midi Information

A MidiInfo object holds a single MIDI sequence and a reference to the sequencer created in MidisLoader. This allows it to play, stop, pause, and resume a clip, and make it loop.

The constructor is passed the sequence's name, filename, and the sequencer reference, and then it loads the sequence using MidiSystem.getSequence(). A sequence is played by loading it into the sequencer and starting the sequence:

```
public void play(boolean toLoop)
{
  if ((sequencer != null) && (seq != null)) {
    try {
      sequencer.setSequence(seq);    // load sequence into sequencer
      sequencer.setTickPosition(0); // reset to the start
      isLooping = toLoop;
      sequencer.start();              // play it
    }
    catch (InvalidMidiDataException e) {
      System.out.println("Invalid midi file: " + filename);
    }
  }
}
```

The Sequencer class has several loop() methods, but they aren't used here. A similar coding technique is employed as in ClipInfo: A global isLooping Boolean is set to true and employed later by tryLooping(). This permits us to trigger a callback in a watcher at the end of each iteration.

Stopping Sequences

Stopping a sequence with Sequencer.stop() causes it to stop at its current position. More importantly, no metaevent is generated unless the stopping coincides with the end of the track. In order to generate an event, my stop() method "winds" the sequence to its end:

```
public void stop()
{
  if ((sequencer != null) && (seq != null)) {
    isLooping = false;
    if (!sequencer.isRunning())    // the sequence may be paused
```

```
        sequencer.start();
      sequencer.setTickPosition( sequencer.getTickLength() );
        // move to end of sequence to trigger end-of-track event
    }
  }
```

This behavior means that meta( ) in MidisLoader is called in two situations: when the sequence reaches its end and when the sequence is stopped. This corresponds to the ways that a LineListener STOP event can be generated for clips.

MidisLoader's meta( ) method calls tryLooping( ) in MidiInfo to determine if the sequence is looping. tryLooping( ) is responsible for restarting the sequence if its isLooping Boolean is true:

```
    public boolean tryLooping()
    {
      if ((sequencer != null) && (seq != null)) {
        if (sequencer.isRunning())
          sequencer.stop();
        sequencer.setTickPosition(0);
        if (isLooping) {     // play it again
          sequencer.start();
          return true;
        }
      }
      return false;
    }
```

Admittedly, this is rather convoluted coding: stop( ) triggers meta( ), which calls tryLooping( ), and then tryLooping( ) restarts a looping sequence.

Part of the problem is that looping isn't implemented with Sequencer.loop( ). Instead, a sequence comes to its end and is started again by tryLooping( ) calling start( ). This allows additional processing in meta( ) (e.g., watcher communication) between the end of the sequence and its restart.

Another aspect is that the sequence control code is located in MidiInfo (stop( ) and tryLooping( )), but the metaevent processing is inside meta( ) in MidisLoader.

Pausing and Resuming Sequences

MidiInfo's pause( ) and resume( ) methods are implemented using the Sequencer class's start( ) and stop( ) methods. These Sequencer methods don't adjust the sequence's playing position:

```
    public void pause()
    { if ((sequencer != null) && (seq != null)) {
        if (sequencer.isRunning())
          sequencer.stop();
      }
    }
```

```
public void resume( )
{ if ((sequencer != null) && (seq != null))
    sequencer.start( );
}
```

LoadersTests as a JAR File

It's straightforward to package the LoadersTests code, its images, and sounds into a JAR file:

```
jar cvmf mainClass.txt LoadersTests.jar *.class Sounds Images
```

```
jar i LoadersTests.jar
```

All the class files and everything in the *Sounds/* and *Images/* subdirectories are packed together.

 The i argument adds indexing information to the JAR file, which will accelerate its execution if it contains many files.

mainClass.txt contains a single line:

```
Main-Class: LoadersTests
```

The JAR file can be started by double-clicking its icon or from the command line:

```
java -jar LoadersTests.jar
```

CHAPTER 9

Audio Effects

This chapter presents different ways of applying effects to existing audio. All of these techniques share one of the key advantages of the Sound API: the ability for a programmer to delve into the low-level details of audio files and affect (to some degree) the audio devices (e.g., the mixer, sequencer, or synthesizer).

You'll see how audio effects can be manipulated with clip and MIDI channel controllers, via sample byte array manipulation and modification of MIDI messages. The discussion is split into two main parts: audio effects for sampled audio and effects for MIDI sequences.

 All the examples can be found in the directory *SoundExamps/ SoundPlayer/*.

Audio Effects on Sampled Audio

There are three approaches for affecting sampled audio:

Precalculation
> Using this approach, you create the audio effect at development time and play the resulting sound clip at execution time.

Byte array manipulation
> Here, you store the sound in a byte array at runtime, permitting it to be modified using array-based operations.

Mixer controls
> A mixer control, such as gain or panning, affects the sound signal passing through the mixer's audio line.

Precalculation

Manipulating audio inside Java can be time-consuming and complicated. If a sound effect is going to be used regularly (e.g., a fading scream, an echoing explosion), then it will probably be better to create it when the game is being developed and save the finished audio to a file for playing at runtime. This moves the overheads associated with sound effect generation out of the application. I've found WavePad useful for various editing, format conversion, and effects tasks (*http://nch.com.au/wavepad/*). Its supported effects include amplification, reverberation, echoing, noise reduction, fading, and sample rate conversion. It offers recording and CD track ripping. It's small (320 KB), free, and has a decent manual.

Many tools are out there: Do a search for "audio editor" at Google or visit a software site such as tucows (*http://www.tucows.com/search*).

Byte Array Manipulation

The most versatile manipulation approach in Java (but potentially tricky to get right) is to load the audio file as a byte array. Audio effects then become a matter of changing byte values, rearranging blocks of data, or perhaps adding new data. Once completed, the resulting array can be passed through a SourceDataLine into the mixer. The *EchoSamplesPlayer.java* application that follows shows how this can be done.

A variant of this approach is to employ streaming. Instead of reading in the entire file as a large byte array, the audio file can be incrementally read, changed, and sent to the mixer. However, this coding style is restricted to effects that only have to examine the sound fragment currently in memory. For example, amplification of the array's contents doesn't require a consideration of the other parts of the sound.

Making a sound clip echo

EchoSamplesPlayer.java completely loads a sound clip into a byte array via an AudioInputStream. Then an echoing effect is applied by creating a new byte array and adding five copies of the original sound to it; each copy is softer than the one before it. The resulting array is passed in small chunks to the SourceDataLine and to the mixer.

EchoSamplesPlayer is an extended version of the BufferedPlayer application described in Chapter 7. The main addition is a getSamples() method: This method applies the effect implemented in echoSamples(). An isRequiredFormat() method exists for checking the input is suitable for modification. The program is stored in *SoundExamps/SoundPlayer/*.

To simplify the implementation, the echo effect is only applied to 8-bit PCM signed or unsigned audio. The choice of PCM means that the amplitude information is stored unchanged in the byte and isn't compressed as in the ULAW or ALAW formats. The 8-bit requirement means a single byte is used per sample, so I don't have to deal with big- or little-endian issues. PCM unsigned data stores values between 0 and $2^8 - 1$ (255), and the signed range is -2^7 to $2^7 - 1$ (–128 to 127). This becomes a concern when I cast a byte into a short prior to changing it.

The main( ) method in EchoSamplesPlayer is similar to the one in BufferedPlayer:

```
public static void main(String[] args)
{ if (args.length != 1) {
    System.out.println("Usage: java EchoSamplesPlayer <clip>");
    System.exit(0);
  }

  createInput("Sounds/" + args[0]);

  if (!isRequiredFormat()) {    // not in SamplesPlayer
    System.out.println("Format unsuitable for echoing");
    System.exit(0);
  }

  createOutput();

  int numBytes=(int)(stream.getFrameLength( )*format.getFrameSize( ));
  System.out.println("Size in bytes: " + numBytes);

  byte[] samples = getSamples(numBytes);
  play(samples);

  System.exit(0);    // necessary in J2SE 1.4.2 and earlier
}
```

The createInput( ) and createOutput( ) methods are unchanged from BufferedPlayer.

isRequiredFormat( ) tests the AudioFormat object that was created in createInput( ):

```
private static boolean isRequiredFormat( )
// Only 8-bit PCM signed or unsigned audio can be echoed
{
  if (((format.getEncoding( )==AudioFormat.Encoding.PCM_UNSIGNED) ||
      (format.getEncoding( ) == AudioFormat.Encoding.PCM_SIGNED))&&
      (format.getSampleSizeInBits( ) == 8))
    return true;
  else
    return false;
}
```

AudioFormat has a selection of get( ) methods for examining different aspects of the audio data. For example, AudioFormat.getChannels( ) returns the number of channels used (1 for mono, 2 for stereo). The echoing effect doesn't need this information; all the frames, independent of the number of channels, will be amplified. Typically, channel information is required if an effect will differentiate between the stereo outputs, as when a sound is panned between speakers.

getSamples( ) adds the echoes after it has extracted the complete samples[] array from the AudioInputStream:

```
private static byte[] getSamples(int numBytes)
{
  // read the entire stream into samples[]
  byte[] samples = new byte[numBytes];
  DataInputStream dis = new DataInputStream(stream);
  try {
    dis.readFully(samples);
  }
  catch (IOException e)
  { System.out.println( e.getMessage( ));
    System.exit(0);
  }
  return echoSamples(samples, numBytes);
}
```

echoSamples( ) returns a modified byte array, which becomes the result of getSamples( ).

 Different audio effects could replace the call to echoSamples( ) at this point in the code.

echoSamples( ) creates a new byte array, newSamples( ), big enough to hold the original sound and ECHO_NUMBER (4) copies. The volume of each one is reduced (decayed) (which is set to by DECAY (0.5) over its predecessor:

```
private static byte[] echoSamples(byte[] samples, int numBytes)
{
  int numTimes = ECHO_NUMBER + 1;
  double currDecay = 1.0;
  short sample, newSample;
  byte[] newSamples = new byte[numBytes*numTimes];

  for (int j=0; j < numTimes; j++) {
    for (int i=0; i < numBytes; i++)  // copy the sound's bytes
      newSamples[i + (numBytes*j)] = echoSample(samples[i], currDecay);
    currDecay *= DECAY;
  }
  return newSamples;
}
```

The nested for loop makes the required copies one byte at a time. echoSample( ) utilizes a byte in the original data to create an "echoed" byte for newSamples[]. The amount of echoing is determined by the currDecay double, which shrinks for each successive copy of the original sound.

echoSample( ) does different tasks depending on if the input data are unsigned or signed PCM. In both cases, the supplied byte is translated into a short so it can be manipulated easily; then, the result is converted back to a byte:

```
private static byte echoSample(byte sampleByte, double currDecay)
{
  short sample, newSample;
  if (format.getEncoding( ) == AudioFormat.Encoding.PCM_UNSIGNED) {
    sample = (short)(sampleByte & 0xff);  // unsigned 8 bit -> short
    newSample = (short)(sample * currDecay);
    return (byte) newSample;
  }
  else if (format.getEncoding( )==AudioFormat.Encoding.PCM_SIGNED){
    sample = (short)sampleByte;   // signed 8 bit -> short
    newSample = (short)(sample * currDecay);
    return (byte) newSample;
  }
  else
    return sampleByte;    //no change; this branch should be unused
}
```

This byte-to-short conversion must be done carefully. An unsigned byte needs masking as it's converted since Java stores shorts in signed form. A short is two bytes long, so the masking ensures that the bits in the high-order byte are all set to 0s. Without the mask, the conversion would add in 1s when it saw a byte value above 127.

 No masking is required for the signed byte to signed short conversion since the translation is correct by default.

Playing

play( ) is similar to the one in *BufferedPlayer.java* in Chapter 7. The difference is that the byte array must be passed through an input stream before it can be sent to the SourceDataLine:

```
private static void play(byte[] samples)
{
  // byte array --> stream
  InputStream source = new ByteArrayInputStream(samples);

  int numRead = 0;
  byte[] buf = new byte[line.getBufferSize( )];

  line.start( );
  // read and play chunks of the audio
```

```
try {
  while ((numRead = source.read(buf, 0, buf.length)) >= 0) {
    int offset = 0;
    while (offset < numRead)
      offset += line.write(buf, offset, numRead-offset);
  }
}
catch (IOException e)
{ System.out.println( e.getMessage( )); }

// wait until all data is played, then close the line
line.drain( );
line.stop( );
line.close( );
}  // end of play( )
```

Utilizing Mixer Controls

The mixer diagram in Figure 9-1 includes a grayish box labeled "Controls." Controls, such as gain and panning, affect the sound signal passing through an audio line. They can be accessed through `Clip` or `SourceDataLine` via a `getControls( )` method that returns an array of available `Control` objects. Each object, suitably subclassed, allows its associated audio control to be manipulated.

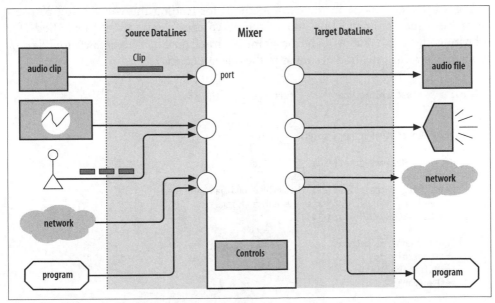

Figure 9-1. Audio I/O to/from the mixer

The bad news is that the default mixer in J2SE 5.0 offers fewer controls than were present in J2SE 1.4.2 since controls tend to have an adverse effect on speed even when they're not being used. However, if a control is present, then it's much easier to apply than the byte array technique.

Adjusting a clip's volume and pan values

PlaceClip plays a clip, allowing its volume and pan settings to be adjusted via command-line parameters. It's called with the following format:

```
java PlaceClip <clip file> [ <volume value> [<pan value>] ]
```

The volume and pan values are optional; if they are both left out, then the clip will play normally.

The volume setting should be between 0.0f (the quietest) and 1.0f (the loudest); –1.0f means that the volume is left unchanged. The pan value should be between –1.0f and 1.0f; –1.0f causes all the sound to be set to the left speaker, 1.0f focuses only on the right speaker, and values in between will send the sound to both speakers with varying weights, as in this example:

```
java PlaceClip dog.wav 0.8f -1.0f
```

This will make the left speaker bark loudly. This mixing of volume and speaker placement is a rudimentary way of placing sounds at different locations in a game.

PlaceClip is an extended version of PlayClip, which was described in Chapter 7. The changes in PlaceClip are in the extra methods for reading the volume and pan settings from the command line and in the setVolume( ) and setPan( ) methods for adjusting the clip controls. The program is stored in *SoundExamps/SoundPlayer/*. PlaceClip's main( ) method is similar to the one in *PlayClip.java*:

```
// globals
private float volume, pan;    // settings from the command line


public PlaceClip(String[] args)
{
  df = new DecimalFormat("0.#");  // 1 dp

  getSettings(args);    // get the volume and pan settings
                        // from the command line
  loadClip(SOUND_DIR + args[0]);

  // clip control methods
  showControls();
  setVolume(volume);
  setPan(pan);

  play();
  try {
    Thread.sleep(600000);   // 10 mins in ms
  }
  catch(InterruptedException e)
  { System.out.println("Sleep Interrupted"); }
}
```

loadClip( ) and play( ) are almost unchanged from PlayClip. (loadClip( ) uses a globally defined AudioFormat variable and has some extra println( )'s.) loadClip( ) includes a call to checkDuration( ), which issues a warning if the clip is one second or less in length. In that case, the clip won't be heard in J2SE 5.0 due to a Java Sound bug.

What controls are available?

showControls( ) displays all the controls available for the clip, which will vary depending on the clip's audio format and the mixer:

```
private void showControls()
{ if (clip != null) {
    Control cntls[] = clip.getControls();
    for(int i=0; i<cntls.length; i++)
      System.out.println( i + ".  " + cntls[i].toString() );
  }
}
```

 getControls( ) returns information once the clip the class represents has been opened.

For the *dog.wav* example, executed using the J2SE 1.4.2 default mixer, showControls( )'s output is given in Example 9-1.

Example 9-1. showControls()'s output

```
0.  Master Gain with current calue: 0.0 dB (range: -80.0 - 13.9794)
1.  Mute Control with current value: Not Mute
2.  Pan with current value: 0.0 (range: -1.0 - 1.0)
3.  Sample Rate with current value: 22000.0 FPS (range: 0.0 - 48000.0)
```

In this case, four controls are available: gain (volume), mute, panning, and sample rate.

Reverberation and balance controls may be available for some types of clips and mixers. In J2SE 5.0, panning, sample rate, and reverberation are no longer supported, and the balance control is only available for audio files using stereo.

In real-world audio gadgets, a pan control distributes *mono input* (input on a single channel) between stereo output lines (e.g., the lines going to the speakers). So, the same signal is sent to both output lines. A balance control does a similar job but for *stereo input*, sending two channels of input to two output lines.

In J2SE 1.4.2 and before, the pan and balance controls could be used with mono or stereo input, i.e., there was no distinction between them. Output lines were always opened in stereo mode. The default J2SE 1.4.2 mixer is the Java Sound Audio Engine.

The default mixer in J2SE 5.0 is the Direct Audio Device, with resulting changes to the controls. If the mixer receives mono input it will open a mono output line and not a stereo one. This means there's no pan control since there's no way to map mono to stereo. There is a balance control, but that's for mapping stereo input to stereo output.

In J2SE 5.0, the example will report that panning is unavailable since *dog.wav* was recorded in mono. The simplest solution is to convert it to stereo using WavePad (*http://nch.com.au/wavepad/*) or similar software. The balance controls will then be available, and setPan( ) can carry out panning by adjusting the balance.

Java audio controls

The various controls are represented by subclasses of the Control class: BooleanControl, FloatControl, EnumControl, and CompoundControl.

BooleanControl is used to adjust binary settings, such as mute on/off. FloatControl is employed for controls that range over floating point values, such as volume, panning, and balance. EnumControl permits a choice between several settings, as in reverberation. CompoundControl groups controls.

 All these controls will function only if the clip is open.

As an example, here's a code fragment that turns mute on and off with a BooleanControl:

```
BooleanControl muteControl =
    (BooleanControl) clip.getControl( BooleanControl.Type.MUTE );
muteControl.setValue(true);      // mute on; sound is switched off
    : // later on
muteControl.setValue(false);     // mute off; sound is audible again
```

Here's another that plays a clip at 1.5 times its normal speed via a FloatControl:

```
FloatControl rateControl =
    (FloatControl) clip.getControl( FloatControl.Type.SAMPLE_RATE );
rateControl.setValue( 1.5f * format.getSampleRate() );
        // format is the AudioFormat object for the audio file
```

Setting the volume in PlaceClip

PlaceClip offers a volume parameter, ranging from 0.0f (off) to 1.0f (on). Additionally, no change to the volume is represented internally by the NO_VOL_CHANGE constant (the float –1.0f).

Unfortunately, the mixer's gain controls use the logarithmic decibel scale (related to the square of the distance from the sound source). Rather than grappling with a realistic mapping from my linear scale (0–1) to the decibel range, I use a linear equation to calculate the new gain:

```
gain = ((range_max - range_min) * input_volume) + range_min
```

`range_min` and `range_max` are the minimum and maximum possible gain values; `input_volume` is the float obtained from the command line.

 The drawback to this approach is that the logarithmic gain scale is being treated like a linear one. In practice, this means that the sound becomes inaudible when the supplied volume setting is 0.5f or less. On balance, this is a small price to pay for greatly simplified code.

`setVolume( )` uses `isControlSupported( )` to check for the volume control's presence before attempting to access/change its setting:

```java
private void setVolume(float volume)
{
  if ((clip != null) && (volume != NO_VOL_CHANGE)) {
    if (clip.isControlSupported(FloatControl.Type.MASTER_GAIN)) {
      FloatControl gainControl = (FloatControl)
            clip.getControl(FloatControl.Type.MASTER_GAIN);

      float range = gainControl.getMaximum( ) - gainControl.getMinimum( );
      float gain = (range * volume) + gainControl.getMinimum( );
      System.out.println("Volume: " + volume + "; New gain: " + gain);
      gainControl.setValue(gain);
    }
    else
      System.out.println("No Volume controls available");
  }
}
```

 `FloatControl` has several potentially useful methods, like `shift( )`, which is meant to change the control value gradually over a specified time period and returns without waiting for the shift to finish. Unfortunately, this particular method has never been fully implemented and currently modifies the control value in one step without any incremental changes in between.

Panning between the speakers in PlaceClip

`setPan( )` is supplied with a pan value between -1.0f and 1.0f—which will position the output somewhere between the left and right speakers—or with `NO_PAN_CHANGE` (0.0f). The method pans first, looks for the balance control if panning is unavailable, and finally gives up if both are unsupported:

```java
private void setPan(float pan)
{
```

```
    if ((clip == null) || (pan == NO_PAN_CHANGE))
      return;    // do nothing

    if (clip.isControlSupported(FloatControl.Type.PAN)) {
      FloatControl panControl =
         (FloatControl) clip.getControl(FloatControl.Type.PAN);
      panControl.setValue(pan);
    }
    else if (clip.isControlSupported(FloatControl.Type.BALANCE)) {
      FloatControl balControl =
         (FloatControl) clip.getControl(FloatControl.Type.BALANCE);
      balControl.setValue(pan);
    }
    else {
      System.out.println("No Pan or Balance controls available");
      if (format.getChannels() == 1)    // mono input
        System.out.println("Your audio file is mono;
                             try converting it to stereo");
    }
  }
}
```

Audio Effects on MIDI Sequences

There are four ways of applying audio effects to MIDI sequences:

Precalculation

> Similar to what you've seen, this involves creating the audio effect at development time and playing the resulting MIDI sequence at execution time.

Sequence manipulation

> Here, the MIDI sequence data structure can be manipulated at runtime using a range of methods from MIDI-related classes.

MIDI channel controllers

> In this approach, a channel plays a particular instrument and has multiple controllers associated with it, which manage such things as volume and panning.

Sequencer methods

> The Sequencer class offers several methods for controlling a sequence, including changing the tempo (speed) of the playback and muting or soloing individual tracks in the sequence.

Precalculation

As with sampled audio, using Java at execution time to modify a sequence can be time-consuming and difficult to implement. Several tools allow you to create or edit

---

MIDI sequences, though you do need an understanding of music and MIDI to use them. Here are some of packages I've tinkered with:

The free version of Anvil Studio (http://www.anvilstudio.com/)
> Supports the capture, editing, and direct composing of MIDI. It handles WAV files.

BRELS MIDI Editor (http://www.tucows.com/search)
> A free, small MIDI editor. It's easiest to obtain from a software site, such as tucows.

Midi Maker (http://www.necrocosm.com/midimaker/)
> Emulates a standard keyboard synthesizer. Available for a free 14-day trial.

Sequence Manipulation

Figure 9-2 shows the internals of a sequence.

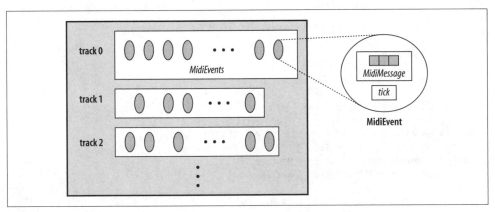

Figure 9-2. The internals of a MIDI sequence

The regularity of the data structure means that it can be easy to modify at runtime, but you're going to need to understand the MIDI specification.

Doubling the sequence volume

Here is the basic code for playing a sequence:

```
Sequence seq = MidiSystem.getSequence(getClass().getResource(fnm));

// change the sequence: double its volume in this case
doubleVolumeSeq(seq);

sequencer.setSequence(seq);   // load changed sequence
sequencer.start();            // start playing it
```

This snippet omits the try/catch blocks you need in an actual code block. Look at *PlayMidi.java* in Chapter 7 for a complete version.

The sequence is modified after being loaded with getSequence( ) and before being assigned to the sequencer with setSequence( ).

Volume doubling is applied to every track in the sequence:

```
private void doubleVolumeSeq(Sequence seq)
{ Track tracks[] = seq.getTracks();      // get all the tracks
  for(int i=0; i < tracks.length; i++)   // iterate through them
     doubleVolume(tracks[i], tracks[i].size());
}
```

doubleVolume( ) examines every MidiEvent in the supplied track, extracting its component tick and MIDI message. If the message is a NOTE_ON, then its volume will double (up to a maximum of 127):

```
private void doubleVolume(Track track, int size)
{
  MidiEvent event;
  MidiMessage message;
  ShortMessage sMessage, newShort;

  for (int i=0; i < size; i++) {
    event = track.get(i);            // get the event
    message = event.getMessage();    // get its MIDI message
    long tick = event.getTick();     // get its tick
    if (message instanceof ShortMessage) {
      sMessage = (ShortMessage) message;

      // check if the message is a NOTE_ON
      if (sMessage.getCommand() == ShortMessage.NOTE_ON) {
        int doubleVol = sMessage.getData2() * 2;
        int newVol = (doubleVol > 127) ? 127 : doubleVol;
        newShort = new ShortMessage();
        try {
          newShort.setMessage(ShortMessage.NOTE_ON,
                              sMessage.getChannel(),
                              sMessage.getData1(), newVol);
          track.remove(event);
          track.add( new MidiEvent(newShort,tick) );
        }
        catch ( InvalidMidiDataException e)
        { System.out.println("Invalid data");  }
      }
    }
  }
} // end of doubleVolume()
```

Each MIDI message is composed from three bytes: a command name and two data bytes. `ShortMessage.getCommand( )` is employed to check the name. If the command name is `NOTE_ON`, then the first byte will be the note number, and the second its velocity (similar to a volume level).

> MIDI messages are encoded using three subclasses of `MidiMessage`: `ShortMessage`, `SysexMessage`, and `MetaMessage`. Each class lists constants representing various commands. The `NOTE_ON` and `NOTE_OFF` messages are `ShortMessage` objects, used to start and terminating note playing.

The volume is obtained with a call to `ShortMessage.getData2( )` and then doubled with a ceiling of 127 since the number must fit back into a single byte. A new `ShortMessage` object is constructed and filled with relevant details (command name, destination channel ID, note number, new volume):

```
newShort.setMessage(ShortMessage.NOTE_ON,
          sMessage.getChannel( ), sMessage.getData1( ), newVol);
```

The old MIDI event (containing the original message) must be replaced by an event holding the new message: a two-step process involving `Track.remove( )` and `Track.add( )`. The new event is built from the new message and the old tick value:

```
track.add( new MidiEvent(newShort,tick) );
```

The tick specifies where the event will be placed in the track.

MIDI Channel Controllers

Figure 9-3 shows the presence of 16 MIDI channels inside the synthesizer; each one acts as a "musician," playing a particular instrument. As the stream of MIDI messages arrive (individually or as part of a sequence), each message is routed to a channel based on its channel setting.

Each channel has a set of controllers associated with it. The set depends on the particular synthesizer; controllers defined in the General MIDI specification should be present, but there may be others. For example, controllers offering the Roland GS enhancements are found on many devices. General MIDI controllers include controls for volume level, stereo balancing, and panning. Popular Roland GS enhancements include reverberation and chorus effects. Each controller is identified by a unique ID, between 0 and 127.

> A list of channel controllers, complete with a short description of each one, can be found at *http://improv.sapp.org/doc/class/MidiOutput/controllers/*. Another site with similar information is *http://www.musicmarkup.info/midi/control.html*.

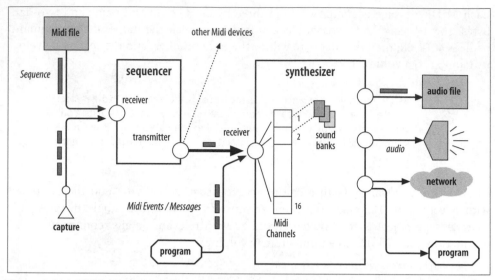

Figure 9-3. A MIDI sequencer and synthesizer

The FadeMidi and PanMidi examples illustrate how to use channel controllers to affect the playback of an existing sequence. They both reuse several methods from *Play-Midi.java*, shown in Chapter 7.

Making a sequence fade away

FadeMidi.java (located in *SoundExamps/SoundPlayer/*) plays a sequence, gradually reducing its volume level to 0 by the end of the clip. The volume settings for all 16 channels are manipulated by accessing each channel's main volume controller (the ID for that controller is the number 7).

 There's a fine-grain volume controller (ID number 39) that's intended to allow smaller change graduations, but many synthesizers don't support it.

The incremental volume reduction is managed by a VolChanger thread, which repeatedly lowers the volume reduction until the sequence has been played to its end.

Figure 9-4 gives the class diagrams for FadeMidi and VolChanger, showing only the public methods.

The main( ) method initializes FadeMidi and starts VolChanger:

```
public static void main(String[] args)
{ if (args.length != 1) {
    System.out.println("Usage: java FadeMidi <midi file>");
    System.exit(0);
  }
```

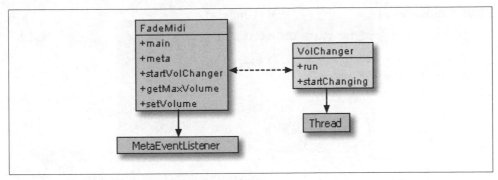

Figure 9-4. Class diagrams for FadeMidi and VolChanger

```
// set up the player and the volume changer
FadeMidi player = new FadeMidi(args[0]);
VolChanger vc = new VolChanger(player);

player.startVolChanger(vc);  // start volume manipulation
}
```

VolChanger is passed a reference to FadeMidi so it can affect the synthesizer's volume settings.

startVolChanger() starts the VolChanger thread running and supplies the sequence duration in milliseconds. The thread needs it to calculate how often to change the volume:

```
public void startVolChanger(VolChanger vc)
{  vc.startChanging( (int)(seq.getMicrosecondLength()/1000) );  }
```

The FadeMidi constructor looks similar to the one in PlayMidi:

```
public FadeMidi(String fnm)
{
 df = new DecimalFormat("0.#");   // 1 dp
  filename = SOUND_DIR + fnm;
  initSequencer();
  loadMidi(filename);
  play();

  /* No need for sleeping to keep the object alive, since
     the VolChanger thread refers to it. */
}
```

initSequencer() and loadMidi() are identical to the methods of the same name in PlayClip, and play() is slightly different. The most significant change is the absence of a call to sleep(), which keeps PlayMidi alive until its sequence has finished. Sleeping is unnecessary in FadeMidi because the object is referred to by the VolChanger thread, which keeps calling its setVolume() method.

play( ) initializes a global array of MIDI channels:

```
private static final int VOLUME_CONTROLLER = 7;

// global holding the synthesizer's channels
private MidiChannel[] channels;


private void play( )
{ if ((sequencer != null) && (seq != null)) {
    try {
      sequencer.setSequence(seq);  // load MIDI into sequencer
      sequencer.start( );   // play it
      channels = synthesizer.getChannels( );
      // showChannelVolumes( );
    }
    catch (InvalidMidiDataException e) {
      System.out.println("Invalid midi file: " + filename);
      System.exit(0);
    }
  }
}


private void showChannelVolumes( )
// show the volume levels for all the synthesizer channels
{
  System.out.println("Syntheziser Channels: " + channels.length);
  System.out.print("Volumes: {");
  for (int i=0; i < channels.length; i++)
    System.out.print( channels[i].getController(VOLUME_CONTROLLER) + " ");
  System.out.println("}");
}
```

 The references to the channels shouldn't be obtained until the sequence is playing (i.e., after calling sequencer.start( )) or their controllers will not respond to changes. This seems to be a bug in the Java Sound implementation.

Channels in the array are accessed using the indices 0 to 15 though the MIDI specification numbers them 1 to 16. For instance, the special percussion channel is MIDI number 10, but it is represented by channels[9] in Java.

In showChannelVolumes( ), MidiChannel.getController( ) obtains the current value of the specified controller. Supplying it with the ID for the volume controller (7) will cause it to return the current volume setting. A controller stores the data in a single byte, so the returned value will be in the range 0 to 127.

Getting and setting the volume

FadeMidi contains two public methods for getting and setting the volume, both used by VolChanger:

```
public int getMaxVolume( )
// return the max level for all the volume controllers
{ int maxVol = 0;
  int channelVol;
  for (int i=0; i < channels.length; i++) {
    channelVol = channels[i].getController(VOLUME_CONTROLLER);
    if (maxVol < channelVol)
      maxVol = channelVol;
  }
  return maxVol;
}


public void setVolume(int vol)
// set all the controller's volume levels to vol
{ for (int i=0; i < channels.length; i++)
    channels[i].controlChange(VOLUME_CONTROLLER, vol);
}
```

getMaxVolume( ) returns a single volume, rather than all 16; this keeps the code simple. setVolume( ) shows how MidiChannel.controlChange( ) is used to change a specified controller's value. The data should be an integer between 0 and 127.

Changing the volume

VolChanger gets started when its startChanging( ) method is called. At this point, the sequence will be playing, and the MIDI channel controllers are available for manipulation:

```
// globals
// the amount of time between changes to the volume, in ms
private static int PERIOD = 500;

private FadeMidi player;
private int numChanges = 0;


public void startChanging(int duration)
/* FadeMidi calls this method, supplying the duration of
   its sequence in ms. */
{
  // calculate how many times the volume should be adjusted
  numChanges = (int) duration/PERIOD;
  start();
} // end of startChanging( )
```

VolChanger adjusts the volume every PERIOD (500 ms), but how many times? The duration of the sequence is passed in as an argument to startChanging( ) and is used to calculate the number of volume changes.

run( ) implements a volume reduction/sleep cycle:

```
public void run( )
{
  /* calculate stepVolume, the amount to decrease the volume
     each time that the volume is changed. */
  int volume = player.getMaxVolume( );
  int stepVolume = (int) volume / numChanges;
  if (stepVolume == 0)
    stepVolume = 1;
  System.out.println("Max Volume: " + volume + ", step: " + stepVolume);
  int counter = 0;
  System.out.print("Fading");
  while(counter < numChanges){
    try {
      volume -= stepVolume;     // reduce the required volume level
      if ((volume >= 0) && (player != null))
        player.setVolume(volume);    // change the volume
      Thread.sleep(PERIOD);          // delay a while
    }
    catch(InterruptedException e) {}
    System.out.print(".");
    counter++;
  }
  System.out.println( );
}
```

The MIDI volume bug

FadeMid.java doesn't work with J2SE 5.0 due to a bug associated with the volume adjustment of a sequencer. The offending line is in initSequencer( ):

```
sequencer = MidiSystem.getSequencer( );
```

The sequencer is retrieved, but subsequent volume changes have no effect. The solution is to explicitly request the sequencer by finding it in on the list of available MIDI devices for the machine. This is packaged inside obtainSequencer( ):

```
private Sequencer obtainSequencer( )
{
  MidiDevice.Info[] mdi = MidiSystem.getMidiDeviceInfo( );
  int seqPosn = -1;
  for(int i=0; i < mdi.length; i++) {
    System.out.println(mdi[i].getName( ));
    if (mdi[i].getName( ).indexOf("Sequencer") != -1) {
      seqPosn = i;     // found the Sequencer
      System.out.println("  Found Sequencer");
    }
  }

  try {
    if (seqPosn != -1)
      return (Sequencer) MidiSystem.getMidiDevice( mdi[seqPosn] );
    else
```

```
        return null;
    }
    catch(MidiUnavailableException e)
    { return null; }
} // end of obtainSequencer()
```

The position of the sequencer in the MIDI device information array, mdi[], will vary depending on the audio devices attached to a given machine and the J2SE version, so some searching is required. The list printed on a test machine running J2SE 5.0 is shown in Example 9-2.

Example 9-2. MIDI device information in J2SE 5.0

```
Roland MPU-401
MIDI Mapper
Microsoft GS Wavetable SW Synth
Roland MPU-401
Real Time Sequencer
  Found Sequencer
Java Sound Synthesizer
```

The list generated on a different machine, using J2SE 1.4.2, is shown in Example 9-3.

Example 9-3. MIDI device information in J2SE 1.4.2

```
Java Sound Synthesizer
Java Sound Sequencer
  Found Sequencer
MIDI Mapper
Microsoft GS Wavetable SW Synth
```

The sequencer is obtained in initSequencer() by calling obtainSequencer():

```
sequencer = obtainSequencer();
```

The problem, which has been reported by several users in the Java Sound forums (e.g., at *http://archives.java.sun.com/cgi-bin/wa?A0=javasound-interest*), only seems to occur when the volume needs to be changed. For example, this extra work isn't required in PanMidi (the next example): the sequencer it obtains with MidiSystem.getSequencer() does respond to panning changes.

 I'm at a loss as to why my workaround works since the sequencer object returned by MidiSystem.getSequencer() and the one obtained with my obtainSequencer() method appear to be the same.

Panning the sequence

PanMidi repeatedly switches its sequence from the left to the right speaker and back again. A PanChanger thread switches the pan settings in all the channel controllers at periodic intervals during the playing of the sequence.

PanMidi and PanChanger can be found in *SoundExamps/SoundPlayer/*.

The class diagrams for PanMidi and PanChanger are given in Figure 9-5.

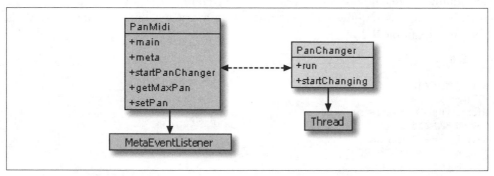

Figure 9-5. Class diagrams for PanMidi and PanChanger

The main( ) method initializes the player and the thread, and then it calls PanMidi's startPanChanger( ) to start the thread running. startPanChanger( ) passes the duration of the sequence to the thread, so it can calculate the number of changes it will make.

The PanMidi pan methods used by PanChanger are getMaxPan( ) and setPan( ):

```
// global constants
// private static final int BALANCE_CONTROLLER = 8; //not working?
private static final int PAN_CONTROLLER = 10;

public int getMaxPan( )
// return the max value for all the pan controllers
{ int maxPan = 0;
  int channelPan;
  for (int i=0; i < channels.length; i++) {
    channelPan = channels[i].getController(PAN_CONTROLLER);
    if (maxPan < channelPan)
      maxPan = channelPan;
  }
  return maxPan;
}

public void setPan(int panVal)
// set all the controller's pan levels to panVal
{ for (int i=0; i < channels.length; i++)
    channels[i].controlChange(PAN_CONTROLLER, panVal);
}
```

The only real difference in PanMidi from FadeMidi is the use of the PAN_CONTROLLER controller number.

The balance controller should work in this situation, but it didn't on my test machines. This bug has been reported by several people, so we may see a fix soon.

Changing the pan value

Unlike VolChanger, PanChanger carries out a cyclic series of changes to the pan value. However, the core of run( ) is still a loop repeatedly calling setPan( ) and sleeping for an interval.

The series of pan values that make up a single cycle are defined in a panVals[] array:

```
// time to move left to right and back again
private static int CYCLE_PERIOD = 4000;  // in ms

// pan values used in a single cycle
// (make the array's length integer divisible into CYCLE_PERIOD)
private int[] panVals = {0, 127};

// or try
// private int[] panVals = {0, 16, 32, 48, 64, 80, 96, 112, 127,
//                           112, 96, 80, 64, 48, 32, 16};
```

The run( ) method cycles through the panVals[] array until it has executed for a time equal to the sequence's duration:

```
public void run( )
{ /* Get the original pan setting, just for information. It
     is not used any further. */
  int pan = player.getMaxPan( );
  System.out.println("Max Pan: " + pan);

  int panValsIdx = 0;
  int timeCount = 0;
  int delayPeriod = (int) (CYCLE_PERIOD / panVals.length);

  System.out.print("Panning");
  while(timeCount < duration){
    try {
      if (player != null)
        player.setPan( panVals[panValsIdx] );
      Thread.sleep(delayPeriod);    // delay
    }
    catch(InterruptedException e) {}
    System.out.print(".");
    panValsIdx = (panValsIdx+1) % panVals.length;
                          // cycle through the array
    timeCount += delayPeriod;
  }
  System.out.println( );
}
```

Sequencer Methods

The Sequencer has methods that can change the tempo (speed) of playback. The easiest to use is probably setTempoFactor( ), which scales the existing tempo by the supplied float:

```
sequencer.setTempoFactor(2.0f);    // double the tempo
```

Tempo adjustments only work if the sequence's event ticks are defined in the PPQ (ticks per beat) format since tempo affects the number of beats per minute. Sequencer. getTempoFactor( ) can be employed after calling Sequencer.setTempoFactor( ) to check whether the requested change has occurred. The Sequence class offers getDivisionType( ), which returns a float representing the sequence's division type. Sequence.PPQ for PPQ, or one of the many Society of Motion Picture and Television Engineers (SMPTE) types, use ticks per frame. This information can be used to determine if setTempoFactor( ) would work on the sequence.

Sequencer has two methods that act upon the sequence's tracks: setTrackMute( ), and setTrackSolo( ). Here's a fragment of code that sets and tests the mute value:

```
sequencer.setTrackMute(4, true);
boolean muted = sequencer.getTrackMute(4);
if (!muted)
  // muting failed
```

CHAPTER 10

Audio Synthesis

The synthesis of new audio during a game's execution can be useful, especially in response to unforeseen or rare events. In this chapter, I look at how to generate tone sequences for sampled audio and how to create MIDI sequences at runtime. The discussion is split into two main parts: synthesis of sampled audio and synthesis of sequences. I finish by describing additional libraries and APIs that can help with audio generation.

Sampled Audio Synthesis

Sampled audio is encoded as a series of samples in a byte array, which is sent through a SourceDataLine to the mixer. In previous examples, the contents of the byte array came from an audio file though you saw that audio effects can manipulate and even add to the array. In sampled audio synthesis, the application generates the byte array data without requiring any audio input. Potentially, any sound can be generated at runtime.

Audio is a mix of sine waves, each one representing a tone or a note. A pure note is a single sine wave with a fixed amplitude and frequency (or pitch). Frequency can be defined as the number of sine waves that pass a given point in a second. The higher the frequency, the higher the note's pitch; the higher the amplitude, the louder the note.

Before I go further, it helps to introduce the usual naming scheme for notes; it's easier to talk about note names than note frequencies.

Note Names

Notes names are derived from the piano keyboard, which has a mix of black and white keys, shown in Figure 10-1.

Keys are grouped into octaves, each octave consisting of 12 consecutive white and black keys. The white keys are labeled with the letters A to G and an octave number.

Figure 10-1. Part of the piano keyboard

For example, the note named C4 is the white key closest to the center of the keyboard, often referred to as middle C. The 4 means that the key is in the fourth octave, counting from the left of the keyboard.

A black key is labeled with the letter of the preceding white key and a sharp (#). For instance, the black key following C4 is known as C#4.

 A note to musicians: for simplicity's sake, I'll be ignoring flats in this discussion.

Figure 10-2 shows the keyboard fragment of Figure 10-1 again but labeled with note names. I've assumed that the first white key is C4.

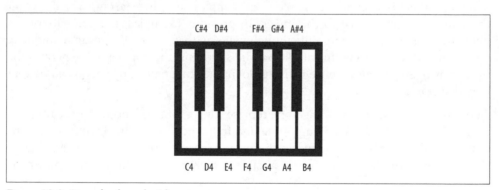

Figure 10-2. Piano keyboard with note names

Figure 10-2 utilizes the C Major scale, where the letters appear in the order C, D, E, F, G, A, and B.

 There's a harmonic minor scale that starts at A, but I won't be using it in these examples.

After B4, the fifth octave begins, starting with C5 and repeating the same sequence as in the fourth octave. Before C4 is the third octave, which ends with B3.

Having introduced the names of these notes, it's possible to start talking about their associated frequencies or pitches. Table 10-1 gives the approximate frequencies for the C4 Major scale (the notes from C4 to B4).

Table 10-1. Frequencies for the C4 major scale

Note name	Frequency (in Hz)
C4	261.63
C#4	277.18
D4	293.66
D#4	311.13
E4	329.63
F4	349.23
F#4	369.99
G4	392.00
G#4	415.30
A4	440.00
A#4	466.16
B4	493.88

When I move to the next octave, the frequencies double for all the notes; for instance, C5 will be 523.26 Hz. The preceding octave contains frequencies that are halved, so C3 will be 130.82 Hz.

A table showing all piano note names and their frequencies can be found at *http://www.phys.unsw.edu.au/~jw/notes.html*. It includes the corresponding MIDI numbers, which I consider later in this chapter.

Playing a Note

A note can be played by generating its associated frequency and providing an amplitude for loudness. But how can this approach be implemented in terms of a byte array suitable for a SourceDataLine?

A pure note is a single sine wave, with a specified amplitude and frequency, and this sine wave can be represented by a series of samples stored in a byte array. The idea is shown in Figure 10-3.

This is a simple form of analog-to-digital conversion. So, how is the frequency converted into a given number of samples, i.e., how many lines should the sample contain?

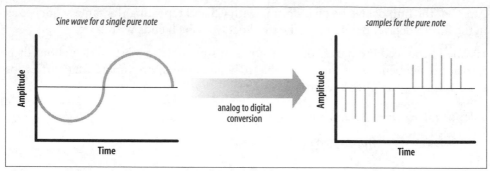

Figure 10-3. From single note to samples

A `SourceDataLine` is set up to accept a specified audio format, which includes a sample rate. For example, a sample rate of 21,000 causes 21,000 samples to reach the mixer every second. The frequency of a note, e.g., 300 Hz, means that 300 copies of that note will reach the mixer per second.

The number of samples required to represent a single note is one of the following

```
samples/note  = (samples/second) / (notes/sec)
samples/note  =  sample rate / frequency
```

For the previous example, a single note would need 21,000/300 = 70 samples. In other words, the sine wave must consist of 70 samples. This approach is implemented in sendNote( ) in the *NotesSynth.java* application, which is explained next.

Synthesizing Notes

NotesSynth generates simple sounds at runtime without playing a clip. The current version outputs an increasing pitch sequence, repeated nine times, each time increasing a bit faster and with decreasing volume.

 NotesSynth.java is stored in *SoundExamps/SynthSound/*.

Here is the main( ) method:

```
public static void main(String[] args)
{ createOutput( );
  play( );
  System.exit(0);    // necessary for J2SE 1.4.2 or earlier
}
```

createOutput( ) opens a SourceDataLine that accepts stereo, signed PCM audio, utilizing 16 bits per sample in little-endian format. Consequently, 4 bytes must be used for each sample:

```
// globals
private static int SAMPLE_RATE = 22050;      // no. of samples/sec
```

```
    private static AudioFormat format = null;
    private static SourceDataLine line = null;



    private static void createOutput()
    {
      format = new AudioFormat(AudioFormat.Encoding.PCM_SIGNED,
                               SAMPLE_RATE, 16, 2, 4, SAMPLE_RATE, false);
    /* SAMPLE_RATE    // samples/sec
       16          // sample size in bits, values can be -2^15 - 2^15-1
       2           // no. of channels, stereo here
       4           // frame size in bytes (2 bytes/sample * 2 channels)
       SAMPLE_RATE    // same as frames/sec
       false       // little endian     */

      System.out.println("Audio format: " + format);

      try {
        DataLine.Info info = new DataLine.Info(SourceDataLine.class, format);
        if (!AudioSystem.isLineSupported(info)) {
          System.out.println("Line does not support: " + format);
          System.exit(0);
        }
        line = (SourceDataLine) AudioSystem.getLine(info);
        line.open(format);
      }
      catch (Exception e)
      {  System.out.println( e.getMessage());
         System.exit(0);
      }
    }  // end of createOutput()
```

play( ) creates a buffer large enough for the samples, plays the pitch sequence using sendNote( ), and then closes the line:

```
    private static void play()
    {
      // calculate a size for the byte buffer holding a note
      int maxSize = (int) Math.round((SAMPLE_RATE * format.getFrameSize())/MIN_FREQ);
                       // the frame size is 4 bytes
      byte[] samples = new byte[maxSize];

      line.start();

      /* Generate an increasing pitch sequence, repeated 9 times, each
         time increasing a bit faster, and the volume decreasing */
      double volume;
      for (int step = 1; step < 10; step++)
        for (int freq = MIN_FREQ; freq < MAX_FREQ; freq += step) {
          volume = 1.0 - (step/10.0);
          sendNote(freq, volume, samples);
        }
```

```
     // wait until all data is played, then close the line
     line.drain();
     line.stop();
     line.close();
   } // end of play()
```

maxSize must be big enough to store the largest number of samples for a generated note, which occurs when the note frequency is the smallest. Therefore, the MIN_FREQ value (250 Hz) is divided into SAMPLE_RATE.

Creating samples

sendNote() translates a frequency and amplitude into a series of samples representing that note's sine wave. The samples are stored in a byte array and sent along the SourceDataLine to the mixer:

```
// globals
private static double MAX_AMPLITUDE = 32760;       // max loudness
                // actual max is 2^15-1, 32767, since I'm using
                // PCM signed 16 bit

// frequence (pitch) range for the notes
private static int MIN_FREQ = 250;
private static int MAX_FREQ = 2000;

// Middle C (C4) has a frequency of 261.63 Hz; see Table 10-1


private static void sendNote(int freq, double volLevel, byte[] samples)
{
  if ((volLevel < 0.0) || (volLevel > 1.0)) {
    System.out.println("Volume level should be between 0 and 1, using 0.9");
    volLevel = 0.9;
  }
  double amplitude = volLevel * MAX_AMPLITUDE;

  int numSamplesInWave = (int) Math.round( ((double) SAMPLE_RATE)/freq );
  int idx = 0;
  for (int i = 0; i < numSamplesInWave; i++) {
    double sine = Math.sin(((double) i/numSamplesInWave) *
                                         2.0 * Math.PI);
    int sample = (int) (sine * amplitude);
    // left sample of stereo
    samples[idx + 0] = (byte) (sample & 0xFF);          // low byte
    samples[idx + 1] = (byte) ((sample >> 8) & 0xFF);   // high byte
    // right sample of stereo (identical to left)
    samples[idx + 2] = (byte) (sample & 0xFF);
    samples[idx + 3] = (byte) ((sample >> 8) & 0xFF);
    idx += 4;
  }

  // send out the samples (the single note)
  int offset = 0;
```

```
    while (offset < idx)
      offset += line.write(samples, offset, idx-offset);
  }
```

numSamplesInWave is obtained by using the calculation described above, which is to divide the note frequency into the sample rate.

A sine wave value is obtained with Math.sin( ) and split into two bytes since 16-bit samples are being used. The little-endian format determines that the low-order byte is stored first, followed by the high-order one. Stereo means that I must supply two bytes for the left speaker, and two for the right; in my case, the data are the same for both.

Extending NotesSynth

A nice addition to NotesSynth would be to allow the user to specify notes with note names (e.g., C4, F#6), and translate them into frequencies before calling sendNote( ). Additionally, play( ) is hardwired to output the same tones every time it's executed. It would be easy to have it read a notes files, perhaps written using note names, to play different tunes.

Another important missing element is timing. Each note is played immediately after the previous note. It would be better to permit periods of silence as well.

 Consider these challenges more than deficiencies. It's easy to implement this functionality in NotesSynth.

MIDI Synthesis

I'll consider three approaches to synthesizing MIDI sound at runtime:

- Send note-playing messages to a MIDI channel. The MidiChannel class offers noteOn( ) and noteOff( ) methods that transmit NOTE_ON and NOTE_OFF MIDI messages.

- Send MIDI messages to the synthesizer's receiver port. This is a generalization of the first approach. The advantages include the ability to deliver messages to different channels, and the ability to send a wider variety of messages.

- Create a sequence, which is passed to the sequencer. This is a generalization of the second approach. Rather than send individual notes to the synthesizer, I build a complete sequence.

These approaches are labeled in the MIDI devices diagram in Figure 10-4.

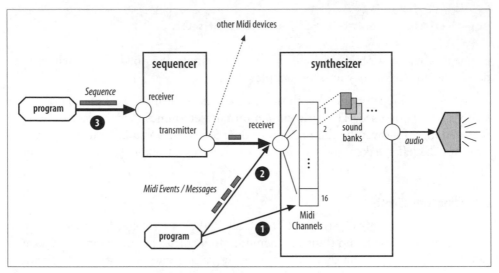

Figure 10-4. Different MIDI synthesis approaches

There is a good Java Tech Tip on these topics at *http://java.sun.com/jdc/JDCTechTips/2003/tt0805.html*.

Sending Note-Playing Message to a MIDI Channel

The MidiChannel class offers noteOn( ) and noteOff( ) methods that correspond to the NOTE_ON and NOTE_OFF MIDI messages:

```
void noteOn(int noteNumber, int velocity);
void noteOff(int noteNumber, int velocity);
void noteOff(int noteNumber);
```

The note number is the MIDI number assigned to a musical note, and velocity is equivalent to the loudness. A note will keep playing after a noteOn( ) call until it's terminated with noteOff( ). The two-argument form of noteOff( ) can affect how quickly the note fades away.

MIDI notes can range between 0 and 127, extending well beyond the piano's scope, which includes 88 standard keys. This means that the note-naming scheme gets a little strange below note 12 (C0) since we have to start talking about octave −1 (e.g., (see the table *at http://www.harmony-central.com/MIDI/Doc/table2.html*). Additionally, a maximum value of 127 means that note names only go up to G9; there is no G#9. Table 10-2 shows the mapping of MIDI numbers to notes for the fourth octave.

Table 10-2. MIDI numbers and note names

MIDI number	Note name
60	C4
61	C#4
62	D4
63	D#4
64	E4
65	F4
66	F#4
67	G4
68	G#4
69	A4
70	A#4
71	B4

 A table showing the correspondence between MIDI numbers and note names can be found at *http://www.phys.unsw.edu.au/~jw/notes.html*.

A channel is obtained in the following way:

```
Synthesizer synthesizer = MidiSystem.getSynthesizer( );
synthesizer.open( );
MidiChannel drumChannel = synthesizer.getChannels( )[9];
```

Channel 9 plays different percussion and audio effect sounds depending on the note numbers sent to it.

Playing a note corresponds to sending a NOTE_ON message, letting it play, and then killing it with a NOTE_OFF message. This can be wrapped up in a playNote( ) method:

```
public void playNote(int note, int duration)
{
  drumChannel.noteOn(note, 70);  // 70 is the volume level
  try {
    Thread.sleep(duration*1000);    // secs --> ms
  }
  catch (InterruptedException e) {}
  drumChannel.noteOff(note);
}
```

The following will trigger applause:

```
for (int i=0; i < 10; i++)
  playNote(39, 1);  // 1 sec duration for note 39
```

Note 39, used here as an example, corresponds to a hand clap sound. A list of the mappings from MIDI numbers to drum sounds can be found at *http://www.midi.org/about-midi/gm/gm1sound.shtml*.

MidiChannel supports a range of useful methods aside from noteOn( ) and noteOff( ), including setMute( ), setSolo( ), setOmni( ), and setPitchBend( ). The two MidiChannel.programChange( ) methods allow the channel's instrument to be changed, based on its bank and program numbers:

```
synthesizer.getChannels( )[0].programChange(0, 15);
    /* change the instrument used by channel 0 to
       a dulcimer - located at bank 0, program 15 */
```

Instruments and soundbanks are explained in more detail later in this chapter.

Sending MIDI Messages to the Synthesizer's Receiver Port

This approach is functionally similar to the channel technique in the last section, except that I use MIDI messages directly. The advantages include the ability to direct messages to different channels and send more kinds of messages than just NOTE_ON and NOTE_OFF.

Lists of MIDI messages can be found at *http://www.borg.com/~jglatt/tech/midispec.htm* and *http://users.chariot.net.au/~gmarts/midi.htm*.

The receiver port for the synthesizer is obtained first:

```
Synthesizer synthesizer = MidiSystem.getSynthesizer( );
synthesizer.open( );
Receiver receiver = synthesizer.getReceiver( );
```

As before, sending a note is two messages, separated by a delay to give the note time to play. You can conclude this logic in another version of the playNote(|) method:

```
public void playNote(int note, int duration, int channel)
{
  ShortMessage msg = new ShortMessage( );
  try {
    msg.setMessage(ShortMessage.NOTE_ON, channel, note, 70);
                           // 70 is the volume level
    receiver.send(msg, -1);  // -1 means play immediately

    try {
      Thread.sleep(duration*1000);
    } catch (InterruptedException e) {}
```

```
      // reuse the ShortMessage object
      msg.setMessage(ShortMessage.NOTE_OFF, channel, note, 70);
      receiver.send(msg, -1);
    }
    catch (InvalidMidiDataException e)
    { System.out.println(e.getMessage()); }
}
```

The receiver expects MIDI events, so the MIDI message must be sent with a time-stamp. -1, used here, means that the message should be processed immediately.

The following sets up more applause:

```
for (int i=0; i < 10; i++)
  playNote(39, 1, 9); // note 39 sent to the drum channel, 9
```

A drawback with this technique, and the previous one, is the timing mechanism, which depends on the program sleeping. It would be better if the synthesizer managed the time spacing of MIDI messages by working with MIDI events that use real timestamps (called *tick values*). This approach is explained later in the chapter.

Control change messages

The FadeMidi and PanMidi examples in Chapter 9 show how to access channel controllers via the synthesizer and MIDI channels, such as in this example:

```
MidiChannel[] channels = synthesizer.getChannels();

// Set the volume controller for channel 4 to be full on (127)
int channelVol = channels[4].getController(VOLUME_CONTROLLER);
channels[4].controlChange(VOLUME_CONTROLLER, 127);
```

Another approach is to construct a MIDI message aimed at a particular channel and controller and to send it to the synthesizer's receiver.

```
// Set the volume controller for channel 4 to be full on (127)
ShortMessage volMsg = new ShortMessage();
volMsg.setMessage(ShortMessage.CONTROL_CHANGE, 4, VOLUME_CONTROLLER, 127);
receiver.send(volMsg, -1);
```

The second argument of the ShortMessage.setMessage() is the channel ID (an index between 0 and 15, not 1 and 16), the third argument is the channel controller ID, and the fourth is the message value itself.

Creating a Sequence

Rather than send individual notes to the synthesizer, the SeqSynth application creates a complete sequence that is passed to the sequencer and then to the synthesizer.

The generation of a complete sequence is preferable if the music is going to be longer than just a few notes. However, this technique requires the programmer to understand the internals of a sequence. A graphical representation of a sequence's structure is given in Figure 10-5.

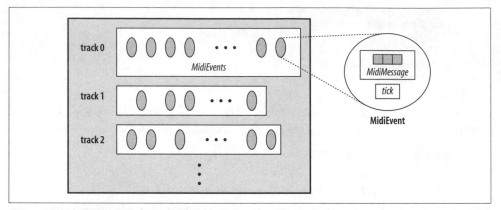

Figure 10-5. The internals of a MIDI sequence

SeqSynth plays the first few notes of "As Time Goes By" from the movie *Casablanca*. The application can be found in the directory *SoundExamps/SynthSound/*.

 The original MIDI note sequence was written by Heinz M. Kabutz (see *http://www.javaspecialists.co.za/archive/Issue076.html*).

The application constructs a sequence of MidiEvents containing NOTE_ON and NOTE_OFF messages for playing notes, and PROGRAM_CHANGE and CONTROL_CHANGE messages for changing instruments. The speed of playing is specified in terms of the ticks per beat (also called pulses per quarter [PPQ] note) and beats/minute (the tempo setting). The sequence only communicates with channel 0 (i.e., it only uses one musician), but this could be made more flexible.

Notes can be expressed as MIDI numbers or as note names (e.g., F4#). See *http://www.phys.unsw.edu.au/~jw/notes.html* for a chart linking the two. This support for note names by SeqSynth is the beginning of an application that could translate a text-based score into music.

Here's SeqSynth's constructor:

```
public SeqSynth( )
{
  createSequencer( );
  // listInstruments( );
  createTrack(4);        // 4 is the PPQ resolution

  makeSong( );
  // makeScale(21);      // the key is "A0"

  startSequencer(60);    // tempo: 60 beats/min

  // wait for the sound sequence to finish playing
  try {
```

```
    Thread.sleep(600000);    // 10 mins in ms
  }
  catch(InterruptedException e)
  { System.out.println("Sleep Interrupted"); }
  System.exit(0);
} // end of SeqSynth( )
```

createSequencer( ) is nothing new: It initializes the sequencer and synthesizer objects, which are assigned to global variables.

Instruments and soundbanks

listInstruments( ) is a utility for listing all the instruments currently available to the synthesizer. The range of instruments depends on the currently loaded soundbank. The default soundbank is *soundbank.gm*, located in *$J2SE_HOME/jre/lib/audio* and *$J2RE_HOME/lib/audio*. It's possible to change soundbanks, for example, to improve the quality of the instruments. This is explained in the *Java Tech Tip* at *http://java.sun.com/developer/JDCTechTips/2004/tt0309.html*.

A soundbank, which is shown as a gray rectangle in Figure 10-4, can be viewed as a 2D-array, as in Figure 10-6.

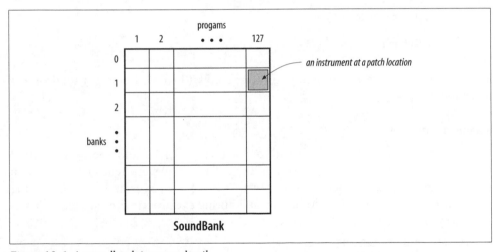

Figure 10-6. A soundbank in more detail

Each box in the soundbank is an instrument (represented by an Instrument object), with its array location stored in a Patch object. To utilize an instrument at runtime, it must be referred to using its Patch details. A patch holds two values: a bank number and a program number.

The General MIDI specification defines a set of instrument names that must be supported in bank 0, for program numbers 0 to 127 (e.g., see *http://www.midi.org/about-midi/gm/gm1sound.shtml*). These will be available on all MIDI synthesizers. The contents of banks 1, 2, etc., can vary.

Even within bank 0, only the names are prescribed, not the actual sound, so the output can differ from one synthesizer to another.

The General MIDI specification actually talks about banks 1–128 and programs 1–128, while Java uses 0–127 for bank and program numbers. For example, the dulcimer is in bank 1, program 16 in the specification, but it is accessed using <0,15> in Java.

Listing instruments

listInstruments( ) prints out the names and patch details for the extensive set of instruments in the default soundbank:

```
private void listInstruments( )
{
  Instrument[] instrument = synthesizer.getAvailableInstruments( );
  System.out.println("No. of Instruments: " + instrument.length);
  for (int i=0; i < instrument.length; i++) {
    Patch p = instrument[i].getPatch( );
    System.out.print("(" + instrument[i].getName( ) +
               " <" + p.getBank( ) + "," + p.getProgram( ) + ">) ");
    if (i%3 ==0)
      System.out.println( );
  }
  System.out.println( );
} // end of listInstruments( )
```

The output on my machine reports on four banks (0 to 3), holding a total of 411 instruments.

Making a sequence

createTrack( ) creates a sequence with a single empty track and specifies its MIDI event timing to be in ticks per beat (PPQ). This allows its tempo to be set in startSequencer( ) using Sequencer.setTempoInBPM( ). (BPM stands for beats per minute.) It permits the tempo to be changed during execution with methods such as Sequencer.setTempoFactor( ):

```
private void createTrack(int resolution)
{ try {
    sequence = new Sequence(Sequence.PPQ, resolution);
  }
  catch (InvalidMidiDataException e) {
    e.printStackTrace( );
  }
  track = sequence.createTrack( );  // track is global
}
```

The other common timestamp format is based on ticks per frame and FPS.

makeSong( ) fills the sequence's single track with MIDI events. In this case, the code is concerned with reproducing the first few notes of "As Time Goes By":

```java
private void makeSong()
{ changeInstrument(0,33);     // set bank and program; bass
  addRest(7);

  add("F4"); add("F4#"); add("F4"); add("D4#");
  add("C4#"); add("D4#", 3);  add("F4"); add("G4#");
  add("F4#"); add("F4"); add("D4#"); add("F4#", 3);
  add("G4#"); add("C5#"); add("C5"); add("A4#");
  add("G4#"); add("A4#", 4); add("G4", 4); add("G4#", 2);

  changeInstrument(0,15);   // dulcimer
  addRest(1);

  add("C5"); add("D5#"); add("C5#"); add("C5"); add("A4#");
  add("C5", 2); add("C5#", 2); add("G4#", 2); add("G4#", 2);
  add("C4#", 2); add("D4#", 2); add("C4#", 2);

  addRest(1);
}
```

changeInstrument( ) is supplied with bank and program numbers to switch the instrument. addRest( ) inserts a period of quiet into the sequence, equal to the supplied number of ticks. add( ) adds a note, with an optional tick duration parameter.

Commented out in *SeqSynth.java* is a simpler example; makeScale( ) plays a rising scale followed by a falling one:

```java
private void makeScale(int baseNote)
{
  for (int i=0; i < 13; i++) {   // one octave up
    add(baseNote);
    baseNote++;
  }
  for (int i=0; i < 13; i++) {   // one octave down
    add(baseNote);
    baseNote--;
  }
}
```

makeScale( ) is called with the MIDI number 21 (note A0), and subsequent notes are calculated using addition and subtraction. This version of add( ) takes an integer argument rather than a string.

For the musically adept out there, this is a useful feature. In any key, you can calculate the notes of the scale numerically and not worry about note names. For example, a major scale is whole step (+2 from the root of the scale), whole step (+2), half step (+1), whole step (+2), whole step (+2), whole step (+2), half step (+1). Using those numerical values is a lot easier than remembering if E# is part of the C# major scale.

Playing the sequence

startSequencer( ) is the final method called from the constructor. It plays the sequence built in the preceding call to makeSong( ) (or makeScale( )):

```
private void startSequencer(int tempo)
/* Start the sequence playing.
   The tempo setting is in BPM (beats per minute),
   which is combined with the PPQ (ticks / beat)
   resolution to determine the speed of playing. */
{
  try {
    sequencer.setSequence(sequence);
  }
  catch (InvalidMidiDataException e) {
    e.printStackTrace( );
  }
  sequencer.addMetaEventListener(this);
  sequencer.start( );
  sequencer.setTempoInBPM(tempo);
} // end of startSequencer( )


public void meta(MetaMessage meta)
// called when a meta event occurs during sequence playing
{
  if (meta.getType( ) == END_OF_TRACK) {
    System.out.println("End of the track");
    System.exit(0);    // not required in J2SE 5.0
  }
}
```

startSequence( ) sets the tempo and adds a meta-event listener. The listener calls meta( ) when the track finishes playing, allowing the application to exit immediately instead of waiting for the full 10 minutes allocated by the constructor.

The add( ) methods

The add( ) methods must deal with note name or MIDI number input and with an optional note-playing period:

```
// global used to timestamp the MidiEvent messages
private int tickPos = 0;
```

```
private void add(String noteStr)
{  add(noteStr, 1);  }

private void add(int note)
{ add(note, 1);  }

private void add(String noteStr, int period)
// convert the note string to a numerical note, then add it
{ int note = getKey(noteStr);
  add(note, period);
}

private void add(int note, int period)
{ setMessage(ShortMessage.NOTE_ON, note, tickPos);
  tickPos += period;
  setMessage(ShortMessage.NOTE_OFF, note, tickPos);
}

private void addRest(int period)
// this will leave a period of no notes (i.e., silence) in the track
{ tickPos += period; }
```

The note name is converted into a MIDI number with getKey( ). The core add( )
method takes a MIDI number and tick period, and it creates two MIDI events with
setMessage( )—one a NOTE_ON message and the other a NOTE_OFF. These events are
timestamped, so they are separated by the required interval.

setMessage( ) builds a MIDI message, places it inside a MIDI event, and adds it to
the track:

```
// globals
private static final int CHANNEL = 0;  // always use channel 0
private static final int VOLUME = 90;  // fixed volume for notes

private void setMessage(int onOrOff, int note, int tickPos)
{
  if ((note < 0) || (note > 127)) {
    System.out.println("Note outside MIDI range (0-127): " + note);
    return;
  }

  ShortMessage message = new ShortMessage( );
  try {
    message.setMessage(onOrOff, CHANNEL, note, VOLUME);
    MidiEvent event = new MidiEvent(message, tickPos);
    track.add(event);
  }
  catch (InvalidMidiDataException e) {
    e.printStackTrace( );
  }
} // end of setMessage( )
```

Changing an instrument

changeInstrument( ) is supplied with the bank and program numbers of the instrument that should be used by the channel from this point on:

```
private void changeInstrument(int bank, int program)
{
  Instrument[] instrument = synthesizer.getAvailableInstruments( );

  for (int i=0; i < instrument.length; i++) {
    Patch p = instrument[i].getPatch( );
    if ((bank == p.getBank( )) && (program == p.getProgram( ))) {
      programChange(program);
      bankChange(bank);
      return;
    }
  }
  System.out.println("No instrument of type <" + bank +
                                      "," + program + ">");
}
```

 The validity of these two numbers are checked before they're processed.

Program and bank change

programChange( ) places a PROGRAM_CHANGE MIDI message onto the track:

```
private void programChange(int program)
{
  ShortMessage message = new ShortMessage( );
  try {
    message.setMessage(ShortMessage.PROGRAM_CHANGE, CHANNEL, program, 0);
                         // the second data byte (0) is unused
    MidiEvent event = new MidiEvent(message, tickPos);
    track.add(event);
  }
  catch (InvalidMidiDataException e) {
    e.printStackTrace( );
  }
}
```

bankChange( ) is similar but uses the bank selection channel controller (number 0), so a CONTROL_CHANGE message is placed on the track:

```
// global
// channel controller name for changing an instrument bank
private static final int BANK_CONTROLLER = 0;

private void bankChange(int bank)
{
  ShortMessage message = new ShortMessage( );
  try {
```

```
          message.setMessage(ShortMessage.CONTROL_CHANGE,
                             CHANNEL, BANK_CONTROLLER, bank);
        MidiEvent event = new MidiEvent(message, tickPos);
        track.add(event);
      }
      catch (InvalidMidiDataException e) {
        e.printStackTrace();
      }
    }
}
```

From note name to MIDI number

The note name syntax used by SeqSynth is simple, albeit nonstandard. Only one letter-single octave combination is allowed (e.g., "C4," "A0"), so it's not possible to refer to the −1 octave. A sharp can be included, but only after the octave number (e.g., "G4#"); the normal convention is that a sharp follows the note letter. No notation for flats is included here though you can represent any flatted note with the "sharped" version of the note below it; for example, D flat is equivalent to C sharp.

The calculations done by getKey( ) use several constants:

```
private static final int[] cOffsets = {9, 11, 0, 2, 4, 5, 7};
                          // A   B  C  D  E  F  G

private static final int C4_KEY = 60;
      // C4 is the "C" in the 4th octave on a piano

private static final int OCTAVE = 12;    // note size of an octave
```

The note offsets in cOffsets[ ] use the C Major scale, which is ordered C D E F G A B, but the offsets are stored in an A B C D E F G order to simplify their lookup by getKey( ).

getKey( ) calculates a MIDI note number by examining the note letter, octave number, and optional sharp character in the supplied string:

```
private int getKey(String noteStr)
/* Convert a note string (e.g., "C4", "B5#" into a key. */
{
  char[] letters = noteStr.toCharArray();

  if (letters.length < 2) {
    System.out.println("Incorrect note syntax; using C4");
    return C4_KEY;
  }

  // look at note letter in letters[0]
  int c_offset = 0;
  if ((letters[0] >= 'A') && (letters[0] <= 'G'))
    c_offset = cOffsets[letters[0] - 'A'];
  else
    System.out.println("Incorrect: " + letters[0] + ", using C");
```

```
    // look at octave number in letters[1]
    int range = C4_KEY;
    if ((letters[1] >= '0') && (letters[1] <= '9'))
      range = OCTAVE * (letters[1] - '0' + 1);
    else
      System.out.println("Incorrect: " + letters[1] + ", using 4");

    // look at optional sharp in letters[2]
    int sharp = 0;
    if ((letters.length > 2) && (letters[2] == '#'))
      sharp = 1;     // a sharp is 1 note higher
    int key = range + c_offset + sharp;

    return key;
  } // end of getKey()
```

Extending SeqSynth

SeqSynth would be more flexible if it could read song operations (i.e., a score) from a text file instead of having those operations hard-coded and passed into methods such as makeSong( ).

The range of musical notation understood by SeqSynth could be enlarged. For example, David Flanagan's PlayerPiano application from *Java Examples in a Nutshell* (O'Reilly) covers similar ground to SeqSynth and supports flats, chords (combined notes), volume control, and the damper pedal (*http://www.onjava.com/pub/a/onjava/excerpt/jenut3_ch17/index1.html*). The resulting sequence can be played or saved to a file.

Several ASCII notations represent scores, such as the abc language (*http://www.gre.ac.uk/~c.walshaw/abc/*). abc is widely used for notating and distributing music. Many tools exist for playing abc notated music, converting it into MIDI sequences or sheet music, and so on. Wil Macaulay has written Skink, a Java application, which supports the abc 1.6 standard with some extensions. It can open, edit, save, play, and display abc files (*http://www.geocities.com/w_macaulay/skink.html*). Skink generates a MIDI sequence using similar techniques as in SeqSynth.

Audio Synthesis Libraries

The sampled audio synthesis carried out by NotesSynth and the MIDI sequence generation in SeqSynth could be expanded to turn the applications into general-purpose synthesis tools, classes, or libraries. However, Java audio synthesis libraries exist but not as part of J2SE.

JSyn (*http://www.softsynth.com/jsyn/*) generates sound effects by employing inter-connected unit generators. It includes an extensive library of generators, including oscillators, filters, envelopes, and noise generators. For example, a wind sound can be built by connecting a white noise generator to a low pass filter modulated by a random contour generator. JSyn comes with a graphical editor, called Wire, for connecting unit generators together. The result can be exported as Java source code.

jMusic (*http://jmusic.ci.qut.edu.au/*) is aimed at musicians rather than engineers. Its libraries provide a music data structure based around note and sound events, with associated methods. jMusic can read and write MIDI and audio files.

CHAPTER 11

Sprites

A game's active entities are often encoded as sprites. A *sprite* is a moving graphical object, which may represent the player (and so respond to key presses and mouse actions) or may be driven by "intelligent" code in the game. The Sprite class developed in this chapter holds a sprite's position, its speed (coded as incremental steps in the x and y directions), and it uses the image classes (ImagesLoader, ImagesPlayer) from Chapter 6 to manage its graphical presence. Sprite's subclasses add user and environmental interactions and audio effects. The coding of these classes is helped by specifying them first with UML statecharts.

Many elements are utilized from earlier chapters: the animation framework from Chapters 2 and 3, the image loader classes from Chapter 6, and the audio loaders from Chapter 8.

Bats, Balls, and Sprites

The BugRunner example allows the user to control a sprite in the shape of an ant. The objective is to move the sprite left and right across the base of the gaming pane to stop falling ball sprites from hitting the floor. Figure 11-1 shows BugRunner in action.

The screenshot is a little misleading because the futuristic cityscape and the flying car are part of the game's background image and aren't active elements in the game. The gameplay components are the ant at the bottom of the screen and the falling yellow and red ball near the center of the panel.

The ant is controlled with the arrow keys or by clicking with the mouse. The left arrow key makes the ant move to the left, the right arrow key makes it go right, and the down key stops it. If the mouse is clicked when the cursor is to the left of the ant, it makes the ant walk to the left; when the cursor is to the ant's right, then the ant will go right. The ant's legs even move as it walks.

Figure 11-1. The BugRunner application

Once the ant is set in motion, it continues moving until its direction is changed or it is stopped. When the ant reaches the left or right walls, it continues walking off screen until it has disappeared and then appears again at the other edge.

To make things more interesting, a ball is dropped at varying speeds and trajectories from the top of the panel. If the ball touches a wall, it rebounds. If the ball reaches the floor, it continues off screen, and the number of returns is decremented. This number is displayed in the top-left corner of the screen as a total out of 16. When it drops to 0, the game is over.

If the player manages to position the ant under the ball, it will rebound, and the number of returns will be incremented as the ball disappears off the top. When the number of returns reaches 16, the game finishes. The ant sprite is being used as a bat (in the sense of a tennis bat) to prevent the ball from reaching the floor.

 One ball is sent falling at a time, and the ball graphic varies each time, cycling through several possibilities.

A MIDI sequence (the *BladeRunner* theme by Vangelis) is continuously played in the background, and various thumps, bangs, and boings are heard when the ball hits the walls or the ant. The game finishes with applause (no matter what the score).

The ant images come from the SpriteLib sprite library by Ari Feldman at *http://www.arifeldman.com/games/spritelib.html*.

Class Diagrams for BugRunner

Figure 11-2 shows the class diagrams for BugRunner application. The class names and public methods are given for the new classes, but only class names are supplied for the imaging and audio classes, which are unchanged from earlier chapters.

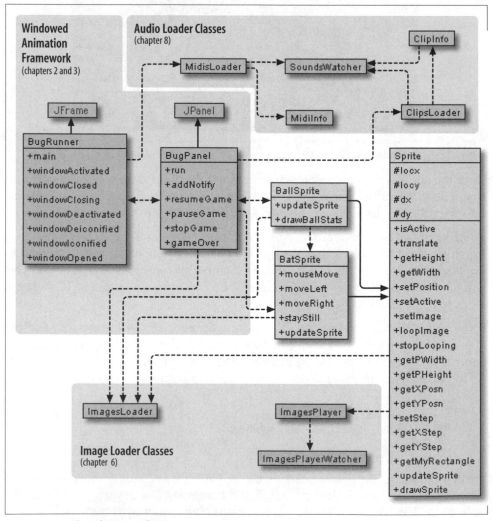

Figure 11-2. Class diagrams for BugRunner

The image and audio loader classes won't be explained again in any detail, so if you've skipped ahead to this chapter, you may want to go back and review Chapters 6 and 8.

The top-level JFrame (BugRunner) and the games panel (BugPanel) use the windowed animation framework developed in Chapters 2 and 3. In particular, the complicated run() method in BugPanel is almost identical to the one in WormPanel in Chapter 3. If you're unfamiliar with it, then you should look at Chapter 3 before continuing.

The new material is mostly concentrated in the Sprite class and its subclasses, BallSprite and BatSprite. BallSprite manages each ball, and BatSprite handles the ant.

The choice of the name BatSprite may seem a tad strange since the sprite image is an ant. Bat refers to the ant's role in the game,, i.e., to bat away balls and stop them from reaching the floor. In truth, the accompanying image could be anything: a mockingbird, Guadalupe bass, armadillo, or longhorn.

The code for the BugRunner game can be found in the *BugRunner/* directory.

The Bug Starts Running

BugRunner fixes the frame rate to be 40 FPS; anything faster makes it almost impossible to move the ant quickly enough to intercept a dropping ball.

The application's constructor loads and starts the *BladeRunner* sequence:

```
// load the background MIDI sequence
midisLoader = new MidisLoader();
midisLoader.load("br", "blade_runner.mid");
midisLoader.play("br", true);   // repeatedly play it
```

Since BugRunner plays one sequence at a time, it's loaded directly via a call to load() rather than being specified in a MIDI information file. MidisLoader assumes the sequence is in the *Sounds/* subdirectory.

Using a well-known piece of music, like the *BladeRunner* theme, is a bad idea for a game intended for widespread distribution. The thorny issue of copyright is bound to come up. I've thrown caution to the wind since *BladeRunner* is one of my favorite sci-fi movies, and the music is great.

BugRunner sets up window listener methods for pausing and resuming the game in a similar manner to the WormChase application in Chapter 3. windowClosing( ) is different:

```
public void windowClosing(WindowEvent e)
{  bp.stopGame( );
   midisLoader.close( );
}
```

The call to close( ) in MidisLoader ensures the sequence is stopped at termination time.

The Animation Framework

BugPanel is a subclass of JPanel that implements the animation framework described in Chapters 2 and 3; BugPanel closely resembles the WormPanel class. The constructor sets up keyboard and mouse listeners, prepares the ImagesLoader and ClipsLoader objects, and creates the bat and ball sprites:

```
public BugPanel(BugRunner br, long period)
{
  bugTop = br;
  this.period = period;

  setDoubleBuffered(false);
  setBackground(Color.black);
  setPreferredSize( new Dimension(PWIDTH, PHEIGHT));

  setFocusable(true);
  requestFocus( );     // now has focus, so receives key events

  addKeyListener( new KeyAdapter() {
    public void keyPressed(KeyEvent e)
    { processKey(e);  }   // handle key presses
  });

  // load the background image
  ImagesLoader imsLoader = new ImagesLoader(IMS_INFO);
  bgImage = imsLoader.getImage("bladerunner");

  // initialise the clips loader
  clipsLoader = new ClipsLoader(SNDS_FILE);

  // create game sprites
  bat = new BatSprite(PWIDTH, PHEIGHT, imsLoader,
                              (int)(period/1000000L) ); // in ms
  ball = new BallSprite(PWIDTH, PHEIGHT, imsLoader,
                          clipsLoader, this, bat);

  addMouseListener( new MouseAdapter() {
    public void mousePressed(MouseEvent e)
    { testPress(e.getX()); }  // handle mouse presses
  });
```

```
      // set up message font
      msgsFont = new Font("SansSerif", Font.BOLD, 24);
      metrics = this.getFontMetrics(msgsFont);

    } // end of BugPanel()
```

The image loaded by ImagesLoader is stored in the global bgImage and later used as the game's background image (see Figure 11-1).

BladeRunner fans will recognize the background image as a still from the movie, so would be another source of copyright problems in a commercial game.

The ClipsLoader object is stored in BugPanel and passes as an argument to the ball sprite, which plays various clips when its ball hits the walls or bat. The clips information file SNDS_FILE (*clipsInfo.txt*) is assumed to be in the *Sounds/* subdirectory. It contains:

```
hitBat jump.au
hitLeft clack.au
hitRight outch.au
gameOver clap.wav
```

The gameOver clip is used by BugPanel when the game finishes; the others are utilized by BallSprite.

User Interaction

The game panel supports user input via the keyboard and mouse, which is dealt with by processKey( ) and testPress( ). They are attached to the listeners in the BugPanel() constructor.

processKey( ) handles two kinds of key operations: those related to termination (e.g., Ctrl-C) and those affecting the ant (the arrow keys):

```
private void processKey(KeyEvent e)
{
  int keyCode = e.getKeyCode();

  // termination keys
  if ((keyCode==KeyEvent.VK_ESCAPE) || (keyCode==KeyEvent.VK_Q) ||
      (keyCode == KeyEvent.VK_END) ||
      ((keyCode == KeyEvent.VK_C) && e.isControlDown()) )
    running = false;

  // game-play keys
  if (!isPaused && !gameOver) {
    if (keyCode == KeyEvent.VK_LEFT)
      bat.moveLeft();
    else if (keyCode == KeyEvent.VK_RIGHT)
      bat.moveRight();
```

```
    else if (keyCode == KeyEvent.VK_DOWN)
      bat.stayStill( );
  }
} // end of processKey( )
```

The game-related keys are normally mapped to calls to BatSprite methods but are ignored if the game has been paused or finished. These extra tests aren't applied to the termination keys since it should be possible to exit the game, whatever its current state.

testPress( ) passes the cursor's x-coordinate to BatSprite to determine which way to move the ant:

```
private void testPress(int x)
{ if (!isPaused && !gameOver)
    bat.mouseMove(x);
}
```

The Animation Loop

BugPanel implements the Runnable interface, allowing its animation loop to be placed in the run( ) method. run( ) is almost the same as the one in the WormPanel class without the overheads of FPS statistics gathering:

```
public void run( )
/* The frames of the animation are drawn inside the while loop. */
{
  long beforeTime, afterTime, timeDiff, sleepTime;
  long overSleepTime = 0L;
  int noDelays = 0;
  long excess = 0L;

  gameStartTime = J3DTimer.getValue( );
  beforeTime = gameStartTime;

  running = true;

  while(running) {
    gameUpdate( );
    gameRender( );
    paintScreen( );

    afterTime = J3DTimer.getValue( );
    timeDiff = afterTime - beforeTime;
    sleepTime = (period - timeDiff) - overSleepTime;

    if (sleepTime > 0) {    // some time left in this cycle
      try {
        Thread.sleep(sleepTime/1000000L);  // nano -> ms
      }
      catch(InterruptedException ex){}
      overSleepTime = (J3DTimer.getValue( ) - afterTime) - sleepTime;
    }
```

```
    else {      // sleepTime <= 0; frame took longer than period
      excess -= sleepTime;  // store excess time value
      overSleepTime = 0L;

      if (++noDelays >= NO_DELAYS_PER_YIELD) {
        Thread.yield();   // give another thread a chance to run
        noDelays = 0;
      }
    }

    beforeTime = J3DTimer.getValue();

    /* If frame animation is taking too long, update the game state
       without rendering it, to get the updates/sec nearer to
       the required FPS. */
    int skips = 0;
    while((excess > period) && (skips < MAX_FRAME_SKIPS)) {
      excess -= period;
      gameUpdate();      // update state but don't render
      skips++;
    }
  }
  System.exit(0);    // so window disappears
} // end of run()
```

 The Java 3D timer is used mainly because it's an excellent timer for J2SE 1.4.2 across a range of platforms. However, as J2SE 5.0 gains popularity, a better choice may be System.nanoTime( ). Porting the code is a matter of replacing calls to J3DTimer.getValue( ) with System.nanoTime( ).

The application-specific elements of the animation are located in gameUpdate( ) and gameRender( ). A new gameStartTime variable is initialized at the start of run( ); it's used later to calculate the elapsed time displayed in the game panel.

gameUpdate( ) updates the active game entities—the ball and bat sprites:

```
private void gameUpdate()
{ if (!isPaused && !gameOver) {
    ball.updateSprite();
    bat.updateSprite();
  }
}
```

gameRender( ) draws the background, the sprites, and the game statistics (the number of rebounds and the elapsed time):

```
private void gameRender()
{
  if (dbImage == null){
    dbImage = createImage(PWIDTH, PHEIGHT);
    if (dbImage == null) {
      System.out.println("dbImage is null");
      return;
```

```
   }
   else
      dbg = dbImage.getGraphics();
}

// draw the background: use the image or a black screen
if (bgImage == null) {  // no background image
   dbg.setColor(Color.black);
   dbg.fillRect (0, 0, PWIDTH, PHEIGHT);
}
else
   dbg.drawImage(bgImage, 0, 0, this);

// draw game elements
ball.drawSprite(dbg);
bat.drawSprite(dbg);

reportStats(dbg);

if (gameOver)
   gameOverMessage(dbg);
}  // end of gameRender()
```

gameUpdate( ) and gameRender( ) show the main way that the sprites are utilized. First their states are updated via calls to updateSprite( ), and then they're drawn by invoking drawSprite( ).

reportStats( ) calculates and renders the current time and the number of rebounds:

```
private void reportStats(Graphics g)
{
   if (!gameOver)    // stop incrementing timer once game is over
      timeSpentInGame =
         (int) ((J3DTimer.getValue() - gameStartTime)/1000000000L);
                  // ns --> secs

   g.setColor(Color.yellow);
   g.setFont(msgsFont);

   ball.drawBallStats(g, 15, 25);  // ball sprite reports ball stats
   g.drawString("Time: " + timeSpentInGame + " secs", 15, 50);

   g.setColor(Color.black);
}
```

The number of rebounds is reported by the ball sprite, which is passed the graphics context in the drawBallStats( ) call.

Finishing the Game

The game is terminated when the gameOver boolean is set to true. This stops any further updates to the active entities via gameUpdate( ) and disables the processing of keyboard and mouse actions. However, the screen is still periodically redrawn, and the background music keeps playing until the application is closed.

The gameOver boolean is set by the BallSprite object calling gameOver( ) in BugPanel:

```
public void gameOver()
{ int finalTime =
        (int) ((J3DTimer.getValue() - gameStartTime)/1000000000L);
                    // ns --> secs
  score = finalTime;   // could be more fancy!
  clipsLoader.play("gameOver", false);   // play clip once
  gameOver = true;
}
```

A score is calculated and the gameOver clip (polite applause) is played.

Defining a Sprite

A general-purpose Sprite class is hard to design since many of its features depend on the application and the gaming context.

For example, a sprite's on-screen movement greatly depends on the type of game. In Tetris, Breakout, and Space Invaders (and many more), the sprite moves within the gaming area while the background scenery remains stationary. In some of these games, the sprite may be unable to move beyond the edges of the panel, while in others it can wrap around to the opposite edge. In side-scrolling games, such as Super Mario, the sprite hardly moves (perhaps only up and down); instead the background shifts behind it.

A sprite must monitor the game environment, for example, reacting to collisions with different sprites or stopping when it encounters an obstacle. Collision processing can be split into two basic categories: collision detection and collision response, with the range of responses being application specific. Many varieties of collision detection exist: a sprite may be represented by a single bounding box, a reduced size bounding box, or several bounding areas. Examples of each are shown in Figure 11-3 where the bounding regions are the dashed boxes around the pigeon and donkey.

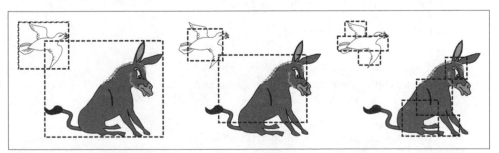

Figure 11-3. Three types of collision detection

A single bounding box is simple to manipulate but prone to inaccuracy. The reduced bounding box is better, but choosing a suitable reduction factor is difficult. The greatest accuracy can be achieved with several boxes for each sprite at the expense of additional calculations.

Sometimes a 2D sprite will have a z-coordinate (or z-level) that dictates its drawing position (or order) on screen, which the user perceives as depth. For instance, if two sprites have the same z-level, then they'll be unable to move past each other, so they will collide. However, a sprite with a smaller z-level is conceptually "in front" of a sprite with a larger z-level, so can pass by without collision. Sprites are drawn in decreasing z-level order, so sprites in the foreground appear in front of those further back.

The visual appearance of a sprite typically changes over time in response to important events (e.g., being shot out of the sky) or by cycling through a series of images (e.g., moving its arms and legs as it walks about). Associated audio effects (e.g., a gunshot sound) may be triggered by events, or played periodically.

Coding a Sprite

The Sprite class is simple, storing little more than the sprite's current position, its speed specified as step increments in the x- and y- directions, with imaging managed by ImagesLoader and ImagesPlayer objects. The ImagesPlayer class allows the sprite to show a sequence of images repeatedly since this is how the ant moves its legs.

The Sprite subclasses, BatSprite and BallSprite in BugRunner, manage user interactions, environment concerns (e.g., collision detection and response), and audio effects. These elements are too application specific to be placed in Sprite.

The Sprite Constructor

A sprite is initialized with its position, the size of the enclosing panel, an ImagesLoader object, and the name of an image:

```
// default step sizes (how far to move in each update)
private static final int XSTEP = 5;
private static final int YSTEP = 5;


private ImagesLoader imsLoader;
private int pWidth, pHeight;   // panel dimensions


// protected vars
protected int locx, locy;      // location of sprite
protected int dx, dy;          // amount to move for each update
```

```
public Sprite(int x, int y, int w, int h, ImagesLoader imsLd, String name)
{ locx = x; locy = y;
  pWidth = w; pHeight = h;
  dx = XSTEP; dy = YSTEP;
  imsLoader = imsLd;
  setImage(name);     // the sprite's default image is 'name'
}
```

The sprite's coordinate (locx, locy) and its step values (dx, dy) are stored as integers. This simplifies certain tests and calculations but restricts positional and speed precision. For instance, a ball can't move 0.5 pixels at a time.

 The alternative is to use floats or doubles to hold the coordinates and velocities. However, this adds complexity and is unnecessary in this example. floats would be useful when the calculations require greater accuracy, for example, for rotations using matrix multiplication.

locx, locy, dx, and dy are protected rather than private due to their widespread use in Sprite subclasses. They have getter and setter methods, so they can be accessed and changed by objects outside of the Sprite hierarchy.

Sprite only stores (x, y) coordinates: there's no z-coordinate or z-level; such functionality is unnecessary in BugRunner. Simple z-level functionality can be achieved by ordering the calls to drawSprite( ) in gameRender( ). Currently, the code is simply:

```
ball.drawSprite(dbg);
bat.drawSprite(dbg);
```

The ball is drawn before the bat, so will appear behind it if they happen to overlap on-screen. In an application where you had 5, 10, or more sprites, this won't work, especially if the objects move in a way that changes their z-level.

A Sprite's Image

setImage( ) assigns the named image to the sprite:

```
// default dimensions when there is no image
private static final int SIZE = 12;


// image-related globals
private ImagesLoader imsLoader;
private String imageName;
private BufferedImage image;
private int width, height;     // image dimensions

private ImagesPlayer player;   // for playing a loop of images
private boolean isLooping;
```

```
public void setImage(String name)
{
  imageName = name;
  image = imsLoader.getImage(imageName);
  if (image == null) {    // no image of that name was found
    System.out.println("No sprite image for " + imageName);
    width = SIZE;
    height = SIZE;
  }
  else {
    width = image.getWidth();
    height = image.getHeight();
  }
  // no image loop playing
  player = null;
  isLooping = false;
}
```

setImage( ) is a public method, permitting the sprite's image to be altered at runtime.

An ImagesPlayer object, player, is available to the sprite for looping through a sequence of images. Looping is switched on with the loopImage( ) method:

```
public void loopImage(int animPeriod, double seqDuration)
{
  if (imsLoader.numImages(imageName) > 1) {
    player = null;    // for garbage collection of previous player
    player = new ImagesPlayer(imageName, animPeriod, seqDuration,
                                    true, imsLoader);
    isLooping = true;
  }
  else
    System.out.println(imageName + " is not a sequence of images");
}
```

The total time for the loop is seqDuration seconds. The update interval (supplied by the enclosing animation panel) is animPeriod milliseconds.

Looping is switched off with stopLooping( ):

```
public void stopLooping()
{ if (isLooping) {
    player.stop();
    isLooping = false;
  }
}
```

A Sprite's Bounding Box

Collision detection and collision response is left to subclasses. However, the bounding box for the sprite is available through the getMyRectangle( ) method:

```
public Rectangle getMyRectangle()
{  return  new Rectangle(locx, locy, width, height);  }
```

Sprite uses the simplest form of bounding box, but it wouldn't be difficult to introduce a reduction factor. The reduced bounded box would have a smaller width and height and would need to be positioned so its center coincided with the center of the image's full-size bounding rectangle.

Updating a Sprite

A sprite is updated by adding its step values (dx, dy) to its current location (locx, locy):

```
// global
private boolean isActive = true;
// a sprite is updated and drawn only when active


public void updateSprite()
{
  if (isActive()) {
    locx += dx;
    locy += dy;
    if (isLooping)
      player.updateTick();   // update the player
  }
}
```

The isActive boolean allows a sprite to be (temporarily) removed from the game since the sprite won't be updated or drawn when isActive is false. There are public isActive() and setActive() methods for manipulating the boolean.

No attempt is made in updateSprite() to test for collisions with other sprites, obstacles, or the edges of the gaming pane. These must be added by the subclasses when they override updateSprite().

Sprites are embedded in an animation framework that works hard to maintain a fixed frame rate. run() calls updateSprite() in all the sprites at a frequency as close to the specified frame rate as possible. For example, if the frame rate is 40 FPS (as it is in BugRunner), then updateSprite() will be called 40 times per second in each sprite.

This allows me to make assumptions about a sprite's update timing. For instance, if the x-axis step value (dx) is 10, then the sprite will be moved 10 pixels in each update. This corresponds to a speed of $10 \times 40 = 400$ pixels per second along that axis. This calculation is possible because the frame rate is tightly constrained to 40 FPS.

An alternative approach is to call updateSprite() with an argument holding the elapsed time since the previous call. This time value can be multiplied to a velocity value to get the step amount for this particular update. This technique is preferably in animation frameworks, where the frame rate can vary during execution.

Drawing a Sprite

The animation loop will call updateSprite( ) in a sprite, followed by drawSprite( ) to draw it:

```
public void drawSprite(Graphics g)
{
  if (isActive( )) {
    if (image == null) {    // the sprite has no image
      g.setColor(Color.yellow);    // draw a yellow circle instead
      g.fillOval(locx, locy, SIZE, SIZE);
      g.setColor(Color.black);
    }
    else {
      if (isLooping)
        image = player.getCurrentImage( );
      g.drawImage(image, locx, locy, null);
    }
  }
}
```

If the image is null, then the sprite's default appearance is a small yellow circle. The current image in the looping series is obtained by calling ImagesPlayer's getCurrentImage( ) method.

Specifying a Sprite with a Statechart

A sprite is a reactive object: it responds dynamically to events, changing its state and modifying its behavior. For all but the simplest example, specify the sprite's behavior before becoming entangled in writing code. The UML statechart is an excellent tool for defining a sprite, and there are even utilities for automatically generating Java code from statecharts.

The rest of this section gives a brief introduction to statecharts and explains how they can be translated to Java. However, this isn't a book about UML, so I refer the interested reader to *UML Distilled* (Addison-Wesley Professional) by Martin Fowler. For a UML text with a Java slant, check out *UML for Java Programmers* (Prentice Hall) by Robert C. Martin (*http://www.objectmentor.com*). Martin's web site offers SMC, a translator that takes textual statechart information and generates Java (or C++) code.

A simple statechart for a subway turnstile is shown in Figure 11-4. (This example comes from a tutorial by Robert C. Martin.)

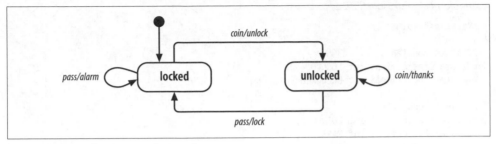

Figure 11-4. A subway turnstile statechart

The states are inside rounded rectangles; the transitions (arrows) indicate how the system responds to events. The syntax for a transition is:

```
event [ condition ] / action
```

An event arrives when the system is in a given state, causing the associated transition to be executed. First, the condition is evaluated if one is present. If the result is true, the associated action is carried out and the system follows the transition to a new state. The solid black circle points to the starting state for the system.

The statechart in Figure 11-4 specifies what happens when a pass or coin event occurs in the locked or unlocked states for a turnstile. A coin event corresponds to a customer placing a coin in the turnstile; a pass event is generated when the turnstile rotates to allow the customer to pass through.

Statecharts can be more sophisticated than this example. For instance, they can represent activities carried out when a state is entered and exited, states can be nested to form hierarchies, states can be grouped together to model concurrent actions, and there is a history mechanism.

Translating a Statechart to Code

There are various approaches for translating a statechart into executable code. One of the simplest is to convert the graphical notation into table form, called a State Transition Table (STT). Table 11-1 shows the STT for the turnstile statechart.

Table 11-1. Turnstile STT

Current state	Event	Action	New state
Locked	Coin	Unlock	Unlocked
Locked	Pass	Alarm	Locked
Unlocked	Coin	Thanks	Unlocked
Unlocked	Pass	Lock	Locked

An imperative-style translation of the table converts it to a series of if statements (see makeTransition( ) in Example 11-1).

Example 11-1. Turnstile STT as code

```java
public class TurnStile
{
  // state constants
  private static final int LOCKED = 0;
  private static final int UNLOCKED = 1;

  // event constants
  private static final int COIN = 2;
  private static final int PASS = 3;


  public static void main(String args[])
  {
    int currentState = LOCKED;
    int event;
    while (true) {
      event = /* get the next event */;
      currentState = makeTransition(currentState, event);
    }
  } // end of main( )


  private static int makeTransition(int state, int event)
  // a translation of Table 1
  {
    if ((state == LOCKED) && (event == COIN)) {
      unlock( );
      return UNLOCKED;
    }
    else if ((state == LOCKED) && (event == PASS)) {
      alarm( );
      return LOCKED;
    }
    else if ((state == UNLOCKED) && (event == COIN)) {
      thanks( );
      return UNLOCKED;
    }
    else if ((state == UNLOCKED) && (event == PASS)) {
      lock( );
      return LOCKED;
    }
    else {
      System.out.println("Unknown state event");
      System.exit(0);
    }
  } // end of makeTransition( )


  // methods for the actions: unlock, alarm, thanks, lock

} // end of Turnstile class
```

The translation strategy is to represent states and events as integers and transition actions as method calls. If a transition has a condition, it will be added to the if-test for that transition. The drawback of this approach is the generation of long sequences of if tests, often with multiple conditions. Fortunately, the code can often be rewritten to make it easier to understand, e.g., makeTransition( ) could be divided into several smaller methods.

As states become more complex (e.g., hierarchical, with internal activities), it's more natural to map a state to a class and a transition to a method. The SMC translator takes this approach (*http://www.objectmentor.com/resources/downloads/*).

A third coding solution is to employ a set of existing statechart classes (e.g., State, Transition), subclassing them for the particular application. Excellent examples of this approach can be found in *Practical Statecharts in C/C++* (CMP Books) by Miro Samek (*http://www.quantum-leaps.com*). As the book's title suggests, its emphasis is on C and C++, but the author's web site contains a Java version of the software, which requires a password generated from the book.

The Ball Sprite

I begin with a textual specification of what a ball sprite should do, then I will translate this into a statechart, and then manually convert it into BallSprite, a subclass of Sprite.

Textual Specification

In the following discussion, I'll refer to the ant sprite as the bat, since that's its function: the ant is used to knock away balls, preventing them from reaching the floor.

The ball drops from the top of the panel at varying speeds and angles of trajectory. It'll bounce off a wall if it hits one, reversing its x-axis direction. If the ball hits the bat, it will rebound and disappear off the top of the panel. If the ball passes the bat, it will disappear through the panel's base.

 Remember, bat refers to the ant—which could be drawn as anything, but always functions as a bat.

After leaving the panel, the ball is reused: it's placed back at the top of the panel and put into motion again. The image associated with the ball is changed.

The number of returned balls is incremented when the ball bounces off the bat (numRebounds is incremented). When the ball drops off the bottom, numRebounds is decremented. If `numRebounds` reaches `MAX_BALLS_RETURNED`, the game is over. If `numRebounds` reaches 0, the game also terminates.

Sound effects are played when the ball hits the walls and the bat.

Statechart Specification

The statechart in Figure 11-5 specifies the actions of the ball sprite.

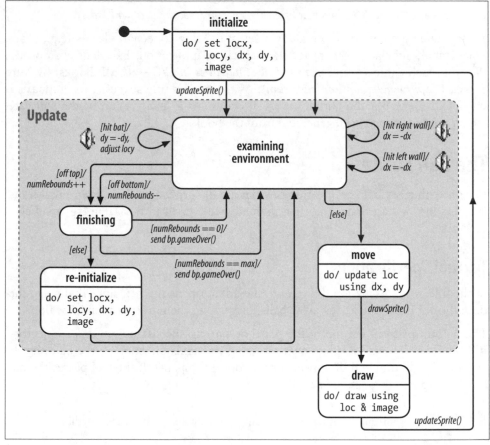

Figure 11-5. The BallSprite statechart

The statechart uses an update *superstate*, which is a state that encapsulates the states that modify the sprite's location, step sizes, and other values before the ball is moved and drawn. The *update* superstate highlights the sprite's update/draw cycle, which is driven by the method calls `updateSprite()` and `drawSprite()`, originating from `BugPanel`'s animation loop.

A do/ activity inside a state is carried out as the sprite occupies that state.

The "do" is what the state "does" when execution is in that state.

The *examining environment* state deals with the unusual situations that may occur as the ball descends through the JPanel. The transitions leaving examining environment are triggered by tests on the sprite's current location. Hitting the left or right walls causes a change in direction along the x-axis. Moving past the top or bottom edges of the panel places the ball in a finishing state. This may result in the sprite notifying the BugPanel object (bp) that the game is over or the ball may be reused. When none of the special environmental conditions apply, the sprite is moved and redrawn.

The speaker icons next to the *[hit bat]*, *[hit right wall]*, and *[hit left wall]* conditional transitions indicate that a sound effect will be played when the condition evaluates to true.

Translating the Statechart

The *initialize* state is covered by BallSprite's constructor:

```
// images used for the balls
private static final String[] ballNames =
            {"rock1", "orangeRock", "computer", "ball"};

// reach this number of balls to end the game
private static final int MAX_BALLS_RETURNED = 16;


// globals
private ClipsLoader clipsLoader;
private BugPanel bp;
private BatSprite bat;
private int numRebounds;



public BallSprite(int w, int h, ImagesLoader imsLd, ClipsLoader cl,
                                    BugPanel bp, BatSprite b)
{ super( w/2, 0, w, h, imsLd, ballNames[0]);
   // the ball is positioned in the middle at the top of the panel
  clipsLoader = cl;
  this.bp = bp;
  bat = b;

  nameIndex = 0;
  numRebounds = MAX_BALLS_RETURNED/2;
      // the no. of returned balls starts half way to the maximum
  initPosition( );
}
```

The names of four ball images are fixed in ballNames[]; they are the names of four GIF files stored in the *Images/* subdirectory.

BallSprite stores a reference to the BugPanel so it can notify the panel when the game is over. The BatSprite reference is used for collision detection (carried out by the *[hit bat]* condition for the examining environment). The ClipsLoader reference enables the sprite to play sounds when it hits the bat or rebounds from the walls.

The numRebounds variable performs the same task as the variable in the statechart. It begins with a value halfway between 0 and the maximum number of returns required for winning the game.

initPosition( ) initializes the ball's image, position and step values:

```
private void initPosition()
{
  setImage( ballNames[nameIndex]);
  nameIndex = (nameIndex+1)%ballNames.length;

  setPosition( (int)(getPWidth() * Math.random()), 0);
                            // somewhere along the top

  int step = STEP + getRandRange(STEP_OFFSET);
  int xStep = ((Math.random() < 0.5) ? -step : step);
                                  // move left or right
  setStep(xStep, STEP + getRandRange(STEP_OFFSET));   // move down
}


private int getRandRange(int x)
// random number generator between -x and x
{   return ((int)(2 * x * Math.random())) - x;  }
```

setImage( ), setPosition( ), and setStep( ) are all methods inherited from Sprite.

Updating the sprite

The update superstate is represented by an overridden updateSprite( ):

```
public void updateSprite()
{
  hasHitBat();
  goneOffScreen();
  hasHitWall();

  super.updateSprite();
}
```

The calls to hasHitBat( ), goneOffScreen( ), and hasHitWall( ) roughly correspond to the examining environment, finishing, and reinitialize states and transitions, while the call to Sprite's updateSprite( ) implements the *move* state.

The looping behavior of the examining environment has been simplified to a sequential series of tests. This is possible since the special conditions (e.g., hit a wall, hit the bat) don't occur more than once during a single update and are independent of each other. However, such optimizations should be done carefully to avoid changing the sprite's intended behavior.

hasHitBat( ) implements the *[hit bat]* conditional transition:

```
private void hasHitBat( )
{
  Rectangle rect = getMyRectangle( );
  if (rect.intersects( bat.getMyRectangle( ) )) {  // bat collision?
    clipsLoader.play("hitBat", false);
    Rectangle interRect = rect.intersection(bat.getMyRectangle( ));
    dy = -dy;        // reverse ball's y-step direction
    locy -= interRect.height;    // move the ball up
  }
}
```

Collision detection is a matter of seeing if the bounding boxes for the ball and the bat intersect. A sound effect is played if they overlap and the ball is made to bounce by having its y-step reversed.

The ball's y-axis location is moved up slightly so it no longer intersects the bat. This rules out the (slim) possibility that the collision test of the ball and bat during the next update will find them still overlapping. This would occur if the rebound velocity were too small to separate the objects within one update.

 The collision algorithm could be improved. For instance, some consideration could be given to the relative positions and speeds of the ball and bat to determine the direction and speed of the rebound. This would complicate the coding but improve the ball's visual appeal.

Hitting a wall

hasHitWall( ) handles the *[hit right wall]* and *[hit left wall]* conditional transitions:

```
private void hasHitWall( )
{
  if ((locx <= 0) && (dx < 0)) {  // touching lhs and moving left
    clipsLoader.play("hitLeft", false);
    dx = -dx;    // move right
  }
  else if ((locx+getWidth( ) >= getPWidth( )) && (dx > 0)) {
                              // touching rhs and moving right
    clipsLoader.play("hitRight", false);
    dx = -dx;    // move left
  }
}
```

hasHitWall() is made easier to understand by having it directly referring to the sprite's x-axis location (locx) and step sizes (dx and dy). They are protected variables, inherited from Sprite.

The if tests illustrate a common form of testing: a combination of location and direction tests. It isn't enough to examine the sprite's location; you must determine whether the sprite is heading out of the panel. This will correctly exclude a recently rebounded sprite, which is still near an edge but moving away from it.

A subtle coding assumption is that the boundaries of the BufferedImage correspond to the visible edges of the image on the screen. For example, a sprite surrounded by a large transparent border, as shown in Figure 11-6, would not seem to be touching the panel's left edge when its top-left x-coordinate (locx) is at pixel 0.

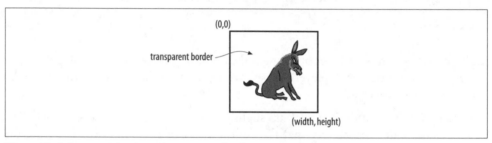

Figure 11-6. Image with a large transparent border

The simplest solution is to ensure that images are cropped to have as small a transparent border as possible. Alternatively, bounding box calculations could use a reduction factor to shrink the bounding region.

Leaving the screen

goneOffScreen() implements the *[off top]* and *[off bottom]* conditional transitions and implements the *finishing* and *re-initialize* states connected to them:

```
private void goneOffScreen()
{
  if (((locy+getHeight()) <= 0) && (dy < 0)) {
    numRebounds++;         // off top and moving up
    if (numRebounds == MAX_BALLS_RETURNED)
      bp.gameOver();       // finish
    else
      initPosition();      // start the ball in a new position
  }
  else if ((locy >= getPHeight()) && (dy > 0)) {
    numRebounds--;         // off bottom and moving down
    if (numRebounds == 0)
      bp.gameOver();
    else
      initPosition();
  }
}
```

The finishing state and its exiting transitions have been mapped to the bodies of the if tests. The reinitialize state has been implemented by reusing initPosition(), which is part of the initialize code.

Drawing the sprite

The draw state in BallSprite's statechart has no equivalent method in the BallSprite class. It's handled by the inherited drawSprite() method from Sprite.

Defining the Bat

I'll define and implement the bat in the same way as the ball sprite. I'll write a textual specification of what a bat should do, translate it into a statechart, and then manually convert it into BatSprite, a subclass of Sprite. Once again, I'll refer to the ant sprite as a bat since that's what it does; that's why its class is BatSprite. The ant image is irrelevant to the game play since it could be anything.

Textual Specification

The bat can only move horizontally across the floor, controlled by arrow keys and mouse presses. Once the bat is set in motion, it continues moving until its direction is changed or it is stopped. As the bat leaves one side of the panel, it appears on the other side. The bat is assigned a left-facing and right-facing set of images (a walking ant), which are cycled through as the bat moves.

Statechart Specification

A statechart for BatSprite's actions appears in Figure 11-7.

The new statechart element in Figure 11-7 is the concurrent state diagram with two concurrent sections: user-based reactions and time-based reactions. Concurrent state diagrams allow the modeling of concurrent activities using this section notation. Concurrent activities are present in all sprites controlled by the user.

The time-based reactions section illustrates the update/draw cycle carried out by the animation loop. The user-based reactions section encapsulates the changes made to the sprite by the user pressing the arrow keys and/or the mouse. A move right transition occurs when the user presses the right arrow key or clicks the mouse to the right of the bat. The move left transition handles the left arrow key and a mouse press to the left of the bat. The stop transition deals with the down arrow key and a mouse press over the bat. The implementation of user-based reactions uses listener methods, which are processed in Swing's event thread. This means there's no need for explicit threaded coding in the BatSprite class.

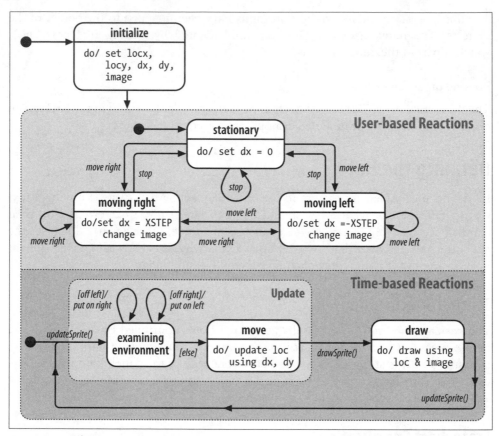

Figure 11-7. The BatSprite statechart

The statechart nicely highlights an important issue with user-controlled sprites: the concurrent sharing of data between the animation loop and the event processing code. The statechart shows that the shared data will be the sprite's x-axis step size (dx) and the current image.

Translating the Statechart

The initialize state is covered by BatSprite's constructor:

```
// globals
private static final int FLOOR_DIST = 41;
    // distance of ant's top from the floor


private int period;
  /* in ms. The game's animation period used by the image
     cycling of the bat's left and right facing images. */
```

```
public BatSprite(int w, int h, ImagesLoader imsLd, int p)
{
  super( w/2, h-FLOOR_DIST, w, h, imsLd, "leftBugs2");
      // positioned at the bottom of the panel, near the center
  period = p;
  setStep(0,0);   // no movement
}
```

User-based reactions

The key presses that trigger move left, move right, and stop events are caught by
BugPanel's key listener, which calls processKey( ). Inside processKey( ), the code for
responding to the arrow keys is:

```
if (!isPaused && !gameOver) {
  if (keyCode == KeyEvent.VK_LEFT)
    bat.moveLeft( );
  else if (keyCode == KeyEvent.VK_RIGHT)
    bat.moveRight( );
  else if (keyCode == KeyEvent.VK_DOWN)
    bat.stayStill( );
}
```

moveLeft( ) implements the moving left state in Figure 11-7:

```
// global
private static final int XSTEP = 10;
    // step distance for moving along x-axis


public void moveLeft( )
{ setStep(-XSTEP, 0);
  setImage("leftBugs2");
  loopImage(period, DURATION);    // cycle through leftBugs2 images
}
```

> *leftBugs2* is the name for a GIF file in *Images/*, which contains an
> image strip of ants walking to the left.

moveRight( ) handles the moving right state in Figure 11-7:

```
public void moveRight( )
{ setStep(XSTEP, 0);
  setImage("rightBugs2");
  loopImage(period, DURATION);   // cycle through the images
}
```

The stationary state is encoded by stayStill( ):

```
public void stayStill( )
{ setStep(0, 0);
  stopLooping( );
}
```

This translation of the statechart is possible because of a property of the events. A move left event always enters the moving left state, a move right event always enters moving right, and stop always goes to the stationary state. This means that I don't need to consider the current state to determine the next state when a given event arrives; the next state is always determined solely by the event.

Mouse responses

Move left, move right, and stop events can be triggered by mouse actions. BugPanel employs a mouse listener to call testPress() when a mouse press is detected:

```
private void testPress(int x)
{ if (!isPaused && !gameOver)
    bat.mouseMove(x);
}
```

BatSprite's mouseMove() calls one of its move methods depending on the cursor's position relative to the bat:

```
public void mouseMove(int xCoord)
{
  if (xCoord < locx)  // click was to the left of the bat
    moveLeft();        // make the bat move left
  else if (xCoord > (locx + getWidth()))  // click was to the right
    moveRight();       // make the bat move right
  else
    stayStill();
}
```

Time-based reactions

The update superstate in the time-based reactions section is coded by overriding updateSprite() (in a similar way to in BallSprite):

```
public void updateSprite()
{
  if ((locx+getWidth() <= 0) && (dx < 0))    // almost gone off lhs
    locx = getPWidth()-1;      // make it just visible on the right
  else if ((locx >= getPWidth()-1)&&(dx>0)) // almost gone off rhs
    locx = 1 - getWidth();     // make it just visible on the left

  super.updateSprite();
}
```

The looping behavior of the examining environment has been simplified so that the *[off left]* and *[off right]* conditional transitions are implemented as two sequential if tests. The move state is handled by calling Sprite's updateSprite().

The draw state in BatSprite's statechart has no equivalent method in the BatSprite class. As in BallSprite, it's handled by the inherited drawSprite() method from Sprite.

Concurrently shared data

BatSprite makes no attempt to synchronize the accesses made to the data shared between the user-based reactions and time-based reactions sections. The shared data is the sprite's x-axis step size (dx), and the current image.

The step size is modified by moveLeft( ), moveRight( ), and stayStill( ) when they call the inherited setStep( ) method. Possibly at the same time, the step is used by Sprite's updateSprite( ) method.

Fortunately, Java guarantees that an assignment to a variable (other than a long or double) is atomic, as is the accessing of the variable's value. This means that simple reads and writes of variables (other than longs and doubles) won't interfere with each other.

moveLeft( ) and moveRight( ) assign a new object to the image reference by calling the inherited setImage( ) method. Meanwhile, in Sprite, drawSprite( ) passes the reference to drawImage( ) to draw the image on the screen. This amounts to a simple assignment and a dereference of the variable, both of which will be atomic, so they won't interfere with each other.

Concurrent state diagrams highlight synchronization issues in sprite design, which will always be present when the sprite can be updated by the user and affected by the game at the same time. The decision on whether to add synchronization code to the implementation depends on tradeoffs between speed and safety. Locking and unlocking code at runtime will affect the speed, especially for operations being carried out 50 times (or more) a second.

CHAPTER 12
A Side-Scroller

The player's sprite in a side-scrolling game usually travels left or right through a landscape that extends well beyond the limits of the gaming pane. The landscape scrolls past in the background while the player jumps (or perhaps flies) over various obstacles and bad guys, landing safely on platforms to collect treasure, food, or rescue Princess Peach. Of course, the quintessential side-scroller is *Super Mario Bros.*, still available today in many versions on many platforms.

Most side-scrollers implement their backgrounds using *tile maps*: the tiles can be square, rectangular, or any shape once transparent GIFs are brought in. Tiles can be unchanging blocks, animated, or they can behave like (clever) sprites.

Backgrounds are often composed of several tile map *layers*, representing various background and foreground details. They may employ *parallax scrolling*, in which layers "further back" in the scene scroll past at a slower rate than layers nearer the front.

 Tiling is a versatile technique: *Super Mario* (and its numerous relatives) present a side view of the game world, but tiles can offer bird's eye viewpoints looking down on the scene from above and can offer isometric views, as in *Civilization*, to create a pseudo-3D environment. You'll see how to implement a basic isometric game in Chapter 13.

This chapter describes JumpingJack, a side-scroller in the *Super Mario* mold—albeit considerably simpler—that illustrates tile maps, layers, parallax scrolling, and a jumping hero called Jack who has to dodge exploding fireballs.

JumpingJack has some unusual elements: the foreground is a tile map, which Jack scrambles over, but the other layers are large GIFs. The background layers and tiles wrap around the drawing area, so if Jack travels long enough he returns to his starting point. An introductory startup screen doubles as a help screen, toggled by pressing "h."

Two screenshots of JumpingJack are shown in Figure 12-1.

Figure 12-1. Two JumpingJack screenshots

The arrow keys make Jack move left, right, stand still, and jump. Once Jack starts moving (when the user presses the left or right arrow keys), he keeps moving until he hits a brick. To prevent him from stopping, the user should press the jump key (up arrow) to make him hop over bricks in his path.

Fireballs shoot out from the right edge of the panel, heading to the left, unaffected by bricks in their way. If a fireball hits Jack, the number of hits reported in the top-left of the panel is incremented; when it reaches 20, the game is over and a score is reported. (As a slight relief, only a single fireball is shot at Jack at a time, which simplifies the coding).

An instrumental version of "Jumping Jack Flash" by The Rolling Stones repeatedly plays in the background, occasionally punctuated by an explosion audio clip when a fireball hits Jack.

JumpingJack in Layers

The easiest way of understanding JumpingJack's coding design is to consider the graphical layers making up the on-screen image. Figure 12-2 shows the various parts, labeled with the classes that represent them.

The scenic background is made from three GIFs (*mountains.gif*, *houses.gif*, and *trees.gif* in *Images/*), all wider than the JPanel, and moving at different speeds behind the bricks layer and sprites. The images are drawn to the JPanel in back-to-front order and are easily combined since *houses.gif* and *trees.gif* contain large transparent areas. Each image is maintained by a Ribbon object, and these are collectively managed by a RibbonsManager object.

The bricks layer is composed of bricks, positioned on the screen according to a bricks map created by the programmer. Each brick is assigned a GIF, which can be any rectangular shape. Other shapes can be faked by using transparency, showing only a portion of the rectangle. Each brick is represented by a Brick object, grouped

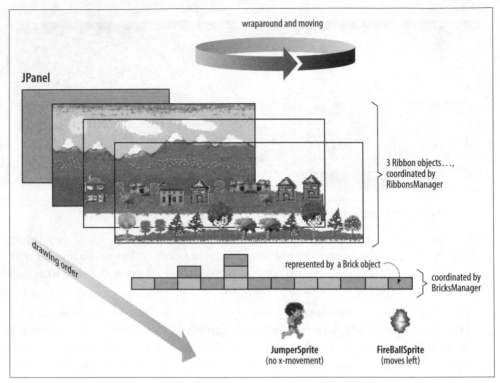

Figure 12-2. The visual layers in JumpingJack

together and managed by BricksManager. The brick layer is wider than the JPanel and wraps around in a similar way to the Ribbon backgrounds. Jack walks or jumps over the bricks.

A strange feature of side-scrollers, which is hard to believe unless you watch a game carefully, is that the hero sprite often doesn't move in the x-direction. The sprite's apparent movement is achieved by shifting the background. For example, when Jack starts going right, he doesn't move at all (aside from his little legs flapping). Instead, the scenery (the GIF ribbons and the bricks layer) move left. Similarly, when Jack appears to move left, it's the scenery moving right.

When Jack jumps, the sprite moves up and down over the space of one to two seconds. However, the jump's arc is an illusion caused by the background moving.

Class Diagrams for JumpingJack

Figure 12-3 shows the class diagrams for the JumpingJack application. Only the class names are shown.

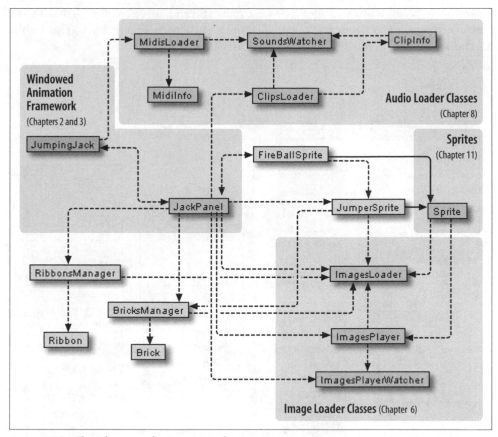

Figure 12-3. Class diagrams for JumpingJack

 This large number of classes is daunting, but many of them can be ignored since they're unchanged from earlier chapters.

The image loaders read in the GIFs used by the Ribbon objects and by the tile and sprite images. ImagesPlayer animates Jack's legs and the fireball explosion. The audio loaders play the "Jumping Jack Flash" MIDI sequence, the explosion, and the applause clips. (Always applaud the users even when they lose.)

The JumperSprite object handles Jack, and FireBallSprite handles the fireball; both are subclasses of the Sprite class that were introduced in Chapter 11. The JumpingJack JFrame and the JackPanel JPanel implement the windowed animation framework of Chapters 2 and 3. BugRunner of Chapter 11 uses the same technique.

If you strip away the unchanged classes from earlier chapters, you're left with the more manageable collection of class diagrams shown in Figure 12-4. The public methods, and any public or protected data, are shown.

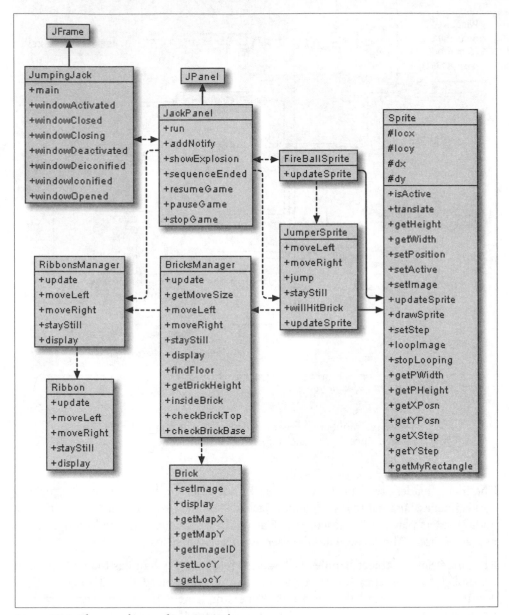

Figure 12-4. The core classes of JumpingJack

The Sprite class is included since JumperSprite and FireBallSprite use many of its methods, but it's unchanged from Chapter 11.

The code for the JumpingJack example can be found in *JumpingJack/*.

Start Jack Jumping

JumpingJack fixes the frame rate at 30 FPS; anything faster makes it almost impossible to control Jack. The illusion of speed is governed by how fast the bricks and image ribbons move, which is controlled by a single moveSize variable in the BricksManager class. moveSize specifies the distance that the bricks layer should be shifted in each update of the animation loop.

It loads and starts playing a "Jumping Jack Flash" MIDI file using the MidisLoader class developed in Chapter 8:

```
// global
private MidisLoader midisLoader;

midisLoader = new MidisLoader();
midisLoader.load("jjf", "jumping_jack_flash.mid");
midisLoader.play("jjf", true);    // repeatedly play it
```

The file is played repeatedly until it's stopped as the application window closes:

```
// global
private JackPanel jp;   // where the game is drawn

public void windowClosing(WindowEvent e)
{ jp.stopGame();  // stop the game
  midisLoader.close();
}
```

JumpingJack sets up window listener methods for pausing and resuming the game, in a similar way to the BugRunner application in Chapter 11. For example, window iconification/deiconification causes the game in the JackPanel object, jp, to be paused/resumed:

```
public void windowIconified(WindowEvent e)
{  jp.pauseGame(); }   // jp is the JackPanel object

public void windowDeiconified(WindowEvent e)
{  jp.resumeGame();  }
```

The Animation Framework

JackPanel is a subclass of JPanel and implements the animation framework described in Chapters 2 and 3; JackPanel resembles the BugPanel class of Chapter 11.

The JackPanel( ) constructor in Example 12-1 creates the game entities: the RibbonsManager, BricksManager, JumperSprite, and FireBallSprite objects. It prepares the explosion animation and the title/help screen.

Example 12-1. The JackPanel constructor

```
// some of the globals
private JumpingJack jackTop;
private JumperSprite jack;           // the sprites
private FireBallSprite fireball;
private RibbonsManager ribsMan;      // the ribbons manager
private BricksManager bricksMan;     // the bricks manager

// to display the title/help screen
private boolean showHelp;
private BufferedImage helpIm;

// explosion-related
private ImagesPlayer explosionPlayer = null;
private boolean showExplosion = false;
private int explWidth, explHeight;   // image dimensions
private int xExpl, yExpl;    // coords where image is drawn


public JackPanel(JumpingJack jj, long period)
{
  jackTop = jj;
  this.period = period;

  setDoubleBuffered(false);
  setBackground(Color.white);
  setPreferredSize( new Dimension(PWIDTH, PHEIGHT));

  setFocusable(true);
  requestFocus();     // so receives key events

  addKeyListener( new KeyAdapter() {
    public void keyPressed(KeyEvent e)
    { processKey(e); }
  });

  // initialise the loaders
  ImagesLoader imsLoader = new ImagesLoader(IMS_INFO);
  clipsLoader = new ClipsLoader(SNDS_FILE);

  // initialise the game entities
  bricksMan = new BricksManager(PWIDTH, PHEIGHT, BRICKS_INFO, imsLoader);
  int brickMoveSize = bricksMan.getMoveSize();

  ribsMan = new RibbonsManager(PWIDTH, PHEIGHT,  brickMoveSize, imsLoader);

  jack = new JumperSprite(PWIDTH, PHEIGHT, brickMoveSize,
          bricksMan, imsLoader, (int)(period/1000000L) ); // in ms
```

Example 12-1. The JackPanel constructor (continued)

```
    fireball = new FireBallSprite(PWIDTH, PHEIGHT,
                                  imsLoader, this, jack);

    // prepare the explosion animation
    explosionPlayer =  new ImagesPlayer("explosion",
                    (int)(period/1000000L), 0.5, false, imsLoader);
    BufferedImage explosionIm = imsLoader.getImage("explosion");
    explWidth = explosionIm.getWidth( );
    explHeight = explosionIm.getHeight( );
    explosionPlayer.setWatcher(this)      // report anim end back here

    // prepare title/help screen
    helpIm = imsLoader.getImage("title");
    showHelp = true;     // show at start-up
    isPaused = true;

    // set up message font
    msgsFont = new Font("SansSerif", Font.BOLD, 24);
    metrics = this.getFontMetrics(msgsFont);
}  // end of JackPanel( )
```

The BricksManager object is created first, so a brickMoveSize variable can be initialized. This will contain the number of pixels that the bricks map is shifted when the sprite appears to move. brickMoveSize is used as the basis for the move increments employed by the Ribbon objects managed in RibbonsManager and is used by the JumperSprite. However, the fireball travels at its own rate, independent of the background, so it doesn't require the move size.

JackPanel is in charge of a fireball's animated explosion and its associated audio, rather than FireBallSprite. The explosion animation in *explosion.gif* is loaded into an ImagesPlayer (see Figure 12-5 for its contents), and the dimensions of its first image are recorded. When the sequence is finished, ImagesPlayer will call sequenceEnded( ) back in JackPanel.

Figure 12-5. The images strip in explosion.gif

The title/help image (in *title.gif*; see Figure 12-6) is loaded into the global helpIm, and the values of the Booleans showHelp and isPaused are set. isPaused causes the game's execution to pause and was introduced in the basic game animation framework; showHelp is a new Boolean, examined by gameRender( ) to decide whether to draw the image.

Figure 12-6. title.gif: the title/help screen in JumpingJack

gameRender( ) displays the image centered in the JPanel, so the image should not be too large or its borders may be beyond the edges of the panel. If the image is the same size as the JPanel, it will totally obscure the game window and look more like a screen rather than an image drawn on the game surface.

 Clever use can be made of transparency to make the image an interesting shape though it's still a rectangle as far as drawImage( ) is concerned.

Switching on isPaused while the help image is visible requires a small change to the resumeGame( ) method:

```
public void resumeGame( )
{ if (!showHelp)      // CHANGED
    isPaused = false;
}
```

This method is called from the enclosing JumpingJack JFrame when the frame is activated (deiconified). Previously, resumeGame( ) is always set isPaused to false, but now this occurs only when the help screen isn't being displayed.

If the game design requires distinct title and help screens, then two images and two Booleans will be needed. For example, you would need showHelp for the help image and showTitle for the titles, which would be examined in gameRender( ). Initially, showTitle would be set to true and showHelp assigned a false value. When the titles or the help is on-screen, isPaused would be set to true.

Dealing with Input

Only keyboard input is supported in JumpingJack. A key press triggers a call to processKey( ), which handles three kinds of input: termination keys, help controls, and game-play keys:

```
private void processKey(KeyEvent e)
{
  int keyCode = e.getKeyCode( );
```

```
// termination keys
// listen for esc, q, end, ctrl-c on the canvas to
// allow a convenient exit from the full screen configuration
if ((keyCode==KeyEvent.VK_ESCAPE) || (keyCode==KeyEvent.VK_Q) ||
    (keyCode == KeyEvent.VK_END) ||
    ((keyCode == KeyEvent.VK_C) && e.isControlDown()) )
  running = false;


// help controls
if (keyCode == KeyEvent.VK_H) {
  if (showHelp) {  // help being shown
    showHelp = false;  // switch off
    isPaused = false;
  }
  else {  // help not being shown
    showHelp = true;     // show it
    isPaused = true;
  }
}


// game-play keys
if (!isPaused && !gameOver) {
  // move the sprite and ribbons based on the arrow key pressed
  if (keyCode == KeyEvent.VK_LEFT) {
    jack.moveLeft();
    bricksMan.moveRight();    // bricks and ribbons move other way
    ribsMan.moveRight();
  }
  else if (keyCode == KeyEvent.VK_RIGHT) {
    jack.moveRight();
    bricksMan.moveLeft();
    ribsMan.moveLeft();
  }
  else if (keyCode == KeyEvent.VK_UP)
    jack.jump();      // jumping has no effect on bricks/ribbons
  else if (keyCode == KeyEvent.VK_DOWN) {
    jack.stayStill();
    bricksMan.stayStill();
    ribsMan.stayStill();
  }
}
}  // end of processKey()
```

The termination keys are utilized in the same way as in earlier examples. The help key (h) toggles the showHelp and isPaused Booleans on and off. The arrow keys are assigned to be the game play keys. When the left or right arrow keys are pressed, the scenery (the bricks and ribbons) is moved in the opposite direction from Jack. You'll see that the calls to moveLeft() and moveRight() in Jack don't cause the sprite to move at all.

Multiple Key Presses/Actions

A common requirement in many games is to process multiple key presses together. For example, it should be possible for Jack to jump and move left/right at the same time. There are two parts to this feature: implementing key capture code to handle simultaneous key presses and implementing simultaneous behaviors in the sprite.

JumpingJack has the ability to jump and move left/right simultaneously: it was wired into the JumperSprite class at the design stage, as you'll see. If Jack is currently moving left or right, then an up arrow press will make him jump. A related trick is to start Jack jumping from a stationary position, causing him to rise and fall over 1 to 2 seconds. During that interval, the left or right arrow keys can be pressed to get him moving horizontally through the air or to change his direction in mid-flight!

Though Jack can jump and move simultaneously, this behavior is triggered by distinct key presses. First, the left/right arrow key is pressed to start him moving, and then the up arrow key makes him jump. Alternatively, the up arrow key can be pressed first, followed by the left or right arrow keys. If you want to capture multiple key presses at the same time, then modifications are needed to the key listener code.

The main change would be to use keyPressed( ) and keyReleased( ) and to introduce new Booleans to indicate when keys are being pressed. The basic coding strategy is shown here:

```
// global Booleans, true when a key is being pressed
private boolean leftKeyPressed = false;
private boolean rightKeyPressed = false;
private boolean upKeyPressed = false;


public JackPanel(JumpingJack jj, long period)
{
  ... // other code
  addKeyListener( new KeyAdapter() {
    public void keyPressed(KeyEvent e)
    { processKeyPress(e);  }
    public void keyReleased(KeyEvent e)
    { processKeyRelease(e); }
  });
  ... // other code
}


private void processKeyPress(KeyEvent e)
{
  int keyCode = e.getKeyCode();

  // record the key press in a Boolean
  if (keyCode == KeyEvent.VK_LEFT)
    leftKeyPressed = true;
  else if (keyCode == KeyEvent.VK_RIGHT)
```

```
    rightKeyPressed = true;
  else if (keyCode == KeyEvent.VK_UP)
    upKeyPressed = true;

  // use the combined key presses
  if (leftKeyPressed && upKeyPressed)
    // do a combined left and up action
  else if (rightKeyPressed && upKeyPressed)
    // do a combined right and up action

  ...  // other key processing code
} // end of processKeyPress()


private void processKeyRelease(KeyEvent e)
{
  int keyCode = e.getKeyCode();

  // record the key release in a Boolean
  if (keyCode == KeyEvent.VK_LEFT)
    leftKeyPressed = false;
  else if (keyCode == KeyEvent.VK_RIGHT)
    rightKeyPressed = false;
  else if (keyCode == KeyEvent.VK_UP)
    upKeyPressed = false;
} // end of processKeyRelease()
```

Key presses cause the relevant Booleans to be set, and they remain set until the user releases the keys at some future time. The combination of key presses can be detected by testing the Booleans in processKeyPress().

This coding effort is only needed for combinations of "normal" keys (e.g., the letters, the numbers, and arrow keys). Key combinations involving a standard key and the shift, control, or meta keys can be detected more directly by using the KeyEvent methods isShiftDown(), isControlDown(), and isMetaDown(). This coding style can be seen in the termination keys code in processKey():

```
if (...||((keyCode==KeyEvent.VK_C) && e.isControlDown())) //ctrl-c
  running = false;
```

The Animation Loop

The animation loop is located in run() and is unchanged from earlier examples. For example, it's the same run() method seen in BugRunner in Chapter 11. Essentially, it is:

```
public void run()
{ // initialization code
  while (running) {
    gameUpdate();
    gameRender();
    paintScreen();
```

```
    // timing correction code
  }
  System.exit(0);
}
```

gameUpdate( ) updates the various game elements (the sprites, the brick layers, and Ribbon objects):

```
private void gameUpdate( )
{
  if (!isPaused && !gameOver) {
    if (jack.willHitBrick( )) { // collision checking first
      jack.stayStill( );     // stop jack and scenery
      bricksMan.stayStill( );
      ribsMan.stayStill( );
    }
    ribsMan.update( );    // update background and sprites
    bricksMan.update( );
    jack.updateSprite( );
    fireball.updateSprite( );

    if (showExplosion)
      explosionPlayer.updateTick( );  // update the animation
  }
}
```

The new element here is dealing with potential collisions: if Jack is to hit a brick when the current update is carried out, then the update should be cancelled. This requires a testing phase before the update is committed, embodied in willHitBrick( ) in JumperSprite. If Jack is to hit a brick with his next update, it will be due to him moving (there are no animated tiles in this game), so the collision can be avoided by stopping Jack (and the backgrounds) from moving.

The fireball sprite is unaffected by Jack's impending collision: it travels left regardless of what the JumperSprite is doing.

The showExplosion Boolean is set to true when the explosion animation is being played by the ImagesPlayer (explosionPlayer), so updateTick( ) must be called during each game update.

Rendering order

gameRender( ) draws the multiple layers making up the game. Their ordering is important because rendering must start with the image farthest back in the scene and work forward. This ordering is illustrated in Figure 12-2 for JumpingJack:

```
private void gameRender( )
{
  if (dbImage == null){
    dbImage = createImage(PWIDTH, PHEIGHT);
    if (dbImage == null) {
      System.out.println("dbImage is null");
      return;
```

```
    }
  else
    dbg = dbImage.getGraphics( );
}

// draw a white background
dbg.setColor(Color.white);
dbg.fillRect(0, 0, PWIDTH, PHEIGHT);

// draw the game elements: order is important
ribsMan.display(dbg);          // the background ribbons
bricksMan.display(dbg);        // the bricks
jack.drawSprite(dbg);          // the sprites
fireball.drawSprite(dbg);

if (showExplosion)        // draw the explosion (in front of jack)
  dbg.drawImage(explosionPlayer.getCurrentImage( ),
                                  xExpl, yExpl, null);
reportStats(dbg);
if (gameOver)
  gameOverMessage(dbg);

if (showHelp)      // draw help at the very front (if switched on)
  dbg.drawImage(helpIm, (PWIDTH-helpIm.getWidth( ))/2,
                  (PHEIGHT-helpIm.getHeight( ))/2, null);
}  // end of gameRender( )
```

gameRender( ) relies on the RibbonsManager and BricksManager objects to draw the multiple Ribbon objects and the individual bricks. The code order means that Jack will be drawn behind the fireball if they are at the same spot, i.e., when the fireball hits him. An explosion is drawn in front of the fireball, and the game statistics, the Game Over message, and the help screen is layered on top.

Handling an Explosion

The fireball sprite passes the responsibility of showing the explosion animation and its audio clip to JackPanel, by calling showExplosion( ):

```
// names of the explosion clips
private static final String[] exploNames =
                        {"explo1", "explo2", "explo3"};

public void showExplosion(int x, int y)
// called by FireBallSprite
{
  if (!showExplosion) {  // only allow a single explosion at a time
    showExplosion = true;
    xExpl = x - explWidth/2;    // (x,y) is center of explosion
    yExpl = y - explHeight/2;

    /* Play an explosion clip, but cycle through them.
       This adds variety, and gets around not being able to
```

```
         play multiple instances of a clip at the same time. */
    clipsLoader.play( exploNames[ numHits%exploNames.length ],
                                                    false);

    numHits++;
  }
} // end of showExplosion()
```

The (x, y) coordinate passed to showExplosion( ) is assumed to be where the center of the explosion should occur, so the top-left corner of the explosion image is calculated and placed in the globals (xExpl, yExpl). These are used to position the explosion in gameRender( ).

The use of a single Boolean (showExplosion) to determine if an explosion appears onscreen is adequate only if a single explosion animation is shown at a time. This means that if a fireball hits Jack while an explosion sequence is playing (as a result of a previous fireball that hit him), a second animation will not be rendered. This restriction allows me to use a single ImagesPlayer object instead of a set containing one ImagesPlayer for each of the current explosions.

play( ) in ClipsLoader eventually calls start( ) for the Clip object. A design feature of start( ) is that when a clip is playing, further calls to start( ) will be ignored. This makes it impossible to play multiple instances of the same Clip object at the same time and means that while the explosion clip is playing (for 1 to 2 seconds), another explosion can't be heard. This absence is quite noticeable (more so than the lack of multiple explosion animations, for some reason). Also, the game just seems more fun if there's a crescendo of explosions as Jack gets pummeled.

Therefore, I've gone for a *set* of explosion clips, stored in exploNames[], and the code cycles through them. A set of three seems enough to deal with even the highest rate of fireball hits to Jack. Since these names represent separate Clips stored in the ClipsLoader, they can be played simultaneously.

The clips are different from each other, so there's a pleasing interplay of noises as multiple explosions go off. The order the sounds are played isn't relevant, at least in this game.

 I found the clips by searching for sound filenames containing the word "explosion," "bomb," and similar, using the FindSounds site (*http:// www.findsounds.com/*). I looked for small clips, lasting 1–2 seconds, to roughly match the duration of the explosion animation.

Once an explosion animation has finished playing, its ImagesPlayer object calls sequenceEnded( ) in JackPanel:

```
public void sequenceEnded(String imageName)
// called by ImagesPlayer when the expl. animation finishes
{
  showExplosion = false;
  explosionPlayer.restartAt(0);   // reset animation for next time
```

```
    if (numHits >= MAX_HITS) {
      gameOver = true;
      score = (int) ((J3DTimer.getValue() -
                              gameStartTime)/1000000000L);
      clipsLoader.play("applause", false);
    }
  }
```

sequenceEnded( ) resets the animation, so it's ready to be played next time, and checks the game over condition. If the number of fireball hits equals or exceeds MAX_HITS, then the game over flag is set, causing the game to terminate.

The main question about sequenceEnded( ) is why it is being used at all. The answer is to make the game terminate at a natural time, just after an explosion has finished. For instance, if the game over condition was tested at the end of showExplosion( ), the game might have been terminated while ImagesPlayer was in the middle of displaying the explosion animation. This might seem a bit odd to a player, especially one who likes to see explosions run their course.

Managing the Ribbons

RibbonsManager is mainly a router, sending move method calls and update( ) and display( ) calls to the multiple Ribbon objects under its charge. Initially, it creates the Ribbon objects, so it acts as a central storage for their GIFs and move factors.

The initialization phase is carried out in the constructor:

```
// globals
private String ribImages[] = {"mountains", "houses", "trees"};
private double moveFactors[] = {0.1, 0.5, 1.0};
    // applied to moveSize
    // a move factor of 0 would make a ribbon stationary

private Ribbon[] ribbons;
private int numRibbons;
private int moveSize;
    // standard distance for a ribbon to 'move' each tick


public RibbonsManager(int w, int h, int brickMvSz, ImagesLoader imsLd)
{ moveSize = brickMvSz;
        // the basic move size is the same as the bricks map

  numRibbons = ribImages.length;
  ribbons = new Ribbon[numRibbons];

  for (int i = 0; i < numRibbons; i++)
     ribbons[i] = new Ribbon(w, h, imsLd.getImage( ribImages[i] ),
                              (int) (moveFactors[i]*moveSize));
} // end of RibbonsManager( )
```

The choice of GIFs is hardwired into ribImages[], and the constructor loops through the array creating a Ribbon object for each one.

The basic move size is the same as that used by the bricks layer but multiplied by a fixed moveFactors[] value to get a size suitable for each Ribbon.

 A *move size* is the amount that a background layer moves in each animation period.

A move factor will usually be less than one, to reduce the move size for a Ribbon in comparison to the bricks layer. The Ribbons move more slowly, reinforcing the illusion that they're further back in the scene.

The other methods in RibbonsManager are routers. For example, moveRight( ) and display( ):

```
public void moveRight()
{ for (int i=0; i < numRibbons; i++)
    ribbons[i].moveRight();
}

public void display(Graphics g)
/* The display order is important.
   Display ribbons from the back to the front of the scene. */
{ for (int i=0; i < numRibbons; i++)
    ribbons[i].display(g);
}
```

 moveLeft( ), stayStill( ), and update( ) are similar to moveRight( ).

The calls from display( ) ensure that the display of the Ribbons is carried out in a back-to-front order; in this case, mountains, houses, and then trees are displayed.

Wraparound Ribbons

A Ribbon object manages a wraparound, movable image, which should be wider than the game panel. This width requirement is important for the amount of work needed to draw the image as it wraps around the JPanel.

A wide image means that its display on-screen requires, at most, two drawImage( ) calls (with associated calculations for the coordinates and image dimensions): one to draw the tail of the image on the left side and the other for its start on the right. If the image is narrower than the panel, then three drawImage( ) calls (or more) might be needed, with an increase in the number of calculations.

Furthermore, if the panel width is constant, as here, then some parts of the calculations need only be carried out once and can be reused after that.

The constructor of this class initializes the graphic, its moveSize value, two movement flags, and a position variable called xImHead:

```
// globals
private BufferedImage im;
private int width;        // the width of the image (>= pWidth)
private int pWidth, pHeight;    // dimensions of display panel

private int moveSize;        // size of the image move (in pixels)
private boolean isMovingRight;  // movement flags
private boolean isMovingLeft;

private int xImHead;    // panel position of image's left side


public Ribbon(int w, int h, BufferedImage im, int moveSz)
{
  pWidth = w; pHeight = h;

  this.im = im;
  width = im.getWidth();    // no need to store the height
  if (width < pWidth)
    System.out.println("Ribbon width < panel width");

  moveSize = moveSz;
  isMovingRight = false;    // no movement at start
  isMovingLeft = false;
  xImHead = 0;
}
```

xImHead holds the x-coordinate in the panel where the left side of the image (its head) should be drawn.

The isMovingRight and isMovingLeft flags determine the direction of movement for the Ribbon image (or whether it is stationary) when its JPanel position is updated. The flags are set by the moveRight( ), moveLeft( ), and stayStill( ) methods:

```
public void moveRight()
// move the ribbon image to the right on the next update
{ isMovingRight = true;
  isMovingLeft = false;
}
```

update( ) adjusts the xImHead value depending on the movement flags. xImHead can range between -width to width (where width is the width of the image):

```
public void update()
{ if (isMovingRight)
    xImHead = (xImHead + moveSize) % width;
  else if (isMovingLeft)
    xImHead = (xImHead - moveSize) % width;
}
```

As xImHead varies, the drawing of the ribbon in the JPanel will usually be a combination of the image's tail followed by its head.

Drawing the Ribbon's Image

The display() method does the hard work of deciding where various bits of the image should be drawn in the JPanel.

One of the hard aspects of display() is that it utilizes two different coordinate systems: JPanel coordinates and image coordinates. This can be seen in the many calls to Graphics' 10-argument drawImage() method:

```
boolean drawImage(Image img, int dx1, int dy1, int dx2, int dy2,
                  int sx1, int sy1, int sx2, int sy2,
                  ImageObserver observer);
```

Figure 12-7 shows that the eight integers represent two regions: the destination JPanel and source image.

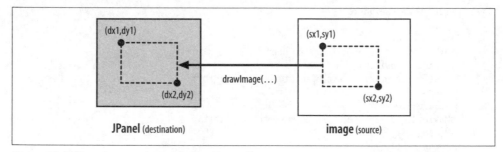

Figure 12-7. Drawing a region with drawImage()

Fortunately, in JumpingJack, the regions are always the same height, starting at the top edge of the JPanel (y == 0) and extending to its bottom (y == pHeight). However, dx1 and dx2 vary in the JPanel, and sx1 and sx2 vary in the image.

The x-coordinates are derived from the current xImHead value, which ranges between *width* and *-width* as the image is shifted right or left across the JPanel. As the image moves right (or left), there will come a point when it'll be necessary to draw the head and tail of the image to cover the JPanel.

These considerations lead to display() consisting of five cases; each is detailed in the following sections:

```
public void display(Graphics g)
{
  if (xImHead == 0)   // draw im start at (0,0)
    draw(g, im, 0, pWidth, 0, pWidth);
  else if ((xImHead > 0) && (xImHead < pWidth)) {
    // draw im tail at (0,0) and im start at (xImHead,0)
    draw(g, im, 0, xImHead, width-xImHead, width);   // im tail
    draw(g, im, xImHead, pWidth, 0, pWidth-xImHead);  // im start
```

```
      }
    else if (xImHead >= pWidth)    // only draw im tail at (0,0)
      draw(g, im, 0, pWidth,
                   width-xImHead, width-xImHead+pWidth);  // im tail
    else if ((xImHead < 0) && (xImHead >= pWidth-width))
      draw(g, im, 0, pWidth, -xImHead, pWidth-xImHead);  // im body
    else if (xImHead < pWidth-width) {
        // draw im tail at (0,0) and im start at (width+xImHead,0)
      draw(g, im, 0, width+xImHead, -xImHead, width);  // im tail
      draw(g, im, width+xImHead, pWidth,
                   0, pWidth-width-xImHead);  // im start

    }
  } // end of display()


  private void draw(Graphics g, BufferedImage im,
                    int scrX1, int scrX2, int imX1, int imX2)
  /* The y-coords of the image always starts at 0 and ends at
     pHeight (the height of the panel), so are hardwired. */
  { g.drawImage(im, scrX1, 0, scrX2, pHeight,
                    imX1, 0,  imX2, pHeight, null);

  }
```

Case 1: Draw the image at JPanel (0,0)

The relevant code snippet from display( ):

```
    if (xImHead == 0)    // draw im start at (0,0)
      draw(g, im, 0, pWidth, 0, pWidth);
```

Figure 12-8 illustrates the drawing operation.

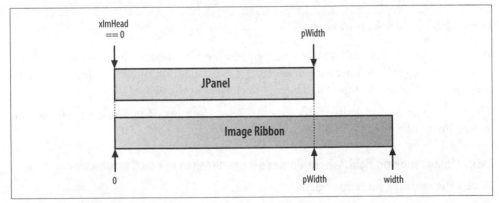

Figure 12-8. Case 1 in Ribbon's display()

Case 1 occurs at startup time, when the scene is first drawn, and reoccurs when Jack has run around the width of the image and xImHead is back at 0.

draw( ) is a simplified interface to drawImage( ), hiding the fixed y-coordinates (0 to pHeight). Its third and fourth arguments are the x-coordinates in the JPanel (the positions pointed to in the top gray box in Figure 12-8). The fifth and sixth arguments are the positions pointed to in the image ribbon (the box at the bottom of the figure).

Case 2: Image moving right, where xImHead is less than pWidth

Here's the code fragment from display( ) for this case:

```
if ((xImHead > 0) && (xImHead < pWidth)) {
    // draw im tail at (0,0) and im head at (xImHead,0)
    draw(g, im, 0, xImHead, width-xImHead, width);   // im tail
    draw(g, im, xImHead, pWidth, 0, pWidth-xImHead);  // im head
}
```

Figure 12-9 illustrates the drawing operations.

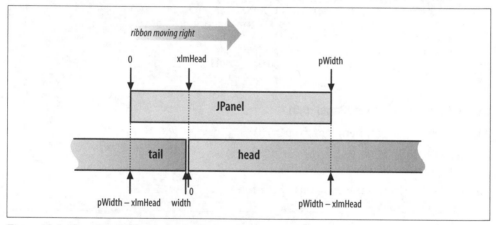

Figure 12-9. Case 2 in Ribbon's display( )

When the image moves right (caused by the sprite apparently moving left), the JPanel drawing will require two drawImage( ) calls: one for the tail of the image and the other for the head (which still begins at xImHead in the JPanel).

The tricky part is calculating the x-coordinate of the start of the image's tail and the x-coordinate of the end of the head.

Case 3: Image moving right, where xImHead is greater than or equal to pWidth

Here's the relevant piece of code:

```
if (xImHead >= pWidth)   // only draw im tail at (0,0)
    draw(g, im, 0, pWidth, width-xImHead, width-xImHead+pWidth);
```

Figure 12-10 shows the drawing operation.

Case 3 happens after Case 2 as the image moves even further to the right and xImHead travels beyond the right edge of the JPanel. This means only one drawImage( ) call is

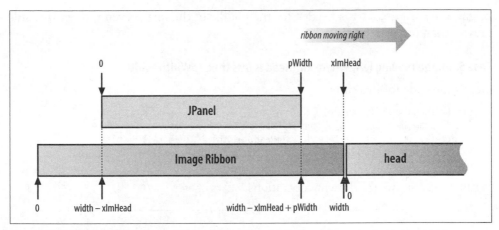

Figure 12-10. Case 3 in Ribbon's display()

necessary to draw the middle part of the image into the JPanel. The tricky x-coordinates are the start and end points for the image's middle.

Case 4: Image moving left, where xImHead is greater than or equal to (pWidth-width)

This is the relevant code snippet:

```
if ((xImHead < 0) && (xImHead >= pWidth-width))
    draw(g, im, 0, pWidth, -xImHead, pWidth-xImHead);  // im body
```

Figure 12-11 illustrates the drawing operation.

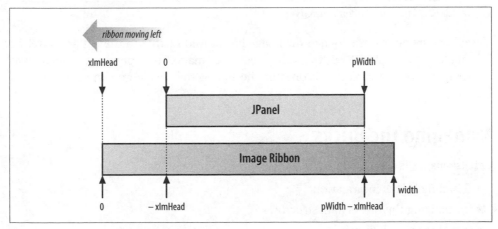

Figure 12-11. Case 4 in Ribbon's display()

Case 4 occurs when the image is moving left, which happens when the sprite apparently travels to the right. xImHead will become negative since it's to the left of JPanel's origin. One `drawImage( )` is needed for the middle of the image even though it is still greater than (pWidth − width).

Case 5. Image moving left, where xImHead is less than (pWidth-width)

Here's the code for this case:

```
if (xImHead < pWidth-width) {
    // draw im tail at (0,0) and im head at (width+xImHead,0)
    draw(g, im, 0, width+xImHead, -xImHead, width);  // im tail
    draw(g, im, width+xImHead, pWidth, 0, pWidth-width-xImHead);  // im head
}
```

Figure 12-12 shows the drawing operations.

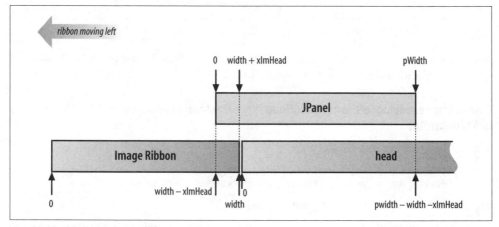

Figure 12-12. Case 5 in Ribbon's display( )

Case 5 occurs after Case 4 when the image has moved further to the left and `xImHead` is smaller than (pWidth-width). This distance marks the point at which two `drawImage( )` calls are required, one for the tail of the image and the other for its head.

Managing the Bricks

`BricksManager` is separated into five broad groups of methods:

- Loading bricks information.
- Initializing the bricks data structures.
- Moving the bricks map.
- Drawing the bricks.
- `JumperSprite`-related tasks. These are mostly various forms of collision detection between the sprite and the bricks.

BricksManager reads a bricks map and creates a Brick object for each brick. The data structure holding the Brick objects is optimized so drawing and collision detection can be carried out quickly.

Moving and drawing the bricks map is analogous to the moving and drawing of an image by a Ribbon object. However, the drawing process is complicated by the ribbon consisting of multiple bricks instead of a single GIF.

Jack, the JumperSprite object, uses BricksManager methods to determine if its planned moves will cause it to collide with a brick.

Loading Bricks Information

BricksManager calls loadBricksFile( ) to load a bricks map; the map is assumed to be in *bricksInfo.txt* from *Images/*.

The first line of the file (ignoring comment lines) is the name of the image strip:

```
s tiles.gif 5
```

This means that *tiles.gif* holds a strip of five images. The map is a series of lines containing numbers and spaces. Each line corresponds to a row of tiles in the game. A number refers to a particular image in the image strip, which becomes a tile. A space means that no tile is used in that position in the game.

 The map file may contain empty lines and comment lines (those starting with //), which are ignored.

bricksInfo.txt is:

```
// bricks information

s tiles.gif 5

// -----------
44444
                              222222222
                      111
                      2222
                  11111
            444
            444
      22222         444                111
      1111112222222    23333  2     33     44444444
00 0001113333300000002222222233333  333 2222222223333301
00000000011100000000002220000000003300001111111222222234
// -----------
```

The images strip in *tiles.gif* is shown in Figure 12-13.

Figure 12-13. The images strip in tiles.gif

The images strip is loaded with an `ImagesLoader` object, and an array of `BufferedImages` is stored in a global variable called `brickImages[]`.

This approach has several drawbacks. One is the reliance on single digits to index into the images strip. This makes it impossible to utilize strips with more than 10 images (images can only be named from 0 to 9), which is inadequate for a real map. The solution probably entails moving to a letter-based scheme (using A–Z and/or a–z) to allow up to 52 tiles.

`loadBricksFile()` calls `storeBricks()` to read in a single map line, adding `Brick` objects to a `bricksList` ArrayList:

```
    private void storeBricks(String line, int lineNo, int numImages)
    {
      int imageID;
      for(int x=0; x < line.length(); x++) {
        char ch = line.charAt(x);
        if (ch == ' ')    // ignore a space
          continue;
        if (Character.isDigit(ch)) {
          imageID = ch - '0';     // Assume a digit is 0-9
          if (imageID >= numImages)
            System.out.println("Image ID "+imageID+" out of range");
          else    // make a Brick object
            bricksList.add( new Brick(imageID, x, lineNo) );
        }
        else
          System.out.println("Brick char " + ch + " is not a digit");
      }
    }
```

A `Brick` object is initialized with its image ID (a number in the range 0 to 9); a reference to the actual image is added later. The brick is passed its map indices (x, lineNo). lineNo starts at 0 when the first map line is read and is incremented with each new line.

Figure 12-14 shows some of the important variables associated with a map, including example map indices.

Initializing the Bricks Data Structures

Once the `bricksList` ArrayList has been filled, `BricksManager` calls `initBricksInfo()` to extract various global data from the list and to check if certain criteria are met. For instance, the maximum width of the map should be greater than the width of the

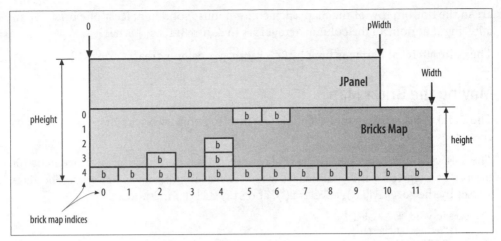

Figure 12-14. Brick map variables

panel (*width* ≥ pWidth). initBricksInfo( ) calls checkForGaps( ) to check that no gaps are in the map's bottom row. The presence of a gap would allow Jack to fall down a hole while running around, which would necessitate more complex coding in JumperSprite. If checkForGaps( ) finds a gap, the game terminates after reporting the error. The bricksList ArrayList doesn't store its Brick objects in order, which makes finding a particular Brick time-consuming. Unfortunately, searching for a brick is a common task and must be performed every time that Jack is about to move to prevent it from hitting something.

A more useful way of storing the bricks map is ordered by column, as illustrated in Figure 12-15.

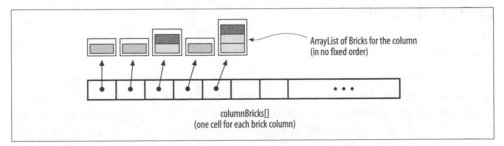

Figure 12-15. Bricks stored by column

This data structure is excellent for brick searches where the column of interest is known beforehand since the array allows constant-time access to a given column.

A column is implemented as an ArrayList of Bricks in no particular order, so a linear search looks for a brick in the selected column. However, a column contains few bricks compared to the entire map, so the search time is acceptable. Since no gaps are in the bottom row of the map, each column must contain at least one brick, guaranteeing that none of the column ArrayLists in columnBricks[] is null.

The columnBricks[] array is built by BricksManager calling createColumns().

Moving the Bricks Map

The BricksManager uses the same approach to moving its bricks map as the Ribbon class does for its GIF.

The isMovingRight and isMovingLeft flags determine the direction of movement for the bricks map (or if it is stationary) when its JPanel position is updated. The flags are set by the moveRight(), moveLeft(), and stayStill() methods:

```
public void moveRight()
{ isMovingRight = true;
  isMovingLeft = false;
}
```

update() increments an xMapHead value depending on the movement flags. xMapHead is the x-coordinate in the panel where the left edge of the bricks map (its head) should be drawn. xMapHead can range between -width to width (where width is the width of the bricks map in pixels):

```
public void update()
{ if (isMovingRight)
    xMapHead = (xMapHead + moveSize) % width;
  else if (isMovingLeft)
    xMapHead = (xMapHead - moveSize) % width;
}
```

Drawing the Bricks

The display() method does the hard work of deciding where the bricks in the map should be drawn in the JPanel.

As in the Ribbon class, several different coordinate systems are combined: the JPanel coordinates and the bricks map coordinates. The bad news is that the bricks map uses two different schemes. One way of locating a brick is by its pixel position in the bricks map; the other is by using its map indices (see Figure 12-14). This means that three coordinate systems are utilized in display() and its helper method drawBricks():

```
public void display(Graphics g)
{
  int bCoord = (int)(xMapHead/imWidth) * imWidth;
  // bCoord is the drawing x-coord of the brick containing xMapHead
  int offset;    // offset is distance between bCoord and xMapHead
  if (bCoord >= 0)
    offset = xMapHead - bCoord;   // offset is positive
  else  // negative position
    offset = bCoord - xMapHead;   // offset is positive
```

```
    if ((bCoord >= 0) && (bCoord < pWidth)) {
      drawBricks(g, 0-(imWidth-offset), xMapHead,
                              width-bCoord-imWidth);    // bm tail
      drawBricks(g, xMapHead, pWidth, 0);  // bm start
    }
    else if (bCoord >= pWidth)
      drawBricks(g, 0-(imWidth-offset), pWidth,
                              width-bCoord-imWidth);  // bm tail
    else if ((bCoord < 0) && (bCoord >= pWidth-width+imWidth))
      drawBricks(g, 0-offset, pWidth, -bCoord);        // bm tail
    else if (bCoord < pWidth-width+imWidth) {
      drawBricks(g, 0-offset, width+xMapHead, -bCoord);  // bm tail
      drawBricks(g, width+xMapHead, pWidth, 0);      // bm start
    }
  } // end of display()
```

The details of drawBricks() will be explained later in the chapter. For now, it's enough to know the meaning of its prototype:

```
    void drawBricks(Graphics g, int xStart, int xEnd, int xBrick);
```

drawBricks() draws bricks into the JPanel starting at xStart, ending at xEnd. The bricks are drawn a column at a time. The first column of bricks is the one at the xBrick pixel x-coordinate in the bricks map.

display() starts by calculating a brick coordinate (bCoord) and offset from the xMapHead position. These are used in the calls to drawBricks() to specify where a brick image's left edge should appear. This should become clearer as you consider the four drawing cases.

Case 1. Bricks map moving right and bCoord is less than pWidth

This is the relevant code snippet in display():

```
    if ((bCoord >= 0) && (bCoord < pWidth)) {
      drawBricks(g, 0-(imWidth-offset), xMapHead,
                              width-bCoord-imWidth);    // bm tail
      drawBricks(g, xMapHead, pWidth, 0);  // bm start
    }  // bm means bricks map
```

Figure 12-16 illustrates the drawing operations:

Case 1 occurs as the bricks map moves right since the sprite is apparently moving left. xMapHead will have a value between 0 and pWidth (the width of the JPanel). Two groups of bricks will need to be drawn, requiring two calls to drawBricks(). The first group starts near the left edge of the JPanel, and the second starts at the xMapHead position. I've indicated these groups by drawing the bricks map area occupied by the left group in gray in Figure 12-16 and the righthand group's area with stripes.

The positioning of the bricks in the gray area of the bricks map in Figure 12-16 poses a problem. The drawing of a column of bricks requires the x-coordinate of the column's

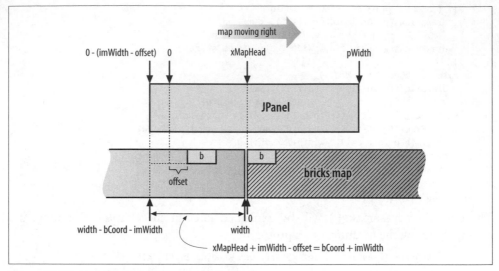

Figure 12-16. Case 1 in BricksManager's display()

left edge. What is that coordinate for the first column drawn in the gray area of the bricks map?

The left edge of that column will usually not line up with the left edge of the panel, most likely occurring somewhere to its left and off screen. The required calculation (`width-bCoord-imWidth`) is shown in Figure 12-16, next to the leftmost arrow at the bottom of the figure.

The drawing of a group of bricks is packaged up in `drawBricks()`. The second and third arguments of that method are the start and end x-coordinates for a group in the `JPanel`. These are represented by arrows pointing to the `JPanel` box at the top of Figure 12-16. The fourth argument is the x-coordinate of the left column of the group in the bricks map. These coordinates are represented by the arrows at the bottom of Figure 12-16.

`drawBricks()` is called twice in the code snippet shown earlier: once for the group in the lefthand gray area of the bricks map in Figure 12-16, and once for the group in the righthand striped area.

Case 2. Bricks map moving right and bCoord is greater than pWidth

Here's the code piece:

```
if (bCoord >= pWidth)
   drawBricks(g, 0-(imWidth-offset), pWidth,
                        width-bCoord-imWidth);  // bm tail
```

Figure 12-17 shows the operation.

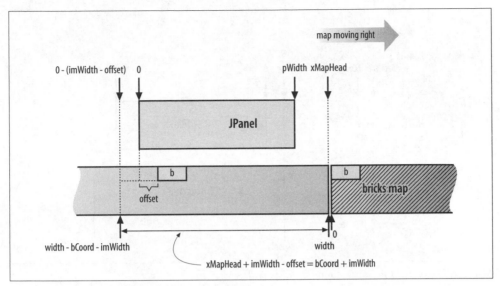

Figure 12-17. Case 2 in BricksManager's display( )

Case 2 happens some time after Case 1, when xMapHead has moved farther right, beyond the right edge of the JPanel. The drawing task becomes simpler since only a single call to drawBricks( ) is required to draw a group of columns taken from the middle of the bricks map. I've indicated that group's area in gray in the bricks map in Figure 12-17.

Case 2 has the same problem as Case 1 in determining the x-coordinate of the left column of the gray group in the bricks map. The value is shown next to the leftmost bottom arrow in Figure 12-17.

Case 3. Bricks map moving left and bCoord is greater than (pWidth-width+imWidth)

The relevant code fragment is shown here:

```
if ((bCoord < 0) && (bCoord >= pWidth-width+imWidth))
   drawBricks(g, 0-offset, pWidth, -bCoord);             // bm tail
```

Figure 12-18 illustrates the drawing operation.

Case 3 applies when the bricks map is moving left, as the sprite is apparently traveling to the right. xMapHead goes negative, as does bCoord, but the calculated offset is adjusted to be positive.

Until bCoord drops below (pWidth-width+imWidth), the bricks map will only require one drawBricks( ) call to fill the JPanel.

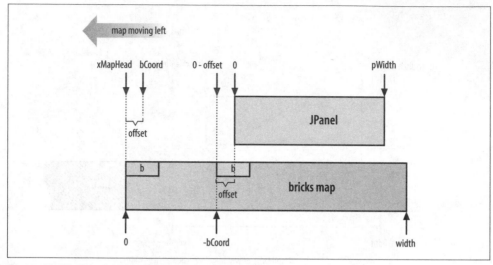

Figure 12-18. Case 3 in BricksManager's display()

Case 4. Bricks map moving left and bCoord is less than (pWidth-width+ imWidth)

Here's the code:

```
if (bCoord < pWidth-width+imWidth) {
  drawBricks(g, 0-offset, width+xMapHead, -bCoord);  // bm tail
  drawBricks(g, width+xMapHead, pWidth, 0);     // bm start
}
```

Figure 12-19 shows the operations.

Case 4 occurs after xMapHead has moved to the left of (pWidth-width+imWidth). Two drawBricks() calls are needed to render two groups of columns to the JPanel. The group's areas are shown in solid gray and striped in the bricks map in Figure 12-19.

The drawBricks( ) method

drawBricks() draws bricks into the JPanel between xStart and xEnd. The bricks are drawn a column at a time, separated by imWidth pixels. The first column of bricks drawn is the one at the xBrick pixel x-coordinate in the bricks map:

```
private void drawBricks(Graphics g, int xStart, int xEnd, int xBrick)
{ int xMap = xBrick/imWidth;    // get column position of the brick
                                // in the bricks map
  ArrayList column;
  Brick b;
  for (int x = xStart; x < xEnd; x += imWidth) {
    column = columnBricks[ xMap ];   // get the current column
    for (int i=0; i < column.size(); i++) {   // draw all bricks
```

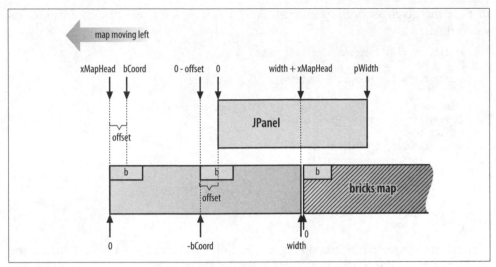

Figure 12-19. Case 4 in BricksManager's display()

```
        b = (Brick) column.get(i);
        b.display(g, x);    // draw brick b at JPanel posn x
    }
    xMap++;  // examine the next column of bricks
  }
}
```

drawBricks( ) converts the xBrick value, a pixel x-coordinate in the bricks map, into a map x index. This index is the column position of the brick, so the entire column can be accessed immediately in columnBricks[ ]. The bricks in the column are drawn by calling the display( ) method for each brick.

Only the JPanel's x-coordinate is passed to display( ) with the y-coordinate stored in the Brick object. This is possible since a brick's y-axis position never changes as the bricks map is moved horizontally over the JPanel.

JumperSprite-Related Methods

The BricksManager has several public methods used by JumperSprite to determine or check its position in the bricks map. The prototypes of these methods are:

```
    int findFloor(int xSprite);
    boolean insideBrick(int xWorld, int yWorld);
    int checkBrickBase(int xWorld, int yWorld, int step);
    int checkBrickTop(int xWorld, int yWorld, int step);
```

Finding the floor

When Jack is added to the scene, his x-coordinate is in the middle of the JPanel, but what should his y-coordinate be? His feet should be placed on the top-most brick at or near the given x-coordinate. findFloor() searches for this brick, returning its y-coordinate:

```
public int findFloor(int xSprite)
{
  int xMap = (int)(xSprite/imWidth);    // x map index

  int locY = pHeight;      // starting y pos (largest possible)
  ArrayList column = columnBricks[ xMap ];
  Brick b;
  for (int i=0; i < column.size(); i++) {
    b = (Brick) column.get(i);
    if (b.getLocY() < locY)
      locY = b.getLocY();    // reduce locY (i.e., move up)
  }
  return locY;
}
```

Matters are simplified by the timing of the call: findFloor() is invoked before the sprite has moved and, therefore, before the bricks map has moved. Consequently, the sprite's x-coordinate in the JPanel (xSprite) is the same x-coordinate in the bricks map.

xSprite is converted to a map x index to permit the relevant column of bricks to be accessed in columnBricks[].

Testing for brick collision

JumperSprite implements collision detection by calculating its new position after a proposed move and by testing if that point (xWorld, yWorld) is inside a brick. If it is, then the move is aborted and the sprite stops moving.

The point testing is done by BricksManager's insideBrick(), which uses worldToMap() to convert the sprite's coordinate to a brick map index tuple:

```
public boolean insideBrick(int xWorld, int yWorld)
// Check if the world coord is inside a brick
{
  Point mapCoord = worldToMap(xWorld, yWorld);
  ArrayList column = columnBricks[ mapCoord.x ];
  Brick b;
  for (int i=0; i < column.size(); i++) {
    b = (Brick) column.get(i);
    if (mapCoord.y == b.getMapY())
      return true;
  }
  return false;
}  // end of insideBrick()
```

worldToMap() returns a Point object holding the x and y map indices corresponding to (xWorld, yWorld). The relevant brick column in columnBricks[] can then be searched for a brick at the y map position.

The conversion carried out by worldToMap() can be understood by referring to Figure 12-14. Here's the code:

```
private Point worldToMap(int xWorld, int yWorld)
// convert world coord (x,y) to a map index tuple
{
  xWorld = xWorld % width;    // limit to range (width to -width)
  if (xWorld < 0)             // make positive
    xWorld += width;
  int mapX = (int) (xWorld/imWidth);   // map x-index

  yWorld = yWorld - (pHeight-height);  // relative to map
  int mapY = (int) (yWorld/imHeight);  // map y-index

  if (yWorld < 0)    // above the top of the bricks
    mapY = mapY-1;   // match to next 'row' up

  return new Point(mapX, mapY);
}
```

xWorld can be any positive or negative value, so it must be restricted to the range (0 to *width*), which is the extent of the bricks map. The coordinate is then converted to a map a index.

The yWorld value uses the JPanel's coordinate system, so it is made relative to the y-origin of the bricks map (some distance down from the top of the JPanel). The conversion to a map y index must take into account the possibility that the sprite's position is above the top of the bricks map. This can occur by having the sprite jump upward while standing on a platform at the top of the bricks map.

Jumping and hitting your head

When Jack jumps, his progress upward will be halted if he is about to pass through the base of a brick. The concept is illustrated in Figure 12-20.

The sprite hopes to move upward by a step amount, but this will cause it to enter the brick. Instead, it will travel upward by a smaller step, step-(imHeight-topOffset), placing its top edge next to the bottom edge of the brick.

checkBrickBase() is supplied with the planned new position (xWorld, yWorld)—labeled as (x, y) in Figure 12-20—and the step. It returns the step distance that the sprite can move without passing into a brick:

```
public int checkBrickBase(int xWorld, int yWorld, int step)
{
  if (insideBrick(xWorld, yWorld)) {
    int yMapWorld = yWorld - (pHeight-height);
    int mapY = (int) (yMapWorld/imHeight);  // map y- index
    int topOffset = yMapWorld - (mapY * imHeight);
    return (step - (imHeight-topOffset));   // a smaller step
  }
  return step;   // no change
}
```

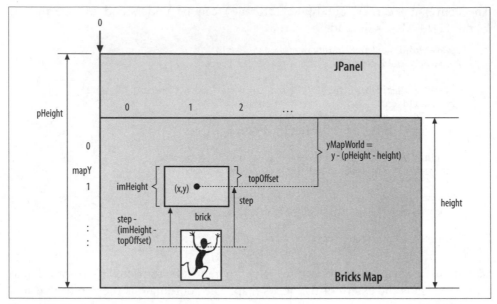

Figure 12-20. A rising sprite hitting a brick

Falling and sinking into the ground

As a sprite descends, during a jump or after walking off the edge of a raised platform, it must test its next position to ensure that it doesn't pass through a brick on its way down. When a brick is detected beneath the sprite's feet, the descent is stopped, ensuring that the Jack lands on top of the brick. Figure 12-21 illustrates the calculation.

The sprite moves downward by a step amount on each update, but when a collision is detected, the step size is reduced to step-topOffset so it comes to rest on top of the brick:

```
public int checkBrickTop(int xWorld, int yWorld, int step)
{
  if (insideBrick(xWorld, yWorld)) {
    int yMapWorld = yWorld - (pHeight-height);
    int mapY = (int) (yMapWorld/imHeight);  // map y- index
    int topOffset = yMapWorld - (mapY * imHeight);
    return (step - topOffset);    // a smaller step
  }
  return step;   // no change
}
```

The intended new position for the sprite (xWorld, yWorld) is passed to checkBrickTop( ), along with the step size. The returned value is the step the sprite should take to avoid sinking into a brick.

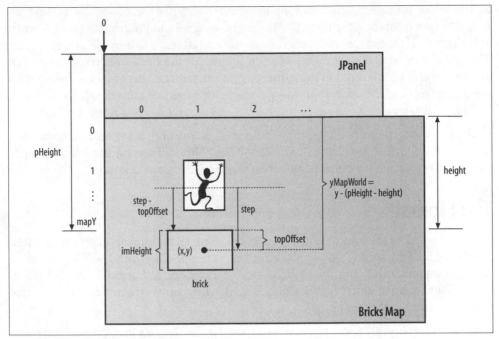

Figure 12-21. A falling sprite hitting a brick

Storing Brick Information

The Brick class stores coordinate information for a brick and a reference to its image. The coordinate details are the brick's map indices and its y-axis pixel position inside the map.

 The x-axis position isn't stored since it changes as the bricks map is moved horizontally.

Brick's display( ) method is short:

```
public void display(Graphics g, int xScr)
// called by BricksManager's drawBricks()
{  g.drawImage(image, xScr, locY, null);  }
```

 xScr is the current JPanel x coordinate for the brick.

The capabilities of the Brick class could be extended. One common feature in side-scrollers is animated tiles, such as flames and rotating balls. If the animation is local to the tile's allocated map location, then the effect can be coded by adding an ImagesPlayer to Brick. One issue is whether to assign a unique ImagesPlayer to each Brick (costly if there are many bricks) or to store a reference to a single ImagesPlayer. The drawback with the reference solution is that all the bricks referring to a given animation will be animated in the same way on the screen. This can look overly regimented in most games. A compromise is to create an AnimatedBrick subclass, which will be used rarely, so it can support the overhead of having its own ImagesPlayer.

If tiles can move about in the game world (e.g., a platform that moves up and down), then bricks will need more sprite-like capabilities. This will complicate BricksManager as a Brick object can no longer be relied on to stay in the same column.

The Fireball

A fireball starts at the lower righthand side of the panel and travels across to the left. If it hits Jack, the fireball will explode and a corresponding sound will be heard. A fireball that has traveled off the lefthand side of the panel, or has exploded, is reused. The FireBallSprite object is repositioned somewhere on the right edge of the game panel and fired at Jack again.

Only a single fireball is on the screen at a time, so JumpingJack creates only one FireBallSprite object. It is declared in JackPanel's constructor:

```
fireball = new FireBallSprite(PWIDTH, PHEIGHT, imsLoader, this, jack);
```

The fourth argument is a reference to JackPanel allowing the fireball to call its methods; the fifth argument is a reference to the JumperSprite object, jack, allowing the fireball to call its methods.

As the fireball moves left, it keeps checking whether it has hit Jack. If a collision occurs, JackPanel will be asked to display an explosion as FireBallSprite resets its position.

Statechart Specification

The statechart in Figure 12-22 is a useful way of specifying the design needs of FireBallSprite.

 Statecharts were introduced in Chapter 11.

The update/draw cycle driven by JackPanel's animation loop is visible. There are two special cases to consider: when the fireball hits Jack and when it leaves the left side of the panel.

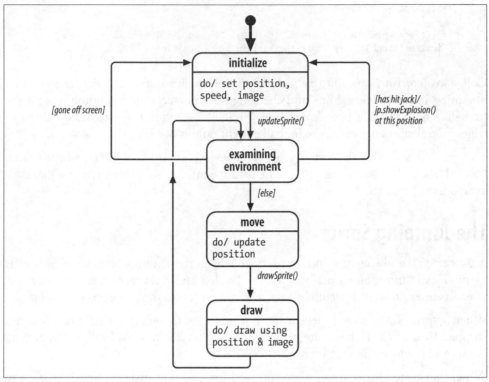

Figure 12-22. The FireBallSprite statechart

The examining environment and move states are represented by updateSprite():

```
public void updateSprite()
{ hasHitJack();
  goneOffScreen();
  super.updateSprite();
}


private void hasHitJack()
/* If the ball has hit jack, tell JackPanel (which will
   display an explosion and play a clip), and begin again.
*/
{ Rectangle jackBox = jack.getMyRectangle();
  jackBox.grow(-jackBox.width/3, 0);    // make bounding box thinner

  if (jackBox.intersects( getMyRectangle() )) {      // collision?
    jp.showExplosion(locx, locy+getHeight()/2);
            // tell JackPanel, supplying it with a hit coordinate
    initPosition();
  }
} // end of hasHitJack()
```

```
private void goneOffScreen()
{
  if (((locx+getWidth()) <= 0) && (dx < 0)) // gone off left
    initPosition();   // start the ball in a new position
}
```

Collision detection (the *[has hit jack]* condition in the statechart) is carried out by obtaining Jack's bounding box and checking if it intersects the bounding box for the fireball. The bounding box dimensions for Jack are temporarily reduced a little to trigger a collision only when the fireball is right on top of him.

The *move* state is dealt with by Sprite's updateSprite(), which is called from FireBallSprite's updateSprite(). The *draw* state is implemented by Sprite's drawSprite() method.

The Jumping Sprite

A JumperSprite object can appear to move left or right, jump, and stand still. The sprite doesn't move horizontally at all, but the left and right movement requests will affect its internal state. It maintains its current world coordinates in (xWorld, yWorld).

When a sprite starts moving left or right, it will keep traveling in that direction until stopped by a brick. If the sprite runs off a raised platform, it will fall to the ground below and continue moving forward.

When the sprite jumps, it continues upward for a certain distance and falls back to the ground. The upward trajectory is stopped if the sprite hits a brick.

Statechart Specification

The JumperSprite statechart is given in Figure 12-23.

The statechart models JumperSprite as three concurrent activities: its horizontal movement in the top section, its vertical movement in the middle section, and the update/draw cycle in the bottom section.

 The effects of an updateSprite() event have been distributed through the diagram, rather than placing them together in an *examining environment* state.

The horizontal movement section shows that a new updateSprite() event doesn't change the current state, be it moving right, moving left, or stationary. Movement stops when the user sends a stop event or when the sprite hits a brick.

The vertical movement section utilizes three states: not jumping, rising, and falling. Rising is controlled by an upCount counter, which limits how long an upward move can last. Rising may be stopped by the sprite hitting a brick. Falling is triggered when

---

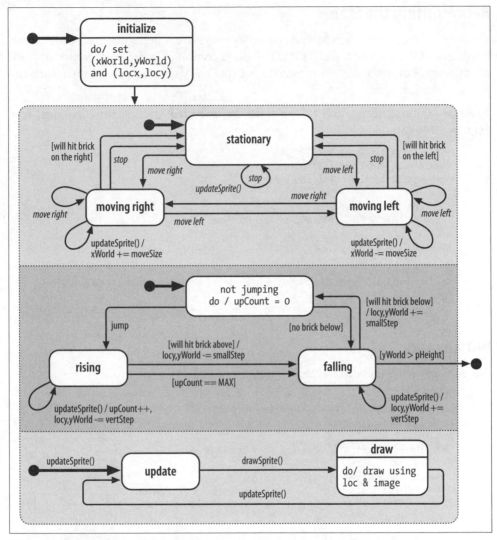

Figure 12-23. The JumperSprite statechart

rising finishes and when no brick is underneath the sprite. This latter condition becomes true when the sprite moves horizontally off a raised platform.

The falling state can lead to termination if the sprite drops below the bottom of the panel (yWorld > pHeight). In fact, this transition led to a redesign of BricksManager to reject a bricks map with a gap in its floor. Consequently, dropping off the panel cannot occur in JumpingJack.

Though the statechart is clear, I want to avoid the complexity of multiple threads in JumperSprite. Instead, the concurrent activities are interleaved together in my code, making it somewhat harder to understand but easier to write.

Representing the States

The moving right, moving left, and stationary states are represented indirectly as two Booleans—isFacingRight and isStill—which combine to define the current horizontal state. For instance, when isStill is false and isFacingRight is true, then the sprite is moving right.

The not jumping, rising, and falling states are encoded as constants, assigned to a vertMoveMode variable:

```
private static final int NOT_JUMPING = 0;
private static final int RISING = 1;
private static final int FALLING = 2;

private int vertMoveMode;
  /* can be NOT_JUMPING, RISING, or FALLING */

private boolean isFacingRight, isStill;
```

 In J2SE 5.0, vertMoveMode could be defined using an enumerated type.

Initialization

The *initialize* state is coded in JumperSprite's constructor:

```
// some globals
private int vertStep;    // distance to move vertically in one step
private int upCount;

private int moveSize;    // obtained from BricksManager

private int xWorld, yWorld;
  /* the current position of the sprite in 'world' coordinates.
     The x-values may be negative. The y-values will be between
     0 and pHeight. */


public JumperSprite(int w, int h, int brickMvSz, BricksManager bm,
                                  ImagesLoader imsLd, int p)
{
  super(w/2, h/2, w, h, imsLd, "runningRight");
     // standing center screen, facing right
  moveSize = brickMvSz;
        // the move size is the same as the bricks ribbon

  brickMan = bm;
  period = p;
  setStep(0,0);      // no movement
```

```
    isFacingRight = true;
    isStill = true;

    /* Adjust the sprite's y- position so it is
       standing on the brick at its mid x- position. */
    locy = brickMan.findFloor(locx+getWidth()/2)-getHeight();
    xWorld = locx; yWorld = locy;    // store current position

    vertMoveMode = NOT_JUMPING;
    vertStep = brickMan.getBrickHeight()/2;
             // the jump step is half a brick's height
    upCount = 0;
  }  // end of JumperSprite()
```

The (xWorld, yWorld) coordinates and the sprite's position and speed are set. The state variables isFacingRight, isStill, and vertMoveMode define a stationary, non-jumping sprite, facing to the right.

BricksManager's findFloor() method is used to get a y location for the sprite that lets it stand on top of a brick. The method's input argument is the sprite's midpoint along the x-axis, which is its leftmost x-coordinate plus half its width (locx+getWidth()/2).

Key Event Processing

The events move left, move right, stop, and jump in the statechart are caught as key presses by the key listener in JackPanel, triggering calls to the JumperSprite methods moveLeft(), moveRight(), stayStill(), and jump().

moveLeft(), moveRight(), and stayStill() affect the horizontal state by adjusting the isFacingRight and isStill variables. The animated image associated with the sprite changes:

```
    public void moveLeft()
    { setImage("runningLeft");
      loopImage(period, DURATION);   // cycle through the images
      isFacingRight = false;  isStill = false;
    }

    public void moveRight()
    { setImage("runningRight");
      loopImage(period, DURATION);   // cycle through the images
      isFacingRight = true;  isStill = false;
    }

    public void stayStill()
    { stopLooping();
      isStill = true;
    }
```

The jump( ) method represents the transition from the not jumping to the rising state in the statechart. This is coded by changing the value stored in vertMoveMode. The sprite's image is modified:

```
public void jump( )
{ if (vertMoveMode == NOT_JUMPING) {
    vertMoveMode = RISING;
    upCount = 0;
    if (isStill) {     // only change image if the sprite is 'still'
      if (isFacingRight)
        setImage("jumpRight");
      else
        setImage("jumpLeft");
    }
  }
}
```

JackPanel Collision Testing

The *[will hit brick on the right]* and *[will it brick on the left]* conditional transitions in the statechart are implemented as a public willHitBrick( ) method called from JackPanel's gameUpdate( ) method:

```
private void gameUpdate( )
{
  if (!isPaused && !gameOver) {
    if (jack.willHitBrick()) { // collision checking first
      jack.stayStill();      // stop everything moving
      bricksMan.stayStill();
      ribsMan.stayStill();
    }
    ribsMan.update();    // update background and sprites
    bricksMan.update();
    jack.updateSprite();
    fireball.updateSprite();

    if (showExplosion)
      explosionPlayer.updateTick();  // update the animation
  }
}
```

The reason for placing the test in JackPanel's hands is so it can coordinate the other game entities when a collision occurs. The JumperSprite and the background layers in the game are halted:

```
public boolean willHitBrick( )
{
  if (isStill)
    return false;    // can't hit anything if not moving

  int xTest;   // for testing the new x- position
  if (isFacingRight)   // moving right
    xTest = xWorld + moveSize;
```

```
      else // moving left
        xTest = xWorld - moveSize;

      // test a point near the base of the sprite
      int xMid = xTest + getWidth( )/2;
      int yMid = yWorld + (int)(getHeight( )*0.8);     // use y posn

      return brickMan.insideBrick(xMid,yMid);
    }  // end of willHitBrick( )
```

willHitBrick( ) represents two conditional transitions, so the isFacingRight flag is used to distinguish how xTest should be modified. The proposed new coordinate is generated and passed to BricksManager's insideBrick( ) for evaluation.

The vertical collision testing in the middle section of the statechart, *[will hit brick below]* and *[will hit brick above]*, is carried out by JumperSprite, not JackPanel, since a collision affects only the sprite.

Updating the Sprite

The statechart distributes the actions of the updateState( ) event around the state-chart: actions are associated with the moving right, moving left, rising, and falling states. These actions are implemented in the updateState( ) method, and the functions it calls:

```
    public void updateSprite( )
    {
      if (!isStill) {      // moving
        if (isFacingRight)  // moving right
          xWorld += moveSize;
        else // moving left
          xWorld -= moveSize;
        if (vertMoveMode == NOT_JUMPING)    // if not jumping
          checkIfFalling( );   // may have moved out into empty space
      }

      // vertical movement has two components: RISING and FALLING
      if (vertMoveMode == RISING)
        updateRising( );
      else if (vertMoveMode == FALLING)
        updateFalling( );

      super.updateSprite( );
    }  // end of updateSprite( )
```

The method updates its horizontal position (xWorld) first, distinguishing between moving right or left by examining isStill and isFacingRight. After the move, checkIfFalling( ) decides whether the *[no brick below]* transition from not jumping to falling should be applied. The third stage of the method is to update the vertical states.

Lastly, the call to Sprite's updateSprite( ) method modifies the sprite's position and image. updateSprite( ) illustrates the coding issues that arise when concurrent activities (in this case, horizontal and vertical movement) are sequentialized. The statechart places no restraints on the ordering of the two types of movement, but an ordering must be imposed when it's programmed as a sequence. In updateSprite( ), the horizontal actions are carried out before the vertical ones.

Falling?

checkIfFalling( ) determines whether the not jumping state should be changed to falling:

```
private void checkIfFalling( )
{
  // could the sprite move downwards if it wanted to?
  // test its center x-coord, base y-coord
  int yTrans = brickMan.checkBrickTop( xWorld+(getWidth( )/2),
                     yWorld+getHeight( )+vertStep, vertStep);
  if (yTrans != 0)    // yes it could
    vertMoveMode = FALLING;    // set it to be in falling mode
}
```

The test is carried out by passing the coordinates of the sprite's feet, plus a vertical offset downward, to checkBrickTop( ) in BricksManager.

Vertical Movement

updateRising( ) deals with the updateSprite( ) event associated with the *rising* state, and tests for the two conditional transitions that leave the state: rising can stop either when upCount = MAX or when *[will hit brick above]* becomes true. Rising will continue until the maximum number of vertical steps is reached or the sprite hits the base of a brick. The sprite then switches to falling mode. checkBrickBase( ) in BricksManager carries out the collision detection:

```
private void updateRising( )
{ if (upCount == MAX_UP_STEPS) {
    vertMoveMode = FALLING;    // at top, now start falling
    upCount = 0;
  }
  else {
    int yTrans = brickMan.checkBrickBase(xWorld+(getWidth( )/2),
                           yWorld-vertStep, vertStep);
    if (yTrans == 0) {    // hit the base of a brick
      vertMoveMode = FALLING;    // start falling
      upCount = 0;
    }
    else {    // can move upwards another step
      translate(0, -yTrans);
```

```
        yWorld -= yTrans;   // update position
        upCount++;
      }
    }
  }  // end of updateRising( )
```

updateFalling( ) processes the updateSprite( ) event associated with the falling state, and deals with the *[will hit brick below]* transition going to the not jumping state. checkBrickTop( ) in BricksManager carries out the collision detection.

The other conditional leading to termination is not implemented since the bricks map cannot contain any holes for the sprite to fall through:

```
private void updateFalling( )
{ int yTrans = brickMan.checkBrickTop(xWorld+(getWidth( )/2),
                     yWorld+getHeight( )+vertStep, vertStep);
  if (yTrans == 0)   // hit the top of a brick
    finishJumping( );
  else {      // can move downwards another step
    translate(0, yTrans);
    yWorld += yTrans;   // update position
  }
}

private void finishJumping( )
{ vertMoveMode = NOT_JUMPING;
  upCount = 0;
  if (isStill) {     // change to running image, but not looping yet
    if (isFacingRight)
      setImage("runningRight");
    else     // facing left
      setImage("runningLeft");
  }
}
```

Other Side-Scroller Examples

JumpingJack could be improved in many areas, including adding multiple levels, more bad guys (enemy sprites), and complex tiles.

A good source of ideas for improvements can be found in other side-scrolling games. *ArcadePod.com* (*http://arcadepod.com/java/*) lists 64 scroller games though none of the ones I tried came with source code.

The following is a list of side-scrollers, which do include source and were written in the last two to three years:

- *Meat Fighter: The Wiener Warrior* (*http://www.meatfighter.com/*). The web site includes an article about the implementation, which appeared in *Java Developers Journal*, March 2003, Vol. 8, No. 3.

- *Frogma* (*http://sourceforge.net/projects/frogma/*).

- *VideoToons* (*http://sourceforge.net/projects/videotoons/*).
- *Mario Platformer* (*http://www.paraduck.net/misterbob/Platformer1.1/classes/*). Only the compiled classes are available for this applet.

Chapter 5 of *Developing Games in Java* (New Riders Publishing) by David Brackeen, Bret Barker, and Laurence Vanhelswue is about a side-scroller (a 2D platform game). (The source code for this book's examples can be obtained from *http://www.brackeen.com/javagamebook/*.) He develops a wider range of bad guys than I have and includes things for the hero to pick up. However, the game doesn't have multiple scrolling backgrounds.

A good place for articles about tile-based games is the "Isometric and Tile-based Games" reference section at *GameDev* (*http://www.gamedev.net/reference/list.asp?categoryid=44*).

Tiling Software

One of the time-consuming aspects of side-scroller creation is the building of the tile map. A realistic game will require a much larger collection of tiles, including ones for smoothing the transition between one type of tile and another.

Tile map editors let you visually edit tiles and build a map using drawing tools. Here are two popular, free tools:

- Tile Studio (*http://tilestudio.sourceforge.net/*)
- Mappy for PC (*http://www.tilemap.co.uk/mappy.php*)

Functionally, they're similar, but Mappy has additional support for creating hexagonal and isometric tiles. It's possible to customize how TileStudio exports its data by creating a Tile Studio Definition (TSD), which defines the output file format.

Tile Studio is used with Java (actually J2ME) in Chapter 11 of *J2ME Game Programming* by Martin Wells (Muska and Lipman/Premier-Trade). In the example, Tile Studio exports several tile maps to a TSD-defined file, and Java is used to read them. This chapter is available online at *http://www.courseptr.com/ptr_detail.cfm?isbn=1592001181*.

Mappy places a lot of emphasis on playback libraries/APIs, allowing its maps to be loaded, manipulated, and displayed. The Mappy web site offers two Java playback libraries. JavaMappy (*http://www.alienfactory.co.uk/javamappy/*) is an open source Java playback library for Mappy. It includes pluggable renderers for J2ME and J2SE 1.4. The download includes several examples and documentation.

CHAPTER 13

An Isometric Tile Game

AlienTiles is a basic *isometric tile* game consisting of one player who must pick up a cup, flower pot, and a watch before four nasty aliens catch and hit him three times (see Figure 13-1).

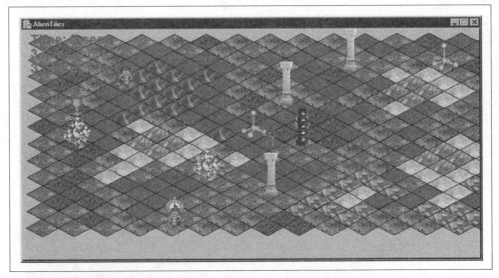

Figure 13-1. AlienTiles in action

The player is represented by a little blue man with a red cap in the center of the screen. The orange aliens (with red hair) are a bit easier to see in Figure 13-1, though one is mostly hidden by the black and white column just to the right of the player, and two of the aliens are momentarily occupying the same tile, so one is obscured.

Isometric Tiles

Isometric tiles are the basis of many real-time strategy (RTS) games, war games, and simulations (e.g., *Civilization II, Age of Empires*, and *SimCity* variants), though the tiling of the game surface is usually hidden.

Isometric tiles give an artificial sense of depth as if the player's viewpoint is somewhere up in the sky, looking down over the playing area. Of course, this view is artificial since no perspective effects are applied; the tiles in the row "nearest" the viewer are the same size and shape as the tiles in the most "distant" row at the top of the screen. This is where the term isometric comes from: an *isometric projection* is a 3D projection that doesn't correct for distance.

The illusion that each row of tiles is further back inside the game is supported by the z-ordering of things (sprites, objects) drawn in the rows. An object on a row nearer the front is drawn after those on rows further back, hiding anything behind it. This is the case in Figure 13-1, where the black and white column partially hides the alien standing two rows behind it.

There are various ways of labeling the x-axis and y-axis of a isometric tile map. I'll use the standard *staggered-map* approach illustrated in Figure 13-2.

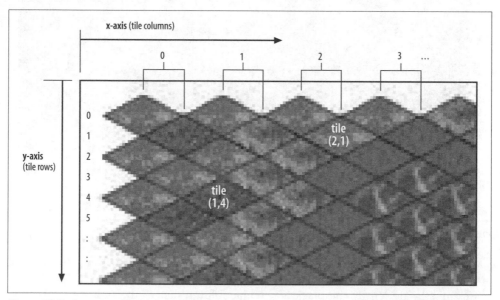

Figure 13-2. A staggered isometric tile map

Odd and even rows are offset from each other, which means that the tile coordinates can be a little tricky to work out as a sprite moves between rows.

`AlienTiles` uses tile coordinates to position sprites and other objects on the surface. However, the surface isn't made from tiles; instead, it's a single medium size GIF (216 KB), as shown in Figure 13-3.

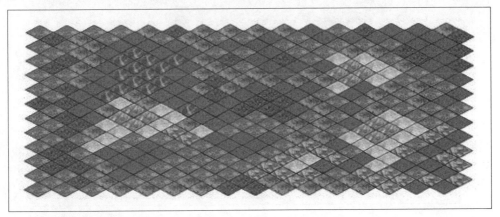

Figure 13-3. The surface.gif image

Most isometric games construct the surface from individual tiles, which allows the floor space to be rendered incrementally and to change dynamically over time. The drawback is the increased complexity (and time) in drawing the tiles to the screen. Drawing the individual tiles in back-to-front row order is necessary, with each diamond represented by a rectangular GIF with transparent corners. The coding problems are like the difficulties detailed in Chapter 12, with positioning bricks correctly on screen as the `JumpingSprite` moved around. And do you want to go through all of that again?

Often, the surface will be a composite of several layers of tile of different sizes. For example, there may be several large green tiles for the terrain, partially covered over with smaller grass, dirt, and sand tiles to create variety. *Fringe tiles* are employed to break up the regularity of the edges between two large areas, such as the land and the sea. The graphic on a fringe tile represents the edge (or fringe) of one kind of tile, and the start of another.

Movement

`AlienTiles` offers four directions for a sprite to follow: northeast, southeast, southwest, and northwest, as illustrated by Figure 13-4.

The user interface maps these directions to the four corners of the numbers keypad: to the keys 9, 3, 1, and 7. Pressing one of these keys makes the sprite move one step to the corresponding adjacent tile. An obvious extension is to offer north, east, south, and west movement.

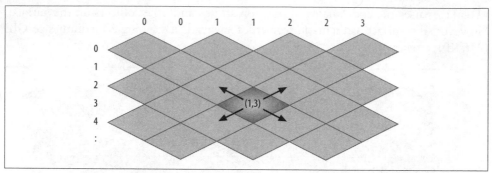

Figure 13-4. Directions of movement for a sprite

The range of directions is dictated by the tile shape, to a large extent, and diamonds aren't the only possibility. For instance, a number of strategy games use hexagons to form a *Hex* map (Figure 13-5), which allows six compass directions out of a tile.

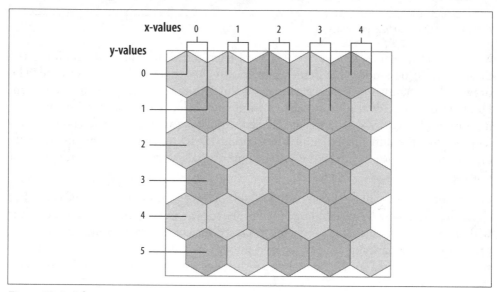

Figure 13-5. A hex map

Movement around an isometric tile surface is often based on single steps between tiles. It's not possible for a sprite to move about inside a tile; the sprite can only stand still on a tile or make a single step to an adjacent tile. In AlienTiles, a key press causes a single step, and the user must hold down the key to make the sprite sprint across several tiles. A key press triggers a method call to update the sprite's position, which is updated onscreen at 40 FPS.

This rate is fast enough to deal with the user keeping a key constantly held down.

Though I talk about a player moving around the surface, the truth is that the user's sprite doesn't move at all. Instead, the surface moves in the opposite direction, together with the other objects and sprites. For instance, when the player moves to the northeast, the user's sprite stays still but the ground underneath it shifts to the southwest.

This nonmovement is only true for the user's sprite; the alien sprites do move from one tile to another.

As with a side-scroller, this approach keeps the user's sprite center stage at all times. In commercial games, a player's sprite does sometimes move to the edge of the screen, usually as a prelude to entering a new game level.

Placing a Sprite/Object

Care must be taken with object placement so the illusion of an object standing on top a tile is maintained. Figure 13-6 shows that the positioning of a sprite's top-left corner, so planting its "feet" on the tile's surface can be a little hard to calculate:

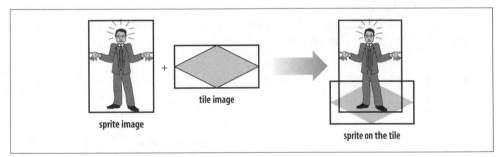

Figure 13-6. Placing a sprite onto a tile

The sprite can occupy screen space above the tile but should not overlap the bottom left and right edges of the diamond. If it does, the image will seem to be partly in the next row, weakening the row ordering effect. I'll implement this placement rule in my code later.

The Tile Map Surface

The `AlienTiles` surface contains no-go areas that the sprites cannot enter. These include the ocean around the edges of the tiled surface, a lake, a pond, and four red squares (all visible in Figure 13-1). The no-go areas are defined in a configuration file read in by `AlienTiles` at start-up.

The game surface has two kinds of objects resting on it: *blocks* and *pickups*. A block fully occupies a tile, preventing a sprite from moving onto it. The block image can be anything; I employ various columns and geometric shapes. A player can remove a pickup from the surface when it's standing on the same tile by pressing 2 on the numeric keypad.

Blocks and pickups are harder to implement than no-go areas since they occupy space on the game surface. This means that a sprite can move behind one and be partially hidden. Pickups pose more problems than blocks since they can be removed from a tile.

More sophisticated games have a much greater variety of surface objects. Two common types are *walls* and *portals* (doors). A wall between two tiles prevents a sprite from moving between the tiles. A portal is often used as a way of moving between tile maps, for example when moving to the next game level or entering a building with its own floor plan.

The Aliens

`AlienTiles` offers two types of aliens: those that actively chase after the player (`AlienAStarSprite` objects) and those that congregate around the pickup that the player is heading toward (`AlienQuadSprite` objects).

 The `AlienAStarSprite` class uses A* (pronounced "A star") pathfinding to chase the player, which will be explained later in this chapter.

In general, alien design opens the door to intelligent behavior code, often based on Artificial Intelligence (AI) techniques. Surprisingly though, quite believable sprite behavior can often be hacked together with the use of a few random numbers and conventional loops and branches, and `AlienQuadSprite` is an illustration.

Class Diagrams for AlienTiles

Figure 13-7 shows a simplified set of class diagrams for `AlienTiles`. The audio and image classes (e.g., `MidisLoader`, `ClipsLoader`, and `ImagesLoader`) have been edited away, and the less important links between the remaining classes have been pruned back for clarity.

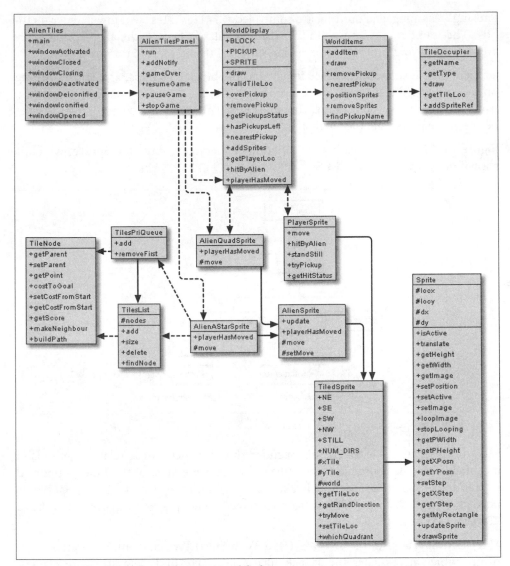

Figure 13-7. AlienTiles classes diagram (simplified)

The AlienTiles JFrame and the AlienTilesPanel JPanel implement the windowed animation framework introduced in Chapters 2 and 3, BugRunner of Chapter 11, and JumpingJack of Chapter 12 use the same technique.

Pausing, resuming, and quitting are controlled via `AlienTiles`' window listener methods. The frame rate is set to 40 FPS, which is still too fast for the alien sprites; they are slowed down further by code in `AlienQuadSprite` and `AlienAStarSprite`.

`WorldDisplay` displays the surface image and the blocks, pickups, and sprites resting on the surface. The tile coordinates for the entities are stored in a `WorldItems` object, using a `TileOccupier` object for each one. `WorldDisplay` acts as a communication layer between the player and the aliens.

Figure 13-7 includes a small sprite inheritance hierarchy, rooted at `Sprite`, which is shown on its own in Figure 13-8.

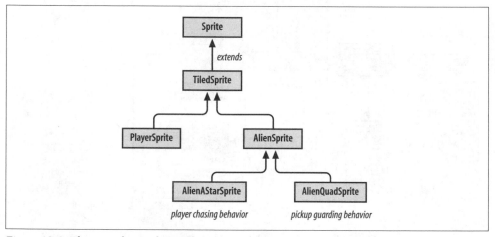

Figure 13-8. The sprite hierarchy in AlienTiles

Most of the methods in `Sprite` are extended or overridden by tile-related methods in its subclasses. Tile coordinates are utilized by the game most of the time, supported by methods in `TiledSprite` though a sprite's pixel location (maintained by `Sprite`) is needed when it's being drawn to the screen. The player is represented by a `PlayerSprite` object.

`AlienAStarSprite` uses the A* JWS (Java Web Start):JWS and other libraries algorithm, which necessitates the `TilesPriQueue` and `TilesList` data structure classes; they maintain sequences of `TileNode` objects.

 The code for the `AlienTiles` game can be found in the *AlienTiles/* directory.

The Animation Framework

`AlienTilesPanel` is similar to `JackPanel` in Chapter 12; it uses an active rendering animation loop driven by Java 3D's timer. It displays an introductory image when the game starts, which doubles as a help screen during the course of play. While the help screen is being shown, the game pauses.

Managing the Game World

AlienTilesPanel creates the various game elements in createWorld( ):

```
// globals game entities
private WorldDisplay world;
private PlayerSprite player;
private AlienSprite aliens[];


private void createWorld(ImagesLoader imsLoader)
// create the world display, the player, and aliens
{
  world = new WorldDisplay(imsLoader, this);

  player = new PlayerSprite(7,12, PWIDTH, PHEIGHT,
                   clipsLoader, imsLoader, world, this);
                   // sprite starts on tile (7,12)

  aliens = new AlienSprite[4];
  aliens[0] = new AlienAStarSprite(10, 11, PWIDTH, PHEIGHT,
                                        imsLoader, world);
  aliens[1] = new AlienQuadSprite(6, 21, PWIDTH, PHEIGHT,
                                        imsLoader, world);
  aliens[2] = new AlienQuadSprite(14, 20, PWIDTH, PHEIGHT,
                                        imsLoader, world);
  aliens[3] = new AlienAStarSprite(34, 34, PWIDTH, PHEIGHT,
                                        imsLoader, world);
   // use 2 AStar and 2 quad alien sprites
   // the 4th alien is placed at an illegal tile location (34,34)

  world.addSprites(player, aliens);
                     // tell the world about the sprites
} // end of createWorld( )
```

Tile coordinates are passed to the sprites, rather than pixel locations in the JPanel. The two A* and two quad sprites are stored in an aliens[] array to make it easier to send messages to all of them as a group.

The player and aliens do not communicate directly; instead, they call methods in the WorldDisplay object, world, which passes the messages on. This requires that sprite references be passed to world via a call to addSprites( ).

Dealing with Input

The game is controlled from the keyboard only; no mouse events are caught. As in previous applications, the key presses are handled by processKey( ), which deals with termination keys (e.g., Ctrl-C), toggling the help screen, and player controls. The code related to the player keys is:

```
private void processKey(KeyEvent e)
// handles termination, help, and game-play keys
{
  int keyCode = e.getKeyCode( );

  // processing of termination and help keys
  ...

  // game-play keys
  if (!isPaused && !gameOver) {
    // move the player based on the numpad key pressed
    if (keyCode == KeyEvent.VK_NUMPAD7)
      player.move(TiledSprite.NW);    // move north west
    else if (keyCode == KeyEvent.VK_NUMPAD9)
      player.move(TiledSprite.NE);    // north east
    else if (keyCode == KeyEvent.VK_NUMPAD3)
      player.move(TiledSprite.SE);    // south east
    else if (keyCode == KeyEvent.VK_NUMPAD1)
      player.move(TiledSprite.SW);    // south west
    else if (keyCode == KeyEvent.VK_NUMPAD5)
      player.standStill( );                // stand still
    else if (keyCode == KeyEvent.VK_NUMPAD2)
      player.tryPickup( );        // try to pick up from this tile
  }
}  // end of processKey( )
```

Three `PlayerSprite` methods are called: move( ), standStill( ), and tryPickup( ). These correspond to the three things a sprite can do: move to another tile, stand still, and pick up something. The "standing still" action is fairly trivial: it only changes the sprite's image.

The Animation Loop

The animation loop is located in run( ) and unchanged from earlier examples:

```
public void run( )
{ // initialization code
  while (running) {
    gameUpdate( );
    gameRender( );
    paintScreen( );
    // timing correction code
  }
  System.exit(0);
}
```

gameUpdate( ) updates the changing game entities (the four mobile aliens):

```
private void gameUpdate()
{ if (!isPaused && !gameOver) {
    for(int i=0; i < aliens.length; i++)
      aliens[i].update();
  }
}
```

gameRender( ) relies on the WorldDisplay object to draw the surface and its contents:

```
private void gameRender()
{
  // create the dbg graphics context

  // a light blue background
  dbg.setColor(lightBlue);
  dbg.fillRect(0, 0, PWIDTH, PHEIGHT);

  // draw the game elements: order is important
  world.draw(dbg);
  /* WorldDisplay draws the game world: the tile floor, blocks,
     pickups, and the sprites. */

  reportStats(dbg);
    // report time spent playing, number of hits, pickups left

  if (gameOver)
    gameOverMessage(dbg);

  if (showHelp)    // draw the help at the very front (if switched on)
    dbg.drawImage(helpIm, (PWIDTH-helpIm.getWidth())/2,
                          (PHEIGHT-helpIm.getHeight())/2, null);
}  // end of gameRender()
```

Ending the Game

The game finishes (gameOver is set to true) when the player has been hit enough times or when all the pickups (a cup, flower pot, and watch) have been gathered. The first condition is detected by the PlayerSprite object and the second by the WorldDisplay object; both of them call gameOver( ) to notify AlienTilesPanel when the game should be stopped:

```
public void gameOver()
{  if (!gameOver) {
     gameOver = true;
     score = (int) ((J3DTimer.getValue() -
                          gameStartTime)/1000000000L);
     clipsLoader.play("applause", false);
   }
}
```

Managing the World

`WorldDisplay` manages:

- The moving tile floor, represented by a single GIF
- No-go areas on the floor
- Blocks occupying certain tiles
- Pickups occupying certain tiles
- Communication between the player and aliens sprites

The communication between the player and sprites in the game is rudimentary, mainly involving the transmission of position information and the number of pickups left. However, the coding technique of passing this information through the `WorldDisplay` is a useful one since it allows `WorldDisplay` to monitor and control the interactions between the sprites. `WorldDisplay` utilizes three main data structures:

- An `obstacles[][]` Boolean array specifying which tiles are no-go's or contain blocks
- A `WorldItems` object that stores details on blocks, pickups, and sprites in tile row order to make them easier to draw with the correct z-ordering
- A `numPickups` counter to record how many pickups are still left to be picked up

These are simply declared as variables in the class:

```
private boolean obstacles[][];
private WorldItems wItems;
private int numPickups;
```

`WorldDisplay`'s methods fall into five main groups, which I'll consider in detail in the following subsections:

- The loading of floor information, which describes where the tiles, rows, and columns are located on the floor
- The loading of world entity information, which gives the tile coordinates of the no-go areas, blocks, and pickups
- Pickup-related methods
- Player-related methods
- Drawing the world

Loading Floor Information

The floor image is a single GIF, so additional information must state where the odd and even tile rows are located and give the dimensions for a tile (a diamond). These details are shown in Figure 13-9.

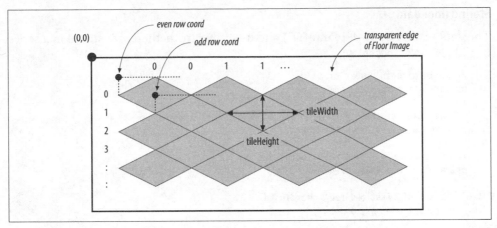

Figure 13-9. Floor information

The relevant information is stored in *worldInfo.txt* in the *World/* subdirectory and read in by loadWorldInfo( ). The file contains the following:

```
// name of the GIF (surface.gif) holding the floor image
image surface

// number of tiles (x,y)
numTiles  16 23

// pixel dimensions of a single tile (width, height)
dimTile 56 29

// 'start of first even row' (x,y) coordinate
evenRow 12 8

// 'start of first odd row' (x,y) coordinate
oddRow 40 23
```

Lines beginning with // are comments.

The image used is *surface.gif*, which should be in the *Images/* subdirectory below the *AlienTiles/* directory. There are 16 columns of tiles, and 23 rows. Each tile is 56 pixels wide, at its widest point, and 29 pixels high. The first even row (row 0) starts at pixel coordinate (12,8), the first odd row (row 1) at (40,23). The starting point is taken to be the top-left corner of the rectangle that surrounds the diamond. With this information, translating any tile coordinate into a pixel location in the floor image is possible.

Storing floor data

The data read in by loadFloorInfo( ) and its secondary methods are stored in a series of globals in WorldDisplay:

```
// world size in number of tiles
private int numXTiles, numYTiles;

// max pixel width/height of a tile
private int tileWidth, tileHeight;

// 'start of first even row' coordinate
private int evenRowX, evenRowY;

// 'start of first odd row' coordinate
private int oddRowX, oddRowY;
```

Most of them are used only to initialize the WorldItems object:

```
WorldItems wItems = new WorldItems(tileWidth, tileHeight,
                         evenRowX, evenRowY, oddRowX, oddRowY);
```

The WorldItems object organizes details about the surface entities (blocks, pickups, and sprites) by tile row to ensure they are drawn to the JPanel with the correct z-ordering. The floor information is required so an entity's tile coordinates can be translated to pixel locations.

Creating obstacles

The number of tiles on the surface is used to initialize the obstacles[][] array:

```
private void initObstacles()
// initially there are no obstacles in the world
{
  obstacles = new boolean[numXTiles][numYTiles];
  for(int i=0; i < numXTiles; i++)
    for(int j=0; j < numYTiles; j++)
      obstacles[i][j] = false;
}
```

Obstacles are registered (i.e., particular cells are set to true) as WorldDisplay loads entity information (see the next section for details).

Sprites utilize validTileLoc( ) to check if a particular tile (x, y) can be entered:

```
public boolean validTileLoc(int x, int y)
// Is tile coord (x,y) on the tile map and not contain an obstacle?
{
  if ((x < 0) || (x >= numXTiles) || (y < 0) || (y >= numYTiles))
    return false;
  if (obstacles[x][y])
    return false;
  return true;
}
```

Loading World Entity Information

Rather than specify the entity positions as constants in the code, the information is read in by `loadWorldObjects( )` from the file *worldObjs.txt* in the subdirectory *World/*.

The data come in three flavors—no-go areas, blocks, and pickups—placed at a given tile coordinate and unable to move. Sprites aren't included in this category since their position can change during game play. Consequently, *worldObjs.txt* supports three data formats:

```
// no-go coordinates
n <x1>-<y1> <x2>-<y2> .....
.... #

// block coordinates for blockName
b <blockName>
  <x1>-<y1> <x2>-<y2> .....
  .... #

// pickup coordinate for pickupName
p <pickupName> <x>-<y>
```

An n is for no-go, followed by multiple lines of (x, y) coordinates defining which tiles are inaccessible. The sequence of coordinates is terminated with a #. A b line starts with a block name, which corresponds to the name of the GIF file for the block, and is followed by a sequence of tile coordinates where the block appears. The name on a p line is mapped to a GIF file name but is followed only by a single coordinate. A pickup is assumed to only appear once on the floor.

The GIFs referenced in this file should be in the subdirectory *Images/* below the *AlienTiles/* directory.

Here is a fragment of *worldObjs.txt*:

```
// bottom right danger zone (red in the GIF)
n 12-13 12-14 13-14 12-15 #

// blocks
b column1
9-3 7-7 7-18 #

b pyramid
1-12 5-16 #

b statue
14-13 #

// pickups
p cup 1-8
```

A quick examination of the *Images/* subdirectory will show the presence of *column1.gif*, *pyramid.gif*, *statue.gif*, and *cup.gif*.

As the information is parsed by loadWorldObjects( ) and its helper methods, the obstacles[][] array and the WorldItems objects are passed through the entity details. For instance, in getsBlocksLine( ), the following code fragment is executed when a (x, y) coordinate for a block has been found:

```
wItems.addItem( blockName+blocksCounter, BLOCK, coord.x, coord.y, im);
obstacles[coord.x][coord.y] = true;
```

addItem( ) adds information about the block to the WorldItems object. The relevant obstacles[][] cell is set to true.

Similar code is executed for a pickup in getPickup( ):

```
wItems.addItem( pickupName, PICKUP, coord.x, coord.y, pickupIm);
numPickups++;
```

The obstacles[][] array is not modified since a sprite must be able to move to a tile occupied by a pickup (so it can pick it up). BLOCK, PICKUP, and SPRITE are constants used by WorldItems to distinguish between tile entities.

Pickup Methods

WorldDisplay offers a range of pickup-related methods used by the sprites. For example, the PlayerSprite object calls removePickup( ) to pick up a named item:

```
public void removePickup(String name)
{ if (wItems.removePickup(name)) {  // try to remove it
    numPickups--;
    if (numPickups == 0)   // player has picked up everything
      atPanel.gameOver( );
  }
  else
    System.out.println("Cannot delete unknown pickup: " + name);
}
```

WorldDisplay communicates with its WorldItems object to attempt the removal and decrements of its numPickups counter. If the counter reaches 0, then the player has collected all the pickups and AlienTilesPanel (atPanel) can be told the game is over.

Player Methods

The player sprite and the aliens don't communicate directly; instead, their interaction is handled through WorldDisplay. This allows code in WorldDisplay the potential to modify, add, or delete information. For example, WorldDisplay might not pass the player's exact position to the aliens, thereby making it harder for them to find him.

This version of the application doesn't change or limit information transfer, but that sort of behavior could be introduced without much difficulty.

One of the more complicated player methods is playerHasMoved( ) called by the PlayerSprite object when it moves to a new tile.

```
public void playerHasMoved(Point newPt, int moveQuad)
{
  for(int i=0; i < aliens.length; i++)
    aliens[i].playerHasMoved(newPt);    // tell the aliens
  updateOffsets(moveQuad);    // update world's offset
}
```

The player passes in a Point object holding its new tile coordinate, as well as the quadrant direction that brought the sprite to the tile. The moveQuad value can be the constant NE, SE, SW, NW, or STILL, which correspond to the four possible compass directions that a sprite can use, plus the no-movement state.

The new tile location is passed to the aliens, which can use it to modify their intended destination. The quadrant direction is passed to updateOffsets( ) to change the surface image's offset from the enclosing JPanel.

As mentioned earlier, the player sprite doesn't move at all. A careful examination of AlienTiles during execution shows that the sprite always stays at the center of the game's JPanel. The floor image and its contents (blocks, pickups, aliens) move instead. For instance, when the player sprite is instructed to move northwest (the quadrant direction NW), the sprite does nothing, but the floor and its contents shifts southeast.

The floor offset is maintained in two globals:

```
private int xOffset = 0;
private int yOffset = 0;
```

xOffset and yOffset hold the pixel offsets for drawing the top-left corner of the floor image (and its contents) relative to the top-left corner (0,0) of the JPanel, as shown in Figure 13-10. The offsets may have negative values.

The offsets are the final part of the mapping required to translate a tile coordinate into an on-screen pixel location.

This approach means that a stationary block or pickup, always positioned on the same tile, will be drawn at different places inside the JPanel as the xOffset and yOffset values change.

The offsets are adjusted by updateOffsets( ):

```
private void updateOffsets(int moveQuad)
{
  if (moveQuad == TiledSprite.SW) {    // offset to NE
    xOffset += tileWidth/2;
    yOffset -= tileHeight/2;
  }
```

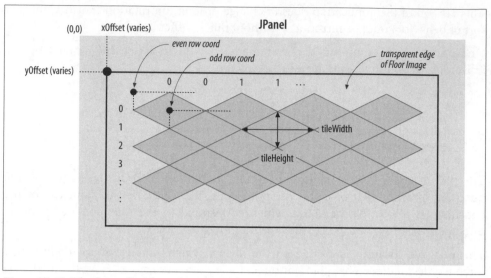

Figure 13-10. The floor offset from the JPanel

```
    else if (moveQuad == TiledSprite.NW) {  // offset to SE
      xOffset += tileWidth/2;
      yOffset += tileHeight/2;
    }
    else if (moveQuad == TiledSprite.NE) {  // offset to SW
      xOffset -= tileWidth/2;
      yOffset += tileHeight/2;
    }
    else if (moveQuad == TiledSprite.SE) {  // offset to NW
      xOffset -= tileWidth/2;
      yOffset -= tileHeight/2;
    }
    else if (moveQuad == TiledSprite.STILL) {  // do nothing
    }
    else
      System.out.println("moveQuad error detected");
  }
```

Drawing the World

AlienTilesPanel delegates the world drawing task to draw( ) in WorldDisplay:

```
  public void draw(Graphics g)
  {
    g.drawImage(floorIm, xOffset, yOffset, null); // draw floor image
    wItems.positionSprites(player, aliens);        // add the sprites
    wItems.draw(g, xOffset, yOffset);              // draw entities
    wItems.removeSprites( );                        // remove sprites
  }
```

WorldDisplay draws the floor GIF, suitably offset, but the entities resting on the floor (the blocks, pickups, and sprites) are left to WorldItems to render.

During WorldDisplay's loading phase, the WorldItems object is initialized with the locations of the blocks and pickups, but not sprites. The reason is that sprites move about at run time, so they would have to be reordered repeatedly in WorldItems' internal data structures.

Instead, whenever the game surface needs to be drawn, the sprites' current positions are recorded temporarily in WorldItems by calling positionSprites( ). After the drawing is completed, the sprite data are deleted with removeSprites( ).

This approach simplifies the housekeeping tasks carried out by WorldItems, as you'll soon see. A drawback to this approach, though, is the need for repeated insertions and deletions of sprite information. However, there are only five sprites in AlienTiles, so the overhead isn't excessive.

If the number of sprites were considerably larger, then you might have to rethink this approach, as the cost of adding and removing the sprites would become significant. The data structures used by WorldItems would need to be made more sophisticated, so moveable items could be permanently stored there and found quickly.

Managing WorldItems

WorldItems maintains an ArrayList of TileOccupier objects (called items) ordered by increasing tile row. Figure 13-10 shows that row 0 is the row furthest back in the game, and the last row is nearest the front. When the ArrayList objects are drawn, the ones in the rows further back will be drawn first, matching the intended z-ordering of the rows.

A TileOccupier object can represent a block, pickup, or sprite.

The ArrayList changes over time. The most frequent change is to add sprites temporarily, so they can be drawn in their correct positions relative to the blocks and pickups. Pickups are deleted as they are collected by the player.

The WorldItems constructor stores floor information. This is used to translate the tile coordinates of the TileOccupiers into pixel locations on the floor:

```
// max pixel width/height of a tile
private int tileWidth, tileHeight;

// 'start of first even row' coordinate
private int evenRowX, evenRowY;
```

```
// 'start of first odd row' coordinate
private int oddRowX, oddRowY;

private ArrayList items;
        // a row-ordered list of TileOccupier objects


public WorldItems(int w, int h, int erX, int erY, int orX, int orY)
{ tileWidth = w; tileHeight = h;
  evenRowX = erX; evenRowY = erY;
  oddRowX = orX; oddRowY = orY;
  items = new ArrayList( );
}
```

Adding an Entity

Adding an entity (a pickup or a block) requires the creation of a TileOccupier object
and its placement in the items ArrayList sorted by its row/column position:

```
public void addItem(String name, int type, int x, int y,
                                        BufferedImage im)
{ TileOccupier toc;
  if (y%2 == 0) // even row
    toc = new TileOccupier(name, type, x, y, im,
                              evenRowX, evenRowY,
                              tileWidth, tileHeight);
  else
    toc = new TileOccupier(name, type, x, y, im,
                              oddRowX, oddRowY,
                              tileWidth, tileHeight);
  rowInsert(toc, x, y);
}
```

Each TileOccupier object must calculate its pixel location on the floor, which
requires the tile coordinate of the occupier (x, y), the dimensions of a tile (tileWidth
and tileHeight), and the start coordinate of the first even or odd row. If the
TileOccupier is positioned on an even row (i.e., y%2 = 0), then it's passed to the
even row coordinate; if not, it is passed to the odd coordinate.

addItem( ) only deals with blocks or pickups, so the type argument will be BLOCK or
PICKUP. The creation of a SPRITE entity is handled by a separate method, posnSprite( ),
which is similar to addItem( ). posnSprite( ) adds a sprite reference to the information
in the TileOccupier object. rowInsert( ) inserts the TileOccupier object into the
ArrayList in increasing row order. Within a row, the objects are ordered by increasing
column position.

Drawing Entities

WorldDisplay's draw( ) displays all the entities using a z-ordering that draws the rows further back first. Since the TileOccupier objects are stored in the ArrayList in increasing row order, this is achieved by cycling through them from start to finish:

```
public void draw(Graphics g, int xOffset, int yOffset)
{
  TileOccupier item;
  for(int i = 0; i < items.size( ); i++) {
    item = (TileOccupier) items.get(i);
    item.draw(g, xOffset, yOffset);    // draw the item
  }
}
```

The TileOccupier draw( ) call is passed the x- and y-offsets of the floor image from the JPanel's top-left corner. They are used to draw the entity offset by the same amount as the floor.

Pickup Methods

WorldItems contains several pickup-related methods. They all employ a similar algorithm, involving a loop through the items list looking for a specified pickup. Then a method is called upon the located TileOccupier object instance.

As a concrete example, I'll consider the implementation of nearestPickup( ). It's supplied with a tile coordinate and returns the coordinate of the nearest pickup:

```
public Point nearestPickup(Point pt)
{
  double minDist = 1000000;    // dummy large value (a hack)
  Point minPoint = null;
  double dist;
  TileOccupier item;
  for(int i=0; i < items.size( ); i++) {
    item = (TileOccupier) items.get(i);
    if (item.getType( ) == WorldDisplay.PICKUP) {
      dist = pt.distanceSq( item.getTileLoc( ) );
                              // get squared dist. to pickup
      if (dist < minDist) {
        minDist = dist;                  // store smallest dist
        minPoint = item.getTileLoc( );  // store associated pt
      }
    }
  }
  return minPoint;
}  // end of nearestPickup( )
```

The pickups are found by searching for the PICKUP type. The square of the distance between the input point and a pickup is calculated, thereby avoiding negative lengths, and the current minimum distance and the associated pickup point is stored.

The Tile Occupier

A tile occupier has a unique name, a type value (BLOCK, PICKUP, or SPRITE), a tile coordinate (xTile, yTile), and a coordinate relative to the top-left corner of the floor image (xDraw, yDraw), where the occupier's image should be drawn. The relationship between these coordinates is shown in Figure 13-11.

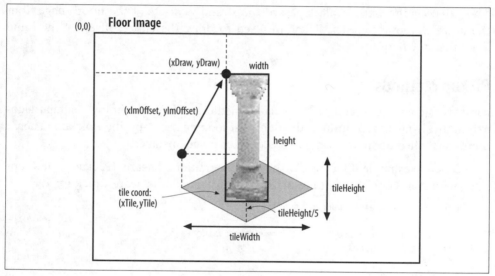

Figure 13-11. Positioning a tile occupier in a tile

xDraw and yDraw are relative to the floor image, so floor offsets must be added to them before the image is drawn into the JPanel. The constructor initializes the coordinate details and calls calcPosition( ) to calculate xDraw and yDraw:

```
// globals
private String name;
private int type;       // BLOCK, PICKUP, or SPRITE
private BufferedImage image;
private int xTile, yTile;    // tile coordinate
private int xDraw, yDraw;
        // coordinate relative to the floor image where the tile
        // occupier should be drawn

private TiledSprite sprite = null;
  // used when the TileOccupier is a sprite
```

```
public TileOccupier(String nm, int ty, int x, int y,
         BufferedImage im, int xRowStart, int yRowStart,
                      int xTileWidth, int yTileHeight)
{ name = nm;
  type = ty;
  xTile = x; yTile = y;
  image = im;
  calcPosition(xRowStart, yRowStart, xTileWidth, yTileHeight);
}
```

If this object is in an even row, then xRowStart and yRowStart will hold the pixel location of the first even row; otherwise, the location of the first odd row is used. The (x, y) arguments give the tile's location.

calcPosition( ) calculates the (xDraw, yDraw) coordinate relative to the floor image:

```
private void calcPosition(int xRowStart, int yRowStart,
                   int xTileWidth, int yTileHeight)
{
  // top-left corner of image relative to its tile
  int xImOffset = xTileWidth/2 - image.getWidth( )/2;   // in middle
  int yImOffset = yTileHeight - image.getHeight( ) - yTileHeight/5;
                  // up a little from bottom point of the diamond

  // top-left corner of image relative to floor image
  xDraw = xRowStart + (xTile * xTileWidth) + xImOffset;
  if (yTile%2 == 0)    // on an even row
    yDraw = yRowStart + (yTile/2 * yTileHeight) + yImOffset;
  else        // on an odd row
    yDraw = yRowStart + ((yTile-1)/2 * yTileHeight) + yImOffset;
}
```

The (xDraw, yDraw) coordinate will cause the TileOccupier's image to be rendered so its base appears to be resting on the tile, centered in the x-direction, and a little forward of the middle in the y-direction.

Additional Sprite Information

When a TileOccupier object is created for a sprite, the addSpriteRef( ) method is called to store a reference to the sprite:

```
public void addSpriteRef(TiledSprite s)
{ if (type == WorldDisplay.SPRITE)
    sprite = s;
}
```

addSpriteRef( ) is used by the draw( ) method, as explained below.

Drawing a Tile Occupier

When the draw( ) method is called, the (xDraw, yDraw) coordinate relative to the floor image is known. Now the x- and y- offsets of the floor image relative to the JPanel must be added to get the image's position in the JPanel.

One complication is drawing a sprite. A sprite may be animated and will be represented by several images, so which one should be drawn? The task is delegated to the sprite, by calling its draw( ) method:

```
public void draw(Graphics g, int xOffset, int yOffset)
{
  if (type == WorldDisplay.SPRITE) {
    sprite.setPosition( xDraw+xOffset, yDraw+yOffset);
                          // set its position in the JPanel
    sprite.drawSprite(g);   // let the sprite do the drawing
  }
  else     // the entity is a PICKUP or BLOCK
    g.drawImage( image, xDraw+xOffset, yDraw+yOffset, null);
}
```

 Prior to the draw, the sprite's pixel position must be set.

draw( ) in TileOccupier is the only place where the pixel coordinates maintained by the Sprite class are manipulated. Tile coordinates, held in the TiledSprite subclass, are utilized in the rest of AlienTiles.

A Sprite on a Tile

A TiledSprite represents a sprite's position using tile coordinates (xTile, yTile); its most important method allows a sprite to move from its current tile to an adjacent one using a compass direction (quadrant): NE, SE, SW, NW. One assumption of TiledSprite is that a sprite cannot move around inside a tile—the sprite can only step from one tile to another.

The constructor initializes a sprite's tile position after checking its validity with WorldDisplay:

```
protected int xTile, yTile;     // tile coordinate for the sprite
protected WorldDisplay world;


public TiledSprite(int x, int y, int w, int h,
                       ImagesLoader imsLd, String name,
                       WorldDisplay wd)
{ super(0, 0, w, h, imsLd, name);
```

```
    setStep(0, 0);      // no movement
    world = wd;

    if (!world.validTileLoc(x, y)) {  // is tile (x,y) valid
      System.out.println("Alien tile location (" + x + "," + y +
                                    ") not valid; using (0,0)");

      x = 0; y = 0;
    }
    xTile = x; yTile = y;
  } // end of TiledSprite( )
```

Moving to Another Tile

AlienTiles' staggered tile layout means that the coordinates of the four tiles adjacent to the current one are obtained in different ways, depending on if the current tile is on an even or odd row. Figures 13-12 and 13-13 show examples of the two possibilities.

The highlighted tile in Figure 13-12 is in row 3 (odd), and the one in Figure 13-13 is in row 2 (even). The coordinates of the adjacent tiles are calculated differently in these two cases.

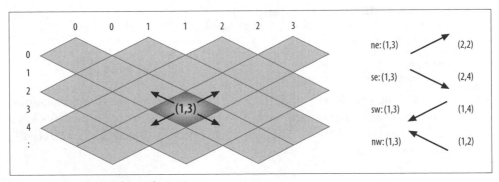

Figure 13-12. Moving from tile (1,3)

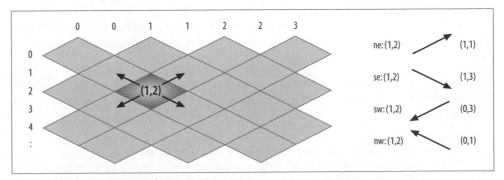

Figure 13-13. Moving from tile (1,2)

tryMove( ) calculates a new tile coordinate based on the current location and the supplied quadrant. A four-way branch deals with the four possible directions, and each branch considers whether the starting point is on an even or odd row:

```
public Point tryMove(int quad)
{
  Point nextPt;
  if (quad == NE)
    nextPt = (yTile%2 == 0)? new Point(xTile,yTile-1) :
                             new Point(xTile+1,yTile-1);
  else if (quad == SE)
    nextPt = (yTile%2 == 0)? new Point(xTile,yTile+1) :
                             new Point(xTile+1,yTile+1);
  else if (quad == SW)
    nextPt = (yTile%2 == 0)? new Point(xTile-1,yTile+1) :
                             new Point(xTile,yTile+1);
  else if (quad == NW)
    nextPt = (yTile%2 == 0)? new Point(xTile-1,yTile-1) :
                             new Point(xTile,yTile-1);
  else
    return null;

  if (world.validTileLoc(nextPt.x, nextPt.y))
    // ask WorldDisplay if proposed tile is valid
    return nextPt;
  else
   return null;
} // end of tryMove( )
```

The method is called tryMove( ) since there is a possibility that the desired quadrant direction is invalid because the new tile is a no-go area (it is occupied by a block) or the coordinate lies off the surface. These cases are checked by called validTileLoc( ) in WorldDisplay.

The Player Sprite

PlayerSprite represents the player and is a subclass of TiledSprite. The statechart for PlayerSprite in Figure 13-14 shows that the sprite performs three concurrent activities.

The move( ) and tryPickup( ) transitions are triggered by the user from the keyboard. The hitByAlien( ) transition is initiated by the WorldDisplay object when an alien tells it that it has hit the player.

 The transitions in Figure 13-14 are labeled with method names; this is a practice that I'll use when there's a direct mapping from a transition to a method call. This makes it easier to see the mapping from the statechart to the corresponding code.

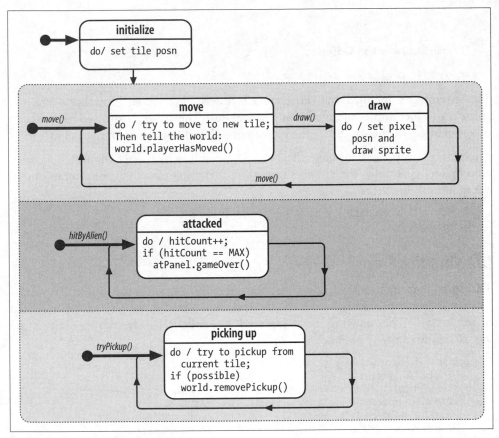

Figure 13-14. PlayerSprite statechart

Moving (and Standing Still)

A PlayerSprite tries to move when the user presses one of the quadrant keys (9, 3, 1, or 7):

```
public void move(int quad)
{
  Point newPt = tryMove(quad);
  if (newPt == null) {    // move not possible
    clipsLoader.play("slap", false);
    standStill();
  }
  else {    // move is possible
    setTileLoc(newPt);    // update the sprite's tile location
    if (quad == NE)
      setImage("ne");
    else if (quad == SE)
      setImage("se");
    else if (quad == SW)
```

```
      setImage("sw");
    else // quad == NW
      setImage("nw");
    world.playerHasMoved(newPt, quad);
  }
} // end of move()
```

The attempt is handled by TiledSprite's inherited tryMove( ) method, and the sprite's tile location is updated if it's successful. The move is dressed up with an image change for the sprite and the playing of a sound effect if the move is blocked.

The player can press 5 to make the sprite stand still, which only changes its associated image. Normally, the sprite is poised in a running position, pointing in one of the quadrant directions.

```
public void standStill( )
{ setImage("still"); }
```

Drawing the Player

The statechart includes a draw state, triggered by a draw( ) transition. The draw activity is implemented by using the setPosition( ) and draw( ) methods inherited from Sprite. The drawing isn't initiated by code in PlayerSprite but is by WorldDisplay's draw( ) method:

```
public void draw(Graphics g)
// in WorldDisplay
{ g.drawImage(floorIm, xOffset, yOffset, null); // draw floor image
  wItems.positionSprites(player, aliens);      // add sprites
  wItems.draw(g, xOffset, yOffset);            // draw things
  wItems.removeSprites( );                      // remove sprites
}
```

As explained earlier, all the sprites, including the player, are added to WorldItems temporarily so they can be drawn in the correct z-order. Each sprite is stored as a TileOccupier object, and setPosition( ) and draw( ) are called from there.

Being Hit by an Alien

PlayerSprite maintains a hit counter, which is incremented by a call to hitByAlien( ) from the WorldDisplay object:

```
public void hitByAlien( )
{ clipsLoader.play("hit", false);
  hitCount++;
  if (hitCount == MAX_HITS)    // player is dead
    atPanel.gameOver( );
}
```

When hitCount reaches a certain value (MAX_HITS), it's all over. The sprite doesn't terminate though; it only notifies AlienTilePanel. This allows AlienTilesPanel to carry out "end of game" tasks, which in this case are reporting the game score and playing a sound clip of applause. `AlienTilesPanel` could do a lot more, such as ask users if they wanted to play another game. These kinds of game-wide activities should be done at the game panel level and not by a sprite.

Trying to Pick Up a Pickup

The user tries to pick up an item by pressing 2 on the numbers keypad. The hard work here is determining if the sprite's current tile location contains a pickup and to remove that item from the scene. The two operations are handled by `WorldDisplay` methods:

```
public boolean tryPickup()
{
  String pickupName;
  if ((pickupName = world.overPickup( getTileLoc())) == null) {
    clipsLoader.play("noPickup", false);      // nothing to pickup
    return false;
  }
  else {       // found a pickup
    clipsLoader.play("gotPickup", false);
    world.removePickup(pickupName);      // tell WorldDisplay
    return true;
  }
}
```

The name of the pickup on the current tile is obtained and used in the deletion request. If the tile is empty, a sound clip will be played instead.

The Alien Sprite

`AlienSprite` implements the basic behavior of an alien sprite and is subclassed to create the `AlienAStarSprite` and `AlienQuadSprite` classes. `AlienSprite` is a subclass of `TiledSprite`.

Alien behavior can best be understood by considering the statechart in Figure 13-15.

The plan move state is entered by the `WorldDisplay` object, notifying the alien that the player has moved. This gives it the opportunity to recalculate its current direction or destination, but the precise algorithm will vary from one `AlienSprite` subclass to another.

The other activity is the usual update/draw cycle driven by the animation loop in `AlienTilesPanel`. The alien tries to hit the player while in the attack state. A successful hit is reported to the `WorldDisplay` object, and the alien stays where it is. Otherwise, the alien updates its position, in the hope of getting closer to the player. In the draw state, the sprite's tile coordinates are mapped to a pixel location and the sprite's image is rendered.

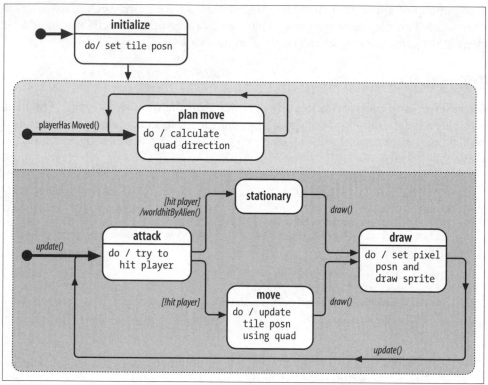

Figure 13-15. Alien statechart

Responding to a player's movement is sprite-specific, so playerHasMoved( ) is empty in AlienSprite:

```
public void playerHasMoved(Point playerLoc)
{ }
```

PlayerLoc contains the current tile coordinates for the PlayerSprite object.

Updating the AlienSprite

The attack, stationary, and move states are encapsulated in update( ):

```
// globals
private final static int UPDATE_FREQ = 30;
private int updateCounter = 0;


public void update()
{
  updateCounter = (updateCounter+1)%UPDATE_FREQ;
  if (updateCounter == 0) {    // reduced update frequency
```

```
      if (!hitPlayer())
        move();
    }
  }
```

update( ) is called from `AlienTilesPanel`'s animation loop, which executes at 40 FPS. This makes the aliens respond too quickly. The solution is to use a counter to reduce the update frequency.

This issue only became apparent when the game was first tested without the alien movement being slowed down. At 40 FPS, the aliens always caught the user's sprite quickly, even when the user kept the move keys constantly pressed.

The A* pathfinding algorithm in `AlienAStarSprite` becomes deadly accurate when it's recalculated so frequently. There's no way to avoid capture, even if the user randomly changes direction at frequent intervals.

hitPlayer( ) checks if the alien is on the same tile as the player. If it is, then the `WorldDisplay` object will be informed of a hit:

```
private boolean hitPlayer()
{
  Point playerLoc = world.getPlayerLoc();
  if (playerLoc.equals( getTileLoc() )) {
    world.hitByAlien();  // whack!
    return true;
  }
  return false;
}
```

The details of the move state will vary from one alien to another, which translates to the alien subclasses overriding the move( ) method.

`AlienSprite`'s move( ) carries out a random walk. getRandDirection( ) (a method inherited from `TiledSprite`) returns a quadrant, and this is tried out with `TiledSprite`'s tryMove( ) method:

```
protected void move()
{
  int quad = getRandDirection();
  Point newPt;
  while ((newPt = tryMove(quad)) == null)
    quad = getRandDirection();
    // the loop could repeat for a while,
    // but it should eventually find a direction
  setMove(newPt, quad);
}
```

The new tile coordinate is use to update the sprite's position in setMove( ):

```
protected void setMove(Point newPt, int quad)
{
  if (world.validTileLoc(newPt.x, newPt.y)) {    // should be ok
    setTileLoc(newPt);
    if ((quad == NE) || (quad == SE))
      setImage("baddieRight");
    else if ((quad == SW) || (quad == NW))
      setImage("baddieLeft");
    else
      System.out.println("Unknown alien quadrant: " + quad);
  }
  else
    System.out.println("Cannot move alien to (" + newPt.x +
                                  ", " + newPt.y + ")");
} // end of doMove()
```

setMove( ) double-checks the validity of the new tile and changes the sprite's appearance. The method is protected since only subclasses of AlienSprite will use it (as part of the subclasses' versions of move( )).

update( ) handles the attack, stationary, and move states of the alien statechart. This leads to the question: Where is the *draw* state processed? As with the PlayerSprite class, this task is part of the drawing operation carried out by WorldDisplay through its WorldItems object.

The Quadrant-Based Alien Sprite

AlienQuadSprite is a subclass of AlienSprite and overrides the playerHasMoved( ) and move( ) methods. AlienQuadSprite has the same basic statechart as AlienSprite (shown in Figure 13-15), but the plan move and move states are different.

In the plan move state, the alien calculates a quadrant direction (NE, SE, SW, or NW). The direction is chosen by finding the nearest pickup point to the player, and then calculating that pickup's quadrant direction relative to the alien. This gives the alien a "pickup-guarding" behavior, as the alien then moves towards the pickup that the player (probably) wants to collect.

Planning a Move

playerHasMoved( ) calculates a quadrant direction for the sprite:

```
// global
private int currentQuad;


public void playerHasMoved(Point playerLoc)
{
  if (world.hasPickupsLeft()) {
```

```
        Point nearPickup = world.nearestPickup(playerLoc);
              // return coord of nearest pickup to the player
        currentQuad = calcQuadrant(nearPickup);
  }
}

private int calcQuadrant(Point pickupPt)
/* Roughly calculate a quadrant by comparing the
   pickup's point with the alien's position. */
{
  if ((pickupPt.x > xTile) && (pickupPt.y > yTile))
    return SE;
  else if ((pickupPt.x > xTile) && (pickupPt.y < yTile))
    return NE;
  else if ((pickupPt.x < xTile) && (pickupPt.y > yTile))
    return SW;
  else
    return NW;
  } // end of calcQuadrant( )
```

calcQuadrant( ) could be more complex, but the emphasis is on speed.
playerHasMoved( ) and calcQuadrant( ) will be called frequently—whenever the
player moves—so there is no need to spend a large amount of time processing a single move.

This is an example of the common tradeoff between accuracy and speed.
calcQuadrant( ) is called often, so should be fast and doesn't need to be accurate
since any errors will be smoothed out by subsequent calls. Also, I don't want to
make the alien's behavior too sophisticated or the player will always be caught,
which isn't much fun.

This kind of deliberately inaccurate algorithm needs to be tested in real gameplay to
ensure that it's not too inadequate, and perhaps to see if it can be simplified more.

Moving the AlienQuadSprite

The sprite tries to move in the currentQuad direction. If that direction leads to a no-
go tile or a tile holding a block, then the sprite randomly will try another direction.

```
protected void move( )
{ int quad = currentQuad;
  Point newPt;
  while ((newPt = tryMove(quad)) == null)
    quad = getRandDirection( );
    // the loop could repeat for a while,
    // but it should eventually find a way
  setMove(newPt, quad);
}
```

The use of a randomly chosen direction when the sprite is blocked may lead to it repeatedly picking a blocked direction, especially if it's stuck in a cul-de-sac. This is unlikely to be a problem for long, and this kind of suboptimal behavior is endearing to a player who is use to being chased at close quarters by deadly aliens.

The A*-Based Alien Sprite

In a similar manner to AlienQuadSprite, AlienAStarSprite is a subclass of AlienSprite and overrides its superclass's playerHasMoved( ) and move( ) methods.

The alien calculates a path to the player using the A* pathfinding algorithm. The path is stored as a sequence of tile coordinates that need to be visited to reach the player. In each call to move( ), the sprite moves to the next coordinate in the sequence, giving it a "player-chasing" behavior.

Planning a Move

Every time the user presses one of the move keys, the PlayerSprite object moves to an adjacent tile, and it notifies WorldDisplay by calling playerHasMoved( ). You don't want to recalculate a path after every player move since the change will be minimal but expensive to generate. Instead, the path is generated only when the player has moved MAX_MOVES steps. This saves on computation and makes things a bit easier for the player:

```
// globals
private final static int MAX_MOVES = 5;

private int numPlayerMoves = 0;
private ArrayList path;     // tile coords going to the player
private int pathIndex = 0;


public void playerHasMoved(Point playerLoc)
{ if (numPlayerMoves == 0)
    calcNewPath(playerLoc);
  else
    numPlayerMoves = (numPlayerMoves+1)%MAX_MOVES;
}


private void calcNewPath(Point playerLoc)
{ path = aStarSearch( getTileLoc(), playerLoc );
  pathIndex = 0;   // reset the index for the new path
}
```

The A* Algorithm

A* search finds a path from a start node to a goal node; in AlienTiles, the starting point is the alien's current tile position and the goal is the player's tile. The algorithm maintains a set of tiles it has seen but not visited. It chooses the highest scoring tile from that set and moves there. The search is finished if that tile holds the player; otherwise, it stores the locations of the adjacent tiles in its set of seen-but-not-visited tiles. The algorithm then repeats until the player's tile is found. The algorithm scores a tile (for algorithmic purposes, called a *node*) by estimating the cost of the best path that starts at the alien's position, goes through the node being examined, and finishes at the player's tile. The scoring formula is expressed using two functions, usually called g() and h(). I'll break with tradition and call them getCostFromStart() and costToGoal() for clarity's sake:

    score(node) = node.getCostFromStart() + node.costToGoal()

getCostFromStart() is the smallest cost of arriving at node from the starting tile (the alien's current position). costToGoal() is a heuristic estimate (an educated guess) of the cost of reaching the goal tile (the player's location) from node.

A* search is popular because it's guaranteed to find the shortest path from the start to the goal as long as the heuristic estimate, costToGoal(), is admissible. Admissibility means that the node.costToGoal() value is always less than (or equal to) the actual cost of getting to the goal from the node. The A* algorithm has been proven to make the most efficient use of costToGoal(), in the sense that other search techniques cannot find an optimal path by checking fewer nodes.

If costToGoal() is inaccurate—it returns too large a value—then the search will become unfocused, examining nodes which won't contribute to the final path. The generated path may not be the shortest possible. However, a less accurate costToGoal() function may be easier (and faster) to calculate, so path generation may be quicker. Speed might be preferable, as long as the resulting path isn't excessively meandering. A less accurate path gives the player more of a chance to evade capture (and death).

In visual terms, an optimal path goes directly to the goal, examining only the nodes along the edges of that path. A suboptimal path wanders about, with many more nodes examined on either side. The A* demo applet by James Macgill at *http://www.ccg.leeds.ac.uk/james/aStar/* allows the costToGoal() function to be varied, and the incremental generation of the path is displayed.

Figure 13-16 shows the applet's calculations to find a path from a start node at the top of a grid to a goal node at the bottom, with few wasteful operations.

Figure 13-17 shows the result when the applet uses an estimation function that is much worse, resulting in unnecessary computation, though a path was found eventually.

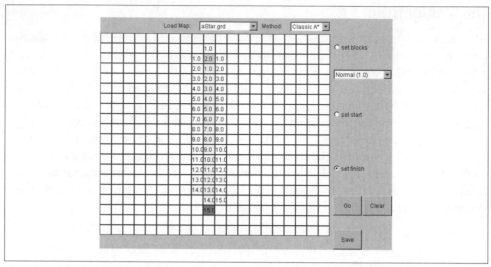

Figure 13-16. A* applet path calculations with a good estimator

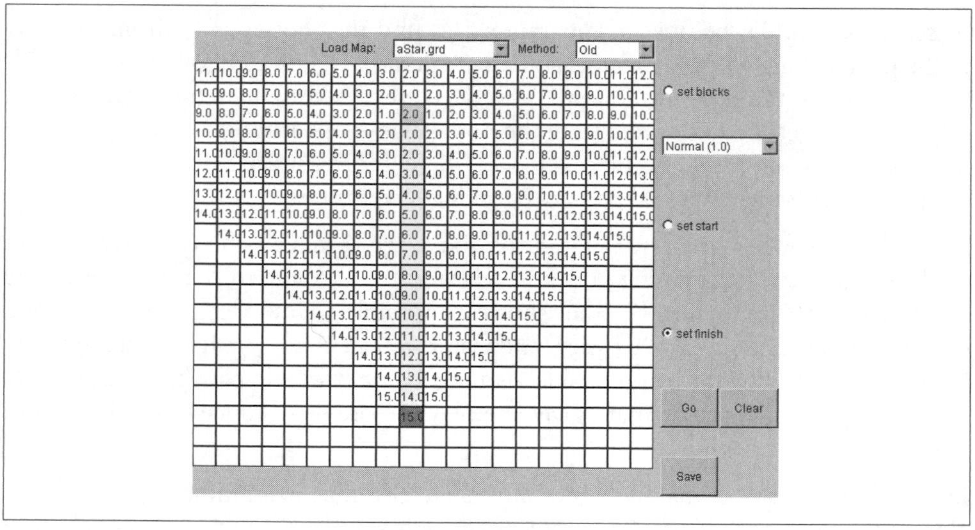

Figure 13-17. A* applet path calculations with a bad estimator

getCostFromStart( ) and costToGoal( ) rely on calculating a cost of moving from one tile to another. Various costing approaches are possible, including the distance between the tiles, the cost in time, the cost of fuel, or weights based on the terrain type. AlienTiles ignores these factors (you don't want this chapter to be longer, do you?) and uses raw distance.

A* employs two list data structures, usually called open and closed. open is a list of tiles that have not yet been examined (i.e., their adjacent tiles have not been scored). closed contains the tiles which have been examined. The tiles in *open* are sorted by decreasing score, so the most promising tile is always the first one. The following pseudocode shows how the A* search progresses:

```
add the start tile to open;
create an empty closed list;

while (open isn't empty) {
  get the highest scoring tile x from open;
  if (x is the goal tile)
    return a path to x;    // I'm done
  else {
    for (each adjacent tile y to x) {
      calculate the costFromStart() value for y;
      if ((y is already in open or closed) and
          (value is no improvement))
        continue;    // ignore y
      else {
        delete old y from open or close (if present);
        calculate costToGoal() and the total score for y;
        store y in open;
      }
    }
  }
  put x into closed;  // since I'm finished with it
}
report no path found;
```

 This pseudocode is based on code in "The Basics of A* for Path Planning" by Bryan Stout, from *Game Programming Gems* (Charles River Media), edited by Mike DeLoura.

The translation of the pseudocode to the aStarSearch( ) method is quite direct:

```
private ArrayList aStarSearch(Point startLoc, Point goalLoc)
{
  double newCost;
  TileNode bestNode, newNode;

  TileNode startNode = new TileNode(startLoc);  // set start node
  startNode.costToGoal(goalLoc);

  // create the open queue and closed list
  TilesPriQueue open = new TilesPriQueue(startNode);
  TilesList closed = new TilesList();

  while (open.size() != 0) {  // while some node still left
    bestNode = open.removeFirst();
    if (goalLoc.equals( bestNode.getPoint() ))   // reached goal
      return bestNode.buildPath();    // return a path to that goal
    else {
      for (int i=0; i < NUM_DIRS; i++) {    // try every direction
        if ((newNode = bestNode.makeNeighbour(i, world)) != null) {
          newCost = newNode.getCostFromStart();
```

```
            TileNode oldVer;
            // if this tile already has a cheaper open or closed node
            // then ignore the new node
            if (((oldVer=open.findNode(newNode.getPoint())) !=null)&&
                (oldVer.getCostFromStart() <= newCost))
              continue;
            else if (((oldVer = closed.findNode( newNode.getPoint()))
                                                    != null) &&
                (oldVer.getCostFromStart() <= newCost))
              continue;
            else {    // store new/improved node, removing old one
              newNode.costToGoal(goalLoc);
              // delete the old details (if they exist)
              closed.delete( newNode.getPoint());   // may do nothing
              open.delete( newNode.getPoint());    // may do nothing
              open.add(newNode);
            }
          }
        } // end of for block
      } // end of if-else
      closed.add(bestNode);
    }
    return null;    // no path found
  }  // end of aStarSearch( )
```

The code is simplified by being able to rely on the TilesList and TilesPriQueue classes to represent the closed and open lists. They store tile information as TileNode objects. TilesList is essentially a wrapper for an ArrayList of TileNode objects, with additional methods for finding and deleting a node based on a supplied coordinate. TilesPriQueue is a subclass of TilesList and stores TileNodes sorted by decreasing node score (i.e., the highest scoring node comes first).

Moving the AlienAStarSprite

AlienAStarSprite overrides AlienSprite's move( ) method, so the next move is to the next tile in the path calculated by the A* algorithm:

```
protected void move( )
{
  if (pathIndex == path.size( ))  // current path is used up
    calcNewPath( world.getPlayerLoc( ) );
  Point nextPt = (Point) path.get(pathIndex);
  pathIndex++;
  int quad = whichQuadrant(nextPt);
  setMove(nextPt, quad);
}
```

If move( ) finds the destination of the current path has been reached (i.e., the sprite has reached the goal node), it will initiate the calculation of a new path by calling calcNewPath( ).

Storing Tile Details

A `TileNode` object stores details about a particular tile node, which are used by the A* algorithm when it looks at that node. The most important are values for the `getCostFromStart()` and `costToGoal()` functions so the overall score for the node can be worked out.

As explained in the last section, the `getCostFromStart()` function is the cost of the path that leads to this node from the starting tile. This algorithm's precise definition will vary from game to game, but I use the simplest measure—the length of the path—with the step between adjacent tiles assigned a value of 1. `costToGoal()` estimates the cost of going from this tile node to the goal.

 This is a little harder to calculate in `AlienTiles` due to the staggered layout of the tiles as detailed below.

Each `TileNode` stores a reference to its parent, the tile node that was visited before it. The sequence of nodes from this particular tile node back to the starting tile defines the sprite's path (in reverse).

Calculating the Cost to the Goal

`costToGoal()` treats the tile coordinates of the current tile and the goal as points on the XY plane and calculates the length of the floor of the straight line between them:

```
public void costToGoal(Point goal)
{ double dist = coord.distance(goal.x, goal.y);
  costToGoal = Math.floor(dist);
}
```

However, the tiles are positioned in staggered rows, which means the straight line distance can be an inaccurate measure. Therefore, the `costToGoal()` value may not be less than or equal to the cheapest path, so the path found by A* may not be optimal. However, the calculation is simple and fast, and the path is sufficient for `AlienTiles`.

 This "sufficiency" was checked by playing the game and seeing how quickly and accurately the `AlienAStarSprite` sprites closed in on the player. The algorithm is arguably still too good since the aliens almost always take the shortest path to the player and are very fast.

The reason for using `Math.floor()` can be justified by considering an example. Figure 13-18 shows the four adjacent tiles to tile (1,3).

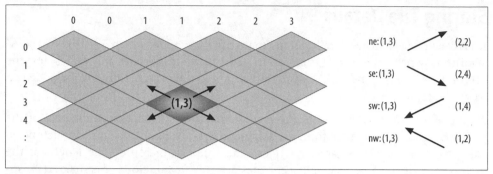

Figure 13-18. Tiles adjacent to (1,3)

Figure 13-19 maps the five tile points to a rectangular grid and shows the straight line distances between them.

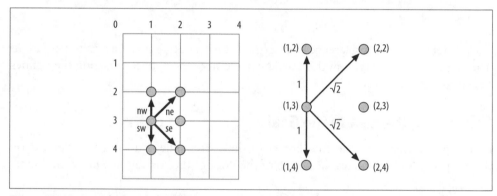

Figure 13-19. Straight-line distances between the tiles in Figure 13-18

The cost of moving to a neighbor is 1 in all cases. However, the straight-line distances to two of the tiles (the north east and south east ones) are the square root of two. Fortunately, the floor of all the distances is one (1.414 is rounded down to one), which makes the cost function optimal.

The Math.floor() solution works for adjacent tiles but is less successful when the straight-line distances span multiple tiles.

Further Reading

The Isometrix Project (*http://www.isometrix.org/*; *http://isometrix.tsx.org/*) concentrates on isometric tile games. The articles section covers topics such as map formats, tile layout, placing objects, and lighting. The engines section lists code sources, tools, and demos.

I mentioned GameDev.net's "Isometric and Tile-based Games" section at the end of the last chapter (*http://www.gamedev.net/reference/list.asp?categoryid=44*). It contains over 30 articles on tile-based gaming.

A good introductory book is *Isometric Game Programming with DirectX 7.0* (Muska and Lipman/Premium-Trade) by Ernest Pazera. The first 230 or so pages are about Windows programming, and the examples use C. However, there's good stuff on the basics of rectangular and isometric games tile plotting, drawing, world and map coordinate systems, and moving about a map.

Some modern Java isometric or tile games examples, which come with source code, are:

Javagaming.org: Scroller (http://sourceforge.net/projects/jgo-scroller/)
A full-screen isometric scrolling game intended to illustrate how to write high-performance 2D games in J2SE 1.4.

haphazard (http://haphazard.sourceforge.net/)
A role-playing game set in an isometric world.

CivQuest (http://civquest.sourceforge.net/)
A strategy game inspired by *Civilization*, including game play against AI opponents. The coding is at an earlier stage.

IsometricEngine (http://sourceforge.net/projects/jisoman/)
An isometric game engine written by Jason Gauci, with support for line-of-sight calculations, entity and terrain objects, a tile map and wall map. It has a graphically mode for designing maps.

JTBRPG (http://jtbrpg.sourceforge.net/)
Includes tools for creating role-playing isometric game content and an engine for making it playable.

YARTS (http://www.btinternet.com/~duncan.jauncey/old/javagame/)
YARTS (Yet Another Real Time Strategy game) is a 2D rectangular tile-based real-time strategy game. The source code for the first version is available.

Hephaestus (http://kuoi.asui.uidaho.edu/~kamikaze/Hephaestus/)
A role-playing game construction kit based around 2D rectangular tiles.

Mappy for PC (*http://www.tilemap.co.uk/mappy.php*) can create isometric and hexagonal tile maps, and there are several Java-based playback libraries, including JavaMappy (*http://www.alienfactory.co.uk/javamappy/*).

The surface image created for `AlienTiles` (shown in Figure 13-3) was hacked together using MS PowerPoint and Paint—a reasonable approach for demos but not recommended for real maps.

A* Information

The workings of the A* algorithm can be hard to visualize. The A* Demo page (*http://www.ccg.leeds.ac.uk/james/aStar/*) by James Macgill, lets the user create a search map and watch the scoring process in action. The applet source code can be downloaded.

The pseudocode I used is based on code from "The Basics of A* for Path Planning" by Bryan Stout, from *Game Programming Gems* (Charles River Media), edited by Mike DeLoura. There are other articles in *Game Programming Gems* related to A* optimization worth checking out as well.

An online version of another A* article by Bryan Stout, "Smart Moves: Intelligent Path-finding," is available at *http://www.gamasutra.com/features/19970801/pathfinding.htm*. It includes a PathDemo application which graphically illustrates several search algorithms, including A*.

The A* algorithm tutor (*http://www.geocities.com/SiliconValley/Lakes/4929/astar.html*) by Justin Heyes-Jones offers a detailed account of the algorithm.

Amit J. Patel's web site on games programming (*http://www-cs-students.stanford.edu/~amitp/gameprog.html*) covers several relevant topics, including pathfinding (with a bias towards A*), tile games, and the use of hexagonal grids.

Information on A* can be found at game AI sites, usually under the pathfinding heading. Two excellent sources are:

- Game AI Site (*http://www.gameai.com/*)
- GameDev's AI section (*http://www.gamedev.net/reference/list.asp?categoryid=18*)

A modern AI textbook, which discusses several search algorithms (including A*), is *Artificial Intelligence: A Modern Approach* (Prentice Hall) by Stuart Russell and Peter Norvig. Many of the pseudocode examples from the book have been rewritten in Java (including those for doing searches), and they're available from the web site, *http://aima.cs.berkeley.edu/*.

CHAPTER 14

Introducing Java 3D

The next 15 chapters will be about programming 3D games using Java 3D, Java's *scene graph* API. A scene graph makes 3D programming easier for novices (and for experienced programmers) because it emphasizes scene design, rather than rendering, by hiding the graphics pipeline. The scene graph supports complex graphical elements such as 3D geometries, lighting modes, picking, and collision detection. Java 3D is a scene graph API.

I'll summarize the main elements of Java 3D in this chapter, leaving program examples aside for the moment. Then, as in Chapter 1, I'll examine Java 3D's suitability for games programming by considering the criticisms leveled against it.

Java 3D

The Java 3D API provides a collection of high-level constructs for creating, rendering, and manipulating a 3D scene graph composed of geometry, materials, lights, sounds, and more. Java 3D was developed by Sun Microsystems, and the most recent stable release is Version 1.3.1.

There is a Version 1.3.2, but it's a bug fix release under review as I write this in December 2004. For example, a rarely occurring bug with the J3DTimer class has been fixed.

By the time you read this, Version 1.3.2 will have been finalized (an FCS release will be available).

There are two Java 3D variants: one implemented on top of OpenGL, and the other above DirectX Graphics. OpenGL is a popular software API for writing 3D (and 2D) graphics applications across a wide range of hardware and operating systems (*http://www.opengl.org/*). It's a low-level API based around a graphics pipeline for pixel and vertex manipulation.

Prior to the 1.3.2 bug fix release, a programmer had to choose whether to download the OpenGL version of Java 3D or the DirectX implementation since they were offered as separate installers. With Version 1.3.2 (build 7 and later), both versions are in a single download.

DirectX Graphics supports a traditional graphics pipeline, describing all geometry in terms of vertices and pixels. It's part of DirectX, a collection of related gaming modules aimed at MS Windows (*http://www.microsoft.com/directx*). The other DirectX APIs support 3D audio, networking, input device integration, multimedia, and installation management.

DirectX or OpenGL?

Often, the debate about which version of Java 3D is better is a debate about the relative merits of DirectX Graphics and OpenGL.

In most technical areas, DirectX Graphics and OpenGL are almost equivalent since both are based on the same graphics pipeline architecture and ideas flow between the two. The most significant differences between the two APIs are unrelated to their functionality. OpenGL is ported to a wide range of platforms and OSs, and DirectX is limited to PCs running Windows and the Xbox. DirectX is controlled by Microsoft alone, and the OpenGL Architecture Review Board (ARB) allows input from many partners.

The Direct X Graphics version of Java 3D is only available for Windows, where some users report that it's marginally faster than the OpenGL implementation. However, I've never noticed any difference when I've tried both systems.

The future seems brightest for the OpenGL version, which is the main focus of the current "bug fix" release of Java 3D, Version 1.3.2. I'll use the stable OpenGL version (1.3.1) in the rest of this book. It can be downloaded from *http://java.sun.com/products/java-media/3D/*, together with ample documentation and a long tutorial.

 The FCS release of Version 1.3.2 will be available by the time you read this. You can obtain it from *https://java3d.dev.java.net/*.

The Scene Graph

Java 3D uses a scene graph to organize and manage a 3D application. The underlying graphics pipeline is hidden, replaced by a tree-like structure built from nodes representing 3D models, lights, sounds, the background, the camera, and many other scene elements.

The nodes are typed, the main division being between Group and Leaf nodes. A Group node is one with child nodes, grouping the children so operations such as translations, rotations, and scaling can be applied en masse. Leaf nodes are the leaves of the graph (did you guess that?), which often represent the visible things in the scene such as the models, but may be nontangible entities, such as lighting and sounds. Additionally, a Leaf node (e.g., for a 3D shape) may have node components, specifying color, reflectivity, and other attributes of the leaf.

The scene graph can contain behaviors, nodes holding code that can affect other nodes in the graph at runtime. Typical behavior nodes move shapes, detect and respond to shape collisions, and cycle lighting from day to night.

Scene graph is used, rather than *scene tree*, because it's possible for nodes to be shared (i.e., have more than one parent).

Before looking at a real Java 3D scene graph, Figure 14-1 shows how the scene graph idea can be applied to defining the contents of an office.

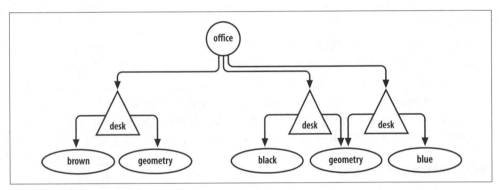

Figure 14-1. Scene graph for an office

The office Group node is the parent of Leaf nodes representing a desk and two chairs. Each Leaf utilizes geometry (shape) and color node components, and the chair geometry information is shared. This sharing means that both chairs will have the same shape but will be colored differently.

The choice of symbols in Figure 14-1 comes from a standard symbol set (shown in Figure 14-2), used in all of this book's Java 3D scene graph diagrams. I'll explain the VirtualUniverse and Locale nodes and the Reference relationship in due course.

Some Java 3D scene graph nodes

The Java 3D API can be viewed as a set of classes that subclass the Group and Leaf nodes in various ways. The Leaf class is subclassed to define different kinds of 3D shapes and *environmental* nodes (i.e., nodes representing lighting, sounds, and behaviors).

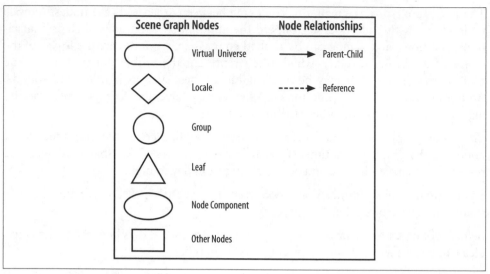

Figure 14-2. Scene graph symbols

The main shape class is called Shape3D, which uses two node components to define its geometry and appearance; these classes are called Geometry and Appearance.

The Group class supports basic node positioning and orientation for its children and is subclassed to extend those operations. For instance, BranchGroup allows children to be added or removed from the graph at runtime; TransformGroup permits the position and orientation of its children to be changed.

The HelloUniverse scene graph

The standard first example for Java 3D programmers is HelloUniverse. (It appears in Chapter 1 of Sun's Java 3D tutorial.) It displays a rotating colored cube, as in Figure 14-3.

The scene graph for this application is given in Figure 14-4.

VirtualUniverse is the top node in every scene graph and represents the virtual world space and its coordinate system. Locale acts as the scene graph's location in the virtual world. Below the Locale node are two subgraphs—the left branch is the *content branch graph*, holding program-specific content such as geometry, lighting, textures, and the world's background. The content branch graph differs significantly from one application to another.

The ColorCube is composed from a Shape3D node and associated Geometry and Appearance components. Its rotation is carried out by a Behavior node, which affects the TransformGroup parent of the ColorCube's shape.

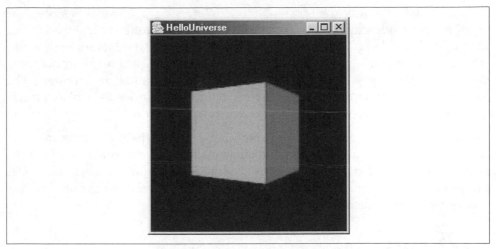

Figure 14-3. A rotating colored cube

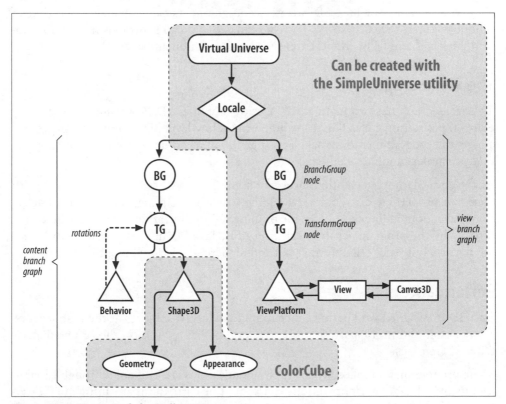

Figure 14-4. Scene graph for HelloUniverse

The righthand branch below `Locale` is the *view branch graph*, which specifies the users' position, orientation, and perspective as they look into the virtual world from the physical world (e.g., from in front of a monitor). The `ViewPlatform` node stores the viewer's position in the virtual world; the `View` node states how to turn what the viewer sees into a physical world image (e.g., a 2D picture on the monitor). The `Canvas3D` node is a Java GUI component that allows the 2D image to be placed inside a Java application or applet.

The `VirtualUniverse`, `Locale`, and view branch graph often have the same structure across different applications since most programs use a single `Locale` and view the virtual world as a 2D image on a monitor. For these applications, the relevant nodes can be created with Java 3D's `SimpleUniverse` utility class, relieving the programmer much graph construction work.

Java 3D Strengths

The core strengths of Java 3D are its scene graph, its performance, collection of unique features, the fact that it's Java and can call upon an enormous number of support packages and APIs, and its extensive documentation and examples.

The Scene Graph

The scene graph has two main advantages: it simplifies 3D programming and accelerates the resulting code. The scene graph hides low-level 3D graphics elements and allows the programmer to manage and organize a 3D scene. A scene graph supports many complex graphical elements.

At the Java 3D implementation level, the scene graph is used to group shapes with common properties, carry out view culling, occlusion culling, level of detail selection, execution culling, and behavior pruning, all optimizations that must be coded directly by the programmer in lower-level APIs. Java 3D utilizes Java's multithreading to carry out parallel graph traversal and rendering, both useful optimizations.

Performance

Java 3D is designed with performance in mind, which it achieves at the high level by scene graph optimizations and at the low level by being built on top of OpenGL or DirectX Graphics.

Some programmer-specified scene graph optimizations are available through capability bits, which state what operations can/cannot be carried out at runtime (e.g., prohibiting a shape from moving). Java 3D also permits the programmer to bypass the scene graph, either totally by means of an immediate mode, or partially via the mixed mode. Immediate mode gives the programmer greater control over rendering and scene management, but it isn't often required. Retained mode programs only use the scene graph API. All the examples in this book employ retained mode.

Unique Features

Java 3D's view model separates the virtual and physical worlds through the ViewPlatform and View nodes. This makes it straightforward to reconfigure an application to utilize many output devices, from a monitor, to stereo glasses, to CAVEs.

Virtual world behavior is coded with Behavior nodes in the scene graph and is triggered by events. Among other things, this offers a different style of animation based on responding to events instead of the usual update redraw/cycle you've seen in all my 2D games programs.

The core Java 3D API package, javax.media.j3d, supports basic polygons and triangles within a scene graph; the com.sun.j3d packages add a range of utility classes including ColorCube and SimpleUniverse, mouse and keyboard navigation behaviors, audio device handling, and loaders for several 3D file formats.

Geometry compression is possible, often reducing size by an order of magnitude. When this is combined with Java's NIO and networking, it facilitates the ready transfer of large quantities of data between applications such as multiplayer games.

Java 3D allows 2D and 3D audio output, ambient and spatialized sound. Unfortunately, the sound system has bugs. Consequently, spatialized sound isn't available by default in Java 3D 1.3.2. Version 1.4 may offer a JOALMixer class instead, i.e., a JOAL-based audio device. JOAL is a Java binding for a 3D audio API called OpenAL, which is supported by many sound cards.

Java Integration

Java 3D is Java and offers object orientation (classes, inheritance, polymorphism), threads, exception handling, and more. Java 3D can easily make use of other Java APIs, such as JMF and JAI. The Java Media Framework (JMF) includes mechanisms for playing audio and video segments and can be extended to support new forms or audio and video (*http://java.sun.com/products/java-media/jmf*). Java Advanced Imaging (JAI) provides many advanced image processing features, including over 100 imaging operators, tiling of large images, network-based capabilities, and the means to add new image processing features (*http://java.sun.com/products/java-media/jai*).

Documentation and Examples

The Java 3D distribution comes with about 40 small to medium examples. They're a great help but somewhat lacking in documentation. Fortunately, more resources are online. Sun's Java 3D tutorial is available at *http://java.sun.com/products/java-media/3D/ collateral/*. The tutorial is a good introduction to Java 3D but can confuse beginners.

Ben Moxon has a good introductory Java 3D tutorial based around getting a MilkShape 3D figure to move over a hilly terrain (*http://www.newview.co.uk/e/tutorials/java3d/index.jsp*) and is called *The Little Purple Dude Walks.*

Reading Up

I recommend three Java 3D textbooks as supplemental reading:

- *Java 3D API Jump-Start* by Aaron E. Walsh and Doug Gehringer (Prentice Hall)
- *Java 3D Programming* by Daniel Selman (Manning)
- *Java Media APIs: Cross-Platform Imaging, Media, and Visualization* by Alejandro Terrazas, John Ostuni, and Michael Barlow (Sams)

The Walsh and Gehringer text is an excellent overview, using code snippets rather than pages of listings. It complements the Java 3D tutorial.

The Selman book is more advanced. For the games enthusiast, Selman describes a Doom-like world, utilizing first-person perspective keyboard navigation and scene creation from a 2D map. The world contains bookcases, pools of water, flaming torches, and animated guards.

Terrazas is involved in VR research and business, so there's a heavy slant in the 3D part of his book toward less common topics such as sensors, head tracking, and a bit on CAVEs. There's an example combining Java 3D and JMF to create a streaming 3D chat room.

Criticisms of Java 3D for Games Programming

The misconceptions and complaints about Java 3D closely match those used against Java, which we discussed in Chapter 1:

- Java 3D is too slow for games programming.
- Java 3D is too high-level.
- Java 3D isn't supported on games consoles, so why bother using it?
- No one uses Java 3D to write real games.
- Sun Microsystems isn't interested in supporting Java 3D.

Java 3D Is Too Slow for Games

This claim comes with almost no evidence. Jacob Marner did the only serious test (2002). Marner carried out comparative performance tests on OpenGL and Java 3D versions of the same 3D noninteractive space of randomly positioned, scaled and rotated boxes. He used the C++ and GL4Java bindings for OpenGL, and used

Version 1.3.0 beta 1 of Java 3D. His master's thesis, *Evaluating Java for Game Development*, can be obtained from *http://www.rolemaker.dk/articles/evaljava/*.

The C++ version was fastest, the GL4Java implementation a little slower, and Java 3D about 2.5 times slower. However, the slowdown was due to a performance bug in that version of Java 3D and a poorly optimized scene graph. The timings haven't been repeated with the latest version of Java 3D or with more recent Java bindings to OpenGL such as JOGL or LWJGL.

Marner's code highlights some striking differences between Java 3D and OpenGL. The C++ and GL4Java programs are of comparable sizes (about 10 classes and 30 pages of code with documentation), but the Java 3D application is smaller (5 classes and 11 pages). Marner comments on the complexity of the OpenGL code, which requires a kd-tree data structure, a culling algorithm around the view frustum, and preprocessing vertex operations. All of these capabilities are built into Java 3D, so they didn't need to be implemented in the Java 3D application. In the GL4Java source, the optimized view frustum algorithm is hard to understand but is responsible for an order of magnitude speedup over the simpler version.

The OpenGL applications could have been considerable faster if extensions available on the graphics card were employed.

Another outcome of Marner's work is that it shows a negligible overhead for JNI: GL4Java uses JNI to interface Java to OpenGL, and its performance is slightly less than the C++ binding.

Java 3D is slow because Java is slow

Java 3D performance is often equated with Java performance: the myth of Java's slowness somehow demonstrates the slowness of Java 3D. Since Java 3D relies on OpenGL or DirectX for rendering, much of the graphics processing speed of Java 3D is independent of Java.

History suggests that performance will become a less important consideration as the base speed of hardware keeps increasing. Many successful games rely less on special effects, more on gaming characterization and story. Of course, games will always need performance, but the real bottleneck will not be the platform but the network as multiplayer games begin to dominate.

Performance should be considered alongside issues such as code complexity, productivity, maintainability, and portability. These criteria strongly influence a move toward higher-level APIs, as typified by Java 3D.

Java 3D Is Too High-Level

Java 3D's scene graph is often considered an unreasonable overhead, especially by programmers with experience in OpenGL or DirectX. Though Java 3D's scene graph does introduce some overhead, this overhead should be compared to the optimizations that comes along. These can be implemented in a low-level API by an experienced programmer but at what cost in time and maintainability?

Most large OpenGL and DirectX applications need a data structure like a scene graph to manage code complexity, so the scene graph versus no scene graph argument is often invalid.

A powerful, high-level, and flexible 3D graphics API needs a scene graph and a way to access the graphics pipeline efficiently. These mechanisms are aimed at different levels in 3D graphics programming, sometimes called the entity level and the rendering level. An application's entity level requires a data structure for organizing the scene objects, and the rendering level handles light mapping, shadows, radiosity, vertex shading, and so on. Great games are designed at the entity level, in terms of game play, characters, scenarios, and story elements. The look and feel of a great game, the light and dark, the atmosphere, is created at the rendering level.

Though Java 3D has highly developed tools for entity level programming, its deficit is at the rendering level. For example, the current version of Java 3D cannot perform vertex and pixel shading. Part of this is due to the desire to support Java 3D portability across OpenGL and DirectX, preventing it from making assumptions about which low-level features are present. Nevertheless, it is possible to achieve some striking rendering effects in Java 3D by employing multi-textures. The next major Java 3D release, Version 1.4, is scheduled to support two shader languages (Cg and GLSL); a beta version is due out in the middle of 2005.

The high-level nature of the scene graph makes Java 3D code harder to tune for speed unlike programs using OpenGL or DirectX directly. However, a programmer does have the option of moving to Java 3D's mixed or immediate modes.

Hiding low-level graphics API makes programming code around bugs harder in the APIs or the drivers.

Lack of Console Support

The lack of a console implementation for Java 3D is a serious problem, but if Java and OpenGL are available on a game machine, then Java 3D should be readily portable. The Game Cube already uses OpenGL.

Linux for the PlayStation 2 includes OpenGL support (*http://playstation2-linux.com/projects/openglstuff/*). There's an old alpha version of an OpenGL for the PlayStation 2, implemented by DataPlus (*http://www.dataplus.co.jp/OpenGL4ps2.html*). However, the future for OpenGL on consoles and other small devices is probably OpenGL ES, a subset of OpenGL (*http://www.khronos.org/opengles/*).

A Java binding is being developed for OpenGL ES, managed by JSR 239 (*http://www.jcp.org/en/jsr/detail?id=239*). A JSR is a Sun-sanctioned process for defining a new Java API. Much of the work is derived from JSR 231, which will be based on JOGL and/or LWJGL (both are explained in the section "Java Bindings to OpenGL"). JSR 239 is scheduled to be finished early in 2005.

No Real Java 3D Games

Java 3D has been employed in relatively few games, but they include bestsellers and award winners. I mentioned the commercial games in Chapter 1.

- *Law and Order II* by Legacy Interactive (*http://www.lawandordergame.com/index2.htm*).
- *Pernica* by Starfire Research (*http://www.starfireresearch.com/pernica/pernica.html*).
- *Cosm* by Navtools, Inc. (*http://www.cosm-game.com/*).
- *Roboforge* by Liquid Edge Games (*http://www.roboforge.com*).
- *FlyingGuns* (*http://www.flyingguns.com/*).
- *CazaPool3D* (*http://cazapool3d.sourceforge.net/cazapooljws/Pool.html*).
- *Out Of Space* (*http://www.geocities.com/Psionic1981*).
- *Cassos* (*http://www.la-cfd.com/cassos/english/index.php*). Racing monkeys, with a dragon.
- Immediate Mode Interactive (*http://www.imilabs.com/*) has built several impressive game demos with Java 3D over the years, including *Java 3D Grand Prix* (a racing game), *JAMID* (a first-person shooter in the Quake mold), and *Underworld Assault* (a two-person fighting game). Pictures and videos of these games can be found at the web site.
- *The Virtual Fishtank* (*http://www.virtualfishtank.com/main.html*). A distributed simulation of a 24,000-gallon aquarium rendered to 13 large projection screens and running on 15 networked machines. The fish migrate from server to server as they swim from screen to screen. It was shown at the Boston Museum of Science and the St. Louis Science Center to teach children about emergent self-organizing behavior in decentralized rule-based systems.
- *DALiWorld* (*http://www.dalilab.com/*). Another distributed aquatic virtual world inhabited by autonomous artificial life.

The "Other Sites" page at j3d.org (*http://www.j3d.org/sites.html*) is a good source for Java 3D examples and includes games and demos sections with many links.

The Java Games Factory (JGF), *http://grexengine.com/sections/externalgames/*, places its games into 2D and 3D categories, with the 3D examples further subdivided by the 3D API being used, such as Java 3D, JOGL, and LWJGL.

The third year Computer Graphics course in the Computer Science Department of the University of Applied Sciences in Biel, Switzerland, maintains a site of student projects using Java 3D (*http://www.hta-bi.bfh.ch/~swc/DemoJ3D/*). Several of them have been games, including Battleship3D-Net (networked Battleships), Billard-3D (pool), Glymp3D (role playing action), JBomba (based on Bomberman), and TriChess (3D networked chess).

A good strategy for finding Java 3D games and source code is to visit SourceForge (*http://sourceforge.net/search/*) and FreshMeat.com (*http://freshmeat.net/*) and search for keywords such as "Java," "3d," and "game."

Two very exciting Java 3D projects, which aren't really games:

Project Looking Glass (https://lg3d.dev.java.net/)
> A prototype 3D desktop offering rotating, transparent windows, multiple desktop workspaces, and an API for developing applications. It received much attention at JavaOne in 2004.

The Mars Rover Mission (http://www.sun.com/aboutsun/media/features/mars.html)
> Java 3D and JAI are being used to render and interpret the real-time images captured by the rover. A rover simulator is implemented in Java 3D, which is sort of a game.

Java 3D loaders for games

A loader is an essential tool for quickly populating a game with people, artifacts, and scenery. All the model loaders listed below are for popular games formats, and all support animation.

Quake Loaders (http://www.newdawnsoftware.com/)
> Supports Id Software's Quake 2 MD2 and BSP and Quake 3 MD3 formats. A morphing animation example using the MD3 loader can be found at *http://www. la-cfd.com/cassos/test/md3/index.html*.

JAVA is DOOMED (http://javaisdoomed.sourceforge.net/)
> A complete 3D engine, including loaders for Quake 2 MD2 and 3D Studio Max 3DS files.

The Java XTools (http://www.3dchat.org/dev.php) package
> Offers a range of Java 3D extras, including loaders for Renderware, Caligari TrueSpace, Alias/Wavefront Maya OBJ, and MTL files. Other elements include a lens flare mechanism, a text-to-texture converter, and a skybox class.

Salamander3D (https://skinandbones.dev.java.net/)
> Supports a file format for specifying 3D worlds and levels, character animations, collision objects, sensor objects, and other useful aspects of game scenes.

NWN Java 3D utilities (http://nwn-j3d.sourceforge.net/)
> Handles Neverwinter Night models, including animation and emitters.

Java 3D 3DS Loader (http://sourceforge.net/projects/java3dsloader/)
> Supports 3D Studio Max models, including cameras, point and directional lights, animation, and hierarchy textures.

Anim8or Loader (http://anim8orloader.sourceforge.net/)
> Can load 3D models and scenes saved in the Anim8or file format. Anim8or is a 3D-modeling and character animation program (*http://www.anim8or.com/main/index.html*).

Xj3D (http://www.xj3d.org/)
> Implements the X3D standard, a successor to VRML 97, and provides for key-frame animation. Xj3D also contains it own OpenGL renderer, which is reportedly much faster than the one inside Java 3D.

Add-ons for gaming

- Yaarq (*http://www.sbox.tugraz.at/home/w/wkien/*), by Wolfgang Kienreich, offers APIs for several gaming-related features, including texturing, bump maps, reflection maps, overlays, and particle systems. It also demonstrates how to achieve stable frame rates.

- Lighting Effects (*http://planeta.terra.com.br/educacao/alessandroborges/java3d.html*). Java 3D is often criticized for lacking sophisticated lighting effects. Alessandro Borges has developed several examples that show how to use bump maps to generate irregular surface lighting and cube map textures for reflection effects. Florin Herinean has also developed a series of texture examples, available at *http://www.seelenbinder-schule.de/~fherinean/*.

- Toon shaders (*http://www.antiflash.net/java3d/comicshader.html*) demonstrates how simple cartoon-style shading can be added to shapes.

- A library for building 3D geometries using meshes, NURBS, and subdivision surfaces (*https://jgeom.dev.java.net/*).

- A CSG API, by Danilo Balby Silva Castanheira, for geometry Boolean operators is available at *http://www.geocities.com/danbalby/*.

- A skeletal animation and skinning system, by Mark McKay, can be found at *https://skinandbones.dev.java.net/*.

- Java 3D Game SDK (*https://java3dgamesdk.dev.java.net/*). The extra functionality includes a menu to let the user choose between full-screen and window mode, a game mouse, and a collision box for the precise steering of objects.

- JXInput (*http://www.hardcode.de/jxinput*). This game supports joysticks and other input devices on Windows via Java 3D's Sensor class. It's also possible to interface Java 3D with JInput for game controller discovery and polled input (*https://jinput.dev.java.net/*).

- The j3d.org Code Repository (*http://code.j3d.org/*) includes code (or partial code) for ROAM terrain rendering, particle systems, and 2D overlays.

- The j3d-incubator project (*https://j3d-incubator.dev.java.net/*) on java.net is for sharing examples and utility code.

Sun Doesn't Support Java 3D

Perhaps this statement was true in 2003, but Java 3D is now a community project managed by the Advanced Software Development Group at Sun. If support means a pool of knowledgeable people ready to offer advice and large archives of technical information, then Java 3D has an abundance of support.

In the middle of 2003, Doug Twilleager issued the now infamous message "Java 3D 1.4 is currently in a holding pattern" (read it in full at *http://www.javagaming.org/cgi-bin/ JGNetForums/YaBB.cgi?board=3D;action=display;num=1054567731*). Doug Twilleager is the chief architect of the Game Technologies Group at Sun and one of the designers of Java 3D.

His message appeared just before JavaOne 2003, a conference that emphasized the JOGL, JOAL, and JInput APIs. Many people interpreted this as meaning that Java 3D was heading for the dustbin of history.

A possible reason for the holding pattern was Java 3D's development origins in the 3D Graphics Hardware Group at Sun. As graphics cards from companies such as ATI and nVidia caught up and surpassed Sun's hardware, the group started to become less profitable. Layoffs occurred and unprofitable group projects, such as Java 3D, were given low priority.

In March 2004, Doug Twilleager was back, this time announcing that Sun was making Java 3D available through a public source license at *https://java3d.dev.java.net/*.

The reemergence of Java 3D is due to the work of a few key people, including Doug Twilleager, and high-profile uses in Sun projects such as *Mars Rover* and *Looking Glass*. Java 3D has moved to the Advanced Software Development Group, a unit within Sun that is actively supported by upper management.

The new Java 3D project site (*https://java3d.dev.java.net/*) hosts the source code for Java 3D 1.3.2, a bug fix release. The version that was stable while I was writing was 1.3.1, which is used in this book.

Java 3D's license allows developers to download the source code and to contribute bug fixes and utilities. Modifications are allowed for research purposes, and a no-fee commercial license is available.

An expert group is being formed to define and implement future versions of the Java 3D API. An important point is that much of the implementation work is expected to come from the community, a strategy successfully employed to develop the JOGL, JOAL, and JInput APIs.

Four new Java 3D mailing lists exist:

- interest@java3d.dev.java.net
- announce@java3d.dev.java.net

- issues@java3d.dev.java.net
- cvs@java3d.dev.java.net

A new Java Desktop 3D Forum is at: *http://www.javadesktop.org/forums/forum. jspa?forumID=55*.

Older Java 3D information sources are still around:

- The Java 3D Product Page (*http://java.sun.com/products/java-media/3D/*), with links to demos, a basic FAQs page, and several application sites such as the Virtual Fishtank.
- The Java 3D Gaming Forum (*http://www.javagaming.org/cgi-bin/JGNetForums/ YaBB.cgi?board=3D*).
- The Java 3D Interest Mailing list can be searched at (*http://archives.java.sun.com/ archives/java3d-interest.html*). Subscription is possible from this site. A searchable-only interface can be found at *http://www.mail-archive.com/java3d-interest@java.sun.com/*.
- The Java Technology Forum for Java 3D (*http://forum.java.sun.com/forum. jsp?forum=21*).
- A Java 3D Programming Forum hosted at Manning Publications (*http://www. manning-sandbox.com/forum.jspa?forumID=31*). This is a good place to contact Daniel Selman, the author of *Java 3D Programming* (Manning).
- The best independent Java 3D site is *j3d.org* (*http://www.j3d.org*). It has a great FAQs page, and a large collection of tutorials, utilities, and a code repository.
- Java 3D at VirtualWorlds (*http://java3d.virtualworlds.de/index.php*) is a German/English site with sections on loaders, input devices, add-on libraries, documentation links, and a Java 3D Wiki (at an early stage).
- The USENET newsgroup *comp.lang.java.3d* can be searched and mailed to from Google's Groups page (*http://groups.google.com/groups?group=comp.lang.java.3d*).

Roadmaps for the future

A feature-complete beta version of Java 3D 1.4 may be released by mid-2005 and will include programmable shaders and other features that can be quickly added.

The shader support will be able to process descriptions written in the Cg or the GLSL shader languages. There is an active forum thread on this topic at *http:// www.javadesktop.org/forums/thread.jspa?threadID=5056*.

There have been discussions about using JOAL to replace Java 3D's buggy sound and to add in character animation, terrain utilities, improved collision detection and avoidance, NURBs, CSG (geometry Boolean operators), and more loaders. As mentioned in the sections "Java 3D loaders for games" and "Add-ons for gaming," many of these extensions exist.

The Java 3D team at Sun has a web page containing proposed Version 1.4 (and later) API changes: *https://j3d-core.dev.java.net/j3d1_4/proposed-changes.html*.

Whether these plans for Version 1.4 bear fruit depends on the Java 3D developer community; Sun is involved mainly as a manager and adjudicator. The signs for the future look bright since the community is involved in the bug fix release, Version 1.3.2.

It's interesting to look at the future plans list for *Project Looking Glass* (*https://lg3d. dev.java.net/*), which is built on top of Java 3D. It includes some of the Java 3D wish list, a physics engine (perhaps using odejava, *https://odejava.dev.java.net/*), and a particle system.

Java 3D 1.5 (or perhaps 2.0) will take longer to arrive since major changes are planned, such as pluggable renderers and extensibility. Athomas Goldberg, the head of the Game Technologies Group, has remarked that JOGL and JOAL may come into the picture at this stage.

The eventual release dates for Java 3D will probably be closely linked to those for Java. J2SE 5.1 (code-named "Dragon Fly") in the middle of 2005, Version 6 ("Mustang") in early 2006, Version 7 (Dolphin) in late 2007. Snapshot releases of the Mustang project can be accessed at *https://j2se.dev.java.net*.

Alternatives to Java 3D

There are a large number of ways of programming in 3D with Java without employing Java 3D. I've divided them into three categories: Java bindings to OpenGL, scene graph APIs, and game engine bindings.

Java Bindings to OpenGL

Several Java OpenGL bindings have been released over the years, but they tend to be incomplete, contain bugs, lack support and documentation, and often disappear suddenly. A (slightly out of date) list of Java bindings is maintained at the OpenGL site, *http://www.opengl.org/resources/java/*. It includes links to JOGL, LWJGL, Java 3D, GL4Java, and a few older projects. I'll describe only the active ones here.

GL4Java

GL4Java (*http://gl4java.sourceforge.net/*), known as "OpenGL for Java Technology," was one of the most popular OpenGL bindings until the arrival of JOGL. It can be used with AWT and Swing and has links to OpenGL 1.3 and vendor extensions.

Lightweight Java Game Library (LWJGL)

LWJGL (*http://www.lwjgl.org/*) utilizes OpenGL 1.5 with vendor extensions. It works with the latest versions of Java, so it can use the NIO and full-screen capabilities of

J2SE 1.4. However, it doesn't support AWT or Swing. LWJGL is quite small, as the name suggests, so it is suitable for devices with limited resources.

The documentation for LWJGL is a little scanty though ports of the Nehe OpenGL tutorials have started to appear; they're at the end of the original Nehe tutorials (*http://nehe.gamedev.net*).

JOGL

JOGL (*https://jogl.dev.java.net/*) is the most recent of the Java bindings for OpenGL, and promoted by the Game Technologies Group at Sun. Like LWJGL, it supports the latest versions of Java, OpenGL, and extensions. It differs in being integrated with AWT and Swing, and it is considerably larger.

JOGL will be the starting point for the Java OpenGL reference binding being developed as part of Sun's JSR 231 specification process (*http://www.jcp.org/en/jsr/detail?id=231*). JSR 231 will become the official Java binding for OpenGL. A few details about its status as of December 2004 is at *http://www.javagaming.org/cgi-bin/JGNetForums/YaBB.cgi?board=jogl;action=display;num=1102990415*.

The amount of tutorial material on JOGL is growing. The JOGL Forum at java-gaming.org is a rich information source (*http://www.javagaming.org/cgi-bin/JGNetForums/YaBB.cgi?board=jogl*). One good JOGL introduction, by Gregory Pierce, can be found at *http://www.javagaming.org/cgi-bin/JGNetForums/YaBB.cgi?board=jogl;action=display;num=1058027992*. Another introductory article, "Jumping into JOGL," by Chris Adamson is at *http://today.java.net/pub/a/today/2003/09/11/jogl2d.html*.

The eBook *Learning Java Bindings for OpenGL (JOGL)* (Kagi) by Gene Davis is available from *http://www.genedavissoftware.com/books/jogl/*. It starts with basic JOGL examples, suitable for beginners. Several chapters and appendixes are free online.

All the Nehe OpenGL tutorials have been ported to JOGL and can be downloaded from *http://nehe.gamedev.net* or *http://pepijn.fab4.be/nehe/*.

JOGL's access to OpenGL and its extensions means it can utilize shading languages for special effects like fish eyes and spherization, and it can generate various types of shadow using textures. Java 3D 1.3.1. can mimic a few of these (see the section "Add-ons for gaming"), and Java 1.4 will include a shader language. A crucial difference is that JOGL employs program code to affect the graphics pipeline dynamically, whereas Java 3D mostly uses capability bits and get/set methods.

A posting to the Java Desktop 3D forum (*http://www.javadesktop.org/forums/thread.jspa?threadID=3222*) describes the use of JOGL's GLCanvas class to create a HUD (heads-up display) within a Java 3D application. The canvas can be manipulated in the pre- or post-rendering phases of Java 3D's immediate mode.

Scene Graph APIs

The creation of scene graph APIs for Java is something of a growth area, aided by the existence of lower-level OpenGL bindings. Most of the systems are open source.

Xith3D

Xith3D (*http://xith.org*) uses the same basic scene graph structure as Java 3D but can directly call OpenGL operations. This means it supports functionality like shadow volumes and vertex and fragment programs. This is the ideal situation for a 3D graphics API, making Xith3D a strong contender as an alternative to Java 3D.

Since the high-level APIs of Xith3D and Java 3D are similar, porting Java 3D code over to Xith3D is fairly straightforward. Versions of Xith3D run on top of JOGL or LWJGL.

A good tutorial for Xith3D beginners is at *http://xith.org/tiki-index.php?page=Docs*. There is a Xith3D forum at javagaming.org: *http://www.javagaming.org/cgi-bin/ JGNetForums/YaBB.cgi*.

Two problems with Xith3D are its restriction to OpenGL (with no DirectX version), and the lack of scene graph thread safety.

OpenMind

The OpenMind API (*http://sourceforge.net/projects/open-mind/*) contains the expected elements, including hierarchical scene management and object transforms, dynamic cameras, lights, and fog. OpenMind is implemented on top of JOGL (it formerly used GL4Java).

jME graphics engine

jME (*http://www.mojomonkeycoding.com/*) was inspired by the scene graph engine described in *3D Game Engine Design* (Morgan Kaufmann) by David H. Eberly (*http:// www.magic-software.com/Books.html*). Currently, jME is built on top of LWJGL, with plans for JOGL support in the near future.

Jist3D

The alpha version of this engine will be released in 2005 (*http://www.imilabs.com/*). Many of its features are described in *Practical Java Game Programming* (Charles River Media) by Clingman, et al.

A key element of Jist3D is its utilization of JOGL, JOAL, and JInput. The rendering engine uses JOGL to support the scene graph and includes utilities for working with Java 3D graphs, a collision system, and 2D overlays.

JiD

JiD (*http://javaisdoomed.sourceforge.net*) includes loaders for Quake 2 MD2 and 3D Studio Max 3DS files. The implementation uses JOGL. The distribution includes Escape, a Doom-like game.

Aviatrix3D

Aviatrix3D (*http://aviatrix3d.j3d.org/*) is a retained-mode Java scene graph API above JOGL. Its tool set is aimed at data visualization rather than gaming and supports CAVEs, domes, and HMDs.

Kahlua

Kahlua (*http://www.igd.fhg.de/CP/kahlua/*) is a Java wrapper for Open Inventor (*http://www.sgi.com/software/inventor/*), a scene graph API available on the Unix/Linux and Windows platforms.

jFree-D2

jFree-D2 (*http://sourceforge.net/projects/jfreed2/*) is a reincarnation of the open source Java 3D implementation JFree-D, developed by Jean-Christophe Taveau in 1999. It provides a workable (but incomplete) implementation of Java 3D on top of GL4Java. Support for JOGL is planned in the future.

Game Engine Bindings

The following APIs emulate well-known game engines (e.g., Quake) or are Java wrappers around existing engines.

Auriga3D

Auriga3D (*http://www.auriga3d.org/*) works with Quake3 maps. There are versions on top of JOGL and LWJGL.

Jake2

Jake2 (*http://www.bytonic.de/html/jake2.html*) is a port of the GPL'd Quake2 game engine. It uses JOGL for the graphics and JOAL for the 3D sound. In tests, it achieves better than 85% of the speed of the original C:210 FPS compared to 245 FPS.

Ogre4J

Ogre4J (*http://www.bytelords.de/cowiki/427.html*) is a binding for the OGRE 3D Engine (*http://www.ogre3d.org/*) using JNI. OGRE 3D supports Direct3D and OpenGL and runs on all the main desktop platforms.

Jirr

Jirr (*http://sourceforge.net/projects/jirr/*) is a binding of the open source Irrlicht game engine (*http://irrlicht.sourceforge.net/*), which is written in C++. Jirr is in the early stages of development.

Odejava

Odejava (*https://odejava.dev.java.net/*) is a binding around the Open Dynamics Engine (ODE), an industrial quality library for simulating articulated rigid body dynamics. Typical applications include ground vehicles, legged creatures, and moving objects in VR environments. ODE is coded in C. The project contains tools for linking Odejava into Xith3D, OpenMind, and jME. A Java 3D binding is currently being developed as an offshoot of Project Looking Glass.

CHAPTER 15

A 3D Checkerboard: Checkers3D

This chapter describes Checkers3D with a Java 3D example that creates a scene consisting of a dark green and blue tiled surface with labels along the x- and z-axes, a blue background, and a floating sphere lit from two different directions. The user (viewer) can travel through the scene by moving the mouse.

The lefthand screenshot in Figure 15-1 shows the initial view; the picture on the right shows the scene after the user has moved around a bit.

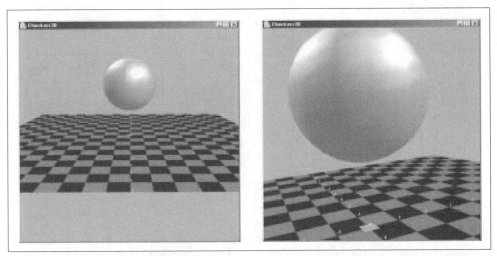

Figure 15-1. Initial view, and later

Checkers3D illustrates many of the common, and sometimes tricky, aspects of programming with Java 3D. For example, the 3D scene is displayed using the Java 3D Canvas3D class, which must be integrated with Java's Swing components. All Java 3D applications require a scene graph, and Checkers3D shows how to add basic shapes, lighting (ambient and directional), and a background. The scene graph diagram acts as a visual form of documentation, and a textual version of its information can be generated easily, with the help of Daniel Selman's Java3dTree package. (I'll supply details at the end of this chapter).

The floor and sphere utilize Java 3D's QuadArray, Text2D, and Sphere geometry classes: the floor is a series of quadrilaterals in a QuadArray, and labels are placed along the main axes of the floor using Text2D objects. The sphere shows how a 3D shape is colored, lit, and positioned in space. The user looks into the 3D world from a viewpoint. You'll see how it can be initially positioned, and how it can be moved during execution by using Java 3D's OrbitBehavior class.

Class Diagrams for Checkers3D

The class diagrams in Figure 15-2 show all the public and private data and methods for the Checkers3D application.

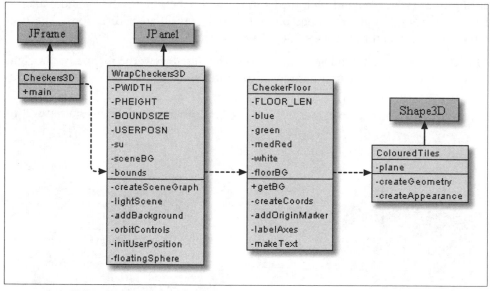

Figure 15-2. Class diagrams for Checkers3D

Checkers3D is the top-level JFrame for the application. WrapCheckers3D is a JPanel holding the scene graph, which is viewable via a Canvas3D object. CheckerFloor creates the subgraph for the floor (e.g., tiles, axes, etc.), with all the same colored tiles represented by a single ColoredTiles object.

 The source code for this example is in the *Checkers3D/* directory.

Integrating Java 3D and Swing

Checkers3D is a JFrame where GUI controls, such as Swing text fields and buttons, would be placed if necessary. In this example, it creates an instance of WrapCheckers3D (a JPanel) and places it in the center of a BorderLayout:

```
c.setLayout( new BorderLayout() );
WrapCheckers3D w3d = new WrapCheckers3D();    // panel for 3D canvas
c.add(w3d, BorderLayout.CENTER);
```

The Canvas3D view onto the scene is created inside WrapCheckers3D:

```
public WrapCheckers3D()
{
  setLayout( new BorderLayout() );
  // other initialization code

  GraphicsConfiguration config =
          SimpleUniverse.getPreferredConfiguration();
  Canvas3D canvas3D = new Canvas3D(config);
  add("Center", canvas3D);

  // other initialization code}
```

Some care must be taken when using Canvas3D since it's a heavyweight GUI element (a thin layer over an OS-generated window). Heavyweight components aren't easily combined with Swing controls, which are lightweight; the controls are mostly generated by Java. Problems are avoided if the Canvas3D object is embedded in a JPanel; then the panel can be safely integrated with the rest of the Swing-built application.

 There's a detailed discussion of the issues related to combining Canvas3D and Swing at j3d.org (*http://www.j3d.org/tutorials/quick_fix/swing.html*).

Compared to applications in earlier chapters, there's no update/draw animation loop. This is unnecessary because Java 3D contains its own mechanism for monitoring changes in the scene and initiating rendering. Here is the algorithm in pseudocode form:

```
while(true) {
  process user input;
  if (exit request) break;
  perform behaviors;
  if (scene graph has changed)
    traverse scene graph and render;
}
```

Behaviors are scene graph nodes containing code that can influence other parts of the graph, such as moving shapes or changing the lighting. They may be used for monitoring the graph, passing details to the non-3D parts of the application.

The details are more complicated than this pseudocode suggests for example, Java 3D uses multithreading to carry out parallel traversal and rendering. However, having a general idea of the process will help you work through the code in the rest of this chapter.

Scene Graph Creation

The scene graph is created by the constructor for WrapCheckers3D:

```
public WrapCheckers3D()
{
  // initialization code

  GraphicsConfiguration config =
            SimpleUniverse.getPreferredConfiguration();
  Canvas3D canvas3D = new Canvas3D(config);
  add("Center", canvas3D);
  canvas3D.setFocusable(true);      // give focus to the canvas
  canvas3D.requestFocus();

  su = new SimpleUniverse(canvas3D);

  createSceneGraph();
  initUserPosition();         // set user's viewpoint
  orbitControls(canvas3D);    // controls for moving the viewpoint

  su.addBranchGraph( sceneBG );
}
```

The Canvas3D object is initialized with a configuration obtained from getPreferredConfiguration(); this method queries the hardware for rendering information. Some older Java 3D programs don't bother initializing a GraphicsConfiguration object, using null as the argument to the Canvas3D constructor instead. This is bad programming practice.

canvas3D is given focus so keyboard events will be sent to behaviors in the scene graph. Behaviors are often triggered by key presses and releases, but they may be triggered by timers, frame changes, and events generated by Java 3D internally. There aren't any behaviors in Checkers3D, so it's not necessary to set the focus. I've left these lines in since they're needed in almost every other program we'll consider.

The su SimpleUniverse object creates a standard view branch graph and the VirtualUniverse and Locale nodes of the scene graph. createSceneGraph() sets up the lighting, the sky background, the floor, and floating sphere; initUserPosition() and orbitControls() handle viewer issues. The resulting BranchGroup is added to the scene graph at the end of the method:

```
private void createSceneGraph()
{
  sceneBG = new BranchGroup();
  bounds = new BoundingSphere(new Point3d(0,0,0), BOUNDSIZE);
```

```
    lightScene();          // add the lights
    addBackground();       // add the sky
    sceneBG.addChild( new CheckerFloor().getBG() );  // add floor

    floatingSphere();      // add the floating sphere

    sceneBG.compile();     // fix the scene
  } // end of createSceneGraph()
```

Various methods add subgraphs to sceneBG to build the content branch graph. sceneBG is compiled once the graph has been finalized to allow Java 3D to optimize it. The optimizations may involve reordering the graph and regrouping and combining nodes. For example, a chain of TransformGroup nodes containing different translations may be combined into a single node. Another possibility is to group all the shapes with the same appearance properties together, so they can be rendered more quickly.

bounds is a global BoundingSphere used to specify the influence of environment nodes for lighting, background, and the OrbitBehavior object. The bounding sphere is placed at the center of the scene and affects everything within a BOUNDSIZE units radius. Bounding boxes and polytopes are available in Java 3D.

The scene graph by the end of WrapCheckers3D() is shown in Figure 15-3.

The "Floor Branch" node is my invention to hide some details until later. Missing from Figure 15-3 is the view branch part of the scene graph.

Lighting the Scene

One ambient and two directional lights are added to the scene by lightScene(). An ambient light reaches every corner of the world, illuminating everything equally.

```
Color3f white = new Color3f(1.0f, 1.0f, 1.0f);
// Set up the ambient light
AmbientLight ambientLightNode = new AmbientLight(white);
ambientLightNode.setInfluencingBounds(bounds);
sceneBG.addChild(ambientLightNode);
```

The color of the light is set, the ambient source is created along with bounds and added to the scene. The Color3f() constructor takes Red/Green/Blue values between 0.0f and 1.0f (1.0f being "full-on").

A directional light mimics a light from a distant source, hitting the surfaces of objects from a specified direction. The main difference from an ambient light is the requirement for a direction vector.

```
Vector3f light1Direction  = new Vector3f(-1.0f, -1.0f, -1.0f);
    // left, down, backwards
DirectionalLight light1 =  new DirectionalLight(white, light1Direction);
light1.setInfluencingBounds(bounds);
sceneBG.addChild(light1);
```

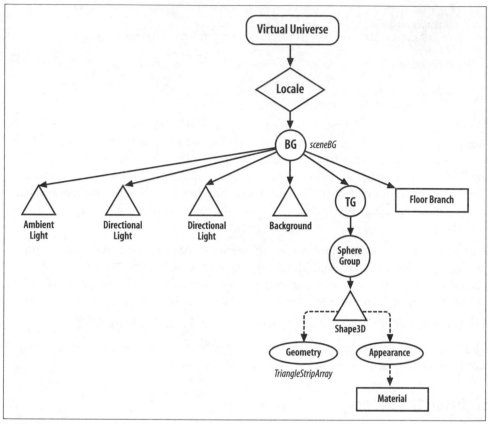

Figure 15-3. Partial scene graph for Checkers3D

The direction is the vector between (0, 0, 0) and (–1, –1, –1); the light can be imagined to be multiple parallel lines with that direction, originating at infinity.

Point and spot lights are the other forms of Java 3D lighting. Point lights position the light in space, emitting in all directions. Spot lights are focused point lights, aimed in a particular direction.

The Scene's Background

A background for a scene can be specified as a constant color (as shown here), a static image, or a texture-mapped geometry such as a sphere:

```
Background back = new Background();
back.setApplicationBounds( bounds );
back.setColor(0.17f, 0.65f, 0.92f);    // sky color
sceneBG.addChild( back );
```

Floating Spheres

Sphere is a utility class from Java 3D's com.sun.j3d.utils.geometry package, a subclass of the Primitive class, which is a Group node with a Shape3D child (see Figure 15-3). Its geometry is stored in a Java 3D TriangleStripArray, which specifies the sphere as an array of connected triangles. I don't have to adjust this geometry, but the sphere's appearance and position do require changes.

The Appearance node is a container for references of to much information, including coloring, line, point, polygon, rendering, transparency, and texture attributes.

ColouringAttributes fixes the color of a shape and is unaffected by scene lighting. For a shape requiring interaction between color and light, the Material component is employed. For light to affect a shape's color, three conditions must be met:

- The shape's geometry must include normals.
- The shape's Appearance node must have a Material component.
- The Material component must have enabled lighting with setLightingEnable( ).

The utility Sphere class can automatically creates normals, so the first condition is easily satisfied.

Coloring the Spheres

The Java 3D Material component controls what color a shape exhibits when lit by different kinds of lights:

```
Material mat = new Material(ambientColor, emissiveColor,
                           diffuseColor, specularColor, shininess);
```

The ambient color argument specifies the shape's color when lit by ambient light: this gives the object a uniform color. The emissive color contributes the color that the shape produces (as for a light bulb); frequently, this argument is set to black (equivalent to off). The diffuse color is the color of the object when lit, with its intensity depending on the angle the light beams make with the shape's surface.

 The diffuse and ambient colors are often set to be the same, which matches the way real-world objects are colored when lit.

The intensity of the specular color parameter is related to how much the shape reflects from its shiny areas. This is combined with the shininess argument, which controls the size of the reflective highlights.

The specular color is often set to white, matching the specular color produced by most objects in the real world.

In Checkers3D, there are two directional lights, which create two shiny patches on the top of the floating sphere (see Figure 15-1). The floor tiles are unlit since their color is set in the shape's geometry (more on this later in the chapter).

The code in floatingSphere( ) that handles the sphere's appearance is shown here:

```
Color3f black = new Color3f(0.0f, 0.0f, 0.0f);
Color3f blue = new Color3f(0.3f, 0.3f, 0.8f);
Color3f specular = new Color3f(0.9f, 0.9f, 0.9f); // near white

Material blueMat= new Material(blue, black, blue, specular, 25.0f);
blueMat.setLightingEnable(true);

Appearance blueApp = new Appearance();
blueApp.setMaterial(blueMat);
```

Positioning the Spheres

Positioning a shape is almost always done by placing its scene graph node below a TransformGroup (see the sphere Group in Figure 15-3). A TransformGroup can be used to position, rotate, and scale the nodes which lie beneath it, with the transformations defined with Java 3D Transform3D objects:

```
Transform3D t3d = new Transform3D();
t3d.set( new Vector3f(0,4,0));      // place at (0,4,0)
TransformGroup tg = new TransformGroup(t3d);
tg.addChild(new Sphere(2.0f, blueApp));
        // set the sphere's radius and appearance
        // and its normals by default
sceneBG.addChild(tg);
```

The set( ) method positions the sphere's center at (0, 4, 0) and resets any previous rotations or scalings. set( ) can be used to scale and rotate while resetting the other transformations. The methods setTranslation( ), setScale( ), and setRotation( ) only affect the given transformation.

Unlike some 3D drawing packages, the y-axis in Java 3D is in the vertical direction, while the ground is being defined by the XZ plane, as shown in Figure 15-4.

The position of the sphere is Checkers3D is set to be (0, 4, 0), which places its center four units above the XZ plane.

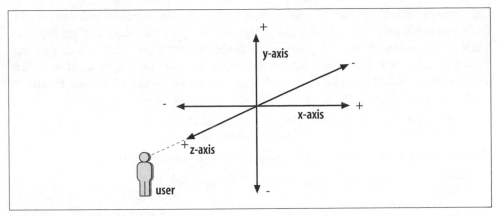

Figure 15-4. Axes in Java 3D

The Floor

The floor is made of tiles created with my ColouredTiles class, and axis labels made with the Java 3D Text2D utility class. Figure 15-5 shows the floor branch, previously hidden inside a "Floor Branch" box in Figure 15-3.

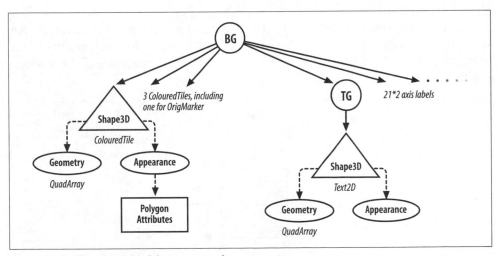

Figure 15-5. Floor branch of the scene graph

The floor subgraph is constructed with an instance of my CheckerFloor class and made available via the getBG( ) method:

```
sceneBG.addChild( new CheckerFloor().getBG() );   // add the floor
```

The CheckerFloor() constructor uses nested for loops to initialize two ArrayLists. The blueCoords list contains all the coordinates for the blue tiles, and greenCoords holds the coordinates for the green tiles. Once the ArrayLists are filled, they are passed to ColouredTiles objects, along with the color that should be used to render the tiles. A ColouredTiles object is a subclass of Shape3D, so can be added directly to the floor's graph:

```
floorBG.addChild( new ColouredTiles(blueCoords, blue) );
floorBG.addChild( new ColouredTiles(greenCoords, green) );
```

The red square at the origin (visible in Figure 15-1) is made in a similar way:

```
Point3f p1 = new Point3f(-0.25f, 0.01f, 0.25f);
Point3f p2 = new Point3f(0.25f, 0.01f, 0.25f);
Point3f p3 = new Point3f(0.25f, 0.01f, -0.25f);
Point3f p4 = new Point3f(-0.25f, 0.01f, -0.25f);

ArrayList oCoords = new ArrayList();
oCoords.add(p1); oCoords.add(p2);
oCoords.add(p3); oCoords.add(p4);

floorBG.addChild( new ColouredTiles(oCoords, medRed) );
```

The square is centered at (0, 0) on the XZ plane and raised a little above the y-axis (0.01 units) so it's visible above the tiles.

Each side of the square is the length of 0.5 units. The four Point3f points in the ArrayList are stored in a counterclockwise order. This is true for each group of four points in blueCoords and greenCoords. Figure 15-6 shows the ordering of the square's points.

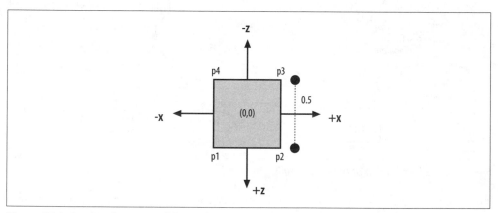

Figure 15-6. OrigMarker, viewed from above

The Colored Tiles

My ColouredTiles class extends Shape3D and defines the geometry and appearance of tiles with the same color. The geometry uses a Java 3D QuadArray to represent the tiles as a series of quadrilaterals (quads). The constructor is

```
QuadArray(int vertexCount, int vertexFormat);
```

The vertex format is an ORed collection of static integers, which specify the different aspects of the quad to be initialized later, such as its coordinates, color, and normals. In ColouredTiles, the QuadArray plane is created using this line of code:

```
plane = new QuadArray(coords.size( ),
                GeometryArray.COORDINATES | GeometryArray.COLOR_3 );
```

The size( ) method returns the number of coordinates in the supplied ArrayList. The coordinate and color data is supplied in createGeometry( ):

```
int numPoints = coords.size( );
Point3f[] points = new Point3f[numPoints];
coords.toArray( points );   // ArrayList-->array
plane.setCoordinates(0, points);

Color3f cols[] = new Color3f[numPoints];
for(int i=0; i < numPoints; i++)
  cols[i] = col;
plane.setColors(0, cols);
```

The order in which a quad's coordinates are specified is significant. The front of a polygon is the face where the vertices form a counterclockwise loop. Knowing front from back is important for lighting and hidden face culling, and by default, only the front face of a polygon will be visible in a scene. In this application, the tiles are oriented so their fronts are facing upward along the y-axis.

It's necessary to ensure that the points of each quad from a convex, planar polygon, or rendering may be compromised. However, each quad in the coordinates array doesn't need to be connected or adjacent to the other quads, which is the case for these tiles.

Since a quad's geometry doesn't include normals information, a Material node component can't be used to specify the quad's color when lit. I could use a ColoringAttributes, but a third alternative is to set the color in the geometry, as done here (plane.setColors(0, cols);). This color will be constant, unaffected by the scene lighting.

Once finalized, the Shape3D's geometry is set with:

```
setGeometry(plane);
```

The shape's appearance is handled by createAppearance( ), which uses a Java 3D PolygonAttribute component to switch off the culling of the back face. PolygonAttribute can be employed to render polygons in point or line form (i.e., as wire frames), and to flip the normals of back facing shapes:

```
Appearance app = new Appearance( );
PolygonAttributes pa = new PolygonAttributes( );
pa.setCullFace(PolygonAttributes.CULL_NONE);
app.setPolygonAttributes(pa);
```

Once the appearance has been fully specified, it's fixed in the shape with

```
setAppearance(app);
```

The Floor's Axis Labels

The floor's axis labels are generated with the labelAxes( ) and makeText( ) methods in CheckerFloor( ). labelAxes( ) uses two loops to create labels along the x and z. Each label is constructed by makeText( ) and then added to the floor's BranchGroup (see Figure 15-5):

```
floorBG.addChild( makeText(pt,""+i) );
```

makeText( ) uses the Text2D utility class to create a 2D string of a specified color, font, point size, and font style:

```
Text2D message = new Text2D(text, white, "SansSerif", 36, Font.BOLD);
                    // 36 point bold Sans Serif
```

A Text2D object is a Shape3D object with a quad geometry (a rectangle), and appearance given by a texture map (image) of the string, placed on the front face. By default, the back face is culled; if the user moves behind an axis label, the object becomes invisible.

The point size is converted to virtual-world units by dividing by 256. Generally, it's a bad idea to use too large a point size in the Text2D( ) constructor since the text may be rendered incorrectly. Instead, a TransformGroup should be placed above the shape and used to scale it to the necessary size.

The positioning of each label is done by a TransformGroup above the shape:

```
TransformGroup tg = new TransformGroup( );
Transform3D t3d = new Transform3D( );
t3d.setTranslation(vertex);    // the position for the label
tg.setTransform(t3d);
tg.addChild(message);
```

setTranslation( ) only affects the position of the shape. The tg TransformGroup is added to the floor scene graph.

Viewer Positioning

The scene graph in Figure 15-3 doesn't include the view branch graph; that branch is shown in Figure 15-7.

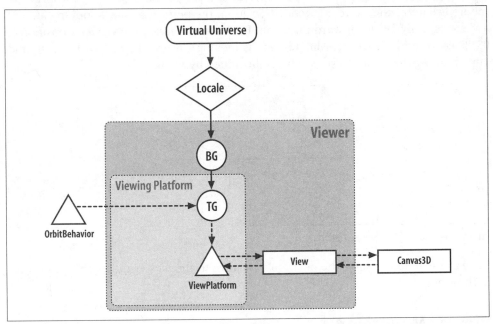

Figure 15-7. The view branch graph

The branch is created by a call to the SimpleUniverse constructor in the WrapCheckers3D( ) constructor:

```
su = new SimpleUniverse(canvas3D);
```

SimpleUniverse offers simplified access to the view branch graph via the ViewingPlatform and Viewer classes, which are mapped to the graph (shown as dotted rectangles in Figure 15-7).

ViewingPlatform is used in initUserPosition( ) to access the TransformGroup above the ViewPlatform node:

```
ViewingPlatform vp = su.getViewingPlatform( );
TransformGroup steerTG = vp.getViewPlatformTransform( );
```

steerTG corresponds to the TG node in Figure 15-7. Its Transform3D component is extracted and changed with the lookAt( ) and invert( ) methods:

```
Transform3D t3d = new Transform3D( );
steerTG.getTransform(t3d);
```

```
t3d.lookAt( USERPOSN, new Point3d(0,0,0), new Vector3d(0,1,0));
t3d.invert( );

steerTG.setTransform(t3d);
```

lookAt( ) is a convenient way to set the viewer's position in the virtual world. The method requires the viewer's intended position, the point that she is looking at, and a vector specifying the upward direction. In this application, the viewer's position is USERPOSN (the (0, 5, 20) coordinate); she is looking toward the origin (0, 0, 0), and "up" is along the positive y-axis. This is illustrated by Figure 15-8.

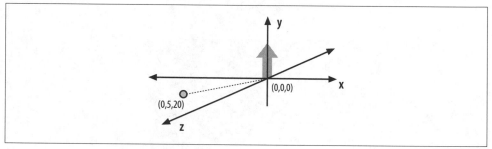

Figure 15-8. lookAt( ) depicted graphically

invert( ) is required since the position is relative to the viewer rather than an object in the scene.

Viewer Movement

The user is able to move through the scene by utilizing the Java 3D OrbitBehavior utility class in the view graph. A combination of control keys and mouse button presses move and rotate (or *orbits*) the viewer's position.

The behavior is set up in orbitControls( ) in WrapCheckers3D:

```
OrbitBehavior orbit = new OrbitBehavior(c, OrbitBehavior.REVERSE_ALL);
orbit.setSchedulingBounds(bounds);
ViewingPlatform vp = su.getViewingPlatform( );
vp.setViewPlatformBehavior(orbit);
```

The REVERSE_ALL flag ensures that the viewpoint moves in the same direction as the mouse.

 Numerous other flags and methods affect the rotation, translation, and zooming characteristics, explained in the OrbitBehavior class documentation.

MouseRotate, MouseTranslate, and MouseZoom are similar behavior classes that appear in many Java 3D examples; their principal difference from OrbitBehavior is that they affect the objects in the scene rather than the viewer.

 Most games, such as first-person shooters (FPS), require greater control over the viewer's movements than these utility behaviors can offer, so I'll be implementing my own behaviors in later chapters.

Viewing the Scene Graph

This chapter has used scene graphs to illustrate the discussed coding techniques, and scene graphs are a useful way of understanding (and checking) code.

I received help with my drawings by using Daniel Selman's Java3dTree package. It creates a JFrame holding a textual tree representation of the scene graph (Figure 15-9).

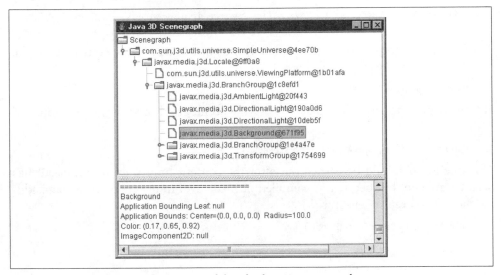

Figure 15-9. Java3dTree representation of the Checkers3D scene graph

The tree (a JTree object) is initially minimized, and branches can be examined by clicking on the subfolder icons. Information about the currently selected node appears in the bottom window. The package is available in *j3dtree.jar* as part of the source code downloadable from *http://www.manning.com/selman/* for Selman's *Java 3D Programming* text.

Augmenting code to generate the JTree is simple. WrapCheckers3D must import the j3dtree package and declare a global variable for the JFrame tree display:

```
import com.sun.j3d.utils.behaviors.vp.*;

private Java3dTree j3dTree;
```

The WrapCheckers3D( ) constructor creates the j3dTree object:

```
public WrapCheckers3D( )
{
  // other code
  su = new SimpleUniverse(canvas3D);

  j3dTree = new Java3dTree( );    // create a display tree for the SG

  createSceneGraph( );
  initUserPosition( );
  orbitControls(canvas3D);
  su.addBranchGraph( sceneBG );

  j3dTree.updateNodes( su );      // build the tree display window
}
```

After the scene graph has been completed, (i.e., at the end of the constructor), the tree display is built with a single line:

```
j3dTree.updateNodes( su );
```

However, prior to this, the capabilities of the scene graph nodes must be adjusted with:

```
j3dTree.recursiveApplyCapability( sceneBG );
```

This operation should be carried out after the content branch group (sceneBG) has been completed, but before it is compiled or made live. In my code, this means adding the line to createSceneGraph( ):

```
private void createSceneGraph( )
{
  sceneBG = new BranchGroup( );
  // other code to create the scene

  j3dTree.recursiveApplyCapability( sceneBG );

  sceneBG.compile( );
}
```

Unfortunately, you can't just call:

```
j3dTree.recursiveApplyCapability( su );
```

without generating errors because the SimpleUniverse( ) constructor has made the ViewingPlatform live, which prevents further changes to its capabilities.

Since only the capabilities in the content branch have been adjusted, the call to updateNodes( ) will generate some warning messages when the view branch below the Locale node is encountered.

Compilation and execution must include *j3dtree.jar* in the classpath. My preferred approach is to do this via command line arguments:

```
javac -classpath "%CLASSPATH%;j3dtree.jar" *.java

java -cp "%CLASSPATH%;j3dtree.jar" Checkers3D
```

 If typing the classpath repeatedly isn't to your taste, command lines like these can be hidden inside batch files or shell scripts.

The Java3dTree object is a textual representation of the scene, which means that I had to draw the scene graph myself. But the plus side is that tree generation has negligible impact on the rest of the program.

Another solution is to use the Java 3D Scene Graph Editor (*http://java3d.netbeans.org/j3deditor_intro.html*). This displays a graphical version of the scene graph but has the downside that its installation and usage are complicated and the memory requirements may be severe on some machines.

CHAPTER 16

Loading and Manipulating External Models

It's possible to build complex geometries in Java 3D by using the `GeometryArray` class or one of its subclasses (e.g., a `QuadArray` or `TriangleStripArray`). This amounts to calculating 3D coordinates for yourself and ensuring they're ordered correctly inside the geometry objects. This is almost impossible to do manually for anything but the simplest shapes (such as boxes or cones). It makes much more sense to create an object using 3D modeling software and then load that object into your Java 3D application at runtime. I'll refer to objects as *external models* since their geometry and appearance (e.g., their color and texture) are created outside of Java 3D.

This chapter describes two Java 3D programs that load external models, and then details placing those models into the checkerboard scene (discussed in Chapter 15). This illustrates many of the typical tasks a Java 3D program will perform: analyzing the contents of a model, adjusting its appearance, and repositioning the model in a scene.

LoaderInfo3D.java shows how a loaded object can be examined and its component shapes manipulated to change color, transparency, texture, and other attributes. Figure 16-1 shows two screenshots: the left one a robot with its original colors, the right one the same model after being turned blue.

Loader3D.java, the other application examined in this chapter, shows how a loaded model's position, orientation, and size can be adjusted. This information can be saved to a text file and applied to the model when it's next loaded.

Figure 16-2 shows two screenshots: the one on the left is of a small castle that, when first loaded, is half hidden below the checkered floor. The screenshot on the right is after the castle has been moved, rotated, and scaled. I've moved the viewpoint back a considerable distance so all of the model can be seen.

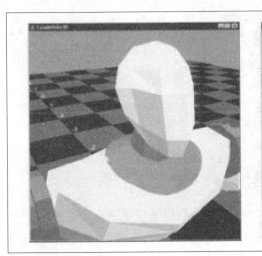

Figure 16-1. A robot turned blue

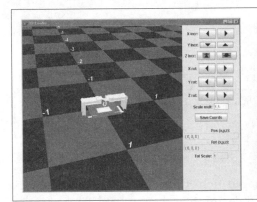
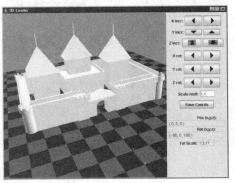

Figure 16-2. A repositioned and scaled castle

This chapter will discuss the following Java 3D techniques:

External model loading (using NCSA `Portfolio`*)*
> `Portfolio` collects several loaders for different 3D file formats into a single, convenient package.

Shape modification
> You'll see five different modifications to a shape's appearance: changing its color, rendering the shape as a wireframe, setting a transparency level, wrapping a texture around it, and modulating (combining) a texture with the shape's color.

Scene graph traversal
> This is required by the shape modification code since a shape node has to be found in the graph before its appearance can be changed.

Integrating GUI controls with the Java 3D canvas
> This follows on from the brief discussion at the start of Chapter 15 about the care needed in combining Java 3D's Canvas3D class with Swing components. Loader3D uses several Swing components, as shown in Figure 16-2.

Shape positioning, scaling, and rotation
> These operations are often required for shapes loaded from external models, which may appear in the Java 3D scene in the wrong position, may be badly orientated, or scaled incorrectly.

An Overview of LoaderInfo3D

The class diagrams for LoaderInfo in Figure 16-3 show only the classes' public methods.

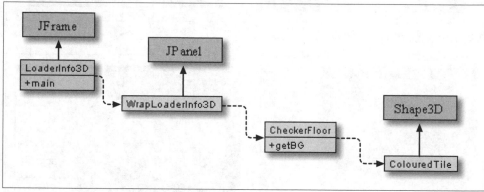

Figure 16-3. Class diagrams for LoaderInfo3D

CheckerFloor and ColouredTile are unchanged from Chapter 15: CheckerFloor creates the floor using ColouredTile objects. LoaderInfo3D is the top-level JFrame for the application and is similar to Checkers3D, except that it takes two arguments from the command line (the name of the file to load and an adaptation number) and passes them to WrapLoaderInfo3D:

```
java -cp "%CLASSPATH%;ncsa\portfolio.jar" LoaderInfo3D Coolrobo.3ds 0
```

This renders the robot model stored in *Coolrobo.3ds* in blue, as in Figure 16-1. The classpath argument is used to include the loaders package stored in *portfolio.jar*.

 The source code for this example can be found in *LoaderInfo3D/* directory.

You may be wondering about the mysterious adaptation number; it's an integer representing the appearance modification that should be applied to the model. The meaning of the integer values are:

0   Makes the shape blue

1   Draws the shape in outline

2   Renders the shape almost transparent

3   Lays a texture over the shape

4   Makes the shape blue and adds a texture

Anything else
    Makes no changes at all

WrapLoaderInfo3D creates the scene in a similar way to the WrapCheckers3D class in Chapter 15. I always use a Wrap class to build the scene in the chapters on Java 3D. WrapLoaderInfo3D performs two other tasks: examining the model and modifying the shape according to the user's supplied adaptation number.

The methods for WrapLoaderInfo3D are shown in Figure 16-4, grouped into three categories:

Create Scene methods
    These methods build the scene by adding the checkerboard floor, lights, background, and viewer's OrbitBehavior. There are methods for loading the model (loadModel( ) and calcScaleFactor( )).

Examine Model methods
    These methods traverse the model's scene graph and save the collected information into a text file. The information is about what shapes are present in the loaded model (a model may be made from multiple shapes), together with geometry and appearance details.

 The details are sent to a text file rather than the screen because of the quantity of information generated. Placing it in a text file makes it easier to examine later.

Change Model Shapes methods
    These methods traverse the scene graph looking for Shape3D nodes and modify them according to the adaptation number supplied on the command line. Once a shape is found, it's turned blue (makeBlue( )), drawn in outline (drawOutline( )), made almost transparent (makeAlmostTransparent( )), draped with a texture (addTexture( )), or turned blue and given a texture (makeBlue( ) and addTexture( )).

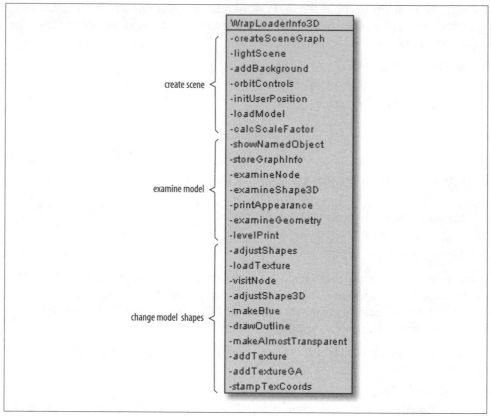

Figure 16-4. WrapLoaderInfo3D methods

Loaders in Java 3D

Before WrapLoaderInfo3D can traverse or change the external model's scene graph, the model has to be loaded. Java 3D supports external model loading through its Loader interface and the Scene class. Loader takes as input the model's filename and flags for enabling and disabling the loading of certain elements of the model, such as light nodes, sound nodes, and view graphs.

Java 3D's utilities package includes two subclasses of Loader aimed at particular file formats: Lw3dLoader handles Lightwave 3D scene files, and ObjectFile processes Wavefront OBJ files. A third subclass, LoaderBase, implements the Loader interface in a generic way to encourage the building of loaders for other 3D formats through subclassing.

The Scene class uses a Loader object to extract details about a model, the most significant being its BranchGroup, usually for the purpose of adding it to the application scene. Information about other aspects of the model may be available, including the model's light nodes, object names, viewpoints, and behavior nodes. However, not all loaders supply this information, i.e., the relevant methods may return nothing.

There's a wide range of Java 3D loaders for different file formats, written by third-party developers. A good list is maintained at *http://www.j3d.org/utilities/loaders.html*.

 Loaders specifically aimed at gaming are listed in Chapter 14.

In this and other chapters, I employ the loaders in the NCSA Portfolio package (available from *http://www.ncsa.uiuc.edu/~srp/Java3D/portfolio/* or at the web site for this book: *http://fivedots.coe.psu.ac.th/~ad/jg/portfolio.jar*). Using a single ModelLoader interface, the package supports many formats, including 3D Studio Max (3DS files), AutoCAD (DXF), Digital Elevation Maps (DEMs), TrueSpace (COB), and VRML 97 (WRL). The drawbacks of Portfolio are its advanced age (the current version is 1.3, from 1998) and its relatively simple support of the formats: often only the geometry and shape colors are loaded, without textures, behaviors, or lights. Portfolio offers more than just loaders, though, since it has interfaces for several kinds of input devices and makes it easy to take snapshots of the 3D canvas and convert them into video clips.

Alternate Loaders

Inspector3ds is an up-to-date 3DS loader, developed by John Wright at Starfire Research (*http://www.starfireresearch.com*). The loader handles geometry, materials, textures, and normals.

The popular modeling package ac3d (*http://www.ac3d.org*) has a loader written by Jeremy Booth, available at *http://www.newdawnsoftware.com/*.

Programmers wishing to utilize a modern VRML loader should consider the Xj3D loader (*http://www.web3d.org*), which is actively being developed and covers most of the VRML 2.0 standard. The actual aim is to load X3D files, which extend VRML with XML functionality.

For the artistically impaired (e.g., yours truly), many web sites offer 3D models. A good starting point is the Google directory on 3D models *http://directory.google.com/Top/Computers/Software/Graphics/3D/Models/*. One site with many free models is 3D Cafe (*http://www.3dcafe.com/asp/freestuff.asp*).

Using NCSA Portfolio Loaders

The ModelLoader interface is used by WrapLoaderInfo3D in loadModel( ). First, a Loader object is obtained, which loads a Scene object. If this is successful, then a call to getSceneGroup( ) extracts the model's BranchGroup (into loadedBG).

```
import ncsa.j3d.loaders.*;      // Portfolio loaders
import com.sun.j3d.loaders.Scene;


private Scene loadedScene = null;   // globals
private BranchGroup loadedBG = null;


public void loadModel(String fn)
{
  FileWriter ofw = null;
  System.out.println( "Loading: " + fn );

  try {
    ModelLoader loader = new ModelLoader();
    loadedScene = loader.load(fn);    // the model's scene
    if(loadedScene != null ) {
      loadedBG = loadedScene.getSceneGroup();  // model's BG
      // code to manipulate the model
    }
  }
  catch( IOException ioe )
  { System.err.println("Could not find object file: " + fn); }
} // end of loadModel( )
```

The compilation of the LoaderInfo3D classes requires *portfolio.jar* which contains the Portfolio packages:

```
javac -classpath "%CLASSPATH%;ncsa\portfolio.jar" *.java
```

Displaying a Model

Once a model is loaded, it's displayed inside the scene. This simple task is complicated by the need to make sure that the model is positioned, oriented, and scaled so the user can see all of it.

I've simplified the problem by making some assumptions about how the model should be reoriented and scaled: a loaded model is always rotated clockwise around the x-axis by 90 degrees and scaled to be no bigger than 10 world units across. I don't bother repositioning the model since all the examples I tested were located close to the origin after they'd been scaled.

Why the rotation? Most of the models I'm using were created with 3D Studio Max, which uses a different axis system from Java 3D. The axes in 3D Studio Max use the XY plane as the floor, with the z-axis as the vertical; Java 3D treats the XZ plane as the floor and the y-axis as the vertical. The difference can be seen by considering a vector displayed in the two systems. The vertical vector (0, 0, 1) in 3D Studio Max will point forward in Java 3D (see Figure 16-5).

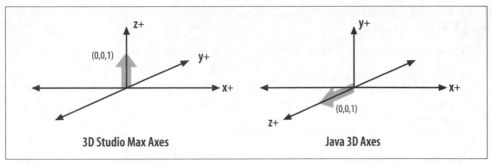

Figure 16-5. The vector (0,0,1) in 3D Studio Max and Java 3D

A model that's upright in 3D Studio Max will be displayed face down when loaded into a Java 3D scene. The solution? Rotate the model clockwise around the x-axis by 90 degrees to bring it back upright.

The rotation and the scaling operations are applied to the model via a TransformGroup node placed between the model's BranchGroup node (loadedBG in Figure 16-6) and the sceneBG BranchGroup node (the top-level node of the scene). Figure 16-6 shows the scene graph fragment for the model. In practice, the model subgraph below loadedBG will be more complex than the one shown here.

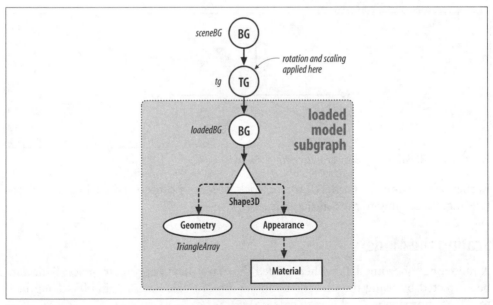

Figure 16-6. Scene graph fragment for the loaded model

The code that creates this graph is located in `loadModel()` and executed just after the model has been loaded:

```
loadedBG = loadedScene.getSceneGroup();      // model's BG

Transform3D t3d = new Transform3D();
t3d.rotX( -Math.PI/2.0 );          // rotate
Vector3d scaleVec = calcScaleFactor(loadedBG);  // scale
t3d.setScale( scaleVec );
TransformGroup tg = new TransformGroup(t3d);

tg.addChild(loadedBG);
sceneBG.addChild(tg);    // add (tg->loadedBG) to scene
```

The code is simple since it applies a rotation to every loaded model, even those that are correctly oriented.

The rotation operation is

```
t3d.rotX(-Math.PI/2.0);
```

This specifies a negative rotation of 90 degrees about the x-axis according to Java 3D's righthand rule for rotations: place your closed right hand with its thumb pointing in the direction of the positive axis of interest, (the x-axis in this case) and your fingers will be bent in the direction of a positive rotation (see Figure 16-7).

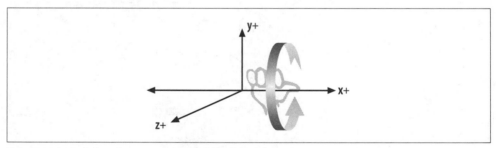

Figure 16-7. Righthand, positive rotation for the x-axis

In this case, I want the model to rotate clockwise around the x-axis, which is a negative angle according to the righthand rule.

Scaling the Model

A model may become large when loaded into Java 3D's coordinate space. This can be corrected by using the object's bounding box to calculate a suitable scaling factor. This approach is employed in calcScaleFactor():

```
private Vector3d calcScaleFactor(BranchGroup loadedBG)
{
    BoundingBox boundbox = new BoundingBox( loadedBG.getBounds() );
```

```
    // obtain the upper and lower coordinates of the box
    Point3d lower = new Point3d( );
    boundbox.getLower( lower );
    Point3d upper = new Point3d( );
    boundbox.getUpper( upper );

    // calculate the maximum dimension
    double max = 0.0;
    if( (upper.x - lower.x ) > max )
      max = (upper.x - lower.x );

    if( (upper.y - lower.y ) > max )
      max = (upper.y - lower.y );

    if( (upper.z - lower.z ) > max )
      max = (upper.z - lower.z );

    double scaleFactor = 10.0/max;

    // limit the scaling so that a big model isn't scaled too much
    if( scaleFactor < 0.0005 )
        scaleFactor = 0.0005;
    return new Vector3d(scaleFactor, scaleFactor, scaleFactor);
  } // end of calcScaleFactor( )
```

The scaling factor will leave the model at most 10 units wide, high, or deep, which is comparable to the size of the floor (20 units square).

The scale factor reduction is constrained so a large model isn't shrunk too much. This problem occurs when one dimension of the model is large (for example, its height), but the other dimensions are small. An unconstrained reduction applied to the height will leave the width and depth so small that the model will be almost invisible.

Examining a Model's Scene Graph

After loading the model, WrapLoaderInfo3D's next main task is to traverse the model's scene graph and report on its structure. Walking over the graph is easy due to the parent-child relationship between the nodes and that all the nodes are subclasses of a single superclass, SceneGraphObject. A simplified inheritance hierarchy is shown in Figure 16-8.

As mentioned in Chapter 14, Leaf nodes are subclassed in various ways to obtain Shape3D and environment nodes for lighting, backgrounds, sound, and so on. The subclasses of Group include BranchGroup and TransformGroup, which may have their own children (Group and/or Leaf nodes). NodeComponent objects are used to store information in nodes, such as Geometry and Appearance attributes, and may be shared between nodes.

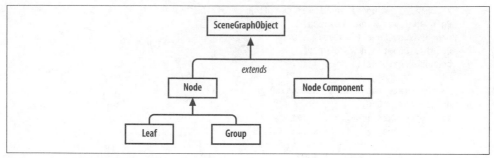

Figure 16-8. Some subclasses of SceneGraphObject

A simple algorithm for traversing a scene graph is shown here:

```
examineNode(node) {
  if the node is a Group {
    print Group info;
    for each child of the node
      examineNode(child);  // recursive call
  }
  else if the node is a Leaf
    if the node is a Shape3D {
      examine its appearance;
      examine its geometry;
    }
    else print Leaf info
  }
  else print general node info;
}
```

This pseudocode is the heart of the examineNode() and examineShape3D() methods in WrapLoaderInfo3D. The algorithm is simplified by concentrating on a few node types, principally Shape3D, and by considering the graph as a tree. Shape3D details are often the most important since they store the model's geometry, and there's little point looking for environmental data since they are frequently not converted to Java 3D by the loader.

examineShape3D() calls printAppearance() to examine the model's appearance, which is confined to reporting Java 3D ColouringAttributes and/or Material details.

 Many other Appearance components could be considered, such as point, line, and polygon characteristics and rendering attributes.

examineShape3D() calls examineGeometry() to examine the model's geometry, which checks out the possible subclasses of the Geometry object. Loaded models almost always use a subclass of GeometryArray (e.g., TriangleArray, QuadArray), and examineGeometry() reports the number of vertices in the array.

examineShape3D( ) is made more complicated by dealing with the possibility that several geometries may be assigned to a single shape.

Two useful methods for the traversal code are Object.getClass( ), which returns the class name of the object, and the infix operation instanceof that tests for membership in a class (or superclass).

Graph Traversal Output

examineNode( ) is called from StoreGraphInfo( ), which first sets up a FileWriter object linked to the text file *examObj.txt*. The output of the traversal is redirected into the file, as shown below (when a model containing three dolphins is examined):

```
Group: class javax.media.j3d.BranchGroup
3 children
  Leaf: class javax.media.j3d.Shape3D
  Material Object:AmbientColor=(0.7, 0.7, 0.7) EmissiveColor=(0.0, 0.0, 0.0)
  DiffuseColor=(0.3, 0.3, 0.3) SpecularColor=(1.0, 1.0, 1.0) Shininess=0.6
  LightingEnable=true ColorTarget=2
    Geometry: class javax.media.j3d.TriangleArray
    Vertex count: 1692

  Leaf: class javax.media.j3d.Shape3D
  Material Object:AmbientColor=(0.7, 0.7, 0.7) EmissiveColor=(0.0, 0.0, 0.0)
  DiffuseColor=(0.3, 0.3, 0.3) SpecularColor=(1.0, 1.0, 1.0) Shininess=0.6
  LightingEnable=true ColorTarget=2
    Geometry: class javax.media.j3d.TriangleArray
    Vertex count: 1692

  Leaf: class javax.media.j3d.Shape3D
  Material Object:AmbientColor=(0.7, 0.7, 0.7) EmissiveColor=(0.0, 0.0, 0.0)
  DiffuseColor=(0.3, 0.3, 0.3) SpecularColor=(1.0, 1.0, 1.0) Shininess=0.6
  LightingEnable=true ColorTarget=2
    Geometry: class javax.media.j3d.TriangleArray
    Vertex count: 1692
```

The three dolphins are represented by a BranchGroup with three Shape3D children. These store TriangleArrays for each dolphin's geometry and have the same Material colors.

The on-screen rendering of the dolphins is shown in Figure 16-9.

Adjusting a Model's Shape Attributes

After reporting on the model's scene graph, WrapLoaderInfo3D's last task is to modify the model's appearance according to the user's supplied adaptation number. Many aspects of a model can be easily changed once its individual Shape3D nodes are accessible. This

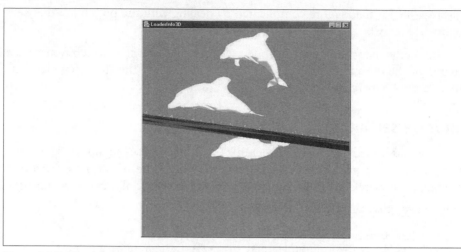

Figure 16-9. The dolphins modeldD

can be done with a variant of the examineNode( ) pseudocode, concentrating only on Leaf nodes that are Shape3Ds:

```
visitNode(node) {
  if the node is a Group {
    for each child of the node
      visitNode(child);  // recursive call
  }
  else if the node is a Shape3D
    adjust the node's attributes;
}
```

This pseudocode is the basis of visitNode( ) in WrapLoaderInfo3D.

The manipulation of the shape's attributes is initiated in adjustShape3D( ), which uses the adaptation number entered by the user to choose between six possibilities:

0   Makes the shape blue with makeBlue( )

1   Draws the shape in outline with drawOutline( )

2   Renders the shape almost transparent with makeAlmostTransparent( )

3   Lays a texture over the shape with addTexture( )

4   Makes the shape blue and adds a texture by calling makeBlue( ) and addTexture( )
Anything else
    Makes no changes at all

Turning the Shape Blue

Figure 16-10 shows the rendering of the dolphins model after being turned blue.

Figure 16-10. Blue dolphins

The Material node used in makeBlue( ) is:

```
Material blueMat = new Material(black, black, blue, white, 20.0f);
```

The use of black as the ambient color (Color3f(0.0f, 0.0f, 0.0f)) means unlit parts of the shape are rendered in black, which looks like shadow on the model. However, the model doesn't cast shadows onto other surfaces, such as the floor:

```
private void makeBlue(Shape3D shape)
{
  Appearance app = shape.getAppearance( );
  Material blueMat = new Material(black, black, blue, white, 20.0f);
  blueMat.setLightingEnable(true);
  app.setMaterial(blueMat);
  shape.setAppearance(app);
}
```

The appearance is obtained from the shape, its material attribute changed, and then the appearance component assigned back to the shape; only the attribute of interest is modified.

Drawing a Shape in Outline

Figure 16-11 shows a VRML model of a box, cone, and sphere rendered in outline:

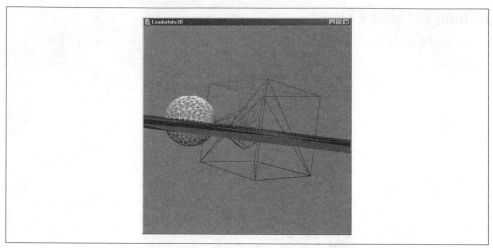

Figure 16-11. Shapes in outline

The original colors of the three objects (yellow, red, blue) are still visible in their line colors.

The effect is achieved by setting the POLYGON_LINE mode in PolygonAttribute in drawOutline( ):

```
private void drawOutline(Shape3D shape)
{
  Appearance app = shape.getAppearance( );
  PolygonAttributes pa = new PolygonAttributes( );
  pa.setCullFace( PolygonAttributes.CULL_NONE );
  pa.setPolygonMode( PolygonAttributes.POLYGON_LINE );
  app.setPolygonAttributes( pa );
  shape.setAppearance(app);
}
```

Culling is disabled so that the lines are visible from every direction.

Making a Shape Almost Transparent

Figure 16-12 shows a model of the gun rendered almost transparent.

This is done in makeAlmostTransparent( ) by setting the TransparencyAttributes of the shape's Appearance:

```
private void makeAlmostTransparent(Shape3D shape)
{
  Appearance app = shape.getAppearance( );
```

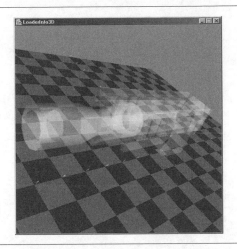

Figure 16-12. Semi-transparent gun

```
        TransparencyAttributes ta = new TransparencyAttributes();
        ta.setTransparencyMode( TransparencyAttributes.BLENDED );
        ta.setTransparency(0.8f);      // 1.0f is totally transparent
        app.setTransparencyAttributes( ta );
        shape.setAppearance(app);
    }
```

Various transparency mode settings affect how the original color of the shape is mixed with the background pixels. For example, *blended transparency* (used here) mixes the color of the transparent shape with the color of the background pixels. *Screen door transparency* (`TransparencyAttributes.SCREEN_DOOR`) renders a mesh-like pattern of pixels with the color of the transparent shape, leaving gaps where the background pixels show through. More details can be found in the documentation for the `TransparencyAttributes` class.

A comparison of the last three examples shows the general strategy for manipulating a shape: create an attribute setting, and add it to the existing `Appearance` component of the shape.

Adding a Texture to a Shape

Figure 16-13 shows a castle with a rock texture wrapped over it.

A quick look at Figure 16-13 reveals some of the texturing is unrealistic: clear stripes of textures run down the walls. Once you understand how the texture is mapped, the reasons for this striping will be clear.

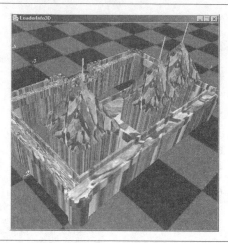

Figure 16-13. Castle rock

A texture is made in two stages. First, a TextureLoader object is created for the file holding the texture image, then the texture is extracted from the object:

```
private Texture2D texture = null;  // global


private void loadTexture(String fn)
{
  TextureLoader texLoader = new TextureLoader(fn, null);
  texture = (Texture2D) texLoader.getTexture();
  if (texture == null)
    System.out.println("Cannot load texture from " + fn);
  else {
    System.out.println("Loaded texture from " + fn);
    texture.setEnable(true);
  }
}
```

The call to setEnable( ) switches on texture mapping, which allows the texture to be wrapped around a shape.

TextureLoader can handle JPEGs and GIFs (which are useful if transparency is required), and it can be employed in conjunction with Java Advanced Imaging (JAI) to load other formats, such as BMP, PNG, and TIFF files. The loader can include various flags, such as one for creating textures at various levels of resolution for rendering onto small areas. Aside from Textures, the loader can return ImageComponent2D objects, the Java 3D format for images used in backgrounds and rasters.

Textures can be 2D (as shown here) or 3D: Texture3D objects are employed for volumetric textures, typically in scientific applications and visualization.

The if test in loadTexture( ) checks if the texture was successfully created. A common reason for the texture being null is that the source image's dimensions are invalid. The image must be square, with its dimensions a power of two. Keeping this in mind, I made the rock image's size 256×256 pixels.

For a texture to be applied to a shape, three conditions must be met:

- The shape must have texture coordinates, either set through its geometry or using a TexCoordGeneration object (as detailed in the next section).
- The shape's appearance must have been assigned a Texture2D.
- The texture must be enabled (which was done in loadTexture( )).

Texture coordinates

Texture2D coordinates are measured with (s, t) values that range between 0 and 1. Texture mapping is the art of mapping (s, t) values (sometimes called texels) onto geometry coordinates (x, y, z) to create a realistic looking effect.

One mapping approach is to tile the texture in one-by-one patches over the geometry's surface. However, tiling may create excessive repetition of the pattern, and after the geometry has been scaled down for the Java 3D world, the texture's details may be too small to see.

A more flexible mapping approach is to utilize a TexCoordGeneration object, which lets the programmer define equations stating how geometry coordinates (x, y, z) values are converted into texels (s, t). The simplest equations are linear, of these forms:

- s = (x*planeS.xc) + (y*planeS.yc) + (z*planeS.zc) + (planeS.w)
- t = (x*planeT.xc) + (y*planeT.yc) + (z*planeT.zc) + (planeT.w)

planeS and planeT are vectors that contain the xc, yc, zc, and w constants, which define the equations. Specifying these equations can be tricky, so I'll use a simple technique based on the bounding box for the shape.

Figure 16-14 shows a shape's bounding box, with its upper and lower points highlighted. The upper point contains the maximum x, y, and z values, and the lower point has the minima. Texture mapping becomes a matter of mapping the (x, y, z) coordinates of the box to the (s, t) coordinates of the texture.

The height and width of the bounding box is easily calculated:

- height = $y_{max} - y_{min}$
- width = $x_{max} - x_{min}$

Two simple equations for s and t are then given:

- s = x/width – x_{min}/width
- t = y/height – y_{min}/height

This is expressed in vector form:

- planeS = [1/width, 0, 0, –x_{min}/width]
- planeT = [0, 1/height, 0, –y_{min}/height]

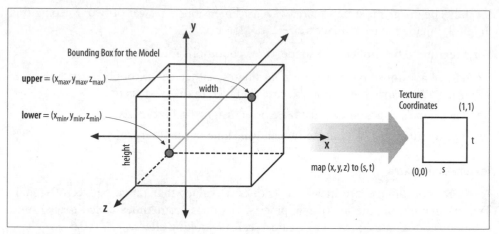

Figure 16-14. From bounding box to texture

 Unfortunately, the z-coordinate isn't used in the equations. I'll explain what this means in a moment.

This bounding box algorithm is implemented in stampTexCoords( ):

```
private TexCoordGeneration stampTexCoords(Shape3D shape)
{
  BoundingBox boundBox = new BoundingBox( shape.getBounds( ) );
  Point3d lower = new Point3d( );
  Point3d upper = new Point3d( );
  boundBox.getLower(lower);  boundBox.getUpper(upper);

  double width = upper.x - lower.x;
  double height = upper.y - lower.y;
  Vector4f planeS = new Vector4f( (float)(1.0/width), 0.0f, 0.0f,
                                        (float)(-lower.x/width));
  Vector4f planeT = new Vector4f( 0.0f, (float)(1.0/height), 0.0f,
                                        (float)(-lower.y/height));

  // generate texture coordinates
  TexCoordGeneration texGen = new TexCoordGeneration( );
  texGen.setPlaneS(planeS);
  texGen.setPlaneT(planeT);

  return texGen;
} // end of stampTexCoords( )
```

The (s, t) equations are encoded as two Java 3D Vector4f objects: planeS and planeT. They're used to initialize a TexCoordGeneration object, which becomes the return result of the method.

A tendency to strip

Figure 16-13 shows stripes of textures running down the castle walls. However, this orientation is due to the model being rotated 90 degrees clockwise around the x-axis. In fact, the stripes are running along the z-axis of the model.

This z-striping is the visible consequence of not using the z-coordinate in the (s, t) equations. It means that (x, y, z) coordinates with the same (x, y) value but different z-values will all map to the same (s, t) texel.

Applying the texture to the shape

The texture is applied to the shape by the addTextureGA( ) method, which has four main duties:

- To switch off face culling so the texture appears on all sides of the shape
- To generate a TexCoordGeneration object, using stampTexCoords( )
- To modulate the texture mode so the underlying color and texture are combined
- To assign the texture to the shape, done by calling setTexture( )

Here is the code:

```
private void addTextureGA(Shape3D shape)
{
  Appearance app = shape.getAppearance();

  // make shape two-sided, so texture appears on both sides
  PolygonAttributes pa = new PolygonAttributes();
  pa.setCullFace( PolygonAttributes.CULL_NONE );
  app.setPolygonAttributes( pa );

  // generate texture coords
  app.setTexCoordGeneration( stampTexCoords(shape) );

  // modulate texture with color and lighting of underlying surface
  TextureAttributes ta = new TextureAttributes();
  ta.setTextureMode( TextureAttributes.MODULATE );
  app.setTextureAttributes( ta );

  // apply texture to shape
  if (texture != null) {    // loaded at start, from adjustShapes( )
    app.setTexture(texture);
    shape.setAppearance(app);
  }
}  // end of addTextureGA( )
```

The modulation task utilizes a Java 3D TextureAttributes object to control how the texture is combined with the surface colors of the shape.

There are four texture modes:

REPLACE
> The texture replaces any shape color.

MODULATE
> The texture and color are combined (as here).

DECAL
> The transparent areas of the texture aren't drawn onto the shape.

BLEND
> A varying mix of texture and color is possible.

The MODULATE mode is often used to combine an underlying Material with a texture, which allows lighting and shading effects to be seen alongside the texture. Figure 16-15 shows the dolphins models turned blue and with a texture.

Figure 16-15. Textured, blue dolphins

 This effect should be compared with the purely blue dolphins of Figure 16-10.

An Overview of Loader3D

Like LoaderInfo3D, Loader3D loads an external model with the Porfolio loader but it is mostly concerned with how the model can be moved, rotated, and scaled once it's loaded.

The model is displayed in a 3D canvas on the lefthand side of the application, and a series of buttons (and a text field) on the right allow the model to be manipulated. Details of the model's new configuration can be saved to a text file, which can be loaded with the model next time, so the model begins with the given location, orientation, and size.

The class diagrams for the Loader3D application are shown in Figure 16-16; only the public methods are shown.

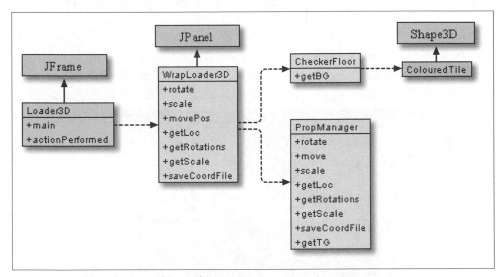

Figure 16-16. Class diagrams for Loader3D

The CheckerFloor and ColouredTile classes are the same as in previous examples.

The earlier Java 3D examples have simple GUIs: basically just a Java 3D Canvas3D object embedded in a JPanel, with mouse actions to move the viewpoint. Loader3D manages a more complicated GUI and send the user's input to WrapLoader3D, which passes it onto PropManager. PropManager is in charge of altering the model's position, orientation, and scale.

PropManager will play a prominent role in several later chapters, when I want to load a model into a scene.

  The code for these classes is located in the *Loader3D/* directory.

Using Loader3D

Loader3D can be called in two ways:

```
java -cp "%CLASSPATH%;ncsa\portfolio.jar Loader3D" <filename>
```

or:

```
java -cp "%CLASSPATH%;ncsa\portfolio.jar Loader3D" -c <filename>
```

The application searches the *models/* subdirectory for the filename and loads the file. If the –c option is included, Loader3D will attempt to load the text file *replaceable Coords.txt*, which contains translation, rotation, and scaling values (called *coords data*) that should be applied to the model.

Figure 16-17 shows the *Coolrobo.3ds* model initially loaded into the application.

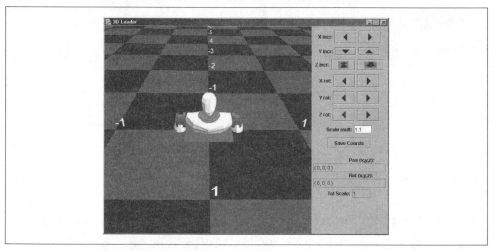

Figure 16-17. Coolrobo.3ds first loaded

Figure 16-18 shows the model after it has been moved, rotated, and scaled in various ways.

The user's viewpoint has been moved in Figures 16-17 and 16-18 to make the images bigger on-screen. The changes to the robot can be observed by comparing the model to the red square in both figures, which is centered at (0, 0) on the XZ plane.

The bottom half of the GUI pane in Figure 16-18 shows the current configuration: the (x, y, z) position is (–1.9, 3.9, 0), which is the distance of the model's center from its starting point. The rotation values are (0, 70, 0), which means a 70-degree positive rotation around the y-axis. The model has been scaled by a factor of 2.594.

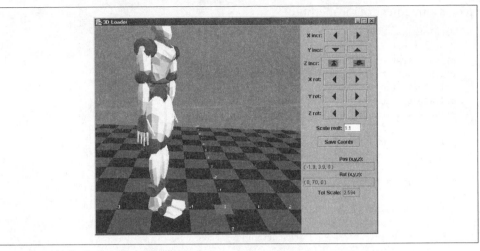

Figure 16-18. Coolrobo.3ds after manipulation

When the Save Coords button is pressed, the current coords data is saved to a text file in the subdirectory *models/*. The contents of the file generated for *Coolrobo.3ds* (*CoolroboCoords.txt*) are:

```
Coolrobo.3ds
-p -1.9 3.9 0
-r 3333333
-s 2.594
```

The –p line gives the (x, y, z) translation, the –r line contains a series of rotation numbers (explained later), and the –s value is for scaling.

The methods defined in Loader3D are given in Figure 16-19.

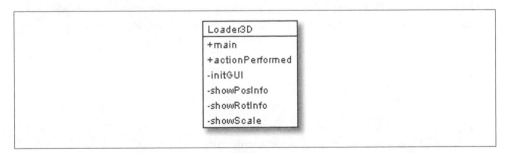

Figure 16-19. Loader3D methods

Loader3D creates its GUI control panel with initGUI(). actionPerformed() handles the various GUI events triggered by pressing buttons and typing in the text field. Depending on the user request, actionPerformed() calls movePosn(), rotate(), scale(), or saveCoordsFile() in the WrapLoader3D class to request changes to the model's position, rotation, scaling, or to save its coords data.

Here is a fragment of the method:

```
// globals
// constants for specifying moves and rotations
private static final int X_AXIS = 0;
private static final int Y_AXIS = 1;
private static final int Z_AXIS = 2;
private static final int INCR = 0;
private static final int DECR = 1;

private WrapLoader3D w3d;     // the loader canvas


public void actionPerformed(ActionEvent e)
{
  if (e.getSource() == saveBut)    // save coord info
    w3d.saveCoordFile();
  else if (e.getSource() == xPosLeftBut)    // an X move
    w3d.movePos(X_AXIS, DECR);
  else if (e.getSource() == xPosRightBut)
    w3d.movePos(X_AXIS, INCR);
  else if (e.getSource() == yPosLeftBut)    // a Y move
    w3d.movePos(Y_AXIS, DECR);
  else if (e.getSource() == yPosRightBut)
    w3d.movePos(Y_AXIS, INCR);
   ...
  // more branches dealing with a Z move, X rotation,
  // Y rotation, Z rotation, and scaling

  showPosInfo();    // update on-screen display
  showRotInfo();
  showScale();
}
```

At the end of actionPerformed( ), showPosInfo( ), showRotInfo( ), and showScale( ) communicate with WrapLoader3D to obtain the current coords data and to update the GUI display. For example, here's showPosInfo( ):

```
// global
private JTextField xyzTF;


private void showPosInfo()
{
  Vector3d loc = w3d.getLoc();  // get coords data
  xyzTF.setText("( " + df.format(loc.x) + ", " +
      df.format(loc.y) + ", " + df.format(loc.z) + " )");
}
```

Creating the Scene

As with previous Wrap classes, WrapLoader3D creates the scene (the checkerboard, the lights, the background, the mouse controls and viewpoint). It offers methods that Loader3D can call to set and get the model's coordinates.

Figure 16-20 shows the methods defined in WrapLoader3D.

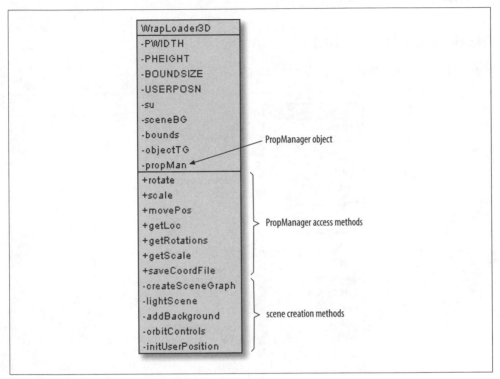

Figure 16-20. WrapLoader3D methods

The public methods pass requests sent from the GUI through to a PropManager object, propMan:

```
// global
private PropManager propMan;

public void movePos(int axis, int change)
{  propMan.move(axis, change);  }
```

PropManager manipulates the model. WrapLoader3D is acting as a facade, hiding implementation details from the application's GUI layer. This coding approach allows WrapLoader3D to carry out its own checking on the GUI inputs though it currently doesn't do that.

The `PropManager` object is created in `WrapLoader3D`'s constructor:

```
propMan = new PropManager(filename, hasCoordsInfo);
```

The call includes the model's filename and a Boolean indicating if a coords datafile is available.

The top-level `TransformGroup` for the model is accessed in `createSceneGraph( )`:

```
sceneBG.addChild( propMan.getTG( ) );
```

Managing the Model

Figure 16-21 shows `PropManager`'s methods.

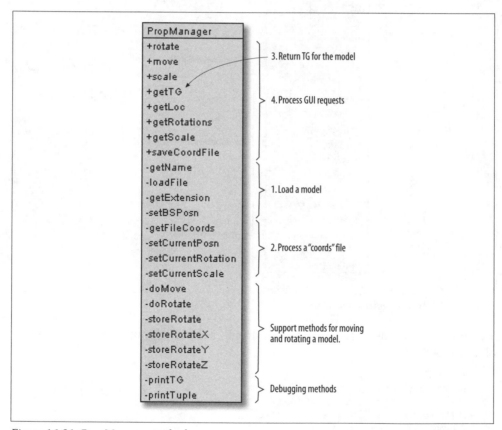

Figure 16-21. PropManager methods

There are four main tasks carried out by a `PropManager` object (indicated in Figure 16-21 with the same numbering scheme):

1. It loads the specified model, scales to a standard size, and rotates the model if it's been saved as a 3D Studio Max (3DS) file.

2. It loads a coords datafile if requested and applies the translations, rotations, and scaling values in that file to the model.

3. It makes the top-level `TransformGroup` for the model available.

> In this program, the subgraph is added to the scene by `WrapLoader3D`.

4. At runtime, the `PropManager` object accepts commands to modify the model's position, orientation, and size, causing alterations to the model's scene graph.

> In this application, these commands come from the GUI, via `WrapLoader3D`.

Building the Model's Scene Graph

Figure 16-22 shows the scene graph after *dolphins.3ds* has been loaded (the three dolphins model). The `PropManager` object creates the long branch shown on the right of the figure, consisting of a chain of four `TransformGroup` nodes and a `BranchGroup` with three `Shape3D` children. The loaded model was translated into the `BranchGroup` and its children (each dolphin in *dolphins.3ds* is represented by a `Shape3D` node).

`PropManager` utilizes four `TransformGroups` to deal with different aspects of the model's configuration:

moveTG
: Handles the translations

rotTG
: For rotations

scaleTG
: For scaling

objBoundsTG
: Carries out the scaling and possible rotation of the model when it's first loaded

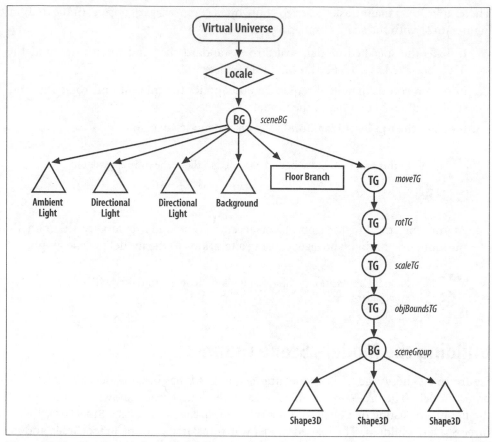

Figure 16-22. Scene graph for loaded dolphins

The reason for this separation is to process distinct operations in different nodes in the graph. This reduces the overall complexity of the coding because I can take advantage of the hierarchy of local coordinate systems used by the TransformGroup nodes.

A TransformGroup's local coordinate system means it always starts at (0, 0, 0) with no rotation or scaling. However, when Java 3D renders the node into the virtual world, it must obtain its global coordinates (i.e., its virtual world position). It does this by calculating the combined effects of all the ancestor TransformGroup nodes operations upon the node.

For example, if the moveTG node is moved to coordinate (1, 5, 0) from its starting point of (0, 0, 0), then all the TransformGroup nodes below it in the scene graph are repositioned as well. Java 3D generates this effect at render time but, as far as the child nodes are concerned, they are still at (0, 0, 0) in their local coordinate systems.

This mechanism greatly simplifies the programmer's task of writing TransformGroup transformations. For instance, a rotation of 70 degrees around the y-axis for rotTG is applied in its local coordinate system, so it is a straightforward rotation around the center. If the transformations of its parent (grandparent, great-grandparent, etc.) had to be taken into account, then the rotation operation would be much more complicated since the code would need to undo all the transformations, rotate around the center, and then apply the transformations again. The advantage of splitting the translation and rotation effects so the translation component (in moveTG) is above the rotation (in rotTG) is that rotational changes only apply to rotTG and its children.

For instance, a positive rotation of 90 degrees around the y-axis turns the XZ plane so the x- and z-axes are pointing in new directions. Subsequently, if a child of rotTG moves two units in the positive x direction, it will appear on screen as a 2-unit move in the negative z direction!

Fortunately, since moveTG is above rotTG, the axes' changes made by rotTG don't trouble moveTG: an x direction move applied to moveTG is always carried out along the x-axis as expected by the user.

Loading the Model

The scene graph is created in PropManager's loadFile( ). First, the model is loaded with ModelLoader, and its BranchGroup is extracted into the sceneGroup variable. The chain of four TransformGroups are then created. The following code snippet shows the creation of objBoundsTG and scaleTG, and how scaleTG is linked to objBoundsTG:

```
// create a transform group for the object's bounding sphere
TransformGroup objBoundsTG = new TransformGroup( );
objBoundsTG.addChild( sceneGroup );

// resize loaded object's bounding sphere (and maybe rotate)
String ext = getExtension(fnm);
BoundingSphere objBounds = (BoundingSphere) sceneGroup.getBounds( );
setBSPosn(objBoundsTG, objBounds.getRadius( ), ext);

// create a transform group for scaling the object
scaleTG = new TransformGroup( );
scaleTG.setCapability(TransformGroup.ALLOW_TRANSFORM_READ);
scaleTG.setCapability(TransformGroup.ALLOW_TRANSFORM_WRITE);
scaleTG.addChild( objBoundsTG );   // link TGs
```

 The capability bits of scaleTG (and rotTG and moveTG) must be set to allow these nodes to be adjusted after the scene has been made live.

Included in the code fragment is the call to setBSPosn( ). It scales the model so its bounding sphere has a unit radius; this avoids problems with the model being too big or small.

This is a variant of the bounding box technique used in LoaderInfo3D.

If the file extension is *.3ds*, then the model is rotated –90 degrees around the x-axis to compensate for the axes differences between 3DS and Java 3D, as outlined earlier.

Loading and Applying the Coords Data

The coords datafile requires parsing to extract its translation, rotation, and scaling values. getFileCoords( ) opens the file and reads in lines of text. These are passed to setCurrentPosn( ), setCurrentRotation( ), or setCurrentScale( ) depending on the character following the - at the start of a line.

setCurrentPosn( ) extracts the (x, y, z) values and calls doMove( ) with the values packaged as a Vector3d object. doMove( ) adds the translation to the current value:

```
private void doMove(Vector3d theMove)
{ moveTG.getTransform(t3d);       // get current posn from TG
  chgT3d.setIdentity( );          // reset change TG
  chgT3d.setTranslation(theMove); // setup move
  t3d.mul(chgT3d);                // 'add' move to current posn
  moveTG.setTransform(t3d);       // update TG
}
```

 chgT3d is a global Transform3D and is reinitialized before use by setting it to be an identity matrix.

The addition of the new translation is done using multiplication since I'm dealing with matrices inside the Transform3D objects.

setCurrentScale( ) is similar in that it extracts a single value and then calls scale( ) to apply that value to the scene graph:

```
public void scale(double d)
{ scaleTG.getTransform(t3d);      // get current scale from TG
  chgT3d.setIdentity( );          // reset change Trans
  chgT3d.setScale(d);             // set up new scale
  t3d.mul(chgT3d);                // multiply new scale to current one
  scaleTG.setTransform(t3d);      // update the TG
  scale *= d;                     // update scale variable
}
```

The coding style of scale( ) is the same as doMove( ).

Handling Rotation

Dealing with rotation is more complicated due to the mathematical property that rotations about different axes are noncommutative. For example, a rotation of 80 degrees around the x-axis followed by 80 degrees about the z-axis (see Figure 16-23) produces a different result if carried out in the opposite order (see Figure 16-24).

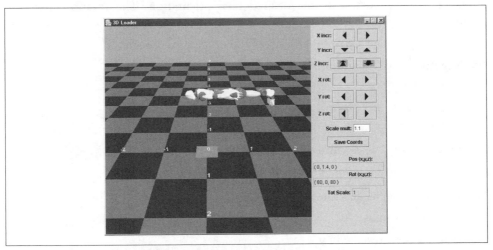

Figure 16-23. Rotation order: x-axis rotation then z-axis

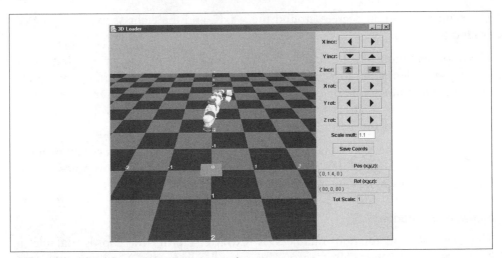

Figure 16-24. Rotation order: z-axis rotation then x-axis

Though the GUI displays are too small to read in the figures, they show the rotation values to be (80, 0, 80).

This rotation property means that the coords datafile cannot store the rotation information as three total rotations. Storing the order in which the rotations were carried out is necessary. The solution to this problem relies on a simplification of the user interface: a click of a rotation button always results in a rotation of 10 degrees (negative or positive, around the x-, y-, or z-axes). Then the user's rotation commands can be represented by a sequence of rotation numbers, which must be executed in sequence order to duplicate the desired final orientation. The rotation numbers range between 1 and 6:

1   Positive ROT_INCR around the x-axis

2   Negative ROT_INCR around the x-axis

3   Positive ROT_INCR around the y-axis

4   Negative ROT_INCR around the y-axis

5   Positive ROT_INCR around the z-axis

6   Negative ROT_INCR around the z-axis

ROT_INCR is a constant defined in PropManager (10 degrees).

This approach means that the rotation information for Figure 16-23 is encoded as:

    -r 1111111155555555

Figure 16-24 is represented by:

    -r 5555555511111111

The eight 1s mean 80 degrees around the x-axis, and the eight 5s mean 80 degrees around the z-axis.

This representation has the drawback that it may lead to long strings, but this is unlikely considering the application. Usually, a model only needs turning through 90 or 180 degrees along one or perhaps two axes. However, if the user makes lots of adjustments to the rotation, they are all stored; in that case, it's probably better to exit the application and start over.

An advantage of the representation is the simple way that the sequence can be modified manually through editing the coords datafile in a text editor. This holds true for the position and scaling data, which can be changed to any value.

Applying the rotation

The sequence of rotation numbers is extracted form the coords datafile in PropManager's setCurrentRotation( ). The method calls rotate( ) to carry out a rotation for each rotation number.

rotate( ) calls doRotate( ) to change the scene graph and one of storeRotateX( ), storeRotateY( ), or storeRotateZ( ) to record the rotation in an ArrayList of rotation numbers and to update the total rotations for the x-, y-, or z-axes. The doRotate( ) method is shown here:

```
private void doRotate(int axis, int change)
{
  double radians = (change == INCR) ? ROT_AMT : -ROT_AMT;
  rotTG.getTransform(t3d);      // get current rotation from TG
  chgT3d.setIdentity();         // reset change Trans
  switch (axis) {               // setup new rotation
    case X_AXIS: chgT3d.rotX(radians); break;
    case Y_AXIS: chgT3d.rotY(radians); break;
    case Z_AXIS: chgT3d.rotZ(radians); break;
    default: System.out.println("Unknown axis of rotation"); break;
  }
  t3d.mul(chgT3d);       // 'add' new rotation to current one
  rotTG.setTransform(t3d);      // update the TG
}
```

The coding style is similar to doMove( ) and scale( ): the existing Tranform3D value is extracted from the TransformGroup node, updated to reflect the change and then stored back in the node.

Making the Model Available

As Figure 16-22 shows, the top level of the model's scene graph is the moveTG TransformGroup. This can be accessed by calling getTG( ):

```
public TransformGroup getTG( )
{  return moveTG; }
```

The one subtlety here is that the moveTG, rotTG, and scaleTG nodes will almost certainly be modified after the model's graph has been added to the scene. This means that their capability bits must be set to permit runtime access and change when the nodes are created:

```
// create a transform group for scaling the object
scaleTG = new TransformGroup( );
scaleTG.setCapability(TransformGroup.ALLOW_TRANSFORM_READ);
scaleTG.setCapability(TransformGroup.ALLOW_TRANSFORM_WRITE);
scaleTG.addChild( objBoundsTG );

// create a transform group for rotating the object
rotTG = new TransformGroup( );
rotTG.setCapability(TransformGroup.ALLOW_TRANSFORM_READ);
rotTG.setCapability(TransformGroup.ALLOW_TRANSFORM_WRITE);
rotTG.addChild( scaleTG );

// create a transform group for moving the object
moveTG = new TransformGroup( );
moveTG.setCapability(TransformGroup.ALLOW_TRANSFORM_READ);
moveTG.setCapability(TransformGroup.ALLOW_TRANSFORM_WRITE);
moveTG.addChild( rotTG );
```

Modifying the Model's Configuration at Runtime

User requests to move, rotate, scale, or save the coords data are passed from the GUI in Loader3D through WrapLoader3D to the PropManager object. The relevant methods are move( ), rotate( ), scale( ), and saveCoordFile( ).

I've described rotate( ) and scale( ); they're employed when the coords data are being applied to the model. move( )'s main purpose is to translate the data supplied by the GUI (an axis and direction) into a vector, which is passed to doMove(|).

saveCoordFile( ) is straightforward, but relies on global variables holding the current configuration information.

Another aspect of Loader3D's GUI is that it displays the current configuration. This is achieved by calling getLoc( ), getRotations( ), and getScale( ) in PropManager via WrapLoader3D. For example, in Loader3D:

```
// global
private WrapLoader3D w3d;

private void showPosInfo( )
{ Vector3d loc = w3d.getLoc( );
  xyzTF.setText("( " + df.format(loc.x) + ", " +
      df.format(loc.y) + ", " + df.format(loc.z) + " )");
}
```

In WrapLoader3D:

```
// global
private PropManager propMan;

public Vector3d getLoc( )
{  return propMan.getLoc( );  }
```

In PropManager:

```
public Vector3d getLoc( )
{ moveTG.getTransform(t3d);
  Vector3d trans = new Vector3d( );
  t3d.get(trans);
  return trans;
}
```

CHAPTER 17

Using a Lathe to Make Shapes

I've run up against the lack of useful shapes in Java 3D many times: there's only so much that can be done with the Box, Cone, Cylinder, and Sphere classes. One way of getting past this limitation is to use Java 3D's GeometryArray (or one of its sub-classes) to specify a geometry in terms of separate arrays of positional coordinates, colors, normals, and texture coordinates. This is pretty daunting, and I like to avoid it if possible.

An alternative to this low-level shape building is to follow the approach outlined in Chapter 16: create the shape in a 3D modeling package and load it into Java 3D. The drawback is that you need to learn the modeling software. Most of these packages have so many bells and whistles that it's hard to get what you need done.

This chapter describes a compromise between the complexity of Java 3D GeometryArrays and the loading of ready-made models. The edge of a shape is defined in terms of straight lines and simple curves. This edge (or lathe curve) is rotated around the y-axis to create a 3D volume, called a lathe shape. This approach, often called surface or sweep revolution, is packaged up in a LatheShape3D class.

Color or texture information can be added easily. A lathe shape is pink by default, but this can be changed to a different color or texture. In both cases, the shape will reflect light (i.e., a shape's faces always have normals). A color is defined using two Color3f objects: one for ambient illumination (typically a dark hue) and the other for diffuse lighting.

 A mix of two colors generally makes the shape look more realistic than using just one.

A texture is wrapped around the shape starting from the middle of the shape's back (the side facing away from the camera position), continuing counterclockwise around the front, and ending back where it started. The texture is stretched in the y-direction, ensuring it covers the shape vertically.

Figure 17-1 shows a selection of LatheShape3D objects.

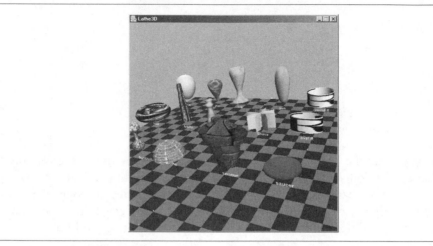

Figure 17-1. LatheShape3D objects

 LatheShape3D was designed with Chapter 20 in mind, where I will describe how to animate an articulated moveable figure. LatheShape3D is ideal for creating body parts, such as arms, legs, and a torso.

This chapter illustrates the following features:

A shape's lathe curve employs Hermite curves

Hermite curves are used to represent the curve sequences inside a lathe curve. I chose Hermite curves since they're simple to specify and (after making a few assumptions about the shape) can be generated automatically.

A lathe shape is created using surface revolution

A QuadArray shape is made by revolving a lathe curve around the y-axis. This was low-level shape creation, but done by the code rather than myself (the way I like it).

Texture coordinate calculation

The calculation of texture coordinates (s, t) is based on the shape's (x, y, z) coordinates, without using a Java 3D TexCoordGeneration object (TexCoordGeneration was introduced in Chapter 16). It's possible to automate these calculations after making some simple assumptions about how the texture should be wrapped over a shape.

Normals calculated with Java 3D utilities

Normals are generated for the quadrilaterals (quads) in the QuadArray with the aid of Java 3D's GeometryInfo and NormalGenerator classes. This allows the shape to reflect light without having to do the hard work of generating the normals.

Subclassing of shapes

LatheShape3D can be subclassed to modify the surface revolution. In other words, the 3D volume doesn't need to be created solely from a circular rotation around the y-axis, and the path can be elliptical or stranger (as you'll see).

Class Diagrams for Lathe3D

Figure 17-2 shows the class diagrams for the Lathe3D application. The class names, as well as the public and protected methods, are shown.

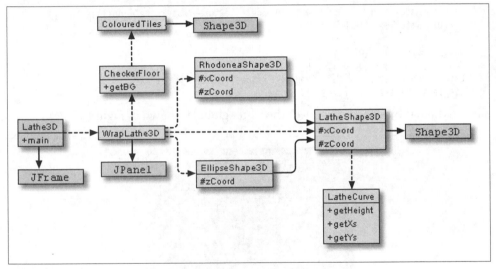

Figure 17-2. Class diagrams for Lathe3D

Much of this Lathe3D application is scenery to show off various lathe shapes.

Lathe3D is the top-level JFrame and similar to earlier examples: It's the application window holding a 3D canvas made by WrapLathe3D. WrapLathe3D sets up the 3D world like previous wrap classes: it creates the checkerboard, the lights, background, and mouse controls. The only change is a large method called addLatheShapes() that makes multiple calls to LatheShape3D (and its subclasses) to create the shapes shown in Figure 17-1. CheckerFloor and ColouredTiles are unchanged from previous chapters. LatheShape3D creates a shape using a LatheCurve object to create the lathe curve. The subclasses of LatheShape3D (EllipseShape3D and RhodoneaShape3D) are examples showing how the rotation path employed by LatheShape3D can be modified.

 The code for these classes can be found in *Lathe3D/*.

Creating the Scene

The novel parts of the scene creation carried out by WrapLathe3D are located in addLatheShapes( ), which generates the lathe shapes on the checkerboard:

```
TextureLoader texLd3 =  new TextureLoader("textures/water.jpg", null);
Texture waterTex = texLd3.getTexture( );

double xsIn15[] = {0, 0.1, 0.7, 0};
double ysIn15[] = {0, 0.1, 1.5, 2};
LatheShape3D ls2 = new LatheShape3D( xsIn15, ysIn15, waterTex);
displayLathe(ls2, -3.5f, -5.0f, "drip");
```

This particular bit of code produces the water globule, shown in Figure 17-3.

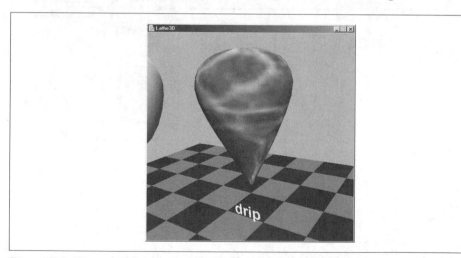

Figure 17-3. Water globule

The coordinates for the lathe curve are supplied as two arrays: one for the x-values and one for the y-values. Figure 17-4 shows the four coordinates plotted against the x- and y-axes.

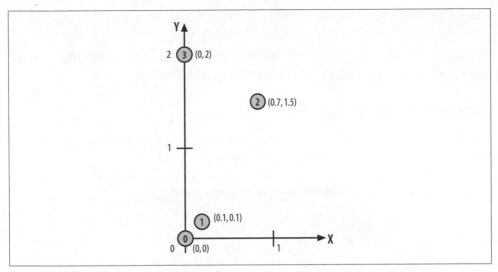

Figure 17-4. Coordinates for the water globule

These coordinates are ordered by increasing the y-value, indicated by the numbered circles in the figure.

The x- and y-values must be greater than or equal to 0, and the first y-value must be 0. These restrictions simplify the calculation of the shape's height, which is used when mapping a texture over the shape's surface. Since the shape always starts at 0 on the y-axis, and there are no negative values, the shape's height is the largest y-value. An x-value may use a negative sign, but this has a special meaning (explained below).

displayLathe( ) positions the shape at a given (x, z) location, 1.5 units above the XZ plane (the floor of the scene). The shape's label is displayed as a Text2D object, a little below the shape:

```
private void displayLathe(LatheShape3D ls, float x, float z, String label)
{
  // position the LatheShape3D object
  Transform3D t3d = new Transform3D( );
  t3d.set( new Vector3f(x, 1.5f, z));
  TransformGroup tg1 = new TransformGroup(t3d);
  tg1.addChild( ls );
  sceneBG.addChild(tg1);

  // position the label for the shape
  Text2D message = new Text2D(label, white, "SansSerif", 72, Font.BOLD );
  t3d.set( new Vector3f(x-0.4f, 0.75f, z) );
  TransformGroup tg2 = new TransformGroup(t3d);
  tg2.addChild(message);
  sceneBG.addChild(tg2);
}
```

Due to the ordering of the coordinates, the base of a lathe shape is its origin (most Java 3D utilities have their origins at their centers).

displayLathe( ) shows that a LatheShape3D instance can be used in the same way as a Shape3D object due to LatheShape3D being a subclass of Shape3D.

Shapes with Curves and Lines

A LatheShape3D object can be built from a lathe curve made up of curve segments and straight lines as illustrated by the cup in Figure 17-5.

Figure 17-5. A cup with curves and straight edges

 By the way, it's possible to create lathe shapes purely from straight lines if you want. Those are pretty boring, so I've boogied on down to more interesting shapes.

The code for this shape is:

```
TextureLoader texLd10 = new TextureLoader("textures/swirled.jpg", null);
Texture swirledTex = texLd10.getTexture( );

double xsIn2[] = {-0.001, -0.7, -0.25, 0.25, 0.7, -0.6, -0.5};
double ysIn2[] = { 0,      0,    0.5,  1,    2.5, 3,    3};
LatheShape3D ls3 = new LatheShape3D( xsIn2, ysIn2, swirledTex);
displayLathe(ls3, -1.0f, -5.0f, "cup");
```

 This code fragment (and the others in this section) come from addLatheShapes( ) in WrapLathe3D.

A confusing aspect of this fragment is the use of negative x-values, especially the starting value of -0.001. A plot of these points should ignore the negative signs, resulting in Figure 17-6. This hack will be explained momentarily.

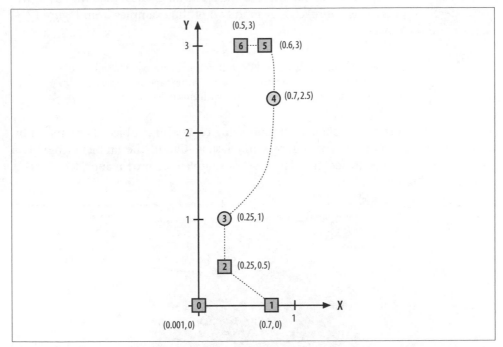

Figure 17-6. Coordinates for a cup

Points with negative x-values are represented by squares in the figure. Dotted lines have been added to indicate the curve segments or straight lines between the points.

The LatheCurve class (which LatheShape3D utilizes) can link points together with curves or lines. If a coordinate has a negative x-value, then a straight line is drawn from it to the next point in the sequence; otherwise, a curve is created. Once this choice about the next segment has been made, any negative sign is discarded.

The negative sign labeling is admittedly a bit confusing but keeps the specification of the shape's coordinates simple without the need to introduce additional data structures or classes. The drawback is shown in Figure 17-6: how can you make a coordinate with an x-value equal to 0 be treated as negative and, therefore, result in a straight line being drawn? The solution is to use a small negative x-value (-0.001). This leaves a tiny hole in the base of the cup when the shape is rotated, but the hole is too little to be visible.

Shapes with Colors

Figure 17-5 shows the texture is rendered on both sides of the lathe shape. If no texture is supplied (or the texture loading stage fails, returning null), then the shape will be rendered in pink. This approach is seen in two of the examples from Figure 17-1: the egg and the flower.

 I like pink because it is a good default color for limbs. The moveable figure in Chapter 20 is constructed from LatheShape3D shapes, so I'm preparing the groundwork in advance with this coloring.

The shape coloring can be changed by supplying two Color3f objects: one for ambient lighting and the other for diffuse illumination. Often, the ambient color is a darker version of the diffused one. The saucer example uses brown and then a darker brown as in Figure 17-7.

Figure 17-7. Brown saucer

The code that creates the saucer is:

```
Color3f brown = new Color3f( 0.3f, 0.2f, 0.0f);
Color3f darkBrown = new Color3f(0.15f, 0.1f, 0.0f);

double xsIn10[] = {0, 0.75, 0.9, 0.75, 0};
double ysIn10[] = {0, 0.23, 0.38, 0.53, 0.75};
LatheShape3D ls14 = new LatheShape3D( xsIn10, ysIn10, darkBrown, brown);
displayLathe(ls14, 6.0f, 5.0f, "saucer");
```

Different Curve Rotations

LatheShape3D rotates each point in the lathe curve around the y-axis, marking out a circular path back to the point's starting position. However, it's possible to subclass LatheShape3D to modify the path. EllipseShape3D sends the points in an elliptical orbit, and RhodoneaShape3D makes the points trace the outlines of petals.

Figure 17-8 shows two shapes: the LatheShape3D object at the back of the picture is a rotation of a single straight line in a circular orbit covered with a texture of the letter "R." The object in the foreground is an EllipseShape3D object made with the same line but forming an ellipse. The same "R" texture dresses the shape.

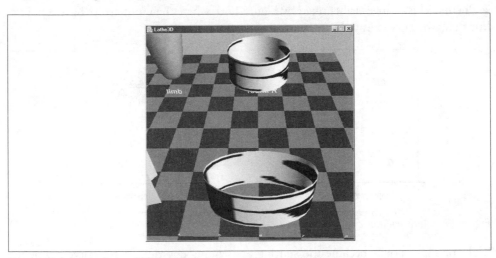

Figure 17-8. Circular and elliptical Rs

Here's the code that creates these shapes:

```
TextureLoader texLd1 = new TextureLoader("textures/r.gif", null);
Texture rTex = texLd1.getTexture( );

double xsIn3[] = {-1, -1};    // straight line
double ysIn3[] = {0, 1};

LatheShape3D ls5 = new LatheShape3D( xsIn3, ysIn3, rTex);
displayLathe(ls5, 6.0f, -5.0f, "round R");

EllipseShape3D ls6 = new EllipseShape3D( xsIn3, ysIn3, rTex);
displayLathe(ls6, 6.0f, 0, "oval R");
```

These examples show that the texture is stretched over a shape, rather than being tiled (i.e., repeatedly applied to the shape like a wallpaper stencil). The left side of the texture is attached to the middle of the back of the shape and wrapped around it in a counterclockwise direction. The texture is stretched in the vertical direction to cover the shape from its base (at y == 0) to its maximum height. The decision to stretch the texture over the shape means the texture image should contain all the detail for the shape.

The Lathe Curve

LatheCurve takes two arrays of x- and y-values as input, and creates two new arrays of x- and y-values representing the curve. The difference between the two pairs of arrays is the addition of interpolated points in the second group to represent curve segments. This change is illustrated by Figure 17-9, where the input arrays have 3 points, but the lathe curve arrays have 13.

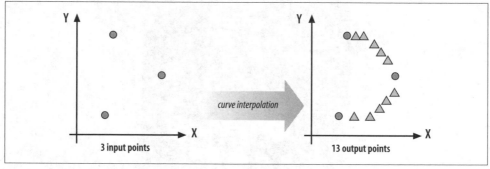

Figure 17-9. Interpolating curves

If all the input points became the starting and ending coordinates for curve segments, then the size of the output arrays would be (*<number of points>* – 1)*(*<STEP>* + 1) + 1, where STEP is the number of introduced interpolation points.

Unfortunately, the sizes of the output arrays is a more complicated matter since points connected by straight lines don't require any additional points. The size calculation is implemented in countVerts( ), which checks the sign of each x value in the input array (xsIn[]) to decide on the number of output points:

```
private int countVerts(double xsIn[], int num)
{
  int numOutVerts = 1;
  for(int i=0; i < num-1; i++) {
    if (xsIn[i] < 0)    // straight line starts here
      numOutVerts++;
    else    // curve segment starts here
      numOutVerts += (STEP+1);
  }
  return numOutVerts;
}
```

Specifying Curve Segments

A crucial problem is how to interpolate the curve segment. Possible methods include Bezier interpolation and B-splines. I use *Hermite curves*: a curve segment is derived from the positions and tangents of its two endpoints. Hermite curves are simple to calculate and can be generated with minimal input from the user. For a given curve segment, four vectors are required:

P0   The starting point of the curve segment

T0   The tangent at P0, analogous to the direction and speed of the curve at that position

P1   The endpoint of the curve segment

T1   The tangent at P1

Figure 17-10 illustrates the points and vectors for a typical curve.

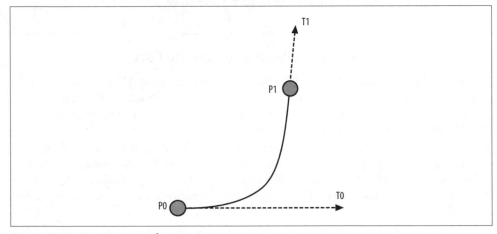

Figure 17-10. Hermite curve data

The longer a tangent vector, the more the curve is "pulled" in the direction of the vector before it begins to move towards the endpoint. Figure 17-11 shows this effect as tangent T0 is made longer.

Four *blending functions* control the interpolations:

- $fh1(t) = 2t^3 - 3t^2 + 1$
- $fh2(t) = -2t^3 + 3t^2$
- $fh3(t) = t^3 - 2t^2 + t$
- $fh4(t) = t^3 - t^2$

Blending functions specify how the intervening points and tangents between the starting and ending points and tangents are calculated as functions of an independent variable t. As t varies from 0 to 1, $fh1(t)$ and $fh2(t)$ control the transition from P0 to P1;

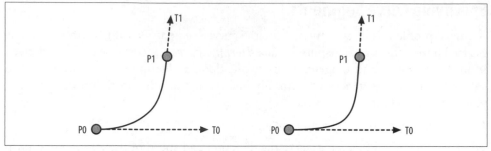

Figure 17-11. How lengthening the tangent vector T0 affects a curve

fh3(t) and fh4(t) manage the transition from T0 to T1. The resulting x- and y-values are calculated like so:

- x = fh1(t)*P0.x + fh2(t)*P1.x + fh3(t)*T0.x + fh4(t)*T1.x
- y = fh1(t)*P0.y + fh2(t)*P1.y + fh3(t)*T0.y + fh4(t)*T1.y

Blending Functions and Hermite Curves

You may be wondering where the blending functions come from. The math is straight-forward and can be found in any good computer graphics textbook, for example, *Foley and Van Dam* (Addison-Wesley). I don't discuss it here as this is meant to be a jovial gaming pandect rather than a graphics tome.

A good online explanation on Hermite curve interpolation can be found at *http://www.cubic.org/~submissive/sourcerer/hermite.htm*, written by Nils Pipenbrinck. A Java applet, coded by Lee Holmes, allows the user to play with natural splines, Bezier curves, and Hermite curves and is located at *http://www.leeholmes.com/projects/grapher/*.

Implementation

The Hermite curve interpolation points are calculated in makeHermite() in LatheCurve. The points are placed in xs[] and ys[], starting at index position startPosn. The P0 value is represented by x0 and y0, P1 by x1 and y1. The tangents are two Point2d objects, t0 and t1:

```
private void makeHermite(double[] xs, double[] ys, int startPosn,
        double x0, double y0, double x1, double y1,
        Point2d t0, Point2d t1)
{
  double xCoord, yCoord;
  double tStep = 1.0/(STEP+1);
  double t;
```

```
if (x1 < 0)        // next point is negative to draw a line, make it
  x1 = -x1;        // +ve while making the curve

for(int i=0; i < STEP; i++) {
  t = tStep * (i+1);
  xCoord = (fh1(t) * x0) + (fh2(t) * x1) +
           (fh3(t) * t0.x) + (fh4(t) * t1.x);
  xs[startPosn+i] = xCoord;

  yCoord = (fh1(t) * y0) + (fh2(t) * y1) +
           (fh3(t) * t0.y) + (fh4(t) * t1.y);
  ys[startPosn+i] = yCoord;
}

xs[startPosn+STEP] = x1;
ys[startPosn+STEP] = y1;
}
```

The loop increments the variable t in steps of 1/(STEP+1), where STEP is the number of interpolated points to be added between P0 and P1. The division is by (STEP+1) since the increment must include P1. The loop does not add P0 to the arrays since it will have been added as the endpoint of the previous curve segment or straight line.

The Java equivalents of the blending functions are shown here:

```
private double fh1(double t)
{   return (2.0)*Math.pow(t,3) - (3.0*t*t) + 1;  }

private double fh2(double t)
{   return (-2.0)*Math.pow(t,3) + (3.0*t*t); }

private double fh3(double t)
{   return Math.pow(t,3) - (2.0*t*t) + t; }

private double fh4(double t)
{   return Math.pow(t,3) - (t*t);  }
```

All this code allows me to flesh out the data points supplied by the user, but it requires each data point to have an associated tangent. Where do these tangents come from?

Calculating the Tangents

A tangent is required for each point in the input sequence. The aim is to reduce the burden on the user as much as possible, so LatheCurve is capable of generating all the tangents by itself.

The first and last tangents of a curve are obtained by making some assumptions about a typical shape. The primary aim is to make limb-like shapes, which are defined by curves starting at the origin, curving out to the right and up, and ending by curving back to the left to finish on the y-axis. This kind of shape is convex, with its starting tangent pointing to the right and the last tangent going to the left.

Both tangents should have a large magnitude to ensure the curve is suitably rounded at the bottom and top. These assumptions are illustrated in Figure 17-12.

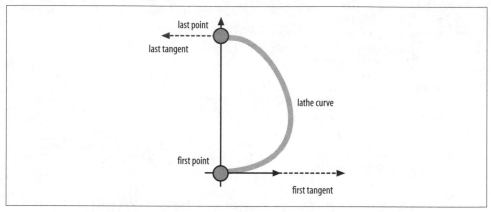

Figure 17-12. Typical lathe curve with tangents

The code that handles all of this is located in LatheCurve's constructor:

```
Point2d startTangent =
  new Point2d((Math.abs(xsIn[1]) - Math.abs(xsIn[0]))*2, 0);

Point2d endTangent =
  new Point2d((Math.abs(xsIn[numVerts-1]) -
            Math.abs(xsIn[numVerts-2]))*2, 0);
```

The xsIn[] array stores the user's x-values, and numVerts is the size of the array. The use of Math.abs() around the x-values is to ignore any negative signs due to the points being used to draw straight lines. The tangents are then each multiplied by 2 to pull the curve outwards making it more rounded.

The intermediate tangents can be interpolated from the data points, using the *Catmull-Rom* spline equation:

$$T_i = 0.5 * (P_{i+1} - P_{i-1})$$

This grandiose equation obtains a tangent at point i by combining the data points on either side of it, at points i-1 and i+1. setTangent() implements this:

```
private void setTangent(Point2d tangent, double xsIn[], double ysIn[], int i)
{
  double xLen = Math.abs(xsIn[i+1]) - Math.abs(xsIn[i-1]);
  double yLen = ysIn[i+1] - ysIn[i-1];
  tangent.set(xLen/2, yLen/2);
}
```

Building the Entire Curve

The for loop in makeCurve( ) iterates through the input points (stored in xsIn[ ] and ysIn[ ]) building new arrays (xs[ ] and ys[ ]) for the resulting curve:

```
private void makeCurve(double xsIn[], double ysIn[],
            Point2d startTangent, Point2d endTangent)
{
  int numInVerts = xsIn.length;
  int numOutVerts = countVerts(xsIn, numInVerts);
  xs = new double[numOutVerts];    // seq after adding extra pts
  ys = new double[numOutVerts];

  xs[0] = Math.abs(xsIn[0]);    // start of curve is initialised
  ys[0] = ysIn[0];
  int startPosn = 1;

  // tangents for the current curve segment between two points
  Point2d t0 = new Point2d( );
  Point2d t1 = new Point2d( );

  for (int i=0; i < numInVerts-1; i++) {
    if (i == 0)
      t0.set( startTangent.x, startTangent.y);
    else    // use previous t1 tangent
      t0.set(t1.x, t1.y);

    if (i == numInVerts-2)    // next point is the last one
      t1.set( endTangent.x, endTangent.y);
    else
      setTangent(t1, xsIn, ysIn, i+1);    // tangent at pt i+1

    // if xsIn[i] < 0 then use a line to link (x,y) to next pt
    if (xsIn[i] < 0) {
      xs[startPosn] = Math.abs(xsIn[i+1]);
      ys[startPosn] = ysIn[i+1];
      startPosn++;
    }
    else {    // make a Hermite curve
      makeHermite(xs, ys, startPosn, xsIn[i], ysIn[i],
                            xsIn[i+1], ysIn[i+1], t0, t1);
      startPosn += (STEP+1);
    }
  }
}  // end of makeCurve( )
```

The loop responds differently if the current x-value is positive or negative. If it's negative, the coordinates will be copied over to the output arrays unchanged (to represent a straight line). If the x-value is positive, then makeHermite( ) will be called to generate a series of interpolated points for the curve. This is the place where the negative number hack is implemented: if a coordinate has a negative x-value, then a straight line will be drawn from it to the next point in the sequence; otherwise, a curve will be created.

The two tangents, t0 and t1, are set for each coordinate. Initially, t0 will be the starting tangent, and then it will be the t1 value from each previous calculation. At the end, t1 will be assigned the endpoint tangent.

The new arrays of points, and the maximum height (largest y-value), are made accessible through public methods:

```
public double[] getXs()
{  return xs;  }

public double[] getYs()
{  return ys;  }

public double getHeight()
{  return height;  }
```

The Lathe Shape

A LatheShape3D object first creates a lathe curve using the points supplied by the user and then decorates it with color or a texture. The choice between color and texture is represented by two constructors:

```
public LatheShape3D(double xsIn[], double ysIn[], Texture tex)
{ LatheCurve lc = new LatheCurve(xsIn, ysIn);
  buildShape(lc.getXs(), lc.getYs(), lc.getHeight(), tex);
}

public LatheShape3D(double xsIn[], double ysIn[],
                Color3f darkCol, Color3f lightCol)
// two colors required: a dark and normal version of the color
{ LatheCurve lc = new LatheCurve(xsIn, ysIn);
  buildShape(lc.getXs(), lc.getYs(), lc.getHeight(),
                           darkCol, lightCol);
}
```

Both versions of buildShape() call createGeometry() to build a QuadArray for the shape. Then the four-argument version of buildShape() lays down a texture, and the five-argument version calls createAppearance() to add color.

Creating the Geometry

createGeometry() passes the lathe curve coordinates to surfaceRevolve(), which returns the coordinates of the resulting shape. The coordinates are used to initialize a QuadArray, complete with normals (to reflect light) and texture coordinates if a texture is going to be wrapped around the shape:

```
private void createGeometry(double[] xs, double[] ys, boolean usingTexture)
{
  double verts[] = surfaceRevolve(xs, ys);
```

```
    // use GeometryInfo to compute normals
    GeometryInfo geom = new GeometryInfo(GeometryInfo.QUAD_ARRAY);
    geom.setCoordinates(verts);

    if (usingTexture) {
      geom.setTextureCoordinateParams(1, 2);    // set up tex coords
      TexCoord2f[] texCoords = initTexCoords(verts);
      correctTexCoords(texCoords);
      geom.setTextureCoordinates(0, texCoords);
    }

    NormalGenerator norms = new NormalGenerator();
    norms.generateNormals(geom);

    setGeometry( geom.getGeometryArray() );    // back to geo array
  }
```

The calculation of the normals is carried out by a NormalGenerator object, which requires that the coordinates be stored in a GeometryInfo object.

setTextureCoordinatesParams( ) specifies how many texture coordinate sets will be used with the geometry and specifies their dimensionality (Java 3D offers 2D, 3D, and 4D texture coordinates). The actual texture coordinates are calculated by initTexCoords( ) and added to the geometry with setTextureCoordinates( ).

 You'll encounter NormalGenerator again, as well as other geometry utilities, in Chapter 26.

You Say You Want a Revolution

surfaceRevolve( ) generates the shape's coordinates by revolving the lathe curve clockwise around the y-axis in angle increments specified by ANGLE_INCR. This results in NUM_SLICES columns of points around the y-axis:

```
private static final double ANGLE_INCR = 15.0;
        // the angle turned through to create a face of the solid
private static final int NUM_SLICES = (int)(360.0/ANGLE_INCR);
```

The coordinates in adjacent slices are organized into quadrilaterals (quads). Each quad is specified by four points, with a point represented by three floats (for the x-, y-, and z-values). The points are organized in counterclockwise order so the quad's normal is facing outward.

Figure 17-13 shows how two quads are defined. Each point is stored as three floats.

The surfaceRevolve( ) method is shown here:

```
private double[] surfaceRevolve(double xs[], double ys[])
{
  checkCoords(xs);
  double[] coords = new double[(NUM_SLICES) * (xs.length-1) *4*3];
```

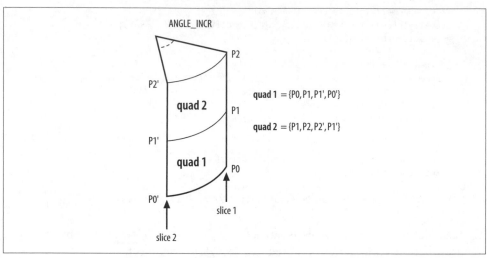

Figure 17-13. Quads creation

```
int index=0;
for (int i=0; i < xs.length-1; i++) {
  for (int slice=0; slice < NUM_SLICES; slice++) {
    addCorner( coords, xs[i], ys[i],slice,index); // bottom right
    index += 3;

    addCorner( coords, xs[i+1],ys[i+1],slice,index); // top right
    index += 3;

    addCorner( coords, xs[i+1],ys[i+1],slice+1,index); //top left
    index += 3;

    addCorner( coords, xs[i],ys[i],slice+1,index); // bottom left
    index += 3;
  }
}
return coords;
}
```

The generated coordinates for the shape are placed in the coords[] array. surfaceRevolve( )'s outer loop iterates through the coordinates in the input arrays, which are stored in increasing order. The inner loop creates the corner points for all the quads in each slice clockwise around the y-axis. This means that the quads are built a ring at a time, starting at the bottom of the shape and working up.

addCorner( ) rotates an (x, y) coordinate around to the specified slice and stores its (x, y, z) position in the coords[] array:

```
private void addCorner(double[] coords, double xOrig, double yOrig,
                       int slice, int index)
{ double angle = RADS_DEGREE * (slice*ANGLE_INCR);
```

```
    if (slice == NUM_SLICES)  // back at start
      coords[index] = xOrig;
    else
      coords[index] = xCoord(xOrig, angle);  // x

    coords[index+1] = yOrig;    // y

    if (slice == NUM_SLICES)
      coords[index+2] = 0;
    else
      coords[index+2] = zCoord(xOrig, angle);    // z
  }
```

The x- and z-values are obtained by treating the original x-value (xOrig) as a hypotenuse at the given angle and projecting it onto the x- and z-axes (see Figure 17-14).

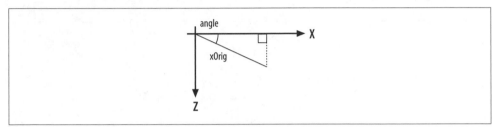

Figure 17-14. Obtaining new x- and z-values

The xCoord( ) and zCoord( ) methods are simple:

```
protected double xCoord(double radius, double angle)
{   return radius * Math.cos(angle);  }

protected double zCoord(double radius, double angle)
{   return radius * Math.sin(angle);  }
```

These methods carry out a mapping from Polar coordinates (radius, angle) to Cartesian ones (x, y). Since the radius argument (xOrig) never changes, the resulting coordinates will always be a fixed distance from the origin and, therefore, be laid out around a circle. These methods are protected, so it's possible to override them to vary the effect of the radius and/or angle.

 The algorithm in surfaceRevolve( ) and addCorner( ) comes from the SurfaceOfRevolution class by Chris Buckalew, which is part of his *FreeFormDef.java* example (see *http://www.csc.calpoly.edu/~buckalew/ 474Lab6-W03.html*).

Creating Texture Coordinates

In Chapter 16, a TexCoordGeneration object mapped (s, t) values onto geometry coordinates (x, y, z). Unfortunately, the simplest TexCoordGeneration form only supports planar equations for the translation of (x, y, z) into s and t. Planar equations can produce repetitive patterns on a shape, especially shapes with flat areas. These problems can be avoided if the mapping from (x, y, z) to (s, t) is quadratic or cubic, but the design of the equation becomes harder. In those cases, it's arguably simpler to calculate s and t directly (as in this chapter) without utilizing the TexCoordGeneration class.

The s value 0 is mapped to the shape's back face and increased in value around the edge of the shape in a counterclockwise direction until it reaches the back face again when it equals 1. t is given the value 0 at the base of the shape (where y equals 0) and increased to 1 until it reaches the maximum y-value. This has the effect of stretching the texture vertically.

Figure 17-15 shows the s mapping applied to a circle, from a viewpoint looking down toward the XZ plane.

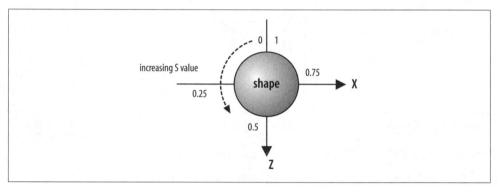

Figure 17-15. The s mapping from above

Figure 17-15 gives a hint of how to calculate s: its value at a given (x, z) coordinate can be obtained from the angle that the point makes with the z-axis. This will range between π and -π (see Figure 17-16), which is converted into a value between 0 and 1.

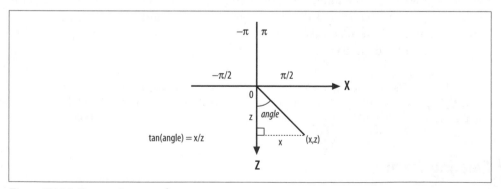

Figure 17-16. From point to angle

Here's the code for `initTexCoords( )` that makes all this happen:

```java
private TexCoord2f[] initTexCoords(double[] verts)
{
    int numVerts = verts.length;
    TexCoord2f[] tcoords = new TexCoord2f[numVerts/3];

    double x, y, z;
    float sVal, tVal;
    double angle, frac;

    int idx = 0;
    for(int i=0; i < numVerts/3; i++) {
        x = verts[idx];  y = verts[idx+1];   z = verts[idx+2];

        angle = Math.atan2(x,z);       // -PI to PI
        frac = angle/Math.PI;          // -1.0 to 1.0
        sVal = (float) (0.5 + frac/2);   // 0.0f to 1.0f

        tVal = (float) (y/height);   // 0.0f to 1.0f; uses height

        tcoords[i] = new TexCoord2f(sVal, tVal);
        idx += 3;
    }
    return tcoords;
}
```

The texture coordinates are stored in an array of TexCoord2f objects, each object holding a (s, t) pair. The angles for the shape's vertices are obtained by calling Math. atan2( ), and their range of values (π to −π) is scaled and translated to (0 to 1).

A Thin Problem

The mapping described in the last subsection has a flaw, which occurs in any quad spanning the middle of the shape's back face. Figure 17-17 shows the round R example, with this problem visible as a thin R stretched down the middle of the shape's back. In short, there are two Rs, when there should only be one. The extra letter is also reversed when viewed from the back (remember that I'm placing the texture on the *outside* surface of the shape). Figure 17-17 should be compared with the round R example in Figure 17-8, rendered after the flaw was fixed.

The same effect is apparent in all the other texture-wrapped shapes (although some shapes and textures make it harder to see). The problem is that the quads which span the middle of the back face have coordinates at angles on either side of the −z-axis. An example shows the problem in Figure 17-18.

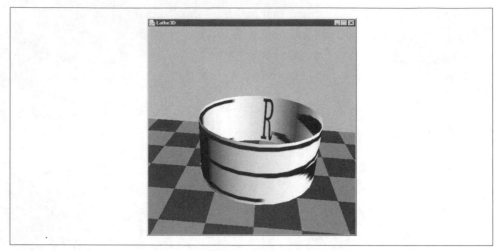

Figure 17-17. An extra R

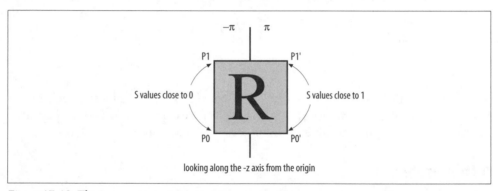

Figure 17-18. The incorrect s mapping

P0 and P1 have angles near to $-\pi$ and, therefore, s values close to 0; P0' and P1' have angles closer to π and, therefore, s values closer to 1. Consequently, the s component of the texture will be drawn in its entirety in that one quad, as seen in Figure 17-17.

The solution is something of a hack. Each quad generates four TexCoord2f objects corresponding to the order of the coordinates of the quad (P0, P1, P1', P0'). In correctly textured quads, the s value for P0 is greater than P0', and P1 is greater than P1'. This is due to the surfaceRevolve( ) method rotating points clockwise around the y-axis. In incorrectly textured quads, the reverse is true: P0 is less than P0' and P1 is less than P1'.

In correctTexCoords( ), every group of four TexCoord2f objects is examined for this condition, and the offending textured coordinates for P0 and P1 are adjusted to be greater than those for P0' and P1'. The code to take care of this is:

```
private void correctTexCoords(TexCoord2f[] tcoords)
{
  for(int i=0; i < tcoords.length; i=i+4) {
    if( (tcoords[i].x < tcoords[i+3].x) &&
        (tcoords[i+1].x < tcoords[i+2].x)) { // should not increase
      tcoords[i].x = (1.0f + tcoords[i+3].x)/2 ; // between x & 1.0
      tcoords[i+1].x = (1.0f + tcoords[i+2].x)/2 ;
    }
  }
}
```

Making an Appearance

The createAppearance( ) method has two versions. One of them colors the shape with two colors: one for the light's ambient component and the other for diffuse illumination. This is achieved with a Material object:

```
Appearance app = new Appearance( ):

Material mat = new Material(darkCol, black, lightCol, black, 1.0f);
        // sets ambient, emissive, diffuse, specular, shininess
mat.setLightingEnable(true);     // lighting switched on
app.setMaterial(mat);
setAppearance(app);
```

The other createAppearance( ) method sets the texture and uses a white Material object. The texture is combined with the color using the MODULATE mode (see Chapter 16 for more details on modulation), which allows lighting and shading effects to be blended with the texture:

```
Appearance app = new Appearance( );

// mix the texture and the material color
TextureAttributes ta = new TextureAttributes( );
ta.setTextureMode(TextureAttributes.MODULATE);
app.setTextureAttributes(ta);

Material mat = new Material( );   // set a default white material
mat.setSpecularColor(black);     // no specular color
mat.setLightingEnable(true);
app.setMaterial(mat);

app.setTexture( tex );

setAppearance(app);
```

Subclassing the Lathe Shape

Figure 17-2 shows that LatheShape3D can be subclassed. The aim is to override its xCoord() and zCoord() methods, which control the shape of the path made by the lathe curve when it's rotated. These methods appear in LatheShape3D as shown here:

```
protected double xCoord(double radius, double angle)
{  return radius * Math.cos(angle);  }

protected double zCoord(double radius, double angle)
{  return radius * Math.sin(angle);  }
```

radius is the x-value of the point being rotated around the y-axis, and angle is the angle of rotation currently being applied. xCoord() and zCoord() return the new x- and z-values after the rotation has been applied.

An Elliptical Shape

An ellipse resembles a circle stretched in one direction. Another (more formal) way of characterizing the ellipse is that its points all have the same sum of distances from two fixed points (called the *foci*).

The line that passes through the foci is called the *major axis*, and is the longest line through the ellipse. The *minor axis* is the line that passes through the center of the ellipse, perpendicular to the major axis. The *semi-major axis* is half the length of the major axis: it runs from the center of the ellipse to its edge. There's also a *semi-minor axis* (half of the minor axis). See Figure 17-19 for illustrations of all of these concepts.

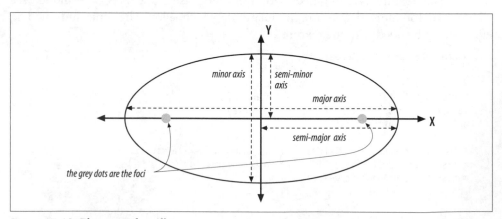

Figure 17-19. Elements of an ellipse

Figure 17-20 shows an ellipse with a semi-major axis of 4 and a semi-minor axis of length 2.

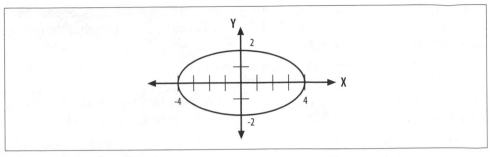

Figure 17-20. Another ellipse

The semi-major and semi-minor axes can be used to calculate the (x, y) coordinates of the ellipse:

```
x = semiMajorAxis * cos(angle)
y = semiMinorAxis * sin(angle)
```

In the case of the ellipse in Figure 17-20, these calculations would result in the following:

```
x = 4 * cos(angle)
y = 2 * sin(angle)
```

The y equation can be rephrased by writing the semi-minor axis value as a scale factor applied to the semi-major axis number:

```
x = 4 * cos(angle)
y = 0.5 * 4 * sin(angle)
```

The scale factor is 0.5 since 0.5×4 is 2, the semi-minor axis value. This means that the semi-minor axis is half the length of the semi-major, as illustrated by Figure 17-20.

I've been talking about x and y equations, but now it's time to change the axes. A lathe shape is made by rotating a lathe curve over the floor (the XZ plane). This means that my ellipses are drawn on the x- and z-axes, not the x- and y-axes. As a consequence, the y equation becomes the z equation:

```
z = 0.5 * 4 * sin(angle)
```

The x and z equations use the semi-major axis number (4). Is there a way of obtaining this from the radius value supplied as an argument to the xCoord( ) and zCoord( ) methods? Yes, when the angle is 0, the x-value is the semi-major axis, which is the radius:

```
radius = semiMajorAxis * cos(0),    so radius = semiMajorAxis.
```

This means I can use the radius as a replacement for the semi major axis value in the x and z equations. The equations become:

```
x = radius * cos(angle)
z = scaleFactor * radius * sin(angle)
```

The x equation is the same as the xCoord( ) method in LatheShape3D, so doesn't need to be overridden. The zCoord( ) method does need changing and becomes the following in the EllipseShape3D class:

```
protected double zCoord(double radius, double angle)
{  return  0.5 * radius * Math.sin(angle);   }
```

The scale factor is set to 0.5, which makes the semi-minor axis half the semi-major axis, which can be confirmed by examining the oval R example in Figure 17-8.

A weakness of this approach is that the user cannot set the scale factor via a parameter of EllipseShape3D's constructor. The reason is that the xCoord( ) and zCoord( ) methods are called (indirectly) by the LatheShape3D constructor, so must be fully specified before any code in the EllipseShape3D constructor is executed. In other words, the scale factor (e.g., 0.5) must be hardwired into the EllipseShape3D class as a constant in zCoord( ).

The armor example uses EllipseShape3D:

```
double xsIn9[] = {-0.01, 0.5, -1, -1.2, 1.4, -0.5, -0.5, 0};
double ysIn9[] = {0, 0, 1.5, 1.5, 2, 2.5, 2.7, 2.7};

EllipseShape3D ls13 = new EllipseShape3D( xsIn9, ysIn9, plateTex);
displayLathe(ls13, 3.0f, 5.0f, "armour");
```

Figure 17-21 shows the rendering of armor.

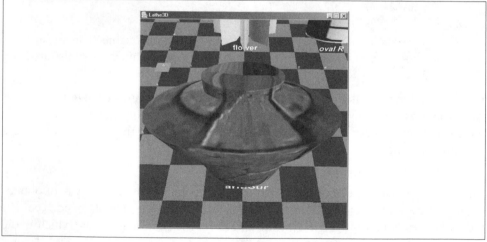

Figure 17-21. The armor ellipse

A Rhodonea Shape

A rhodonea curve resembles the petals of a rose. The simplest way to define one is with an equation using polar coordinates:

```
r = a * cos(k*angle)
```

This lays down a curve with k or 2k petals, depending if k is an odd or even integer. a is the amplitude, affecting the length of the petals. Some examples of rhodonea curves with different k values are given in Figure 17-22.

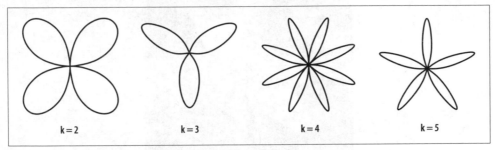

Figure 17-22. Some rhodonea curves

Once r is obtained for a given angle, it can be translated to Cartesian coordinates with:

```
x = r * cos(angle)
y = r * sin(angle)
```

I store the initial x value in radius, which is the length of the first petal when the angle is 0:

```
radius = a * cos(0),    so radius = a
```

The rhodonea equation then becomes:

```
r = radius * cos(k*angle)
```

In the RhodoneaShape3D class, k is set to be 4, and xCoord( ) and yCoord( ) must be overridden:

```
protected double xCoord(double radius, double angle)
{ double r = radius * Math.cos(4 * angle);    // 8 petals
  return  r * Math.cos(angle);
}

protected double zCoord(double radius, double angle)
{ double r = radius * Math.cos(4 * angle);
  return  r * Math.sin(angle);
}
```

RhodoneaShape3D is used in the flower example, which is defined as:

```
double xsIn3[] = {-1, -1};
double ysIn3[] = {0, 1};

RhodoneaShape3D ls7 = new RhodoneaShape3D(xsIn3, ysIn3, null);
displayLathe(ls7, 3.0f, 0, "flower");
```

A vertical straight line of unit length is rotated and then colored pink. The resulting curve is shown in Figure 17-23.

Figure 17-23. A rough RhodoneaShape3D shape

The curve is rather rough due to the ANGLE_INCR setting in LatheShape3D (15 degrees between each slice). If this is reduced to 5 degrees, the result will be more pleasing (see Figure 17-24).

Figure 17-24. A smoother RhodoneaShape3D shape

 The drawback of reducing the ANGLE_INCR value is the increase in the number of vertices generated for each shape.

CHAPTER 18

3D Sprites

In this chapter, I'll develop a Sprite3D class, which can be subclassed to create different kinds of sprites. The user's sprite (a robot) and a chasing sprite (a hand) are shown in action in Figure 18-1 sharing the checkerboard with some scenery (a palm tree and castle) and obstacles (the red poles).

Figure 18-1. 3D sprites in action

Features illustrated by the Tour3D application include:

Sprite behavior

> The sprites are controlled by Behavior subclasses.

A third-person camera

> A simple third-person camera automatically adjusts the user's viewpoint as the user's sprite moves around the scene. The camera can be zoomed in and out by keyboard controls.

Obstacles

The scene contains obstacles that a sprite can't pass through. (They're represented by cylinders in Figure 18-1.) Sprites are prevented from moving off the checkered floor.

Collision detection

Collision detection between a sprite and the obstacles is implemented by bounds checking.

Scenery configuration

A "tour" text file loaded at start time contains obstacle and scenery information. The scenery models (e.g., the castle and the palm tree in this example) are loaded with PropManager objects.

A background image

The scene's background is drawn using a scaled JPEG.

Full-screen display

The application is configured to be full-screen.

Class Diagrams for Tour3D

Figure 18-2 shows class diagrams for Tour3D. Only class names are shown here, to reduce the complexity of the diagram.

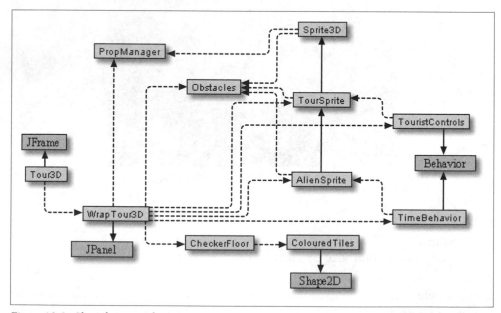

Figure 18-2. Class diagrams for Tour3D

Tour3D is the top-level JFrame for the application. WrapTour3D creates the 3D scene and is similar to earlier Wrap classes in that it creates the checkered floor and sets up the lighting. This version loads the scenery and obstacles and creates the sprites.

PropManager is unchanged from the class in the Loader3D application in Chapter 16. CheckerFloor and ColouredTiles are the same classes as in previous examples. The Obstacles class is new: it stores information about the scene's obstacles.

The sprites are subclasses of Sprite3D. The robot is an instance of TourSprite, and the hand is an AlienSprite object. TourSprite is controlled by TouristControls, and TimeBehavior updates AlienSprite. TouristControls and TimeBehavior are subclasses of Java 3D's Behavior class.

 The code for the Tour3D example can be found in the *Tour3D/* directory.

Creating the Scene

Figure 18-3 shows the methods defined in WrapTour3D.

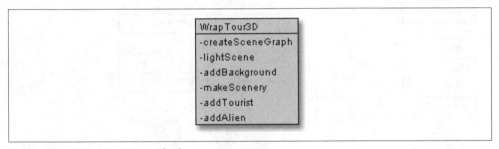

Figure 18-3. WrapTour3D methods

WrapTour3D sets up the checkered floor and lights (similar to previous Wrap classes). However, addBackground( ) uses a scaled image, and there are three new methods: makeScenery( ), addTourist( ), and addAlien( ). These methods are called by createSceneGraph( ) to add scenery, obstacles, and sprites to the scene.

The application's scene graph is shown in Figure 18-4. Its details will be explained in subsequent sections.

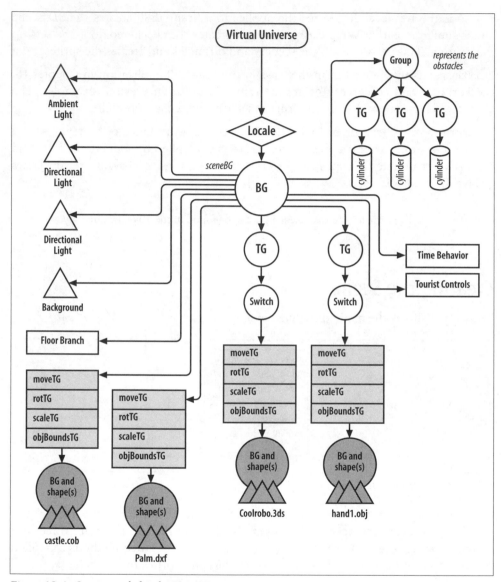

Figure 18-4. Scene graph for the Tour3D scene

Adding a Background Image

A Java 3D Background node can use a solid color, an image, or a geometric shape (e.g., a sphere or a box) with an image rendered onto it. Here, the application utilizes a picture of a hazy sky, 400×400 pixels in size, stored in *bigSky.jpg*:

```
TextureLoader bgTexture = new TextureLoader("models/bigSky.jpg", null);
Background back = new Background(bgTexture.getImage());
back.setImageScaleMode(Background.SCALE_FIT_MAX);   // fit the display
```

```
back.setApplicationBounds( bounds );
sceneBG.addChild( back );
```

The image is loaded as a texture and then converted to ImageComponent2D form for the Background object. Java 3D 1.3 added several scaling modes to Background; the one employed here scales the image to fit the display window. This can cause significant distortion, which is why I haven't used a detailed image (haze looks pretty much the same even after being distorted).

Another scaling mode is Background.SCALE_REPEAT, which tiles the image over the display area. This avoids the distortion caused by scaling but introduces repetition and joins between the tiles. With careful design, tile edges can be hidden, and if the image is large, the repetition will be less obvious.

A drawback of using a background image is it remains stationary in the background even when the viewpoint moves. Chapter 25 (about the mysterious maze) shows a way around this by using a shape as the background and placing a texture over it. As the user moves around, she sees different parts of the geometry and, therefore, different parts of the background. Chapter 27 (on terrain generation) places stars in the sky with the same technique.

Full-Screen Display

There are two approaches to making a full-screen application in Java 3D: the display window's dimensions can be set to match those of the monitor or full-screen exclusive mode (FSEM) can be deployed. These techniques were explained in Chapter 4, in the context of 2D Java games.

When writing a Java 3D application, which technique is preferable? In terms of speed, the two are similar since Java 3D passes most graphics processing to OpenGL or DirectX.

One advantage of using FSEM is control over screen resolution. A minor disadvantage is that FSEM interacts poorly with Swing components, minor because most full-screen games don't utilize Swing controls. Another limitation is that GraphicsDevice.isFullScreenSupported() may return false (e.g., on some versions of Unix). On systems where FSEM is unavailable, FSEM will appear to work by falling back to using a full-size window.

In this chapter, I'll use a fixed-size window that fills the screen and grapple with FSEM in the next chapter.

The resizing of the display window requires three pieces of code. In the Tour3D class, the menu bars and other JFrame decoration must be turned off:

```
setUndecorated(true);
```

In WrapTour3D, the panel must be resized to fill the monitor:

```
setPreferredSize( Toolkit.getDefaultToolkit().getScreenSize() );
```

A full-screen application with no menu bar raises the question of how to terminate the program. The usual approach is to add a KeyAdapter anonymous class to the window that has keyboard focus, which is the Canvas3D object in this application:

```
canvas3D.setFocusable(true);
canvas3D.requestFocus();

canvas3D.addKeyListener( new KeyAdapter() {
// listen for Esc, q, end, Ctrl-c on the canvas to
// allow a convenient exit from the full screen configuration
  public void keyPressed(KeyEvent e)
  { int keyCode = e.getKeyCode();
    if ((keyCode == KeyEvent.VK_ESCAPE) ||
        (keyCode == KeyEvent.VK_Q) ||
        (keyCode == KeyEvent.VK_END) ||
        ((keyCode == KeyEvent.VK_C) && e.isControlDown()) ) {
      win.dispose();
      System.exit(0);    // exit() isn't sufficient usually
    }
  }
});
```

Catching KeyEvents in WrapTour3D doesn't preclude their use in other parts of the application. As you'll see, the TouristControls class utilizes KeyEvents to govern the movement of the robot sprite and to adjust the user's viewpoint.

The unusual aspect of my coding is the Window.dispose( ) call, applied to win, a reference to the top-level JFrame created in Tour3D. This is preferable to shutting things down with exit( ) only; a call to exit( ) kills the application but often fails to clear the application's image from the monitor.

Adding Scenery and Obstacles

Tour3D makes a distinction between scenery and obstacles: scenery comes from external models (e.g., the castle, palm tree) and is loaded via PropManager objects. Obstacles are red columns generated by the code, requiring only a (x, z) location to position them on the floor.

A crucial attribute of scenery is its intangibility: the robot and hand sprites can move right through it if they wish. In contrast, a sprite is disallowed from passing through an obstacle.

Scenery and obstacle data are read from a text file whose name is supplied on the command line when Tour3D is started. For example, the following call uses the *ctour. txt* tour file:

```
java -cp %CLASSPATH%;ncsa\portfolio.jar Tour3D ctour.txt
```

The extension of the classpath is to utilize the loaders in the NCSA Portfolio package.

The format of a tour file is simple: each line contains the filename of a model or a sequence of coordinates for positioning obstacles. The sequences are prefixed by -o to make them easy to find when the data are read in.

The *ctour.txt* file used to decorate the scene in Figure 18-1 contains:

```
Castle.cob
-o (4,4) (6,6)
Palm.dxf
-o (-2,3)
```

Any number of coordinates can be in an -o sequence; two -o lines are in *ctour.txt* as an example.

 Alternatively, the three points could be listed on a single -o line.

The obstacle coordinates are passed to the Obstacle object, which creates the necessary data structures, including the three on-screen red cylinders.

The model filenames are assumed to be located in the *models/* subdirectory and to come with coord datafiles for positioning them in the scene. Coord datafiles were introduced in Chapter 16, and they're generated by the Loader3D application as a loaded model that is translated, rotated, and scaled. These details can be stored in a coord datafile for the model and utilized later by the PropManager class in Loader3D when the model is loaded. PropManager is being reused in Tour3D to place a correctly positioned, rotated, and sized model in the scene. The loading of the tour file is done by makeScenery() in WrapTour3D. Here's the relevant code fragment from that method:

```
obs = new Obstacles();     // initialise Obstacle object
PropManager propMan;
... // other nonrelevant code

BufferedReader br =  new BufferedReader( new FileReader(tourFile));
String line;
while((line = br.readLine()) != null) {
  if (line.startsWith("-o"))    // save obstacle info
    obs.store( line.substring(2).trim() );
  else {     // load scenery
    propMan = new PropManager(line.trim(),true);
    sceneBG.addChild( propMan.getTG() );    // add to scene
  }
}
br.close();
sceneBG.addChild( obs.getObsGroup() );  // add obs to scene
```

A PropManager object creates a scene graph branch containing a chain of TransformGroups. In Figure 18-4, the chains above the BranchGroups for the castle and palm tree are drawn as rectangles. A chain of TransformGroups may be considered too much overhead for loading a model, but the overhead (and the chain) can be removed fairly easily: PropManager must be extended with a method which switches off the capability bits in the TransformGroups:

```
moveTG.clearCapability(TransformGroup.ALLOW_TRANSFORM_READ);
moveTG.clearCapability(TransformGroup.ALLOW_TRANSFORM_WRITE);
```

This should be done before the branch is added to the main scene and compiled. Compilation will optimize the chain away to a single TransformGroup since Java 3D will notice that none of the chain's nodes can be transformed at runtime. However, I haven't made these coding changes since I prefer to leave PropManager unchanged from its first appearance in Chapter 16.

Obstacles

The Obstacle object created by makeScenery( ) maintain three types of information:

- A 2D array of Booleans called obs, which indicates if a particular (x, z) location is occupied by an obstacle
- A 2D array of Java 3D BoundingSphere objects called obsBounds, which specifies the influence of an obstacle at a given (x, z) location
- A Group node called obsGroup, which holds the cylinders representing the obstacles

A class diagram for Obstacles is given in Figure 18-5.

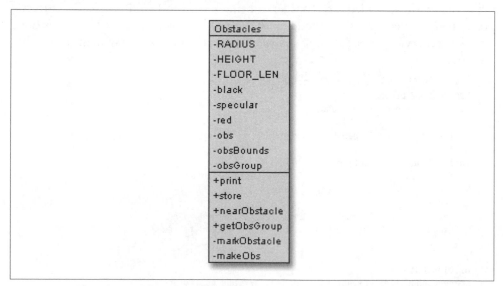

Figure 18-5. Class diagram for Obstacles

The coding of the class is simplified by restricting the obstacles to integer positions on the checkerboard, which permits array-based data structures and algorithms to be employed.

A given (x, z) coordinate is checked for obstacles with nearObstacle( ), called by the sprites from the Sprite3D class. It returns false if the supplied position is outside the floor area or too near an obstacle. Nearness testing is done by determining if a bounding sphere centered at the coordinate intersects with any of the bounding spheres in obsBounds:

```
BoundingSphere bs = new BoundingSphere( pos, radius);
for (int z=0; z <= FLOOR_LEN; z++)
  for(int x=0; x <= FLOOR_LEN; x++)
    if (obs[z][x]) {    // does (x,z) have an obstacle?
      if (obsBounds[z][x].intersect(bs))
        return true;
    }
return false;
```

The bounding sphere is created using Java 3D's BoundingSphere class and is defined by a center point and radius. The bounding spheres for the obstacles are generated as their coordinates are read in from the tour file and stored in the obsBounds[] array. I utilize BoundingSphere's intersect( ) method, which returns true if two bounding volumes intersect.

The algorithm given above is exhaustive in that it tests every obstacle against the supplied position (pos). It might be more efficient to use the pos value to limit the number of obstacles considered, but then I would have to store the obstacle information in a more structured, ordered form. That seems overly complicated for this example.

Each obstacle is displayed as a red cylinder and placed below a TransformGroup to orient it on screen, as shown in the scene graph in Figure 18-4. The TransformGroup moves the cylinder upward by HEIGHT/2, so its base is resting on the floor at the (x, z) coordinate specified for that obstacle in the tour file.

The Basic 3D Sprite

Sprite3D is the base class for creating 3D sprites. The TourSprite subclass is used to create the user's robot sprite, and AlienSprite is a subclass of TourSprite for the alien hand.

TourSprite is controlled by TouristControls, which monitors user key presses and can adjust the sprite's position or the user's viewpoint as needed. AlienSprite is periodically updated by the TimeBehavior class to make the alien hand chase the user's sprite.

Figure 18-6 shows the public methods of the Sprite3D and Behavior classes and the relationships between them.

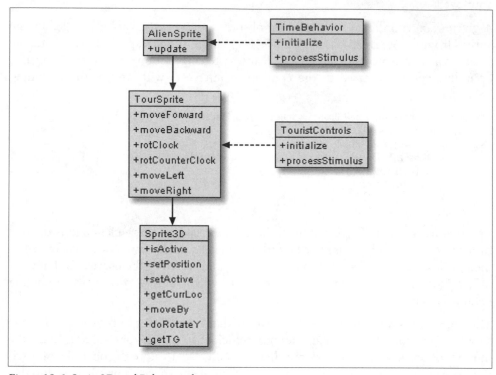

Figure 18-6. Sprite3D and Behavior classes

Sprite3D represents a model able to move about the XZ plane, rotate around the y-axis, and detect obstacles and floor boundaries. The sprite can be made inactive, which will cause it to disappear from the scene.

The constructor for Sprite3D utilizes PropManager to load the model representing the sprite. It then adds a Switch node and TransformGroup above the model's graph. The result can be seen in the branches for the robot (*Coolrobo.3ds*) and alien hand (*hand1.obj*) in Figure 18-4. Here is the relevant code:

```
PropManager propMan = new PropManager(fnm, true);

visSwitch = new Switch();   // for sprite visibility
visSwitch.setCapability(Switch.ALLOW_SWITCH_WRITE);
visSwitch.addChild( propMan.getTG() );     // add obj to switch
visSwitch.setWhichChild( Switch.CHILD_ALL );   // make visible

objectTG = new TransformGroup();  // for sprite moves
objectTG.setCapability(TransformGroup.ALLOW_TRANSFORM_READ);
objectTG.setCapability(TransformGroup.ALLOW_TRANSFORM_WRITE);
objectTG.addChild( visSwitch );    // add switch to TG
```

The objectTG node is made available to the application's scene via getTG( ), which is called by WrapTour3D.

Visibility

The Switch node is used to control the image branch's visibility. This is done in the setActive( ) method of Sprite3D:

```
public void setActive(boolean b)
{ isActive = b;
  if (!isActive)
     visSwitch.setWhichChild( Switch.CHILD_NONE ); //make invisible
  else if (isActive)
     visSwitch.setWhichChild( Switch.CHILD_ALL );   // make visible
}
```

In Java 3D, the visibility of a model can be controlled in at least three ways:

- Use setWhichChild( ) on a Switch above the model (as here).
- Use setVisible( ) on the model's rendering attributes.
- Use Java 3D TransparencyAttributes, as detailed in the LoaderInfo3D application in the section "Making a Shape Almost Transparent" in Chapter 16.

The overhead of manipulating rendering or transparency attributes can be high and will continue to produce an overhead during rendering. A Switch node placed above the model in the scene graph means that rendering doesn't need to visit the model at all when the Switch node is set to CHILD_NONE, a clear gain in efficiency.

Another advantage of Switch is it can be placed above Group nodes to control the visibility of subgraphs in the scene. The subgraph might be a group of shapes (e.g., a group of soldiers) who should all disappear at the same time when zapped by a laser. Attribute approaches only apply to individual Shape3D nodes.

Movement and Rotation

The addition of another TransformGroup to a model's scene branch (labeled as TG in Figure 18-4) is for coding simplicity. It means that a Sprite3D object can be moved and rotated without the code having to delve into the graph structure returned by PropManager's getTG( ).

A sprite can be moved with setPosition( ) and moveBy( ) and can be rotated with doRotateY( ). These methods affect the objectTG TransformGroup, which corresponds to the TG node above each model in Figure 18-4.

The movement and rotation methods affect the same TransformGroup so that rotations will influence movement. For example, when a sprite moves "forward," it *will* move forward according to the direction it is currently facing. In other words, the sprite's rotation affects its movement. doMove( ) makes the sprite move by the distance specified in a vector:

```
private void doMove(Vector3d theMove)
// move the sprite by the amount in theMove
{
  objectTG.getTransform( t3d );
  toMove.setTranslation(theMove);    // overwrite previous trans
  t3d.mul(toMove);
  objectTG.setTransform(t3d);
}
```

The Transform3D objects t3d and toMove are declared globally and created in the constructor of Sprite3D for efficiency reasons. The alternative would be to create a Transform3D object inside doMove( ) each time it was called. This would generate a lot of temporary objects over time, which would need to be garbage collected, causing the application to slow down while the objects were removed by the JVM.

doRotateY( ) is similar to doMove( ) and uses another global Transform3D object called toRot:

```
public void doRotateY(double radians)
// rotate the sprite by radians around its y-axis
{
  objectTG.getTransform( t3d );
  toRot.rotY(radians);    // overwrite previous rotation
  t3d.mul(toRot);
  objectTG.setTransform(t3d);
}
```

Obstacle and Boundary Detection

The sprite should not pass through obstacles or move off the floor. This behavior is achieved by utilizing a Obstacles object, called obs. A reference to obs is passed into the sprite at creation time and used in moveBy( ). moveBy( ) is the public movement method for the sprite and accepts a (x, z) step:

```
public boolean moveBy(double x, double z)
// Move the sprite by offsets x and z, but only if within
// the floor and there is no obstacle nearby.
{
  if (isActive( )) {
    Point3d nextLoc = tryMove(new Vector3d(x, 0, z));
    if (obs.nearObstacle(nextLoc, radius*OBS_FACTOR))  // ask Obstacles object
      return false;
    else {
      doMove( new Vector3d(x,0,z) );
      return true;
    }
  }
  else  // not active
    return false;
}
```

moveBy( ) calculates its next position by calling tryMove( ), which is almost the same as doMove( ) except that it does not adjust the position of objectTG. The possible new location, nextLoc, is passed to Obstacles's nearObstacle( ) for testing. If the new location is acceptable, the step will be made by calling doMove( ).

This approach nicely separates the issues of obstacle and boundary detection from the sprite, placing them in the Obstacles class. Another aim was to implement this form of collision detection without utilizing features in Java 3D.

Java 3D can be employed for collision detection in two main ways:

- Java 3D can generate an event when one shape intersects with another, which is processed by a Behavior object. The drawback is that such events only occur once the shapes have intersected. What is required is an event just before the shapes intersect.

- Java 3D picking can query whether moving the user's viewpoint will result in a collision with an object in the scene. Picking is a technique for selecting shapes inside the scene by shooting a line (or cone) from the viewer's location, through the mouse position, into the scene. When the line intersects with a shape in the scene, the shape's been picked. This approach is suitable for first-person games where the viewpoint represents the player. Tour3D is the beginnings of a third-person game, where the viewer is distinct from the player (the robot). I'll return to this picky question when I look at first-person games in Chapter 24.

Updating the Sprite

A comparison of Sprite (the 2D sprite class from Chapter 11) and Sprite3D highlights an important difference between the 2D and 3D games programming styles. The 2D games all use an update redraw cycle, with timer calculations to control the cycle's frequency. Sprite3D has no redraw method, and no explicit timer control of its redraw rate.

The difference is due to the high-level nature of Java 3D's scene graph. Java 3D controls graph rendering, so it handles redraws, including their frequency. At the programming level, you only have to change the scene (e.g., by adjusting the objectTG node) and let Java 3D do its thing. If you do want direct control, you can switch from Java 3D's default retained mode to immediate mode, but I won't explore that approach here. Immediate mode allows the programmer to specify when a scene should be rendered, but it's also the programmer's responsibility to manage the rendering scene data, which is a considerable amount of work.

The User's Touring Sprite

TourSprite subclasses Sprite3D to specify the movement step and rotation amounts of the user's sprite. Here are the relevant methods:

```
private final static double MOVERATE = 0.3;
private final static double ROTATE_AMT = Math.PI / 16.0;

public TourSprite(String fnm, Obstacles obs)
{ super(fnm, obs);  }

public boolean moveForward()
{ return moveBy(0.0, MOVERATE); }

public void rotClock()
{ doRotateY(-ROTATE_AMT); }  // clockwise
```

TourSprite doesn't contain any behavior code to specify when the move and rotation methods should be called and is placed in a separate Behavior class (TouristControls for TourSprite). Behavior classes are explained after the next section.

The Alien Sprite

A TimeBehavior object drives AlienSprite's chasing behavior by calling AlienSprite's update() method periodically. update() uses the alien's and robot's current positions to calculate a rotation that makes the alien turn to face the robot. Then the alien moves toward the robot. Once the alien is sufficiently close to the robot, an exciting message is printed to standard output (this is, after all, just a demo).

update() is defined as follows:

```
public void update()
// called by TimeBehaviour to update the alien
{ if (isActive()) {
    headTowardsTourist();
    if (closeTogether(getCurrLoc(), ts.getCurrLoc()))
      System.out.println("Alien and Tourist are close together");
  }
}
```

headTowardsTourist() rotates the sprite then attempts to move it forward:

```
private void headTowardsTourist()
{
  double rotAngle = calcTurn( getCurrLoc(), ts.getCurrLoc());
  double angleChg = rotAngle-currAngle;
  doRotateY(angleChg);   // rotate to face tourist
  currAngle = rotAngle;  // store new angle for next time
  if (moveForward())
    ;
  else if (moveLeft())
    ;
```

```
    else if (moveRight())
      ;
    else if (moveBackward())
      ;
    else
      System.out.println("Alien stuck!");
  }
```

`AlienSprite` extends `TourSprite` and uses the movement and rotation methods defined in that class.

A complication with the chasing behavior is how to deal with obstacles. If a move is blocked by an obstacle, then the move method (i.e., `moveForward()`, `moveLeft()`) returns `false`. `headTowardsTourist()` tries each method until one succeeds. This may lead to the sprite moving about in an inefficient manner due to the lack of any path planning, but this behavior is satisfactory (and fast) in a scene with few obstacles.

 Path planning using the A* algorithm is described in the 2D context in Chapter 13.

`calcTurn()` deals with seven possible positional relationships between the alien and the robot, which can be understood by referring to Figure 18-7.

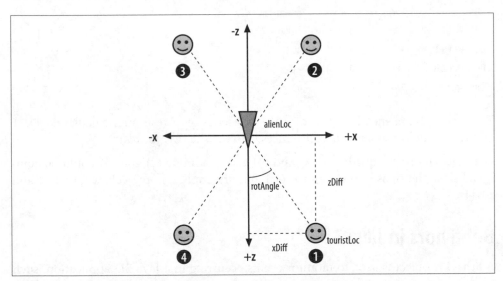

Figure 18-7. Possible angles between the alien and robot

The alien begins by facing along the positive z-axis, toward the user's viewpoint. The rotation (stored in `rotAngle`) is calculated relative to that starting angle so the rotation change from the previous orientation can be obtained by subtraction. The start of headTowardsTourist() contains this code:

```
double rotAngle = calcTurn( getCurrLoc(), ts.getCurrLoc());
double angleChg = rotAngle-currAngle;
doRotateY(angleChg);    // rotate to face tourist
currAngle = rotAngle;   // store new angle for next time
```

The tourist may be in any of the four quadrants marked in Figure 18-7, it may be on the positive or negative x-axes (i.e., with a zero z value), or may be at the same spot as the alien; altogether, there are seven possibilities.

 A positive rotation around the y-axis is counterclockwise.

The possibilities for rotAngle are shown in Table 18-1.

Table 18-1. Positions for the robot relative to the alien

Quadrant	x loc	z loc	rotAngle
(1)	+ve	+ve	arctan x/z
(2)	+ve	−ve	pi + arctan x/−z
(3)	−ve	−ve	pi + arctan −x/−z
(4)	−ve	+ve	arctan −x/z
On the +x axis	+ve	0	pi/2
On the −x axis	−ve	0	−pi/2
Same spot	0	0	0

These choices are encoded in calcTurn() as a series of if tests after calculating xDiff and zDiff (the x-axis and z-axis distances between the two sprites).

The calculations for quadrants (1) and (4) and quadrants (2) and (3) could be combined since the signs of the x and z locations are implicit in the values for xDiff and zDiff.

Behaviors in Java 3D

A Behavior object is used to monitor events occurring in a Java 3D application, such as key presses, the rendering of frames, the passage of time, the movement of the user's viewpoint, Transform3D changes, and collisions. These events, called *wakeup criteria*, activate the Behavior object so it can carry out specified tasks.

A typical Behavior subclass has the following format:

```
public class FooBehavior extends Behavior
{
  private WakeupCondition wc;     // what will wake the object
  // other global variables

  public FooBehavior(...)
  { // initialise globals
     wc = new ... //  create the wakeup criteria
  }

  public void initialize()
  // register interest in the wakeup criteria
  {  wakeupOn(wc);  }


  public void processStimulus(Enumeration criteria)
  {
     WakeupCriterion wakeup;
     while (criteria.hasMoreElements() ) {
       wakeup = (WakeupCriterion) criteria.nextElement();
       // determine the type of criterion assigned to wakeup;
       // carry out the relevant task;
     }
     wakeupOn(wc);  // reregister interest
  } // end of processStimulus()

} // end of FooBehavior class
```

A subclass of Behavior must implement initialize() and processStimulus().
initialize() should register the behavior's wakeup criteria, but other initialization
code can be placed in the constructor for the class. processStimulus() is called by
Java 3D when an event (or events) of interest to the behavior is received. Often,
processStimulus() being called is enough to decide what task should be carried out,
e.g., TimeBehavior. In more complex classes, the events passed to the object must be
analyzed. For example, a key press may be the wakeup condition, but the code will
need to determine which key was pressed.

 A common error when implementing processStimulus() is to forget to
re-register the wakeup criteria at the end of the method:

```
wakeupOn(wc);  // reregister interest
```

If this is skipped, the behavior won't be triggered again.

A WakeupCondition object can be a combination of one or more WakeupCriterion. There are many subclasses of WakeupCriterion, including:

WakeupOnAWTEvent

For AWT events such as key presses and mouse movements. WakeupOnAWTEvent is used in TouristControls.

WakeupOnElapsedFrames

An event can be generated after a specified number of renderings. This criterion should be used with care since it may result in the object being triggered many times per second.

WakeupOnElapsedTime

An event can be generated after a specified time interval. WakeupOnElapsedTime is used in TimeBehavior.

Another common mistake when using Behaviors is to forget to specify a scheduling volume (or region) with setSchedulingBounds( ). A Behavior node is only active (and able to receive events) when the user's viewpoint intersects a Behavior object's scheduling volume. If no volume is set, then the Behavior will never be triggered.

Controlling the Touring Sprite

The TouristControls object responds to key presses by moving the robot sprite or by changing the user's viewpoint. As the sprite moves, the viewpoint is automatically adjusted so the sprite and viewpoint stay a fixed distance apart. This is a simple form of third-person camera.

What's a Third-Person Camera?

A third-person camera is a viewpoint that semiautomatically or automatically tracks the user's sprite as it moves through a game. This is difficult to automate since the best vantage point for a camera depends on the sprite's position and orientation and on the location of nearby scenery and other sprites, as well as the focal point for the current action. A common solution is to offer the player a selection of several cameras.

Tour3D is simpler: the camera stays at a certain distance from the sprite, offset along the positive z-axis. This distance is maintained as the sprite moves forward, backward, left, and right. The only permitted adjustment to the camera is a zoom capability that reduces or increases the offset. Though this approach is simple, it is quite effective. The coding can be extended to support more complex changes in the camera's position and orientation.

As an added bonus, having a camera means that I no longer need to use Java 3D's OrbitBehavior class.

Setting Up TouristControls

The TourSprite and TouristControls are created and linked inside addTourist() in WrapTour3D:

```
private void addTourist()
{
  bob = new TourSprite("Coolrobo.3ds", obs);    // sprite
  bob.setPosition(2.0, 1.0);
  sceneBG.addChild( bob.getTG() );

  ViewingPlatform vp = su.getViewingPlatform();
  TransformGroup viewerTG = vp.getViewPlatformTransform();
                  // TransformGroup for the user's viewpoint

  TouristControls tcs = new TouristControls(bob, viewerTG);
                // sprite's controls
  tcs.setSchedulingBounds( bounds );
  sceneBG.addChild( tcs );
}
```

The TouristControls object (tcs) requires a reference to the TourSprite (called bob) to monitor and change its position, and a reference to the user's viewpoint TransformGroup (viewerTG) to move the viewpoint in line with the TourSprite's position.

The WakeupCondition for TouristControls is an AWT key press, which is specified in the constructor:

```
keyPress = new WakeupOnAWTEvent( KeyEvent.KEY_PRESSED );
```

The key press is then registered in initialize():

```
wakeupOn( keyPress );
```

processStimulus() checks that the criterion is an AWT event and responds to key presses:

```
public void processStimulus(Enumeration criteria)
{ WakeupCriterion wakeup;
  AWTEvent[] event;

  while( criteria.hasMoreElements() ) {
    wakeup = (WakeupCriterion) criteria.nextElement();
    if( wakeup instanceof WakeupOnAWTEvent ) {  // is it AWT?
      event = ((WakeupOnAWTEvent)wakeup).getAWTEvent();
      for( int i = 0; i < event.length; i++ ) { // many events
```

```
        if( event[i].getID() == KeyEvent.KEY_PRESSED )
          processKeyEvent((KeyEvent)event[i]);  // do something
      }
    }
  }
  wakeupOn( keyPress );  // re-register
}
```

All the testing and iteration through the event[] array leads to a call to processKeyEvent( ), which reacts to the key press.

Keys Understood by TouristControls

The user sprite can move in four directions: forward, backward, left, and right; it can also rotate left or right around the y-axis. The down, up, left, and right arrow keys cover forward, backward, rotate left, and rotate right. The Alt key combined with the left and right arrows support left and right movement (a sort of sidestepping).

One subtlety here is the choice of keys to denote direction. The down arrow key is most natural for representing forward when the sprite is facing out of the world, along the +z axis but is less appealing when the sprite has been rotated by 180 degrees and is facing into the scene. For this reason, it may be better to use letter keys such as f, b, l, and r for movement; however, I'm not convinced that letters are easier to remember (e.g., does r mean reverse or right?). The arrow keys have the advantage of being placed together on the keyboard.

The viewpoint can be zoomed in and out along the z-axis; those two operations are activated by the i and o keys.

processKeyEvent( )'s definition is shown here:

```
private void processKeyEvent(KeyEvent eventKey)
{ int keyCode = eventKey.getKeyCode();
  if( eventKey.isAltDown() )
    altMove(keyCode);
  else
    standardMove(keyCode);

  viewerMove();
}
```

Every key has a unique key code constant; each is listed at length in the documentation for the KeyEvent class. Checking for modifier keys, such as alt and shift, can be done by testing the KeyEvent object, e.g., see the isAltDown( ) test in processKeyEvent( ).

standardMove( ) calls the relevant methods in the TourSprite (called bob) depending on which key is pressed:

```
if(keycode == forwardKey )
  bob.moveForward();
else if(keycode == backKey )
  bob.moveBackward();
```

forwardKey and backKey (and others) are constants defined in TouristControls:

```
private final static int forwardKey = KeyEvent.VK_DOWN;
private final static int backKey = KeyEvent.VK_UP;
```

Viewpoint Initialization

The initial positioning of the user's viewpoint is done in TouristControls in the setViewer( ) method:

```
private void setViewer( )
{ bobPosn = bob.getCurrLoc();    // start location for bob
  viewerTG.getTransform( t3d );
  t3d.lookAt( new Point3d(bobPosn.x, HEIGHT, bobPosn.z + ZOFFSET),
          new Point3d(bobPosn.x, HEIGHT, bobPosn.z),
          new Vector3d(0,1,0));
  t3d.invert( );
  viewerTG.setTransform(t3d);
}
```

Transform3D.lookAt( ) specifies the viewer's position, the point being looked at, and the up direction. The coordinates are obtained from the TourSprite's original position. The viewpoint is raised HEIGHT units up the y-axis and ZOFFSET units away down the positive z-axis to give an overview of the robot.

It's important that the vector between the user's viewpoint and the sprite is at right angles to the XY plane. This means that a translation applied to the sprite will have the same effect when applied to the viewpoint. This issue is a consequence of the translation and rotation components of the viewer being applied to a single TransformGroup.

Moving the Camera

The camera is moved by viewerMove( ), which is called at the end of processKeyEvent( ) after the sprite's position or orientation has been altered.

viewerMove( ) obtains the new position of the sprite and calculates the translation relative to the previous position. This translation is then applied to the viewer:

```
private void viewerMove( )
{ Point3d newLoc = bob.getCurrLoc();
  Vector3d trans = new Vector3d( newLoc.x - bobPosn.x,
                      0, newLoc.z - bobPosn.z);
  viewerTG.getTransform( t3d );
  toMove.setTranslation(trans);
  t3d.mul(toMove);
  viewerTG.setTransform(t3d);
  bobPosn = newLoc;    // save for next time
}
```

Figure 18-8 shows two screenshots of Tour3D with the sprite in different locations and orientations, but the viewpoint is in the same relative position in both pictures.

Figure 18-8. Sprite movement affects the viewpoint

Zooming the Camera

Camera zooming is achieved by adjusting the z-axis distance between the viewpoint and the sprite. When the user presses i or o, shiftViewer( ) is called inside standardMove( ):

```
// other key processing in standardMove( )
else if(keycode == inKey)    // letter 'i'
  shiftViewer(-ZSTEP);
else if(keycode == outKey)   // letter 'o'
  shiftViewer(ZSTEP);
```

ZSTEP is set to be 1.0. shiftViewer( ) moves the TransformGroup by the required amount along the z-axis:

```
private void shiftViewer(double zDist)
{ Vector3d trans = new Vector3d(0,0,zDist);
  viewerTG.getTransform( t3d );
  toMove.setTranslation(trans);
  t3d.mul(toMove);
  viewerTG.setTransform(t3d);
}
```

Figure 18-9 shows the result of pressing i five times. Compare the viewpoint's position with the images in Figure 18-8 to see the effect of zooming.

Rotating the Camera

The TouristControls class doesn't support viewpoint rotation, but it's interesting to discuss the issues involved in implementing some form of rotation.

Figure 18-9. A closer view of the sprite

The first problem is to make sure that the rotations and translations applied to the sprite are echoed by the same rotations and translations of the viewpoint. If the viewpoint rotates by a different amount, then the sprite's translations will have a different effect on the viewpoint since it will be facing in a different direction. This echoing is best implemented by duplicating the Sprite3D methods for translation and rotation inside TouristControls. The coding will require some modifications since the viewpoint is facing toward the sprite, so its notions of forward, backward, left, and right are different.

Even if the rotations of the sprite and viewpoint are always aligned, problems will still occur. For instance, a 180-degree rotation of the sprite will cause a 180-degree rotation of the viewpoint, and the viewpoint will now be facing away from the sprite. This is a result of rotating the sprite and the viewpoint around their own centers, and the rotation of the viewpoint must use the sprite's position as its center of rotation.

Figure 18-10 shows the desired viewpoint rotation after the sprite has rotated 30 degrees.

In coding terms, this requires the viewpoint TransformGroup to be translated to the sprite's position, rotated, and then translated back. The translation back will be the negative of the first translation since the viewpoint's coordinate system will have been changed by the rotation.

A more fundamental question still remains: does rotation give the user a better view of the sprite? Unfortunately, the answer is "maybe." The problem is that the rotation may move the viewpoint inside a piece of scenery or otherwise block the view in some way. One solution is to offer the user several alternative viewpoints, in the hope that at least one of them will be useful. You'll learn how to implement multiple viewpoints in the Maze3D application in Chapter 25.

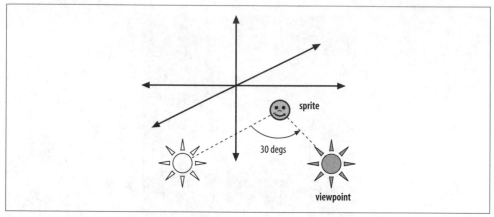

Figure 18-10. Viewpoint rotation

Updating the Alien Sprite

TimeBehavior acts as a Timer-like object for calling the update( ) method in AlienSprite every 500 milliseconds. The two are linked together by WrapTour3D in its addAlien( ) method:

```
private void addAlien( )
{
  AlienSprite al =  new AlienSprite("hand1.obj", obs, bob);   // alien
  al.setPosition(-6.0, -6.0);
  sceneBG.addChild( al.getTG( ) );

  TimeBehavior alienTimer = new TimeBehavior(500, al);  // alien's controls
  alienTimer.setSchedulingBounds( bounds );
  sceneBG.addChild( alienTimer );
}
```

The TimeBehavior class is simpler than TouristControls since its processStimulus( ) method being called is enough to trigger the call to update( ):

```
public class TimeBehavior extends Behavior
{
  private WakeupCondition timeOut;
  private AlienSprite alien;

  public TimeBehavior(int timeDelay, AlienSprite as)
  { alien = as;
    timeOut = new WakeupOnElapsedTime(timeDelay);
  }

  public void initialize( )
  { wakeupOn( timeOut );  }
```

```
    public void processStimulus( Enumeration criteria )
    { alien.update();        // ignore criteria
      wakeupOn( timeOut ); // re-register
    }
}
```

The wakeup criterion is an instance of WakeupOnElapsedTime.

CHAPTER 19

Animated 3D Sprites

This chapter and the next deal with sprite animation. The Sprite3D class of Chapter 18 possesses a rudimentary kind of animation, allowing the entire sprite to be moved over the XY plan and rotated around the y-axis. The kind of animation we'll be discussing here allows parts of the figure to move; for example, to have a robot wave its arms, jump, or turn its head.

There are three common animation approaches:

- Keyframe animation
- Figure articulation
- Figure articulation with skinning

Keyframe animation is similar to the technique used in the 2D Sprite class from Chapter 11. However, instead of using a sequence of 2D images, a sequence of 3D models is used. Each model is represented by the same figure but is positioned slightly differently; rapid switching between the models creates the illusion of sprite movement. Poses can be organized into an *animation sequence*, so, for example, walking is represented by a sequence of different leg positions. A sequence is typically triggered by the user pressing a key (e.g., the down arrow, to move the sprite forward) or by other external events. A simple keyframe animation system is developed in this chapter.

Figure articulation represents a figure (or any articulated model) as a series of interconnected components. These components typically represent the limbs of a figure and can be moved and rotated. The movement of one limb affects the limbs connected to it, usually through the process of forward or inverse kinematics. Figure articulation with forward kinematics is detailed in Chapter 20.

Figure articulation with skinning extends the articulation technique by layering a mesh (skin) over the limbs (bones). As limbs move, the mesh is automatically moved and distorted to keep the components covered. Links and further information on skinning are provided in Chapter 20.

Keyframe Animation in This Chapter

The main example in this chapter, AnimSprite3D, loads several models, representing different positions for the sprite, including standing and walking poses. The poses are organized into an animation sequence managed by an Animator object.

 This application runs in a medium-sized window. At the end of the chapter, though, you'll see how to modify it to use Full-Screen Exclusive Mode (FSEM), and you'll learn how to modify the display mode for the monitor with FSEM.

Figure 19-1 contains two screenshots: the image on the left shows the sprite (a "stick child") walking, and the right hand image has the sprite punching.

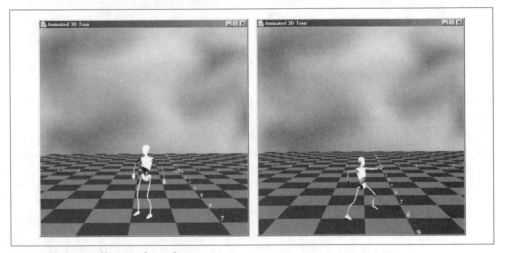

Figure 19-1. A walking and punching sprite

 The application in this chapter does not include a chasing alien sprite, scenery, or any obstacles. However, these could be added by using the techniques described in Chapter 18.

Class Diagrams for AnimTour3D

Figure 19-2 shows the class diagrams for the classes in the AnimTour3D application. Only the class names are shown to reduce the amount of detail.

AnimTour3D is the top-level JFrame for the application. WrapAnimTour3D creates the 3D scene and is similar to the earlier Wrap classes in that it creates the checkered floor and lighting. It loads the stick child sprite and sets up the sprite's controlling behaviors. PropManager is unchanged from the class in the Loader3D application in Chapter 16. CheckerFloor and ColouredTiles are unchanged from previous examples.

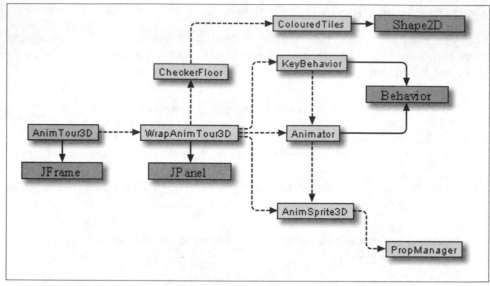

Figure 19-2. Class diagrams for AnimTour3D

KeyBehavior and Animator are subclasses of Behavior. KeyBehavior is triggered by key presses, like those used in the Tour3D from Chapter 18. It responds by requesting that the Animator object adds animation sequences to its animation schedule. Animator wakes up periodically and processes the next animation in its schedule, thereby altering the sprite.

 The code for this application is in *AnimTour3D/*.

Creating the Scene

Figure 19-3 shows all the methods in WrapAnimTour3D Class.

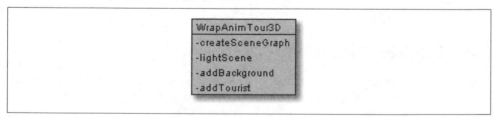

Figure 19-3. WrapAnimTour3D methods

The Scene-creation Code In WrapAnimTour3D is almost identical to previous Wrap classes with the exception of the addTourist( ) method. It sets up the sprite, the KeyBehavior, and Animator objects, and links them together as shown in the application's class diagram (see Figure 19-2):

```
private void addTourist( )
{ // sprite
  AnimSprite3D bob = new AnimSprite3D( );
  bob.setPosition(2.0, 1.0);
  sceneBG.addChild( bob.getTG( ) );

  // viewpoint TG
  ViewingPlatform vp = su.getViewingPlatform( );
  TransformGroup viewerTG = vp.getViewPlatformTransform( );

  // sprite's animator
  Animator animBeh = new Animator(20, bob, viewerTG);
  animBeh.setSchedulingBounds( bounds );
  sceneBG.addChild( animBeh );

  // sprite's input keys
  KeyBehavior kb = new KeyBehavior(animBeh);
  kb.setSchedulingBounds( bounds );
  sceneBG.addChild( kb );
} // end of addTourist( )
```

The AnimSprite3D object is responsible for loading the multiple models that represent the sprite's various poses. Animator is in charge of adjusting the user's viewpoint and so is passed the ViewingPlatform's TransformGroup node. The Animator is set to wake up every 20 milliseconds through the first argument of its constructor.

The scene graph for the application is shown in Figure 19-4. Since there's no alien sprite, scenery, or obstacles, it's simpler than the scene graph in Chapter 18.

The Animated 3D Sprite

Figure 19-5 shows the visible methods of AnimSprite3D.

The interface of this class is almost identical to Sprite3D (from the Tour3D application in Chapter 18). The setPosition( ), moveBy( ), and doRotateY( ) operations adjust the position and orientation of the sprite, isActive( ) and setActive( ) relate to the sprite's activity (i.e., whether it is visible on the screen or not), getCurrLoc( ) returns the sprite's position, and getTG( ) returns its top-level TransformGroup.

The only new method is setPose( ), which takes a pose name as an argument and changes the displayed model accordingly. Its implementation is explained later in this section.

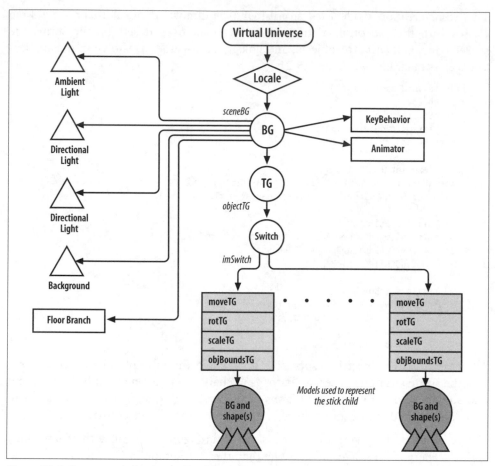

Figure 19-4. Scene graph for the application

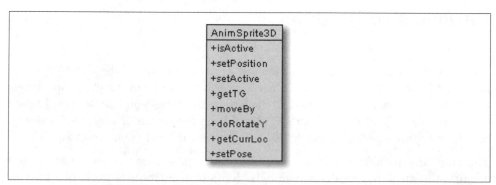

Figure 19-5. The public methods of AnimSprite3D

Loading the Poses

The choice of models is hardwired into AnimSprite3D, which makes things simpler than having to deal with arbitrary input. The names of the models are predefined in the poses[] array:

```
private final static String poses[] =
        {"stand", "walk1", "walk2", "rev1", "rev2", "rotClock",
         "rotCC", "mleft", "mright", "punch1", "punch2"};
```

The names in poses[] are used by loadPoses() to load the same-named 3D Studio Max files using PropManager. The loaded models (the different sprite poses) are attached to the scene using a Java 3D Switch node:

```
private void loadPoses()
{ PropManager propMan;

  imSwitch = new Switch(Switch.CHILD_MASK);
  imSwitch.setCapability(Switch.ALLOW_SWITCH_WRITE);

  maxPoses = poses.length;
  for (int i=0; i < maxPoses; i++) {
    propMan = new PropManager(poses[i] + ".3ds", true);
    imSwitch.addChild( propMan.getTG() );   // add obj to switch
  }

  visIms = new BitSet( maxPoses );     // bitset used for switching
  currPoseNo = STAND_NUM;  // sprite standing still
  setPoseNum( currPoseNo );
}
```

The Switch node (imSwitch) is shown in the scene graph in Figure 19-4. It's a child of the objectTG TransformGroup, which is used for positioning and rotating the sprite. The purpose of the Switch node is to allow the sprite to strike up a different pose by choosing one from the selection hanging below the Switch.

imSwitch is created with the CHILD_MASK value, which permits pose switching to be carried out using a Java 3D BitSet object (visIms). The bits of the BitSet are mapped to the children of the Switch: bit 0 corresponds to child 0, bit 1 to child 1, and so on. BitSet offers various methods for clearing bits and setting them.

The bit manipulation is hidden inside the setPoseNum() method, which takes as its input the bit index that should be turned on in imSwitch:

```
private void setPoseNum(int idx)
{ visIms.clear();
  visIms.set( idx );   // show child with index idx
  imSwitch.setChildMask( visIms );
  currPoseNo = idx;
}
```

The model stored in the idx position below the Switch node is made visible when setChildMask( ) is called.

The runtime adjustment of the Switch requires its write capability to be turned on.

Where Did These Models Come From?

I created the models using Poser (*http://www.curiouslabs.com*), which specializes in 3D figure creation and animation and includes a range of predefined models, poses, and animation sequences. Poser fans should check out the collection of links in the Google directory: *http://directory.google.com/Top/Computers/Software/Graphics/3D/ Animation_and_Design_Tools/Poser/*. I used one of Poser's existing figures, the stick child, and exported different versions of it in various standard poses to 3DS files. Poser animation sequences weren't utilized; each file only contains a single figure.

> Though I used Poser, any 3D modeling tool would be fine. MilkShape 3D, for example, is a good shareware product (*http://www.swissquake.ch/ chumbalum-soft/ms3d/*).

The models were loaded into the Loader3D application (developed in Chapter 16) to adjust their position and orientation. Poser exports 3DS models oriented with the XZ plane as their base, which means that the model is lying flat on its back when loaded into Loader3D.

> Each 3DS file is about 20 KB due to the choice of a simple model.

Setting a Pose

A sprite's pose is changed by calling setPose( ), which takes a pose name as its input argument. The method determines the index position of that name in the poses[ ] array and calls setPoseNum( ):

```
public boolean setPose(String name)
{ if (isActive()) {
    int idx = getPoseIndex(name);
    if ((idx < 0) || (idx > maxPoses-1))
      return false;
    setPoseNum( idx );
    return true;
  }
  else
    return false;
}
```

The code is complicated by the need to check for sprite activity. An inactive sprite is invisible, so there's no point changing its pose.

 The use of a name as the setPose( ) argument means that the caller must know the pose names used in poses[]. The alternative would be to use the child index position in the Switch node, which is harder to remember.

Sprite Activity

Sprite activity can be toggled on and off by calls to setActive( ) with a Boolean argument:

```
public void setActive(boolean b)
{ isActive = b;
  if (!isActive) {
    visIms.clear();
    imSwitch.setChildMask( visIms );   // display nothing
  }
  else if (isActive)
    setPoseNum( currPoseNo );   // make visible
}
```

This approach requires a global integer, currPoseNo, which records the index of the current pose. It's used to make the sprite visible after a period of inactivity.

Floor Boundary Detection

The movement and rotation methods in AnimSprite3D are unchanged from Sprite3D except in the case of the moveBy( ) method. The decision not to use obstacles means there's no Obstacle object available for checking if the sprite is about to move off the floor. This is remedied by a beyondEdge( ) method, which determines if the sprite's (x, z) coordinate is outside the limits of the floor:

```
public boolean moveBy(double x, double z)
// move the sprite by an (x,z) offset
{ if (isActive()) {
    Point3d nextLoc = tryMove( new Vector3d(x, 0, z));
    if (beyondEdge(nextLoc.x) || beyondEdge(nextLoc.z))
      return false;
    else {
      doMove( new Vector3d(x, 0, z) );
      return true;
    }
  }
  else    // not active
    return false;}  // end of moveBy( )
```

```
private boolean beyondEdge(double pos)
{ if ((pos < -FLOOR_LEN/2) || (pos > FLOOR_LEN/2))
    return true;
  return false;
}
```

Controlling the Sprite

The sprite's movements are controlled by key presses, caught by a KeyBehavior object. KeyBehavior is a version of the TouristControls class of Chapter 18 but without the key processing parts. What remains is the testing of the key press to decide which method of the Animator class to call. standardMove( ) shows how a key press (actually its key code) is converted into different calls to the Animator object (called animBeh):

```
private void standardMove(int keycode)
{ if(keycode == forwardKey )
    animBeh.moveForward( );
  else if ...  // more if-tests of keycode
    ...
  else if(keycode == activeKey)
    animBeh.toggleActive( );
  else if(keycode == punchKey)
    animBeh.punch( );
  else if(keycode == inKey)
    animBeh.shiftInViewer( );
  else if(keycode == outKey)
    animBeh.shiftOutViewer( );
}
```

The activeKey key code, the letter a, is used for toggling the sprite's activity. When the sprite is active, it's visible in the scene and can be affected by key presses. When it's inactive, the sprite is invisible and nothing affects it (apart from the a key).

The punchKey key code (the letter p) sets the sprite into punching pose, as illustrated by the righthand image in Figure 19-1.

Animating the Sprite

Figure 19-6 shows the visible methods in Animator.

Animator performs three core tasks:

- It adds animation sequences to its schedule in response to calls from the KeyBehavior object.
- It periodically removes an animation operation from its schedule and executes it. The execution typically changes the sprite's position and pose. A removal is triggered by the arrival of a Java 3D WakeupOnElapsedTime event.
- It updates the user's viewpoint in response to calls from KeyBehavior.

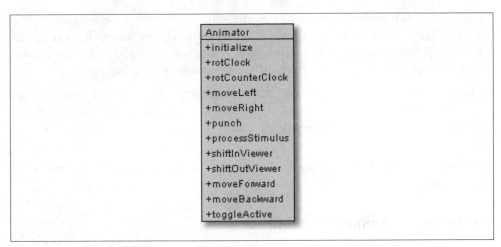

Figure 19-6. Public methods in the Animator class

Adding an Animation Sequence

The majority of the public methods in Animator (rotClock( ), rotCounterClock( ), moveLeft( ), moveRight( ), punch( ), moveForward( ), moveBackwards( ), and toggleActive( )) execute in a similar way when called by the KeyBehavior object. They add a predefined animation sequence to a schedule (which is implemented as an ArrayList called animSchedule):

```
public void moveForward( )
{ addAnims(forwards); }
```

forwards is an array of strings, which represents the animation sequence for moving the sprite forward one step:

```
private final static String forwards[] = {"walk1", "walk2", "stand"};
```

"walk1", "walk2", and so forth are the names of the 3DS files holding the sprite's pose This correspondence is used to load the models when AnimTour3D starts.

A requirement of an animation sequence is that it ends with "stand". One reason for this is that a sequence should end with the model in a neutral position, so the next sequence can follow on smoothly from the previous one. The other reason is the Animator object uses "stand" to detect the end of a sequence.

addAnims( ) adds the sequence to the end of animSchedule and increments seqCount, which stores the number of sequences currently in the schedule:

```
synchronized private void addAnims(String ims[])
{ if (seqCount < MAX_SEQS) {   // not too many animation sequences
    for(int i=0; i < ims.length; i++)
      animSchedule.add(ims[i]);
    seqCount++;
  }
}
```

The maximum number of sequences in the schedule at any time is restricted to MAX_SEQS. This ensures that a key press (or, equivalently, an animation sequence) isn't kept waiting too long in the schedule before being processed. This would happen if the user pressed a key continuously, causing a long schedule to form.

By limiting the number of sequences, the Animator briefly ignores key presses when the waiting animation sequence gets too long. However, once the animation sequence gets smaller (after some of it has been processed), key presses will be accepted.

addAnims() is synchronized so it's impossible for the animSchedule to be read while being extended.

Processing an Animation Operation

The Animator constructor creates a WakeupCondition object based on the time delay passed to it from WrapAnimTour3D:

```
public Animator(int td, AnimSprite3D b, TransformGroup vTG)
{   timeDelay = new WakeupOnElapsedTime(td);
    // the rest of Animator's initialization
}
```

This condition is registered in initialize() so processStimulus() will be called every td milliseconds:

```
public void processStimulus( Enumeration criteria )
{ // don't bother looking at the criteria
  String anim = getNextAnim();
  if (anim != null)
    doAnimation(anim);
  wakeupOn( timeDelay );
}
```

processStimulus() is short since there's no need to examine the wake-up criteria. Since it's been called is enough because a call occurs every td milliseconds.

getNextAnim() wants to remove an animation operation from animSchedule. However, the ArrayList may be empty, so the method can return null:

```
synchronized private String getNextAnim()
{ if (animSchedule.isEmpty())
    return null;
  else {
    String anim = (String) animSchedule.remove(0);
    if (anim.equals("stand"))    // end of a sequence
      seqCount--;
    return anim;
  }
}
```

getNextAnim() is synchronized to enforce mutual exclusion on animSchedule. If the retrieved operation is "stand", then the end of an animation sequence has been reached, and seqCount is decremented. My defense of this wonderful design is that "stand" performs two useful roles: it signals the end of a sequence (as here), and changes the sprite pose to a standing position, which is a neutral stance before the next sequence begins.

doAnimation( ) can process an animation operation (represented by a String) in two ways: the operation may trigger a transformation in the user's sprite (called bob), and/or cause a change to the sprite's pose. In addition, it may be necessary to update the user's viewpoint if the sprite has moved:

```
private void doAnimation(String anim)
{ /* Carry out a transformation on the sprite.
    Note: "stand", "punch1", "punch2" have no transforms
  */
  if ( anim.equals("walk1") || anim.equals("walk2"))    // forward
    bob.moveBy(0.0, MOVERATE/2);        // half a step
  else if ( anim.equals("rev1") || anim.equals("rev2"))  // back
    bob.moveBy(0.0, -MOVERATE/2);       // half a step
  else if (anim.equals("rotClock"))
    bob.doRotateY(-ROTATE_AMT);         // clockwise rot
  else if (anim.equals("rotCC"))
    bob.doRotateY(ROTATE_AMT);          // counterclockwise rot
  else if (anim.equals("mleft"))        // move left
    bob.moveBy(-MOVERATE,0.0);
  else if (anim.equals("mright"))       // move right
    bob.moveBy(MOVERATE,0.0);
  else if (anim.equals("toggle")) {
    isActive = !isActive;       // toggle activity
    bob.setActive(isActive);
  }

  // update the sprite's pose, except for "toggle"
  if (!anim.equals("toggle"))
    bob.setPose(anim);

  viewerMove();     // update the user's viewpoint
} // end of doAnimation()
```

The first part of doAnimation( ) specifies how an animation operation is translated into a sprite transformation. One trick is shown in the processing of the forward and backwards sequences. These sequences are defined as:

```
private final static String forwards[] = {"walk1","walk2","stand"};
private final static String backwards[] = {"rev1","rev2","stand"};
```

The forwards sequence is carried out in response to the user pressing the down arrow. What happens? The sequence is made up of three poses ("walk1", "walk2", and "stand"), so the sequence will be spread over three activations of processStimulus( ). This means that the total sequence will take 3*<time delay> to be evaluated, which is about 60 ms. Multiple steps forward are achieved by adding multiple copies of the forward sequence to the Animator's scheduler list.

The punching animation sequence is defined as:

```
private final static String punch[] =
        {"punch1", "punch1", "punch2", "punch2", "stand"};
```

Since `"punch1"` and `"punch2"` appear twice, they will be processed twice by `processStimulus()`, which means their effects will last for 2*<time delay>. Consequently, the poses will be on the screen for twice the normal time, suggesting that the sprite is holding its stance.

Updating the User's Viewpoint

`Animator` uses the viewpoint manipulation code developed in `TouristControls` (in Chapter 18). As a sprite moves, the viewpoint sticks with it, staying a constant distance away unless the user zooms the viewpoint in or out.

The initial viewpoint is set up in `Animator`'s constructor via a call to `setViewer()`, which is the same method as in `TouristControls`.

The new problem with `Animator` is when to update the viewpoint. It shouldn't be updated until the animation operation (e.g., `"walk1"`) is executed. For that reason, the viewpoint update method, `viewerMove()`, is called at the end of `doAnimation()`.

The final aspects of viewpoint adjustment are the keys i and o, which zoom the viewpoint in and out. The keys are immediately processed in `Animator` by `shiftViewer()`, which changes the viewpoint based on the sprite's current position:

```
public void shiftInViewer()
{  shiftViewer(-ZSTEP); }    // move viewer negatively on z-axis

public void shiftOutViewer()
{  shiftViewer(ZSTEP); }

private void shiftViewer(double zDist)
// move the viewer inwards or outwards
{ Vector3d trans = new Vector3d(0,0,zDist);
  viewerTG.getTransform( t3d );
  toMove.setTranslation(trans);
  t3d.mul(toMove);
  viewerTG.setTransform(t3d);
}
```

The shift operations aren't scheduled like the other sprite movement commands. As a consequence, the `Animator` changes the viewpoint immediately, even if a large number of sprite movement key presses precede the i or o keys. This behavior may be disconcerting to a user since the viewpoint seems to change too soon before earlier sprite moves have been carried out.

An obvious question is why do I support this strange behavior? Why not schedule the viewpoint zooming along with the sprite animation? The answer is to illustrate that viewpoint and sprite changes can be separated.

Full-Screen Exclusive Mode (FSEM)

FSEM was introduced back in J2SE 1.4 as a way of switching off Java's windowing system and allowing direct drawing to the screen. The principal reason for this is speed, an obvious advantage for games. Secondary benefits include the ability to control the bit depth and size of the screen (its display mode). Advanced graphics techniques such as page flipping and stereo buffering are often only supported by display cards when FSEM is enabled.

FSEM was discussed in the context of 2D games in Chapter 4. The code described in this section uses *passive rendering*, which means that Java 3D is left in control of when to render to the screen.

 An excellent Java tutorial on FSEM is at *http://java.sun.com/docs/ books/tutorial/extra/fullscreen/*, which includes good overviews of topics like passive and active rendering, page flipping, and display modes. A few examples include the useful *CapabilitiesTest.java* program, which allows you to test your machine for FSEM support.

A Full-Screen Version of the Application

The `AnimTourFS` application is essentially `AnimTour3D`, but with the original `AnimTour3D` and `WrapAnimTour3D` classes replaced by a single new class, `AnimTourFS`. `AnimTourFS` contains the new FSEM-related code. The rest of the classes are unchanged, as Figure 19-7 shows.

Application invocation must include the option -Dsun.java2d.noddraw=true:

```
java -cp %CLASSPATH%;ncsa\portfolio.jar  -Dsun.java2d.noddraw=true AnimTourFS
```

The `noddraw` property switches off the use of Window's DirectDraw for drawing AWT elements and off-screen surfaces. This avoids a problem which first appeared when using the OpenGL version of Java 3D 1.3 with J2SE 1.4 and DirectX 7.0. Version numbers have moved on since then, so you may want to see what happens without the `noddraw` option.

Creating the Full-Screen Scene

Figure 19-8 shows all the methods in the `AnimTourFS` class and should be compared with Figure 19-3, which lists the methods in the old `WrapAnimTour3D` class.

`main( )` is new; all the other changes are inside the `AnimTourFS( )` constructor (with the addition of some new private global variables).

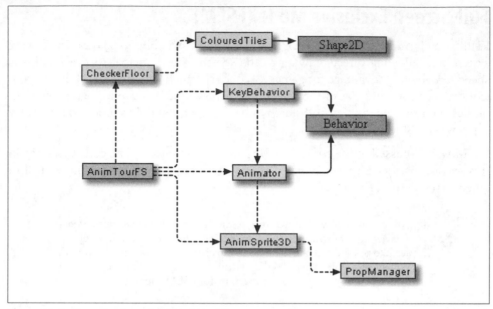

Figure 19-7. Class diagrams for AnimTourFS

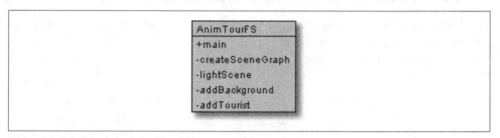

Figure 19-8. Methods in AnimTourFS

FSEM works poorly with Swing components, so AnimTourFS( ) uses a Frame object as the top-level window and embeds the Canvas3D GUI inside it:

```
private Frame win;   // global, required at quit time

GraphicsConfiguration config =
        SimpleUniverse.getPreferredConfiguration( );

win = new Frame("AnimTourFS", config);   // use SU's preference
win.setUndecorated(true) ;
           // no menu bar, borders, etc. or Swing components
win.setResizable(false);    // fixed size display


Canvas3D canvas3D = new Canvas3D(config);    // set up canvas3D
win.add(canvas3D);
```

The graphics configuration of the Frame is set to the one preferred by Java 3D. FSEM likes a fixed-size window with no decoration.

FSEM is handled through a GraphicsDevice object representing the screen, which is accessed via a GraphicsEnvironment reference. There may be several GraphicsDevice objects for a machine if, for example, it uses dual monitors. However, for the normal single-monitor system, the getDefaultScreenDevice( ) method is sufficient:

```
private GraphicsDevice gd;    // global


GraphicsEnvironment ge =
  GraphicsEnvironment.getLocalGraphicsEnvironment( );
gd = ge.getDefaultScreenDevice( );
```

Once the GraphicsDevice object (gd) has been obtained, it's a good idea to check if FSEM is supported by the user's OS before attempting to use it:

```
if (!gd.isFullScreenSupported( )) {
  System.out.println("FSEM not supported.") ;
  System.out.println("Device = " + gd) ;
  System.exit(0) ;
}


gd.setFullScreenWindow(win); // set FSEM
if (gd.getFullScreenWindow( ) == null)
  System.out.println("Did not get FSEM");
else
  System.out.println("Got FSEM") ;
```

If GraphicsDevice.setFullScreenWindow( ) cannot switch to FSEM mode, then it will position the window at (0,0) and resize to fit the screen, so the application can continue without being overly affected.

The final task is to switch off FSEM when the program terminates, which is done as part of the response to a quit key being pressed:

```
canvas3D.addKeyListener( new KeyAdapter( ) {
  public void keyPressed(KeyEvent e)
  { int keyCode = e.getKeyCode( );
    if ((keyCode == KeyEvent.VK_ESCAPE) || (keyCode == KeyEvent.VK_Q) ||
        (keyCode == KeyEvent.VK_END) ||
        ((keyCode == KeyEvent.VK_C) && e.isControlDown( )) ) {
      gd.setFullScreenWindow(null);  // exit FSEM
      win.dispose( );
      System.exit(0);
    }
  }
});
```

Figure 19-9 shows the FSEM in operation. Note the absence of a window frame or any other decoration.

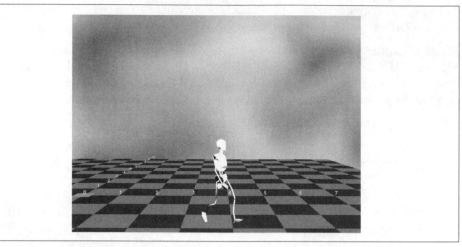

Figure 19-9. AnimTourFS in action

Changing the Display Mode

Once an application is in FSEM, further performance gains may be available by adjusting the screen's display mode (i.e., its bit depth, height, width, and refresh rate). *Bit depth* is the number of bits per pixel, and *refresh rate* is how frequently the monitor updates itself. Reducing the bit depth will increase rendering speed, but there may be an impact on the quality of the textures and other images in the scene.

A crucial thing to do when changing the display mode is to store the original version so it can be restored at the end of execution, as shown in the following code. In AnimTourFS( ), you should change the display mode after FSEM has been initiated:

```
private DisplayMode origDM = null;  // global


if (gd.isDisplayChangeSupported()) {
  origDM = gd.getDisplayMode();
  gd.setDisplayMode(
      new DisplayMode( origDM.getWidth(), origDM.getHeight(),
              origDM.getBitDepth()/2,
              origDM.getRefreshRate() ));
}
```

The code checks if display changing is supported via a call to GraphicsDevice. isDisplayChangeSupported( ), stores the original display mode, and updates the mode using the original screen dimensions and refresh rate but halving the bit depth (with the aim of increasing the rendering speed).

This reduces the bit depth of my machine from 32 to 16 bits.

The original display mode is restored at the end of the program by two extra lines in the quit key listener:

```
if ((keyCode == KeyEvent.VK_ESCAPE) || (keyCode == KeyEvent.VK_Q) ||
    (keyCode == KeyEvent.VK_END) ||
    ((keyCode == KeyEvent.VK_C) && e.isControlDown()) ) {
  if (origDM != null)  // original was saved
    gd.setDisplayMode(origDM);
  gd.setFullScreenWindow(null);
  win.dispose( );
  System.exit(0);
}
```

Figure 19-10 shows `AnimTourFS` with its reduced bit depth.

Figure 19-10. Reduced bit depth AnimTourFS

The 24-bit JPEG used for the background has become rather pixilated as you would expect with only 16 bits per pixel. I didn't notice any acceleration in rendering, but that may be because the scene is already so easy to render.

 The Java FSEM tutorial (*http://java.sun.com/docs/books/tutorial/extra/fullscreen/*) includes a section on display modes and an example showing how to use them.

Pros and Cons of Keyframe Animation

The advantage of using multiple models is they can be designed and created outside of Java 3D with software specific to the task (I used Poser). Model creation can be carried out independently of game development, perhaps assigned to someone skilled in 3D modeling. An animation sequence is a combination of poses, which you can mix and match. For example, the poses needed in a fighting game will be different from those in a sports game.

Several Java 3D loaders support keyframe animation. For example, the NWN loader (*http://nwn-j3d.sourceforge.net/loader.about.php*) defines animations as frames sequences which refer to the Never Winter Night models. Playing an animation consists of calling the loader's playAnimation( ) method with the name of the animation sequence. You'll find a list of all the keyframe animation loaders in Chapter 14.

A major drawback is the potential size of each model and the number of models required to cover all the necessary positions. I chose the simplest figure (size 20 KB) and a small number of poses (13), coming to 260 KB, which must be loaded at startup. These numbers could become unmanageable with larger models and more poses, but that depends on the application. One means of reducing the memory requirements is to share poses between the sprites (by using Java 3D SharedGroup nodes), which would be useful for groups of similar sprites, such as soldiers. This would require changes to the implementation detailed in this chapter.

CHAPTER 20

An Articulated, Moveable Figure

This chapter describes the implementation of an *articulated figure* (sprite), composed of moveable and rotatable limbs, which can be instructed to walk, run, and jump around a checkerboard floor.

 This work is based on the first part of a student project carried out for me by Thana Konglikhit in 2003–2004.

Chapter 19 was concerned with sprite animation but used the keyframe animation of multiple models. Advantages of figure articulation over keyframes include the increase in control over the figure and the reduction in memory requirements since only one model is being manipulated.

A disadvantage of articulation is the model will probably be a Java 3D creature of cylinders, spheres, and blocks, which must be "dressed" in some way. This will usually necessitate the loading of 3D models, which may bring back the problem of excessive memory usage.

Another issue is the increased complexity of the control code, which requires some mechanism for coordinating the movement of numerous TransformGroups; for instance, a single step forward will affect many joints, and the exact changes needed aren't obvious. I utilize forward kinematics in this chapter.

There are several ways of extending the basic articulation technique, including the use of mesh deformation, morphing, and skinning, which I briefly mention at the end.

The Articulated Figure Application

The Mover3D application demonstrates the articulated figure approach.

The lefthand picture in Figure 20-1 shows the figure's initial stance and the right-hand one is the position after the following commands have been processed:

```
urLeg f 40, lrLeg f -40, ulArm f 20, llArm f 20, chest t 10, head t -10
```

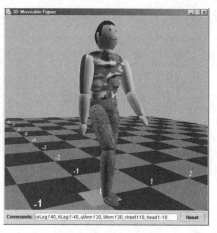

Figure 20-1. Initial position and after limb movement

The commands are typed into a text field at the bottom of the application window and processed when Enter is pressed. All the commands are carried out as a group, causing a single reorientation of the figure.

The first four commands specify forward (f in the command line above) rotations of the limbs representing the upper part of the right leg (urLeg), the lower-right leg (lrLeg), the upper-left arm (ulArm), and the lower part of the left arm (llArm). The chest and head are turned (t) left and right respectively, so the head stays facing forward.

Pressing Enter again repeats the commands, though when a limb reaches its pre-defined maximum positive or negative rotation, operations that would rotate it beyond these limits are ignored. Figure 20-2 shows the result of executing the command line from Figure 20-1 a few more times. Several of the limbs have reached their rotational limits, including the upper-right leg and the upper-left arm.

 The right arm passes through the right leg because Mover3D does not employ collision avoidance to prevent limbs from intersecting.

Aside from commands that influence individual limbs, several affect the entire fig-ure, moving it over the floor and rotating it around the y-axis. These commands can

Figure 20-2. Repeated limb movements

be typed into the text field or entered by pressing arrow keys on the keyboard. Figure 20-3 displays the outcome of the text field commands:

    f, f, c, c, f, f

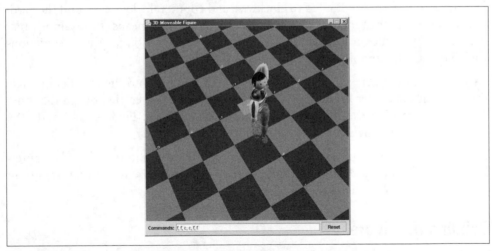

Figure 20-3. Figure movement

This sequence causes the figure to move from its starting position at (0,0) on the floor, forward 0.6 units (2×0.3), 45 degrees to its right (two 22.5 degree turns), and forward another 0.6 units.

The move increment and rotation angle are hardwired into the code. An advantage of 22.5 degrees is that four turns total 90 degrees, and 16 turns bring the figure back to its original orientation.

Figure 20-4 is a view of the scene after repeating the f, f, c, c, f, f commands three times.

Figure 20-4. Repeated figure movement

The figure can move up and down (i.e., it can float), but it can't be lowered below floor level. Rotations are limited to clockwise and counterclockwise around the vertical, with no support for turns about the x- or z-axes. This means, for example, that the figure cannot lie on its back on the floor. The main reason for these restrictions was to reduce the complexity of the implementation.

As with the limb operations, all figure commands entered into the text field update the figure at once after Enter is pressed. The operations are carried out in the order specified by reading the input sequence from left to right. Figures 20-3 and 20-4 show that the entire figure moves and rotates as a single unit.

Figure 20-5 illustrates the result of pressing the Reset button in the GUI: the figure's limbs are rotated back to their starting position, but the figure remains at its current position and orientation on the floor.

Building the Figure

The figure is created by connecting together instances of the Limb class. The shape of a limb is specified using a LatheShape3D object (introduced in Chapter 17), and its appearance is derived from a texture.

As the limbs are connected, they form a parent/child hierarchy. Each limb can be given an initial orientation relative to its parent limb, and it can be rotated around its x-, y-, and z-axes at runtime. A limb may be invisible, which enables it to be used as a connector between other limbs without being rendered. For example, invisible limbs are used to connect the arms to the torso.

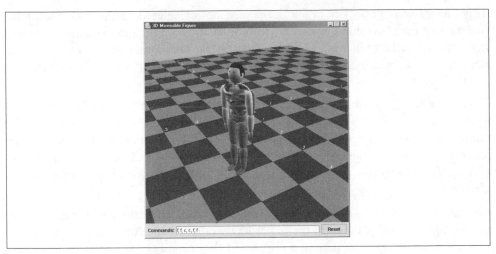

Figure 20-5. Reset limbs

Though the aim is to make a limbed, human figure, the Limb class is sufficiently general to be used to build most kinds of articulated shapes.

Forward and Inverse Kinematics

Before talking about forward and inverse kinematics, it's useful to review the parent-child relationship utilized by the nodes in a Java 3D scene graph. This hierarchy is particularly important for sequences of TransformGroup nodes.

Figure 20-6 shows a simple hierarchy made up of a parent and a child TransformGroup. The parent holds a translation of (1, 1, 2), and the child a translation of (2, 3, 1). However, from the world's viewpoint, the child's translation will be (3, 4, 3), a combination of the parent and child values. Here, the combination is an addition of the local translations, but it becomes more complicated when introducing rotation and scaling elements.

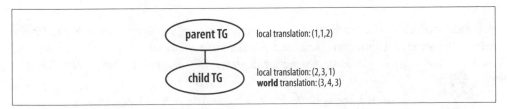

Figure 20-6. A hierarchy of TransformGroups

In general, the world (or scene) view of a TransformGroup is a combination of its translation, rotations, and scaling with those of its ancestors (parent, grandparent, and so on).

This hierarchy is important when developing an articulated figure since each limb contains several `TransformGroups`, and the connection of limbs to make the complete figure creates a large hierarchy of `TransformGroups`. The consequence is that when a limb is moved (by affecting one of its `TransformGroups`), the limbs linked to it as children will also move.

This top-down behavior is at the heart of *forward kinematics*, one of the standard approaches to animating articulated figures. For example, the rotation of a figure's chest can cause its arms and head to turn even though the bottom and legs remain stationary. From a programming point of view, this means less explicit manipulation of `TransformGroups` but requires the arms and head are connected as children to the chest's `TransformGroup`.

Forward kinematics is especially useful for movements that originate at the top-level of a figure and ripple down to the lower-level components. An everyday example is moving a figure: the translation is applied to the top-most `TransformGroup`, and all the other nodes will move as well.

Forward kinematics is less satisfactory for operations that start at lower-level limbs and should ripple up. For instance, the natural way of having a figure touch an object in the scene is to move its hand to the object's location. As the hand is moved, the arm and torso should follow. Unfortunately, this would require that a child `TransformGroup` be able to influence its ancestors, which is impossible in the parent-child hierarchy used by Java 3D.

This ripple-up animation technique is called *inverse kinematics* and is a staple of professional animation packages such as Poser, Maya, and 3D Studio Max. Important low-level nodes are designated as *end-effectors*, and these influence higher-level nodes as they're manipulated. Typically, end-effectors for an articulated human are its hands, feet, and head.

Inverse kinematics has problems specifying top-down effects, so it is often combined with constraints that link end-effectors to other nodes. For instance, when the body moves, the end-effectors can be constrained to stay within a certain distance of the torso.

A good nontechnical introduction to forward and inverse kinematics is Steve Pizel's article "Character Animation: Skeletons and Inverse Kinematics," online at *http://www.intel.com/cd/ids/developer/asmo-na/eng/segments/games/resources/modeling/20433.htm*.

 As far as I know, no Java 3D examples use inverse kinematics. The FAQ at j3d.org contains a few links to discussions of how to implement inverse kinematics in procedural languages (*http://www.j3d.org/faq/techniques.html#ik*).

Forward Kinematics in Mover3D

The Mover3D application in this chapter creates a figure by linking Limb objects together in a parent/child relationship. As I'll explain in detail, each Limb object is a collection of TransfromGroup nodes (and other things) forming a complex hierarchical scene graph.

Limb movement is a matter of translating or rotating TransformGroups in a limb, and changes to those nodes will affect all the child nodes below it (i.e., the child Limb objects). In other words, Mover3D uses forward kinematics.

Class Diagrams for Mover3D

Figure 20-7 shows the class diagrams for the Mover3D application. The class names, public and protected methods, and data are shown.

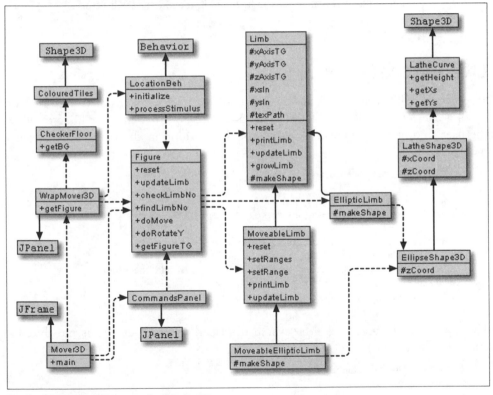

Figure 20-7. Class diagrams for Mover3D

Mover3D is the top-level JFrame for the application, containing two JPanels. The 3D scene is created in WrapMover3D and displayed in its panel, the text field for entering commands and Reset button are managed by CommandsPanel. The LocationBeh behavior deals with user input via the keyboard, and enables the figure to be moved and rotated. WrapMover3D creates the usual checkerboard scene, using the CheckerFloor and ColouredTiles classes (first used in Chapter 15) to create the floor.

The scene contains one Figure object that represents the figure as a series of connected shapes created from the Limb class and its subclasses (MoveableLimb, MoveableEllipticLimb, and EllipticLimb). The shape of a limb is specified using a LatheShape3D or EllipseShape3D object, both described in Chapter 17. The choice depends on the cross-sectional shape you want for a limb: LatheShape3D offers a circular cross-section suitable for arms and legs, and EllipseShape3D is a better choice for a torso (which is closer to elliptical).

 The code for this example can be found in the *Mover3D/* directory.

Creating the Scene

WrapMover3D is like previous Wrap classes: it creates a 3D scene inside a JPanel, made up of a checkerboard floor, blue sky, lighting, and an OrbitBehavior node to allow the user to adjust the viewpoint. Much of this is done in the createSceneGraph() method:

```
private void createSceneGraph()
{
  sceneBG = new BranchGroup();
  bounds = new BoundingSphere(new Point3d(0,0,0), BOUNDSIZE);

  lightScene();          // add the lights
  addBackground();       // add the sky
  sceneBG.addChild( new CheckerFloor().getBG() );  // add the floor
  addFigure();
  sceneBG.compile();   // fix the scene
}
```

The code that distinguishes WrapMover3D from earlier Wrap classes is mostly contained in addFigure():

```
// global: the multilimbed figure
private Figure figure;

private void addFigure()
// add the figure and its behavior to the scene
{
  figure = new Figure();
  sceneBG.addChild( figure.getFigureTG() );  // add figure's TG
```

```
      // add behavior
      LocationBeh locBeh = new LocationBeh( figure );
      locBeh.setSchedulingBounds(bounds);
      sceneBG.addChild(locBeh);
   }
```

The Figure object constructs the articulated figure, and its top-level TransformGroup is added to the scene. The LocationBeh object converts user key presses into figure commands.

Mover3D uses the getFigure() method to obtain a reference to the Figure object, which it passes to the CommandsPanel:

```
   public Figure getFigure()
   { return figure; }
```

Processing User Input

The LocationBeh behavior class deals with user input via the keyboard. The figure can be moved forward, back, left, right, up, or down, and turned clockwise or counterclockwise around the y-axis via the arrow keys. The code in LocationBeh is similar to the code in the TourControls class in Tour3D (from Chapter 18) but simpler in many cases since there's no viewpoint manipulation.

The figure reference is passed in through the constructor:

```
   // globals
   private Figure figure;
   private WakeupCondition keyPress;


   public LocationBeh(Figure fig)
   { figure = fig;
     keyPress = new WakeupOnAWTEvent(KeyEvent.KEY_PRESSED);
   }
```

If a key is pressed along with alt, then altMove() will be called; otherwise, standardMove() will be invoked. (An Alt-key pair is used to move the figure vertically up and down and slide it to the left and right.) Both move methods have a similar style:

```
   // global movement constants
   private final static int FWD = 0;
   private final static int BACK = 1;
   private final static int LEFT = 2;
   private final static int RIGHT = 3;
   private final static int UP = 4;
   private final static int DOWN = 5;

   private final static int CLOCK = 0;   // clockwise turn
   private final static int CCLOCK = 1;  // counter clockwise
```

```
private void standardMove(int keycode)
// moves figure forwards, backwards, rotates left or right
{
  if(keycode == forwardKey)
    figure.doMove(FWD);
  else if(keycode == backKey)
    figure.doMove(BACK);
  else if(keycode == leftKey)
    figure.doRotateY(CLOCK);      // clockwise
  else if(keycode == rightKey)
    figure.doRotateY(CCLOCK);     // counter-clockwise
} // end of standardMove( )

private void altMove(int keycode)
// moves figure up, down, slideleft or right
{
  if(keycode == backKey )
    figure.doMove(UP);
  else if(keycode == forwardKey)
    figure.doMove(DOWN);
  else if(keycode == leftKey)
    figure.doMove(LEFT);
  else if(keycode == rightKey)
    figure.doMove(RIGHT);
  }  // end of altMove( )
```

 The movement and rotation constants (FWD, BACK, etc.) are utilized as unique identifiers to control the move and rotation methods in Figure.

The keys are processed by calling doMove( ) and doRotateY( ) in the Figure object.

The Commands Panel

CommandsPanel creates the panel at the bottom of the GUI containing the text field and Reset button. Much of the code deals with the parsing of the input from the text field, which takes two forms. A *limb command* has the following format:

(<*limbName*> | <*limbNo*>) (fwd | f | turn | t | side | s) [*angleChg*]

A *figure command* has this format:

(fwd | f | back | b | left | l | right | r | up | u | down | d | clock | c | cclock | cc)

Each moveable limb is assigned a name and number, and either one can be used to refer to the limb. As a convenience, the name/number mappings are printed to standard output when Mover3D is started.

The principal difference between the limb and figure commands is that a limb command needs to refer to a particular limb, and a figure command applies to the entire figure. A limb command can include a rotation value (angleChg).

The rotation operations refer to the three axes:

fwd *(or f)*
> Rotation around x-axis

turn *(or t)*
> Rotation around y-axis

side *(or s)*
> Rotation around z-axis

 If an angleChg value isn't included, a rotation of +5 degrees will be carried out.

Each limb has a predefined maximum positive and negative rotation, and a rotation command will only move a limb to the prescribed limit.

An advantage of text field input is the ability to group several limb and/or figure commands together, separated by commas. These are processed before the figure is redrawn. By pressing Enter, a complex sequence of commands is repeated. This can be seen in action in the example that started this chapter when several parts of the figure were rotated in unison.

Processing a Command

The string entered in the text field is tokenized in processComms( ), which separates out the individual commands and extracts the two or three argument limb action or single argument figure operation:

```
private void processComms(String input)
{ if (input == null)
    return;

  String[] commands = input.split(",");  // split into commands
  StringTokenizer toks;
  for (int i=0; i < commands.length; i++) {
    toks = new StringTokenizer( commands[i].trim() );
    if (toks.countTokens( ) == 3)          // three-arg limb command
      limbCommand( toks.nextToken( ), toks.nextToken( ),
                                      toks.nextToken( ) );
    else if (toks.countTokens( ) == 2)     // two-arg limb command
      limbCommand( toks.nextToken( ), toks.nextToken( ), "5");
    else if (toks.countTokens( ) == 1)     // one-arg figure command
      figCommand( toks.nextToken( ) );
    else
      System.out.println("Illegal command: " + commands[i]);
  }
}
```

limbCommand( ) must extract the limb number, the axis of rotation, and the rotation angle from the command string. If a limb name has been entered, then the corresponding number will be obtained by querying the Figure object:

```
private void limbCommand(String limbName, String opStr, String angleStr)
{ // get the limb number
  int limbNo = -1;
  try {
    limbNo = figure.checkLimbNo( Integer.parseInt(limbName) );
  }
  catch(NumberFormatException e)
  { limbNo = figure.findLimbNo(limbName); }    // map name to num
  if (limbNo == -1) {
    System.out.println("Illegal Limb name/no: " + limbName);
    return;
  }

  // get the angle change
  double angleChg = 0;
  try {
    angleChg = Double.parseDouble(angleStr);
  }
  catch(NumberFormatException e)
  { System.out.println("Illegal angle change: " + angleStr); }
  if (angleChg == 0) {
    System.out.println("Angle change is 0, so doing nothing");
    return;
  }

  // extract the axis of rotation from the limb operation
  int axis;
  if (opStr.equals("fwd") || opStr.equals("f"))
    axis = X_AXIS;
  else if (opStr.equals("turn") || opStr.equals("t"))
    axis = Y_AXIS;
  else if (opStr.equals("side") || opStr.equals("s"))
    axis = Z_AXIS;
  else {
    System.out.println("Unknown limb operation: " + opStr);
    return;
  }

  // apply the command to the limb
  figure.updateLimb(limbNo, axis, angleChg);

}    // end of limbCommand( )
```

The handling of possible input errors lengthens the code. The limb number is checked via a call to checkLimbNo( ) in Figure, which scans the limbs to determine if the specified number is used by one of them. The mapping of a limb name to a number is carried out by Figure's findLimbNo( ), which returns -1 if the name is not found amongst the limbs. Once the correct input has been gathered, it is passed to updateLimb( ) in the Figure object.

A figure command is processed by figCommand( ), which uses lots of if/else statements to convert the command into a correctly parameterized call to Figure's doMove( ) or doRotateY( ) method:

```
private void figCommand(String opStr)
{ if (opStr.equals("fwd") || opStr.equals("f"))
    figure.doMove(FWD);
  else if (opStr.equals("back") || opStr.equals("b"))
    figure.doMove(BACK);
  else if (opStr.equals("left") || opStr.equals("l"))
    figure.doMove(LEFT);
  else if (opStr.equals("right") || opStr.equals("r"))
    figure.doMove(RIGHT);
  else if (opStr.equals("up") || opStr.equals("u"))
    figure.doMove(UP);
  else if (opStr.equals("down") || opStr.equals("d"))
    figure.doMove(DOWN);
  else if (opStr.equals("clock") || opStr.equals("c"))
    figure.doRotateY(CLOCK);
  else if (opStr.equals("cclock") || opStr.equals("cc"))
    figure.doRotateY(CCLOCK);
  else {
    System.out.println("Unknown figure operation: " + opStr);
    return;
  }
} // end of figCommand( )
```

Making and Moving the Figure

The Figure class carries out three main tasks:

- It builds the figure by connecting Limb objects. The resulting figure is translated into a Java 3D subgraph.
- It processes limb-related operations, such as updateLimb( ) calls.
- It processes figure movement operations, such as doRotateY( ).

Building the Figure

The construction of the figure starts in Figure( ):

```
//globals
private ArrayList limbs;
  // Arraylist of Limb objects, indexed by limb number
private HashMap limbNames;
  // holds (limb name, limb number) pairs

private TransformGroup figureTG;
  // the top-level TG for the entire figure
```

```
public Figure( )
{
  yCount = 0;      // the figure is on the floor initially
  t3d = new Transform3D( );   // used for repeated calcs
  toMove = new Transform3D( );
  toRot = new Transform3D( );

  limbs = new ArrayList( );
  limbNames = new HashMap( );

  // construct the figure from connected Limb objects
  buildTorso( );
  buildHead( );

  buildRightArm( );
  buildLeftArm( );

  buildRightLeg( );
  buildLeftLeg( );

  printLimbsInfo( );

  buildFigureGraph( );   // convert figure into a Java 3D subgraph
} // end of Figure( )
```

The figure's Limb objects are stored in the limbs ArrayList. Each Limb object has a unique ID (its limb number), which is used as its index position in the ArrayList.

The other important data structure is the limbNames HashMap. The HashMap stores (limb name, limb number) pairs, with the name being the key and the limb number the value. At runtime, the HashMap is employed to determine a limb's number when a name is supplied in a limb command.

Figure 20-8 shows the limbs that comprise the figure, labeled with their names and numbers.

Only moveable limbs have names, which exclude the neck and bottom (bottom as in derriere). Invisible limbs are nameless and are marked as dotted lines in the figure. Two short invisible limbs link the legs to their feet (labeled as 16 and 21 in Figure 20-8). The small gray circles in Figure 20-8 are the joints, the points where limbs connect to each other, and they are positioned to make the limbs overlap.

Figure 20-9 shows the articulated figure again but with emphasis given to the joints. Each arrow shows the positive y-axis in the limb's local coordinate space. A limb's shape extends from the joint, following the arrow's direction.

The first joint in the figure is j0, which is the starting location of the bottom. The chest limb begins at joint j1, the neck at j2, the upper-left arm at j9, the lower-left arm at j10, and so on. The side view of the lower-left leg shows the invisible joint that begins at j20 and extends downward. The foot is attached to it via j21. The arrows on the joints show that the local y-axis for a limb can be rotated significantly

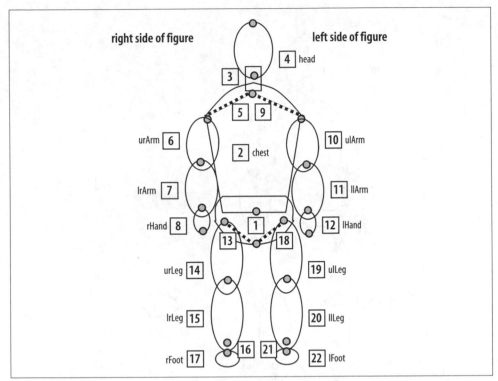

Figure 20-8. The Figure's limbs, named and numbered

when viewed in world coordinates. For example, the base of the upper-left arm is at j9, and the limb's positive y-axis is pointing almost straight down. Several limbs can be attached to one joint. For instance, j0 is the starting point for the bottom limb, as well as two invisible limbs which extend up and to the left and right, respectively.

Each limb utilizes two joints. In the joint's local coordinate system, the *start joint* begins at (0,0) on its XZ plane. The limb's shape is placed at the start joint location and oriented along the positive y-axis. The *end joint* is positioned along the limb's y-axis, 90% of the way toward the end of the limb's shape. For example, the upper-left arm's start joint is j9, and its end joint is j10. The lower-left arm's start joint is j10, thereby linking the lower arm to the upper.

A limb's joints are encoded in Java 3D as TransformGroups. The start joint TransformGroup of a child limb is the end joint TransformGroup of its parent, so linking the child to the parent. Figure 20-10 shows the articulated figure again but in terms of the TransformGroups that encode the joints.

The thick gray lines denote the limbs and hide several TransformGroups and other Java 3D nodes. The visible TransformGroups are for the joints, and are labeled with their joint name and TG. For instance, the limb for the upper-left arm (ulArm) starts at

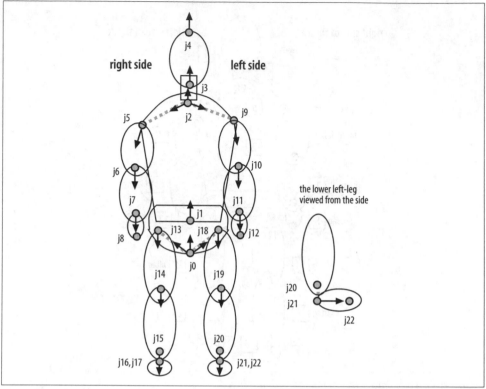

Figure 20-9. The Figure's joints

joint j9, and its end joint is j10. The limb for the lower-left arm (l1Arm) is attached to the TransformGroup for j10 and becomes its child.

> The gray lines labeled with "link" are invisible limbs, which have no names.

Figure 20-10 shows the top-level TransformGroups for the figure: figureTG and offsetTG. figureTG represents the origin for the entire figure and is located on the floor, initially at (0,0). figureTG is affected by figure commands. offsetTG is a vertical offset, up off the floor, which corresponds to the j0 start joint.

The details of Limb creation in the Figure object depend on the type of Limb being created. Figure 20-11 shows the hierarchy for Limb and its subclasses.

Limb defines the appearance of a limb (using a lathe shape) and how it is connected to a parent limb via a joint (TransformGroup). The limb's initial orientation is fixed. Limb and EllipticLimb cannot be moved and do not use limb names.

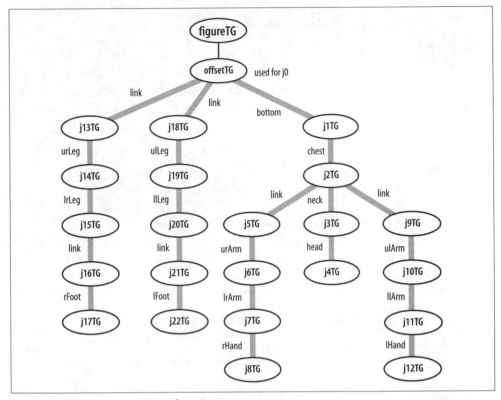

Figure 20-10. The Figure's TransformGroups

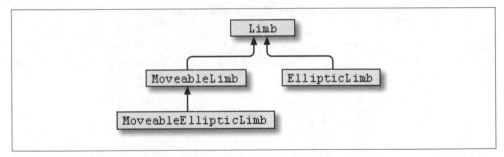

Figure 20-11. The Limb class hierarchy

The MoveableLimb and MoveableEllipticLimb classes are moveable. They have limb names and x-, y-, and z-axis rotation ranges. If a range is not specified, then it is assumed to be 0 (i.e., rotation is not possible around that axis). The lathe shape used in a Limb or MoveableLimb object has a circular cross-section but is elliptical in EllipticLimb and MoveableEllipticLimb.

Lathe shapes were described in Chapter 17.

buildTorso(), from the Figure class, shows the use of EllipticLimb and MoveableEllipticLimb to create the bottom and chest for the figure. The bottom is not moveable, but the chest is:

```
private void buildTorso()
{
  // the figure's bottom
  double xsIn1[] = {0, -0.1, 0.22, -0.2, 0.001};
  double ysIn1[] = {0, 0.03, 0.08, 0.25, 0.25};
  EllipticLimb limb1 = new EllipticLimb(
        1, "j0", "j1", Z_AXIS, 0, xsIn1, ysIn1, "denim.jpg");
  // no movement, so no name or ranges

  // the figure's chest: moveable so has a name ("chest")
  // and rotation ranges
  double xsIn2[] = {-0.001, -0.2, 0.36, 0.001};
  double ysIn2[] = {0, 0, 0.50, 0.68};
  MoveableEllipticLimb limb2 = new MoveableEllipticLimb("chest",
        2, "j1", "j2", Z_AXIS, 0, xsIn2, ysIn2, "camoflage.jpg");
  limb2.setRanges(0, 120, -60, 60, -40, 40);
        // x range: 0 to 120; y range: -60 to 60; z range: -40 to 40

  limbs.add(limb1);
  limbs.add(limb2);

  limbNames.put("chest", new Integer(2)); // store (name,number)
}  // end of buildTorso()
```

The arrays of coordinates passed to the limb1 and limb2 objects define the lathe curves for the bottom and chest. Figure 20-12 shows the graph of points making up the curve for the bottom (limb1).

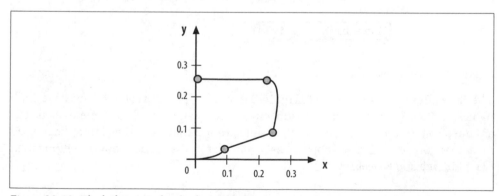

Figure 20-12. The lathe curve for the figure's bottom

A limb requires a limb number, its start and end joint names, an axis of orientation and angle to that axis, and lathe shape coordinates and texture. The lathe shape and texture can be omitted, to signal that the limb should be invisible, but a limb length must be supplied instead. If the limb is moveable (i.e., a MoveableLimb or MoveableEllipticLimb object), then it also requires a name and x-, y-, and z-ranges to restrict its movements.

The bottom limb is defined as:

```
EllipticLimb limb1 = new EllipticLimb(
            1, "j0", "j1", Z_AXIS, 0, xsIn1, ysIn1, "denim.jpg");
```

This is a nonmoveable limb, so it has no name. Its limb number is 1, it starts at joint j0, and its end joint is called j1. It is rotated around the z-axis by 0 degrees (i.e., not rotated at all), and has a lathe shape covered in denim. These details can be checked against the information in Figures 20-9 and 20-10.

The chest limb is:

```
MoveableEllipticLimb limb2 = new MoveableEllipticLimb("chest",
            2, "j1", "j2", Z_AXIS, 0, xsIn2, ysIn2, "camoflage.jpg");
limb2.setRanges(0, 120, -60, 60, -40, 40);
        // x range: 0 to 120; y range: -60 to 60; z range: -40 to 40
```

This moveable limb is called chest, limb number 2. Its start joint is j1 (the end joint of the bottom), so it will become a child of the bottom limb. Its end joint is called j2. It is rotated around the z-axis by 0 degrees (i.e., not rotated at all), and has a lathe shape covered in a camouflage pattern. The permitted ranges for rotation around the x-, y-, and z-axes are set with a call to setRanges().

The end of buildTorso() shows the two limbs being added to the limbs ArrayList. A limb numbered as X can be found in the list by looking up entry X-1.

The limb names (in this case only chest) are added to a limbNames HashMap together with their limb numbers. This data structure is used when a limb is referred to by its name, and its corresponding number must be found. Limb names aren't needed, but they're a lot easier for a user to remember than numbers.

Orientating Limbs

The construction of the left arm illustrates how the initial orientation of a limb can be adjusted. Figure 20-13 shows the construction of the left arm, including the angles between the limbs.

The relevant code is in buildLeftArm():

```
private void buildLeftArm()
{
  // invisible limb connecting the neck and upper-left arm
  Limb limb9 = new Limb(9, "j2", "j9", Z_AXIS, -95, 0.35);
```

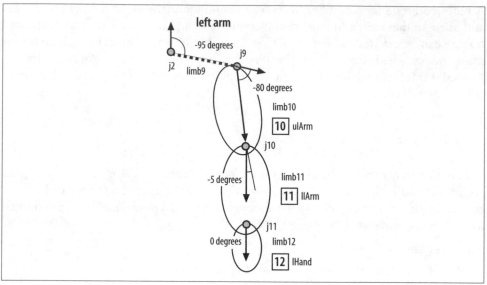

Figure 20-13. The left arm in detail

```
// upper-left arm
double xsIn10[] = {0, 0.1, 0.08, 0};
double ysIn10[] = {0, 0.08, 0.45, 0.55};
MoveableLimb limb10 = new MoveableLimb("ulArm",
    10, "j9", "j10", Z_AXIS, -80, xsIn10, ysIn10, "leftarm.jpg");
limb10.setRanges(-60, 180, -90, 90, -30, 90);

// lower-left arm
double xsIn11[] = {0, 0.08, 0.055, 0};
double ysIn11[] = {0, 0.08, 0.38, 0.43};
MoveableLimb limb11 = new MoveableLimb("llArm",
     11, "j10", "j11", Z_AXIS, -5, xsIn11, ysIn11, "skin.jpg");
limb11.setRanges(0, 150, -90, 90, -90, 90);

// left hand
double xsIn12[] = {0, 0.06, 0.04, 0};
double ysIn12[] = {0, 0.07, 0.16, 0.2};
MoveableEllipticLimb limb12 = new MoveableEllipticLimb("lHand",
    12, "j11", "j12", Z_AXIS, 0, xsIn12, ysIn12, "skin.jpg");
limb12.setRanges(-50, 50, -90, 40, -40, 40);

limbs.add(limb9);
limbs.add(limb10);
limbs.add(limb11);
limbs.add(limb12);

limbNames.put("ulArm", new Integer(10));
limbNames.put("llArm", new Integer(11));
limbNames.put("lHand", new Integer(12));
} // end of buildLeftArm()
```

The invisible limb, limb9, is made 0.35 units long and rotated around the z-axis by 95 degrees:

```
Limb limb9 = new Limb(9, "j2", "j9", Z_AXIS, -95, 0.35);
```

The rotation turns the y-axis of limb9 clockwise by 95 degrees. However, the actual orientation of the limb in world coordinate space depends on the overall orientation of the y-axis specified by its ancestors. In this case, none of its ancestors (bottom and chest) have been rotated, so its world orientation is the same as its local value.

The limb for the upper-left arm is defined as:

```
MoveableLimb limb10 = new MoveableLimb("ulArm",
        10, "j9", "j10", Z_AXIS, -80, xsIn10, ysIn10, "leftarm.jpg");
```

This rotates the y-axis of limb10 clockwise by 80 degrees, which when added to the ancestor rotations (bottom, chest, limb9) means that the shape is almost pointing downward, with a total rotation of 175 degrees. The lower arm (limb11; llArm) is rotated another 5 degrees to point straight down (180 degrees). The left hand (limb12; lHand) has no rotation of its own, so it points downward.

Creating the Scene Graph

The buildXXX() methods (e.g., buildTorso(), buildLeftArm()) create the limb objects and specify how they are linked in terms of joint names. The creation of the scene graph outlined in Figure 20-11 is initiated by buildFigureGraph() after all the limbs have been initialized:

```
private void buildFigureGraph()
{
  HashMap joints = new HashMap();
  /* joints will contain (jointName, TG) pairs. Each TG is the
     position of the joint in the scene.
     A limb connected to a joint is placed in the scene by
     using the TG associated with that joint.
  */
  figureTG = new TransformGroup();
  figureTG.setCapability( TransformGroup.ALLOW_TRANSFORM_READ);
  figureTG.setCapability( TransformGroup.ALLOW_TRANSFORM_WRITE);

  TransformGroup offsetTG = new TransformGroup();
  Transform3D trans = new Transform3D();
  trans.setTranslation( new Vector3d(0, 1.24, 0));
          // an offset from the ground to the first joint
  offsetTG.setTransform( trans );

  joints.put("j0", offsetTG);    // store starting joint j0

  /* Grow the subgraph for each limb object, attaching it
     to the figure's subgraph below offsetTG. */
  Limb li;
  for (int i = 0; i < limbs.size(); i++) {
```

```
      li = (Limb)limbs.get(i);
      li.growLimb(joints);
    }

    figureTG.addChild(offsetTG);
  } // end of buildFigureGraph( )
```

buildFigureGraph( ) initializes figureTG and offsetTG. offsetTG will be the TransformGroup for the first joint, j0, and its name/TransformGroup pair is stored in a HashMap called joints.

A for loop iterates through the Limb objects stored in the limbs ArrayList and calls each limb's growLimb( ) method, passing in the joints HashMap. growLimb( ) creates a Java 3D subbranch for the limb and attaches it to the TransformGroup corresponding to the limb's start joint. This joint/TransformGroup correspondence is found by searching the joints HashMap.

 A subtle assumption of this code is that a child limb is never attached to a joint before the joint has been converted into a TransformGroup. Another way of understanding this is that a parent limb must be converted to a Java 3D subbranch before any of its children.

Processing Limb-Related Operations

The Figure class uses the limbNames HashMap, which contains limb name/limb number pairs to check if a user-supplied limb number is used by the figure and to convert limb names into numbers. If the number or name isn't correct, then an error message is printed and the associated operation is ignored. The operations are carried out by checkLimbNo( ) and findLimbNo( ).

updateLimb( ) is called with a legal limb number, an axis of rotation, and a rotation angle and passes the request on to the limb in question:

```
public void updateLimb(int limbNo, int axis, double angle)
{ Limb li = (Limb) limbs.get(limbNo-1);
  li.updateLimb(axis, angle);   // pass on axis and angle
}
```

reset( ) is called by CommandsPanel when the user presses the reset button. The reset request is sent to every limb:

```
public void reset( )
// restore each limb to its original position in space
{ Limb li;
  for (int i = 0; i < limbs.size( ); i++) {
    li = (Limb)limbs.get(i);
    li.reset( );
  }
}
```

Figure Movement

Figure commands, such as forward and clock, are converted into transforms applied to the figureTG TransformGroup at the root of the figure's subgraph. doMove( ) converts a move request into a translation vector, which is applied in doMoveVec( ):

```
private void doMoveVec(Vector3d theMove)
// Move the figure by the amount in theMove
{
  figureTG.getTransform( t3d );
  toMove.setTranslation(theMove);     // overwrite previous trans
  t3d.mul(toMove);
  figureTG.setTransform(t3d);
}
```

toMove and t3d are global Transform3D variables reused by doMoveVec( ) to avoid the overhead of object creation and garbage collection.

doRotateY( ) converts a rotation request into a rotation around the y-axis, which is carried out by doRotateYRad( ):

```
private void doRotateYRad(double radians)
// Rotate the figure by radians amount around its y-axis
{
  figureTG.getTransform( t3d );
  toRot.rotY(radians);    // overwrite previous rotation
  t3d.mul(toRot);
  figureTG.setTransform(t3d);
}
```

toRot is a global Transform3D variable.

 A drawback of this implementation is the lack of x- and z-axis rotations that make it impossible to position the figure in certain ways. For instance, you cannot make the figure stand on its hands, as that would require a rotation around the x-axis. Adding this functionality would be easy, though. You could add two extra TransformGroups below figureTG so the three rotation axes could be cleanly separated and easily reset. This coding strategy is used for limb rotation, as seen below.

Modeling a Limb

The main job of the Limb class is to convert limb information into a Java 3D subgraph, like the one in Figure 20-14.

The start and end joints are represented by TransformGroups. startLimbTG isn't created by the limb but obtained from the parent limb. It's the parent's endLimbTG, and in this way are children attached to parents. The limb creates endLimbTG, which is positioned along the y-axis, 90 percent of the way along the length of the limb's shape. Child limbs can be attached to endLimbTG, meaning that they will overlap the

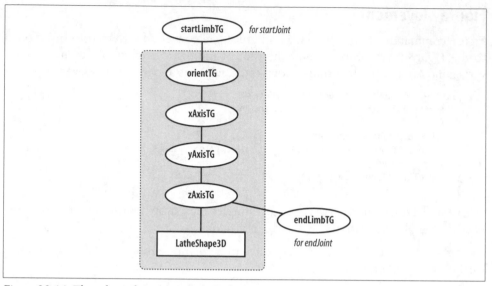

Figure 20-14. The subgraph representing a limb

parent limb shape. This enhances the effect that the limbs are connected, especially when a limb is rotated.

In between the joint `TransformGroups` are four more `TransformGroups` and a `LatheShape3D` node representing the limb shape and its position. These are the details hidden by the thick gray lines between the `TransformGroups` in Figure 20-10. Each of those lines should be expanded into the five nodes surrounded by the gray dotted box in Figure 20-14.

`orientTG` is used to orient the shape initially. The other `TransformGroups` are located below it as its children, so they view the new orientation as pointing along the positive y-axis. The `xAxisTG`, `yAxisTG`, and `zAxisTG` `TransformGroups` are employed to rotate the limb around the x-, y-, and z-axes at runtime. The separation of these rotations into three parts makes it much easier to undo them if the limb is reset.

Though the `Limb` class creates the Figure 20-14 subgraph, it does not allow the `xAxisTG`, `yAxisTG`, or `zAxisTGs` to be affected. The `MoveableLimb` class offers implementations of the methods that adjust these `TransformGroups`.

`Limb` contains various limb data, supplied by its constructor:

```
private int limbNo;
private String startJoint, endJoint;
private int orientAxis;        // limb's axis of initial orientation
private double orientAngle = 0;      // angle to orientation axis

private double limbLen;
private boolean visibleLimb = false;
```

```
protected double xsIn[], ysIn[];      // coordinates of lathe shape
protected String texPath;             // shape's texture filename
```

The `Limb` class doesn't have a limb name; only moveable limbs utilize names. The length of a limb is usually obtained from the lathe shape coordinates. I assume the final value in the lathe shape's y-coordinates is the maximum y-value for the entire shape (i.e., its height). If the limb is to be invisible, then the constructor will have to a limb length, which is directly assigned to `limbLen`.

The `visibleLimb` Boolean is used to distinguish between visible and invisible limbs. The lathe shape coordinates and texture are protected since they need to be accessible by `Limb` subclasses that override the lathe shape creation method, `makeShape( )`.

Growing a Limb

`growLimb( )` starts the process of subgraph creation for the limb:

```
public void growLimb(HashMap joints)
{
  TransformGroup startLimbTG =
        (TransformGroup) joints.get(startJoint);
  if (startLimbTG == null)
    System.out.println("No transform group for " + startJoint);
  else {
    setOrientation(startLimbTG);
    makeLimb(joints);
  }
}
```

The start joint name is used to find the `startLimbTG` TransformGroup in the `joints` HashMap. This should have been created by the parent of this limb.

`setOrientation( )` creates the four rotational TransformGroups (orientTG, xAxisTg, yAxisTG, and zAxisTG) below startLimbTG:

```
private void setOrientation(TransformGroup tg)
{
  TransformGroup orientTG = new TransformGroup( );
  if (orientAngle != 0) {
    Transform3D trans = new Transform3D( );
    if (orientAxis == X_AXIS)
      trans.rotX( Math.toRadians(orientAngle));
    else if (orientAxis == Y_AXIS)
      trans.rotY( Math.toRadians(orientAngle));
    else    // must be z-axis
      trans.rotZ( Math.toRadians(orientAngle));
    orientTG.setTransform(trans);
  }

  xAxisTG = new TransformGroup( );
  xAxisTG.setCapability( TransformGroup.ALLOW_TRANSFORM_READ);
  xAxisTG.setCapability( TransformGroup.ALLOW_TRANSFORM_WRITE);
```

```
yAxisTG = new TransformGroup( );
yAxisTG.setCapability( TransformGroup.ALLOW_TRANSFORM_READ);
yAxisTG.setCapability( TransformGroup.ALLOW_TRANSFORM_WRITE);

zAxisTG = new TransformGroup( );
zAxisTG.setCapability( TransformGroup.ALLOW_TRANSFORM_READ);
zAxisTG.setCapability( TransformGroup.ALLOW_TRANSFORM_WRITE);

// scene graph's sequence of TG's
tg.addChild(orientTG);
orientTG.addChild(xAxisTG);
xAxisTG.addChild(yAxisTG);
yAxisTG.addChild(zAxisTG);
} // end of setOrientation( )
```

The capability bits are set to allow the axis TransformGroups to change during execution, but orientTG remains fixed after being positioned at build time.

makeLimb( ) creates the endLimbTG TransformGroup and may create a lathe shape if the limb is set to be visible:

```
private void makeLimb(HashMap joints)
{
  if (visibleLimb)
    makeShape( );  // create the lathe shape

  TransformGroup endLimbTG = new TransformGroup( );
  Transform3D trans = new Transform3D( );
  trans.setTranslation(
      new Vector3d(0.0, limbLen*(1.0-OVERLAP), 0.0) );
  /* The end position is just short of the actual length of the
     limb so that any child limbs will be placed so they overlap
     with this one. */
  endLimbTG.setTransform(trans);
  zAxisTG.addChild(endLimbTG);

  joints.put(endJoint, endLimbTG);   // store (jointName, TG) pair
}
```

The endLimbTG TransformGroup is stored in the joints HashMap at the end of the method, so it is available for use by this limb's children.

makeShape( ) creates a LatheShape3D object and attaches it to the zAxisTG node:

```
protected void makeShape( )
{
  LatheShape3D ls;
  if (texPath != null) {
    TextureLoader texLd =
            new TextureLoader("textures/"+texPath, null);
    Texture tex = texLd.getTexture( );
    ls = new LatheShape3D(xsIn, ysIn, tex);
  }
  else
    ls = new LatheShape3D(xsIn, ysIn, null);
```

```
    zAxisTG.addChild(ls);  // add the shape to the limb's graph
  } // end of makeShape()
```

makeShape() is a protected method since it may be overridden by Limb's subclasses. For example, EllipticLimb replaces the call to LatheShape3D by EllipseShape3D. This causes the limb to have an elliptical cross-section.

Updating and Resetting

Limb() contains empty updateLimb() and reset() methods:

```
public void updateLimb(int axis, double angleStep) {}
public void reset() {}
```

updateLimb() and reset() affect the position of the limb, so they aren't used in Limb. They are overridden by the MoveableLimb subclass.

Moving a Limb

MoveableLimb allows a limb to be moved around the x-, y-, and z-axes. This is achieved by affecting the xAxisTG, yAxisTG, and zAxisTG TransformGroups in the limb's subgraph.

MoveableLimb maintains range information for the three axes and ignores rotations that would move the limb outside of those ranges. If a range isn't specified, then it will be assumed to be 0 (i.e., rotation is not possible around that axis). The programmer calls setRanges() or setRange() to initialize the range details for different axes:

```
// globals: the axis ranges
private double xMin, xMax, yMin, yMax, zMin, zMax;


public void setRanges(double x1, double x2, double y1, double y2,
                                double z1, double z2)
{ setRange(X_AXIS, x1, x2);
  setRange(Y_AXIS, y1, y2);
  setRange(Z_AXIS, z1, z2);
}


public void setRange(int axis, double angle1, double angle2)
// set the range for axis only
{
  if (angle1 > angle2) {
    System.out.println(limbName + ": wrong order... swapping");
    double temp = angle1;
    angle1 = angle2;
    angle2 = temp;
  }
  if (axis == X_AXIS) {
    xMin = angle1;  xMax = angle2;
```

```
      }
      else if (axis == Y_AXIS) {
        yMin = angle1;   yMax = angle2;
      }
      else {   // Z_AXIS
        zMin = angle1;   zMax = angle2;
      }
    } // end of setRange()
```

The methods initialize the xMin, xMax, yMin, yMax, zMin, and zMax globals and ensure the ranges are given in the right order.

Rotations are processed by updateLimb( ), which is called from the Figure object with axis and angle arguments:

```
    public void updateLimb(int axis, double angleStep)
    // Attempt to rotate this limb by angleStep around axis
    {
      if (axis == X_AXIS)
        applyAngleStep(angleStep, xCurrAng, axis, xMax, xMin);
      else if (axis == Y_AXIS)
        applyAngleStep(angleStep, yCurrAng, axis, yMax, yMin);
      else     // Z_AXIS
        applyAngleStep(angleStep, zCurrAng, axis, zMax, zMin);
    }



    private void applyAngleStep(double angleStep, double currAngle,
                                int axis, double max, double min)
    /* Before any rotation, check that the angle step moves the
       limb within the ranges for this axis.
       If not then rotate to the range limit, and no further. */
    {
      if ((currAngle >= max) && (angleStep > 0)) {  // will exceed max
        System.out.println(limbName + ": no rot; already at max");
        return;
      }
      if (currAngle <= min && (angleStep < 0)) { // will drop below min
        System.out.println(limbName + ": no rot; already at min");
        return;
      }

      double newAngle = currAngle + angleStep;
      if (newAngle > max) {
        System.out.println(limbName + ": reached max angle");
        angleStep = max - currAngle;   // rotate to max angle only
      }
      else if (newAngle < min) {
        System.out.println(limbName + ": reached min angle");
        angleStep = min - currAngle;   // rotate to min angle only
      }
```

```
    makeUpdate(axis, angleStep);     // do the rotation
  }  // end of applyAngleStep()
```

updateLimb() uses the supplied axis value to pass the correct axis range to applyAngleStep(). This method checks that the requested rotation stays within the allowed range. The range extends from some largest negative value to a largest positive angle (referred to by min and max). This may mean ignoring the rotation (if the min or max value has been reached), or reducing the rotation so the limb stops at min or max. Once the actual rotation angle has been calculated (and stored in angleStep), makeUpdate() is called:

```
// globals: the current angle in three axes
private double xCurrAng, yCurrAng, zCurrAng;


private void makeUpdate(int axis, double angleStep)
// rotate the limb by angleStep around the given axis
{
  if (axis == X_AXIS) {
    rotTrans.rotX( Math.toRadians(angleStep));
    xAxisTG.getTransform(currTrans);
    currTrans.mul(rotTrans);
    xAxisTG.setTransform(currTrans);
    xCurrAng += angleStep;
  }
  else if (axis == Y_AXIS) {
    rotTrans.rotY( Math.toRadians(angleStep));
    yAxisTG.getTransform(currTrans);
    currTrans.mul(rotTrans);
    yAxisTG.setTransform(currTrans);
    yCurrAng += angleStep;
  }
  else {  // z-axis
    rotTrans.rotZ( Math.toRadians(angleStep));
    zAxisTG.getTransform(currTrans);
    currTrans.mul(rotTrans);
    zAxisTG.setTransform(currTrans);
    zCurrAng += angleStep;
  }
} // end of makeUpdate()
```

makeUpdate() applies a rotation to xAxisTG, yAxisTG, or zAxisTG depending on the axis value supplied by the user. The rotational transform is multiplied to the current value held in the relevant TransformGroup, which is equivalent to adding the rotation to the current angle. rotTrans and currTrans are global Transform3D variables to save on the cost of object creation and deletion. The new limb angle is stored in xCurrAng, yCurrAng, or zCurrAng.

The limb can be reset to its initial orientation, via a call to reset( ) by the Figure object:

```
public void reset()
{
  rotTrans.rotX( Math.toRadians(-xCurrAng));     // reset x angle
  xAxisTG.getTransform(currTrans);
  currTrans.mul(rotTrans);
  xAxisTG.setTransform(currTrans);
  xCurrAng = 0;

  rotTrans.rotY( Math.toRadians(-yCurrAng));     // reset y angle
  yAxisTG.getTransform(currTrans);
  currTrans.mul(rotTrans);
  yAxisTG.setTransform(currTrans);
  yCurrAng = 0;

  rotTrans.rotZ( Math.toRadians(-zCurrAng));     // reset z angle
  zAxisTG.getTransform(currTrans);
  currTrans.mul(rotTrans);
  zAxisTG.setTransform(currTrans);
  zCurrAng = 0;
}  // end of reset()
```

The rotations maintained by xAxisTG, yAxisTG, and zAxisTG are undone by rotating each one by the negative of their current angle, as stored in xCurrAng, yCurrAng, and zCurrAng. The simplicity of this operation is due to the separation of the three degrees of freedom into three TransformGroups.

Moving an Elliptical Limb

MoveableEllipticLimb shows how little code is required to adjust the limb's shape. Only makeShape( ) must be overridden to use EllipseShape3D instead of the version in the Limb class that utilizes LatheShape3D:

```
protected void makeShape()
{
  EllipseShape3D es;
  if (texPath != null) {
    TextureLoader texLd =
        new TextureLoader("textures/"+texPath, null);
    Texture tex = texLd.getTexture();
    es = new EllipseShape3D(xsIn, ysIn, tex);
  }
  else
    es = new EllipseShape3D(xsIn, ysIn, null);

  zAxisTG.addChild(es);  // add the shape to the limb's graph
}
```

Other Articulated Figures

Several excellent Java 3D articulated figure examples are out on the Web:

Ana

Alessandro Borges has developed an articulated figure with named parts, with a similar joint-based TransformGroup implementation as here but with spheres at the limb intersections (*http://planeta.terra.com.br/educacao/alessandroborges/ana/ana.html*). Movement/rotation commands are grouped together to form keyframe animations. Forward kinematics controls the interaction between the limbs.

The Virtual Drummer

This 3D drummer by Martijn Kragtwijk is coded in a similar way to my figure, but the emphasis is on animating the model by having it play along to the drum parts of music (*http://parlevink.cs.utwente.nl/Projects/virtualdrummer/*). The site contains a number of papers on the work.

The fun idea of animation through music recognition has been extensively developed in Wayne Lytle's Animusic (*http://www.animusic.com/*), which is unfortunately not Java-based.

Robot Simulation

Yuan Cheng wrote a graphical, interactive, physical-based robot control simulation environment using Java 3D (*http://icmit.mit.edu/robot/simulation.html*) back in 1999. The robots are built using a hierarchy of TransformGroups.

H-Anim Working Group

The H-Anim (Humanoid Animation) Working Group (*http://www.h-anim.org/*) has developed a VRML97 specification for representing figures. There is no Java 3D implementation available, but the specification contains numerous good ideas on how to model an articulated figure.

A Joint node defines limb position, orientation, and other attributes such as skin properties. Joints are linked together to form a hierarchy, so Joint is somewhat similar to the Limb class developed here. The Segment node is concerned with the shape of the body part, including its mass, and allows the shape's geometry to be adjusted. Segment could be equated with the LatheShape3D class but has greater functionality. Site nodes are used to attach items to Segments, such as clothing and jewelry. Site nodes may be employed to fix a camera so it stays in a certain position relative to the figure. The Displacer node permits groups of vertices in a Segment to be associated with a higher-level feature of the figure. For example, the location of the nose, eyes, and mouth on a face can be identified with Displacer nodes.

Articulation and Mesh Deformation

An alternative to building a figure from articulated shapes is to create a single mesh (e.g., by using Java 3D's GeometryArray). Mesh deformation can be significantly optimized if carried out by reference, where the mesh data is stored in an array maintained by the program, rather than as part of the scene graph. The array can be modified without the overhead of scene graph accesses, and the on-screen representation is updated by calls to GeometryArray's updateData( ) method.

The standard Java 3D demos contain an example, in the directory *GeometryByReference/*, showing how the shape and color of an object can be changed in this manner. I discuss geometry referencing in Chapter 21, in relation to particle systems.

j3d.org has a small mesh deformation demo, written by Leyland Needham, which bends a cylinder like a human arm (*http://www.j3d.org/utilities/bones.html*). The code gradually updates the cylinder mesh to achieve its effect. Alessandro Borges is planning to add similar mesh deformation elements to his Ana system (*http://planeta.terra.com.br/educacao/alessandroborges/ana/bone.html*).

Articulation and Skinning

Skinning utilizes two elements: a mesh for the figure's skin (or clothes) and an articulated bone model. The vertices of the skin mesh are connected to bone contact points by weights, which specify how the skin adjusts as the bones move.

Salamander

Mark McKay has released a skeletal animation and skinning system as part of his unfinished but useful Salamander Project (*https://skinandbones.dev.java.net/*). Salamander offers keyframe interpolation and multiple animation tracks based on the Maya trax editor.

Skinning VRML loader

Seungwoo Oh has developed a VRML loader that can handle motion data (rotations and translations) and supports geometry skinning (*http://vr.kaist.ac.kr/~redmong/research.htm*). He has utilized this for clothing human figures with convincing results. His site includes Java 3D loaders and articles explaining the concepts behind his software.

H-Anim skinning

A skinned mesh system, derived from the H-Anim specification, is part of Xj3D, a toolkit for VRML 97 and X3D content written in Java (*http://www.xj3d.org/*). There's a version for Aviatrix3D, a Java scene graph API over the top of JOGL (*http://aviatrix3d.j3d.org/*). There's no Java 3D version at the moment (December 2004).

M3G

Java 2 Micro Edition (J2ME) has an optional 3D graphics API package called M3G. It's an interesting mix of high-level and low-level 3D graphics features, developed under JSR 184. M3G includes a SkinnedMesh class, which represents a skeletally polygon mesh.

A good source of M3G documentation, articles, and examples is Nokia (*http://www.forum.nokia.com/java/jsr184*) and the web site for this book (*http://fivedots.coe.psu.ac.th/~ad/jg/*), which includes five chapters about M3G (including one on skinning).

Magicosm

The Magicosm site has a page about its skin and bone capabilities (*http://www.cosm-game.com/dev_skinbones.php*), posted in 2001. The Skeleton class contains a hierarchy of bones and stores active, queued, and dormant animations. A Skin is a collection of sinews, vertices and triangles. Each Sinew object forms a bond between a vertex and a bone with a weight.

Articulation and Morphing

Another animation possibility is *morphing*, which allows a smooth transition between different GeometryArrays. This is done using a Morph node, set up in a similar way to a Switch to access its child geometries but with weights assigned to the shapes. The Morph node combines the geometries into a single aggregate shape based on each GeometryArray's corresponding weight. Typically, Behavior nodes modify the weights to achieve various morphing effects.

The drawback is that the various objects must have similar structures (e.g., the same number of coordinates). Morphing may not be required for rapidly changing poses since our eyes tend to deceive us by filling in the gaps themselves.

Morphing can be used in two ways with the animation techniques I've been discussing. It can be employed as an interpolation mechanism between models in a keyframe sequence or utilized to deform a figure. The former approach is discussed in Chapter 5 of the Java 3D tutorial where a stick figure is animated. Mesh deformation is illustrated by an example in the Java 3D demos, in the directory *Morphing/*, showing how a hand can be made to slowly wave by morphing between three OBJ files.

MD3 loader

A morphing animation example using the MD3 loader from New Dawn Software (*http://www.newdawnsoftware.com/*) can be found at *http://www.la-cfd.com/cassos/test/md3/*.

M3G

J2ME's M3G API (see the previous section) includes a `MorphingMesh` class. An example showing its capabilities can be found at this book's web site, *http://fivedots.coe.psu.ac.th/~ad/jg/*.

Salamander

Articulated figures in McKay's Salamander (see the previous section) originally used morphing for animation, but it was abandoned in favor of the skinning system. Morphing tended to produce unrealistic visual transitions.

CHAPTER 21

Particle Systems

Particle systems are an important component of many 3D games: when you see sparks flying, smoke swirling, fireworks exploding, snow falling, water shooting, or blood spurting, then it's probably being done with a particle system. A *particle system* consists of a large population of individual particles, perhaps hundreds of thousands, though many commercial games use far fewer depending on the effect required. The particle system is in charge of creating and deleting particles and updating their attributes over time.

A particle is typically rendered as a graphics primitive, such as a point or line, as opposed to a full-fledged 3D shape, such as a sphere or cylinder. This means that rendering overheads can be reduced, an important consideration when so many particles are involved. However, with the advent of more powerful graphics cards, particle systems have started to utilize polygons (e.g., particles made from triangles and quadrilaterals [quads]), which allow textures and lighting to be introduced.

The attributes of a particle vary depending on the kind of system required but typically include position, velocity, forces (e.g., gravity), age, color/texture, shape, size, and transparency. The code that updates a system usually affects particle attributes using time-based equations, but other approaches are possible. For instance, a particle's new position may be a random adjustment of its previous position.

Particle systems often have a *generation shape*, which specifies a bounding volume in which particles can be created. For example, a system for a water fountain will create particles within a small space near the fountain's base. Generation shapes have been extended to specify bounding volumes for particle updating and aging. For instance, if a particle moves outside the space, then it will begin to age and age more quickly as it moves further away. The aging could trigger a change in its size or color, all depending on the application's needs.

A central and practical issue with particle systems is efficiency since a system may be made up of so many particles. Efficiency influences how particles are updated, rendered, and reused (e.g., a *dead particle* may be reset to its initial attribute settings and started again). If particles use texturing, then the texture should be applied to the entire system. A particle is a passive entity: its attributes are changed by the particle system.

 An offshoot of particle systems are flocking boids, which I consider in Chapter 22. A boid is more intelligent in the sense that it has its own internal state and behavior. For instance, a boid may examine the attributes of its nearest neighbors in the flock to adjust its velocity to avoid colliding with them.

Three particle systems are developed in this chapter: one where the particles are points, another using lines, and a third using quadrilaterals (quads). Figures 21-1, 21-2, and 21-3 show the three systems in action.

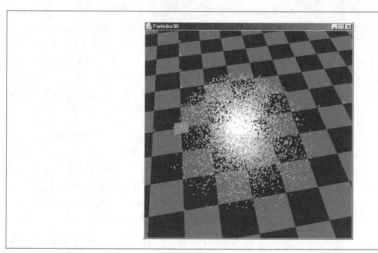

Figure 21-1. A particle system of points

The three systems are part of a single application, Particles3D:

 The example code for this chapter is located in *Particles3D/*.

The coding illustrates the following techniques:

Geometry-based particle systems
   I use Java 3D's PointArray, LineArray, and QuadArray geometries to implement the point-, line-, and quad-based particle systems.

Reduced data copying
   Information is stored in BY_REFERENCE geometries, which avoids the need for a lot of data copying when a geometry is changed.

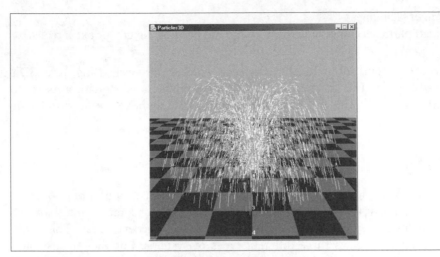

Figure 21-2. A particle system of lines

Figure 21-3. A particle system of quads

Shape management

Shape changes are handled by a subclass of Java 3D's GeometryUpdater interface.

Reusing textures

A single texture is applied to multiple quad particles, as opposed to using one texture for each quad, which would cause a massive increase in memory usage.

Transparent textures

The quad texture has transparent elements, allowing boring quadrilaterals to look more shapely (as in Figure 21-3).

Color and light blending

The quad particles combine texture, color, and lighting effects for extra realism.

The illusion of 3D

A particle system automatically rotates toward the viewer using Java 3D's OrientedShape3D. This means that a 2D geometry, such as a quad, appears to have 3D thickness. This produces the illusion of 3D without the need to create 3D shapes.

Particle Systems in Java 3D

There are several ways of implementing a particle system in Java 3D, but concerns about efficiency mean that many of them are impractical for large systems. In this chapter, particles are represented as elements of a Java 3D GeometryArray. The example in this chapter displays three different types of systems, but they all use subclasses of GeometryArray: a PointArray is employed to store particles as points, a LineArray for particles which are lines, and a QuadArray is used for quads.

The standard approach to using GeometryArray is to make changes to it by copying in new coordinates, colors, etc. This approach introduces two copies of the geometry: one stored internally by Java 3D (the GeometryArray instance) and another in the user's program (usually arrays of coordinates, colors, and so on). When users change their data, they must make sure to update the version maintained by Java 3D. The sample application avoids this approach, since the rapidly changing nature of a particle system and its size would necessitate large amounts of copying, which is just too slow.

The alternative is to link the GeometryArray to the data stored in the user's program. This means users only need to update their version of the data, and Java 3D's GeometryArray will be automatically changed since it's a reference to the user's data. There's no need for copying, and there's a reduction in memory requirements since the data is only stored in one place, in the users' code. This is the approach used in this chapter.

The GeometryArray is created with a BY_REFERENCE flag:

```
// a BY_REFERENCE PointArray with numPoints points
PointArray pointParts = new PointArray(numPoints,
        PointArray.COORDINATES | PointArray.COLOR_3 |
        PointArray.BY_REFERENCE );

// allow things to be read and written by reference
pointParts.setCapability(GeometryArray.ALLOW_REF_DATA_READ);
pointParts.setCapability(GeometryArray.ALLOW_REF_DATA_WRITE);
```

The flag signals that the data managed by the PointArray isn't copied; instead, the PointArray refers to data structures stored in the user's execution space. pointParts will reference two data structures: one maintaining the coordinates of the PointArray and the other the colors of the points at those coordinates.

The next step is to create the local data structures utilized by pointParts. Java 3D 1.3 only supports references to float arrays:

```
private float[] cs, cols;

cs = new float[numPoints*3];    // to store each (x,y,z) coord
cols = new float[numPoints*3];
// fill in the arrays with coordinates and colors

// store coordinates and colors array refs in PointArray
pointParts.setCoordRefFloat(cs);    // use BY_REFERENCE
pointParts.setColorRefFloat(cols);
```

The restriction to float arrays means the coordinates must be stored as individual x-, y-, and z-values, which requires a numPoints*3 size array. Similarly, the red-green-blue components of each color must be stored separately.

Once the arrays have been filled, the references are set up with calls to setCoordRefFloat( ) and setColorRefFloat( ). After these methods have been called, the program need only change the cs and cols arrays to change the PointArray. There's no need to copy the changes into the PointArray.

pointParts becomes the geometry of a scene graph node, such as a Shape3D, with:

```
setGeometry(pointParts);
```

Java 3D will render the shape using the data in PointArray and update the shape when the referenced float arrays are modified.

Referring to Float Arrays

The Java 3D distribution comes with several demos using BY_REFERENCE geometry; the most relevant to understanding referenced geometries is the GeometryByReferenceTest application, available in <JAVA HOME>/demo/java3d/GeometryByReference/. The code sets up references to Point3f and Color3f arrays with the following methods:

```
setCoordRef3f( );
setColorRef3f( );
```

However, these methods—and similar ones for textures and normals—are deprecated in Java 1.3, and the GeometryByReference demo has not been updated. The reason for the deprecation is to reduce the work required by Java 3D to maintain the references.

Synchronization Problems

An important issue is when the user's program should update the float arrays referenced by the geometry. The simple—but wrong—answer is "whenever it wants" as this may lead to synchronization problems. Java 3D will periodically access the arrays to use their information for rendering the geometry, and problems may occur if this examination is intertwined with the arrays being changed by the user's code. The nasty aspect of synchronization bugs is their time-dependency, which makes them hard to detect during testing.

Synchronization worries are avoided by using Java 3D's GeometryUpdater interface to update the geometry:

```
public class PointsUpdater implements GeometryUpdater
{
  public void updateData(Geometry geo)
  { PointArray pa = (PointArray) geo;
    float[] cs = pa.getCoordRefFloat();     // use BY_REFERENCE
    float[] cols = pa.getColorRefFloat();
     // update the cs and cols float arrays
  }

  // other support methods
}
```

Java 3D passes a GeometryArray reference to the updateDate() method when it's safe for the user's program to carry out changes. The reference must be cast to the right type, and then the getCoordRefFloat() and getColorRefFloat() methods are used to return references to the required float arrays. The arrays can be safely modified, and the changes will be utilized by Java 3D when it next renders the geometry.

A GeometryUpdater object is set up like so:

```
PointsUpdater updater = new PointsUpdater();
// I can now request an update of the pointParts PointArray geometry
pointParts.updateData(updater);
```

Rather confusingly, the updating of the pointParts geometry involves *two* Java 3D methods called updateData(), which are doing slightly different things.

The call to updateData() in pointParts is processed by GeometryArray.updateData(), which requests that Java 3D carry out an update. The method argument is the PointsUpdater object, which will be called by Java 3D when it's safe to perform an update. At that point, Java 3D calls the GeometryUpdater.updateData() method implemented in the PointsUpdater class.

The Inner Class Coding Style

A particle system consists of three classes:

- The particle system class containing the BY_REFERENCE geometry (e.g., a PointArray, LineArray, or QuadArray), the float arrays holding the referenced coordinates, colors, and so on. The class will hold the particle attribute initialization code.

- A GeometryUpdater implementation, which carries out an update of the particle system by changing various attributes in the particles. This means accessing and changing the particle system's float arrays.

- A Behavior class which is triggered periodically and then calls the geometry's updateData( ) method, thereby requesting an update.

This functionality requires a substantial amount of shared data between the classes. Consequently, the particle systems detailed in this chapter will use inner classes to implement the Behavior and GeometryUpdater classes. An added benefit of this strategy is the inner classes will be hidden from the user of the particle system.

The coding style is illustrated in Figure 21-4, which shows a simplified class diagram for the PointParticles class, which manages the particle system made of points.

 The details of each of these classes will be explained in subsequent sections.

The other two particle systems in the Particles3D application have the same basic structure.

Class Diagrams for Particles3D

Figure 21-5 shows the class diagrams for the Particles3D program. Only the class names are shown.

Particles3D is the top-level JFrame for the application. WrapParticles3D creates the 3D scene and is similar to the earlier Wrap classes in that it creates the checkered floor and sets up lighting. WrapParticles3D invokes one of the three particle systems (PointParticles, LineParticles, or QuadParticles), depending on user input.

The PointParticles and LineParticles particle systems are subclasses of Shape3D, allowing them to be added to the 3D scene easily. QuadParticles is a subclass of OrientedShape3D and permits its on-screen representation to rotate towards the viewer.

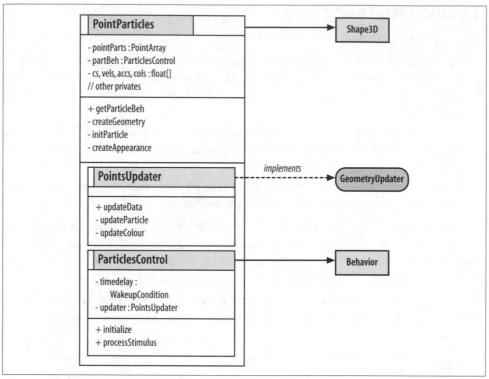

Figure 21-4. Point particle systems class structure

The diagrams for the particle system classes show they use the inner classes approach with GeometryUpdater and Behavior classes. CheckerFloor and ColouredTiles are the same as in previous examples.

Creating the Scene

The WrapParticles3D object is passed two integers from the command line: the number of points to be used when creating a particle system and an integer between 1 and 3, which selects a particular system. The selection is done inside the createSceneGraph( ) method:

```
switch(fountainChoice) {
  case 1: addPointsFountain(numParts); break;
  case 2: addLinesFountain(numParts); break;
  case 3: addQuadFountain(numParts); break;
  default: break;   // do nothing
}
```

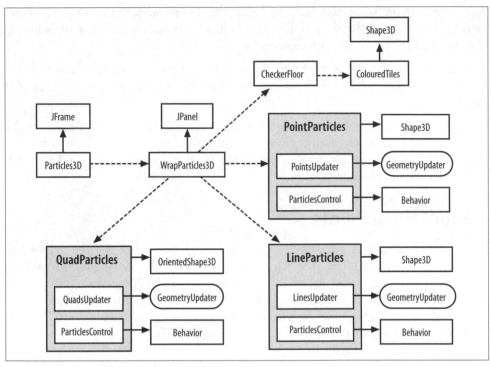

Figure 21-5. The Particles3D classes

The three particle systems all render variants of a fountain, which explains the prevalence of the word "fountain." The three addFountain( ) methods are similar, with addPointsFountain( ) the longest:

```
private void addPointsFountain(int numParts)
{
  PointParticles ptsFountain = new PointParticles(numParts, 20);
  // 20ms time delay between updates

  // move particles start position to (2,0,1)
  TransformGroup posnTG = new TransformGroup( );
  Transform3D trans = new Transform3D( );
  trans.setTranslation( new Vector3d(2.0f, 0.0f, 1.0f) );
  posnTG.setTransform(trans);
  posnTG.addChild(ptsFountain);
  sceneBG.addChild( posnTG );

  // timed behavior to animate the fountain
  Behavior partBeh = ptsFountain.getParticleBeh( );
  partBeh.setSchedulingBounds( bounds );
  sceneBG.addChild(partBeh);
}
```

The particle system (together with its GeometryUpdater and Behavior objects) is created by the PointParticles() constructor, which supplies the number of points to use and the time delay between each update.

The middle part of the addPointFountain() shows that moving the system—as a single Shape3D entity—to a new position is simple. By default, the systems all start at the origin.

Though the Behavior object is created inside PointParticles, it still needs to be attached to the scene graph and given a bounding volume. This is done in the last part of addPointFountain() and requires a public getParticleBeh() method to return a reference to the behavior.

A Fountain of Points

PointsParticles creates a fountain of points, whose points are colored yellow initially but gradually turn red. The particles are emitted from the origin and travel in parabolas of various velocities in any direction across the XZ plane and upwards along the y-axis. The only force applied to the particles is gravity which will affect their acceleration and velocity over time. When a particle drops below the XZ plane, it's reused by having its attributes reset to their initial settings.

A particle has four attributes:

- Its (x, y, z) location
- Its velocity (expressed in x-, y-, and z-directional components)
- Its acceleration (also expressed as three components)
- Its color (as three floats for its Red/Green/Blue parts)

The class diagram for PointParticles is shown in Figure 21-4. The attributes are represented by the float arrays cs, vels, accs, and cols. If the user starts the PointParticles system with numPoints particles, these arrays will be sized at numPoints*3 to accommodate all the necessary data.

The PointParticles() constructor initializes the PointArray as outlined:

```
PointArray pointParts = new PointArray(numPoints,
            PointArray.COORDINATES | PointArray.COLOR_3 |
            PointArray.BY_REFERENCE );

// allow things to be read and written by reference
pointParts.setCapability(GeometryArray.ALLOW_REF_DATA_READ);
pointParts.setCapability(GeometryArray.ALLOW_REF_DATA_WRITE);
```

The constructor creates the GeometryUpdater and Behavior objects:

```
PointsUpdater updater = new PointsUpdater();
partBeh = new PartclesControl(delay, updater);
```

partBeh is a global so it can be returned by getParticleBeh():

```
public Behavior getParticleBeh()
{ return partBeh;  }
```

The constructor calls createGeometry() to initialize the Shape3D's geometry and createAppearance() for its appearance.

The Particle System's Geometry and Appearance

createGeometry() declares the float arrays, initializes them, and sets up references to the coordinate and color float arrays for the PointArray:

```
private void createGeometry()
{ cs = new float[numPoints*3];    // to store each (x,y,z)
  vels = new float[numPoints*3];
  accs = new float[numPoints*3];
  cols = new float[numPoints*3];

  // step in 3's == one (x,y,z) coord
  for(int i=0; i < numPoints*3; i=i+3)
    initParticle(i);

  // store the coordinates and colors in the PointArray
  pointParts.setCoordRefFloat(cs);     // use BY_REFERENCE
  pointParts.setColorRefFloat(cols);

  setGeometry(pointParts);
}
```

pointParts is only set to refer to the cs and cols arrays since these contain the position and color data required for each point. GeometryArrays may be assigned normals and texture coordinates, as you'll see in the QuadParticles class.

initParticles() is called in steps of three, as each iteration is initializing one point, which is equivalent to three values in the float arrays:

```
private void initParticle(int i)
{ cs[i] = 0.0f; cs[i+1] = 0.0f; cs[i+2] = 0.0f;
      // (x,y,z) at origin
  // random velocity in XZ plane with combined vector XZ_VELOCITY
  double xvel = Math.random()*XZ_VELOCITY;
  double zvel = Math.sqrt((XZ_VELOCITY*XZ_VELOCITY) - (xvel*xvel));
  vels[i] = (float)((Math.random()<0.5) ? -xvel : xvel);  // x vel
  vels[i+2] = (float)((Math.random()<0.5) ? -zvel : zvel);// z vel
  vels[i+1] = (float)(Math.random() * Y_VELOCITY);  // y vel

  // unchanging accelerations, downwards in y direction
  accs[i] = 0.0f; accs[i+1] = -GRAVITY; accs[i+2] = 0.0f;

  // initial particle color is yellow
  cols[i] = yellow.x;  cols[i+1] = yellow.y; cols[i+2] = yellow.z;
}
```

The method initializes the cs[], vels[], accs[], and cols[] arrays.

The x-axis velocity is randomly set between -XZ_VELOCITY and XZ_VELOCITY, and the z-axis velocity is assigned the value that makes the magnitude of the combined XZ vector equal XZ_VELOCITY. This means that particles can travel in any direction across the XZ plane, but they all have the same speed.

The only acceleration is a constant, gravity down the y-axis. By including accelerations in the x- and z-directions, forces such as air resistance could be simulated as well.

createAppearance( ) increases the point size of the particles:

```
private void createAppearance( )
{ Appearance app = new Appearance( );
  PointAttributes pa = new PointAttributes( );
  pa.setPointSize( POINTSIZE );  // may cause bugs
  app.setPointAttributes(pa);
  setAppearance(app);
}
```

Point size adjustment, point anti-aliasing, line size adjustment, and line anti-aliasing are poorly supported in Java 3D because of weaknesses in the underlying graphics libraries and/or drivers. Currently, OpenGL and OpenGL-compatible graphics cards can cope, but DirectX-based system often crash.

Updating the Points

The PointsUpdater class utilizes updateData( ) differently than outlined earlier:

```
public void updateData(Geometry geo)
{ // GeometryArray ga = (GeometryArray) geo;
  // float cds[] = ga.getCoordRefFloat( );

  // step in 3's == one (x,y,z) coord
  for(int i=0; i < numPoints*3; i=i+3) {
    if (cs[i+1] < 0.0f)     // particle dropped below y-axis
      initParticle(i);       // reinitialise it
    else          // update the particle
      updateParticle(i);
  }
} // end of updateData( )
```

The commented out lines indicate that no use is made of the Geometry input argument. Instead, the float arrays (cs[], vels[], accs[], and cols[]), which are global, are accessed directly.

 updateData( )'s primary purpose is to be called by Java 3D when it's safe to modify the arrays. It doesn't matter where the array references originate.

updateData( ) implements particle reuse by detecting when a particle has dropped below the y-axis and then reinitializing it by calling PointParticles's initParticle( ) method. This shows the advantage of using an inner class and global float arrays.

Updating Particles

Underpinning the motion of the particles is Newton's second law, which relates force (F) to mass (m) and acceleration (a):

$F = ma$

I can make this simpler by assuming that a particle has a mass of one unit:

$F = a$

In other words, the only force on a particle is constant acceleration, which is gravity for the examples in this chapter.

It's possible to obtain velocity and distance equations from this basic assumption by using Euler's integration algorithm. The acceleration equation can be written as:

$d\ vel/dt = a$

or:

$d\ vel = a\ dt$

Using Euler's method, you can obtain the velocity equation:

$vel(t + dt) = vel(t) + a\ dt$

Integrating again:

$dist(t + dt) = dist(t) + vel(t)\ dt + 1/2\ a\ dt^2$

The equations can be separated into their x-, y-, and z-components. For example:

$vel_x(t+dt) = vel_x(t) + a_x\ dt$
$dist_x(t+dt) = dist_x(t) + vel_x(t)\ dt + 1/2\ a_x\ dt^2$

These equations are embedded in the updateParticle( ) method, where $dist_x$, $dist_y$, and $dist_z$ are cs[i] to cs[i+2], and vel_x, vel_y, and vel_z are vels[i] to vels[i+2]:

```
private void updateParticle(int i)
{ cs[i] += vels[i] * TIMESTEP +
          0.5 * accs[i] * TIMESTEP * TIMESTEP;      // x coord
  cs[i+1] += vels[i+1] * TIMESTEP +
          0.5 * accs[i+1] * TIMESTEP * TIMESTEP;  // y coord
  cs[i+2] += vels[i+2] * TIMESTEP +
          0.5 * accs[i+2] * TIMESTEP * TIMESTEP;  // z coord

  vels[i] += accs[i] * TIMESTEP;      // x vel
  vels[i+1] += accs[i+1] * TIMESTEP;  // y vel
  vels[i+2] += accs[i+2] * TIMESTEP;  // z vel
```

```
      updateColour(i);
    } // end of updateParticle( )
```

The small time step, dt, is fixed as the constant TIMESTEP (0.05f).

updateColor( ) reduces the green and blue components of a point's color. Over time, these will drop to 0, leaving only red:

```
    private void updateColour(int i)
    { cols[i+1] = cols[i+1] - FADE_INCR;    // green part
      if (cols[i+1] < 0.0f)
        cols[i+1] = 0.0f;
      cols[i+2] = cols[i+2] - FADE_INCR;    // blue part
      if (cols[i+2] < 0.0f)
        cols[i+2] = 0.0f;
    }
```

Triggering an Update

The ParticlesControl behavior requests an update to the PointArray every few milliseconds:

```
    public class PartclesControl extends Behavior
    { private WakeupCondition timedelay;
      private PointsUpdater updater;

      public PartclesControl(int delay, PointsUpdater updt)
      {   timedelay = new WakeupOnElapsedTime(delay);
          updater = updt;
      }

      public void initialize( )
      { wakeupOn( timedelay );  }

      public void processStimulus(Enumeration criteria)
      { pointParts.updateData(updater);  // request update of geometry
        wakeupOn( timedelay );
      }
    }  // end of PartclesControl class
```

This behavior is almost the same in each of the particle system classes: only the types of the GeometryArray and GeometryUpdater arguments change.

A Fountain of Lines

The LineParticles class implements a particle system made up of yellow and red lines, which shoot out from the origin with parabolic trajectories. The effect, as seen in Figure 21-2, is something like a firework. The thickness of the lines is increased slightly, and anti-aliasing is switched on. When a line has completely dropped below the y-axis, it's reinitialized, which means the firework never runs out.

The main difference from PointParticles is the extra code required to initialize the lines and update them inside the float arrays. Six values in a float array are necessary to represent a single line, three values for each of the two end points.

The LineParticles constructor creates a LineArray object using BY_REFERENCE geometry for its coordinates and color:

```
lineParts = new LineArray(numPoints, LineArray.COORDINATES |
                          LineArray.COLOR_3 | LineArray.BY_REFERENCE );

lineParts.setCapability(GeometryArray.ALLOW_REF_DATA_READ);
lineParts.setCapability(GeometryArray.ALLOW_REF_DATA_WRITE);
```

Initializing the Particles

The changes start with the initialization of the float arrays inside createGeometry( ):

```
// step in 6's == two (x,y,z) coords == one line
for(int i=0; i < numPoints*3; i=i+6)
  initTwoParticles(i);
```

initTwoParticles( ) initializes the two points. It assigns the same position and velocity to both points and then calls updateParticle( ) to update one of the point's position and velocity. This specifies a line with a point which is one update ahead of the other point. This means that as the particle system is updated, each line will follow a smooth path since one point is following the other.

The color of the line is set to red or yellow by fixing the colors of both points:

```
private void initTwoParticles(int i)
{ cs[i] = 0.0f; cs[i+1] = 0.0f; cs[i+2] = 0.0f;    // origin

  // random velocity in XZ plane with combined vector XZ_VELOCITY
  double xvel = Math.random( )*XZ_VELOCITY;
  double zvel = Math.sqrt((XZ_VELOCITY*XZ_VELOCITY) - (xvel*xvel));
  vels[i] = (float)((Math.random( )<0.5) ? -xvel : xvel);   // x vel
  vels[i+2] = (float)((Math.random( )<0.5) ? -zvel : zvel); // z vel
  vels[i+1] = (float)(Math.random( ) * Y_VELOCITY); // y vel

  // unchanging accelerations, downwards in y direction
  accs[i] = 0.0f; accs[i+1] = -GRAVITY; accs[i+2] = 0.0f;

  // next particle starts the same, but is one update advanced
  cs[i+3] = cs[i]; cs[i+4] = cs[i+1]; cs[i+5] = cs[i+2];
  vels[i+3] =vels[i]; vels[i+4] = vels[i+1]; vels[i+5] = vels[i+2];
  accs[i+3] =accs[i]; accs[i+4] = accs[i+1]; accs[i+5] = accs[i+2];
  updateParticle(i+3);

  // set initial colors for the first particle
  Color3f col = (Math.random( ) < 0.5) ? yellow : red;
  cols[i] = col.x;    cols[i+1] = col.y; cols[i+2] = col.z;
  // the next particle has the same colors
  cols[i+3] = col.x; cols[i+4] = col.y; cols[i+5] = col.z;
} // end of initTwoParticles( )
```

initTwoParticles() is similar to the initParticles() method in PointParticles because they set up a parabolic trajectory for their particles.

The updateParticle() method does the same task as the one in PointParticles but is located in the particle systems class (LineParticles) rather than in GeometryUpdater.

Particle Appearance

createAppearance() adjusts the line width, and switches on anti-aliasing:

```
private void createAppearance()
{ Appearance app = new Appearance();
  LineAttributes la = new LineAttributes();
  la.setLineWidth( LINEWIDTH );    // may cause bugs
  la.setLineAntialiasingEnable(true);
  app.setLineAttributes(la);
  setAppearance(app);
}
```

 As mentioned previously, these features may cause DirectX-based system, or machines with old graphics cards, to respond strangely or crash.

Updating the Particle System

LinesUpdater implements the GeometryUpdater interface, and specifies updateData(). The method ignores the Geometry argument and, instead, uses the global float arrays directly. It makes use of the initTwoParticles() and updateParticle() methods in LineParticles:

```
public void updateData(Geometry geo)
{
  // step in 6's == two (x,y,z) coords == one line
  for(int i=0; i < numPoints*3; i=i+6) {
    if ((cs[i+1] < 0.0f) && (cs[i+4] < 0.0f))
    // both particles in the line have dropped below the y-axis
      initTwoParticles(i);    // reinitialise them
    else {        // update the two particles
      updateParticle(i);
      updateParticle(i+3);
    }
  }
}
```

A Fountain of Quads

Though many particle systems can be modeled with points and lines, quadrilaterals (quads) combined with textures allow more interesting effects. The texture can contain extra surface detail and can be partially transparent to break up the regularity of the quad shape. A quad can be assigned a normal and a `Material` node component to allow it to be affected by lighting in the scene.

The only danger with these additional features is that they may decelerate rendering. The example here only utilizes a single `Texture2D` object and stores all the quads in a single `QuadArray`, thereby reducing the overheads of texture and shape creation considerably.

The effect I'm after with this example is suitably gory: a fountain of blood corpuscles gushing up from the origin. Each "blood" particle is roughly spherical and oscillates slightly as it travels through the air.

Figure 21-3 shows the `QuadParticles` system in action. If the user viewpoint is rotated around the fountain, the particles seem to be rounded on all sides (see Figure 21-6).

Figure 21-6. A fountain of blood from the back

It's a mistake to represent the particles using `GeometryArray` meshes; the number of vertices required for a reasonable blood cell would severely restrict the total number of particles that could be created. Instead the effect is achieved by trickery: the particle system is placed inside an `OrientedShape3D` node, rather than a `Shape3D`.

`OrientedShape3D` nodes automatically face toward the viewer and can be set to rotate about a particular point or axis. Since the particle system is rooted at the origin, it makes the most sense to rotate the system about the y-axis.

`QuadParticles` is made a subclass of `OrientedShape3D`, rather than `Shape3D`, and its constructor specifies the rotation axis:

```
// rotate about the y-axis to follow the viewer
setAlignmentAxis( 0.0f, 1.0f, 0.0f);
```

This means that the illusion of blood globules starts to breaks down if the viewpoint is looking down toward the XZ plane, as in Figure 21-7.

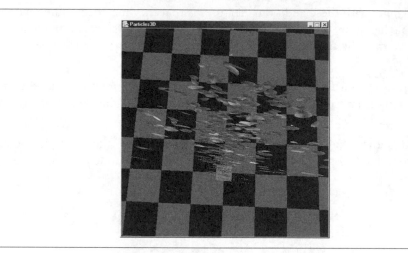

Figure 21-7. The fountain of blood from above

There is a drawback with the y-axis rotation setting in setAlignmentAxis( ): the entire particle system rotates as the viewpoint moves so each particle retains its position relative to the others. This is noticeable with the fountain of blood since each particle is large and moving relatively slowly. It's interesting to experiment with different alignment values, such as rotations around the x- or z-axes, or axis combinations.

Specifying the Geometry

The QuadArray requires information about coordinates, textures, and normals:

```
// BY_REFERENCE QuadArray
quadParts = new QuadArray(numPoints,GeometryArray.COORDINATES |
                    GeometryArray.TEXTURE_COORDINATE_2 |
                    GeometryArray.NORMALS   |
                    GeometryArray.BY_REFERENCE );


// the referenced data can be read and written
quadParts.setCapability(GeometryArray.ALLOW_REF_DATA_READ);
quadParts.setCapability(GeometryArray.ALLOW_REF_DATA_WRITE);
```

Using BY_REFERENCE means there must be float arrays for the coordinates, velocities, and accelerations (as before), and for normals and texture coordinates:

```
private float[] cs, vels, accs, norms;
private float[] tcoords;

cs = new float[numPoints*3];   // to store each (x,y,z)
vels = new float[numPoints*3];
accs = new float[numPoints*3];
```

```
norms = new float[numPoints*3];
tcoords = new float[numPoints*2];
```

Each vertex in the QuadArray (there are numPoints of them) requires a texture coordinate (s, t), where s and t have float values in the range 0 to 1 (see Chapter 16 for the first use of Texture2D).

 As of Java 3D 1.3, the use of a TexCoord2f array to store the texture coordinates of a BY_REFERENCE geometry is no longer encouraged; a float array should be employed. Instead of storing numPoints TexCoord2f objects, numPoints*2 floats are added to a tcoords[] array.

Initializing Particle Movement

A particle is a single quad, made up of four vertices (12 floats). The consequence is that much of the particle initialization and updating code utilizes loops which make steps of 12 through the float arrays. The creation/updating of one quad involves 12 floats at a time.

createGeometry( ) calls initQuadParticle( ) to initialize each quad:

```
for(int i=0; i < numPoints*3; i=i+12)
  initQuadParticle(i);
// refer to the coordinates in the QuadArray
quadParts.setCoordRefFloat(cs);
```

initQuadParticles( ) has a similar style to the initialization methods in PointParticles and LineParticles. The idea is to use the same initial velocity and acceleration for all the vertices and to make the parts of the quad move in the same manner.

The position of a quad is determined by setting its four points to have the values stored in the globals p1, p2, p3, and p4:

```
private float[] p1 = {-QUAD_LEN/2, 0.0f, 0.0f};
private float[] p2 = {QUAD_LEN/2, 0.0f, 0.0f};
private float[] p3 = {QUAD_LEN/2, QUAD_LEN, 0.0f};
private float[] p4 = {-QUAD_LEN/2, QUAD_LEN, 0.0f};
```

The order of these starting points is important: they specify the quad in a counter-clockwise order starting from the bottom-left point. Collectively, the points define a quad of sides QUAD_LEN, facing along the positive z-axis, resting on the XZ plane, and centered at the origin. This is illustrated by Figure 21-8.

The QuadArray will contain quads which all begin at this position and orientation.

Initializing Particle Texture Coordinates

The aim is to add a texture to each particle (each quad) in the QuadArray and to use only one Texture2D object. This is possible by mapping the four vertices of each quad

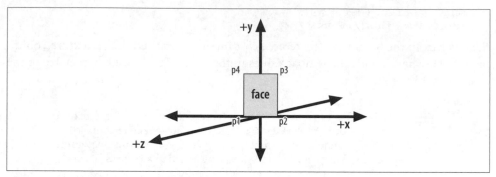

Figure 21-8. Initial quad position

to the same (s, t) texels. Later, when the Texture2D is set in the Appearance node component, it will be applied to all the quads in the QuadArray individually. The mapping of quad coords to texels is represented in Figure 21-9.

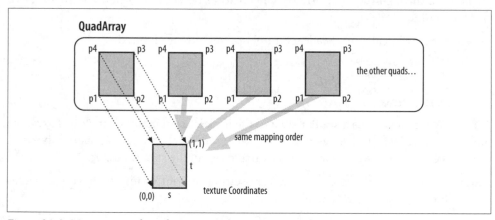

Figure 21-9. Mapping quads to the same texels

The texels should be specified in an counterclockwise order starting at the bottom left so they possess the same ordering as the quad vertices; otherwise, the texture image will appear distorted.

The mapping is done in createGeometry( ):

```
for(int i=0; i < numPoints*2; i=i+8) {
  tcoords[i]   = 0.0f; tcoords[i+1] = 0.0f;  // for one vertex
  tcoords[i+2] = 1.0f; tcoords[i+3] = 0.0f;
  tcoords[i+4] = 1.0f; tcoords[i+5] = 1.0f;
  tcoords[i+6] = 0.0f; tcoords[i+7] = 1.0f;
}
quadParts.setTexCoordRefFloat(0, tcoords);    // use BY_REFERENCE
```

tcoords is filled with a repeating sequence of (s, t) texels (in float format). When this is applied to the QuadArray, Java 3D will map the vertices to the texels.

The code is difficult to understand because the cs[] array (holding the vertices) is bigger than tcoords[] (holding the texels). The reason for the size difference is that a vertex is stored as three floats, but a texel only needs two.

Initializing Particle Normals

For lighting and Material node components to work, normals must be set for the points of each quad. The desired effect is a fountain of globules pumping out in different directions, which can be enhanced by assigning random normals to the quads. This causes each one to reflect light in a different way, giving the impression of surface variations. In fact, the normals won't be completely random: the z-direction should be positive so light is bounced back toward the viewer, but the x- and y- components can be positive or negative. A further restriction is that the normal vector must be unit length (i.e., be normalized).

Here's the code in createGeometry() that does this:

```
Vector3f norm = new Vector3f();
for(int i=0; i < numPoints*3; i=i+3) {
  randomNormal(norm);
  norms[i]=norm.x; norms[i+1]=norm.y; norms[i+2]=norm.z;
}
quadParts.setNormalRefFloat(norms);    // use BY_REFERENCE
```

and:

```
private void randomNormal(Vector3f v)
{ float z = (float) Math.random();       // between 0-1
  float x = (float)(Math.random()*2.0 - 1.0);   // -1 to 1
  float y = (float)(Math.random()*2.0 - 1.0);   // -1 to 1
  v.set(x,y,z);
  v.normalize();
}
```

Particle Appearance

createAppearance() carries out four tasks:

- It switches on transparency blending so the transparent parts of a texture will be invisible inside Java 3D.
- It turns on texture modulation so the texture and material colors will be displayed together.
- It loads the texture.
- It sets the material to a blood red.

Here's the code:

```
private void createAppearance()
{ Appearance app = new Appearance();
```

```
// blended transparency so texture can be irregular
TransparencyAttributes tra = new TransparencyAttributes();
tra.setTransparencyMode( TransparencyAttributes.BLENDED );
app.setTransparencyAttributes( tra );

// mix the texture and the material color
TextureAttributes ta = new TextureAttributes();
ta.setTextureMode(TextureAttributes.MODULATE);
app.setTextureAttributes(ta);

// load and set the texture
System.out.println("Loading textures from " + TEX_FNM);
TextureLoader loader = new TextureLoader(TEX_FNM, null);
Texture2D texture = (Texture2D) loader.getTexture();
app.setTexture(texture);

// set the material: bloody
Material mat = new Material(darkRed, black, red, white, 20.f);
mat.setLightingEnable(true);
app.setMaterial(mat);

setAppearance(app);
}
```

TEX_FNM is the file *smoke.gif*, shown in Figure 21-10. Its background is transparent (i.e., its alpha is 0.0).

Figure 21-10. The smoke.gif texture

createAppearance( ) doesn't switch off polygon culling, which means that the back face of each quad will be invisible (the default action). Will this spoil the illusion when the viewer moves round the back of the particle system? No, because the system is inside an OrientedShape3D node and will rotate to keep its front pointing at the user.

Permitting back face culling improves overall speed since Java 3D only has to render half of the quad.

Updating the Particles

QuadsUpdater is similar to previous GeometryUpdater implementations but works on groups of four points (12 floats) at a time. When a quad has completely dropped below the XZ plane then it's reinitialized: the blood never stops flowing.

Here is updateDate( )'s code:

```
public void updateData(Geometry geo)
{   // step in 12's == 4 (x,y,z) coords == one quad
    for(int i=0; i < numPoints*3; i=i+12)
        updateQuadParticle(i);
}

private void updateQuadParticle(int i)
{ if ((cs[i+1] < 0.0f) && (cs[i+4] < 0.0f) &&
      (cs[i+7] < 0.0f) && (cs[i+10] < 0.0f))
      // all of the quad has dropped below the y-axis
      initQuadParticle(i);
  else {
      updateParticle(i);   // all points in a quad change the same
      updateParticle(i+3);
      updateParticle(i+6);
      updateParticle(i+9);
  }
}
```

updateParticle( ) uses the same position and velocity equations as the point and line-based particle systems but with a slight modification to the position calculation. After the new coordinates for a point have been stored in cs[i], cs[i+1], and cs[i+2], they are adjusted:

```
cs[i] = perturbate(cs[i], DELTA);
cs[i+1] = perturbate(cs[i+1], DELTA);
cs[i+1] = perturbate(cs[i+1], DELTA);
```

perturbate( ) adds a random number in the range -DELTA to DELTA, to the coordinate (DELTA is set to be 0.05f). This has the effect of slightly distorting the quad as it moves through the scene, which causes the texture to twist.

Figure 21-11 shows the particle system with the perturbate( ) calls commented out: each quad looks like a perfect sphere, which is unconvincing. This should be compared to the irregular shapes in Figures 21-3 and 21-6.

Performance Results

Many of the techniques used in this chapter are aimed at increasing performance (balanced against realism and functionality). The obvious question is how fast are these particle systems? Table 21-1 gives average frames per second (FPS) for the PointParticles, LineParticles, and QuadParticles classes, initialized with increasing numbers of points.

Figure 21-11. Particles without perturbation

Table 21-1. Average FPS for the particle system with varying numbers of points

	Number of points					
	1,000	**5,000**	**10,000**	**20,000**	**50,000**	**100,000**
Point particles	19 (50)	19 (35)	19 (24)	12 (14)	7 (7)	4 (4)
Line particles	19 (50)	19 (45)	19 (35)	19 (24)	11 (11)	6 (6)
Quad particles	19 (44)	14 (17)	9 (9)	6 (6)	2 (2)	1 (1)

These averages are for at least five runs of the application. The hardware used was a Pentium IV 1800 MHz, 256 MB RAM, and an old NVIDIA RIVA TNT 2 Model 64 display card. The window size was 512×512 pixels.

The first number in a cell is the FPS reported by FRAPS (a screenshot utility available at *http://www.fraps.com*) when the application was left to run for a minute or so. The number in parentheses is the reported FPS when the mouse was moved rapidly inside the application window. This shows the response rate of the application when it had to carry out some basic processing (responding to mouse movements) at the same time as updating the particle system.

 The results for PointParticles and LineParticles are improved if point size and line size are unchanged and anti-aliasing isn't switched on.

The number of points for each column must be divided by two to obtain the number of lines in the LineParticles row by four to get the number of quads in QuadParticles.

When an FPS speed of about 15 is employed, the particle systems are capable of dealing with many thousands of points—about 15,000 points in the PointParticles system, about 15,000 lines (30,000 points) in LineParticles, and 1,000 quads (4,000 points) in QuadParticles.

More Particle Systems

Chapter 5 of the Java 3D tutorial (*Interaction and Animation*) has a section on the GeometryUpdater interface and illustrates it with a LineArray particle system for a fountain. It's similar to my LineArray example but uses a different algorithm for updating the positions of the lines, and it utilizes the Geometry argument of the updateDate( ) method rather than accessing global float arrays.

Sun's Java 3D Demo page (*http://java.sun.com/products/java-media/3D/demos/*) contains two examples by Jeff White showing the use of lines and points to create a swirl of particles that change color.

A Java 3D package for writing particle systems is available at j3d.org (*http://code.j3d.org/*). It utilizes TriangleArrays or QuadArrays and supports attributes for position, color, texture, aging, wind movement, and forces. It supports collision detection through picking and allows bounding boxes to be set to limit movement. It was written by Daniel Selman (the author of the *Java 3D Programming* text); the package is currently an alpha version.

Artur Biesiadowski has a beautiful particle system demo available at *http://nwn-j3d.sourceforge.net/misc/particles.jar*—a mass of glowing, flickering colored clouds of light speeding around and through a central location in space.

Other Java 3D Approaches

The particle systems in this chapter were coded with BY_REFERENCE geometries and GeometryUpdater, but what other ways are there of writing particle systems?

One possibility is to represent each particle by a separate TransformGroup and Shape3D pair and have the particle system move the shapes by adjusting the TransformGroups. This coding style is utilized in an example by Peter Palombi and Chris Buckalew, which is part of Buckalew's CSc 474 Computer Graphics course (*http://www.csc.calpoly.edu/~buckalew/474Lab5-W03.html*). It has the advantage of being simple to understand but isn't scaleable to large numbers of particles.

Another technique is to store all the particles in a GeometryArray as before, but do the updates directly without the involvement of a GeometryUpdater. Synchronization problems can be avoided by detaching the Shape3D from the scene graph before the updates are made and reattaching it afterward. The detachment of the shape removes it from the rendering cycle, so synchronization problems disappear. There seems little advantage to this approach since the overhead of removing and restoring scene graph nodes is large.

If the application uses mixed mode or immediate mode rendering, then the programmer gains control of when rendering is carried out and can avoid synchronization problems.

The excellent Yaarq demo by Wolfgang Kienreich (downloadable from *http://www.ascendancy.at/downloads/yaarq.zip*) is a mixed mode Java3D example showing off a range of advanced techniques such as bump mapping, reflection mapping, overlays, and particle systems. It utilizes a `BY_REFERENCE` `TriangleArray` and a `GeometryUpdater`. The particle attributes include size, position, direction, gravity, friction, alpha values for transparency, and a texture applied to all the particles.

There are three particle systems available at the WolfShade web site (*http://www.wolfshade.com/technical/3d_code.htm*), coded in retained, mixed, and immediate modes. They don't use `BY_REFERENCE` geometries for storing the particles.

Non–Java 3D Approaches

The basic framework for a particle system is fairly standard, and variations only appear when we decide on a particle's attributes and how they change over time. Ideas for these can be gained by looking at implementations in other languages.

Almost every games programming book seems to have a particle system example. For instance, *OpenGL Game Programming* (Muska and Lipman/Premier-Trade) by Kevin Hawkins and Dave Astle implements a snow storm effect, which can be easily translated from C++ to Java.

A popular particle system API created by David McAllister is downloadable at *http://www.cs.unc.edu/~davemc/Particle/*. Its C++ source code is available, as well as excellent documentation. It uses the interesting notions of actions and action lists. Actions are low-level operations for modifying particles, including gravity, bouncing, orbiting, swirling, heading toward a point, matching velocity with another particle, and avoiding other particles. Action lists are groups of actions which together make more complex effects. Many of the actions employ Euler's integration method, which underpins the workings of the parabolas in my examples. The API has been ported to various Unixes, Windows operating systems, and to parallel machines. The API would make an excellent model for a Java 3D–based package.

Most graphics software, such as Maya and 3DS, have particle system animation packages that can be used for testing effects.

The two papers that introduced particle systems are by William T. Reeves:

- "Particle Systems – a Technique for Modeling a Class of Fuzzy Objects," *Computer Graphics*, 17 (3), p.359–376, 1983.
- "Approximate and Probabilistic Algorithms for Shading and Rendering Structured Particle Systems," *Computer Graphics*, 19 (3), p.313–322, 1985.

The first paper was written after Reeves's work on the movie *Star Trek II: The Wrath of Khan*, for which he created a wall of fire that engulfed a planet with a particle system made of points. The second paper came out of the graphics work for the animated cartoon *The Adventures of Andrew and Wally B*, where the particles were small circles and lines used to model tree, branches, leaves, and grass.

GameDev has a small subsection on particle systems in its "Special Effects" section (*http://www.gamedev.net/reference/list.asp?categoryid=72*).

CHAPTER 22
Flocking Boids

Flocking is a computer model for the coordinated motion of groups (or flocks) of entities called boids. Flocking represents group movement—as seen in bird flocks and fish schools—as combinations of steering behaviors for individual boids, based on the position and velocities of nearby flockmates. Though individual flocking behaviors (sometimes called *rules*) are quite simple, they combine to give boids and flocks interesting overall behaviors, which would be complicated to program explicitly.

Flocking is often grouped with *Artificial Life* algorithms because of its use of *emergence*: complex global behaviors arise from the interaction of simple local rules. A crucial part of this complexity is its unpredictability over time; a boid flying in a particular direction may do something different a few moments later. Flocking is useful for games where groups of things, such as soldiers, monsters, or crowds move in complex, coordinated ways.

 Flocking appears in games such as *Unreal* (Epic), *Half-Life* (Sierra), and *Enemy Nations* (Windward Studios).

Flocking was first proposed by Craig Reynolds in his paper "Flocks, Herd, and Schools: A Distributed Behavioral Model," published in *Computer Graphics*, 21(4), SIGGRAPH'87, pp. 25–34.

The basic flocking model consists of three simple steering behaviors (or rules):

Separation
> Steer to avoid crowding local flockmates.

Alignment
> Steer toward the average heading of local flockmates.

Cohesion
> Steer to move toward the average position of local flockmates.

These rules are illustrated in Figure 22-1.

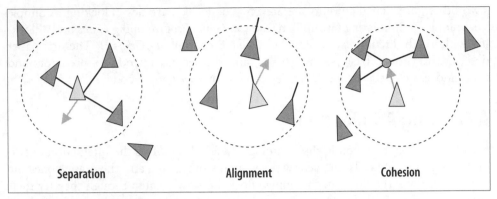

Figure 22-1. Reynolds' steering rules

The circles in Figure 22-1 surround the center boid's local flockmates. Any boids beyond a certain distance of the central boid don't figure in the rule-based calculations.

A more elaborate notion of neighborhood only considers flockmates surrounding the boid's current forward direction (see Figure 22-2). The extent of neighborhood is governed by an arc on either side of the forward vector. This reduced space more closely reflects how real-world flock members interact.

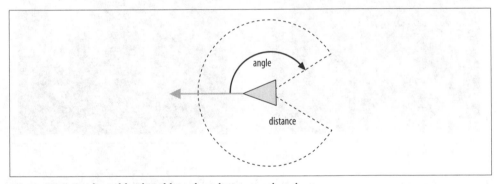

Figure 22-2. Boid neighborhood based on distance and angle

Many other rules have been proposed over the years, including ones for obstacle avoidance and goal seeking. Reynold's web site (*http://www.red3d.com/cwr/boids/*) contains hundreds of links to relevant information, including flocking in games, virtual reality, computer graphics, robotics, art, and artificial life. The plethora of links at Reynold's site can be a tad daunting. A good starting point is Conrad Parker's web page explaining boid algorithms with pseudocode examples (*http://www.vergenet.net/~conrad/boids/pseudocode.html*). He describes Reynolds' steering rules, and additional techniques for goal setting, speed limiting, keeping the flock inside a bounded volume, perching, and flock scattering. His pseudocode was a major influence on the design of my boids' steering rules.

Two other good starting points are Steven Woodcock's articles "Flocking: A Simple Technique for Simulating Group Behavior" in *Game Programming Gems* and "Flocking with Teeth: Predators and Prey" in *Game Programming Gems II*. The first paper describes Reynolds' basic steering rules, and the second introduces predators and prey, and static obstacles. Both articles come with C++ source code.

A Flocking Application

My Flocking3D application is shown in Figure 22-3. It involves the interaction of two different groups of boids: the yellow flock are the predators, and the orange ones the prey. Over time, the boids in the orange flock are slowly eaten though they try their best to avoid it. Both flocks must avoid obstacles and stay within the bounds of the scene.

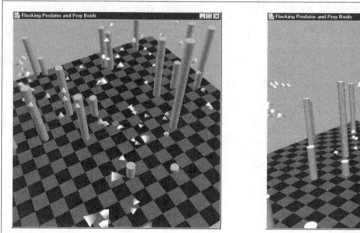

Figure 22-3. Predator and prey flocks in Flocking3D

The lefthand image shows an early stage in the system, when the predators are chasing prey. The righthand image was taken after all the prey have been eaten, and the predators are flying in groups.

 The code in this chapter was developed by one of my students, Miss Sirinart Sakarin, and me; the code can be found in *Flocking3D/*.

Boid behavior includes:

- Reynolds' steering rules for separation, alignment, and cohesion.
- Perching on the ground occasionally.
- Avoiding static obstacles.

- Staying within the scene volume.
- A maximum speed (the prey boids have a higher maximum than the predators).
- When a predator is hungry, it chases prey boids. If it gets close enough to a prey boid, it will eat the prey.
- Prey boids try to avoid predators (they have an aversion to being eaten).

The implementation techniques illustrated in this example include:

Inheritance
Inheritance is used to define the boids (as subclasses of Boid) and their behaviors (as subclasses of FlockingBehavior).

Geometry building
The boid shape (a sort of arrowhead) is built using Java 3D's IndexedTriangleArray.

Synchronized updates
Updates to the boids must be controlled, so changes to the flock in each time interval only become visible when every boid in the flock has been changed.

Scene graph detaching
When a boid is eaten, it's removed from the scene graph by having its BranchGroup detached from its parent node.

Figure 22-4 shows the class diagrams for the application. Only the class names are shown; superclasses that are a standard part of Java or Java 3D (e.g., JPanel, Shape3D) are omitted.

Flocking3D's Ancestor

Flocking3D was influenced by Anthony Steed's Java 3D flocking program, developed back in 1998 as part of a comparison with VRML (*http://www.cs.ucl.ac.uk/staff/A.Steed/ 3ddesktop/*). Each boid in his work is represented as a TransformGroup and utilizes a BoidSet object (a BranchGroup subclass) for a flock. An interesting feature is his use of morphing for wing flapping, implemented as a transition between three TriangleArrays. A FlockBehavior class uses WakeupOnFramesElapsed(0) to trigger boid updates, and a FlapBehavior object for the wings is triggered by WakeupOnTransformChanged events when the boid moves. Flock dynamics include perching, speed limiting, proximity detection, and inertia. There's only one kind of boid, and no obstacles in the scene.

Flocking3D is the top-level JFrame. WrapFlocking3D creates the 3D scene, the predator and prey behaviors, and the obstacles. PreyBehavior and PredatorBehavior can be thought of as flock managers: they initialize the boids that make up their flock and handle rule evaluation at runtime; they're subclasses of the FlockBehavior class.

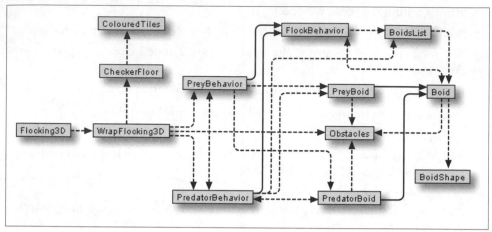

Figure 22-4. The Flocking3D classes

PreyBoid and PredatorBoid represent individual boids and are subclasses of the Boid class. BoidShape is a subclass of Shape3D and manages the boid shape. CheckerFloor and ColouredTiles are the same as in previous examples.

Scene Creation

WrapFlocking3D is like previous Wrap classes in that it creates a 3D scene inside a JPanel, made up of a checkerboard floor, blue sky, lighting, and an OrbitBehavior node to allow the user to adjust the viewpoint.

The additions are the obstacles and the two flocks, both created in addFlockingBoids():

```
private void addFlockingBoids(int numPreds, int numPrey, int numObs)
{ // create obstacles
  Obstacles obs = new Obstacles(numObs);
  sceneBG.addChild( obs.getObsBG() );  // add obstacles to scene

  // make the predator manager
  PredatorBehavior predBeh = new PredatorBehavior(numPreds, obs);
  predBeh.setSchedulingBounds(bounds);
  sceneBG.addChild( predBeh.getBoidsBG() );  // add preds to scene

  // make the prey manager
  PreyBehavior preyBeh = new PreyBehavior(numPrey, obs);
  preyBeh.setSchedulingBounds(bounds);
  sceneBG.addChild( preyBeh.getBoidsBG() );  // add prey to scene

  // tell behaviors about each other
  predBeh.setPreyBeh( preyBeh );
  preyBeh.setPredBeh( predBeh );

} // end of addFlockingBoids()
```

The number of predators, prey, and obstacles are read from the command line in Flocking3D or are assigned default values. The behaviors are passed references to each other so their steering rules can consider neighboring boids of the other type. Here's a typical call to Flocking3D:

```
java Flocking3D 10 200 15
```

This will make addFlockingBoids( ) create 10 predators, 200 prey, and 15 obstacles.

Adding Obstacles

The Obstacles class creates a series of blue cylinders placed at random locations around the XZ plane. The cylinders have a fixed radius, but their heights can vary between 0 and MAX_HEIGHT (8.0f). A cylinder is positioned with a TransformGroup and then added to a BranchGroup for all the cylinders; the BranchGroup is then retrieved by calling getObsBG( ).

At the same time that a cylinder is being created, a BoundingBox is calculated:

```
height = (float)(Math.random( )*MAX_HEIGHT);
lower = new Point3d( x-RADIUS, 0.0f, z-RADIUS );
upper = new Point3d( x+RADIUS, height, z+RADIUS );
bb = new BoundingBox(lower, upper);
```

A boid checks an obstacle's bounding box to avoid colliding with it. The bounding boxes for all the obstacles are added to an ArrayList, which is examined by boids when they call isOverlapping( ). A boid calls isOverlapping( ) with a BoundingSphere object representing its current position:

```
public boolean isOverlapping(BoundingSphere bs)
// Does bs overlap any of the BoundingBox obstacles?
{ BoundingBox bb;
  for (int i=0; i < obsList.size( ); i++) {
    bb = (BoundingBox)obsList.get(i);
    if( bb.intersect(bs) )
      return true;
  }
  return false;
} // end of isOverlapping( )
```

The isOverlapping( ) method sacrifices efficiency for simplicity: the bounding sphere is checked against every obstacle's bounding box in the scene. An obvious improvement would be to order the bounding boxes in some way to reduce the number that needs to be tested. However, this would complicate the code and wouldn't produce much improvement for the small number of obstacles used in my examples.

The boid shape

A boid is represented by a spearhead shape, which is shown from three different directions in Figure 22-5. A prey boid has an orange body with a purple nose, while predators are completely yellow.

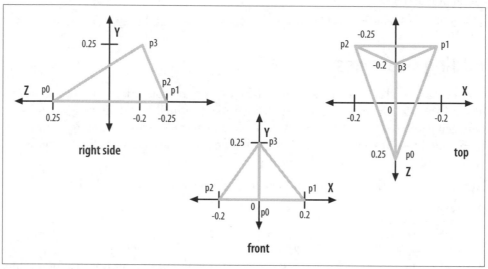

Figure 22-5. CAD sketches for a boid shape

Even with something as simple as this shape, doing a preliminary sketch before resorting to programming is useful. I usually draw a simple side/front/top CAD-style diagram, as in Figure 22-5. The points in the diagrams (p0, p1, etc.) will become the points in the resulting GeometryArray.

Different sides of the shape reuse the same points, which suggests that Java 3D's IndexedGeometry (or a subclass) should represent the shape. IndexedGeometry allows sides to be specified by indices into an array of points, which means fewer points are needed when creating the shape.

The spearhead is made up of four triangles, so my BoidShape class uses a Java 3D IndexedTriangleArray:

```
IndexedTriangleArray plane = new IndexedTriangleArray(NUM_VERTS,
                                GeometryArray.COORDINATES |
                                GeometryArray.COLOR_3, NUM_INDICES);
```

The shape is made from four triangles, but the sharing of sides means there's only four different vertices (labeled as p0, p1, p2, and p3 in Figure 22-5). As a consequence, NUM_VERTS is 4 in the code above. Each vertex has an (x, y, z) coordinate, so the IndexedTriangleArray will use 12 indices (4 vertices each require 3 values). Consequently, NUM_INDICES has the value 12.

First, the points are stored in an array, and then the indices of the points array are used to define the sides in another array:

```
// the shape's coordinates
Point3f[] pts = new Point3f[NUM_VERTS];
pts[0] = new Point3f(0.0f, 0.0f, 0.25f);
pts[1] = new Point3f(0.2f, 0.0f, -0.25f);
pts[2] = new Point3f(-0.2f, 0.0f, -0.25f);
pts[3] = new Point3f(0.0f, 0.25f, -0.2f);

// anti-clockwise face definition
int[] indices = {
    2, 0, 3,      // left face
    2, 1, 0,      // bottom face
    0, 1, 3,      // right face
    1, 2, 3  };   // back face

plane.setCoordinates(0, pts);
plane.setCoordinateIndices(0, indices);
```

Some care must be taken to get the ordering of the indices correct. The points for a face must be listed in counterclockwise order for the front of the face to point toward the viewer. This is an example of the "righthand rule" for orienting normals (discussed back in Chapter 16).

The point colors are set in the same way with an array of Java 3D Color3f objects, and an array of indices into that array:

```
Color3f[] cols = new Color3f[NUM_VERTS];
cols[0] = purple;    // a purple nose
for (int i=1; i < NUM_VERTS; i++)
    cols[i] = col;   // the body color

plane.setColors(0,cols);
plane.setColorIndices(0, indices);
```

The array holding the indices (i.e., indices) can be reused, which may allow some graphics cards to do further optimizations on the shape's internal representation.

My boids don't change shape or color though this is quite common in other flocking systems; perhaps the boid gets bigger as it gets older or eats and changes color to indicate a change to its age or health. From a coding perspective, this requires a mechanism for adjusting the coordinate and/or color values inside BoidShape. The safe way to do this, as discussed in the last chapter, is to use a Java 3D GeometryUpdater, maintained as an inner class of BoidShape. The GeometryArray's updateData() method would be called when the shape and/or its color had to be changed.

Types of Boids

The public and protected methods and data of the Boid class and its PredatorBoid and PreyBoid subclasses are shown in Figure 22-6.

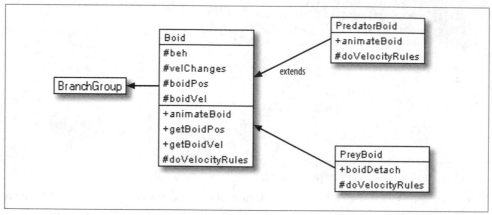

Figure 22-6. The Boid class and subclasses

Boid represents a boid using a BranchGroup, TransformGroup, and BoidShape (a Shape3D node). The TransformGroup moves the boid about in the scene, and the BranchGroup permits the boid to be removed from the scene (e.g., after being eaten). Only a BranchGroup can be detached from a scene graph. The subgraph is built in the Boid( ) constructor:

```
private TransformGroup boidTG = new TransformGroup( );  // global

public Boid(...)
{ // other initialization code, and then ...

  // set TG capabilities so the boid can be moved
  boidTG.setCapability(TransformGroup.ALLOW_TRANSFORM_WRITE);
  boidTG.setCapability(TransformGroup.ALLOW_TRANSFORM_READ);
  addChild(boidTG);   // add TG to Boid BranchGroup

  // add the boid shape to the TG
  boidTG.addChild( new BoidShape(boidColour) );
} // end of Boid( )
```

Boid Movement

The most important attributes for a boid are its current position and velocity. These are set to random values (within a certain range) in the Boid constructor:

```
// globals
protected Vector3f boidPos = new Vector3f( );
protected Vector3f boidVel = new Vector3f( );
```

```
// code in the Boid constructor
boidPos.set(randPosn(),(float)(Math.random()*6.0), randPosn());
boidVel.set( randVel(), randVel(), randVel());
```

The moveBoid( ) method uses them to orient and position the boid in the scene:

```
// global used for repeated calculations
private Transform3D t3d = new Transform3D();

private void moveBoid()
{ t3d.setIdentity();   // reset t3d
  t3d.rotY( Math.atan2( boidVel.x, boidVel.z) );  // around y-axis
        // atan2() handles 0 value input arguments
  t3d.setTranslation(boidPos);
  boidTG.setTransform(t3d);   // move the TG
} // end of moveBoid()
```

The boid position and velocity vectors (boidPos and boidVel) are protected, so subclasses that need to access or change their values can do so easily. moveBoid( ) uses the current velocity to calculate a rotation around the y-axis, and positions the boid with boidPos. A limitation of moveBoid( ) is that the boid doesn't rotate around the x- or z-axes, which means a boid always remains parallel to the XZ plane. For example, a boid can't turn downward into a nose dive or lean over as it turns sharply. This restriction can be removed by adding extra TransformGroup nodes above the boid's current TransformGroup to handle the other forms of rotation.

Animating the Boid

animateBoid( ) is the top-level method for animating a boid and is called by the FlockBehavior class at each update for every boid. animateBoid( ) can be overridden by Boid subclasses (e.g., by PredatorBoid) to modify the animation activities.

animateBoid( ) begins with code related to boid *perching*, which is when a boid is stationary on the floor:

```
// global constants for perching
private final static int PERCH_TIME = 5;     // how long to perch
private final static int PERCH_INTERVAL = 100;  // how long between perches


// global variables for perching
private int perchTime = 0;
private int perchInterval = 0;
private boolean isPerching = false;


public void animateBoid()
{ if (isPerching) {
    if (perchTime > 0) {
      perchTime--;  // perch a while longer
      return;       // skip rest of boid update
    }
```

```
      else {    // finished perching
        isPerching = false;
        boidPos.y = 0.1f;    // give the boid a push up off the floor
        perchInterval = 0;  // reset perching interval
      }
    }
    // update the boid's vel & posn, but keep within scene bounds
    boidVel.set( calcNewVel() );
    boidPos.add(boidVel);
    keepInBounds();
    moveBoid();
  } // end of animateBoid()
```

`keepInBounds()` contains the rest of the perching code:

```
perchInterval++;
if ((perchInterval > PERCH_INTERVAL) &&
     (boidPos.y <= MIN_PT.y)) {    // let the boid perch
  boidPos.y = 0.0f;           // set down on the floor
  perchTime = PERCH_TIME;   // start perching time
  isPerching = true;
}
```

Perching sessions occur at fixed intervals, and each session lasts for a fixed amount of time. During the PERCH_INTERVAL time, the boid must fly about, until the interval is met; then the boid can perch for PERCH_TIME time units before it must start flying again. animateBoid() is called repeatedly by the FlockBehavior object, and perchInterval records the number of calls. When the count exceeds the number stored in PERCH_INTERVAL, perching is initiated.

isPerching is set to true when perching starts, and perchTime is set to PERCH_TIME. Each time that animateBoid() is called after that, perchTime is decremented. When perchTime reaches 0, perching stops. The perchInterval counter is reset to 0, and the perching interval can start being measured off again.

This code illustrates how the timing of boid activities can be implemented using counters. This is possible since animateBoid() is called at fixed intervals by FlockingBehavior.

If the boid is not perching, then calcNewVel() calculates the boid's new velocity and updates boidVel and boidPos with this velocity. keepInBounds() checks these values to decide if they specify a new position for the boid outside the scene's boundaries. If they do, then the values are modified so that when they're applied to the boid, it will stay within the boundary. Back in animateBoid(), the boid in the scene is moved by moveBoid().

Velocity Rules

calcNewVel( ) calculates a new velocity for a boid by executing all of the velocity rules for steering the boid. Each rule returns a velocity, and these velocities are summed by calcNewVel( ) to get a total.

An important design aim is that new velocity rules can be easily added to the system (e.g., by subclassing Boid), so calcNewVel( ) doesn't make any assumptions about the number of velocity rules being executed. Each velocity rule adds its result to a global ArrayList, called velChanges. calcNewVel( ) iterates through the list to find all the velocities.

Two other issues are obstacle avoidance and limiting the maximum speed. If the boid has collided with an obstacle, then the velocity change to avoid the obstacle takes priority over the other velocity rules. The new velocity is limited to a maximum value, so a boid cannot attain the speed of light, or something similar by the combination of the various rules:

```
protected ArrayList velChanges = new ArrayList( ); // globals
protected FlockBehavior beh;


private Vector3f calcNewVel( )
{ velChanges.clear( );    // reset velocities ArrayList

  Vector3f v = avoidObstacles( );        // check for obstacles
  if ((v.x == 0.0f) && (v.z == 0.0f))     // if no obs velocity
    doVelocityRules( );      // then carry out other velocity rules
  else
    velChanges.add(v);      // else only do obstacle avoidance

  newVel.set( boidVel );     // re-initialise newVel
  for(int i=0; i < velChanges.size( ); i++)
    newVel.add( (Vector3f)velChanges.get(i) );  // add vels

  newVel.scale( limitMaxSpeed( ) );
  return newVel;
}  // end of calcNewVel( )


protected void doVelocityRules( )
// override this method to add new velocity rules
{
  Vector3f v1 = beh.cohesion(boidPos);
  Vector3f v2 = beh.separation(boidPos);
  Vector3f v3 = beh.alignment(boidPos, boidVel);
  velChanges.add(v1);
  velChanges.add(v2);
  velChanges.add(v3);
} // end of doVelocityRules( )
```

avoidObstacles( ) always returns a vector even when there is no obstacle to avoid. The "no obstacle" vector has the value (0, 0, 0), which is detected by calcNewVel( ).

 To reduce the number of temporary objects, calcNewVel( ) reuses a global newVel Vector3f object in its calculations.

doVelocityRules( ) has protected visibility so subclasses can readily extend it to add new steering rules. In addition to executing a rule, adding the result to the velChanges ArrayList is necessary. The three rules executed in Boid are Reynolds' rules for cohesion, separation, and alignment.

beh is a reference to the FlockBehavior subclass for the boid. Velocity rules that require the checking of flockmates, or boids from other flocks, are stored in the behavior class, which acts as the flock manager.

Obstacle Avoidance

Obstacle avoidance can be computationally expensive, easily crippling a flocking system involving hundreds of boids and tens of obstacles. The reason is two-fold: the algorithm has to keep looking ahead to detect a collision before the boid image intersects with the obstacle and, therefore, should calculate a rebound velocity that mimics the physical reality of a boid hitting the obstacle.

As usual, a trade-off is made between the accuracy of the real-world simulation and the need for fast computation. In Flocking3D, the emphasis is on speed, so there's no look-ahead collision detection and no complex rebound vector calculation. A boid is allowed to hit (and enter) an obstacle and rebounds in the simplest way possible.

The boid is represented by a bounding sphere, whose radius is fixed but center moves as the boid moves. The sphere is tested for intersection with all the obstacles, and if an intersection is found, then a velocity is calculated based on the negation of the boid's current (x, z) position, scaled by a factor to reduce its effect:

```
private Vector3f avoidObstacles( )
{ avoidOb.set(0,0,0);    // reset
  // update the BoundingSphere's position
  bs.setCenter( new Point3d( (double)boidPos.x,
                    (double)boidPos.y, (double)boidPos.z) );
  if ( obstacles.isOverlapping(bs)) {
    avoidOb.set( -(float)Math.random( )*boidPos.x, 0.0f,
                    -(float)Math.random( )*boidPos.z);
    // scale to reduce distance moved away from the obstacle
    avoidOb.scale(AVOID_WEIGHT);
  }
  return avoidOb;
}
```

There's no adjustment to the boid's y-velocity, which means that if it hits an obstacle from the top, its y-axis velocity will be unchanged (i.e., it'll keep moving downward) but it will change its x- and z-components.

Instead of creating a new temporary object each time obstacle checking is carried out, the code utilizes a global Vector3f object called avoidOb. The bs BoundingSphere object is created when the boid is first instantiated.

Staying in Bounds

keepInBounds() checks a bounding volume defined by two points, MIN_PT and MAX_PT, representing its upper and lower corners. If the boid's position is beyond a boundary, then it's relocated to the boundary, and its velocity component in that direction is reversed.

The following code fragment shows what happens when the boid has passed the upper x-axis boundary:

```
if (boidPos.x > MAX_PT.x) {      // beyond upper x-axis boundary
    boidPos.x = MAX_PT.x;        // put back at edge
    boidVel.x = -Math.abs(boidVel.x);   // move away from boundary
}
```

The same approach is used to check for the upper and lower boundaries along all the axes.

The Prey Boid

A prey boid has an orange body and wants to avoid being eaten by predators. It does this by applying a velocity rule for detecting and evading predators. It has a higher maximum speed than the standard Boid, so it may be able to outrun an attacker.

Since a PreyBoid can be eaten, it must be possible to detach the boid from the scene graph:

```
public class PreyBoid extends Boid
{
  private final static Color3f orange = new Color3f(1.0f,0.75f,0.0f);

  public PreyBoid(Obstacles obs, PreyBehavior beh)
  { super(orange, 2.0f, obs, beh);      // orange and higher max speed
    setCapability(BranchGroup.ALLOW_DETACH);   // prey can be "eaten"
  }

  protected void doVelocityRules()
  // Override doVelocityRules() to evade nearby predators
  { Vector3f v = ((PreyBehavior)beh).seePredators(boidPos);
    velChanges.add(v);
    super.doVelocityRules();
  } // end of doVelocityRules()
```

```
      public void boidDetach()
      { detach(); }
   }
```

The benefits of inheritance are clear, as it's simple to define `PreyBoid`. `doVelocityRules()` in `PreyBoid` adds a rule to the ones present in `Boid` and calls the superclass's method to evaluate those rules as well.

`seePredators()` is located in the `PreyBehavior` object, the manager for the prey flock. The method looks for nearby predators and returns a flee velocity. `seePredators()` is inside `PreyBehavior` because it needs to examine a flock.

The Predator Boid

A predator gets hungry. Hunger will cause it to do two things: eat a prey boid, if one is sufficiently close (as defined by the `eatClosePrey()` method), and trigger a velocity rule to make the predator subsequently pursue nearby prey groups:

```
public class PredatorBoid extends Boid
{ private final static Color3f yellow = new Color3f(1.0f, 1.0f,0.6f);
  private final static int HUNGER_TRIGGER = 3;
                       // when hunger affects behavior
  private int hungerCount;

  public PredatorBoid(Obstacles obs, PredatorBehavior beh)
  { super(yellow, 1.0f, obs, beh);   // yellow boid, normal max speed
    hungerCount = 0;
  }

  public void animateBoid()
  // extend animateBoid() with eating behavior
  { hungerCount++;
    if (hungerCount > HUNGER_TRIGGER)    // time to eat
      hungerCount -= ((PredatorBehavior)beh).eatClosePrey(boidPos);
    super.animateBoid();
  }

  protected void doVelocityRules()
  // extend VelocityRules() with prey attack
  { if (hungerCount > HUNGER_TRIGGER) {  // time to eat
      Vector3f v = ((PredatorBehavior)beh).findClosePrey(boidPos);
      velChanges.add(v);
    }
    super.doVelocityRules();
  }

} // end of PredatorBoid class
```

Eating prey isn't a velocity rule, so it is carried out by extending the behavior of `animateBoid()`. `eatClosePrey()` is located in `PredatorBehavior` because it examines (and modifies) a flock, which means that it's handled by the flock manager. The method returns the number of prey eaten (usually 0 or 1), reducing the predator's hunger.

The movement toward prey is a velocity rule, so it is placed in the overridden doVelocityRules( ) method. Since findClosePrey( ) is looking at a flock, it's carried out by PredatorBehavior.

Grouping the Boids

The FlockBehavior class is a flock manager and, consequently, must maintain a list of boids. The obvious data structure for the task is an ArrayList, but there's a subtle problem: boids may be deleted from the list, as when a prey boid is eaten. This can cause synchronization problems because of the presence of multiple behavior threads in the application.

For example, the PredatorBehavior thread may delete a prey boid from the prey list at the same time that PreyBehavior is about to access the same boid in the list. The solution is to synchronize the deleting and accessing operations so they can't occur simultaneously. This is the purpose of the BoidsList class:

```
public class BoidsList extends ArrayList
{
  public BoidsList(int num)
  {  super(num);  }

  synchronized public Boid getBoid(int i)
  // return the boid if it is visible; null otherwise
  { if (i < super.size( ))
      return (Boid)get(i);
    return null;
  }

  synchronized public boolean removeBoid(int i)
  // attempt to remove the i'th boid
  { if (i < super.size( )) {
      super.remove(i);
      return true;
    }
    return false;
  }

  } // end of BoidsList class
```

Another consequence of the dynamic change of the boids list is that code should not assume that the list's length stays the same. This means, for instance, that for loops using the list size should be avoided. If a for loop was utilized, then a change in the boids list may cause a boid to be processed twice, or skipped, because of its index position changing.

Flock Behavior

The public and protected methods and data of the FlockBehavior class and its PredatorBehavior and PreyBehavior subclasses are shown in Figure 22-7.

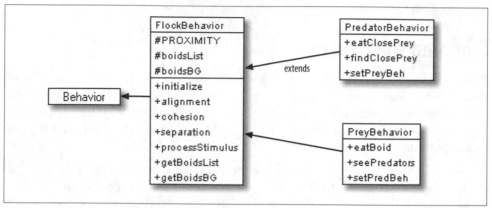

Figure 22-7. FlockBehavior and its subclasses

FlockBehavior has two main tasks:

- To call animateBoid( ) on every boid periodically
- To store the velocity rules, which require an examination of the entire flock

FlockBehavior doesn't create boids since that's handled by its subclasses, and the information required for each type of boid is too specialized to be located in the superclass. PredatorBehavior creates a series of PredatorBoids, and PreyBehavior handles PreyBoids. But the subclass behaviors do use the inherited boidsList list for storage.

Animate the Boids

The calls to animateBoid( ) are carried out in processStimulus( ):

```
public void processStimulus(Enumeration en)
{ Boid b;
  int i = 0;
  while((b = boidsList.getBoid(i)) != null) {
    b.animateBoid( );
    i++;
  }
  wakeupOn(timeOut);   // schedule next update
}
```

Velocity Rules Again

FlockBehavior is a general-purpose flock manager, so it stores the basic velocity methods used by all boids: Reynolds' cohesion, separation, and alignment rules. All the rules have a similar implementation since they examine nearby flockmates and build an aggregate result. This is converted into a velocity and scaled before being returned.

As explained at the start of this chapter, Reynolds' notion of flockmates is based on a distance measure and an angle around the forward direction of the boid. However, the rules in Flocking3D only utilize the distance value, effectively including flock-mates from all around the boid. The angle measure is dropped because of the over-head of calculating it and because the behavior of the boids seems realistic enough without it. A boid using an angle component is only influenced by the boids within its field of vision. The general effect is that a flock is more affected by changes to boids near the front and less affected by changes toward the back.

The cohesion( ) method is shown below. It calculates a velocity that encourages the boid to fly toward the average position of its flockmates:

```
public Vector3f cohesion(Vector3f boidPos)
{ avgPosn.set(0,0,0);      // the default answer
  int numFlockMates = 0;
  Vector3f pos;
  Boid b;

  int i = 0;
  while((b = boidsList.getBoid(i)) != null) {
    distFrom.set(boidPos);
    pos = b.getBoidPos( );
    distFrom.sub(pos);
    if(distFrom.length( ) < PROXIMITY) {    // is boid a flockmate?
      avgPosn.add(pos);// add position to tally
      numFlockMates++;
    }
    i++;
  }
  avgPosn.sub(boidPos);      // don't include the boid itself
  numFlockMates--;

  if(numFlockMates > 0) {    // there were flockmates
    avgPosn.scale(1.0f/numFlockMates);    // calculate avg position
    // calculate a small step towards the avg. posn
    avgPosn.sub(boidPos);
    avgPosn.scale(COHESION_WEIGHT);
  }
  return avgPosn;
}
```

avgPosn and distPosn are global Vector3f objects to reduce the creation of temporary objects when the method is repeatedly executed. The while loop uses getBoid( ) to iterate through the boids list. The loop's complexity is O(n), where n is the number of boids. Since the method is called for every boid, checking the entire flock for cohe-sion is O(n²). If there are m velocity rules, then each update of the flock will have a complexity of $O(m*n^2)$. This is less than ideal and one reason why flocking systems tend to have few boids.

A well-designed boids list data structure will reduce the overhead of the calculations; for example, one simple optimization is to utilize boid position in the list's ordering. A search algorithm using spatial information should find a nearby boid in constant time ($O(1)$), reducing the cost of a flock update to $O(m*n)$. For example, if there are 1,000 boids and 10 rules, then the current algorithm takes time proportional to $O(10^7)$, whereas the improved version would be $O(10^4)$, potentially a 1,000-fold improvement

In cohesion( ), nearness is calculated by finding the absolute distance between the boid (boidPos) and each neigboring boid. The PROXIMITY constant can be adjusted to change the number of neighbors.

The choice of scaling factor (COHESION_WEIGHT in this case) is a matter of trial and error, determined by running the system with various values and observing the behavior of the flock. Part of the difficulty when deciding on a good value is that the rules interact with each other to produce an overall effect. For example, the cohesion rule brings boids together while the separation rules keep them apart. This interplay is what makes boid behavior hard to predict and so interesting.

The Prey's Behavior

PreyBehavior has three tasks:

- To create boids (e.g., PreyBoids) and store them in the boids list
- To store the velocity rules specific to PreyBoids, which require an examination of the entire flock
- To delete a PreyBoid when a predator eats it

Boid creation is done in createBoids( ), called from the class's constructor:

```
private void createBoids(int numBoids, Obstacles obs)
{ // preyBoids can be detached from the scene
  boidsBG.setCapability(BranchGroup.ALLOW_CHILDREN_WRITE);
  boidsBG.setCapability(BranchGroup.ALLOW_CHILDREN_EXTEND);

  PreyBoid pb;
  for(int i=0; i < numBoids; i++){
    pb = new PreyBoid(obs, this);
    boidsBG.addChild(pb);    // add to BranchGroup
    boidsList.add(pb);       // add to BoidsList
  }
  boidsBG.addChild(this);    // store the prey behavior with its BG
}
```

`boidsBG` is the inherited `BranchGroup` holding the boids in the scene; `boidsBG`'s capabilities must allow changes to its children so prey boids can be detached from it at runtime (after they're eaten).

When a `PreyBoid` object is created, it's passed a reference to the obstacles (passed to the behavior from `WrapFlocking3D`) and a reference to the behavior itself, so its velocity rules can be accessed.

`createBoid( )` creates a scene branch such as that shown in Figure 22-8.

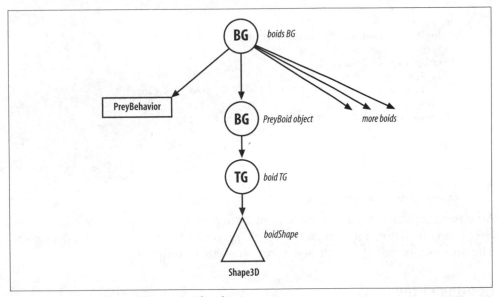

Figure 22-8. Scene branch for PreyBoid nodes

Velocity Rules and Other Flocks

`PreyBehavior`'s second task is complicated by the need to access the other flock (the predators), which means that it must reference the `PredatorBehavior` object. `WrapFlocking3D` delivers the reference via `PreyBehavior`'s `setPredBeh( )`:

```
public void setPredBeh(PredatorBehavior pb)
{ predBeh = pb; }
```

 `predBeh` is a global, used by the `seePredators( )` velocity rule.

`seePredators()` is coded in a similar way to the rules in `FlockBehavior`: a loop tests each of the boids in the predator flock for proximity. If a predator is within range, the velocity will be set to a scaled move in the opposite direction:

```
public Vector3f seePredators(Vector3f boidPos)
{
  predsList = predBeh.getBoidsList();  // refer to pred list
  avoidPred.set(0,0,0);  // reset
  Vector3f predPos;
  PredatorBoid b;

  int i = 0;
  while((b = (PredatorBoid)predsList.getBoid(i)) != null) {
    distFrom.set(boidPos);
    predPos = b.getBoidPos();
    distFrom.sub(predPos);
    if(distFrom.length() < PROXIMITY) {   // is pred boid close?
      avoidPred.set(distFrom);
      avoidPred.scale(FLEE_WEIGHT);  // scaled run away
      break;
    }
    i++;
  }
  return avoidPred;
} // end of seePredators()
```

An important difference in this code from earlier rules is the first line, where a reference to the predators list is obtained by calling `getBoidsList()` in `PredatorBehavior`. The prey examine this list to decide if they should start running.

Goodbye Prey

`PreyBehavior` contains an `eatBoid()` method, called by `PredatorBehavior` when the given boid has been eaten:

```
public void eatBoid(int i)
{ ((PreyBoid)boidsList.getBoid(i)).boidDetach();
  boidsList.removeBoid(i);
}
```

`eatBoid()` deletes a boid by detaching it from the scene graph, and removing it from the boids list.

The Predator's Behavior

`PredatorBehavior` has similar tasks to `PreyBehavior`:

- To create its boids (e.g., `PredatorBoids`) and store them in the boids list
- To store the velocity rules specific to `PredatorBoids`, which require an examination of the entire flock
- To eat prey when they're close enough

Boid creation is almost identical to that done in PreyBehavior, except that PredatorBoids are created instead of PreyBoids. PredatorBoid has a method, setPredBeh( ), which allows WrapFlocking3D to pass it a reference to the PreyBehavior object.

The velocity rule is implemented by findClosePrey( ): the method calculates the average position of all the nearby PreyBoids and moves the predator a small step toward that position. The code is similar to other rules, except that it starts by obtaining a reference to the prey list by calling getBoidsList( ) in PreyBehavior.

```
preyList = preyBeh.getBoidsList( );  // get prey list
int i = 0;
while((b = (PreyBoid)preyList.getBoid(i)) != null) {
  pos = b.getBoidPos( );  // get prey boid position
  // use pos to adjust the predator's velocity
}
```

Lunch Time

The third task for PredatorBehavior—eating nearby prey—isn't a velocity rule but a method called at the start of each predator's update in animateBoid( ). However, the coding is similar to the velocity rules—it iterates through the prey boids checking for those near enough to eat:

```
public int eatClosePrey(Vector3f boidPos)
{ preyList = preyBeh.getBoidsList( );
  int numPrey = preyList.size( );
  int numEaten = 0;
  PreyBoid b;

  int i = 0;
  while((b = (PreyBoid)preyList.getBoid(i)) != null) {
    distFrom.set(boidPos);
    distFrom.sub( b.getBoidPos( ) );
    if(distFrom.length( ) < PROXIMITY/3.0) { // boid v.close to prey
      preyBeh.eatBoid(i);    // found prey, so eat it
      numPrey--;
      numEaten++;
      System.out.println("numPrey: " + numPrey);
    }
    else
       i++;
  }
  return numEaten;
} // end of eatClosePrey( )
```

The reference to PreyBehavior is used to get a link to the prey list and to call eatBoid( ) to remove the ith boid. When a boid is removed, the next boid in the list becomes the new i[th] boid, so the i index mustn't be incremented.

CHAPTER 23

Shooting a Gun

It's an unfortunate fact that shooting (and being shot) is a major part of many types of games. Exact percentages are hard to come by, but I've seen figures which indicate that perhaps 40 percent of the top-selling console games involve shooting, rising to 50 percent for PC games. My own feeling is that the percentages are much higher.

I'm writing this as Christmas 2004 approaches, and the top action games for the PC include *Half-Life 2*, *Doom 3*, *Medal of Honor: Pacific Assault*, *The Lord of the Rings: Battle For Middle Earth*, *Warhammer 40,000: Dawn of War*, *World of Warcraft*, and so on. Where's the peace and harmony gone? Santa better have some serious armor on his sleigh this Yuletide.

Action games can be categorized into third person and first person. Third-person games frequently utilize a viewpoint slightly above and behind the main character as in *Splinter Cell* and *Hitman*. First-person games put the gun in your hand, with a viewpoint linked to the gun, as in *Doom* and *Half-Life*.

This chapter looks at how to get an object in the scene to shoot. This is a prerequisite for third person games and, of course, is needed in first person games when the enemy fires back. Chapter 24 is about first person shooting, where the shot comes from your own gun.

The Shooter3D application contains a gun (a cone mounted on a cylinder) which fires a laser beam at a point on the checkered floor clicked on by the user. The flight of the laser beam (a red cylinder) is accompanied by a suitable sound and followed by an explosion (an animated series of images and another sound).

Figure 23-1 shows three screenshots of Shooter3D. The first one has the laser beam in mid-flight, the second captures the explosion, and the third is another explosion after the user has clicked on a different part of the floor, from a different viewpoint.

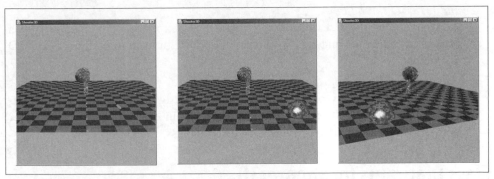

Figure 23-1. The deadly Shooter3D

The cone head rotates to aim at the target point, and the animated explosion always faces the user.

Here are some Java 3D and Java features illustrated by this example:

Picking

The user's clicking on the floor is dealt with by Java 3D *picking*. Picking works by creating a *pick shape* (often a line or cone) extending from the user's view-point, through the mouse location and into the scene. Information can be gathered about the objects in the scene (e.g., the floor) which intersect with the pick shape.

3D sounds

The laser beam and explosion sounds are Java 3D `PointSound` objects. A `PointSound` is a sound source at a given position in the scene.

More complex rotations

The rotations of the cone and the laser beam are handled by axis angles defined using Java 3D's `AxisAngle4d` class. An axis angle specifies a rotation in terms of an angle turned around a vector. The vector can be any direction, not just along one of the axes.

Animation

The explosion visual is created with my `ImagesSeries` class, which simplifies the loading and displaying of a sequence of transparent GIFs as an animation.

Global variables for repeated calculations

Many operations, such as the method to rotate the gun, require Java 3D objects (e.g., `Transform3D` and `Vector3d`). A bad way of coding these methods is to create new, temporary objects each time they're called. Object creation, and subsequent garbage collection, will slow the application down. Instead, I employ global objects, created once at startup and reused throughout the execution.

User and Java 3D threads

The delivery of the laser beam and subsequent explosion are managed by a FireBeam thread, showing how Java threads and the built-in threading of Java 3D can coexist.

The benefits of OOD

The overall complexity of this application is greatly reduced by using object-oriented design (OOD) principles; each of the main entities (the gun, the laser beam, the explosion) are represented by its own class.

Class Diagrams for Shooter3D

Figure 23-2 shows the class diagrams for the Shooter3D application. The class names and public methods are included.

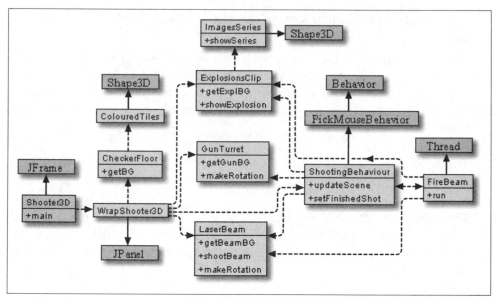

Figure 23-2. Class diagrams for Shooter3D

Shooter3D is the top-level JFrame for the application, and very similar to the JFrame classes in earlier chapters. WrapShooter3D creates the 3D scene (as usual) and adds the gun, laser beam and explosion, as well as their controlling behavior. CheckerFloor and ColouredTiles manage the checkerboard as in previous chapters, but both have been modified to deal with floor picking.

ExplosionsClip represents the explosion, GunTurret the gun, and LaserBeam the laser beam. ExplosionsClip uses ImagesSeries to animate the explosion. ShootingBehaviour contains the behavior triggered when the user clicks on the floor. Its picking capabilities come from being a subclass of PickMouseBehavior, a Java 3D utility class, which is itself a subclass of Behavior. The tasks of firing the laser beam and triggering the explosion are delegated to the FireBeam thread.

 All the code for this example can be found in the *Shooter3D/* directory.

Scene Creation

WrapShooter3D's createSceneGraph( ) calls makeGun( ) to initialize various elements:

```
private void makeGun(Canvas3D canvas3D)
{ // starting vector for the gun cone and beam
  Vector3d startVec = new Vector3d(0, 2, 0);

  // the gun
  GunTurret gun = new GunTurret(startVec);
  sceneBG.addChild( gun.getGunBG() );

  // explosion and sound
  PointSound explPS = initSound("Explo1.wav");
  ExplosionsClip expl = new ExplosionsClip( startVec, explPS);
  sceneBG.addChild( expl.getExplBG() );

  // laser beam and sound
  PointSound beamPS = initSound("laser2.wav");
  LaserBeam laser = new LaserBeam( startVec, beamPS);
  sceneBG.addChild( laser.getBeamBG() );

  // the behavior that controls the shooting
  ShootingBehaviour shootBeh =
      new ShootingBehaviour(canvas3D, sceneBG, bounds,
                  new Point3d(0,2,0), expl, laser, gun );
  sceneBG.addChild(shootBeh);
} // end of makeGun( )
```

The position vector of the gun cone is hardwired to be (0, 2, 0). The same vector is used to place the laser beam (a red cylinder) inside the cone. The hardwiring makes the coding easier and highlights a major simplification of this example: the base of the gun doesn't move.

The Sound of Shooting

Java 3D has three kinds of sound node classes. All three are subclasses of the Sound class.

BackgroundSound

A BackgroundSound node allows a sound to permeate the entire scene, located at no particular place.

PointSound

A PointSound node has a location, so its volume varies as the user moves (or as the sound node moves). I use PointSound nodes for the laser-beam and explosion sounds in Shooter3D.

ConeSound

A ConeSound node is a PointSound that can be aimed in a particular direction.

Before sound nodes can be added to a scene, an audio device must be created and linked to the Viewer object. This is simple if the SimpleUniverse utility class is being used (as in this example):

```
AudioDevice audioDev = su.getViewer().createAudioDevice();
```

 This line of code appears in the WrapShooter3D constructor.

SimpleUniverse was introduced in Chapter 14; it builds the view branch part of the scene graph, which specifies how the user's viewpoint is positioned in the world and includes the Viewer object.

WrapShooter3D uses initSound() to load a WAV sound file and create a PointSound object:

```
private PointSound initSound(String filename)
{ MediaContainer soundMC = null;
  try {
    soundMC = new MediaContainer("file:sounds/" + filename);
    soundMC.setCacheEnable(true);    // load sound into container
  }
  catch (Exception ex)
  {  System.out.println(ex); }

  // create a point sound
  PointSound ps = new PointSound();
  ps.setSchedulingBounds( bounds );
  ps.setSoundData( soundMC );

  ps.setInitialGain(1.0f);  // full on sound from the start

  // allow sound to be switched on/off & its position to be moved
  ps.setCapability(PointSound.ALLOW_ENABLE_WRITE);
  ps.setCapability(PointSound.ALLOW_POSITION_WRITE);

  System.out.println("PointSound created from sounds/" + filename);
  return ps;
} // end of initSound()
```

A Sound node needs a sound source, which is loaded with a MediaContainer object. Loading can be done from a URL, local file, or input stream; the try/catch block handles invalid filenames, as well as problems with opening files. initSound( ) loads its sound from a local file in the subdirectory *sounds/*.

All Sound nodes must be given a bounding region and assigned a sound source:

```
PointSound ps = new PointSound( );
ps.setSchedulingBounds( bounds );
ps.setSoundData( soundMC );
```

To play, the sound node must be enabled with setEnable( ). initSound( ) doesn't call setEnable( ) since the sound isn't played when first loaded. Instead, the node's capability bits are set to allow it to be enabled and disabled during execution:

```
ps.setCapability(PointSound.ALLOW_ENABLE_WRITE);
```

The explosion sound will be positioned at runtime, requiring another capability bit:

```
ps.setCapability(PointSound.ALLOW_POSITION_WRITE);
```

Other sound elements include setting the volume and saying whether the sound should loop (and if so, then how many times). The relevant methods are:

```
void setInitialGain(float volume);
void setLoop(int loopTimes);
```

initSound( ) sets the volume to 1.0f (full-on) and uses the default looping behavior (play once, finish). PointSound nodes have a location in space, given by setPosition( ). They emit sound in all directions, so attenuation factors can be specified in a similar way to Java 3D PointLight nodes.

Problems with Sound

The Sound classes in the current version of Java 3D (v.1.3.1) contain some severe bugs, including poor volume adjustment when the user moves away from a Java 3D PointSound or ConeSound node, strange interactions between multiple sounds at different locations, and anomalies between left and right ear sounds. There are plans to fix these bugs in the next major Java 3D version, 1.4.

Picking Scene Objects

Shooter3D's gun shoots at a point on the floor selected by the user clicking the mouse. The cursor position on the screen is translated into scene coordinates using Java 3D's picking. In general, picking is a more user-friendly way of obtaining input than asking the user to type in a coordinate or the name of an object.

Picking is the selection of a shape (or shapes) in the scene, usually accomplished by having the user click the mouse while the pointer is over a particular shape. This is implemented by projecting a pick shape (a line or ray) into the scene from the user's viewpoint, through the mouse pointer position on screen, to intersect with the nearest object in the scene (see Figure 23-3).

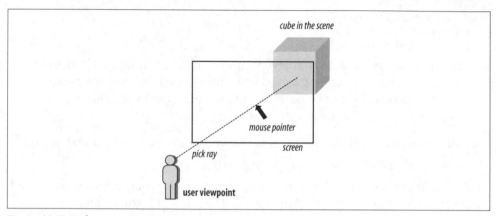

Figure 23-3. Picking using a ray

There are many variations of this idea, such as using a different pick shape instead of a line—a cone or cylinder. Another possibility is to return a list of all the intersected objects rather than the one nearest to the viewer.

The selected object will correspond to a leaf node in the scene graph. Leaf nodes are the visual parts of the scene, such as meshes and models, and internal nodes are typically Group nodes (or subclasses of Group).

By default, leaf nodes, such as Shape3Ds and OrientedShape3Ds, are pickable, so programmers should switch off picking (with setPickable(false)) in as many nodes as possible to reduce the cost of intersection testing. This is an important optimization in a large scene that may contain thousands of visible items.

The information generated by picking can include more than the leaf node: it may include the path from the root of the scene graph (the Locale node) down to the selected node. This can be useful since the path will include the TransformGroup nodes used to position or orient the selected item. However, this requires that the Group nodes have their ENABLE_PICK_REPORTING capability set to true. When picking returns more information (such as the path), processing times increase, and the operation requires the setting of a bewildering range of capability bits. Fortunately, Java 3D's PickTool class offers a simple setCapabilities() method for setting the necessary bits in Java 3D's Shape3D nodes. (The Shape3D class is used to build leaf nodes representing geometric shapes.) The method supports three different types (levels) of picking:

```
static void setCapabilities(Node node, int level);
```

The three levels return increasing amounts of information:

INTERSECT_TEST

A Shape3D node with this level of picking will report if it was intersected by a pick shape.

INTERSECT_COORD

The Shape3D node will report whether it was intersected and supply the intersection coordinates.

INTERSECT_FULL

The node will supply intersection coordinates and details of its geometry's color, normals, and texture coordinates.

What to Pick in Shooter3D?

A consideration of the Shooter3D scene (as shown in Figure 23-1) reveals many potentially pickable shapes:

- Two Shape3D nodes holding the QuadArrays for the blue and green floor tiles
- 42 Text2D axis labels
- The Shape3D red tile at the origin
- The gun cylinder and cone
- The laser-beam cylinder
- The explosion Shape3D

Shooter3D switches off picking for all of these, with the exception of the floor tiles and the red tile at the origin. This matches the intended behavior of the application: the user clicks on a floor tile and the gun shoots at it. Switching off picking capabilities reduces the cost of the intersection calculations and makes the picking result easier to analyze since few things remain that can be picked.

Small changes must be made to the familiar CheckerFloor and ColouredTiles classes to disable the picking of the axis labels and to reduce the amount of picking information gathered for the tiles.

In CheckerFloor, makeText( ) is employed to create an axis label and now includes a call to setPickable( ):

```
private TransformGroup makeText(Vector3d vertex, String text)
// Create a Text2D object at the specified vertex
{
  Text2D message = new Text2D(text, white, "SansSerif", 36, Font.BOLD);
  message.setPickable(false);    // cannot be picked

  TransformGroup tg = new TransformGroup( );
  Transform3D t3d = new Transform3D( );
  t3d.setTranslation(vertex);
  tg.setTransform(t3d);
```

```
    tg.addChild(message);
    return tg;
}
```

In ColouredTile, picking is left on, but the amount of detail returned is set with a call to setCapabilities(). Only intersection coordinates are required—not information about the shape's color, normals, etc.—so the INTERSECT_COORD picking level is sufficient:

```
public ColouredTiles(ArrayList coords, Color3f col)
{ plane = new QuadArray(coords.size(),
                    GeometryArray.COORDINATES | GeometryArray.COLOR_3);
  createGeometry(coords, col);
  createAppearance();
  // set the picking capabilities so that intersection
  // coords can be extracted after the shape is picked
  PickTool.setCapabilities(this, PickTool.INTERSECT_COORD);
}
```

The other objects in the scene—the gun, laser beam, and explosion—contain calls to setPickable(false).

ShootingBehaviour extracts and utilizes the intersection information, so a detailed discussion of that side of picking will be delayed until later. Essentially, the class uses a ray to find the intersection point on a tile nearest to the viewer. There's no need to obtain path information about the Group nodes above it in the graph, so there's no need to set ENABLE_PICK_REPORTING capability bits for Group nodes.

Controlling the Gun

The GunTurret class builds the scene graph branch for the cylinder and cone and has two public methods: getGunBG() and makeRotation(). getGunBG() is used by WrapShooter3D to retrieve a reference to the gun's top-level BranchGroup, gunBG, so it can be added to the scene. makeRotation() is called by ShootingBehaviour to rotate the cone to point at the clicked position.

The scene graph branch built inside GunTurret is shown in Figure 23-4.

The GunTurret constructor is:

```
public GunTurret(Vector3d svec)
{ startVec = svec;
  gunBG = new BranchGroup();
  Appearance apStone = stoneApp();
  placeGunBase(apStone);
  placeGun(apStone);
}
```

startVec contains the position of the gun cone: (0, 2, 0).

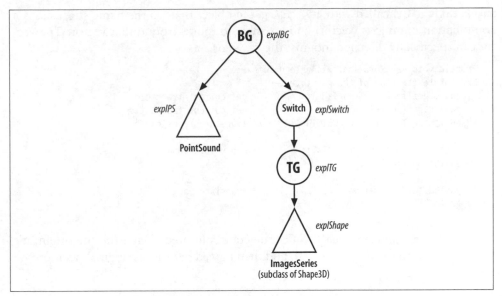

Figure 23-4. Scenegraph branch for GunTurret

There's no particular significance to this coordinate, but it works well, so I've stayed with it.

apStone is a blending of a stone texture and white material, with lighting enabled, which allows lighting effects to be seen on the gun's surfaces. The blending is done using the TextureAttribute.MODULATE setting for the texture mode.

A similar approach was used in Chapter 21 for the texture applied to the particle system of quads.

placeGunBase( ) creates the lefthand side of the subgraph shown in Figure 23-4, and placeGun( ) handles the right side.

The cylinder and cone are unpickable (you only want the gun to shoot at the tiles):

```
cyl.setPickable(false);
cone.setPickable(false);
```

The TransformGroup for the cone (gunTG) will have its rotation details changed at runtime, so its capability bits are set accordingly:

```
gunTG.setCapability(TransformGroup.ALLOW_TRANSFORM_WRITE);
gunTG.setCapability(TransformGroup.ALLOW_TRANSFORM_READ);
```

makeRotation( ) is called with an AxisAngle4d object that, as the name suggests, is a combination of an axis (vector) and an angle to rotate around that vector. The vector can specify any direction, not just the x-, y-, or z-axes :

```
public void makeRotation(AxisAngle4d rotAxis)
// rotate the cone of the gun turret
{ gunTG.getTransform( gunT3d );          // get current transform
  gunT3d.get( currTrans );               // get current translation
  gunT3d.setTranslation( ORIGIN );       // translate to origin

  rotT3d.setRotation( rotAxis );         // apply rotation
  gunT3d.mul(rotT3d);

  gunT3d.setTranslation( currTrans );  // translate back
  gunTG.setTransform( gunT3d );
}
```

The rotation is applied to gunTG. Since the cone is located away from the origin, it's first translated to the origin, rotated, and then moved back to its original position.

Globals for Repeated Calculations

A good optimization technique for Java and Java 3D is to avoid the creation of excessive numbers of temporary objects since the JVM will have to garbage collect them often, slowing down your application in the process.

Temporary objects are usually employed to hold temporary results during a method's execution: they're created at the start of the method, and discarded at its end. If the method is called frequently, then an alternative coding strategy will be to use global variables. They're created once (usually in the classes' constructor) then reinitialized by the method each time they're needed. A multitude of short-lived objects are replaced by a few reusable long-lasting ones.

This coding strategy can be seen in makeRotation( ) in GunTurret, which uses global Transform3D and Vector3d objects (gunT3d, rotT3d, currTrans).

Preparing the Laser Beam

The LaserBeam object is a red cylinder, hidden inside the gun cone when not in use, so there's no need for a Switch or visibility-controlling code. ShootingBehaviour rotates the cylinder (and gun cone) to point at the location picked by the user on the checkerboard. It lets FireBeam handle the shooting of the beam and subsequent explosion.

The laser beam is accompanied by a PointSound, which moves along with it. This means that the sound's volume increases (or diminishes) as the beam travels towards (or away from) the user's viewpoint.

The class diagram for LaserBeam is in Figure 23-5; all public methods are shown.

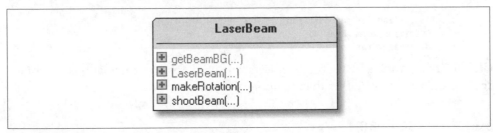

Figure 23-5. LaserBeam's public methods

WrapShooter3D uses getBeamBG( ) to retrieve the beam's BranchGroup for addition to the scene. The scene graph branch built inside LaserBeam (by makeBeam( )) is shown in Figure 23-6.

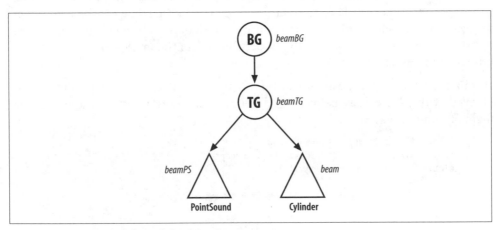

Figure 23-6. Scenegraph branch for LaserBeam

The cylinder is made unpickable, as only the floor should be pickable by the user:

```
beam.setPickable(false);
```

The capability bits of beamTG are set to allow it to be rotated and translated.

ShootingBehaviour rotates the beam with makeRotation( ), which is identical to the method in GunTurret, except that it applies the rotation to the beam's TransformGroup, beamTG.

```
public void makeRotation(AxisAngle4d rotAxis)
// rotate the laser beam
{
```

```
    beamTG.getTransform( beamT3d );          // get current transform
    beamT3d.get( currTrans );                // get current translation
    beamT3d.setTranslation( ORIGIN );        // translate to origin

    rotT3d.setRotation( rotAxis );           // apply rotation
    beamT3d.mul(rotT3d);

    beamT3d.setTranslation( currTrans );     // translate back
    beamTG.setTransform( beamT3d );
  } // end of makeRotation()
```

Global `Transform3D` and `Vector3D` objects are used for the calculations (beamT3d, rotT3d, and currTrans) rather than temporary objects.

Shooting the Beam

`shootBeam( )` is called from `FireBeam` to deliver the beam to the position on the floor clicked on by the user.

What the user sees as a mighty laser beam, is a red cylinder moving along a straight line path from the gun's cone to an intersection point on a tile, taking a few seconds to complete the journey. The intersection coordinate in the scene is called `intercept` in `shootBeam( )` below. It's calculated using picking, which translates the user's mouse click into a coordinate on the floor. (I'll explain the implementation details a little later in this chapter.)

`shootBeam( )` moves the beam toward `intercept`, in incremental steps defined by `stepVec`, with a brief delay between each move of `SLEEP_TIME` ms. As the beam is in flight, a sound is played:

```
    public void shootBeam(Point3d intercept)
    { double travelDist = startPt.distance(intercept);
      calcStepVec(intercept, travelDist);

      beamPS.setEnable(true);            // switch on laser-beam sound

      double currDist = 0.0;
      currVec.set(startVec);
      beamTG.getTransform(beamT3d);      // get current beam transform

      while (currDist <= travelDist) {   // not at destination yet
        beamT3d.setTranslation(currVec); // move the laser beam
        beamTG.setTransform(beamT3d);
        currVec.add(stepVec);
        currDist += STEP_SIZE;
        try {
          Thread.sleep(SLEEP_TIME);      // wait a while
        }
        catch (Exception ex) {}
      }
```

```
          // reset beam to its original coordinates
          beamT3d.setTranslation(startVec);
          beamTG.setTransform(beamT3d);

          beamPS.setEnable(false);    // switch off laser-beam sound
      }  // end of shootBeam( )
```

shootBeam( ) first calculates the distance to be traveled (travelDist) from the starting point to the intercept, as well as a translation increment (stepVec) based on a hard-wired step size constant. These values are shown graphically in Figure 23-7.

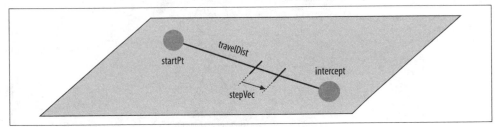

Figure 23-7. Moving the laser beam

The step size affects the user's perception of how fast the laser beam is moving. The larger the step, the quicker the beam reaches intercept. setEnable( ) controls the playing of the sound, which requires the WRITE capability bit to be set in initSound( ).

The beam's current position is stored in currVec and its current distance along the path to the intercept in currDist. currVec is used to update the beam's position by modifying its TransformGroup, beamTG. The while loop continues this process until the required distance has been traveled. When the beam reaches the intercept point, it's reset to its original position at startVec, which hides it from the user back inside the cone.

Causing an Explosion

The explosion is best explained by considering the subgraph created inside ExplosionsClip (see Figure 23-8).

The visual component of the explosion is implemented as a series of transparent GIF images, drawn one after another onto the surface of a QuadArray inside explShape. explTG is utilized to position the explosion shape at the point where the user clicked the mouse and to rotate it around the y-axis to face the user's viewpoint. The Switch node is used to hide the explosion until needed.

The explosion sound is the PointSound node, explPS. The showExplosion( ) method positions it at the intercept point and then enables it (plays it).

The original design for the explosion had the PointSound attached to the explTG TransformGroup, which meant that would automatically move as the explShape node

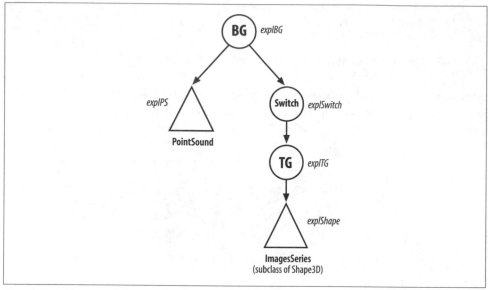

Figure 23-8. Scenegraph branch for ExplosionsClip

moved. Unfortunately, a runtime exception rose as the sound was enabled, making this approach impossible. After some testing, I discovered the exception was caused by the PointSound object being attached below the Switch node, explSwitch. This attachment should be possible; the exception is a bug in Java 3D 1.3.1.

I coded around the problem by moving the PointSound node to a different branch from the Switch node (as shown in Figure 23-8). This avoids the exception but means that the sound node must be explicitly translated to stay with the explShape node as it moves.

The subgraph is created in the constructor for ExplosionsClip, and a reference to explBG is retrieved by WrapShooter3D via calling getExplBG( ).

The explosion is displayed by showExplosion( ), which is called from FireBeam, after the laser beam has reached the click point:

```
public void showExplosion(double turnAngle, Point3d intercept)
// turn to face eye and move to click point
{
  endVec.set(intercept.x, intercept.y, intercept.z);
  rotateMove(turnAngle, endVec);

  explSwitch.setWhichChild( Switch.CHILD_ALL );   // make visible
  explPS.setPosition((float)intercept.x,
                (float)intercept.y, (float)intercept.z);
                // move sound to click point
  explPS.setEnable(true);           // switch on explosion sound
  explShape.showSeries( );          // show the explosion
```

```
    explPS.setEnable(false);        // switch off sound
    explSwitch.setWhichChild( Switch.CHILD_NONE ); // invisible

    // face front again, and reset position
    rotateMove(-turnAngle, startVec);
  } // end of showExplosion( )
```

FireBeam passes the user's click point (intercept) and the turning angle for the explosion (turnAngle) to showExplosion( ). The rotation is handled by rotateMove( ) (explained below), and the animation is triggered by a call to showSeries( ) in the ImagesSeries object.

The PointSound, explPS, requires certain capabilities so it can be positioned and enabled; the capabilities are set by initSound( ). After the explosion has finished, it is hidden, and rotated back to its original orientation.

Rotating the Explosion

rotateMove( ) uses the supplied turning angle to rotate the explosion around the y-axis, so can employ rotY( ) rather than an AxisAngle4d object. As usual, the object must be translated to the origin before the rotation and then translated to its new position afterward:

```
private void rotateMove(double turn, Vector3d vec)
// rotate the explosion around the Y-axis, and move to vec
{
  explTG.getTransform(explT3d);       // get transform info
  explT3d.setTranslation(ORIGIN);     // move to origin

  rotT3d.rotY(turn);           // rotate around the y-axis
  explT3d.mul(rotT3d);

  explT3d.setTranslation(vec);        // move to vector
  explTG.setTransform(explT3d);       // update transform
}
```

Displaying a Series of Images

The constructor for the ImagesSeries class takes a partial filename (e.g., *images/explo*) and a number (e.g., 6) and attempts to loads GIF files which use that name and numbering scheme (e.g., *images/explo0.gif* through *images/explo5.gif*). The images are stored as ImageComponent2D objects in an ims[] array.

ImagesSeries is a Shape3D subclass, containing a QuadArray placed on the XZ plane centered at (0,0). The quad is a single square, of size screenSize, with its front face oriented along the positive z-axis, as in Figure 23-9.

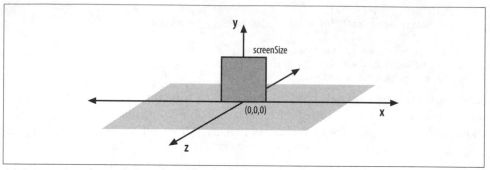

Figure 23-9. The ImagesSeries QuadArray

Implicit in the quad's square shape is the assumption that the GIFs will be square; otherwise, each one will be distorted as it's laid over the face of the quad. The texture coordinates are assigned counterclockwise from the bottom-left coordinate of the quad, so the texture will be the right way up and facing out along the positive z-axis toward the viewer.

The quad's face is covered with a series of transparent GIFs, so the shape's appearance must use blended transparency. This means that the transparent parts of a GIF will remain transparent as the GIF is applied to the shape as a texture:

```
Appearance app = new Appearance( );
// blended transparency so texture can be irregular
TransparencyAttributes tra = new TransparencyAttributes( );
tra.setTransparencyMode( TransparencyAttributes.BLENDED );
app.setTransparencyAttributes( tra );
```

No Material node component is assigned to the shape, which means that lighting cannot be enabled, so the shape is unaffected by the lighting in the scene. This is the code to do this:

```
// mix the texture and the material color
TextureAttributes ta = new TextureAttributes( );
ta.setTextureMode(TextureAttributes.MODULATE);
app.setTextureAttributes(ta);

Material mat = new Material( );      // set material and lighting
mat.setLightingEnable(true);
app.setMaterial(mat);
```

The Texture2D object that holds the texture is based on the size of the first image in ims[]. The code assumes that all the subsequent GIFs are the same size:

```
// Set the texture from the first loaded image
texture = new Texture2D(Texture2D.BASE_LEVEL, Texture.RGBA,
                             ims[0].getWidth( ), ims[0].getHeight( ));
texture.setImage(0, ims[0]);
```

```
texture.setCapability(Texture.ALLOW_IMAGE_WRITE);   // texture can change
app.setTexture(texture);

setAppearance(app);
```

The capability bit allows the texture to be changed by showSeries( ), which is called from ExplosionsClip:

```
public void showSeries()
{ for (int i=0; i < ims.length; i++) {
    texture.setImage(0, ims[i]);
    try {
      Thread.sleep(DELAY);  // wait a while
    }
    catch (Exception ex) {}
  }
}
```

showSeries( ) defines an animation sequence that's played once and then stops. Variants of this idea allow the animation to cycle or to be played from some arbitrary point in the sequence. For example, a cyclic animation might be useful for showing trees waving in the breeze.

Picking with a Mouse Click

Picking projects a pick shape (usually a line or ray) into the scene from the user's viewpoint through the mouse pointer position on screen until it intersects with a shape in the scene (see Figure 23-3).

Java 3D's PickCanvas class is used to turn a mouse click into a ray (a PickShape object). Java 3D finds the pickable shapes that intersect with the PickShape object, returning them as a list of PickResult objects. Returning the PickResult object closest to the viewer is possible.

A single PickResult may contain many PickIntersection objects, which hold the data for each intersection of the shape (e.g., the ray may go through the front and back face of a shape, leading to two intersection points).

The complexity of the picking coding is somewhat alleviated by using Java 3D's PickMouseBehavior utility class, a subclass of Behaviour, which hides much of the picking mechanism. The general format for a subclass of PickMouseBehavior is given in Example 23-1.

Example 23-1. A typical PickMouseBehavior subclass

```
import javax.media.j3d.*;
import com.sun.j3d.utils.picking.PickTool;
import com.sun.j3d.utils.picking.PickResult;
import com.sun.j3d.utils.picking.behaviors.PickMouseBehavior;
```

Example 23-1. A typical PickMouseBehavior subclass (continued)

```
// other imports as necessary...


public class ExamplePickBehavior extends PickMouseBehavior
{
  public PickHighlightBehavior(Canvas3D canvas, BranchGroup bg, Bounds bounds)
  { super(canvas, bg, bounds);
    setSchedulingBounds(bounds);

    pickCanvas.setMode(PickTool.GEOMETRY_INTERSECT_INFO);
       // allows PickIntersection objects to be returned
  }

  public void updateScene(int xpos, int ypos)
  {
    pickCanvas.setShapeLocation(xpos, ypos);
       // register mouse pointer location on the screen (canvas)

    Point3d eyePos = pickCanvas.getStartPosition();
       // get the viewer's eye location

    PickResult pickResult = null;
    pickResult = pickCanvas.pickClosest();
       // get the intersected shape closest to the viewer

    if (pickResult != null) {
      PickIntersection pi = pickResult.getClosestIntersection(eyePos);
          // get the closest intersect to the eyePos point
      Point3d intercept = pi.getPointCoordinatesVW();
          // extract the intersection pt in scene coords space
      // use the intersection pt in some way...
    }
  } // end of updateScene()

} // end of ExamplePickBehavior class
```

The constructor must pass the Canvas3D object, a BranchGroup, and bounds information to the superclass for the superclass to create a PickCanvas object and a PickShape. The PickCanvas object, pickCanvas, is available and can be used to configure the PickShape, such as changing the pick shape from a ray to a cone or adjusting the tolerance for how close a shape needs to be to the PickShape to be picked.

Many subclasses of PickShape (e.g., PickRay, PickCone, PickCylinder) specify different kinds of ray geometries; the default one employed by PickMouseBehavior is a line (PickRay). PickCanvas is intended to make picking based on mouse events easier. It's a subclass of PickTool, which has several additional methods for changing the pick shape and specifying what is returned by the picking operation.

The call to `pickCanvas.setMode()` in `ExamplePickBehavior`'s constructor sets the level of detail for the returned pick and intersection data. The various modes are:

BOUNDS
> This mode tests for intersection using the bounds of the shapes rather than the shapes themselves, so is quicker than the other two modes.

GEOMETRY
> This mode uses the actual shapes in its tests, so is more accurate than the BOUNDS mode. The BOUNDS and GEOMETRY modes return the intersected shapes is.

GEOMETRY_INTERSECT_INFO
> This mode tests for intersection using the shapes and returns details about the intersections, stored in `PickIntersection` objects. The level of detail is controlled by the capabilities set in the shapes using `PickTool`'s `setCapabilities()` method.

From Mouse Click to Picked Object

The `PickMouseBehavior` class contains fully implemented `initialize()` and `processStimulus()` methods, which should not be changed when `PickMouseBehavior` is subclassed. Instead, the programmer should implement the `updateScene()` method, which is called whenever the user clicks the mouse button—this method is passed the (x, y) coordinate of the mouse click on the screen (the `Canvas3D`).

The first step in `updateScene()` is to call `setShapeLocation()` to inform `pickCanvas` of the mouse position so the `PickShape` (the ray) can be cast into the scene. The intersecting shapes can be obtained in various ways: `pickClosest()` gets the `PickResult` object closest to the viewer. There are other methods:

```
PickResult[] pickAll();
PickResult[] pickAllSorted();
PickResult pickAny();
```

The first two return all the intersecting shapes, with the second method sorting them into increasing distance from the viewer. `pickAny()` returns any shape from the ones found, which should be quicker than finding the closest.

Finding Intersections

A `PickResult` will usually refer to a `Shape3D` containing a `GeometryArray` subclass made up of many surfaces. All the intersections between the shape and the ray can be obtained in the following way:

```
PickIntersection pi;
for (int i = 0; i < pickResult.numIntersections(); i++) {
  pi = pickResult.getIntersection(i);
  // use pi in some way...
}
```

More commonly, the intersection closest to some point in the scene is obtained:

```
PickIntersection pi = pickResult.getClosestIntersection(pt);
```

In `ExamplePickBehavior`, the point is the viewer's position, which is extracted from `pickCanvas` with `getStartPosition( )`.

A `PickIntersection` object can hold much information about the `GeometryArray`, such as the point, line, triangle, or quad that was intersected. The intersection point can be retrieved in terms of the picked shape's local coordinate system or in terms of the scene's coordinate system. If the picking level for the shape is `INTERSECT_FULL`, then there will be details about the closest vertex to the intersection point, and the color, normal and texture coordinates at the intersection point.

The call to `getPointCoordinatesVW( )` obtains the intercept point in the scene's coordinate space:

```
Point3d intercept = pi.getPointCoordinatesVW( );
```

Shooting Behavior

`ShootingBehaviour` is a subclass of `PickMouseBehavior`, which controls the various shooting-related entities when the user clicks the mouse. The gun cone and laser beam are rotated to point at the placed clicked on the checkerboard. Then, a `FireBeam` thread is created to move (fire) the beam towards the location and display the explosion.

`ShootingBehaviour`'s central role in the application means that it has passed references to the `GunTurret`, `LaserBeam`, and `ExplosionsClip` objects. In the first version of this class, the code was complex since it dealt directly with the `TransformGroups` and `Shape3Ds` of the shooting elements. Good OOD of the application entities (e.g., hiding subgraph details and computation) leads to a halving of `ShootingBehaviour`'s code length, making it easier to understand, maintain, and modify.

The `ShootingBehaviour` constructor is similar to the constructor in `ExamplePickBehavior`:

```
public ShootingBehaviour(Canvas3D canvas, BranchGroup root,
                          Bounds bounds, Point3d sp, ExplosionsClip ec,
                          LaserBeam lb, GunTurret g)
{ super(canvas, root, bounds);
  setSchedulingBounds(bounds);

  pickCanvas.setMode(PickCanvas.GEOMETRY_INTERSECT_INFO);
  // allows PickIntersection objects to be returned

  startPt = sp; // location of the gun cone
  explsClip = ec;
  laser = lb;
  gun = g;
  // other initialization code...
}
```

updateScene( ) is similar to the one in ExamplePickBehavior since it requires intersection information. updateScene( ) rotates the gun cone and beam to point at the intercept and starts a FireBeam thread to fire the beam and display an explosion:

```
public void updateScene(int xpos, int ypos)
{
  if (finishedShot) {    // previous shot has finished
    pickCanvas.setShapeLocation(xpos, ypos);

    Point3d eyePos = pickCanvas.getStartPosition( );  // viewer loc

    PickResult pickResult = null;
    pickResult = pickCanvas.pickClosest( );

    if (pickResult != null) {
      pickResultInfo(pickResult);  // for debugging

      PickIntersection pi = pickResult.getClosestIntersection(startPt);
              // get intersection closest to the gun cone
      Point3d intercept = pi.getPointCoordinatesVW( );

      rotateToPoint(intercept);      // rotate the cone and beam
      double turnAngle = calcTurn(eyePos, intercept);

      finishedShot = false;
      new FireBeam(intercept, this, laser, explsClip, turnAngle).start( );
        // fire the beam and show explosion
    }
  }
} // end of updateScene( )
```

The finishedShot flag has an important effect on the behavior of the application—it only allows a single laser beam to be in the air at a time. As FireBeam is started, finishedShot is set to false and will remain so until the thread has moved the beam to the intercept point. If the user clicks on the checkerboard while a beam is still traveling, nothing will happen since the if test in updateScene( ) will return false. As a result, the application only requires a single laser-beam object. Otherwise, the coding would have to deal with a user that could quickly click multiple times, each requiring its own laser beam.

The call to getClosestIntersection( ) uses startPt, which is set in the constructor to be the cone's location. The resulting intercept will be the point nearest to the cone.

Debugging Picking

The call to pickResultInfo( ) plays no part in the shooting process; it's used to print extra information about the PickResult object (pr). I use this method to check that the picking code is selecting the correct shape.

getNode( ) is called to return a reference to the shape that the PickResult object represents:

```
Shape3D shape = (Shape3D) pr.getNode(PickResult.SHAPE3D);
```

The code must deal with a possible null result, which occurs if the selected node is not a Shape3D object. However, I've been careful to ensure only Shape3D nodes are pickable in this application, so there shouldn't be any problem.

The PickResult object, pr, contains the scene graph path between the Locale and picked node, which can be employed to access an object above the picked node, such as a TransformGroup. The path is obtained by calling getSceneGraph( ):

```
SceneGraphPath path = pr.getSceneGraphPath();
```

The path may often be empty since internal nodes aren't added to it unless their ENABLE_PICK_REPORTING capability bit is set.

The path can be printed with a for loop:

```
int pathLen = path.nodeCount();
for (int i=0; i < pathLen; i++) {
  Node node = path.getNode(i);
  System.out.println(i + ". Node: " + node);
}
```

println( ) requires that the sceneBG BranchGroup node created in WrapShooter3D sets the necessary capability bit:

```
sceneBG.setCapability(BranchGroup.ENABLE_PICK_REPORTING);
```

Here is the output from the for loop in pickResultInfo( ):

```
0.  Node: javax.media.j3d.BranchGroup@2bcd4b
```

This isn't particularly informative. A typical way of improving the labeling of scene graph nodes is to use the setUserData( ) method from SceneGraphObject, which allows arbitrary objects to be assigned to a node (e.g., a String object):

```
sceneBG.setUserData("the sceneBG node");
```

After a reference to the node has been retrieved, getUserData( ) can be utilized:

```
String name = (String)node.getUserData();
System.out.println(i + ". Node name: " + name);
```

Rotating the Cone

rotateToPoint( ) rotates the gun cone and laser-beam cylinder to point at the intercept. The problem is that a simple rotation about the x-, y-, or z-axis is insufficient since the intercept can be anywhere on the floor. Instead, an AxisAngle4d rotation is utilized, which allows a rotation about any vector. The essential algorithm is illustrated in Figure 23-10.

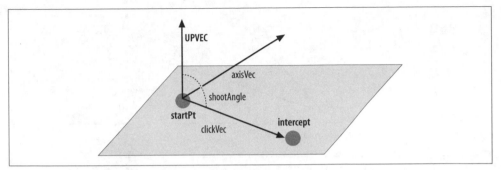

Figure 23-10. Rotating to face the intercept

The cone (and beam) start by pointing in the UPVEC direction at the StartPt location, and they must be rotated to point in the clickVec direction, a rotation of shootAngle radians. The rotation is around the axisVec vector, which is perpendicular to the plane defined by the two vectors UPVEC and clickVec.

startPt and UPVEC values are predefined, and intercept is supplied by updateScene( ) when it calls rotateToPoint( ). clickVec is readily calculated from the startPt and intercept points:

```
clickVec.set( intercept.x-startPt.x, intercept.y-startPt.y,
                                    intercept.z-startPt.z);
```

axisVec is the cross product, and Vector3d contains a cross( ) method which calculates it, given normalized values for UPVEC and clickVec:

```
clickVec.normalize( );
axisVec.cross( UPVEC, clickVec);
```

 The *cross product* of two vectors is a vector in a direction perpendicular to the two original vectors, with a magnitude equal to one (assuming that the original vectors are normalized).

The rotation angle, shootAngle, between UPVEC and clickVec can be easily obtained with Vector3d's angle( ) method:

```
shootAngle = UPVEC.angle(clickVec);
```

shootAngle is related to the *dot product*: the dot product of vectors a and b (often written as a . b) gives the length of the projection of b onto a. For example, a.b = |x| in Figure 23-11.

The angle, theta, between a and b can be expressed as the cosine function in Figure 23-12:

If a and b are unit vectors, as in this code, then:

```
cos theta = a . b
```

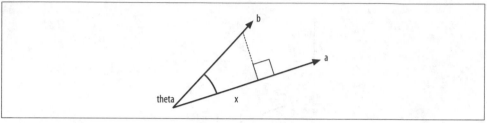

Figure 23-11. The dot product of vectors a and b

$$\cos\ theta\ =\ \frac{a\ \cdot\ b}{|a|\ |b|}$$

Figure 23-12. The cosine function between the vectors

The cosine function can be removed by taking the inverse cosine of both sides (the arc cosine):

```
theta = acos ( a . b )
```

acos( ) is the arc cosine. Since shootAngle is the same as theta, I can obtain it using:

```
shootAngle = Math.acos( UPVEC.dot(clickVec) );
```

Math.dot( ) is the dot product operation, and Math.acos( ) is the arc cosine.

An AxisAngle4d object requires a vector and rotation, which can now be supplied:

```
rotAxisAngle.set(axisVec, shootAngle);
```

This object is used to rotate the cone and laser beam:

```
gun.makeRotation(rotAxisAngle);
laser.makeRotation(rotAxisAngle);
```

A complication is that rotateToPoint( ) assumes that the cone and beam start in the UPVEC direction, which is true at the start of the application. For rotations after the first, the objects must be rotated back to the vertical first. This is achieved by rotating by shootAngle around the negative of the axisVec vector:

```
if (!firstRotation) {    // undo previous rotations
  axisVec.negate( );
  rotAxisAngle.set( axisVec, shootAngle);
  gun.makeRotation(rotAxisAngle);
  laser.makeRotation(rotAxisAngle);
}
```

Making the Explosion Face the Viewer

updateScene( ) calls calcTurn( ) to calculate the angle that the explosion shape should rotate to face the viewer:

```
double turnAngle = calcTurn(eyePos, intercept);
```

The algorithm is illustrated by Figure 23-13.

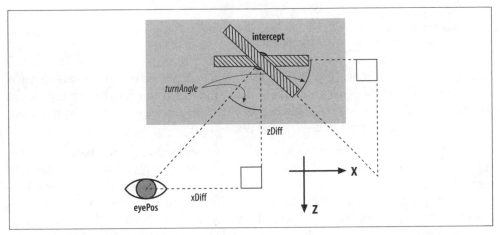

Figure 23-13. Turning to face the viewer

The stripy red bar in Figure 23-13 is the explosion quad, which originally faces along the positive z-axis. I assume the viewer is at the eyePos position, an offset of xDiff units along the x-axis and zDiff units along the z-axis from the quad. A little bit of geometry shows that the angle that eyePos makes with the positive z-axis (called turnAngle) is the same as the angle that the quad should rotate to face the eyePos position.

The eyePos and intercept points are supplied by updateScene( ). turnAngle is readily obtained as the arc tangent of xDiff and zDiff:

```
double zDiff = eyePos.z - intercept.z;
double xDiff = eyePos.x - intercept.x;
double turnAngle = Math.atan2(xDiff, zDiff);
```

Firing the Beam

The FireBeam thread is started from updateScene( ) like so:

```
new FireBeam(intercept, this, laser, explsClip, turnAngle).start( );
```

A basic question is why use a thread? One answer is that by passing the job of beam delivery and explosion to a new thread, the ShootingBehaviour object is free to do other tasks. For example, it could show a puff of animated smoke rising from the gun's cone or have the cone recoil slightly. Shooter3D doesn't do these things, as that would further complicate the example. At present, the threaded implementation allows updateScene( ) to process a user's new pick selection once the finishedShot Boolean has been set to true near the end of run( ) in the FireBeam thread:

```
public void run( )
{
  laser.shootBeam(intercept);
  shooter.setFinishedShot( );      // beam has reached its target
  explsClip.showExplosion(turnAngle, intercept);   // boom!
}
```

The call to setFinishedShot( ) sets finishedShot to true, which permits updateScene( ) to respond to user clicks and, simultaneously, the explosion for the current beam will be initiated from FireBeam. This improves the responsiveness of the application since the explosion animation lasts one to two seconds.

However, there's a problem: what if the explosion animation for the beam (i.e., the current call to showExplosion( )) doesn't finish before the FireBeam thread for the next beam calls showExplosion( ) again? The worst that happens is an interruption to the explosion animation and the truncation of the playing of the sound. However, in the vast majority of situations, the travel time of the laser beam and the explosion animation duration means that the explosion finishes before it's required again.

From a practical point of view, this may be sufficient, but in the next chapter you'll see a better coding approach that allows multiple beams and multiple explosions to coexist safely on screen at the same time.

More on Picking

The Java 3D tutorial (*http://java.sun.com/developer/onlineTraining/java3d/*) has a long section on picking in Chapter 4, "Interaction and Animation," with two examples: *MousePickApp.java* and *PickCallbackApp.java*. The former shows how to use the PickRotateBehavior subclass of PickMouseBehavior to select and rotate shapes. The other predefined subclasses are PickTranslateBehavior and PickZoomBehavior. *Pick-CallbackApp.java* explains how to attach a callback method to the PickRotateBehavior object, which is called automatically when a pick operation takes place. The code is derived from *MousePickApp.java*.

There's not much information in the Java 3D documentation on how to create your own subclasses of MousePickBehavior, but it's possible to look at the source code for these utilities in *java3d-utils-src.jar*. A potential source of confusion is that the JAR contains two copies of each of the picking classes: deprecated ones in com.sun.j3dutils. behaviors.picking and the current versions in com.sun.j3dutils.picking.behaviors.

There are several Java 3D picking demos, in *PickTest/*, *PickText3D/*, and *TickTock-Picking/*. The `TickTockPicking` example involves the picking of cubes and tetrahedrons to change their appearance and utilizes a simple subclass of `PickMouseBehavior` called `PickHighlightBehavior`.

I'll return to picking in Chapter 26 when I use it to determine terrain coordinates below viewers as they move around a landscape. This is a common approach to handling movement over irregular surfaces. The code utilizes a `PickTool` object to fire a ray straight down beneath the viewer to intersect with the shape representing the ground.

CHAPTER 24

A First-Person Shooter

This is the second chapter on 3D shooting. Chapter 23 was about third-person shooting, or when an object in the scene fires at something. This chapter is about first-person shooting (FPS) and puts the gun in the user's hand. There are several new issues to deal with:

Faking the 3D

> There's no need to build 3D models of the user's arm, hand, and gun. The objects always stay in the same spot in front of the user, so a 2D image showing a static view of the gun hand is quite sufficient. In general, a 3D model is only needed if the user is going to move around it or through it. To keep the gun hand image fixed relative to the user's viewpoint, I'll attach the image to the ViewingPlatform component of the scene graph.

Keyboard-based movement

> Up to now, I've been using the Java 3D OrbitBehavior class to change the viewpoint with the mouse, but I'm going to replace it with my own KeyBehavior class (so called because key presses drive the movement). The viewer can move forward, backward, left or right, rotate left or right, and float up or down.

Rapid-fire action

> The gun in Chapter 23 can fire only a single laser beam at a time. Another beam cannot be shot until the current one has disappeared or has been replaced by an explosion. In this chapter, I'll explain how to have *multiple* laser beams and explosions in the scene at the same time. This is important when the user wants to indulge in some rapid firing.

Hitting a target

> Chapter 23 employs Java 3D picking to guide a beam to its target. This chapter utilizes a simpler approach, which detects a hit by comparing the beam's current location with the target's coordinates. A laser beam that misses the target vanishes after traveling a certain distance.

Creating beams and explosions

This chapter reuses (or slightly changes) the techniques of Chapter 23 for creating laser beams (thin red cylinders) and animated explosions, so it's advisable to read that chapter before reading this one.

Figure 24-1 contains two screenshots for the FPShooter3D application: the first has the user strafing a robot with only laser beams that come close enough to the robot explode. The second screenshot shows a similar scene after the user has crept behind and up close to the robot.

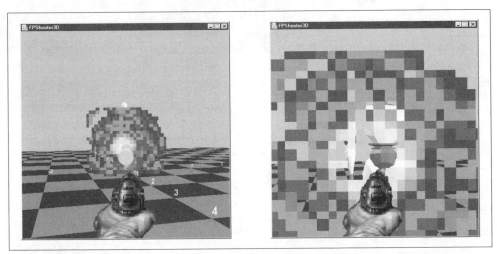

Figure 24-1. FPS diplomacy

A laser beam that misses the target vanishes after traveling a certain distance. To simplify the coding, no sounds are played. The explosions do no harm to the robot, which keeps standing there.

Class Diagrams for FPShooter3D

Figure 24-2 shows the class diagrams for the FPShooter3D application. The class names and public methods are included.

FPShooter3D is the top-level JFrame for the application and similar to earlier JFrame classes. WrapFPShooter3D creates the 3D scene as usual and adds the target and viewer elements. The target (a robot) is loaded with PropManager, a class first seen in Chapter 16 in the Loader3D example. The gun-in-hand image is a transparent GIF loaded and displayed by a TexturedPlane object. CheckerFloor and ColouredTiles manage the checkerboard, as in earlier examples. They were first encountered in Chapter 15, in Checkers3D.

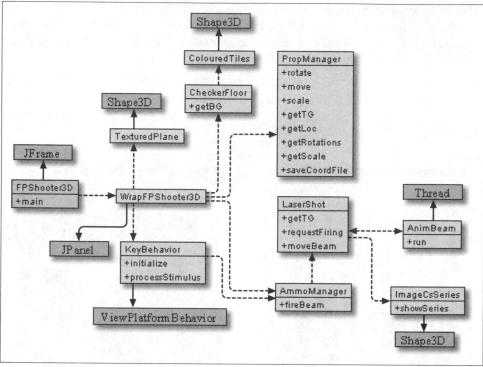

Figure 24-2. Class diagrams for FPShooter3D

A `LaserShot` object represents a single beam and its (possible) explosion. The sequence of explosion images are stored in an `ImageCsSeries` object, a variant of the `ImagesSeries` class from Chapter 23. The animation of the beam and explosion is initiated from an `AnimBeam` thread. `AmmoManager` manages a collection of `LaserShot` objects, which allows the application to display several beams and explosions concurrently.

The code for this application is in the directory *FPShooter3D/*.

Setting Up the Target

`createSceneGraph( )` in `WrapFPShooter3D` loads the target using `PropManager`, places it in the scene, and records its location:

```
PropManager propMan = new PropManager(TARGET, true);
sceneBG.addChild( propMan.getTG( ) );
Vector3d targetVec = propMan.getLoc( );
System.out.println("Location of target: " + targetVec );
```

TARGET is `Coolrobo.3ds`, and the `true` argument to the `PropManager` constructor means that there's a coords datafile that fine-tunes the robot's position. The robot appears facing along the positive z-axis, with its feet resting on the XZ plane, in the middle of the floor. `targetVec` holds the center point of the shape and is used to calculate if a beam is close enough to the robot to trigger an explosion.

Positioning and Moving the User's Viewpoint

The user's viewpoint (sometimes called the application *camera*) is positioned by the view branch part of the scene graph; its main elements are shown in Figure 24-3.

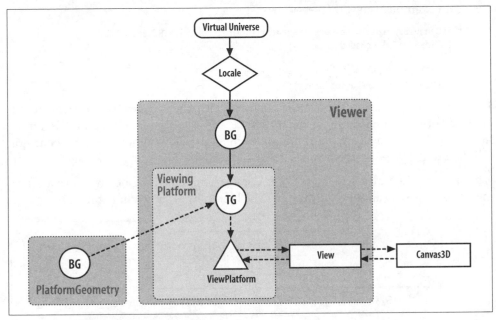

Figure 24-3. The view branch subgraph

You haven't seen the view branch much up to now since it's been built automatically when I've used the `SimpleUniverse` utility class to create the scene graph. However, I need to attach the gun-in-hand image to the viewpoint and move it around in response to user key presses.

The viewpoint is represented by the `ViewPlatform` node in Figure 24-3 (the triangle) and is repositioned by applying transforms to the TG node above it (TG is short for `TransformGroup`). It's possible to add extra `TransformGroups` above the `ViewPlatform` node to implement more complex forms of movements, but I don't need to do that in this example.

A shape is attached to the viewpoint by storing it in a Java 3D `PlatformGeometry` node and connecting it to the `TransformGroup` above the `ViewPlatform`. This is the how I'll place the gun-in-hand image in front of the viewpoint.

`SimpleUniverse` offers access to the view branch via several utility classes: `Viewer`, `ViewingPlatform`, `PlatformGeometry`, and others. You've seen `ViewingPlatform` used several times to move the viewer's starting position.

Viewpoint Behaviors

Java 3D contains several classes that can affect the viewpoint. In previous examples, I've employed an `OrbitBehavior` object attached to the `ViewingPlatform` to convert mouse presses into viewpoint movements (see the end of Chapter 15, for instance). Here's an example using `OrbitBehavior`:

```
OrbitBehavior orbit = new OrbitBehavior(c, OrbitBehavior.REVERSE_ALL);
orbit.setSchedulingBounds(bounds);

ViewingPlatform vp = su.getViewingPlatform( );
vp.setViewPlatformBehavior(orbit);
```

The behavior is attached to `ViewingPlatform` with the `setViewPlatformBehavior( )` method. `ViewingPlatform` hides `ViewPlatform` and its `TransformGroup` and is represented by the rectangle around those nodes in Figure 24-3. When the orbit behavior is linked to the `ViewingPlatform`, it's being connected to the `TransformGroup`.

`OrbitBehavior` is a member of a set of classes for implementing behaviors that affect the `TransformGroup` above `ViewPlatform`. The hierarchy is shown in Figure 24-4.

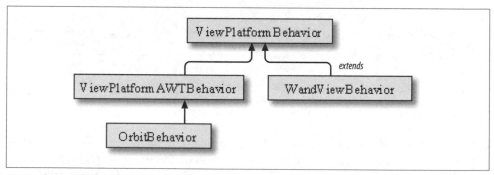

Figure 24-4. ViewPlatformBehavior and subclasses

`ViewPlatformBehavior` is an abstract class that supports basic functionality; it's a subclass of `Behavior`. `ViewPlatformAWTBehavior` catches AWT events and places them in a queue. While pending events or mouse motion are occurring, the behavior will wake up every frame and call `processAWTEvents( )` and `integrateTransforms( )`. `WandViewBehavior` manipulates the transform using a motion-tracked wand or mouse equipped with a six-degrees-of-freedom (6DOF) sensor.

The source code for all these classes can be found in *java3d-utils-src.jar*.

`OrbitBehavior` is mouse-driven, but `FPShooter3D` allows the user to control the viewpoint using key presses. Another Java 3D utility class, `KeyNavigatorBehavior`, does just that. It responds to the arrow keys, +, -, page up, page down, utilizes key presses and releases, and the elapsed time between these key presses. `KeyNavigatorBehavior` makes use of `KeyNavigator`, yet another utility class.

 The source code for both of these classes are in *java3d-utils-src.jar*.

A typical invocation of `KeyNavigatorBehavior`:

```
TransformGroup vpTrans = su.getViewingPlatform( ).getViewPlatformTransform( );
KeyNavigatorBehavior keybehavior = new KeyNavigatorBehavior(vpTrans);
keybehavior.setSchedulingBounds(bounds);
scene.addChild (keybehavior);
```

`KeyNavigatorBehavior` extends `Behavior`, so it requires the `ViewPlatform` `TransformGroup` to be explicitly passed to it. The behavior can be linked to any node in the scene graph, and not just the `ViewPlatform`'s `TransformGroup`.

 `KeyNavigatorBehavior` is employed in *IntersectTest.java* in the *PickTest/* directory of the Java 3D demos. Daniel Selman uses it in his *PlatformTest.java* example in section 6.3 of *Java 3D Programming* (Manning Publications).

`KeyNavigatorBehavior` is a good choice for programs that need keyboard-based navigation but offers too much functionality for this application. I'll use `KeyBehavior` later to build a keyboard navigator from the ground up.

Initializing the User's Viewpoint

`WrapShooter3D` calls `initUserControls( )` to configure the viewpoint. The method carries out four main tasks:

- Sets up the user's gun-in-hand image
- Positions the user's initial viewpoint
- Calls `AmmoManager` to prepare beams and explosions
- Creates a `KeyBehavior` object to process keyboard input

The initUserControls( ) method is:

```
private void initUserControls(Vector3d targetVec)
{
  // add a 'gun in hand' image to the viewpoint
  ViewingPlatform vp = su.getViewingPlatform( );
  PlatformGeometry pg = gunHand( );
  vp.setPlatformGeometry(pg);

  // position starting viewpoint
  TransformGroup steerTG = vp.getViewPlatformTransform( );
  Transform3D t3d = new Transform3D( );
  steerTG.getTransform( t3d );
  t3d.setTranslation( new Vector3d(0, 1, Z_START) );
  steerTG.setTransform(t3d);

  // create ammo (beams and explosions)
  AmmoManager ammoMan = new AmmoManager(steerTG, sceneBG, targetVec);

  // set up keyboard controls
  KeyBehavior keyBeh = new KeyBehavior( ammoMan );
      // keyBeh can ask the ammoManager to fire a beam
  keyBeh.setSchedulingBounds(bounds);
  vp.setViewPlatformBehavior(keyBeh);
}  // end of initUserControls( )
```

Adding an Image to the Viewpoint

The call to gunHand( ) inside initUserControls( ) hides the creation of a TexturedPlane object just in front of and below the user's viewpoint:

```
private PlatformGeometry gunHand( )
{
  PlatformGeometry pg = new PlatformGeometry( );
  // define a square of sides 0.2f, facing along the z-axis
  Point3f p1 = new Point3f(-0.1f, -0.3f, -0.7f);
  Point3f p2 = new Point3f(0.1f, -0.3f, -0.7f);
  Point3f p3 = new Point3f(0.1f, -0.1f, -0.7f);
  Point3f p4 = new Point3f(-0.1f, -0.1f, -0.7f);
  TexturedPlane tp = new TexturedPlane(p1, p2, p3, p4, GUN_PIC);
  pg.addChild( tp );
  return pg;
}
```

The Java 3D PlatformGeometry is nothing more than a detachable BranchGroup (confirmed by looking at its source code in *java3d-utils-src.jar*). It's added to ViewPlatform's TransformGroup by a call to ViewingPlatform's setPlatformGeometry( ).

My TexturedPlane class is a Shape3D holding a four-point QuadArray; the constructor is called with the points and a transparent GIF that will be pasted onto the quad's front face. TexturedPlane is a simplification of the ImagesSeries class of the last chapter, which lays a sequence of GIFs over a quad to exhibit an animation.

The most complicated aspect of using TexturedPlane is determining its scene coordinates. I used trial and error until the image appeared at the bottom edge of the screen. It's helpful to remember that the (x, y) coordinate pair (0, 0) corresponds to the middle of the canvas, and that negative z-coordinates are farther into the scene. For example, look at the following points:

```
Point3f p1 = new Point3f(-0.1f, -0.1f, -1.7f);
Point3f p2 = new Point3f(0.1f, -0.1f, -1.7f);
Point3f p3 = new Point3f(0.1f, 0.1f, -1.7f);
Point3f p4 = new Point3f(-0.1f, 0.1f, -1.7f);
```

These points cause the gun-in-hand image to be located (as shown in Figure 24-5) in the center of the screen, farther into the scene.

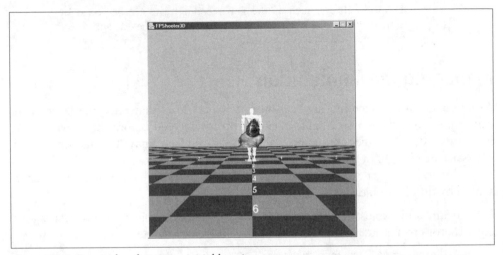

Figure 24-5. Gun-in-hand at a new initial location

An alternative way of placing the image is to use Java 3D's Viewer and ViewerAvatar. A fragment of code illustrates the approach:

```
TexturedPlane tp = new TexturedPlane(p1, p2, p3, p4, GUN_PIC);
ViewerAvatar va = new ViewerAvatar( );
va.addChild( tp );
Viewer viewer = su.getViewer( );
viewer.setAvatar(va);
```

ViewerAvatar plays the same role as PlatformGeometry: it's a subclass of BranchGroup. setAvatar( ) connects it to the TransformGroup above the ViewPlatform node.

 The word *avatar* in this situation means an on-screen representation of the user (or part of the user). Section 6.3 of *Java 3D Programming* (Manning Publications) by Daniel Selman describes two avatar examples (*PlatformTest.java* and *AvatarTest.java*) using the techniques described here. In *PlatformTest.java*, the avatars are cones with text labels, and in *AvatarTest.java* the avatar is a large cube.

Why Use a GIF?

Since any shape can be attached to the viewpoint, why choose a QuadArray acting as a surface for a transparent GIF? One reason is efficiency because it would require a complex shape to represent a hand and a gun, together with suitable coloring and textures. By contrast, the GIF is only 5 KB.

Another advantage is that occlusion is less likely to happen. Occlusion occurs when the image at the viewpoint intersects with a shape in the scene and is partially hidden. Since the GIF is flat, the viewpoint must move right up to a shape before occlusion occurs.

 3D special effects, such as the gun recoiling, can still be coded by using multiple gun-in-hand images and employing a variant of the ImagesSeries class to animate them.

Managing the Ammunition

A drawback of the shooting application in Chapter 23 is that only one laser beam can appear at a time, and if another explosion is triggered before the previous one has finished, then the animation (and sound effects) may be disrupted. My AmmoManager class fixes these problems by creating a collection of beams and explosions; several beam or explosions can appear at the same time because they're represented by different objects.

Each beam and explosion is represented by a LaserShot object, and AmmoManager's constructor creates NUMBEAMS of them (20) and adds them to the scene:

```
public AmmoManager(TransformGroup steerTG,
            BranchGroup sceneBG, Vector3d targetVec)
{
  // load the explosion images
  ImageComponent2D[] exploIms = loadImages("explo/explo", 6);

  shots = new LaserShot[NUMBEAMS];
  for(int i=0; i < NUMBEAMS; i++) {
    shots[i] = new LaserShot(steerTG, exploIms, targetVec);
    // a LaserShot represents a single beam and explosion
    sceneBG.addChild( shots[i].getTG() );
  }
}
```

An explosion animation uses six GIFs, and it would be inefficient if each LaserShot object loaded those images. It's much better to load the images once into an array (exploIms) and pass a reference to that array to each object. In this way each LaserShot object uses the same animation.

Shooting the Gun

A beam is fired from the gun when the user presses the f key. The KeyBehavior object captures the key press and calls fireBeam( ) in AmmoManager.

AmmoManager's managerial role is to hide that there are NUMBEAMS LaserShot objects and, instead, offers a single fireBeam( ) method, which fires a beam if one is available:

```
public void fireBeam( )
{ for(int i=0; i < NUMBEAMS; i++) {
    if( shots[i].requestFiring( ) )
      return;
  }
}
```

The requestFiring( ) method returns true if the beam is free and has been set in motion. It returns false if the beam is already in use (i.e., traveling or exploding).

It's possible for all the LaserShot objects to be busy when the user types f and for nothing to happen. In practice, this situation is unlikely to occur because a beam is busy for no more than 3 to 4 seconds, and 20 LaserShot objects are available. From a gaming point of view, the possibility of running out of beams, albeit temporarily, may make the game play more interesting.

Managing a Laser Beam

Each LaserShot object creates and manipulates a subgraph holding a beam (a thin red cylinder) and explosion (an animation laid over a quad). The subgraph shown in Figure 24-6 is created by makeBeam( ).

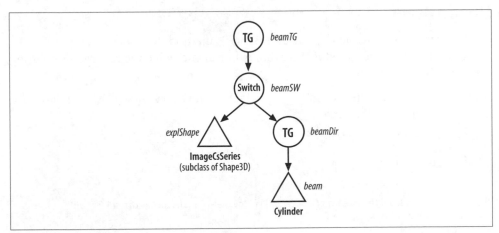

Figure 24-6. Scenegraph branch for LaserShot

The top-level TransformGroup, beamTG, moves the beam (and explosion), and the Switch allows the beam, explosion, or nothing to be displayed. The beamDir TransformGroup initially positions and orients the cylinder so it's pointing into the scene and appears close to the nozzle of the gun image.

The cylinder has a radius of 0.05 units and a height of 0.5; it's rotated by 90 degrees, moved down by 0.3, and into the scene by 0.25 units. This means that the center of its tail is located at (0, –0.3, 0) relative to the coordinate space of beamTG.

The ImagesCsSeries class is almost identical to the ImagesSeries class in Chapter 23. The two differences are:

- The object doesn't load its own GIFs. Instead, an array of ImageComponent2D objects is passed to it in the constructor.
- The shape's position is specified with a center point.

The call to ImageCsSeries's constructor is carried out in makeBeam( ):

```
// create explosion, centered at (0,0,0), size 2.0f
explShape = new ImageCsSeries( new Point3f(), 2.0f, exploIms);
```

The explosion is a child of the same TransformGroup as the beam (beamTG), so placing its center at (0, 0, 0) will make it appear roughly at the same place in beamTG's coordinate space as the tail of the beam.

The positioning of the beam is something of an art since it depends on creating the illusion that it's coming from the gun, which in turn depends on the way that the gun-in-hand is drawn and placed on screen. Similarly, the positioning of the explosion is governed by where the center of the explosion is drawn in the GIF and by where that center should be relative to the beam at explosion time.

Firing a Beam

AmmoManager calls LaserShot's requestFiring( ) method to utilize the beam. The request will only be accepted if the beam is not in use, which is recorded by setting the inUse Boolean.

If the LaserShot is not in use (inUse == false), then LaserShot will start an AnimBeam thread, and inUse is set to true:

```
public boolean requestFiring( )
{ if (inUse)
    return false;
  else {
    inUse = true;
    new AnimBeam(this).start( ); // calls moveBeam( ) inside a thread
    return true;
  }
}
```

The AnimBeam thread is simple: its sole purpose is to call the moveBeam( ) method back in the LaserShot object. By being called in a thread, the method will be executed without causing the rest of the application (e.g., KeyBehavior, AmmoManager) to wait.

moveBeam( ) incrementally moves the beam (and explosion) forward, starting from the current viewer position (steerTG). If the beam gets close to the target, then the explosion is shown; otherwise, the beam disappears after reaching a certain MAX_RANGE distance from the gun.

inUse is set to false again at the end of the method, allowing the LaserShot object to be used again by AmmoManager:

```
public void moveBeam( )
{
  // position the beam at the current viewer position
  steerTG.getTransform( tempT3d );
  beamTG.setTransform( tempT3d);
  showBeam(true);

  double currDist = 0.0;
  boolean hitTarget = closeToTarget( );
  while ((currDist < MAX_RANGE) && (!hitTarget)) {
    doMove(INCR_VEC);
    hitTarget = closeToTarget( );
    currDist += STEP;
    try {
      Thread.sleep(SLEEP_TIME);
    }
    catch (Exception ex) {}
  }

  showBeam(false);      // make beam invisible
  if (hitTarget)
    showExplosion( );   // if a hit, show explosion
  inUse = false;        // shot is finished
}
```

The INCR_VEC vector (0, 0, −1) is repeatedly applied to the beam's TransformGroup, beamTG, by doMove( ) to move the beam away from the viewer's position. This works because the top-level transform for the beam (and explosion), beamTG, is set equal to steerTG before the loop begins, giving it the same starting position and orientation as the viewer.

This means that any movements will be relative to the local coordinate space of the viewer. In particular, the INCR_VEC vector always represents a unit step directly away from the viewpoint, farther into the scene. This is true irrespective of which way the viewpoint is facing in the global coordinate space of the scene. The code for doMove( ) is:

```
private void doMove(Vector3d mv)
{ beamTG.getTransform( tempT3d );
```

```
        toMove.setTranslation( mv );
        tempT3d.mul(toMove);
        beamTG.setTransform( tempT3d );
    }
```

The doMove and tempT3d references are global to avoid the creation of temporary objects.

closeToTarget( ) does a comparison between the current position of the beam and the position of the target. This is complicated because the beam's location in the scene is affected by beamTG *and* by its initial transformation with beamDir.

A general-purpose solution is to use getLocalToVworld( ) on the beam shape to retrieve its overall transformation in terms of the global scene coordinates. This requires a capability bit to be set when the shape is created:

```
    beam.setCapability(Node.ALLOW_LOCAL_TO_VWORLD_READ);
```

The closeToTarget( ) method becomes:

```
    private boolean closeToTarget( )
    /* The beam is close if its current position (currVec)
       is a short distance from the target position (targetVec).
    */
    { beam.getLocalToVworld(localT3d);  // beam's trans in world coords
      localT3d.get(currVec);            // get (x,y,z) component

      currVec.sub(targetVec);     // calc distance between two positions
      double sqLen = currVec.lengthSquared( );
      if (sqLen < HIT_RANGE*HIT_RANGE)
        return true;
      return false;
    }
```

The code tests to see if the beam is within HIT_RANGE units of the center of the target.

Moving the Viewpoint

FPShooter3D moves the viewpoint by attaching a KeyBehavior object to ViewPlatform's TransformGroup:

```
    ViewingPlatform vp = su.getViewingPlatform( );

    KeyBehavior keyBeh = new KeyBehavior( ammoMan );
          // keyBeh can ask the ammoManager to fire a beam
    keyBeh.setSchedulingBounds(bounds);
    vp.setViewPlatformBehavior(keyBeh);
```

KeyBehavior's internals are similar to earlier keyboard-based behaviors developed for the Tour3D and AnimTour3D examples in Chapters 18 and 19. A key press triggers the behavior, and the associated KeyEvent object is used to determine the type of movement to carry out.

Similarities aside though, one difference between KeyBehavior and earlier classes is that this class extends ViewPlatformBehavior so it can work upon ViewPlatform's TransformGroup, called targetTG. targetTG is available to the methods defined in KeyBehavior through inheritance.

Another difference is that the Tour3D and AnimTour3D behaviors pass the responsibility for movement and rotation to objects in the scene (i.e., to the sprites). KeyBehavior carries out those operations for itself, by manipulating targetTG. KeyBehavior detects key presses of the arrow keys, optionally combined with the alt key to move forward, back, left, right, up, down, and rotate around the y-axis. The f key requests beam firing.

processStimulus() calls processKeyEvent() when a key is detected:

```
private void processKeyEvent(KeyEvent eventKey)
{ int keyCode = eventKey.getKeyCode();
  if(eventKey.isAltDown())    // key + <alt>
    altMove(keyCode);
  else
    standardMove(keyCode);
}
```

altMove() and standardMove() are multi-way branches calling doMove() or rotateY() (or AmmoManager's fireBeam(), when the key is f). rotateY() applies a rotation to targetTG:

```
private void rotateY(double radians)
{ targetTG.getTransform(t3d);
  toRot.rotY(radians);
  t3d.mul(toRot);
  targetTG.setTransform(t3d);
}
```

t3d and toRot are globals to avoid the overhead of temporary object creation.

CHAPTER 25

A 3D Maze

The main contributions of the first-person shooter (FPS) in Chapter 24 were a moving viewpoint (controlled by key presses), the use of a 2D image to simulate a gun hand, and the ability to shoot multiple laser beams at once, generating multiple explosions. Though the user could move about, there wasn't any scenery (except the robot target).

This chapter continues the FPS theme but concentrates on letting the user navigate through a complex, realistic looking scene (a 3D maze) without walking through walls or getting too lost:

Key-based navigation

I'll be reusing (with a few changes) the KeyBehavior class from Chapter 24, so the navigation is again controlled from the keyboard. The user can move forward, backward, slide left or right, float up or down but can't walk through walls or descend through the floor. Rotations are limited to 90-degree turns to the left or right, which simplifies the application's position calculations.

A realistic scene

The scene is a 3D maze made from textured, colored blocks and cylinders. The floor is tiled with a texture to make it look more detailed. The background is a textured sphere, which means that the sky looks different when viewed from different locations in the scene. The lighting is deliberately gloomy (there's no ambient light), but a Java 3D Spotlight node is attached to the viewpoint, so the user appears to be carrying a spotlight.

Multiple views to aid navigation

The application offers three views of the maze. The main application panel shows the user's forward facing view (I call this the *main camera*), a smaller panel displays the view directly behind the user (the *back facing camera*), and a third panel offers a schematic overview of the entire maze with the user represented by an arrow pointing in the current forward direction (the *bird's-eye view*). Multiple views are essential in gaming, especially an overview of the entire scene.

Viewpoint adjustments

The viewpoint's field of view (FOV) is widened, so the user can see more of the scene. I adjust the viewpoint's forward and back clip distances, so the player can move close to the maze's blocks and cylinders and still see them.

Using a maze plan

The maze plan is generated by a separate application, which stores it as an ASCII file. The file is read in by the Maze3D application at startup time to generate the 3D structures, create the schematic overview, and use the plan in collision detection code. The utilization of a separate plan allows the maze to be changed quickly and easily.

Figure 25-1 shows a screenshot of the application, Maze3D, which consists of three JPanels. The lefthand side shows the main camera, the top-right panel is the back facing camera, and the bottom-right panel is the bird's-eye view.

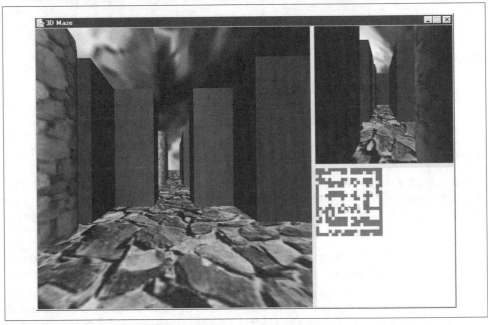

Figure 25-1. Navigating the 3D maze

Class Diagrams for Maze3D

Figure 25-2 gives the class diagrams for the Maze3D application, including the class names and public methods.

Maze3D is the usual top-level JFrame but does a bit more than in previous examples since it builds the GUI interface for the three views of the game.

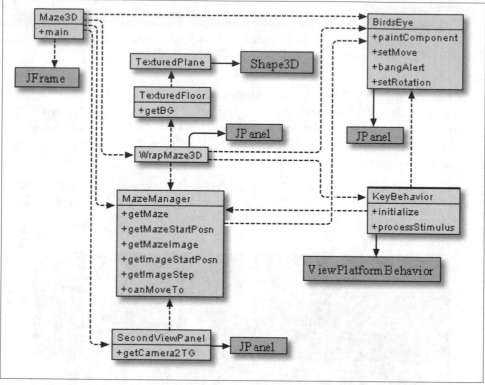

Figure 25-2. Class diagrams for Maze3D

WrapMaze3D is a JPanel that creates the 3D scene including the background, lighting, and the main camera viewpoint. It utilizes maze and floor subgraphs made by other objects, and it invokes a KeyBehavior object. The TexturedFloor and TexturedPlane classes are used to create the floor.

MazeManager reads in the maze plan (a text file) prepared outside of Maze3D and generates two representations: a Java 3D subgraph that is added to the scene and a Java 2D image of the maze passed to the BirdsEye object. BirdsEye draws a 2D overview of the maze and represents the user by moving and rotating an arrow over the top of the maze image. This bird's-eye view is displayed in the bottom righthand JPanel in the GUI. SecondViewPanel creates a second view branch subgraph showing the view behind the user's current position (the back facing camera). The subgraph is added to the main scene, and its Canvas3D object is linked to the top righthand JPanel in the GUI.

KeyBehavior converts key presses into moves and rotations of the two cameras, and it updates to the bird's-eye view.

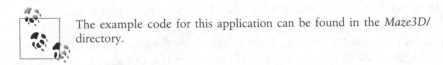

The example code for this application can be found in the *Maze3D/* directory.

Making a Maze Plan

The 3D and 2D maze representations employed in Maze3D are created by the MazeManager object after reading in a maze plan from a text file. Here is the plan in *maze1.txt*:

```
              s
bbbbb bbbbb bbbbb bbbbb
b                     b
b                     b
bbbb  ccccc ccccc  bbbb
   b
   b
   b
```

Figure 25-3 shows that plan realized in Maze3D (via the call java Maze3D maze1.txt).

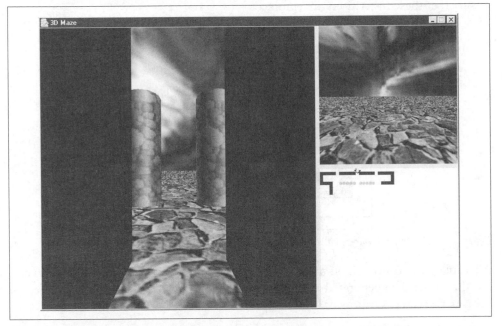

Figure 25-3. Maze3D using maze1.txt

The s character in the text plan specifies the user's starting position in the maze. By default, the viewpoint is set to point along the positive z-axis in the scene, corresponding to downward in the bird's-eye view. The b characters in the maze plan become blue textured blocks, and the c characters are drawn as green textured cylinders.

Generating a Maze Using Software

A maze plan, like the one in *maze1.txt*, can be prepared in various ways, the simplest being to type one manually using a text editor. As an alternative, one of my students, Nawapoom Lohajarernvanich, and I wrote a maze generation application, called *MazeGen.java* (stored in *Maze3D/MazeGen/*). It utilizes a recursive, depth-first search with backtracking to create a maze.

The program generates a maze in a 2D character array. It assumes the array has an even number of rows and columns, and it creates the outer walls of the maze offset by one cell from the left, right, top, and bottom (see Figure 25-4). This means that the maze boundaries are in the odd rows and columns of the array. These restrictions ensure that the maze will have a solid outer wall after the maze has been created. The program adjusts the user's supplied maze width and height values to ensure that these restrictions are enforced.

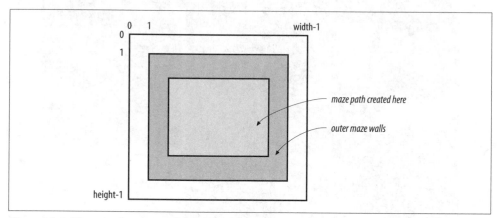

Figure 25-4. The maze's outer walls

A b is placed in every cell on the grid, and the program removes some of them to create the maze. The generated maze is a single, winding path with no disconnected areas (e.g., secret corridors or bricked-up rooms).

The cutting away of the bs to form the maze starts at a randomly chosen even coordinate in the array (e.g., (4, 4)). Then another cell is randomly chosen from the four cells that are two units away in the x- or y-directions. For example, if the current cell is (4, 4), then the next cell could be (2, 4), (6, 4), (4, 6), or (4, 2). The path is made by connecting the cells with spaces, deleting the bs. This process is illustrated in Figure 25-5.

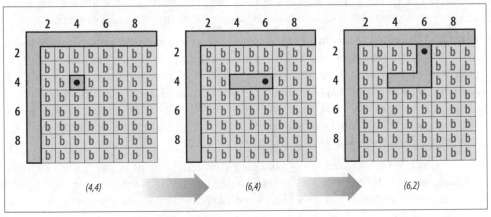

Figure 25-5. Path generation in MazeGen

The path-making process is repeated at the new cell, except that a path cannot return to a cell that's been used or to a position on or outside the maze's outer walls. For example, from (6, 4) the algorithm can use (8, 4), (6, 6), and (6, 2), but not (4, 4). The path cannot revisit a cell that's been visited, so it's not possible to create a maze with loops.

The path is made by joining up cells at even coordinates. Since the outer maze wall is made from cells at odd coordinates, a cell from the outer wall will never be selected to join the maze. This means that the path cannot cut into the maze wall.

The algorithm continues until it reaches a cell that cannot be connected to any further cells. This occurs when all the possible next cells have been utilized or are on or outside the outer walls. At this stage, the algorithm backtracks to the previous cell and looks at it again. Backtracking will continue until a cell has a possible next cell or there is no previous cell to go to (i.e., execution has returned to the starting cell).

The relevant code inside MazeGen is contained in createPath( ):

```
private void createPath(Point cell)
{ RandomInRange rr = new RandomInRange(NUM_DIRS);
  int dir;
  while((dir = rr.getNumber( )) != -1){
    Point nextCell = nextPos(cell, dir);
    if( !beenVisited(nextCell) ){
      visit(nextCell, dir);
      createPath(nextCell);  // recursive creation
    }
  }
}
```

The RandomInRange constructor creates a sequence between 0 and one less than the supplied value, and each call to getNumber() randomly selects a number from that sequence. For this application, NUM_DIRS is 4, so getNumber() can choose from {0, 1, 2, 3}, which represent the four directions leaving a cell (up, down, left, or right).

createPath() passes this number to nextPos() to select the next cell. If the next cell hasn't been visited, then visit() extends the path and the recursive call to createPath() continues the path generation. Backtracking from the recursive call will return to this loop, which will try another direction. getNumber() returns -1 when its sequence is exhausted, causing createPath() to return to an earlier createPath() call. The generated path is remembered by visit() modifying a global maze[][] array, so backtracking won't undo its creation.

The program finishes by randomly changing about 20 percent of the maze's bs to cs, and adds an exit to the top row of the maze. Changing the letter corresponds to replacing some of the 3D maze's blocks with cylinders to make the maze look a bit more interesting.

The starting cell used for path creation is assigned an s to become the starting point for the user. Since the maze has no disconnected parts, we know that it's possible for the player to get from the starting point to the maze's exit.

A typical call to MazeGen, and its output, is shown below:

```
> java MazeGen 21 13
Width: 23; Height: 15 (2 added for borders)
Saving maze to file: maze.txt
Starting point: (2, 20)

bbbbcbbbcb bbbbbbcbcc
b          b  b  sb
b bbbbbccbc b bbb ccb
b       c    b   b b
b bcbbb bbbcbbb cbc b
b   b  c       b   b
b bbb bbb bcbbbbb cbb
b b  b  b      b   b
b c b b bbbbb b b b b
b b b b       b b c b
c b bbccccbbbbb cbb b
b c                 b
cbbbbbbbcbbbbbbbbbbccb

Maze written to file maze.txt
```

The User Interface

Maze3D invokes MazeManager, BirdsEye, SecondViewPanel, and WrapMaze3D objects. The latter three are subclasses of JPanel, which Maze3D organizes using the layout shown in Figure 25-6.

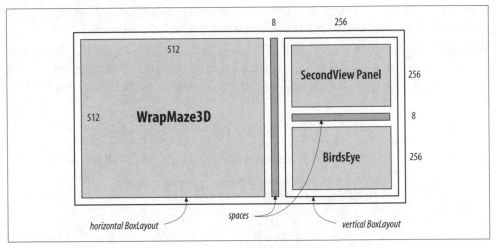

Figure 25-6. Maze3D GUI layout

The fragment of code below contains the invocation of these four objects and shows that MazeManager is required by all the JPanel objects:

```
MazeManager mm = new MazeManager(fnm);    // fnm holds maze plan
BirdsEye be = new BirdsEye(mm);
SecondViewPanel secondVP = new SecondViewPanel(mm);
WrapMaze3D w3d = new WrapMaze3D(mm, be, secondVP.getCamera2TG() );
```

The GUI is made with the BirdsEye object (the bottom-right panel in Figure 25-6), the SecondViewPanel object (the top-right panel in Figure 25-6), and the WrapMaze3D object (the lefthand panel).

Managing the Maze

MazeManager reads in a maze plan and generates two maze representations: a 3D subgraph added to the scene by WrapMaze3D and a 2D image employed by BirdsEye as the background for its moving arrow. The primary aim of MazeManager is to hide the processing of the maze plan from the rest of the application. In addition to serving up 3D and 2D mazes, MazeManager contains the coordinates of the user's starting point and deals with collision detection between the player and the maze walls. MazeManager's readFile( ) initializes maze[][] by reading in the ASCII maze plan, and buildMazeReps( ) creates the on-screen mazes.

When buildMazeReps( ) creates the 3D maze, it has to translate the indices in maze[][] into (x, y, z) coordinates for the blocks and cylinders. The first assumption is that every block and cylinder is standing on the floor, so their y-coordinates are 0. Then, the row's indices of maze[][] are treated as z-axis values and the columns as x-axis values. For example, if maze[3][5] contains a b, then a block will be placed at (5, 0, 3) in the scene.

This approach means that the top-left corner of the maze is located at (0, 0, 0) in the scene, and the rest of the maze extends over the positive XZ quadrant.

When buildMazeReps( ) generates the 2D image, it continues to treat the columns of maze[][] as x-axis numbers, but the rows are viewed as y-axis values. For example, if maze[3][5] contains a b, then a blue square will be drawn at the coordinate (5, 3) in the image.

The 3D scene is a single BranchGroup with TransformGroups hanging off it. There's one TransformGroup for each block (Box node) and cylinder (Cylinder node) to place the shape at its given coordinate. A TransformGroup is created with a call to makeObs( ):

```
private TransformGroup makeObs(char ch,int x,int z,Appearance app)
// place an obstacle (block/cylinder) at (x,z) with appearance app
{
  Primitive obs;
  if (ch == 'b')  // blue textured block
    obs = new Box(RADIUS, HEIGHT/2, RADIUS,
                        Primitive.GENERATE_TEXTURE_COORDS |
                        Primitive.GENERATE_NORMALS, app );
  else    // green textured cylinder
    obs = new Cylinder(RADIUS, HEIGHT,
                        Primitive.GENERATE_TEXTURE_COORDS |
                        Primitive.GENERATE_NORMALS, app );

  // position obstacle so its base is resting on the floor at (x,z)
  TransformGroup posnTG = new TransformGroup( );
  Transform3D trans = new Transform3D( );
  trans.setTranslation( new Vector3d(x, HEIGHT/2, z) );  // move up
  posnTG.setTransform(trans);
  posnTG.addChild(obs);
  return posnTG;
}
```

The overhead of using textured surfaces is reduced by reusing two precalculated Appearance nodes—one for the blocks, one for the cylinders—created with calls to makeApp( ):

```
private Appearance makeApp(Color3f colObs, String texFnm)
{
  Appearance app = new Appearance( );

  // mix the texture and the material color
  TextureAttributes ta = new TextureAttributes( );
  ta.setTextureMode(TextureAttributes.MODULATE);
  app.setTextureAttributes(ta);

  // load and set the texture
  System.out.println("Loading obstacle texture from " + texFnm);
  TextureLoader loader = new TextureLoader(texFnm, null);
  Texture2D texture = (Texture2D) loader.getTexture( );
  app.setTexture(texture);        // set the texture
```

```
    // add a colored material
    Material mat = new Material(colObs,black,colObs,specular,20.f);
    mat.setLightingEnable(true);
    app.setMaterial(mat);
    return app;
}
```

 The Appearance modulates the texture and material and switches on lighting effects.

The intention is that the scene will be poorly lit except for a spotlight "held" by the user. The efficacy of the spot depends on its own parameters, such as its attenuation and concentration, and on the shininess and specular color of the objects, which are set in the Material node component.

 Specular color is the color of a shape when it reflects light from shiny areas. Usually the specular color is white, as in this example.

The 2D image is initialized as a BufferedImage:

```
BufferedImage mazeImg =
    new BufferedImage(IMAGE_LEN, IMAGE_LEN, BufferedImage.TYPE_INT_ARGB);
```

The drawing operations are applied via a graphics context:

```
Graphics g = (Graphics) mazeImg.createGraphics();


drawBlock(g, x, z);      // for a block at (x,y)
// other drawing operations...

drawCylinder(g, x, z);   // for a cylinder at (x,y)


g.dispose();     // when drawing is completed
```

drawBlock( ) and drawCylinder( ) are quite simple:

```
    private void drawBlock(Graphics g, int i, int j)
    // draw a blue box in the 2D image
    { g.setColor(Color.blue);
      g.fillRect(i*IMAGE_STEP, j*IMAGE_STEP, IMAGE_STEP, IMAGE_STEP);
    }

    private void drawCylinder(Graphics g, int i, int j)
    // draw a green circle in the 2D image
    { g.setColor(Color.green);
      g.fillOval(i*IMAGE_STEP, j*IMAGE_STEP, IMAGE_STEP, IMAGE_STEP);
    }
```

IMAGE_STEP is the number of pixels in the 2D image corresponding to a maze cell's dimensions.

Collision Detection

Collision detection is a matter of testing a supplied (x, z) pair against the maze[z][x] cell to see if it contains a b or c. Coordinates beyond the maze's extent must be dealt with:

```
public boolean canMoveTo(double xWorld, double zWorld)
// is (xWorld, zWorld) free of obstacles?
// Called by the KeyBehavior object to test a possible move.
{
  int x = (int) Math.round(xWorld);
  int z = (int) Math.round(zWorld);

  if ((x < 0) || (x >= LEN) || (z < 0) || (z >= LEN))
    return true;     // since outside the possible maze dimensions

  if ((maze[z][x] == 'b') || (maze[z][x] == 'c'))
    return false;    // since loc occupied by block or cylinder

  return true;
} // end of canMoveTo( )
```

The supplied coordinates should be integer values since the user only moves in one-unit steps and rotates by 90 degrees. However, Java 3D transforms utilize floats or doubles, so the coordinates will never be whole, which means they must be rounded before use.

Scenery Creation

WrapMaze3D carries out two main tasks: the creation of scene objects (e.g., the floor, the maze, lighting, background) and the initialization of the viewpoint (e.g., its position, orientation, and geometries linked to the viewpoint). createSceneGraph( ) builds the scene:

```
void createSceneGraph( )
{
  sceneBG = new BranchGroup( );
  bounds = new BoundingSphere(new Point3d(0,0,0), BOUNDSIZE);

  lightScene( );     // add the lights
  addBackground( );  // add the sky

  // add the textured floor
  TexturedFloor floor = new TexturedFloor( );
  sceneBG.addChild( floor.getBG( ) );
```

```
        sceneBG.addChild( mazeMan.getMaze() );
                        // add 3D maze, using MazeManager
        sceneBG.addChild( camera2TG );        // add second camera

        sceneBG.compile();    // fix the scene
    } // end of createScene()
```

lightScene( ) is similar to the lighting code in previous chapters in that it switches on two downward facing lights. However, no ambient light is created, causing the maze's internal walls to be cast into darkness.

Making a Background

WrapMaze3D has two versions of addBackground( ) to choose from, both of which lay a texture over the inside face of a Sphere. The first version makes the Sphere a child of a Background node:

```
    private void addBackground()
    // add a geometric background using a Background node
    {
      System.out.println("Loading sky texture: " + SKY_TEX);
      TextureLoader tex = new TextureLoader(SKY_TEX, null);

      Sphere sphere = new Sphere(1.0f, Sphere.GENERATE_NORMALS |
                Sphere.GENERATE_NORMALS_INWARD |
                Sphere.GENERATE_TEXTURE_COORDS, 4);    // default = 15
      Appearance backApp = sphere.getAppearance();
      backApp.setTexture( tex.getTexture() );

      BranchGroup backBG = new BranchGroup();
      backBG.addChild(sphere);

      Background bg = new Background();
      bg.setApplicationBounds(bounds);
      bg.setGeometry(backBG);

      sceneBG.addChild(bg);
    }
```

A useful way of thinking about a background shape is that it surrounds the scene. This means the user is located inside the background shape and will always see the background shape behind (beyond) the other objects in the scene. This is true even though the Sphere's radius is set to be 1.0f in addBackground( ); the value isn't utilized when the shape is used as a background.

The Sphere is set to create inward normal vectors, which will force the texture to appear on its inside faces—the ones visible within the scene. A normal vector for the surface of a polygon is perpendicular to that surface, usually pointing from the interior of the polygon to the outside. The side of the polygon that faces into the object's interior is called the back (or inward) face, and the outward side is the front face.

The number of divisions, which controls the number of surfaces that make up the sphere, is reduced from 15 (the default) to 4. The number of surfaces is equal to the square of the number of divisions. This reduction makes little difference to the quality of the background but greatly reduces the cost of generating the sphere.

 Another example using this technique can be found in *Background/* in the Java 3D demos directory.

Unfortunately, some bugs are connected with geometric Backgrounds in the current version of Java 3D (1.3.1). Some (older) graphics cards find it hard to display them. The problems manifest themselves as the background not being rendered at all (i.e., the background is left completely black) or parts of it being rendered inconsistently or being clipped.

An alternative is to render an inward facing sphere without using Background:

```
private void addBackground( )
{
  System.out.println("Loading sky texture: " + SKY_TEX);
  TextureLoader tex = new TextureLoader(SKY_TEX, null);

  // create an appearance and assign the texture
  Appearance app =  new Appearance( );
  app.setTexture( tex.getTexture( ) );

  Sphere sphere = new Sphere(100.0f,     // radius to edge of scene
            Sphere.GENERATE_NORMALS_INWARD |
            Sphere.GENERATE_TEXTURE_COORDS, 4, app);

  sceneBG.addChild( sphere );
}
```

The sphere is made as large as the intended radius of the scene and is added to the scene directly.

Tiling the Floor

The floor is a QuadArray made up of a series of quads, which taken together cover the entire floor. Each quad is assigned a texture and an upward facing normal. The sides of the entire floor have the length FLOOR_LEN, and each quad has sides of length STEP, as shown in Figure 25-7.

The paving of the floor starts at the front, leftmost point (-FLOOR_LEN/2, FLOOR_LEN/2) and continues left to right and forward to back. This work is carried out by TexturedFloor's constructor and createCoords( ):

```
public TexturedFloor( )
// create quad coords, make TexturedPlane, add to floorBG
```

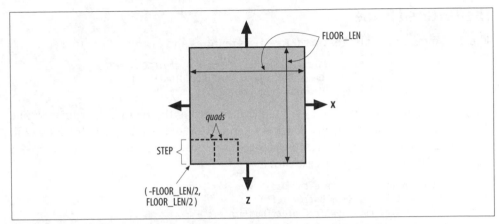

Figure 25-7. The floor and its QuadArray (from above)

```
{
    ArrayList coords = new ArrayList();
    floorBG = new BranchGroup();

    // create coords for the quad
    for(int z=FLOOR_LEN/2; z >= (-FLOOR_LEN/2)+STEP; z-=STEP) {
        for(int x=-FLOOR_LEN/2; x <= (FLOOR_LEN/2)-STEP; x+=STEP)
            createCoords(x, z, coords);
    }

    Vector3f upNormal = new Vector3f(0.0f, 1.0f, 0.0f);    // upwards
    floorBG.addChild( new TexturedPlane(coords,FLOOR_IMG,upNormal) );
}


private void createCoords(int x, int z, ArrayList coords)
{
    // points created in counter-clockwise order, from front left
    // of length STEP
    Point3f p1 = new Point3f(x, 0.0f, z);
    Point3f p2 = new Point3f(x+STEP, 0.0f, z);
    Point3f p3 = new Point3f(x+STEP, 0.0f, z-STEP);
    Point3f p4 = new Point3f(x, 0.0f, z-STEP);
    coords.add(p1); coords.add(p2);
    coords.add(p3); coords.add(p4);
}  // end of createCoords()
```

createCoords() takes one point and creates the four points for a quad, making sure they're in counterclockwise order to place the front face upward on the XZ plane. Once all the coordinates have been calculated, they're passed to a TexturedPlane object, along with the name of a texture file (TEXTURE_IMG) and a vector that will become each quad's normal.

The Textured Plane

The QuadArray created by TexturedPlane uses textures and normals:

```
QuadArray plane = new QuadArray(numPoints, GeometryArray.COORDINATES |
                            GeometryArray.TEXTURE_COORDINATE_2 |
                            GeometryArray.NORMALS );
```

The hardest part of the geometry-related code is setting the texture coordinates. The coordinates in the QuadArray are ordered in groups of four, each specifying a quad in counterclockwise order. The texture coordinates are created in the same way—in groups of four in counterclockwise order:

```
// assign texture coords to each quad
// counter-clockwise, from bottom left
TexCoord2f[] tcoords = new TexCoord2f[numPoints];
for(int i=0; i < numPoints; i=i+4) {
  tcoords[i] = new TexCoord2f(0.0f, 0.0f);    // for 1 point
  tcoords[i+1] = new TexCoord2f(1.0f, 0.0f);
  tcoords[i+2] = new TexCoord2f(1.0f, 1.0f);
  tcoords[i+3] = new TexCoord2f(0.0f, 1.0f);
}
plane.setTextureCoordinates(0, 0, tcoords);
```

The Appearance part of the shape creates a modulated texture with a Material node component so lighting can be enabled. The code is similar to makeApp( ) in MazeManager. The end result is that the texture will be tiled across the floor, with each tile having sides of length STEP. Though there appears to be many textures, there's only one, but it's referenced many times. This optimization means that only one Texture2D object needs to be created by the application.

By varying the STEP constant, the number and size of the tiles can be varied. As the STEP value gets bigger, each tile gets bigger, and fewer tiles are needed to cover the floor. A drawback with a larger tile is that the texture will be stretched over a larger area, so it will become more pixilated. Another point to remember is that STEP should be divisible into the floor length value, FLOOR_LEN.

Viewpoint Creation

Various viewpoint manipulations are carried out by WrapMaze3D's prepareViewPoint( ):

Positioning and orientation
> The viewpoint's position is specified using the maze's starting point (represented by an s in the maze plan). The viewpoint is rotated to face along the positive z-axis. There's no reason for doing this, except to show how I can change the default orientation (which is along the negative z-axis).

Movement control
> A KeyBehavior object is connected to the viewpoint so key presses can move it during execution.

A Spotlight

The maze is cast into stygian gloom, so a Spotlight node is connected to the viewpoint to help the users see what they're doing. It'll move with the viewpoint, giving the impression that the player is holding a spotlight.

Adjustments to the view parameters

The FOV is widened, so the user can see more of the scene in front of them. The front and back clip distances are adjusted, primarily so the user can move right up to a block or cylinder without it being clipped.

An avatar

Many first-person games include a player *avatar* (a visible representation of the user, or part of the user); the "gun-in-hand" image in Chapter 24 is a simple example. I've decided not to include an avatar in the Maze3D application, but I'll discuss how to add one later in this section. The example code adds a 3D cone to the viewpoint.

The FOV

The FOV specifies how much of the scene is visible in terms of an angular spread around the viewpoint. The default is 45 degrees or 22.5 degrees on either side of the perpendicular into the scene (see Figure 25-8).

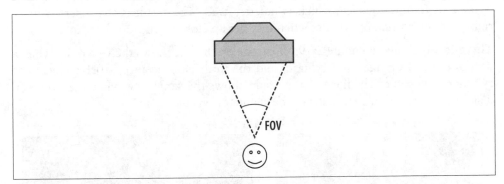

Figure 25-8. Field of view of a user

Increasing the FOV permits the user to see farther to the left and right, which is useful in Maze3D since corridors head off to the left and right. The downside is that a fish-eye effect appearing as the FOV is made larger, distorting the view.

 The camera lovers among you may have come across a *fish-eye lens*, which displays the same effect as a large FOV: the screen image is foreshortened in the center and increasingly distorted at the edges.

Changing the FOV to 90 degrees (from its default of 45 degrees) is straightforward:

```
View userView = su.getViewer().getView();
userView.setFieldOfView( Math.toRadians(90.0)); // wider FOV
```

The user can see more to the left and right, which is useful in a maze for noticing passages leading off to the sides.

Clip Distances

Clip distances specify the closest and farthest objects that can be seen by the viewer. Java 3D's defaults are 0.1 meters for the front clip plane and 10 meters for the back clip, which roughly corresponds to the limitations of human eyesight. These distance are in real-world units, although it's possible to specify values in virtual world units by using the Java 3D `View` class methods `setFrontClipPolicy( )` and `setBackClipPolicy( )` to change the units policy.

The back clip value may be too small for a particular application, resulting in objects disappearing when the viewpoint moves far away from them. This can be tested by moving the viewpoint to some distant location in the game and turning around to see if any parts of the scene have disappeared. In `Maze3D`, I moved the viewpoint out of the maze to the edge of the floor and checked that the maze was still visible.

The default front clip value (0.1 meters) is fine for most applications, but the user is likely to bump into walls in the maze. When this occurs, the front of the block or cylinder will be clipped since the viewpoint is closer than 0.1 meters to the object. What's worse is that the other side of the object will be invisible since the user is looking at its interior face, which is not rendered. The result is that users will see right through a brick or cylinder when they get up close to one.

This effect is shown in Figure 25-9: the image on the left shows the viewpoint when a user is pressed up against a cylinder and the front clip distance is 0.1 meters. The cylinder is invisible. The image on the right shows the same view when the front clip distance is reduced to 0.05 meters. The cylinder is visible again.

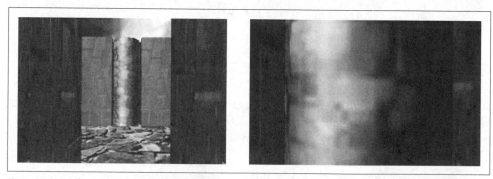

Figure 25-9. The same viewpoint with different front clip distances

Knowing this problem, a programmer may be tempted to set the front clip distance to 0 with the hope that no clipping will occur, no matter how close the user gets to a piece of scenery. What happens is that the depth ordering of objects in the scene breaks down, with far and near objects partially overlapping each other in arbitrary ways.

The breakdown is triggered when the ratio of the back clip to front clip distances becomes too large. The machine's hardware (specifically its depth buffer) is being asked to squeeze too large a range of z-values into too few bits per pixel on screen. The critical ratio depends on the bits per pixel used in the depth buffer: older machines may start to "sweat" at ratios close to 100, but modern cards using 32 bits will be happy with ratios close to 100,000.

After the experimentation mentioned above, I chose a back clip distance of 20 meters and a front clip of 0.05 meters, creating a fairly safe ratio of 400:

```
userView.setBackClipDistance(20);
userView.setFrontClipDistance(0.05);
```

Adding a Spotlight

The spotlight is meant to be in the player's "hand," lighting the way forward as he or she moves around the maze. This means that the spotlight must be connected to the viewpoint and move as it moves. Chapter 24 went into detail about the view branch where the viewpoint is managed, and Figure 25-10 should remind you of its main components.

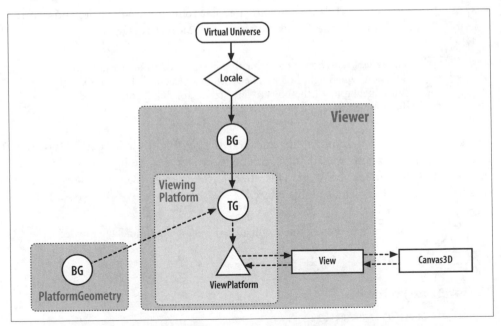

Figure 25-10. The view branch subgraph

The spotlight must be placed inside a `PlatformGeometry` node, then attached to the `TransformGroup` (labeled as TG in Figure 25-10) above the `ViewPlatform`. The code that follows utilizes Java 3D's `ViewingPlatform` utility class to do this.

```
ViewingPlatform vp = su.getViewingPlatform( );


PlatformGeometry pg = new PlatformGeometry( );
pg.addChild( makeSpot( ) );
vp.setPlatformGeometry( pg );
```

The construction of the spotlight is done by `makeSpot( )`.

The Java 3D `SpotLight` node has a position, a direction, and focusing controls for its spread angle and concentration. The spread angle controls the width of the beam; no light is generated outside of the angle. An increased concentration value causes the beam to be focused into a narrower beam, though some light will appear beyond the beam's bounds. The default spread angle is 180 degrees; the default concentration is 0.0, which provides uniform light distribution.

Since `SpotLight` is a subclass of `PointLight`, it inherits other useful attributes, such as the ability to adjust its attenuation (how quickly the light fades away for objects further away).

A spotlight affects an object's diffuse and specular reflection, which depends on the orientation and position of the object's surfaces and on its `Material` node.

The *diffuse reflection* is the color that bounces of an object in random directions when light hits it. The *specular reflection* is the color of the shiny highlights of the object. The size of the highlights depends on the shininess value for the object.

The overall effect of a spotlight depends on the spotlight's parameters (position, direction, concentration, spread angle, attenuation) and on the lighting and material properties of the surfaces being lit. This interplay of so many factors makes it a matter of trial and error to get a suitable effect.

My aim was to have the spotlight cast a faint light, quickly crowded out by darkness.

The `makeSpot( )` method is:

```
private SpotLight makeSpot( )
{
  SpotLight spot = new SpotLight( );
```

```
        spot.setPosition(0.0f, 0.5f, 0.0f);      // a bit above the user
        spot.setAttenuation(0.0f, 1.2f, 0.0f);   // linear attenuation
        spot.setSpreadAngle( (float)Math.toRadians(30.0));  // smaller
        spot.setConcentration(5.0f);             // reduce strength quicker
        spot.setInfluencingBounds(bounds);
        return spot;
    }
```

The 30-degree value for setSpreadAngle( ) corresponds to a spread angle of 60 degrees, 30 degrees on each side of the forward direction. The increased concentration focuses the beam, making the sides of the scene somewhat darker. By making the spread smaller and increasing the concentration, the light becomes weaker.

The setPosition( ) value moves the SpotLight node slightly above the viewpoint, which places the spotlight at a natural looking location relative to the viewpoint.

Adding an Avatar

Chapter 24 describes one way of adding an avatar: by placing a 2D image just in front of the viewpoint. Another solution is to use a 3D model (e.g., a hand, a gun). To illustrate the idea, makeAvatar( ) adds a cone at the viewpoint, rotated by 90 degrees about the x-axis so its apex is pointing forward:

```
    private TransformGroup makeAvatar( )
    {
      Transform3D t3d = new Transform3D( );
      t3d.rotX(Math.PI/2);       // rotate so top of cone is facing front
      TransformGroup userTG = new TransformGroup(t3d);

      userTG.addChild( new Cone(0.35f, 1.0f) );   // a thin cone
      return userTG;
    }
```

The TransformGroup is then linked to PlatformGeometry:

```
    pg.addChild( makeAvatar( ) );
```

If you wanted to add this cone avatar to the viewpoint in Maze3D, the pg.addChild( ) call could be included in the code fragment on the previous page, when the spotlight is added to PlatformGeometry.

Using a 3D model has one major advantage over a 2D image: it can be used as your physical presence in the scene. This is useful if the game contains other players who need to see you (e.g., as in a multiplayer networked application). A 3D model is also a drawback since it may be partially obscured if the viewpoint gets too close to another object in the scene.

Positioning the Viewpoint

The viewpoint's position and orientation are set up by accessing and changing the TransformGroup above ViewPlatform :

```
ViewingPlatform vp = su.getViewingPlatform( );
TransformGroup steerTG = vp.getViewPlatformTransform( );
initViewPosition(steerTG);
```

steerTG is the TransformGroup above the ViewPlatform node shown in Figure 25-10. By default, the initial viewpoint is facing into the scene along the z-axis. initViewPosition( ) rotates it by 180 degrees and moves it to the maze's start position:

```
private void initViewPosition(TransformGroup steerTG)
{
  Transform3D t3d = new Transform3D( );
  steerTG.getTransform(t3d);
  Transform3D toRot = new Transform3D( );
  toRot.rotY(-Math.PI);      // so facing along positive z-axis

  t3d.mul(toRot);
  t3d.setTranslation( mazeMan.getMazeStartPosn() );
  steerTG.setTransform(t3d);
}
```

Since the rotation orients the viewpoint in the positive z-axis direction, the translation value doesn't need to be adjusted.

Keyboard Controls

The keyboard behavior is set up inside prepareViewPoint( ) in WrapMaze3D:

```
ViewingPlatform vp = su.getViewingPlatform( );


KeyBehavior keybeh = new KeyBehavior(mazeMan, be, camera2TG);
keybeh.setSchedulingBounds(bounds);
vp.setViewPlatformBehavior(keybeh);
```

The KeyBehavior class requires a reference to MazeManager (mazeMan), the BirdsEye panel (be), and the TransformGroup for the back facing camera (camera2TG).

The Back Facing Camera

The back facing camera is a second ViewPlatform node, which requires its own Canvas3D object so the view can be displayed. The minimal subgraph for the camera is shown in Figure 25-11.

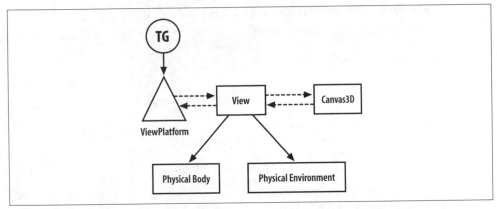

Figure 25-11. The minimal view branch graph

Attributes related to the user's head are defined in PhysicalBody, such as the position of her eyes relative to the scene. PhysicalEnvironment specifies the environment in which the view will be generated, such as whether head-tracking or wall displays are being utilized. I'm using a standard PC configuration, so these objects can be created with their default settings. The ViewPlatform represents the camera's viewpoint, and the TransformGroup above it positions the viewpoint and is the connection point between the camera and the top-level BranchGroup in the main scene.

The SecondViewPanel class creates a subgraph such as the one in Figure 25-11, and makes its TransformGroup, called canvas2TG, visible via the method getCamera2TG( ). The class's other role is to embed its Canvas3D object inside a JPanel so that it can be easily inserted into the Swing-based GUI. SecondViewPanel is a subclass of JPanel, so the attachment of the Canvas3D object is carried out in its constructor:

```
// globals
private static final int PWIDTH = 256;    // size of panel
private static final int PHEIGHT = 256;

private MazeManager mazeMan;
private TransformGroup camera2TG;
    // TG for the camera; will be linked to the main scene

public SecondViewPanel(MazeManager mm)
{ mazeMan = mm;
  setLayout(new BorderLayout( ));
  setOpaque(false);
  setPreferredSize( new Dimension(PWIDTH, PHEIGHT));
  GraphicsConfiguration config =
          SimpleUniverse.getPreferredConfiguration( );
  Canvas3D canvas3D = new Canvas3D(config);
  add("Center", canvas3D);     // add Canvas3D to the JPanel

  initView(canvas3D);
}
```

initView( ) constructs the subgraph:

```
private void initView(Canvas3D canvas3D)
{
  ViewPlatform vp = new ViewPlatform( );

  // create a View node for the ViewPlatform
  // it has the same attributes as the forward facing camera View
  View view = new View( );
  view.setPhysicalBody( new PhysicalBody( ) );
  view.setPhysicalEnvironment( new PhysicalEnvironment( ) );
  view.addCanvas3D(canvas3D);
  view.attachViewPlatform(vp);    // attach the ViewPlatform

  view.setFieldOfView( Math.toRadians(90.0));
  view.setBackClipDistance(20);
  view.setFrontClipDistance(0.05);

  camera2TG = setCameraPosition( );
  camera2TG.addChild(vp);    // add ViewPlatform to camera TG
}
```

The View attributes (FOV, clip distances) are the same as in the forward facing camera. No spotlight is added to the subgraph, causing the view behind the user to be substantially darker than the view ahead.

setCameraPosition( ) sets up the camera's location by creating the top-level TransformGroup and positioning it with lookAt( ):

```
private TransformGroup setCameraPosition( )
{
  Vector3d startVec = mazeMan.getMazeStartPosn( );

  Transform3D t3d = new Transform3D( );
  // args are: viewer posn, where looking, up direction
  t3d.lookAt( new Point3d(startVec.x, startVec.y, startVec.z),
           new Point3d(startVec.x, startVec.y, -10),  //any -z value will do
           new Vector3d(0,1,0));
  t3d.invert( );

  TransformGroup tg = new TransformGroup(t3d);
  tg.setCapability(TransformGroup.ALLOW_TRANSFORM_READ);   // moveable
  tg.setCapability(TransformGroup.ALLOW_TRANSFORM_WRITE);
  return tg;
}
```

lookAt( ) places the camera at the starting position in the maze, pointing along the negative z-axis. An implicit assumption is that the start is somewhere in the positive quadrant of the XZ plane so startVec.z cannot be less than 0. Since the camera's default viewpoint faces into the scene, the transform created with lookAt( ) must be inverted to have the necessary effect.

This back facing camera is now positioned and oriented. However, it has to move at runtime as the user moves through the maze. The forward facing and back facing cameras are controlled by KeyBehavior. For the back facing camera, KeyBehavior affects its TransformGroup (called tg in setCameraPosition( )), so the node's capability bits are set to allow changes

Adding the Second View to the GUI

The creation of the SecondViewPanel and its addition to the GUI is carried out in Maze3D. Maze3D passes a reference to the camera's top-level TransformGroup into WrapMaze3D:

```
public Maze3D(String args[])
{
  // check the args[] array...

  MazeManager mm = new MazeManager(fnm);
  BirdsEye be = new BirdsEye(mm);        // bird's eye view over the maze
  SecondViewPanel secondVP = new SecondViewPanel(mm);
  WrapMaze3D w3d = new WrapMaze3D(mm, be, secondVP.getCamera2TG( ) );

  // GUI creation code ...
  ...
  Box vertBox = Box.createVerticalBox( );
  vertBox.add( secondVP );   // add back-facing camera pane
  c.add(vertBox);

  setDefaultCloseOperation( JFrame.EXIT_ON_CLOSE );
  pack( );
  setResizable(false);    // fixed size display
  show( );
}
```

The TransformGroup, called camera2TG in WrapMaze3D, is added to the scene by the createSceneGraph( ) method:

```
sceneBG.addChild( camera2TG );
```

Moving the Viewpoint

This chapter's KeyBehavior class is similar to the one described in Chapter 24, since both control the user's viewpoint. They both extend ViewPlatformBehavior, so they can access the ViewPlatform's TransformGroup. They both use the same key presses to trigger movement and rotation.

Movement can be forward, backward, left, right, up, or down, by one unit step, excluding jaunts through the walls or floor. Rotations are carried out in 90-degree turns left or right, which simplifies the implementation of the BirdsEye class.

BirdsEye's main task is to calculate the position and orientation of an arrow drawn on top of the overview image when the viewpoint moves or rotates.

KeyBehavior is complicated by being involved in the manipulation of two cameras and the BirdsEye view. The movement/rotation of the cameras are done inside KeyBehavior by affecting their TransformGroups, but the BirdsEye object carries out its own changes. These additional responsibilities can be seen in standardMove() that calls the moveBy() and doRotateY() methods with extra arguments for the extra views:

```
private void standardMove(int keycode)
{
  if(keycode == forwardKey)
    moveBy(VFWD, FORWARD, VBACK);
  else if(keycode == backKey)
    moveBy(VBACK, BACK, VFWD);
  else if(keycode == leftKey)
    doRotateY(ROT_AMT, LEFT);
  else if(keycode == rightKey)
    doRotateY(-ROT_AMT, RIGHT);
}
```

The arguments of moveBy() are constants related to the main camera, the bird's-eye view, and the back facing camera. When the main camera moves in a given direction (e.g., VFWD, meaning forward), then the back facing camera must move in the opposite direction (VBACK, meaning backward). However, both cameras always rotate in the same direction, so no distinction is made between them when doRotateY() is called.

moveBy() implements collision detection by first calculating the expected position after carrying out the requested move. If that position is occupied by an obstacle, then the move isn't executed and a warning is reported:

```
private void moveBy(Vector3d theMove, int dir, Vector3d theMoveC2)
{
  Point3d nextLoc = possibleMove(theMove);
  if (mm.canMoveTo(nextLoc.x, nextLoc.z)) {    // no obstacle there?
    targetTG.setTransform(t3d);  // nasty!
    doMoveC2(theMoveC2);
    be.setMove(dir);
  }
  else  // there is an obstacle
    be.bangAlert();  // tell BirdsEye, so a warning can be shown
}
```

This "try-it-and-see" approach is also employed in the Tour3D application in Chapter 18.

possibleMove( ) retrieves the current transform (into the global t3d) and makes the move but doesn't update the TransformGroup because it's only checking if the move is possible:

```
private Point3d possibleMove(Vector3d theMove)
{
  targetTG.getTransform(t3d);    // targetTG is ViewPlatform's TG
  toMove.setTranslation(theMove);
  t3d.mul(toMove);
  t3d.get(trans);
  return new Point3d( trans.x, trans.y, trans.z);
}
```

The new location is returned to moveBy( ), which checks it by calling canMoveTo( ) in MazeManager. If everything's okay, then targetTG will be updated with t3d. The change is achieved with a global that was set in a different method, so the offending line is commented with the word "nasty!".

moveBy( ) has to change the back facing camera and the bird's-eye view. doMoveC2( ) deals with the camera by applying a move to its TransformGroup:

```
private void doMoveC2(Vector3d theMoveC2)
{
  camera2TG.getTransform(t3d);
  toMove.setTranslation(theMoveC2);
  t3d.mul(toMove);
  camera2TG.setTransform(t3d);
}
```

Rotations of the cameras and bird's-eye view can be carried out immediately without any collision testing, inside doRotateY( ):

```
private void doRotateY(double radians, int dir)
{
  targetTG.getTransform(t3d);    // rotate main camera
  toRot.rotY(radians);
  t3d.mul(toRot);
  targetTG.setTransform(t3d);

  camera2TG.getTransform(t3d);  // rotate back-facing camera
  t3d.mul(toRot);  // reuse toRot value
  camera2TG.setTransform(t3d);

  be.setRotation(dir);  // rotate bird's eye view
}
```

The Bird's-Eye View

The BirdsEye object displays a static image representing the maze as seen from above, and it draws an arrow on top of it to show the user's current position. As the user moves and turns, so does the arrow. If the user hits a wall, then the message "BANG!" appears (see Figure 25-12).

Figure 25-12. The bird's-eye view pane

The arrow switches between four different images, shown in Figure 25-13.

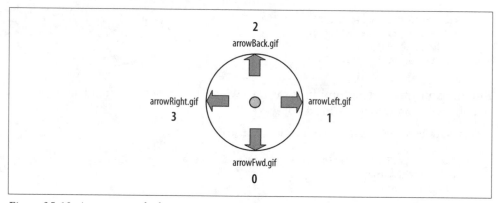

Figure 25-13. Arrows as a clock

Figure 25-13 shows the arrows laid out in a circle, labeled with their filenames and numbers (e.g., the down arrow is in *arrowFwd.gif* and is assigned number 0). The numbering scheme is used to quickly switch between the different arrows when the viewpoint is rotated.

These images are loaded into arrowIms[] at start time, indexed by the numbers shown in Figure 25-13. For instance, arrowIms[0] contains the image from *arrowFwd.gif*:

```
private static final int NUM_DIRS = 4;

private static final int FORWARD = 0;
private static final int LEFT = 1;
private static final int BACK = 2;
private static final int RIGHT = 3;
```

```
Image[] arrowIms = new Image[NUM_DIRS];

arrowIms[FORWARD] = new ImageIcon("images/arrowFwd.gif").getImage( );
arrowIms[LEFT] = new ImageIcon("images/arrowLeft.gif").getImage( );
arrowIms[BACK] = new ImageIcon("images/arrowBack.gif").getImage( );
arrowIms[RIGHT] = new ImageIcon("images/arrowRight.gif").getImage( );
```

The images are ordered in the array so moves and rotations can be calculated using clock arithmetic, as explained below.

moves[] is another important array. It contains the distance offset when the user moves forward, left, backward, or right:

```
private Point moves[];  // global
```

```
private void initMoves( )
{ moves = new Point[NUM_DIRS];
  step = mm.getImageStep( );
  moves[FORWARD] = new Point(0, step);    // move downwards on-screen
  moves[LEFT] = new Point(step, 0);       // right on-screen
  moves[BACK] = new Point(0, -step);      // up on-screen
  moves[RIGHT] = new Point(-step, 0);     // left on-screen
}
```

moves[] stores the offsets in the same order as arrowIms[].

The user's arrow starts at the maze's starting point. The starting direction is along the positive z-axis, which is down the screen when viewed from above in BirdsEye. This information is stored in initPosition( ):

```
private void initPosition( )
{ currPosn = mm.getImageStartPosn( );
  compass = FORWARD;
  userIm = arrowIms[FORWARD];
        // the user's arrow starts by facing down the screen
  showBang = false;
}
```

currPosn is a Point object holding the current (x, y) position of the arrow. compass is the current heading for the user and an index into the arrowIms[] to get the current arrow image.

Moving the Arrow

KeyBehavior calls setMove( ) in BirdsEye to move the arrow and supplies a direction that matches the FORWARD, LEFT, BACK or RIGHT constants defined above. Before the move is made, the actual heading is calculated as the current compass value plus the direction, modulo 4:

```
public void setMove(int dir)
{
  int actualHd = (compass + dir) % NUM_DIRS;
  Point move = moves[actualHd];
```

```
    currPosn.x += move.x;   // update user position
    currPosn.y += move.y;
    repaint();
}
```

For example, if the compass value is LEFT (1) and the direction is BACK (2), then the actual heading will be RIGHT (1 + 2 = 3). In other words, if the users move backward when they're pointing left, then they will move to the right.

After the current position (currPosn) is updated, a repaint is requested, which causes paintComponent() to be called. It draws the maze image first, the arrow at the current position, and finally the "BANG!" text if necessary.

Rotating the Arrow

KeyBehavior calls setRotation() in BirdsEye to rotate the arrow and supplies a LEFT or RIGHT value. As with a move, the heading must be calculated, and this becomes the new compass value and changes the user's arrow:

```
public void setRotation(int dir)
{
   compass = (compass + dir) % NUM_DIRS;
   userIm = arrowIms[compass];  // update user's arrow
   repaint();
}
```

For example, if the compass value is LEFT (1) and the rotation direction is RIGHT (3), then the compass will change to FORWARD (1 + 3 = 4, which becomes 0 when divided modulo 4). This means that when the arrow is pointing left and the user turns right, then the new heading is forward.

The movement and rotation code in BirdsEye is tricky but would be worse if the user could rotate through a wider range of angles. The additional complexity would arise from the need to calculate more distance offsets, which would translate into a larger moves[] array and more images in arrowIms[].

Why Not Use a Bird's-Eye Camera?

An alternative to the schematic view offered by BirdsEye is to create a third camera in a similar way to SecondViewPanel but looking down on the maze from above. This was my original approach, but it proved unsatisfactory. It was almost impossible to see the user's avatar (the cone) due to the darkness of the scene, the texturing on the floor, and the camera's height above the scene. If the camera was moved nearer the ground, then less of the maze would have been visible.

It's useful to present an abstracted picture of the entire scene, which leaves out unnecessary detail such as textures and parts of the scenery. This helps the players maintain a general idea of the game without overloading them with information.

Invariably, this abstraction requires a different kind of modeling than just another Java 3D pane.

Having detailed views and overviews in a game suggests that essential scene information (e.g., the maze plan) should be managed by an object that can supply alternative representations for these views. This is the role played by MazeManager.

Related Approaches to Scene Generation

The idea of using an ASCII plan to generate a 3D maze comes from the excellent "You Build It Virtual Reality" application by Chris Heistad and Steve Pietrowicz, developed while they were in the NCSA Java 3D Group. The scene is defined using a series of ASCII "maps" that specify the location of objects at different heights in the world. This layering approach allows the positioning of things along the y-axis. The notation used in the maps is extensible, so new kinds of objects can be included in the scene, including sounds and animations. The world is networked (using multicasting) with each user represented by an avatar. Communication is via a chat window. Unfortunately, this application is currently unavailable.

Daniel Selman describes a Doom-style application in *Java 3D Programming* (Manning Publications), in section 11.6.3. The map is a GIF, and the colors of its pixels are compared with color values assigned to scenery objects to decide how the scene should be constructed. Interesting elements include animated flaming torches and guards that walk through walls.

CHAPTER 26

Fractal Land

Chapter 25 looked at how to create a realistic setting for a first-person game (a 3D maze). The emphasis was on techniques needed to navigate through the environment, such as multiple views, spotlights, and collision detection. Though the maze's floor was textured, it was quite flat.

This chapter continues the first-person gaming theme but focuses on making the ground more interesting. The terrain can vary from rolling hills to craggy mountains. The key elements of this chapter include:

A fractal landscape

Each time the application begins, a different landscape is generated using a fractal-based algorithm to produce terrain heights. The variation in the heights are controlled by a flatness value entered at the command line when the program is started. The heights are translated into a patchwork of quadrilaterals (quads) which form the landscape.

Figure 26-1 shows two terrains, generated by two separate calls to the application (*FractalLand3D*), with different flatness values.

The ground is surrounded by walls, which prevent the user from leaving the terrain area.

Texturing

Each quad is covered with a texture, the choice of texture being determined by the quad's average height. A highly textured object can start to shimmer when viewed from far away since the texture is being mapped to too small an area of screen pixels. I avoid this problem by using minification filtering and mipmapping, which reduce a texture's resolution depending on the viewpoint's distance from the textured object.

Lighting effects

The quads are affected by lighting, adding interesting shadows to their surfaces. This requires normals to be calculated for each quad, which is done automatically with the aid of Java 3D's GeometryInfo and NormalGenerator classes. Part of the normal generation includes smoothing the creases between the quad's edges, making the edges less visible.

The user's view is obscured by Java 3D fog, which obscures distant parts of the landscape. (I've commented this feature out of the code for the examples in Figure 26-1 so you can see the terrains clearly.)

Key-based navigation (again)

I use another variation of the KeyBehavior class (first seen in Chapter 24) to control navigation from the keyboard. This time the variation allows the viewpoint to follow the lie of the land automatically, moving up hills and down into valleys. This terrain-following technique is implemented using Java 3D's picking.

Landscape construction

The implementation groups the individual quads together based on their average heights, which allows the program to use less geometry and texture objects. At the last stage of landscape creation, the quads are converted into triangle strips by a process called stripification, using Java 3D's Stripifier class. This conversion allows the graphics engine to optimize the rendering of the terrain.

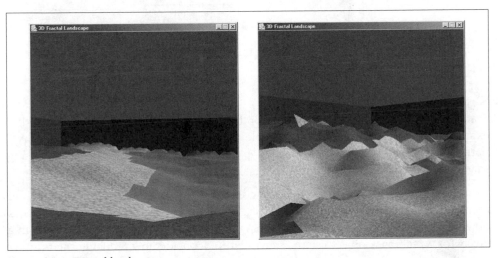

Figure 26-1. Fractal lands

This chapter is the first of two on terrain. Chapter 27 takes a different approach to landscape generation, using data supplied by Terragen, a popular scenery-generation package. This allows me to create a detailed landscape outside of Java 3D, which can be used every time the program is executed.

Another major theme of Chapter 27 is adding scenery to the landscape (3D and 2D objects). The terrain in this chapter is devoid of scenery.

Class Diagrams for the Fractal Land

Figure 26-2 shows the class diagrams for FractalLand3D, including public methods.

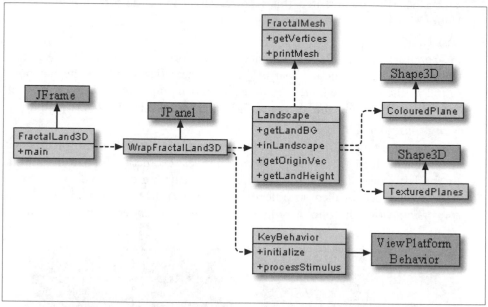

Figure 26-2. Class diagrams for FractalLand3D

FractalLand3D is the top-level JFrame for the application and is similar to earlier examples, except that it extracts a double from the command line to be used as a flatness value by the fractal code. WrapFractalLand3D creates the scene, using Landscape to generate the terrain and walls, and initiates a KeyBehavior object.

Landscape uses FractalMesh to generate a collection of coordinates for the terrain and then converts these coordinates into quads grouped into, at most, five TexturedPlanes objects. The grouping is based on the average heights of the quads. All the quads in a given TexturedPlanes object use the same texture, considerably reducing the number of texture objects needed by the application. Landscape creates the walls around the terrain with four ColouredPlane objects.

Landscape has a getLandHeight( ) method, used by KeyBehavior to calculate the floor height at a given (x, z) location. KeyBehavior employs this information to position the user's viewpoint at the correct height above the floor as it moves.

 The example code for this chapter can be found in *FractalLand3D/*.

What Is Flatness?

The flatness value is passed from FractalLand3D, through WrapFractalLand3D and Landscape, into FractalMesh, where it controls the height variation. By trial and error, I've set this number to be adjustable in the range of 1.6 to 2.5, with 2.3 being the default. A 1.6 value creates a craggy landscape, and 2.5 makes it almost flat.

The number controls the random variation in the height values generated by the fractal algorithm. If the flatness value is above 2, the random fluctuations are dampened down leading to a smoother, flatter terrain. When the flatness value is less than 2, the random component is more important, and the generated ground is more mountainous.

The input flatness number is checked by the FractalLand3D class, and a value outside of the 1.6–2.5 range is ignored. Instead, the default value (2.3) is used, which generates an undulating landscape.

Building the Fractal Land

WrapFractalLand3D is like previous Wrap classes: it creates the 3D scene inside a JPanel. The createSceneGraph( ) method brings the various elements of the scene together:

```
void createSceneGraph(double flatness)
{
  sceneBG = new BranchGroup();
  bounds = new BoundingSphere(new Point3d(0,0,0), BOUNDSIZE);

  lightScene();      // add the lights
  addBackground();   // add the sky
  // addFog();       // add the fog

  // create the landscape: the floor and walls
  land = new Landscape(flatness);
  sceneBG.addChild( land.getLandBG() );

  sceneBG.compile();    // fix the scene
}
```

lightScene( ) creates a single directional light, with no ambient backup, which makes the scene dark (and hopefully mysterious). The sky is set to be dark blue, which is the color used for the fog.

Linear Fog

The examples in Figure 26-1 use the createSceneGraph( ) method shown above, with the call to addFog( ) commented out. When uncommented, the scene looks something like Figure 26-3.

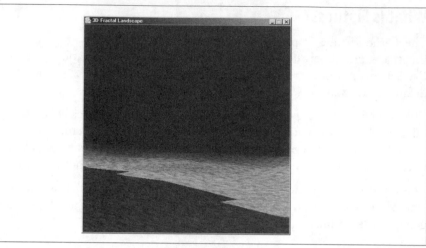

Figure 26-3. A foggy scene

The fog adds to the sinister nature of the landscape. I've commented it out in the example code to allow you to see what the entire landscape looks like.

The addFog( ) method is:

```
private void addFog( )
{ LinearFog fogLinear = new LinearFog( skyColor, 15.0f, 30.0f);
  fogLinear.setInfluencingBounds( bounds );
  sceneBG.addChild( fogLinear );
}
```

The LinearFog node makes the scene start to fade at 15.0f world units from the user and be totally obscured at 30.0f. My choice of numbers is based on the sides of the scene being 64.0f units long, so the fog makes it impossible to see much more than a quarter of the environment at any time. The fog color, skyColour, is also used for the background, creating an effect of things fading away because of their distance from the user.

 Java 3D has an ExponentialFog node which makes a fog that seems heavier and closer, supposedly more akin to real-world fog. When I tried it, the fog seemed too heavy, so I moved back to the linear form.

Though my reason for using fog is to make the terrain seem a bit spookier, there is a good technical reason for employing it: Java 3D culls fog-bound objects (i.e., objects invisible to the user) from the scene, thereby speeding up the rendering of the scene.

User Controls

As I mentioned in the introduction, the user controls are keyboard-based with their processing handled by a variant of the trusty KeyBehavior class. The user can move forward, backward, slide left or right, float up or down but can't descend through the ground. A minor change from KeyBehavior in Chapter 25 is that rotations are in steps of 5 degrees left or right rather than 90 degrees. More importantly, the viewpoint stays a fixed distance above the ground as it moves over the landscape. This greatly enhances the impression that the ground is uneven.

WrapFractalLand3D calls createUserControls( ) to adjust the clip distances and to set up the KeyBehavior object:

```
private void createUserControls( )
{
  // original clips are 10 and 0.1; keep ratio between 100-1000
  View view = su.getViewer( ).getView( );
  view.setBackClipDistance(20);      // can see a long way
  view.setFrontClipDistance(0.05);   // can see close things

  ViewingPlatform vp = su.getViewingPlatform( );
  TransformGroup steerTG = vp.getViewPlatformTransform( );

  // set up keyboard controls (and position viewpoint)
  KeyBehavior keybeh = new KeyBehavior(land, steerTG);
  keybeh.setSchedulingBounds(bounds);
  vp.setViewPlatformBehavior(keybeh);
}
```

The clip distances are adjusted in the same way, and for the same reasons, as in Maze3D in Chapter 25. As you may recall, I reduced the front clip distance so the user could move close to a block or cylinder without seeing through it. I extended the back clip distance so the full extent of the scene could be seen without far parts of it being clipped. In FractalLand3D, if the front clip is left at 0.1 units (the default), then the user can often see through the side of a hill when the viewpoint is positioned directly in front of it and the terrain is steep.

KeyBehavior handles the processing triggered by key presses and sets up the initial viewpoint position; in previous examples, the starting point was managed by the Wrap class itself.

Creating the Landscape

Landscape's initial task is to build the terrain and the four walls around it. The resulting scene graph is shown in Figure 26-4.

The number of TexturedPlanes objects will vary depending on the height of the generated quads. Each TexturedPlanes holds all the quads within a given height range, therefore allowing them to be assigned the same texture. This means that the program only has to create one texture per TexturedPlanes object as opposed to one texture for each quad, a significant reduction in the number of objects.

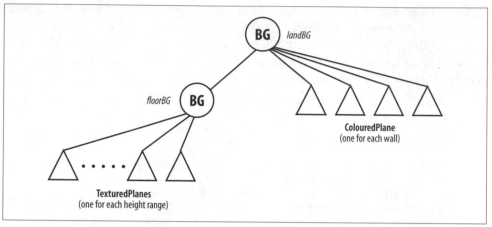

Figure 26-4. Landscape's scene graph

The moving viewpoint hugs the landscape by utilizing Java 3D picking. I'll explain the details later, but it involves shooting a pick ray straight down underneath the viewpoint to hit a quad in the floor. The (x, y, z) coordinate of the intersection with the quad is obtained, and the y-value is used to set the y-axis position of the viewpoint.

The TexturedPlanes are grouped under the floorBG BranchGroup so picking can be localized to everything below floorBG, excluding the walls attached to the landBG BranchGroup.

No TransformGroup nodes are in the graph, and landBG is attached directly to the top-level sceneBG node. This means that the local coordinates used inside the TexturedPlanes and ColouredPlane objects are scene coordinates, and mapping between local and world values is unnecessary. This is an important optimization when picking is employed: it means that the (x, y, z) coordinate returned from the hit quad is the intersection point in world coordinates, so can be used immediately to modify the viewpoint's position.

Creating Floors

Landscape calls on FractalMesh to generate the coordinates for the floor:

```
FractalMesh fm = new FractalMesh(flatness);
// fm.printMesh(1);   // for debugging: x=0; y=1; z=2
vertices = fm.getVertices();
```

The size of the floor is FLOOR_LEN, centered around the origin in the XZ plane.

vertices[] holds Point3d objects organized by FractalMesh into groups of four, each group representing a distinct quad. The four points in a group are specified in counterclockwise order when the points are viewed from above, with the bottom leftmost point first. For example, a possible sequence of points could be (0,5,1), (1,5,1), (1,5,0), (0,5,0), which corresponds to the quad shown in Figure 26-5.

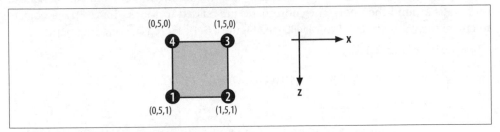

Figure 26-5. A quad from above

The quads in vertices[] are sorted into separate ArrayLists in platifyFloor() based on their average heights and then passed to TexturedPlanes objects:

```
private void platifyFloor()
{
  ArrayList[] coordsList = new ArrayList[NUM_TEXTURES];
  for (int i=0; i < NUM_TEXTURES; i++)
    coordsList[i] = new ArrayList();

  int heightIdx;
  for (int j=0; j < vertices.length; j=j+4) {    // test each quad
    heightIdx = findHeightIdx(j);    //which height applies to quad?
    addCoords( coordsList[heightIdx], j);    // add quad to list
    checkForOrigin(j);         // check if (0,0) in the quad
  }

  // use coordsList and texture to make TexturedPlanes object
  for (int i=0; i < NUM_TEXTURES; i++)
    if (coordsList[i].size() > 0)      // if used
      floorBG.addChild( new TexturedPlanes(coordsList[i],
                        "images/"+textureFns[i]) );  // add to floor
} // end of platifyFloor()
```

platifyFloor() passes a filename to each TexturedPlanes, holding the texture that will be laid over each of the quads. The resulting TexturedPlanes object is a Shape3D, added to floorBG as shown in Figure 26-4.

 Don't bother looking for "platify" in a dictionary; it's my invention, meant to capture the idea that the floor is covered (plated) with textured quads.

platifyFloor() also checks the coordinates in vertices[] to find the one positioned at (0, 0) on the XZ plane, to obtain its height. The coordinate is stored in originVec and made accessible with the public method getOriginVec(). That method is utilized by KeyBehavior to position the viewpoint at (0, 0) and at the correct height.

Creating Walls

addWalls( ) generates eight coordinates that specify the top and bottom corners of the four walls around the floor. The coordinates are passed to four ColouredPlane objects to create the walls attached to landBG (see Figure 26-4). Here is a code fragment:

```
private void addWalls( )
{
    Color3f eveningBlue = new Color3f(0.17f, 0.07f, 0.45f);

    // the eight corner points
    // back, left
    Point3d p1 = new Point3d(-WORLD_LEN/2.0f, MIN_HEIGHT, -WORLD_LEN/2.0f);
    Point3d p2 = new Point3d(-WORLD_LEN/2.0f, MAX_HEIGHT, -WORLD_LEN/2.0f);

    // code for seven more corners, finishing with ...
    // back, right
    Point3d p7 = new Point3d(WORLD_LEN/2.0f, MIN_HEIGHT, -WORLD_LEN/2.0f);
    Point3d p8 = new Point3d(WORLD_LEN/2.0f, MAX_HEIGHT, -WORLD_LEN/2.0f);

    // left wall; its points are specified in counter-clockwise order
    landBG.addChild( new ColouredPlane(p3, p1, p2, p4,
                                new Vector3f(-1,0,0), eveningBlue) );
    // code for three more walls, finishing with ...
    // back wall
    landBG.addChild( new ColouredPlane(p7, p8, p2, p1,
                                new Vector3f(0,0,1), eveningBlue) );
} // end of addWalls( )
```

Take care to supply the points in the right order so the front face of each plane is pointing into the scene. Otherwise, the lighting effects will appear on the face pointing out, hidden from the user.

On the Floor

When the user walks into a wall, any further forward movement is ignored. KeyBehavior prevents the user walking off the edge of the floor by calling the public method inLandscape( ) offered by the Landscape class:

```
public boolean inLandscape(double xPosn, double zPosn)
{
  int x = (int) Math.round(xPosn);
  int z = (int) Math.round(zPosn);
  if ((x <= -WORLD_LEN/2) || (x >= WORLD_LEN/2) ||
      (z <= -WORLD_LEN/2) || (z >= WORLD_LEN/2))
    return false;
  return true;
}
```

Picking a Height

When the user presses a key to move, KeyBehavior can easily calculate the new (x, z) position, but the viewpoint cannot move until the height of the floor at that new spot (its y-value) is obtained. This is the task of getLandHeight( ), by using picking on the floor's BranchGroup. However, before getLandHeight( ) can be employed, a PickTool object is created in Landscape's constructor:

```
private PickTool picker;   // global

picker = new PickTool(floorBG);    // only check the floor
picker.setMode(PickTool.GEOMETRY_INTERSECT_INFO);
```

picker's mode is set so the intersection coordinates can be obtained. It's restricted to the floor's BranchGroup, eliminating the walls from the intersection calculations. getLandHeight( ) uses the (x, z) coordinate as a starting location for a downward pointing pick ray which intersects with the floor. The returned intersection information includes the height of the floor at that (x, z) point, which is passed back to KeyBehavior. The relevant code fragment from the moveBy( ) method in KeyBehavior is shown here:

```
Vector3d nextLoc = tryMove(theMove);    // next (x,?,z) user position
if (!land.inLandscape(nextLoc.x, nextLoc.z))   // if not on landscape
  return;

// Landscape returns floor height at (x,z)
double floorHeight = land.getLandHeight(nextLoc.x, nextLoc.z, currLandHeight);
```

The getLandHeight( ) method is:

```
public double getLandHeight(double x, double z, double currHeight)
{
  Point3d pickStart = new Point3d(x,MAX_HEIGHT*2,z);  // start high
  picker.setShapeRay(pickStart, DOWN_VEC);    // shoot ray downwards

  PickResult picked = picker.pickClosest();
  if (picked != null) {     // pick sometimes misses an edge/corner
    if (picked.numIntersections( ) !=0) { // sometimes no intersects
      PickIntersection pi = picked.getIntersection(0);
      Point3d nextPt;
      try {   // handles 'Interp point outside quad' error
        nextPt = pi.getPointCoordinates( );
      }
      catch (Exception e) {
        // System.out.println(e);
        return currHeight;
      }
      return nextPt.y;
    }
  }
  return currHeight; // if we reach here, return old height
}
```

The downward pointing vector is defined in `DOWN_VEC`:

```
private final static Vector3d DOWN_VEC = new Vector3d(0.0,-1.0, 0.0);
```

`pickClosest()` gets the `PickResult` nearest to the ray's origin, which should be a quad inside a `TexturedPlanes` node. The `PickResult` object is then queried to get a `PickIntersection` object, and the intersection coordinate is accessed with `getPointCoordinates()`. This level of access requires the `TexturedPlanes` objects to have the `INTERSECT_COORD` picking capability:

```
PickTool.setCapabilities(this, PickTool.INTERSECT_COORD);
```

`getLandHeight()` is complicated by having to deal with several error cases:

- No quad is found by the pick ray, so the `PickResult` object is null.
- The `PickResult` object contains no intersections.
- The extraction of the intersection coordinate from the `PickIntersection` object raises an `Interp point outside quad` exception.

None of these errors should occur since the pick ray is aimed straight down at a floor covered entirely by quads. Nevertheless, they do, reflecting the buggy nature of picking in Java 3D 1.3.1. Typically, an error occurs if a ray intersects with a quad at its edge or corner.

My error recovery strategy is to have `KeyBehavior` pass the current floor height into `getLandHeight()` (i.e., the height of the floor where the user will be currently standing). If an error occurs, then that height will be returned.

The effect is that when the user moves, the viewpoint may remain at the same height even if the user is moving up or down a hill. This would seem to be less than ideal since it may mean the user will walk into the side of a hill or off into thin air when descending the hill. In practice, errors occur infrequently, and one move only adjusts the height marginally, so this approach is adequate.

 Another description of this picking technique, with similar code, can be found in Ben Moxon's "The Little Purple Dude Walks," online at *http://www.newview.co.uk/e/tutorials/java3d/index.jsp*.

Issues with Terrain Representation

My approach to representing terrain uses the `Landscape` class to group quads with similar heights together into the same `Shape3D`, so they all share the same `Appearance` node component. This means that the application only has to manage a few geometries and their associated textures at run time. Normal generation and stripification (described in the next section, "Constructing the Ground") only have to be applied to several large geometries, rather than numerous individual quads, which would be less efficient.

However, this approach has some drawbacks, especially if the terrain is large. One issue is view frustum culling, where Java 3D renders only what can be seen in the user's FOV. In effect, Java 3D only displays what the user can see, which may accelerate the overall rendering time. Culling is only carried out if a shape is completely hidden from the user's viewpoint. Unfortunately, the Shape3D objects in FractalLand3D are composed from quads distributed all over the landscape. This means that little culling can be achieved in most situations, resulting in little (or no) rendering gains.

Another problem is the cost of picking, which automatically employs bounds checks to exclude Shape3Ds from more detailed intersection calculations. Again, the grouping of dispersed quads means these checks may not be able to exclude many shapes.

The problems with view frustum culling and picking are caused by the simplistic approach of grouping quads together, based solely on their y-axis positions. Both problems would be alleviated if the quads were grouped based on their x- and z-coordinates. This would allow the culling and picking algorithms to exclude shapes that were located far away from the viewpoint.

Constructing the Ground

Quads with similar heights are grouped together in a TexturedPlanes object (which is a subclass of Shape3D). All the quads in the object are covered with the same texture, thereby adding detail to the landscape. However, a quad cannot be assigned a texture until it has texture coordinates.

I want quads to reflect light, so patterns of light and dark are shown on the landscape. This requires that each quad coordinate has a normal vector, so the direction and intensity of reflected light at each point can be calculated.

Generating these normals manually would be time-consuming, so I use Java 3D's utility class, NormalGenerator, to do the job.

TheTexturedPlanes geometry is a QuadArray, with fields for the (x, y, z) coordinates, texture coordinates, and the normals. The ArrayList of (x, y, z) coordinates (stored in coords) is converted to an array before its points can be used:

```
int numPoints = coords.size();
QuadArray plane = new QuadArray(numPoints,
    GeometryArray.COORDINATES |
    GeometryArray.TEXTURE_COORDINATE_2 |
    GeometryArray.NORMALS );

// obtain points
Point3d[] points = new Point3d[numPoints];
coords.toArray( points );
```

The texture coordinates are created in the same order as the points in a quad and repeated for each quad:

```
TexCoord2f[] tcoords = new TexCoord2f[numPoints];
for(int i=0; i < numPoints; i=i+4) {
  tcoords[i] = new TexCoord2f(0.0f, 0.0f);   // for 1 point
  tcoords[i+1] = new TexCoord2f(1.0f, 0.0f);
  tcoords[i+2] = new TexCoord2f(1.0f, 1.0f);
  tcoords[i+3] = new TexCoord2f(0.0f, 1.0f);
}
```

The calculation of the normals is carried out by a NormalGenerator object, which requires the coordinates and texels to be stored in a Java 3D GeometryInfo object:

```
// create GeometryInfo
GeometryInfo gi = new GeometryInfo(GeometryInfo.QUAD_ARRAY);
gi.setCoordinates(points);
gi.setTextureCoordinateParams(1, 2); // one set of 2D texels
gi.setTextureCoordinates(0, tcoords);

// calculate normals with very smooth edges
NormalGenerator ng = new NormalGenerator();
ng.setCreaseAngle( (float) Math.toRadians(150));  // default is 44
ng.generateNormals(gi);
```

The setTextureCoordinatesParams() specifies how many texture coordinate sets will be used with the geometry and their dimensionality (Java 3D offers 2D, 3D, and 4D texture coordinates).

The NormalGenerator adds vertex normals to the geometry inside GeometryInfo. The crease angle is used to decide when two adjacent quads should be given separate normals. The crease angle is set to some prescribed value (44 degrees is the default), and then the angles between adjacent quads are compared. If the angle between the two quads is less than the crease angle (as in the lefthand pair in Figure 26-6), then the quads will get to share a normal. If the angle between them is greater than the crease angle (as in the righthand pair in Figure 26-6), then the quads will use separate normals. The sharing of normals between the quads creates a lighting effect that smoothes (and nearly hides) the join between them.

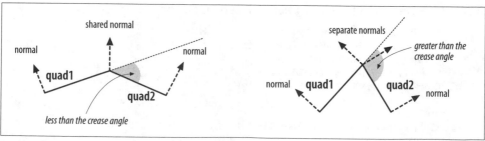

Figure 26-6. Crease angle normals

By increasing the crease angle from 44 to 150 degrees in FractalLand3D, the edges between most quads are made smoother when light is reflected off them; instead of a sharp separation in light and shade at the shared edges, the pattern of light is more diffuse, giving the impression that the underlying geometry is more rounded. This is a useful trick for landscaping since no changes need to be done to the geometry's coordinates; only changes to the normals will be required.

Stripification

Stitching the landscape together from quads has several benefits, including making it easier to generate the (x, y, z) coordinates and map textures to the surface. However, Java 3D's graphics engine (OpenGL or DirectX) can optimize the scene rendering if the shapes are composed from triangle strips. Java 3D offers a Stripifier utility class to convert geometries into triangle strips, a process known as *stripification*.

The geometry chosen for conversion should be supplied to the stripifier in a GeometryInfo object, and the translation will be carried out in place:

```
Stripifier st = new Stripifier();
st.stripify(gi);      // gi is a GeometryInfo object
```

Triangle strips are sequences of triangles where the second and third vertices of one triangle are used as the first and second vertices of the next triangle, as in Figure 26-7.

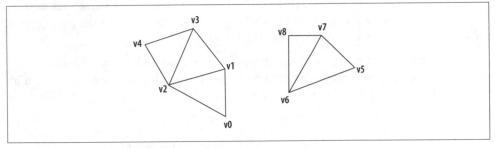

Figure 26-7. Triangle strips examples

The ordering of the points allows the underlying graphics hardware to render the shape more quickly. However, the acceleration depends on the number of triangles in a strip, with larger accelerations when the strip is longer. A TexturedPlanes shape will generally consist of several medium length sequences of quads since the quads are grouped based on similar heights. As a consequence, the rendering gains will generally be modest for this application.

The outcome of stripification is a new geometry stored in the GeometryInfo object. This is the geometry made for the TexturedPlanes object:

```
// extract and use GeometryArray
setGeometry( gi.getGeometryArray() );
```

Texture Minification

The `Appearance` node for the `TexturedPlanes` object is the usual mix of `Texture2D` and `Material` nodes with lighting enabled. However, the size of the landscape means textures appear on quads at a great distance from the viewpoint. In terms of rendering, this requires the texture image to be reduced in size, with a consequent reduction in its resolution. As the viewpoint moves, the quads and textures are redrawn, and this redrawing changes the mix of colors in the screen's pixels. This change is seen by the user as shimmering, which can become annoying in a highly textured environment (as seen here).

Java 3D has a set of texture filtering modes which specify how a texture is made larger or smaller for viewing. *Minification* is the process of reducing the texture's size, and *magnification* is its enlargement. A minification filter is set using the `setMinFilter( )` method:

```
texture.setMinFilter(Texture2D.BASE_LEVEL_LINEAR);
```

The minification specifies that the color in a single pixel should be based on an average of the four nearest texels in the texture. This averaging has the effect of smoothing out the transition of colors from one pixel to another, which reduces the shimmering of the texture as the viewpoint moves.

Unfortunately, minification is only an answer until the viewpoint moves too far from the shape. At some point, the texture will be rendered at so small a size that four or more texels are mapped to a pixel. The flicking will then return since the averaging is no longer smoothing the transition between the pixels.

This problem doesn't occur with *mipmapping*, where several lower resolution versions of the texture are precomputed as the texture is loaded and used as needed at runtime. The relevant code is the following:

```
// load and set the texture; generate mipmaps for it
TextureLoader loader = new TextureLoader(fnm,
                        TextureLoader.GENERATE_MIPMAP, null);

Texture2D texture = (Texture2D) loader.getTexture( );
texture.setMinFilter(Texture2D.MULTI_LEVEL_LINEAR);
```

The `GENERATE_MIPMAP` flag switches on mipmapping, and the `MULTI_LEVEL_LINEAR` mode specifies that the color for a pixel comes from eight texels: the four closest texels from each of the two closest texture resolutions. This averaging approach removes shimmering and replaces the need for runtime scaling of the texture.

 The reduced resolution texture is called a *mip map* (hence the verb mipmapping). The term *mip* is an acronym for the Latin phrase *multum in parvo*, which can be translated as "much on a small object."

Multiple Textures

The edges between one texture and another in FractalLand3D are sharply highlighted by the quad geometry, which tends to destroy the illusion of landscaping. One way to improve the edges is to use multiple textures for each Shape3D. By using a basic ground texture and then adding variations with additional layers of texturing, the edges are smoothed out. Textures representing different kinds of vegetation or even forms of lighting and shading work great for this. The layering of several textures onto a surface is known as *multitexturing*.

The texture attributes for multiple layers are specified with TextureUnitState objects, one for each layer. The setTextureUnitState( ) method is applied to the shape's Appearance node to add the textures. Several texture coordinates can be linked to each vertex of the shape's geometry and mapped to a particular TextureUnitState.

 The Java 3D demo program *TextureTest/MultiTextureTest.java* shows how multitexturing can be utilized.

A drawback with multitexturing is that older graphics cards may not support it. The *QueryProperties.java* utility, in the Java 3D demo directory *PackageInfo/*, prints out several properties related to textures; multiple textures require that textureUnitStateMax be 2 or greater.

Generating a Fractal Landscape

My FractalMesh class utilizes a plasma fractal to generate a mesh of Point3d objects, centered at (0, 0) on the (x, z) plane, at intervals of 1 unit, extending out to WORLD_LEN/2 units in the positive and negative x- and z-directions. (In my code, WORLD_LEN is 64 units.) The y-coordinates of these points become their heights in the scene.

The objects are stored in a 2D array called mesh, with mesh[0][0] storing the back, left-most point in the scene. A row in mesh[][] stores all the points for a given z-value.

The mesh is generated using the algorithm described by Jason Shankel in "Fractal Terrain Generation—Midpoint Displacement" from *Game Programming Gems*. The mesh is seeded with four corner points, and a two-stage process is repeated until sufficient extra points have been created. In the first stage (the *diamond step*), the height of the midpoint of the four corner points is calculated by averaging their heights and adding a random displacement in the range -dHeight/2 to dHeight/2. For example, the height of the E point in Figure 26-8 is calculated this way:

E = (A + B + C + D)/4 + random(-dHeight/2, dHeight/2)

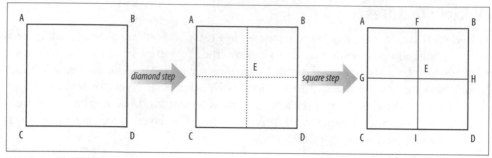

Figure 26-8. Mesh creation: first iteration

The next stage (the *square step*) is to calculate the heights of the midpoints of the four sides (F, G, H, and I in Figure 26-8). For example, G's height is:

G = (A + E + C + E)/4 + random(-dHeight/2, dHeight/2)

If a point is on an edge (as G is), then we can use a neighbor from the opposite edge by thinking of the mesh as wrapping around from left to right, and from top to bottom. That's why G's calculation uses E twice: once as the left neighbor of G and once as its right neighbor.

At the end of the two stages, the mesh can be viewed as four quarter-size squares (AFEG, FBHE, GEIC, EHDI). Now the process begins again, on each of the four smaller squares, as shown in Figure 26-9. The difference is that the sides of the squares are half the length of the original, and dHeight is divided by the flatness value (the number entered by the user at the start of FractalLand3D).

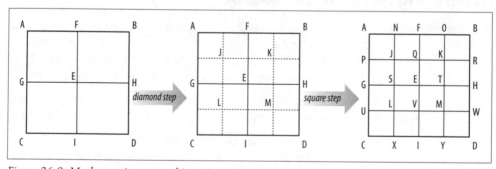

Figure 26-9. Mesh creation: second iteration

When flatness is > 2, dHeight will decrease faster than the sides of the squares, so after the initial creation of hills and valleys, the rest of the terrain will generally consist of smooth slopes between those features. When flatness < 2, the randomness will be a significant component of the height calculations—hills and valleys will be affected by this randomness, resulting in a rockier landscape.

The creation of the corner points is done by makeMesh( ):

```
private void makeMesh( )
{
```

```
      System.out.println("Building the landscape...please wait");
      mesh[0][0] =     // back left
        new Point3d( -WORLD_LEN/2, randomHeight( ), -WORLD_LEN/2 );

      mesh[0][WORLD_LEN] =     // back right
        new Point3d( WORLD_LEN/2, randomHeight( ), -WORLD_LEN/2 );

      mesh[WORLD_LEN][0] =     // front left
        new Point3d( -WORLD_LEN/2, randomHeight( ), WORLD_LEN/2 );

      mesh[WORLD_LEN][WORLD_LEN] =     // front right
        new Point3d( WORLD_LEN/2, randomHeight( ), WORLD_LEN/2 );

      divideMesh( (MAX_HEIGHT-MIN_HEIGHT)/flatness, WORLD_LEN/2);
    }
```

randomHeight( ) selects a random number between the maximum and minimum heights fixed in the class.

divideMesh( ) carries out the diamond and square steps outlined abov, and continues the process by recursively calling itself. Here is the code in outline:

```
    private void divideMesh(double dHeight, int stepSize)
    {
      if (stepSize >= 1) {    // stop recursing once stepSize is < 1
        // diamond step for all midpoints at this level
        // square step for all points surrounding diamonds
        divideMesh(dHeight/flatness, stepSize/2);
      }
    }
```

divideMesh( )'s stepSize value starts at WORLD_LEN/2 and keeps being divided by 2 until it reaches 1. In order for the points to be equally spaced over the XZ plane, WORLD_LEN should be a power of 2 (it's 64 in my code).

divideMesh( ) stores the generated points as Point3d objects in mesh[][]. The Landscape object accesses the points by calling FractalMesh's getVertices( ) method. getVertices( ) creates vertices[] and stores references to mesh[][]'s points inside it, in counterclockwise quad order, starting with the bottom-left corner of the quad. For instance, when considering coordinate (x, z), it will copy the points in the order (x, z + 1), (x + 1, z + 1), (x + 1, z), (x, z). This is somewhat clearer by considering Figure 26-10.

The getVertices( ) method is:

```
    public Point3d[] getVertices( )
    {
      int numVerts = WORLD_LEN*WORLD_LEN*4;
      Point3d vertices[] = new Point3d[numVerts];
      int vPos = 0;
      for(int z=0; z<WORLD_LEN; z++) {
        for(int x=0; x<WORLD_LEN; x++) {
          vertices[vPos++] = mesh[z+1][x];     // counter-clockwise
          vertices[vPos++] = mesh[z+1][x+1];   // from bottom-left
```

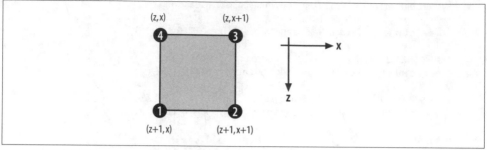

Figure 26-10. Quad ordering for point (x, z)

```
      vertices[vPos++] = mesh[z][x+1];
      vertices[vPos++] = mesh[z][x];
    }
  }
  return vertices;
}
```

Printing the Mesh

FractalMesh contains a printMesh( ) method for debugging purposes: it prints either the x-, y- or z-values stored in mesh[][] to a text file.

This method could easily be extended to store the complete mesh to a file. Landscape could then have the option to create its floor by reading in the mesh from the file rather than by using FractalMesh. This is similar to the way that Maze3D in Chapter 25 reads its maze information from a file created by the MazeGen application.

The advantage of this approach is that FractalLand3D could choose to reuse an existing landscape instead of generating a new one every time it was called.

Fixing the Randomness

The diamond and square steps use a random displacement in the range of –dHeight/2 to dHeight/2. This is implemented in two places in FractalMesh, randomRange( ) and randomHeight( ), using Math.random( ) suitably scaled (e.g., in randomRange( )):

```
    private double randomRange(double h)
    // between -h and h
    {  return ((Math.random( ) * 2 * h) - h);  }
```

This approach means that the landscape is different every time FractalLand3D is called, even when the same flatness value is supplied by the user.

An interesting alternative, suggested to me by Tom Egan, is to employ the Random. nextDouble( ) method instead. The advantage is that a Random object can be created with a specific *seed*, which is a number used to generate the sequence of random numbers. If two instances of Random are created with the same seed, and the same sequence of method calls is made for each, they will generate identical sequences of numbers. This means that the fractal will be the same each time, making the landscape the same as well. This property would be useful in games where the landscape must be fixed. The code changes would require a global Random object in FractalMesh:

```
private Random rnd = new Random(1L);      // use a fixed seed
```

Then randomRange( ) and randomHeight( ) would need their calls to Math.random( ) replaced by rnd.nextDouble( ). For example, randomRange( ) would become:

```
private double randomRange(double h)
// between -h and h
{  return ((rnd.nextDouble( ) * 2 * h) - h);  }
```

Now when FractalLand3D is called with a given flatness value, the same landscape will be generated. However, the terrain will appear to be be random. You can still modify it by adjusting the flatness number.

Responding to Key Presses

KeyBehavior is similar to the KeyBehavior classes I developed for FPShooter3D in Chapter 24 and for Maze3D in Chapter 25. However, this class is given charge of positioning the viewpoint in initViewPosition( ), which asks the Landscape object for the origin's coordinates:

```
private void initViewPosition(TransformGroup steerTG)
// place viewpoint at (0,?,0), facing into scene
{
  Vector3d startPosn = land.getOriginVec( );
  // startPosn is (0, <height of floor>, 0)

  currLandHeight = startPosn.y;   // store current floor height
  startPosn.y += USER_HEIGHT;     // add user's height

  steerTG.getTransform(t3d);      // targetTG not yet available
  t3d.setTranslation(startPosn);  // so use steerTG
  steerTG.setTransform(t3d);
}
```

KeyBehaviour needs to know the current floor height to reposition the viewpoint as it moves.

The operations carried out by KeyBehavior can be grouped into three categories:

- Movements requiring floor height information (i.e., moves forward, backward, to the left, and right)

- Movements requiring height offset information (i.e., moves up and down)

- Rotations around the current location (i.e., turns to the left and right)

Rotations don't require floor height data, so are implemented as rotations of ViewPlatform's TransformGroup.

Movements up and down are made more efficient by KeyBehavior storing a zOffset counter which records how many upward moves have been made by the user. Consequently, a move down will only be allowed if zOffset is > 0. The efficiency gain exists because there's no need to access floor height information.

Movements over the terrain are implemented by a call to moveBy( ), which has three stages:

- The next (x, z) position on the floor is calculated by carrying out the move but not updating ViewPlatform's TransformGroup.

- The resulting (x, z) data are passed to getLandHeight( ) in the Landscape object so that it can look up the floor height for that location.

- The viewpoint's movement along the y-axis is calculated as the change between the current floor height and the height at the new location.

The moveBy( ) method is:

```
private void moveBy(Vector3d theMove)
{
  Vector3d nextLoc = tryMove(theMove);    // next (x,?,z) position
  if (!land.inLandscape(nextLoc.x, nextLoc.z))
    return;

  // Landscape returns floor height at (x,z)
  double floorHeight = land.getLandHeight(nextLoc.x, nextLoc.z, currLandHeight);
  // Calculate the change from the current y-position.
  // Reset any offset upwards back to 0.
  double heightChg = floorHeight - currLandHeight - (MOVE_STEP*zOffset);

  currLandHeight = floorHeight;       // update current height
  zOffset = 0;                        // back on floor, so no offset
  Vector3d actualMove = new Vector3d(theMove.x, heightChg, theMove.z);
  doMove(actualMove);
}
```

The method is a little more complicated than the steps above for two reasons. There is a call to inLandscape( ) to check if the proposed move will take the user off the floor, in which case the move is ignored. Second, a move always cancels out any existing upward offset, returning the user to the floor.

The actual move is carried out by doMove( ) which applies the translation to ViewPlatform's TransformGroup.

Terrain Following and Collision Avoidance

Realistic terrain following must handle issues such as gravity effects (e.g., falling off a cliff), how high to step up/down at a time, holes, and water. The code in KeyBehavior and Landscape doesn't deal with any of these concerns.

A programming style question is whether picking should be used as a walking aid. One reason for employing it is that the same mechanism can help with movement through scenery, such as up and down staircases, so long as the objects can be picked. Picking makes it possible to walk over a terrain without needing a predefined "map."

A downside, until recently, was the large amount of garbage that could accumulate over time because of repeatedly computing intersections. The resulting garbage collection could degrade the application's execution. Fortunately, the `PickRay` and `PickSegment` intersection code was rewritten in Java 3D v.1.3.1 to reduce the overhead, but the other picking shapes, such as `PickCylinderRay`, remain unchanged.

Garbage collection may only become a serious issue when picking is utilized for collision avoidance: the moving object typically sends out multiple rays in several directions at each frame update, each requiring intersection testing. However, this approach is used without problems in the *Pernica* multiplayer role-playing game (*http://www.starfireresearch.com/pernica/pernica.html*) from Starfire Research.

Java XTools (*http://www.3dchat.org/dev.php*) offers a `KeyNavigatorBehavior` class, which implements collision avoidance and terrain following. The online documentation is at *http://www.3dchat.org/doc/com/vwp/j3d/utils/behaviors/keyboard/ KeyNavigatorBehavior.html*.

An interesting article on terrain following and collision detection in Java 3D, written by Justin Couch, can be found at *http://www.j3d.org/tutorials/collision*.

GameDev.net has a good collision-detection section: *http://www.gamedev.net/reference/ list.asp?categoryid=45#99*.

Placing Objects in the Scene

Knowing where to place something in the scene at scene creation time is a question of knowing the height of the ground at a particular (x, z) location. This is problematic because most ground positions will have been extrapolated by Java 3D from the corner points of quads. Picking is useless in this case since we want to position objects before the complete scene is made live.

If a quad is coplanar (i.e., positioned in a single plane), then calculating interior points is straightforward. Unfortunately, most quads are not coplanar. Furthermore, because the underlying graphics hardware works with triangles, the geometry in a `Shape3D` will have been triangulated, and the shape of those triangles is hard to predict when their vertices are highly noncoplanar.

Java 3D uses a subset of the FIST triangulation algorithm (see *http://www.cosy.sbg.ac.at/ ~held/projects/triang/triang.html* for a nontechnical discussion of the algorithm). Each polygon is projected onto a plane, and the 2D projected points are considered using a range of heuristics. One aim is to avoid long, skinny triangles by maximizing the angles within the triangles. The presence of heuristics means that it's sometimes difficult to know how a polygon will be divided.

The example is Figure 26-11, which shows a single quad with two equally likely triangulations. A division along PR will give point pt a height of 0, but if the SQ line is used then the same point will have a height of 5 units.

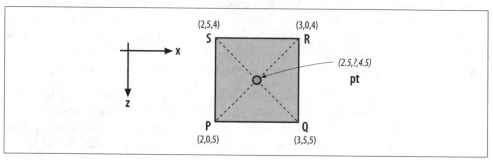

Figure 26-11. A triangulation problem

One way of dealing with this issue is to move away from quadrilaterals and use triangles as the tiling units for the terrain. An equation for the surface delineated by a triangle's three vertices (the *plane equation*) is easily obtained. Consider the points P, Q, and R in the triangle of Figure 26-12.

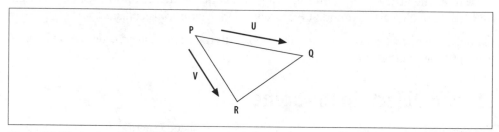

Figure 26-12. A triangle with vectors

The plane equation is defined as:

$$Ax + By + Cz = D$$

where A, B, C, and D are constants.

The normal vector N is calculated with the cross product of the vectors U and V:

$$N = U \times V$$

U and V are obtained by subtracting P from Q and R, respectively.

When is N is normalized (made to have unit length), then A, B, and C are its coefficients.

The distance from the origin to the point on the plane nearest to the origin is equivalent to the plane equation's D constant. D can be calculated as the dot product of the normal and any point on the triangle (e.g., the point P):

$$D = N . P$$

Once we have the plane equation coefficients, the height of any point lying on the triangle is:

$$y = (D - Ax - Cz)/B$$

where (x, z) is the known XZ position of the point.

Here is the Java 3D code for doing this:

```
private void vecsToHeight(Vector3d u, Vector3d v, Vector3d pt)
{
  Vector3d normal = new Vector3d( );
  normal.cross(u, v);
  normal.normalize( );
  double dist = normal.dot(pt);

  System.out.println("A: "+ df.format(normal.x) + ", B: " +
                  df.format(normal.y) + ", C: " + df.format(normal.z) +
                  ", D: " + df.format(dist) );    // Ax + By + Cz = D

  double height = (dist - (normal.x * pt.x) - (normal.z * pt.z)) / normal.y;
  System.out.println("Height for pt: " + df.format(height) );
}
```

A drawback with working with triangles is the distortion apparent in textures laid over the triangles.

Other Fractal Landscapes

Aside from the plasma fractal used in my code, two other popular approaches are the *fault fractal* and the *Fractal Brownian Motion* (FBM) *fractal*.

A fault fractal creates a height map by drawing a random line through a grid and increasing the height values on one side of the line. If this is repeated several hundred times then a reasonable landscape appears. The main drawbacks are the lack of programmer control over the finished product and the length of time required to produce a convincing geography.

An FBM fractal is a combination of mathematical noise functions which generate random height values within a certain range. An important advantage of FBM is that each noise function has several parameters which can be adjusted to alter its effect. C++ code for creating clouds and landscapes with FBMs can be found in the article by Jesse Laeuchi: "Programming Fractals" from *Games Programming Gems 2*, section 2.8, pp.239–246, 2001.

A good online starting point for fractal terrain information is the Virtual Terrain Project page (*http://www.vterrain.org/Elevation/artificial.html*).

The j3d.org code repository (*http://code.j3d.org*) has an extensive set of packages related to terrain creation. There's a FractalTerrainGenerator class in org.j3d.geom.terrain that uses a plasma fractal approach similar to mine in which the heights are generated and converted to geometry with ElevationGridGenerator. Colors are assigned per vertices based on ramp values specified in ColorRampGenerator.

The use of colors at the vertices produces a pleasant blending effect. Unfortunately, it's impossible to combine texture mappings and colored nodes in Java 3D due to restrictions in the underlying OpenGL and DirectX systems.

Merlin Hughes wrote a *JavaWorld* article on plasma fractal terrains in 1998: "3D Graphic Java: Render Fractal Landscapes" (*http://www.javaworld.com/javaworld/jw-08-1998/jw-08-step.html*). He coded in Java without using Java 3D, so the implementation of tessellation, lighting and shading, viewpoint calculations, and rendering are low-level.

Plasma fractals were used by Mike Jacobs in his September 2004 article for *Java Developer Journal* about rendering a Martian landscape with Java 3D (*http://www.sys-con.com/story/?storyid=46231&DE=1*). His terrain utilizes vertex coloring rather than textures.

CHAPTER 27

Terrain Generation with Terragen

This chapter continues the landscape creation theme from Chapter 26 but takes a different approach. A significant drawback of that chapter's FractalLand3D example is the programmer's lack of control over the generated terrain. Most games require mountains, fields, lakes, and so on, to be in fixed, specific places, rather than randomly located in a new landscape each time the program starts. Another weakness of the approach is the lack of scenery (e.g., bushes, trees, buildings).

This chapter explains how to create a detailed, fixed landscape that's the same every time the program uses it and includes scenic dressing. The major topics covered are:

Use of a landscaping tool
> There are numerous tools for terrain building, which are better at creating a realistic looking landscape than a do-it-yourself (DIY) approach coded in Java. I'll be using Terragen, a popular scenery generation package. The landscape is designed with Terragen and then saved as a mesh and texture, which are loaded by my program (Terra3D) at start time. Utilizing specialized modeling software is better than implementing something from scratch.

3D and 2D ground cover
> The landscape can be decorated with two types of scenery: 3D models loaded with the PropManager class (from Chapter 16) and 2D ground cover images (e.g., trees, sagebrush), which stay oriented towards the viewer. The separation into two types is for efficiency: multiple copies of a 2D shape are one instance of that shape shared using Java 3D's SharedGroup class.

Other scenery decorations
> The edges of the landscape are surrounded by walls covered in a mountain range image. This adds to the realism since the user can't peer over the edges of the world or walk out of the scene. The sky is filled with stars represented as a Background geometry (an approach suggested by Kevin Duling).

Configuration files

The landscape isn't hardwired into the Terra3D code: the choice of landscape (its mesh and texture) is determined by a command line argument, and a series of configuration files specify the placement of the 3D and 2D ground cover and the user's starting position.

Terrain following using picking

Picking is employed for terrain following again, as in Chapter 26, but the implementation is complicated by a need to deal with large landscapes. A consequence is that a user can walk "inside" a mountain but will eventually be repositioned on its surface.

The problem is that Java 3D picking is too slow when the terrain is large. My solution is to extend the basic algorithm of Chapter 26 with a HeightFinder thread which separates the slow picking calculation from key processing when the user wants to move.

Figures 27-1 and 27-2 show two landscapes, originally designed with Terragen and then loaded by Terra3D.

Figure 27-1. Green valleys with a castle

The castle in Figure 27-1 is a 3D model, and the trees and sagebrush in Figures 27-1 and 27-2 are 2D ground cover images.

Class Diagrams for Terra3D

Figure 27-3 shows the class diagrams for the Terra3D application. The class names and public methods are included.

Figure 27-2. Desert with sagebrush

Terra3D is the top-level JFrame for the application. WrapTerra3D creates the world, including the lighting and background. However, most of the work is delegated to a Landscape object that loads the landscape (a combination of an OBJ file for the mesh and JPG image for the texture) and places walls around it. Each wall is an instance of TexturedPlane, so a mountain range image can be displayed.

The 3D scenery models are loaded with PropManager objects, and the 2D images are represented by GroundShape objects. A GroundCover object manages the placement of the ground cover and the sharing of the GroundShape objects.

The KeyBehavior class is similar to the one in FractalLand3D in Chapter 26. The user can move forward, backward, left, right, up, down (but not below the ground) and can turn left and right. In addition, the w key prints the user's location in the landscape to System.out.

Terrain picking is handled by a HeightFinder thread, which communicates its answer back to KeyBehavior when the picking is completed.

 The code for this example can be found in the *Terra3D/* directory.

Terragen

Terragen is a scenery-generation package for Windows and the Mac, aimed at producing photorealistic landscape images and animations (*http://www.planetside.co.uk/ terragen/*). It's easy to use, and a beautiful scene can be generated in a few minutes.

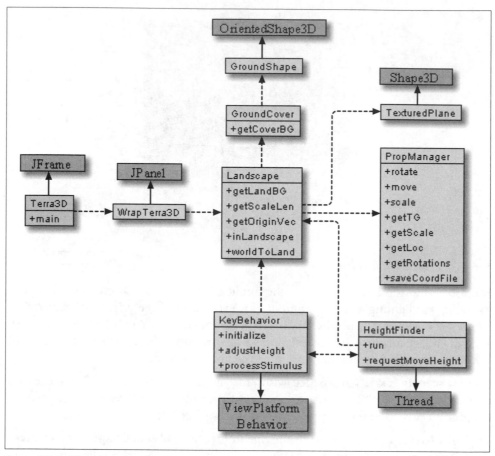

Figure 27-3. Class diagrams for Terra3D

Some examples are at *http://www.planetside.co.uk/terragen/images.shtml* and *http://www.planetside.co.uk/terragen/gallery/gallerymain.php*. Terragen is currently free for personal, noncommercial use, though there are some restrictions on the size and resolution of the scenes that can be built.

A terrain can be created in Terragen using fractals (I talked about fractal terrains in the last chapter), by painting the shape of the landscape, or as a combination of the two. Terragen supports powerful surface and color maps for decorating the landscape, water effects, clouds, atmospheric elements, lighting, and shadows.

Terragen can import and export a wide range of file formats through the use of plug-ins. For example, the Firmament plug-in allows Terragen to read BMPs, STMs, POV-RAY height fields, and U.S. Geological Survey (USGS) DEM (digital elevation model) and spatial data transfer standard (SDTS) files. The For Export Only (FEO) plug-in permits exports to BMP, DXF, OBJ, and RIB files.

My approach requires that Terragen exports its terrain to a Wavefront OBJ file, so the FEO plug-in must be installed (*http://homepages.ihug.co.nz/~jomeder/feo/*). Plug-ins are supported via the `TGPGuiLib` plug-in interface (*http://homepages.ihug.co.nz/~jomeder/tgpguilib/*).

Numerous tools can accept, manipulate, and help create Terragen landscapes. A long list is available at *http://www.planetside.co.uk/terragen/resources.shtml*. For example, 3DEM can read a wide range of USGS and NASA map file formats and save them as Terragen terrains (*http://www.visualizationsoftware.com/3dem.html*). For instance, you could build a Martian terrain using real data from NASA's Mars Surveys.

Using Terragen

A user guide explains the various menu items, dialog boxes, and other GUI elements (*http://www.planetside.co.uk/terragen/guide/*). Carol Brooksbank's tutorial takes a different approach, based around explanations of common tasks (*http://www.caroluk.co.uk/terratut/*). I highly recommended it.

Figure 27-4 shows the Landscape window inside Terragen after a random landscape has been generated with the "Generate Terrain" button. The water level was set at –10 meters with a surface map loaded for light snow. The Rendering Control window is visible behind the Landscape window, showing a preview of the user's current vantage point.

The screenshot in Figure 27-4 was taken from Terragen 0.8.68, Version 0.9 has rearranged some of the Landscape window elements.

Clicking on the Render Image button in the Rendering Control window displays the scene (see Figure 27-5). Varying levels of detail can be selected; more detail takes longer to display.

The landscape mesh can be saved by selecting the FEO Wavefront OBJ item from the Accessories button in the Landscape window. This will only be present if FEO has been installed. Click Ok to save after unchecking the "Swap Y and Z axes" radio box. This will make the floor of the mesh run along the XY plane with heights along the z-axis.

A basic landscape like this one will usually generate a 5-MB OBJ file, taking a few minutes to do so. An advantage of the OBJ file is its ASCII format, which means that any text editor can open it (but the editor must be capable of viewing large files).

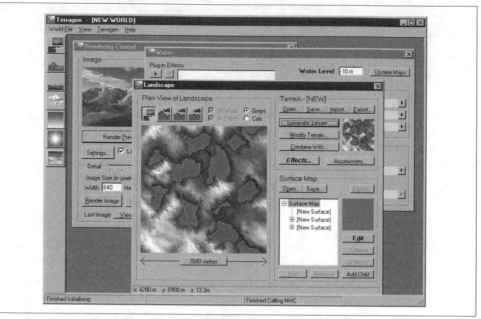

Figure 27-4. Terragen in action

Figure 27-5. Rendered view

The resulting OBJ file (named *test3.obj*) contains two groups of data: the vertices making up the mesh, and face information, with each face made from three vertices. For example, here are the first few lines of vertex data in *test3.obj*:

```
v    0.000000    0.000000   198.037763
v   30.000000    0.000000   190.554714
v   60.000000    0.000000   177.648668
v   90.000000    0.000000   172.938180
v  120.000000    0.000000   170.091105
... // many more lines
```

The mesh's floor is the XY plane; the z-values are the heights. Each vertex is 30 landscape units apart, and the vertices are ordered by increasing column (y-axis) and row (x-axis) values. The bottom-left corner of the XY floor is at coordinate (0, 0).

The last few lines of v data are:

```
... // many lines, and then...
v  7620.000000   7680.000000   217.026916
v  7650.000000   7680.000000   212.388668
v  7680.000000   7680.000000   198.037763
```

The top righthand corner of the floor is at (7680, 7680).

Each v line has an implicit index, starting at 1, and the face lines use them to refer to vertices:

```
f   1 2    258
f   2 259 258
f   2 3    259
f   3 260 259
f   3 4    260
... // many more lines
```

These define triangle strips and will be loaded into a `TriangleStripArray` by Java 3D, a particularly efficient mesh data structure.

A good place to read about OBJ support in Java 3D is the documentation for the `ObjectFile` class, which is used to load an OBJ file. A file may include information about normals, textures, colors, and utilize a separate material file. A specification of the complete OBJ format can be found at *http://www.dcs.ed.ac.uk/home/mxr/gfx/3d/OBJ.spec*.

The OBJ file can be viewed graphically by many packages, including the `ObjLoad` example in the Java 3D demos (which uses `ObjectFile`). One issue is the size of the mesh created by Terragen, which may be too large for some software to handle. For example, `ObjLoad` requires 128 MB of memory to run:

```
java -Xmx128m ObjLoad test3.obj
```

Figure 27-6 shows the landscape as displayed by `ObjLoad`. Face culling is switched on, so the terrain becomes almost invisible if turned over.

Figure 27-6. test3.obj in ObjLoad

The beautiful Terragen surface texturing is missing but can be obtained by separate means.

Extracting a Terragen Texture

The trick for obtaining a texture is to generate an orthographic projection of the terrain when viewed from above. Terragen v.0.9 has an orthographic rendering option in Camera Settings, making it simple to export a texture map. The discussion here is for Version 0.8.68.

The camera's viewpoint must be positioned directly above the terrain, looking straight down. The view will suffer from distortion at the edges due to perspective effects, but the effect can be reduced by setting the camera zoom to 1. Sky rendering and terrain shadows should be switched off. Setting the sun's altitude to 90 degrees (directly overhead) helps to minimize shadow effects on the surface map.

The rendering window should be increased in size (e.g., to 800×800), and rendering set to the highest resolution to produce a detailed image. The result is shown in Figure 27-7.

The image can be saved as a BMP (around 2-MB file sizes seem common) and then converted to a JPG by any number of graphics packages (reducing the image to around 500 KB). The most important aspects of the conversion are to clip away the black background and resize the image to form a square. This will remove some of the terrain surface, but the loss isn't noticeable inside Terra3D.

The image should be saved as a high-quality JPG. Figure 27-8 contains the final image, ready to be used as a texture.

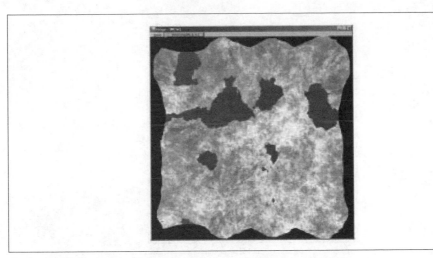

Figure 27-7. The terrain from above

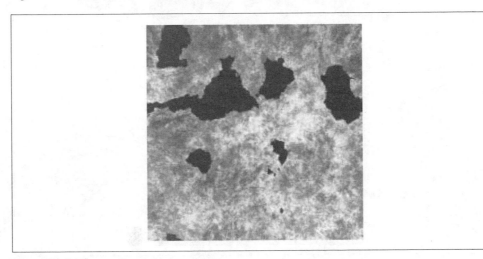

Figure 27-8. The terrain texture

Figure 27-9 shows the terrain as loaded into `Terra3D`, with the user standing in roughly the same position as the view presented in Figure 27-5.

The poor texture resolution compared to the surface maps in Terragen means that a lot of detail is lost, but what is left is sufficient for game play.

Figure 27-10 displays the users' view after they have moved to the other side of the lake and turned to look back toward the viewpoint employed in Figure 27-9.

Figure 27-9. Terra3D's view of the terrain

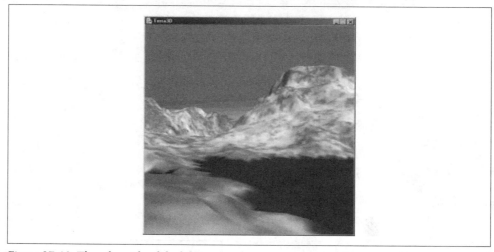

Figure 27-10. The other side of the lake

Scenery Creation

WrapTerra3D sets up the lighting and background, creates a Landscape object, and initializes the KeyControl object for managing user navigation. The background code sets the sky to be medium blue, with stars added to its geometry:

```
private void addBackground( )
{ Background back = new Background( );
  back.setApplicationBounds( bounds );
  back.setColor(0.17f, 0.50f, 0.92f);
  back.setGeometry( addStars( ) );
  sceneBG.addChild( back );
}
```

The background geometry can be any type of Group node, but there are some restrictions on the shapes held inside the group. For example, Shape3D is fine, but OrientedShape3D is prohibited. The geometry is restricted to a unit sphere but drawn as if located at infinity.

addStars() creates a PointArray of coordinates at random places in the hemisphere above the XZ plane (there's no reason to have stars below the horizon). The colors of the points are randomly chosen:

```
private BranchGroup addStars()
{
    PointArray starField =  new PointArray(NUM_STARS,
                  PointArray.COORDINATES |  PointArray.COLOR_3);
    float[] pt = new float[3];
    float[] brightness = new float[3];
    Random rand = new Random();

    for (int i=0; i < NUM_STARS; i++) {
        pt[0] = (rand.nextInt(2) == 0) ? -rand.nextFloat() : rand.nextFloat();
        pt[1] = rand.nextFloat();      // only above the XZ plane
        pt[2] = (rand.nextInt(2) == 0) ? -rand.nextFloat() : rand.nextFloat();
        starField.setCoordinate(i, pt);

        float mag = rand.nextFloat();
        brightness[0] = mag;
        brightness[1] = mag;
        brightness[2] = mag;
        starField.setColor(i, brightness);
    }

    BranchGroup bg = new BranchGroup();
    bg.addChild( new Shape3D(starField) );
    return bg;
}  // end of addStars()
```

 This coding approach was suggested by Kevin Duling in an applet at http://home.earthlink.net/~kduling/Java3D/Stars/.

Setting Up the User's Controls

createUserControls() is similar to the same named method in WrapFractalLand3D in Chapter 26; it adjusts the clip distances and sets up the KeyBehavior object. The front clip distance is adjusted to reduce the chance of the terrain being clipped away when the user's viewpoint is close to it.

An additional line sets up depth sorting for transparent objects in the world:

```
View view = su.getViewer().getView();
view.setTransparencySortingPolicy(View.TRANSPARENCY_SORT_GEOMETRY);
```

Sorting multiple transparent objects is necessary in Terra3D since ground cover objects are implemented as transparent GIFs textured over shapes. It's likely that the user's viewpoint will include many overlapping instances of these. The default behavior of Java 3D is to do no depth sorting, which may cause the transparent objects to be drawn in the wrong order, so trees and bushes in the distance are drawn in front of nearer ones.

The TRANSPARENCY_SORT_GEOMETRY policy only sorts independent geometries (i.e., each Shape3D object must contain only a single geometry). It won't correctly order multiple geometries in a shape, but I've not used this approach; each ground cover shape holds a single quad covered with an image.

Building the Landscape

The Landscape object is created by WrapTerra3D, and is passed a reference to the world's scene (sceneBG) and the filename supplied on the command line (e.g., *test1*).

Landscape's primary purpose is to display a terrain composed from a mesh and a texture. Landscape looks in the *models/* subdirectory for a OBJ file containing the mesh (e.g., *test1.obj*) and for a JPG (e.g., *test1.jpg*) to act as the texture. The OBJ file is loaded, becoming the landBG BranchGroup linked to sceneBG. The texture is laid over the geometry stored within landBG.

Landscape can add two kinds of scenery to the terrain:

3D shapes
> Loaded with PropManager. This type of scenery includes irregular objects that the user can move around and perhaps enter (e.g., the castle shown in Figure 27-1).

Ground cover
> Represented by 2D images that rotate to face the user. This kind of scenery is for simple, symmetrical objects that decorate the ground, such as trees and bushes (see Figures 27-1 and 27-2). Ground cover shapes are managed by a GroundCover object.

The terrain is surrounded by walls covered in a mountain range image.

Loading the Mesh

The Landscape( ) constructor loads the mesh, checks that the resulting Java 3D subgraph has the right characteristics, and extracts various mesh dimensions. At the end of the constructor, the land is added to the world and the texture laid over it:

```
// globals
private BranchGroup sceneBG;
private BranchGroup landBG = null;
private Shape3D landShape3D = null;
```

```
// various mesh dimensions, set in getLandDimensions()
private double landLength, minHeight, maxHeight;
private double scaleLen;


public Landscape(BranchGroup sceneBG, String fname)
{
  loadMesh(fname);        // initialize landBG
  getLandShape(landBG);   // initialize landShape3D

  // set the picking capabilities so that intersection
  // coords can be extracted after the shape is picked
  PickTool.setCapabilities(landShape3D, PickTool.INTERSECT_COORD);

  getLandDimensions(landShape3D);   // extracts sizes from landShape3D

  makeScenery(landBG, fname);       // add any scenery
  addWalls();                       // walls around the landscape
  GroundCover gc = new GroundCover(fname);
  landBG.addChild( gc.getCoverBG() );   // add any ground cover

  addLandtoScene(landBG);
  addLandTexture(landShape3D, fname);
}
```

loadMesh( ) uses Java 3D's utility class, ObjectFile, to load the OBJ file. If the load is
successful, the geometry will be stored in a TriangleStripArray below a Shape3D node
and BranchGroup. loadMesh( ) assigns this BranchGroup to the global landBG:

```
private void loadMesh(String fname)
{
  FileWriter ofw = null;
  String fn = new String("models/" + fname + ".obj");
  System.out.println( "Loading terrain mesh from: " + fn +" ..." );
  try {
    ObjectFile f = new ObjectFile();
    Scene loadedScene = f.load(fn);
    if(loadedScene == null) {
      System.out.println("Scene not found in: " + fn);
      System.exit(0);
    }

    landBG = loadedScene.getSceneGroup();     // the land's BG
    if(landBG == null ) {
      System.out.println("No land branch group found");
      System.exit(0);
    }
  }
  catch(IOException ioe)
  { System.err.println("Terrain mesh load error: " + fn);
    System.exit(0);
  }
}
```

getLandShape( ) checks that the subgraph below landBG has a Shape3D node and the Shape3D is holding a single GeometryArray. The Shape3D node is assigned to the landShape3D global:

```
private void getLandShape(BranchGroup landBG)
{
  if (landBG.numChildren( ) > 1)
    System.out.println("More than one child in land branch group");
  Node node = landBG.getChild(0);
  if (!(node instanceof Shape3D)) {
    System.out.println("No Shape3D found in land branch group");
    System.exit(0);
  }
  landShape3D = (Shape3D) node;
  if (landShape3D == null) {
    System.out.println("Land Shape3D has no value");
    System.exit(0);
  }
  if (landShape3D.numGeometries( ) > 1)
    System.out.println("More than 1 geometry in land BG");
  Geometry g = landShape3D.getGeometry( );
  if (!(g instanceof GeometryArray)) {
    System.out.println("No Geometry Array found in land Shape3D");
    System.exit(0);
  }
}
```

getLandDimensions( ) is called from Landscape's constructor to initialize four globals related to the size of the mesh:

landLength
> The length of the X (and Y) sides of the floor of the landscape.

scaleLen
> The scaling necessary to fit landLength into LAND_LEN units in the world. scaleLen will be used to scale the landscape.

minHeight
maxHeight
> Minimum and maximum heights of the landscape.

The underlying assumptions are that the floor runs across the XY plane, is square, with its lower lefthand corner at (0,0), and the positive z-axis holds the height values:

```
private void getLandDimensions(Shape3D landShape3D)
{
  // get the bounds of the shape
  BoundingBox boundBox = new BoundingBox(landShape3D.getBounds( ));
  Point3d lower = new Point3d( );
  Point3d upper = new Point3d( );
  boundBox.getLower(lower); boundBox.getUpper(upper);
  System.out.println("lower: " + lower + "\nupper: " + upper );
```

```
if ((lower.y == 0) && (upper.x == upper.y)) {
  // System.out.println("XY being used as the floor");
}
else if ((lower.z == 0) && (upper.x == upper.z)) {
  System.out.println("Error: XZ set as the floor; change to XY in Terragen");
  System.exit(0);
}
else {
  System.out.println("Cannot determine floor axes");
  System.out.println("Y range should == X range, and start at 0");
  System.exit(0);
}

landLength = upper.x;
scaleLen = LAND_LEN/landLength;
System.out.println("scaleLen: " + scaleLen);
minHeight = lower.z;
maxHeight = upper.z;
}  // end of getLandDimensions()
```

The lower and upper corners of the mesh can be obtained easily by extracting the BoundingBox for the shape. However, this approach only works correctly if the shape contains a single geometry, which is checked by getLandShape() before getLandDimensions() is called.

Placing the Terrain in the World

The floor of the landscape runs across the XY plane, starting at (0, 0), with sides of landLength units and heights in the z-direction. The world's floor is the XZ plane, with sides of LAND_LEN units and the y-axis corresponding to up and down.

Consequently, the landscape (stored in landBG) must be rotated to lie on the XZ plane and must be scaled to have floor sides of length LAND_LEN. The scaling is a matter of applying the scaleLen global, which equals LAND_LEN/landLength. In addition, the terrain is translated so the center of its floor is at (0, 0) in the world's XZ plane. These changes are illustrated by Figure 27-11.

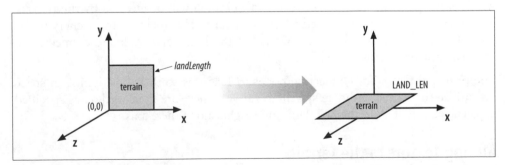

Figure 27-11. Placing the terrain

Here's the relevant code:

```
private void addLandtoScene(BranchGroup landBG)
{
    Transform3D t3d = new Transform3D( );
    t3d.rotX( -Math.PI/2.0 );      // so land's XY resting on XZ plane
    t3d.setScale( new Vector3d(scaleLen, scaleLen, scaleLen) );
    TransformGroup sTG = new TransformGroup(t3d);
    sTG.addChild(landBG);

    // center the land, which starts at (0,0) on the XZ plane,
    // so move it left and forward
    Transform3D t3d1 = new Transform3D( );
    t3d1.set( new Vector3d(-LAND_LEN/2, 0, LAND_LEN/2));
    TransformGroup posTG = new TransformGroup(t3d1);
    posTG.addChild( sTG );

    sceneBG.addChild(posTG);   // add to the world
}
```

The subgraph added to sceneBG is shown in Figure 27-12.

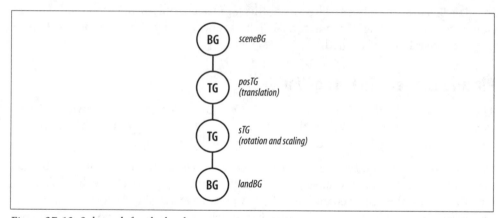

Figure 27-12. Subgraph for the landscape

An essential point is that any nodes added to landBG will be affected by the translation, rotation, and scaling applied to the landscape. This includes the scenery nodes (i.e., the 3D models and ground cover), but the landscape walls are connected to sceneBG and aren't transformed.

The principal reason for connecting nodes to landBG is so their positioning in space can utilize the local coordinate system in landBG. These are the coordinates specified in Terragen: the floor in the XY plane and heights along the z-axis.

Adding Texture to the Terrain

The texture is stretched to fit the terrain stored in landShape3D below landBG. The texture coordinates (s, t), which define a unit square, must be mapped to the (x, y) coordinates of the terrain whose lower lefthand corner is at (0, 0), and the top right-hand corner at landLength, landLength. The intended mapping is captured by Figure 27-13. The simplest way of doing this is define generation planes to translate (x, y) coordinates to (s, t) values.

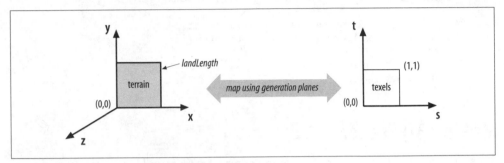

Figure 27-13. Mapping the terrain to the texture

 Generation planes were first seen in Chapter 16.

addLandTexture( ) sets up the generation planes via a call to stampTexCoords( ). It creates an Appearance node for landShape3D and loads the texture:

```
private void addLandTexture(Shape3D shape, String fname)
{
  Appearance app = shape.getAppearance();

  // generate texture coords
  app.setTexCoordGeneration( stampTexCoords(shape) );

  // combine texture with colour and lighting of underlying surface
  TextureAttributes ta = new TextureAttributes();
  ta.setTextureMode( TextureAttributes.MODULATE );
  app.setTextureAttributes( ta );

  // apply texture to shape
  Texture2D tex = loadLandTexture(fname);
  if (tex != null) {
    app.setTexture(tex);
    shape.setAppearance(app);
  }
}
```

The generation planes are specified using the following equations:

s = x/landLength
t = y/landLength

Here's the code that puts this into action:

```
private TexCoordGeneration stampTexCoords(Shape3D shape)
{
  Vector4f planeS = new Vector4f( (float)(1.0/landLength), 0.0f, 0.0f, 0.0f);
  Vector4f planeT = new Vector4f( 0.0f, (float)(1.0/landLength), 0.0f, 0.0f);

  // generate new texture coordinates for GeometryArray
  TexCoordGeneration texGen = new TexCoordGeneration( );
  texGen.setPlaneS(planeS);
  texGen.setPlaneT(planeT);
  return texGen;
}
```

Making 3D Scenery

3D scenes are models which the user may enter, move around, and view from different angles. An example is the castle in the *test2.obj* landscape, as seen in Figures 27-1 and 27-14.

Figure 27-14. The castle in the test2.obj terrain

 The user can enter a model and can walk right through its walls. Terra3D doesn't enforce any constraints on the user's movements around models.

The placement of models and the user's initial position in the terrain are specified in a text file with the same name as the landscape's OBJ file; for this example, the text file is *test2.txt* in the directory *models/*:

```
start 3960 1800 255.64
Castle.cob    4100   4230   220   70
```

```
bldg4.3ds    6780  3840  780  90
hand1.obj    1830  570  781.98   120
```

The file format is:

```
start x y z
<model file>  x y z scale
<model file>  x y z scale
// more model file lines
```

A start line must be included in the file because specifies where the user is initially placed in the landscape, but the scenery objects are optional. The (x, y, z) values are in landscape coordinates, and the scale value is used to adjust the model's size in the terrain.

Each scenery object is loaded with a PropManager object (introduced back in Chapter 16); the code assumes the existence of coords datafiles for the models.

A difficult task is deciding on suitable (x, y, z) and scale values. One approach is to jot down likely coordinates while running Terragen. Another technique is to move over the loaded terrain in Terra3D and print out the current position by pressing the w button (w for "where"). This functionality is supported by KeyBehavior, described later. Yet another possibility is to open the OBJ file with a text editor, and search through the v lines for likely looking coordinates. None of these approaches help with scale factors, which are mostly estimates.

The scenery models are attached to landBG, so will be translated, rotated, and scaled in the same way as the landscape. The scale factor for the terrain is stored in scaleLen (it's 0.0078125 in the test2 example). Thus, to render the model at the same size as it was created, the scaling must be undone by enlarging it by 1/scaleLen (scaleLen is 128 in test2).

Another consideration is the height of the user's viewpoint. In KeyBehavior, the user's height above the XZ plane is set to the USER_HEIGHT constant (0.5 world units), which is equivalent to 0.5/0.0078125, or 64 landscape units. In practice, it's a good idea to start with a scale factor between 64 and 128; 90 seems like a good value.

Landscape's constructor calls makeScenery( ) to add scenery to landBG:

```
makeScenery(landBG, fname);
```

fname is the filename supplied on the command line (e.g., *test2*).

makeScenery( ) parses the scenery file, storing the user's starting position in originVec, and calls placeScenery( ) to place each model in the terrain.

originVec is used by KeyBehavior, so must be specified in world coordinates. However, the input from the scenery file is in terrain coordinates. The translation between the two coordinate systems is done through a call to landToWorld( ):

```
// called in makeScenery( )
originVec = landToWorld(xCoord, yCoord, zCoord);
```

```
private Vector3d landToWorld(double xCoord, double yCoord, double zCoord)
{ double x = (xCoord * scaleLen) - LAND_LEN/2;
  double y = zCoord * scaleLen;      // z-axis -> y-axis
  double z = (-yCoord * scaleLen) + LAND_LEN/2;   // y- -> z-axis
  return new Vector3d(x, y, z);
}
```

landToWorld( ) applies the rotation, scaling, and translation utilized when the terrain is connected to the world, as illustrated in Figure 27-12. The rotation is achieved by swapping the terrain (z, y) values to become world (y, z) coordinates. The scaling must be done before the translation to mimic the ordering of the transforms in Figure 27-12.

Placing the Models

placeScenery( ) attaches a model to landBG. However, some additional transformations must be applied, as shown in Figure 27-15.

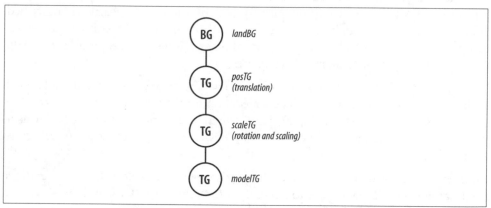

Figure 27-15. A Model subgraph below landBG

The translation and scaling values are supplied for the model in the scenery file. These are given in terms of terrain coordinates because the model is being added to landBG. The rotation is harder to fathom.

The landscape is rotated −90 degrees around the x-axis, and this is applied to the model as well. However, the model is correctly oriented to rest on the XZ plane, so the terrain rotation must be undone by rotating the model +90 degrees back around the x-axis:

```
private void placeScenery(BranchGroup landBG, TransformGroup modelTG,
                          double x, double y, double z, double scale)
{
  modelTG.setPickable(false);    // so not pickable in scene

  Transform3D t3d = new Transform3D( );
  t3d.rotX( Math.PI/2.0 );       // to counter the -ve land rotation
```

```
t3d.setScale( new Vector3d(scale, scale, scale) );    // scaled
TransformGroup scaleTG = new TransformGroup(t3d);
scaleTG.addChild( modelTG );

Transform3D t3d1 = new Transform3D( );
t3d1.set( new Vector3d(x,y,z));  // translated
TransformGroup posTG = new TransformGroup(t3d1);
posTG.addChild( scaleTG );

landBG.addChild( posTG );
}
```

 The model is made unpickable since picking could interact with it if the user went inside the model at run time.

Adding Landscape Walls

The landscape walls surround the terrain and are covered with a mountain range image. Calculating the walls' position in space is somewhat simpler if they are added to sceneBG, which permits world coordinates to be used. The walls surround the terrain after it has been rotated and scaled, so lie in the XZ plane, with lengths LAND_LEN (see Figure 27-16). Their y-axis extent is obtained from the minimum and maximum heights for the terrain, scaled to world size.

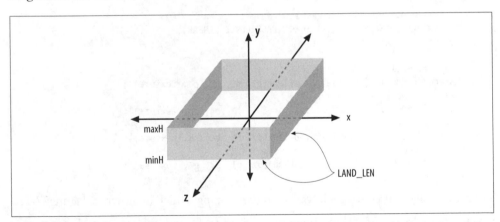

Figure 27-16. Landscape walls

The following code takes care of this:

```
// Landscape globals
private static final double LAND_LEN = 60.0;
        // length of landscape in world coordinates
private static final String WALL_PIC = "models/mountain2Sq.jpg";
```

```
private void addWalls()
{ // heights used for the walls, in world coords
  double minH = minHeight * scaleLen;
  double maxH = maxHeight * scaleLen;

  // the eight corner points
  // back, left
  Point3d p1 = new Point3d(-LAND_LEN/2.0f, minH, -LAND_LEN/2.0f);
  Point3d p2 = new Point3d(-LAND_LEN/2.0f, maxH, -LAND_LEN/2.0f);

  // front, left
  Point3d p3 = new Point3d(-LAND_LEN/2.0f, minH, LAND_LEN/2.0f);
  Point3d p4 = new Point3d(-LAND_LEN/2.0f, maxH, LAND_LEN/2.0f);

  // front, right
  Point3d p5 = new Point3d(LAND_LEN/2.0f, minH, LAND_LEN/2.0f);
  Point3d p6 = new Point3d(LAND_LEN/2.0f, maxH, LAND_LEN/2.0f);

  // back, right
  Point3d p7 = new Point3d(LAND_LEN/2.0f, minH, -LAND_LEN/2.0f);
  Point3d p8 = new Point3d(LAND_LEN/2.0f, maxH, -LAND_LEN/2.0f);

  // load texture; set magnification filter since the image is enlarged
  TextureLoader loader = new TextureLoader(WALL_PIC, null);
  Texture2D texture = (Texture2D) loader.getTexture();
  if (texture == null)
    System.out.println("Cannot load wall image from " + WALL_PIC);
  else {
    System.out.println("Loaded wall image: " + WALL_PIC);
    texture.setMagFilter(Texture2D.BASE_LEVEL_LINEAR);
  }

  // left wall
  sceneBG.addChild( new TexturedPlane(p3, p1, p2, p4, texture));
  // front wall
  sceneBG.addChild( new TexturedPlane(p5, p3, p4, p6, texture));
  // right wall
  sceneBG.addChild( new TexturedPlane(p7, p5, p6, p8, texture));
  // back wall
  sceneBG.addChild( new TexturedPlane(p1, p7, p8, p2, texture));
} // end of addWalls()
```

The same image is used for each wall: *mountain2Sq.jpg*, which is shown in Figure 27-17.

It was originally a wide, thin image but resized to form a square suitable for a texture. It's only 7 KB, so it becomes pixilated when viewed up close inside Terra3D. For that reason, magnification filtering is switched on to smooth the image's enlargement. Another way of improving the image quality is to use a more detailed, larger image.

Figure 27-18 shows one of the walls in the *test1.obj* terrain.

Figure 27-17. mountain2Sq.jpg: the mountain range

Figure 27-18. A landscape wall in Terra3D

A Wall as a Textured Plane

Each wall is an instance of the TexturedPlane class, which is a simplified descendent of TexturedPlanes in FractalLand3D from Chapter 26.

```
// in addWalls( )
// add the left wall to the scene
sceneBG.addChild( new TexturedPlane(p3, p1, p2, p4, texture));
```

The geometry is simpler since only one QuadArray is created to hold the wall's four corners. No normals are specified since the node's appearance doesn't enable lighting or utilize a Material node. The appearance is represented by the texture, with no lighting effects.

The complete TexturedPlane class is shown as Example 27-1.

Example 27-1. The TexturedPlane class

```
public class TexturedPlane extends Shape3D
{
  private static final int NUM_VERTS = 4;

  public TexturedPlane(Point3d p1, Point3d p2, Point3d p3, Point3d p4,
                                  Texture2D tex)
  { createGeometry(p1, p2, p3, p4);

    Appearance app = new Appearance();
    app.setTexture(tex);        // set the texture
    setAppearance(app);
  } // end of TexturedPlane()


  private void createGeometry(Point3d p1, Point3d p2, Point3d p3, Point3d p4)
  {
    QuadArray plane = new QuadArray(NUM_VERTS,
              GeometryArray.COORDINATES |
              GeometryArray.TEXTURE_COORDINATE_2 );

    // anti-clockwise from bottom left
    plane.setCoordinate(0, p1);
    plane.setCoordinate(1, p2);
    plane.setCoordinate(2, p3);
    plane.setCoordinate(3, p4);

    TexCoord2f q = new TexCoord2f();
    q.set(0.0f, 0.0f);
    plane.setTextureCoordinate(0, 0, q);
    q.set(1.0f, 0.0f);
    plane.setTextureCoordinate(0, 1, q);
    q.set(1.0f, 1.0f);
    plane.setTextureCoordinate(0, 2, q);
    q.set(0.0f, 1.0f);
    plane.setTextureCoordinate(0, 3, q);

    setGeometry(plane);
  }  // end of createGeometry()

} // end of TexturedPlane class
```

Creating Ground Cover

Ground cover is the 2D scenery that decorates a landscape. An item of ground cover is represented by a transparent GIF pasted onto a quad that stands on the terrain's surface and is always oriented towards the viewer. The quad is implemented as a four-sided QuadArray inside a GroundShape object (a subclass of OrientedShape3D). The pasting uses blended transparency so the quad is invisible and only the opaque parts of the GIF are rendered.

Typical ground cover includes trees, bushes, and road signs. Such elements will appear many times inside a scene, and it would be inefficient to create a separate shape for each one. Instead, the GroundShape object (e.g., a tree) is embedded in a SharedGroup node, which allows the geometry to be shared by multiple TransformGroups. Each TransfromGroup specifies a location for a particular ground cover element, but the object is a shared node.

The approach is illustrated by Figure 27-19.

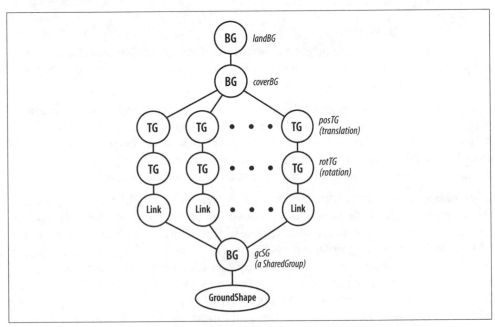

Figure 27-19. A subgraph using a shared GroundShape object

Since a GroundShape object is attached to landBG, terrain coordinates can be used to set its position inside the landscape.

The constructor for Landscape( ) adds ground cover by calling:

```
GroundCover gc = new GroundCover(fname);
landBG.addChild( gc.getCoverBG( ) );
```

The GroundCover object, gc, manages the creation of the subgraph holding the ground cover items. The call to getCoverBG( ) returns the coverBG BranchGroup, the top-level of the subgraph.

The Ground Cover

Information about what ground cover should be added to the terrain is given in a *<fname>GC.txt* text file, where *<fname>* is the name of the landscape OBJ file. For instance, the information for the test2 scene is stored in *test2GC.txt* in *models/*:

```
range 0 500
tree1.gif 90 200
tree2.gif 90 200
tree3.gif 90 200
tree4.gif 90 200
```

Here is the format of a GC file:

```
range [ min max ]
<GS file1> scale1 number1
<GS file2> scale2 number2
// more gs image lines
```

The range line specifies the height range within which ground cover may appear. A range restriction is useful for stopping scenery appearing on the surface of lakes or the tops of mountains.

A GS file contains a transparent GIF image, which is loaded into its own GroundShape object. The scale argument is used to set the size of the screen, and number determines the number of copies of the ground cover placed in the scene. As with 3D models, the best scale value is largely a matter of trial and error, but 90 is a good starting value since it makes the cover a bit taller than the user's viewpoint.

I don't supply terrain coordinates for the scenery, which would further complicate the example. Instead, to keep things simple, the scenery is positioned at random locations. Even this is difficult, since the (x, y, z) data must be obtained from somewhere. The solution used in GroundCover is to read in the OBJ file (e.g., *test2.obj*) as a text file and record the v data (the (x, y, z) coordinates of its mesh) as Vector3d objects in a coords ArrayList. Positioning becomes a matter of randomly selecting a coordinate from the coords list. This approach is surprisingly fast though memory intensive. The selection of the coordinates is done by the code instead of being forced on the programmer. Arguably, this may be a drawback since there's no programmer control over placement, including the inability to clump ground cover together: each mesh coordinate is 30 terrain units apart.

Figure 27-20 gives class diagrams for GroundCover and GroundShape, showing all the data and methods.

In GroundCover, loadCoverInfo( ) loads and parses the GC text file. It calls loadObj( ) and readObj( ) to parse the coordinates information extracted from the OBJ file, storing them in the coords ArrayList. Each GS file line from the GC file triggers a call to loadGC( ), which attaches a subgraph to coverBG similar to the one in Figure 27-19.

```
private void loadGC(String gcFnm, double scale, int gcNo)
{
  String gcFile = new String("models/" + gcFnm);
```

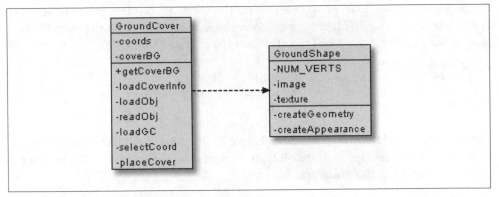

Figure 27-20. GroundCover and GroundShape classes

```
SharedGroup gcSG = new SharedGroup( );
gcSG.addChild( new GroundShape((float) scale, gcFile) );
gcSG.setPickable(false);    // so not pickable in scene

Vector3d coordVec;
for(int i=0; i < gcNo; i++) {   // make multiple TGs using same SG
  coordVec = selectCoord( );
  placeCover(gcSG, coordVec);
}
}
```

The arguments passed to loadGC( ) are the three values supplied on the GS file line in the GC file. A single GroundShape object is created, and multiple transforms are connected to it by repeatedly calling placeCover( ):

```
private void placeCover(SharedGroup gcSG, Vector3d coordVec)
{
  Transform3D t3d = new Transform3D( );
  t3d.rotX( Math.PI/2.0 );      // to counter rotation of the land
  TransformGroup rotTG = new TransformGroup(t3d);
  rotTG.addChild( new Link(gcSG) );

  Transform3D t3d1 = new Transform3D( );
  t3d1.set( coordVec );
  TransformGroup posTG = new TransformGroup(t3d1);
  posTG.addChild( rotTG );

  coverBG.addChild( posTG );
}
```

placeCover( ) creates a single branch down from coverBG to the GroundShape node (see Figure 27-19). A common coding error when using a SharedGroup node is to attempt to link it directly to the rest of the scene graph. Each link must be through a Link node.

Figure 27-19 shows that each branch from coverBG to a Link node holds two TransformGroups. The first (posTG) moves the shape to a location on the terrain's surface; its value comes from a call to selectCoord( ) in loadGC( ):

```
private Vector3d selectCoord()
// randomly select a landscape coordinate
{ int index = (int) Math.floor( Math.random()*coords.size());
  return (Vector3d) coords.get(index);
}
```

The second TransformGroup (rotTG) in Figure 27-19 plays a similar role to the sTG node for 3D models (see Figure 27-12): it counters the −90-degree rotation around the x-axis applied to the landscape.

The Ground Shape

A GroundShape object displays a transparent GIF drawn on the front face of a four-sided QuadArray. The center of the quad's base is at (0, 0, 0) and rests on the ground. It has sides of screenSize and is always oriented toward the viewer. The orientation is achieved by making GroundShape a subclass of OrientedShape3D and setting its axis of rotation to be the y-axis.

GroundShape's createAppearance( ) sets up the necessary transparency attributes for the shape and loads the GIF as a texture:

```
private void createAppearance(String fnm)
{
  Appearance app = new Appearance();

  // blended transparency so texture can be irregular
  TransparencyAttributes tra = new TransparencyAttributes();
  tra.setTransparencyMode( TransparencyAttributes.BLENDED );
  app.setTransparencyAttributes( tra );

  // Create a two dimensional texture with min and mag filtering
  TextureLoader loader = new TextureLoader(fnm, null);
  Texture2D tex = (Texture2D) loader.getTexture();
  if (tex == null)
    System.out.println("Image Loading Failed for " + fnm);
  else {
    tex.setMinFilter(Texture2D.BASE_LEVEL_LINEAR);
    tex.setMagFilter(Texture2D.BASE_LEVEL_LINEAR);
    app.setTexture(tex);
  }

  setAppearance(app);
}  // end of createAppearance()
```

Min filtering improves the texture's appearance when it's reduced in size, while mag-filtering is used when the texture is enlarged.

Moving over the Surface

The KeyBehavior class is similar to the one in FractalLand3D in that it permits the user to move over the surface of the terrain and to float above it. However, there's one small change and one large one. The small change is the addition of the w key, which prints the user's current location on the landscape to System.out.

The major change is that a move doesn't immediately affect the user's vertical position on the terrain. The height calculation is delegated to a HeightFinder object, which may take one or two seconds to obtain the result through picking. In the meantime, KeyBehavior continues to use the old value. As a consequence, the user can move inside mountains, but the vertical position will be corrected. The reason for the slow picking is the large terrain size (e.g., over 66,000 vertices in test2.obj, specifying 131,000 faces), all packaged inside a single GeometryArray.

This approach has the advantage that key processing is decoupled from the height calculation. This means that the KeyBehavior object doesn't have to wait those few seconds after each move-related key press, which would quickly drive the user to distraction. At the end of the chapter, I discuss various alternatives to this coding technique.

Where Am I?

When the user presses the w key, printLandLocation( ) is called:

```
private void printLandLocation()
{ targetTG.getTransform(t3d);
  t3d.get(trans);
  trans.y -= MOVE_STEP*zOffset;  // ignore user floating
  Vector3d whereVec = land.worldToLand(trans);

  System.out.println("Land location: (" + df.format(whereVec.x) + ", " +
              df.format(whereVec.y) + ", " + df.format(whereVec.z) + ")");
}
```

A slight problem is that the KeyBehavior object is attached to sceneBG, so it utilizes world coordinates. However, printing the landscape coordinates is more helpful, and so the (x, y, z) data maintained in KeyBehavior must be transformed. This is achieved by calling worldToLand( ) in Landscape:

```
public Vector3d worldToLand(Vector3d worldVec)
{
  double xCoord = (worldVec.x + LAND_LEN/2) / scaleLen;
  double yCoord = (-worldVec.z + LAND_LEN/2) / scaleLen;
                                  // z-axis --> y-axis
  double zCoord = worldVec.y / scaleLen;   // y-axis --> z-axis
  return new Vector3d(xCoord, yCoord, zCoord);
}
```

The transformations apply the operations implicit in the subgraph in Figure 27-12: the world coordinates are translated, scaled and rotated to make them into terrain coordinates. The rotation (a –90-degree rotation around the x-axis) can be conveniently expressed as a switching of the y- and z-coordinates.

 Another way of understanding worldToLand( ) is as the reverse of landToWorld( ), which is in Landscape.

The w key is quite useful when the programmer is deciding where to place scenery on the terrain. The user can move over the landscape inside Terra3D, and press w when a promising location is encountered. The outputted coordinates can be used in the scenery file to position 3D models.

Strolling Around the Terrain

The principal method for moving is moveBy( ), which is called with a predefined step for moving forward, back, left, or right. The viewpoint is adjusted in four stages:

1. The next (x, z) position on the floor is calculated by carrying out the move but doesn't update the user's actual position. This is done by tryMove( ).
2. The resulting (x, z) data is passed to a HeightFinder thread. HeightFinder uses picking to get the floor height.
3. In the meantime, moveBy( ) uses the current floor height as the height of the new location.
4. Later—perhaps a few seconds later—HeightFinder calls adjustHeight( ) in KeyBehavior. adjustHeight( ) updates the user's height by the difference between the current floor height and the height at the new location.

Here's that sequence of events in code:

```
private void moveBy(Vector3d theMove)
{
  Vector3d nextLoc = tryMove(theMove);    // next (x,?,z) position
  if (!land.inLandscape(nextLoc.x, nextLoc.z))    // not on landscape
    return;

  hf.requestMoveHeight(nextLoc);   // height request to HeightFinder

  Vector3d actualMove = new Vector3d(theMove.x, 0, theMove.z);
                                    // no y-axis change... yet
  doMove(actualMove);
}

public void adjustHeight(double newHeight)
{
  double heightChg = newHeight - currLandHeight - (MOVE_STEP*zOffset);
```

```
        Vector3d upVec = new Vector3d(0, heightChg, 0);
        currLandHeight = newHeight;      // update current height
        zOffset = 0;                     // back on floor, so no offset
        doMove(upVec);
    }
```

moveBy( ) and adjustHeight( ) call doMove( ), which updates the viewpoint position. This method is unchanged from the one in FractalLand3D, except that it is now prefixed with the synchronized keyword. This prevents KeyBehavior and HeightFinder from calling it at the same time.

Finding the Surface Height

KeyBehavior interacts with HeightFinder by calling requestMoveHeight( ), which stores a (x, y, z) coordinate in the global theMove Vector3d object:

```
// globals
private Vector3d theMove;  // current move request from KeyBehavior
private boolean calcRequested;


synchronized public void requestMoveHeight(Vector3d mv)
{ theMove.set(mv.x, mv.y, mv.z);
          // will overwrite any pending request in theMove
  calcRequested = true;
}
```

The (x, z) values in theMove are used for the picking calculation. The calcRequested Boolean signals a pending request.

If the user presses the move keys rapidly, KeyBehavior will call requestMoveHeight( ) frequently, causing theMove to be updated frequently. When HeightFinder processes the next request, it will find only the most recent one in theMove, saving itself unnecessary work. This illustrates the decoupling of key processing from height calculation, so the users can move as fast (or as slow) as they like.

requestMoveHeight( ) returns immediately; KeyBehavior doesn't wait for an answer, or it might be waiting for one or two seconds. Instead, KeyBehavior uses the current y-height for its move. HeightFinder's run( ) method constantly loops, reads the current move request from theMove( ), and then calls getLandHeight( ). At the end of getLandHeight( ), the new height is passed back to KeyBehavior:

```
public void run( )
{ Vector3d vec;
  while(true) {
    if (calcRequested) {
      vec = getMove( );        // get the requested move
      getLandHeight(vec.x, vec.z);   // pick with it
    }
    else {   // no pending request
      try {
```

```
        Thread.sleep(200);      // sleep a little
      }
      catch(InterruptedException e) {}
    }
  }
}
```

The data in theMove is obtained via getMove( ):

```
synchronized private Vector3d getMove()
{ calcRequested = false;
  return new Vector3d(theMove.x, theMove.y, theMove.z);
}
```

The method is synchronized as is requestMoveHeight( ) since the methods access and change theMove( ) and calcRequested( ), and I want to impose mutual exclusion on those operations.

Picking in HeightFinder

getLandHeight( ) in HeightFinder implements picking on the landscape and uses the same code as getLandHeight( ) in the Landscape class in FractalLand3D. Placing the code in the HeightFinder class is a matter of taste: all the height calculations should be located in a single object.

The HeightFinder constructor is passed a reference to the Landscape object so terrain-related data and methods can be accessed:

```
// globals
private Landscape land;
private KeyBehavior keyBeh;
private PickTool picker;
private double scaleLen;

public HeightFinder(Landscape ld, KeyBehavior kb)
{
  land = ld;
  keyBeh = kb;
  picker = new PickTool(land.getLandBG());   //only check landscape
  picker.setMode(PickTool.GEOMETRY_INTERSECT_INFO);

  scaleLen = land.getScaleLen();  // scale factor for terrain
  theMove = new Vector3d();
  calcRequested = false;
}
```

The PickTool object, picker, is configured to examine only landBG. However, 3D models and ground cover are attached to this node, so they should be made unpickable; I'm only interested in obtaining floor coordinates at pick time.

One feature of getLandHeight( ) is the pick ray is specified in world coordinates even though the PickTool is attached to landBG (which uses landscape coordinates):

```java
// global
private final static Vector3d DOWN_VEC = new Vector3d(0.0,-1.0,0.0);


private void getLandHeight(double x, double z)
{
  // high up in world coords; shoot a ray downwards
  Point3d pickStart = new Point3d(x, 2000, z);
  picker.setShapeRay(pickStart, DOWN_VEC);

  PickResult picked = picker.pickClosest();
  if (picked != null) {    // pick sometimes misses at edge/corner
    if (picked.numIntersections() != 0) { //sometimes no intersects
      PickIntersection pi = picked.getIntersection(0);
      Point3d nextPt;
      try {    // handles 'Interp point outside quad' error
        nextPt = pi.getPointCoordinates();
      }
      catch (Exception e) {
        System.out.println(e);
        return;    // don't talk to KeyBehavior as no height found
      }

      double nextYHeight = nextPt.z * scaleLen;
                        // z-axis land --> y-axis world
      keyBeh.adjustHeight(nextYHeight);  //tell KeyBehavior height
    }
  }
}  // end of getLandHeight()
```

The intersection point is obtained in local (i.e., terrain) coordinates by calling PickIntersection.getPointCoordinates( ), which returns the point in world coordinates.

KeyBehavior utilizes world coordinates, so the height value (nextPt.z) must be converted, but this can be done inexpensively by scaling the point directly to give nextYHeight. This value is passed to KeyBehavior by calling adjustHeight( ). The world coordinates are needed since KeyBehavior uses the terrain's height to adjust the user's position in the scene.

Accelerating Terrain Following

The code for terrain following sacrifices accuracy for speed, meaning that users can move quickly over the terrain with the disadvantage that they move straight into the side of a mountain or float off the edge of a cliff. Their vertical position will be corrected, but a temporary position disparity is disconcerting. What can be done? A number of tricks can be utilized without making any fundamental changes to the application.

The step distance used in KeyBehavior is 0.2 world units, which is 26 terrain units (0. 2/0.0078125). As a rough comparison, each mesh coordinate is 30 units apart. If the step distance was reduced, the user would move over the terrain more slowly, and height changes would occur more gradually. This would help the picking code keep up with the height adjustments.

It's possible to increase the user's height, which is 0.5 world unit in KeyBehavior or is 64 terrain units. If the eyeline is higher off the floor, then a larger height change will be required before the users notice that they've sunk beneath the surface.

Two other solutions are to create landscapes with gentler slopes and make it impossible for users to move into rough terrain by imposing restrictions on KeyBehavior. This latter kind of behavior is typical of racing games, where a vehicle can only move a short distance off the racing track.

The terrain and scenery (the 3D and 2D ground cover) are different. Even when the terrain is flat, the problem of walking through castle walls and trees remains. The general approach I've used in previous examples (e.g., the maze walls in Chapter 25) is to store information about the obstacles' location and prevent the user from walking into them.

More Threads?

Since HeightFinder is a thread, why not throw more threads at the task? The single HeightFinder thread takes a couple of seconds to finish a calculation before it can start the next one, which adds a considerable delay to the processing time for the next request. By having several threads, the turnaround time would be reduced since the wait time would be less.

I tried this and discovered that picking on a geometry cannot be threaded. Multiple threads can initiate picking at roughly the same time, but each operation is sequentialized, and extra time is added in the process. Threads may be more successful if the picking is carried out on different GeometryArrays, but I haven't tried it.

Mesh Decomposition

The real problem is the mesh is too large for efficient picking. It should be divided into pieces, perhaps based on the terrain's latitude and longitude. Then, as a user moves over the terrain, the relevant terrain piece can be selected easily and picking would be faster due to the smaller size of the piece.

Multiple pieces lend themselves to the support of multiple levels of detail and dynamic loading. Several of the approaches described in the next section use these ideas.

More on Terrain Generation

A great source for terrain generation information is the Virtual Terrain Project (*http://www.vterrain.org*), which has sections on elevation models, ground detail, rendering, data sources and formats, scenery, software tools, and plants.

GameDev.net has a collection of good articles about landscape modeling at *http://www.gamedev.net/reference/list.asp?categoryid=45#88*.

DEM and Terrain Generation

Though my focus is on gaming, terrain creation is used by simulation and GIS applications. A popular file format for geographic data is the Digital Elevation Model (DEM), which represents grids of regularly spaced elevation values. The USGS produces five primary types of DEM data, which represent different levels of geographical detail: 7.5-minute DEM, 30-minute DEM, 1-degree DEM, 7.5-minute Alaska DEM, and 15-minute Alaska DEM. Here are some useful DEM links:

- *http://www.cis.ksu.edu/~dha5446/topoweb/demtutorial.html*
- *http://www.vterrain.org/Elevation/dem.html*
- *http://edcwww.cr.usgs.gov/products/elevation/dem.html*

Terragen can understand various USGS and NASA file formats when used in conjunction with plug-ins and/or other terrain-based applications, such as 3DEM. This makes the data available to Terra3D once saved as OBJ and JPG files.

j3d.org
> The j3d.org code repository (*http://code.j3d.org*) contains a DEM loader in org.j3d.loaders.dem, but it's poorly documented with no examples of its use. However, the loader is used as part of the GeoSim application, to display DEM files (*http://www.bulletprf.com/lab-index.htm*). The program comes with source code.
>
> The org.j3d.geom.terrain package contains classes for creating height maps from images, and the org.j3d.loaders package supports the loading of grid-aligned data, treating the data as height values.

JLand
> JLand is a Java 3D applet/application for displaying and generating landscapes (*http://www.cyberhipster.com/j3d/jland*). It can read elevation maps stored as compressed (GZIP) or uncompressed PGM, DEM, or POV TGA files. Only the class files are available at the moment.

DEM viewer
> The *JavaWorld* article "Navigate through Virtual Worlds using Java 3D" by Mark O. Pendergast is an excellent tutorial on utilizing DEM files and includes

fly-through navigation controls using the keyboard and mouse, and level-of-detail (LOD) displays of the data (*http://www.javaworld.com/javaworld/jw-07-2003/jw-0704-3d_p.html*). All the source code can be downloaded and includes a Grand Canyon example.

The data is stored internally in `TriangleStripArrays` using interleaving and by-reference, which is the most efficient format in terms of memory and processor usage. Interleaving is utilized to support color and normal information alongside the coordinates. The normals are generated in the code rather than via a `NormalGenerator`. Texturing isn't used. Though interleaved data complicate the coding, the data accelerate rendering.

Rather than using a single `TriangleStripArray` (as in Terra3D), Pendergast employs many arrays so LOD features can be offered. The terrain is divided into segments, with each segment represented by several `TriangleStripArrays` holding varying amounts of (by-reference) mesh detail. *By-reference* means that the mesh data is shared between the various segments, saving considerable space. Switch nodes multiplex between the arrays at runtime: as the user approaches a segment (or moves away from one), more (or less) mesh detail is displayed.

ROAM

A crucial problem for an industrial-strength landscape representation is the enormous amount of memory required for a large map. For example, a height map made up of floats for (x, z) coordinates at 1mm intervals, covering a 10-meter square area, would require about 400 MB of RAM, and that's before the cost of rendering and adding objects to the scene. The obvious answer is to reduce the sampling density, but that will reduce the map's resolution.

A better solution is *adaptive meshing*, as typified by Realtime Optimally Adapting Meshes (ROAM). It's adaptive in the sense that areas that are flat or distant from the viewpoint are covered by low resolution submeshes, and nearby or rocky areas use more detailed grids. Since viewpoints can move, the level of detail apparent at a particular terrain location will vary over time, as users come closer and move away.

ROAM creates its dynamic mesh with triangle bintrees (a close relative of the quadtree), which are split/merged to increase/decrease the resolution. The standard reference on ROAM is the paper by Mark Duchaineau and others: "ROAMing Terrain: Real-time Optimally Adapting Meshes" in *Proc. IEEE Visualization '97*, pp.81–88, 1997 (*http://www.llnl.gov/graphics/ROAM/*).

There's a Java 3D implementation of ROAM in the j3d.org code package `org.j3d.terrain.roam`. Each terrain tile is implemented as a `Shape3D`, so view frustum culling and intersection testing can be accelerated. A tile's geometry is stored in a `TriangleArray` so the overhead of translating down to triangles at the hardware level is reduced. Changes to a tile's geometry is performed with a `GeometryUpdater` object which recalculates its vertices.

`TransformGroups` are avoided; instead a tile is positioned at its intended location directly. This means the shape's coordinate system doesn't need to be mapped to world coordinates when being manipulated, making costly transforms unnecessary.

The ROAM package is explained in Chapter 14 of the textbook *Java Media APIs: Cross-Platform Imaging, Media, and Visualization* by Alejandro Terrazas, John Ostuni, and Michael Barlow (Sams Publishing; *http://www.samspublishing.com/title/0672320940*). I recommend this book for its coverage of other advanced Java 3D topics, such as sensors, stereo viewing, head tracking, and JMF integration.

The CLOD Algorithm

Martin Barbisch implemented a Java 3D application for his student project which illustrates the Continuous Level of Detail (CLOD) algorithm (*http://wwwvis. informatik.uni-stuttgart.de/javatevi/*). The amount of detail visible to the user is adjusted at run time as the viewer moves. The drawback is a "popping" effect as details suddenly appear as the user gets closer to some part of the terrain. The solution is geomorphing, a form of mesh morphing.

Other Java 3D Projects

DTV applet
> Nathan Bower has written a Java 3D applet which displays a UK ordinance survey map, textured over a height field for the same area (*http://www.nathanbower.com/cms?page_id=03_Java3D_Applet.htm&folder=/02_My_Work*). No source code is available, but the information supplied on the web page suggests that he's implemented most of the components himself: the triangulation scheme, viewpoint clipping, the mouse controls. He mentions an application that can display multiple ordinance survey maps, tiled together, sufficient in number to cover the entire UK.

Integrated Data Viewer (IDV)
> IDV is a framework for visualizing and analyzing 2D and 3D geoscience data (*http://my.unidata.ucar.edu/content/software/metapps/*), such as weather satellite imagery and radar. Source code is available.

The Virtual Globe
> The Virtual Globe is a client-server application for displaying large terrain models (*http://globe.sintef.no/*). The terrain database is stored on a server, and the client fetches the data required for generating an image at the required resolution.

JCanyon
> JCanyon is a flight simulator which visualizes its large data set (about 300 MB) using JOGL or GL4Java (often called "OpenGL for Java") rather than Java 3D (*http://java.sun.com/products/jfc/tsc/articles/jcanyon/*).

The terrain is divided into tiles, and multiple samples are prepared for each tile, with varying coordinate and texture resolutions. Only the data for the required resolution is mapped into memory at any given time. Tiles are fetched from the disk in a background thread.

Two novelties of JCanyon are its texture selection technique and a method for eliminating cracks between tiles, called filleting.

The 3D land navigator

The navigator displays land surfaces in 3D and lets the viewer fly over them.

Aerial photos of the landscape must be divided into map cells. Each map cell is then converted into a 3D geometry with texture mapping for the details. As the user flies over the landscape, the map cells near to the user's viewpoint are loaded and displayed. The software is built using the WorldShow3D browser (*http://worldshow3d.home.comcast.net/map3d.html*).

A Java 3D loader for Terragen

Jean-Marc Jung and Pierre Henry have written a loader for Terragen TER height-map files (*http://www.hta-bi.bfh.ch/Projects/diggersim/*). The loader is part of their "Digger Simulation" project for training the pilots of mine clearance vehicles.

CHAPTER 28

Trees That Grow

The last two chapters have been about creating landscapes: the fractal terrain in Chapter 26 was empty, but the Terragen-generated landscape in Chapter 27 was decorated with 3D models and ground cover (2D images that always face the user). This mix of models and images is enough in most situations but still lacking in one area: the scenery doesn't change. For example, the trees don't sway in the wind, and the sagebrush doesn't tumble.

As the title of this chapter suggests, this chapter focuses on making trees grow. Each tree starts from a tiny sampling, then young green shoots turn brown, grow, branch, and sprout leaves. However, the underlying aim is to describe a rule-based approach to animation, which can be applied to many kinds of 3D shapes. This approach has the following characteristics:

Use of `if-then` *rules*

> Each rule is a Java `if-then` statement. If all the conditions of a rule evaluate to true, then the rule's actions are carried out.

 I'm not using a rule-based language such as Prolog, or a Java rules engine such as JESS. There's no need to step beyond standard Java.

Time-based sequential evaluation

> The rules are evaluated at regular intervals during the program's execution. They're executed in a fixed, sequential order, defined by their textual order in the `applyRules()` method in the `GrowthBehavior` class.

Each rule is applied to every tree limb

> When it's time for a rule to be evaluated, it's applied to every tree limb (tree branch) in the scene. For example, for two trees—one with five branches and the other with nine—each rule is executed 14 times (5 + 9), once for each limb.

I can express this idea in more general terms: in each time interval, a rule is applied to every animation component in the scene. The choice of animation component depends on the application domain; in this case, the components are the branches of the trees.

An animation component is an object

In this example, each tree limb is an instance of the TreeLimb class. This approach hiding a tree limb's implementation and most of the rules processing behind the class' methods.

Linked animation components form a hierarchy

Animation components are coupled together to form a hierarchy, where each component has a single parent (except the root component) and zero or more children. This allows rules to talk about parents and children, which adds to their expressiveness. Many 3D models are made from smaller parts, structured into a hierarchy, including trees, humanoids (e.g., the articulated figure in Chapter 20), and buildings (a building is composed of floors and walls).

Rules carry out incremental change

The rules change an animation component. For example, a tree limb will get longer and change color over a period of seconds. It is possible to add and delete animation components (e.g., new branches can start sprouting), but this is less common than changing an existing component.

A rule can behave randomly

A rule must behave randomly to introduce variation into the animation. For instance, the same rule may make one branch shoot up but delay another branch's growth. Randomness is easily achieved with Math.random( ).

The animation is efficiently implemented

Animation efficiency is important since the rules may have to deal with thousands of animation components, each of which is updated 10 or more times a second.

The incremental nature of the rules means that the 3D structures don't need to be generated from scratch in every time interval, which would be time-consuming. Instead, existing structures are modified.

Another optimization is that the geometry of an animation component (e.g., the cylinder representing the tree limb) is unchanged. Instead, changes such as translations, rotations, and scaling are done to TransformGroup nodes connected to the shape. Similarly, changes to the component's appearance are applied to its Appearance node. Since the component's geometry is unaffected, you won't need to employ the complex GeometryUpdater interface used in the particle systems in Chapter 21.

 An approach not used here are rules in the style of a Lindenmayer system (L-system), which suffer from the complexity and inefficiency I've tried to avoid throughout the book. I'll briefly compare my rule mechanism with L-systems in the section "Comparison with L-Systems."

Figure 28-1 shows a sequence of screenshots of the Trees3D application. Five trees grow from saplings, green shoots turn brown, and leaves sprout, all taking place over a period of a few seconds.

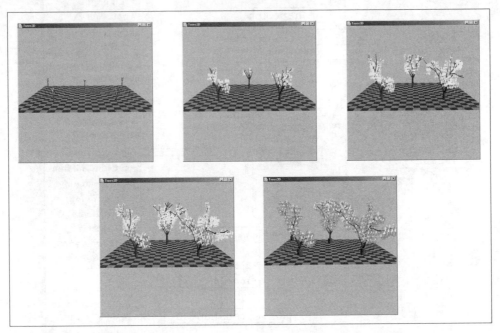

Figure 28-1. Growing trees

Each time Trees3D is executed, the trees will look different, due to random elements in the rules.

Class Diagrams for Trees3D

Figure 28-2 shows the class diagrams for the Trees3D application. The class names and public methods are shown.

Trees3D is the top-level JFrame for the application, and WrapTrees3D sets up the scene. It initially creates five TreeLimb objects, representing five tree limbs. New limbs sprout from these, creating trees like those in Figure 28-1.

TreeLimb encodes the animation component, so it offers many methods for changing a limb (e.g., making it grow longer, thicker, and changing color). The leaves at the end of a tree limb are represented by two ImagesCsSeries screens that show pictures of leaves. The images can be changed to give the effect the leaves are changing.

The rules are implemented in the GrowthBehavior object and evaluated every 100 ms.

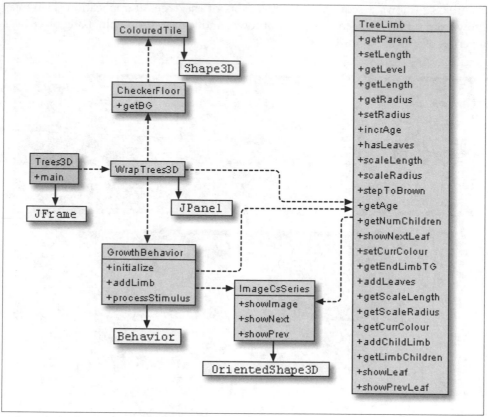

Figure 28-2. Class diagrams for Trees3D

 The application can be found in the *Trees3D/* directory.

Creating the Scene

The WrapTrees3D class creates the scene: the checkerboard floor, the background, the lights, and an OrbitBehavior allow the user to move around.

Most of the tree-related activity is started in growTrees( ), which creates five TransformGroups and five TreeLimb objects. The code fragment shows one of these TransformGroups and TreeLimbs:

```
// starting position for the first tree: (0,0,-5)
Transform3D t3d = new Transform3D( );
t3d.set( new Vector3f(0,0,-5));
TransformGroup tg0 = new TransformGroup(t3d);
sceneBG.addChild(tg0);
```

```
// create the tree
TreeLimb t0 = new TreeLimb(Z_AXIS, 0, 0.05f, 0.5f, tg0, null);
```

The `TransformGroup` reference (tg0) is passed to the `TreeLimb` constructor, where it's used to position the limb.

Loading Leaves

`growTrees()` loads a sequence of leaf images, storing them in an `ImageComponent2D` array. This increases efficiency because each `TreeLimb` will utilize this array if it requires leaves rather than loading its own copy of the images:

```
// load the leaf images used by all the trees
ImageComponent2D[] leafIms = loadImages("images/leaf", 6);
```

The `loadImages()` method is shown here:

```
private ImageComponent2D[] loadImages(String fNms, int numIms)
/* Load the leaf images: they all start with fNms, and there are
   numIms of them.   */
{
  String filename;
  TextureLoader loader;
  ImageComponent2D[] ims = new ImageComponent2D[numIms];
  System.out.println("Loading " + numIms +" textures from "+ fNms);
  for (int i=0; i < numIms; i++) {
    filename = new String(fNms + i + ".gif");
    loader = new TextureLoader(filename, null);
    ims[i] = loader.getImage();
    if(ims[i] == null)
      System.out.println("Load failed for: " + filename);
    ims[i].setCapability(ImageComponent2D.ALLOW_SIZE_READ);
  }
  return ims;
}
```

The leaf images are in the files *images/leaf0-5.gif*, as shown in Figure 28-3.

 The gray and white squares in Figure 28-3 indicate that the GIFs' backgrounds are transparent.

The idea here is that the `ImageCsSeries` screens will iterate through the images from *leaf0.gif* to *leaf5.gif*. The resulting effect will be growing leaves, turning darker.

The drawing style has some room for artistic improvement. However, the effect is still good, especially when viewed at some distance, with many leaves overlapping. Later images were created by modifying earlier ones, so the transition from one image to the next is smooth.

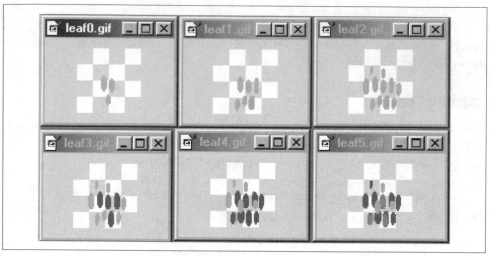

Figure 28-3. The leaf images in leaf0-5.gif

Depth-Sorting for Transparency

Since the scene will contain numerous semi-transparent textures wrapped over quads (i.e., the leaves on the trees), it's necessary to turn on Java 3D's depth-sorting of transparent objects on a per-geometry basis:

```
View view = su.getViewer( ).getView( );
view.setTransparencySortingPolicy(View.TRANSPARENCY_SORT_GEOMETRY);
```

This is carried out in the WrapTrees3D( ) constructor. If depth-sorting isn't switched on, the relative ordering of the leaf images will frequently be wrong as the viewer moves around the trees.

Getting Ready for Growth

WrapTrees3D's growTrees( ) initializes the GrowthBehavior object:

```
// the behavior that manages the growing of the trees
GrowthBehavior grower = new GrowthBehavior(leafIms);
grower.setSchedulingBounds( bounds );

// add the trees to GrowthBehavior
grower.addLimb(t0);
grower.addLimb(t1);
grower.addLimb(t2);
grower.addLimb(t3);
grower.addLimb(t4);

sceneBG.addChild( grower );
```

Building a Tree Limb

Each tree limb is represented by a `TreeLimb` object, which internally builds a sub-graph such as the one in Figure 28-4.

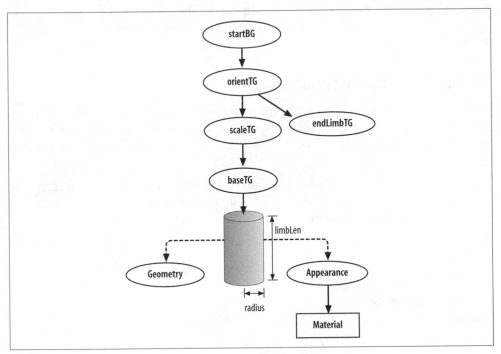

Figure 28-4. The TreeLimb subgraph

Several of the `TransformGroup` nodes (those with "TG" in their name) are used to support translation, rotation, and scaling effects, leaving the basic geometry (a cylinder) unaffected. This means that I could avoid using the complicated `GeometryUpdater` interface.

The `startBG` `BranchGroup` is linked to a parent limb via the parent's `endLimbTG` node. Since the link is made at execution time, Java 3D requires the use of a `BranchGroup`.

`orientTG` holds the orientation of the limb (its initial axis of rotation and angle to that axis). Once set, this cannot change during execution. This restriction is in place to simplify the class's implementation. `scaleTG` manages the scaling of the x-, y-, and z-dimensions of the cylinder. The x- and z-values are kept the same (they represent the radius); the y-axis is for the length.

The center point for Java 3D's `Cylinder` is its middle, but I want the origin to be its base at the place where the cylinder connects to the parent limb. `baseTG` moves the cylinder up the y-axis by `length/2` to achieve it. The capabilities for the `Cylinder`'s `Material` node component are set so that its color can be adjusted at runtime.

Child limbs or leaves are attached to this limb through endLimbTG. The transform inside endLimbTG is an offset of almost the cylinder's scaled length. It is a little less than the length, so child limbs will overlap with their parent. This partly hides any gaps between the limbs when a child is oriented at an extreme angle.

The endLimbTG node is unattached to Cylinder since that would make it prone to scaling, which would affect any child limbs attached to endLimbTG. Scaling is restricted to the limb's cylinder.

Storing Tree Limb Information

Aside from the subgraph data structure, TreeLimb maintains various other information related to a tree limb, including a reference to its parent, current color, current age, level in the overall tree (the first branch is at level 1), and whether it is showing leaves.

The age is a counter, set to 0 when the limb is created, and incremented in each time interval by the GrowthBehavior object. Each limb will have a different age depending on when it was added to the tree.

The large number of public methods in TreeLimb can be roughly classified into five groups:

- Scaling of the cylinder's radius or length
- Color adjustment
- Parent and children methods
- Leaf-related
- Others (e.g., for accessing the limb's current age)

To simplify matters, many of the parameters used by these methods (e.g., scale factors, color changes) are hardwired into the rules found in the GrowthBehavior object (which I explain later). The arguments passed to the TreeLimb constructor are concerned with the new limb's size, position, and orientation relative to its parent:

```
public TreeLimb(int axis, double angle, float rad, float len,
                TransformGroup startLimbTG, TreeLimb par)
```

axis and angle are used by orientTG; rad and len become the radius and length of the new cylinder. startLimbTG will be assigned the TransformGroup of the parent limb where this limb will be attached. par is a reference to the parent as a TreeLimb object.

Subgraph Creation

The subgraph in Figure 28-4 is constructed by buildSubgraph( ):

```
private void buildSubgraph(TransformGroup startLimbTG)
/* Create the scene graph.
   startLimbTG is the parent's endLimbTG. */
```

```
{
  BranchGroup startBG = new BranchGroup( );

  // set the limb's orientation
  TransformGroup orientTG = new TransformGroup( );
  if (orientAngle != 0) {
    Transform3D trans = new Transform3D( );
    if (orientAxis == X_AXIS)
      trans.rotX( Math.toRadians(orientAngle));
    else if (orientAxis == Y_AXIS)
      trans.rotY( Math.toRadians(orientAngle));
    else     // must be z-axis
      trans.rotZ( Math.toRadians(orientAngle));
    orientTG.setTransform(trans);
  }

  // scaling node
  scaleTG = new TransformGroup( );
  scaleTG.setCapability( TransformGroup.ALLOW_TRANSFORM_READ);
  scaleTG.setCapability( TransformGroup.ALLOW_TRANSFORM_WRITE);

  // limb subgraph's sequence of TGs
  startBG.addChild(orientTG);
  orientTG.addChild(scaleTG);
  scaleTG.addChild( makeLimb( ) );

  TransformGroup endLimbTG = locateEndLimb( );
  orientTG.addChild(endLimbTG);

  startBG.compile( );

  startLimbTG.addChild(startBG);    //connect to parent's endLimbTG
} // end of buildSubgraph( )
```

The cylinder and its components are built inside makeLimb( ):

```
private TransformGroup makeLimb( )
// a green cylinder whose base is at (0,0,0)
{
  // fix limb's start position
  TransformGroup baseTG = new TransformGroup( );
  Transform3D trans1 = new Transform3D( );
  trans1.setTranslation( new Vector3d(0, limbLen/2, 0) );
                                      // move up length/2
  baseTG.setTransform(trans1);

  Appearance app = new Appearance( );
  limbMaterial = new Material(black, black, green, brown, 50.f);
  limbMaterial.setCapability( Material.ALLOW_COMPONENT_READ);
  limbMaterial.setCapability( Material.ALLOW_COMPONENT_WRITE);
    // can change colors; only the diffuse color will be altered

  limbMaterial.setLightingEnable(true);
```

```
      app.setMaterial( limbMaterial );
      Cylinder cyl = new Cylinder( radius, limbLen, app);

      baseTG.addChild( cyl );
      return baseTG;
  } // end of makeLimb( )
```

The Material's capabilities must be set since color change will be carried out at runtime. Initially, the limb is green.

The radius and length of the cylinder are stored in the radius and limbLen globals. They will never change (the cylinder's geometry isn't updated). Instead, scaling is applied to the cylinder through the scaleTG node.

The endLimbTG node is connected to the subgraph in locateEndLimb( ):

```
      private TransformGroup locateEndLimb( )
      {
        // fix limb's end position, and store in endLimbTG
        endLimbTG = new TransformGroup( );
        endLimbTG.setCapability( TransformGroup.ALLOW_CHILDREN_EXTEND );
        endLimbTG.setCapability( TransformGroup.ALLOW_TRANSFORM_READ );
        endLimbTG.setCapability( TransformGroup.ALLOW_TRANSFORM_WRITE );

        Transform3D trans2 = new Transform3D( );
        trans2.setTranslation(new Vector3d(0, limbLen*(1.0-OVERLAP), 0));
        /* The end position is just short of the actual length of the
           limb so that any child limbs will be placed so they overlap
           with this one. */
        endLimbTG.setTransform(trans2);

        return endLimbTG;
      } // end of locateEndLimb( )
```

It's important to set the necessary capabilities in locateEndLimb( ). The ALLOW_CHILDREN_EXTEND bit will permit BranchGroup nodes to be attached to this node.

Scaling

The public scaling methods employ a scale factor or scale so the radius (or length) becomes a desired value. Consider setLength( ), which scales the cylinder's length until it's the specified amount:

```
      // global for storing scaling info
      private Vector3d scaleLimb;


      public void setLength(float newLimbLen)
      // change the cylinder's length to newLimbLen
      // (by changing the scaling)
      { double scaledLimbLen = ((double) limbLen) * scaleLimb.y;
        double lenChange = ((double) newLimbLen) / scaledLimbLen;
        scaleLength( lenChange );
      }
```

To simplify the calculations, the current scaling factors (in the x-, y-, and z-directions) are maintained in scaleLimb. The current scaled limb length is stored in scaledLimbLen. The desired scaling is the factor to take the length from scaledLimbLen to the required newLimbLen value.

The scaling is done by scaleLength( ):

```
public void scaleLength(double yChange)
{ scaleLimb.y *= yChange;
  applyScale( );
}

private void applyScale( )
{
  moveEndLimbTG( scaleLimb.y);

  scaleTG.getTransform(currTrans);
  currTrans.setScale(scaleLimb);
  scaleTG.setTransform(currTrans);
}
```

applyScale( ) applies the new scaling to scaleTG, which changes the perceived length of the cylinder. However, this change won't automatically affect the endLimbTG node (the node that represents the end of the limb) since it's unattached to the graph below scaleTG. The call to moveEndLimbTG( ) adjusts the node's position so it stays located at the end of the cylinder:

```
private void moveEndLimbTG( double yScale)
/* yScale is the amount that the Cylinder is about to
   be scaled. Apply it to the y- value in endLimbTG  */
{
  endLimbTG.getTransform( currTrans );
  currTrans.get( endPos );          // current posn of endLimbTG
  double currLimbLen = endPos.y;
    // current y-posn, the cylinder length including scaling

  double changedLen =
      ((double) limbLen*(1.0-OVERLAP) * yScale) - currLimbLen;
    // change in the y- value after scaling has been applied

  endPos.set(0, changedLen, 0);        // store the length change
  toMove.setTranslation( endPos );     // overwrite previous trans
  currTrans.mul(toMove);
  endLimbTG.setTransform(currTrans);   // move endLimbTG
} // end of moveEndLimbTG( )
```

endLimbTG's (x, y, z) position is extracted to the endPos vector. This position corresponds to the end of the scaled cylinder.

The necessary position change is calculated by multiplying the cylinder's physical length by the new scale factor in yScale, and subtracting the endPos y-value. I factor in an overlap, which cause limbs to overlap when linked together.

Changing the Limb's Color

The capabilities for changing the limb's Material were set up in makeLimb( ), described earlier. A global, limbMaterial, stores a reference to the node to make it simple to change:

```java
public void setCurrColour(Color3f c)
// Change the limb's color to c.
{ currColor.x = c.x;
  currColor.y = c.y;
  currColor.z = c.z;
  limbMaterial.setDiffuseColor( currColour );
}
```

To achieve an aging effect, the limb's color is changed from green to brown incrementally, spread out over several frames. This is achieved by precalculating red, green, and blue transitions that will change the RGB values for green to brown over the course of MAX_COLOR_STEP steps:

```java
// globals
private final static int MAX_COLOR_STEP = 15;

private final static Color3f green = new Color3f(0.0f, 1.0f, 0.1f);
private final static Color3f brown = new Color3f(0.35f, 0.29f, 0.0f);

// incremental change in terms of RGB to go from green to brown
private float redShift = (brown.x - green.x)/((float) MAX_COLOR_STEP);
private float greenShift = (brown.y - green.y)/((float) MAX_COLOR_STEP);
private float blueShift = (brown.z - green.z)/((float) MAX_COLOR_STEP);
```

The redShift, greenShift, and blueShift values are utilized in stepToBrown( ):

```java
public void stepToBrown( )
// Incrementally change the limb's color from green to brown
{
  if (colorStep <= MAX_COLOR_STEP) {
    currColor.x += redShift;
    currColor.y += greenShift;
    currColor.z += blueShift;
    limbMaterial.setDiffuseColor( currColour );
    colorStep++;
  }
}
```

stepToBrown( ) will be repeatedly called until the limb has turned brown.

Leaves on Trees

Two ImageCsSeries objects display leaves at the end of a branch. This makes the mass of the leaves seem greater, especially since the images are offset from each other. The two objects are connected to the limb via BranchGroup nodes since the links are formed at runtime:

```
public void addLeaves(ImageCsSeries fls, ImageCsSeries bls)
// Leaves are represented by two ImageCsSeries 'screens'
{
  if (!hasLeaves) {
    frontLeafShape = fls;
    backLeafShape = bls;

    // add the screens to endLimbTG, via BranchGroups
    BranchGroup leafBG1 = new BranchGroup();
    leafBG1.addChild(frontLeafShape);
    endLimbTG.addChild(leafBG1);

    BranchGroup leafBG2 = new BranchGroup();
    leafBG2.addChild(backLeafShape);
    endLimbTG.addChild(leafBG2);

    hasLeaves = true;
  }
}
```

The positioning of the ImageCsSeries objects is done when they are created, inside GrowthBehavior.

The other leaf-related methods in TreeLimbs pass requests to the ImageCsSeries objects; the requests change the image currently being displayed:

```
public void showNextLeaf()
// show the next leaf image
{ if (hasLeaves) {
    frontLeafShape.showNext();
    backLeafShape.showNext();
  }
}
```

Executing the Rules

The rules are located in the GrowthBehavior class, a subclass of Behavior. The GrowthBehavior object created by WrapTrees3D maintains an ArrayList of TreeLimb objects and an ImageComponent2D array of leaf pictures. The pictures are passed to it at construction time, while storing the first five TreeLimb objects via calls to addLimb():

```
// globals
private final static int TIME_DELAY = 100;  //ms

private WakeupCondition timeOut;
private ArrayList treeLimbs;          // of TreeLimb objects
private ImageComponent2D[] leafIms;   // a sequence of leaf images
```

```
public GrowthBehavior(ImageComponent2D[] lfIms)
{ timeOut = new WakeupOnElapsedTime(TIME_DELAY);
  treeLimbs = new ArrayList();
  leafIms = lfIms;
}

public void addLimb(TreeLimb limb)
{ treeLimbs.add(limb);  }
```

processStimulus( ) is called every TIME_DELAY milliseconds (100 ms), which calls
applyRulesToLimbs( ). applyRulesToLimbs( ) cycles through the TreeLimb objects in
the ArrayList, calling applyRules( ) for each one:

```
private void applyRulesToLimbs()
{
  TreeLimb limb;
  for(int i=0; i < treeLimbs.size(); i++) {
    limb = (TreeLimb) treeLimbs.get(i);
    applyRules(limb);
    limb.incrAge();   // a limb gets older after each iteration
  }
}
```

Seven rules controlling the modification of a tree limb are placed in applyRules( ):

```
private void applyRules(TreeLimb limb)
// Apply rules to the tree limb.
{
  // get longer
  if ((limb.getLength() < 1.0f) && !limb.hasLeaves())
    limb.scaleLength(1.1f);

  // get thicker
  if ((limb.getRadius() <= (-0.05f*limb.getLevel()+0.25f))
          && !limb.hasLeaves())
    limb.scaleRadius(1.05f);

  // get more brown
  limb.stepToBrown();

  // spawn some child limbs
  int axis;
  if ((limb.getAge() == 5) && (treeLimbs.size() <= 256)
        && !limb.hasLeaves() &&  (limb.getLevel() < 10)) {
    axis = (Math.random() < 0.5) ? Z_AXIS : X_AXIS;
    if (Math.random() < 0.85)
      makeChild(axis, randomRange(10,30), 0.05f, 0.5f, limb);

    axis = (Math.random() < 0.5) ? Z_AXIS : X_AXIS;
    if (Math.random() < 0.85)
      makeChild(axis, randomRange(-30,-10), 0.05f, 0.5f, limb);
  }

  // start some leaves
  if ( (limb.getLevel() > 3) && (Math.random() < 0.08) &&
```

```
        (limb.getNumChildren( ) == 0) && !limb.hasLeaves( ) )
    makeLeaves(limb);

    // grow the leaves
    if (limb.getAge( )%10 == 0)
      limb.showNextLeaf( );

    // turn the base limb into a "blue bucket"
    if ((limb.getAge( ) == 100) && (limb.getLevel( ) == 1)) {
      limb.setRadius( 2.0f*limb.getRadius( ));
      // limb.setLength( 2.0f*limb.getLength( ));
      limb.setCurrColour( new Color3f(0.0f, 0.0f, 1.0f));
    }
  }  // end of applyRules( )
```

Almost all the rules have an if-then form, where the action is only carried out if the conditions evaluate to true for the current limb. Due to the repeating nature of GrowthBehavior, each rule will be applied to each tree limb in each time interval. This means that the rules express change in incremental terms.

The rule controlling a limb's thickness looks like this:

```
    if ((limb.getRadius( ) <= (-0.05f*limb.getLevel( )+0.25f))
            && !limb.hasLeaves( ))
      limb.scaleRadius(1.05f);
```

The equation $-0.05*limb.getLevel( )+0.25$ relates the maximum radius to the limb's level. For example, a limb touching the ground (level = 1) can have a larger maximum radius than a branch higher up the tree. This means that branches will get less thick the higher up the tree they appear as in nature. The hasLeaves( ) part of the condition stops branches from growing thicker once they have leaves.

The rule for generating child limbs looks like this:

```
    if ((limb.getAge( ) == 5) && (treeLimbs.size( ) <= 256)
            && !limb.hasLeaves( ) &&  (limb.getLevel( ) < 10)) {
      axis = (Math.random( ) < 0.5) ? Z_AXIS : X_AXIS;
      if (Math.random( ) < 0.85)
        makeChild(axis, randomRange(10,30), 0.05f, 0.5f, limb);

      axis = (Math.random( ) < 0.5) ? Z_AXIS : X_AXIS;
      if (Math.random( ) < 0.85)
        makeChild(axis, randomRange(-30,-10), 0.05f, 0.5f, limb);
    }
```

The four conditions only permit a child limb to appear if the parent is at least five time intervals old, the total number of limbs in the scene is less or equal to 256, the parent has no leaves, and the branch isn't too far up the tree.

Math.random( ) is used to randomize the orientation axis and make it less certain that two children will be spawned. randomRange( ) returns a random number (in this case, an angle) in the specified range.

makeChild( )'s definition is:

```
private void makeChild(int axis, double angle, float rad,
                                float len, TreeLimb par)
{ TransformGroup startLimbTG = par.getEndLimbTG( );
  TreeLimb child = new TreeLimb(axis, angle, rad, len, startLimbTG, par);
  treeLimbs.add(child);    // add new limb to the ArrayList
} // end of makeChild( )
```

Leaves are spawned with the following rule:

```
if ( (limb.getLevel( ) > 3) && (Math.random( ) < 0.08) &&
     (limb.getNumChildren( ) == 0) && !limb.hasLeaves( ) )
  makeLeaves(limb);
```

If a limb is far enough up the tree and has no children or existing leaves, then it will
have a small chance of bursting into leaf. makeLeaves( ) packages up the creation of
two ImageCsSeries objects, which are passed to the TreeLimb object:

```
private void makeLeaves(TreeLimb limb)
{
  ImageCsSeries frontLeafShape = new ImageCsSeries(0.5f, 2.0f, leafIms);
  ImageCsSeries backLeafShape = new ImageCsSeries(-0.5f, 2.0f, leafIms);
  limb.addLeaves(frontLeafShape, backLeafShape);
}
```

Displaying Leaves

An ImagesCsSeries object is a quadrilateral (quad), centered at (0, 0, 0), that can display an image from a series passed to it in an ImageComponent2D array. Only the
opaque parts of the image are shown, and the quad is invisible. The quad is a subclass of OrientedShape3D, configured to rotate around the point (0, 0, zCoord) relative
to its origin.

The first image in the array is automatically displayed, but then methods must be
called to change the picture; there is no default animation.

A version of ImageCsSeries with animation can be found in FPShooter3D
in Chapter 24.

The constructor sets up the rotation point:

```
public ImageCsSeries(float zCoord, float screenSize, ImageComponent2D[] ims)
{ this.ims = ims;
  imIndex = 0;
  numImages = ims.length;
```

```
        // set the orientation mode
    setAlignmentMode(OrientedShape3D.ROTATE_ABOUT_POINT);
    setRotationPoint(0.0f, 0.0f, zCoord);

    createGeometry(screenSize);
    createAppearance( );
}
```

A look back at the makeLeaves( ) method, used by the leaf creation rule, shows that
two ImageCsSeries screens are created with different rotation points: one 0.5 units in
front of its location and the other 0.5 units behind. This means that the two screens
will rotate differently as the user's viewpoint moves around a tree. This creates a
much larger mass of leaves that always seems to surround the tree limb, as illustrated by Figure 28-5.

Figure 28-5. Leaves around each limb

The createGeometry( ) and createAppearance( ) methods are unchanged from the
version of the class in FPShooter3D in Chapter 24. The geometry is a mix of coordinates and texture information. The appearance employs a blended form of transparency so transparent parts of the image won't be rendered.

The ImageCsSeries class in FPShooter3D uses a time-delayed loop triggered by a call to
showSeries( ). The Trees3D version has several methods for replacing the currently
displayed image with another one. Here is one example:

```
    public void showNext( )
    // show the next image in the sequence
    { if (imIndex < numImages-1) {
        imIndex++;
        texture.setImage(0, ims[imIndex]);
      }
    }
```

Comparison with L-Systems

L-systems consist of rewrite rules and have been widely used for plant modeling and simulation. Perhaps surprisingly, there is a direct mapping between the string expansions of a rule system and the visual representation of a plant. An example, using a bracketed L-system, will give an idea of how this works.

The L-system contains one start string F and rewrite rule:

```
F --> F [-F] F [+F] F
```

The start symbol represents the initial plant form; in this case, F is a single plant limb. The rewrite rule specifies how the symbol on the left of the --> should be replaced or expanded to create the longer sequence of symbols on the right of the -->. The rewrite rule replaces F with the sequence F[-F]F[+F].

The visual characterization is obtained by thinking of each F in the sequence as a limb of the plant. The bracketed notation is viewed as a branch-creation operator; the - is a rotation to the right for the branch, and the + is a left rotation. Consequently, the rewrite of F to F[-F]F[+F] can be seen as the plant expansion in Figure 28-6.

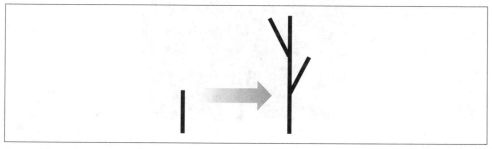

Figure 28-6. First rewrite of F

The rewrite rule can be applied again to each F symbol in the F[-F]F[+F]sequence, producing a longer sequence. Repeated application of the rewrite rule creates ever larger sequences with more complex plant-like shapes as in Figure 28-7.

Perhaps the richest L-system language is cpfg, available from *http://www.cpsc. ucalgary.ca/Research/bmv/*. It includes a full range of programming constructs, data structures, library functions, and various extensions, such as parameterized L-system symbols and sub-L-systems.

Two good introductions to L-Systems, both available online, are "An Introduction to Lindenmayer Systems" by Gabriela Ochoa (*http://www.cogs.susx.ac.uk/lab/nlp/ gazdar/teach/atc/1998/web/ochoa/*) and "Simulating Plant Growth" by Marco Grubert in *ACM Crossroads Student Magazine* (*http://www.acm.org/crossroads/xrds8-2/ plantsim.html*).

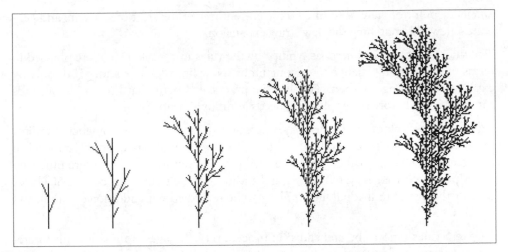

Figure 28-7. A sequence of rewrites

Java 3D and L-Systems

Java 3D was used by René Gressly to implement L-systems for growing bushes, trees, and flowers in a landscape. The user chooses where to place plants and then walks around the scene as the plants grow (*http://www.hta-bi.bfh.ch/~swc/DemoJ3D/VirtualPlants/*).

Chris Buckalew implemented a Java 3D L-Systems engine that uses recursion to parse the start string and replace string elements. It's part of a lab exercise in his CSC 474 Computer Graphics course (*http://www.csc.calpoly.edu/~buckalew/474Lab7-W02.html*).

Scott Teresi has written code that reads a 2D L-System and renders it in 3D (*http://teresi.us/html/main/programming.html*)

So Why Not Use L-Systems?

The truth is that originally I did use L-systems. A student and I developed code along the lines of Chris Buckalew's example. Unfortunately, the heavy use of recursion meant that only one or two trees of perhaps 10 or so levels could be generated before Java required a major memory extension.

The real problem is with the L-system formalism, which has difficulty representing incremental change using L-system rewrite rules. As Figure 28-7 indicates, each expansion creates a more complex tree, but it is hard to see how the fancier tree has grown out of the simpler one. What part of the current tree is new wood, and which is old wood that has grown a bit?

An L-system sees growth as a new tree completely replacing the old one. That doesn't matter when the tree is a mathematical abstraction but has consequences when implementing growth in Java 3D. The natural approach, and the most disastrous from an efficiency point of view, is to discard the current tree at the start of a rewrite and generate a new one matching the new string expansion.

The rules notation used here, as typified by the rules in applyRules( ), are phrased in terms of incremental change to existing limbs. New limbs can be added, but only by explicitly spawning children. This has the practical benefit that thousands of limbs can be created before the application needs additional heap space.

Another drawback of the Lindenmayer notation is its lack of tree nomenclature. For instance, it's impossible to talk about the parent of a node, its children, its level in the tree, and so on. To be fair, some of these capabilities can be programmed by using parameterized L-system rules, and basic L-systems have no notion of global time or the age of individual limbs. This can be remedied with additional parameters in rules.

L-system rules tend to be embedded in procedural languages, so it's difficult to create new plant node types (or classes) with their own data, operators, and behavior. This presents no problem to Java of course; I could start by subclassing TreeLimb.

Networking Basics

This chapter runs through networking fundamentals and explains basic network programming with sockets, URLs, and servlets. It serves as background for the next three chapters on networked games. Chapter 30 is about online chat, the "hello world" of network programming. I will look at three chat variants: one using a client/server model, one employing multicasting, and one illustrating chatting with servlets. Chapter 32 describes a networked version of the FourByFour application, a turn-based game demo in the Java 3D distribution and revisits the Tour3D application in Chapter 18 (the robot walking about a checkerboard landscape) and adds networking to allow multiple users to share the world. I will discuss some of the advanced issues concerning networked virtual environments (NVEs), of which NetTour3D is a simple example.

This chapter provides:

- Descriptions of the core attributes of network communication
- Explanations of IP, User Datagram Protocol (UDP), Transmission Control Protocol (TCP), network addresses, and sockets
- Overviews of the client/server and peer-to-peer models
- Four client/server applications, illustrating the sequential, threaded, nonblocking multiplexing, and UDP multiplexing techniques
- A small peer-to-peer application, as an example of UDP multicasting
- A discussion of the programming problems caused by firewalls, motivating an introduction to URLs and servlets for HTTP tunneling
- A few words about Java networking with JSSE, RMI, and Jini

 The various programming examples in this chapter can be found in the *NetBasics/* directory.

The Elements of Network Communication

Network communication is often characterized by five attributes: topology, bandwidth, latency, reliability, and protocol. I'll consider each one briefly.

Topology

Topology is the interconnection shape of machines linked over a network. Popular shapes are the ring, star, and all-to-all, illustrated by Figure 29-1.

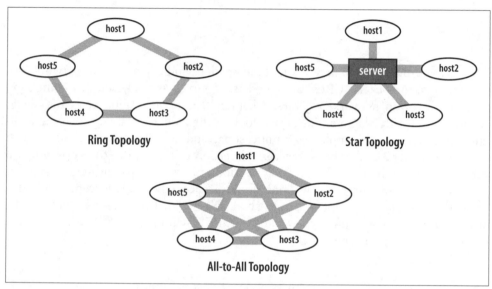

Figure 29-1. Some network topologies

Choosing the best topology for an application is a complicated matter depending on many network characteristics, such as bandwidth, latency, and the particular communication patterns inherent in the system.

The star topology, present in client/server applications, is the most popular; the all-to-all topology appears (in modified forms) in peer-to-peer systems.

Bandwidth

Bandwidth is the rate at which the network can deliver data from a sender to the destination host. Modems can typically deliver anywhere from 14,400 to 56,000 bits per second (14.4 to 56 Kbps), Ethernet can attain 10 to 100 Mbps (million bits per second), with newer technologies offering 1 Gbps (gigabits per second). Fiber-optic cable exhibits speeds of up to 10 Gbps.

Dial-up usage is declining rapidly in the United States, but 49.31% of users still connect with modems, according to July 2004 figures from Nielsen/NetRatings (*http://www.nielsen-netratings.com/*). Specifically, 40.49% use 56-Kbps modems, 6.22% have 28/33.3 Kbps, and 2.60% are stuck with 14.4-Kbps modems. Also, 66.2% of people used modems the previous year, in March 2003.

An estimated 150 million broadband lines were in place worldwide by the end of 2004, including all kinds of mass-market broadband services, such as DSL, cable modems, and fiber optic. Usage is growing even faster than the uptake of mobile phones (*http://www.internetworldstats.com/articles/art030.htm*).

Research by Bolt Lab from January 2005 indicates that 70% of the Gen-Y group (15–22-year-olds) in the United States use broadband to access the Internet (*http://biz.yahoo.com/prnews/050114/nyf005_1.html*). Of those teens, 50% use a cable modem, 44% use DSL, and 6% a T1/T3 line.

Nevertheless, 56 Kbps is probably a realistic bandwidth estimate for most users, at least for 2005.

Bandwidth restricts the number of players in a game: too many participants will swamp the network with data traffic. However, the nature of the extra load depends on topology. For example, a message sent around a ring will have to travel through many links, occupying bandwidth for a longer amount of time. A message traveling through a star topology only requires two links to go from any sender to any receiver, and a message in an all-to-all topology goes directly to its destination.

A knowledge of the available bandwidth allows us to estimate upper limits for the amount of data that can be transferred per each frame rendered in a game and to suggest a likely maximum for the number of users.

A 56-Kbps modem means 7,000 bytes can be transferred per second. I'll assume that the game updates at 30 frames per second (FPS), and each player sends and receives data from all the other players during each frame update. The total amount of data that can be transferred to each frame is 7,000/30 ≈ 233 bytes per frame. This is about 117 bytes for output, 117 bytes for input.

If there are n players, then each player will send (n – 1) output messages and receive (n – 1) input messages at each frame update. As n increases, the 117 bytes limit will be quickly reached.

I can estimate the maximum number of users by starting with a lower bound for the amount of data that must be transferred during each frame update. For instance, if the lower bound is 20 bytes and there's 117 bytes available for output, then a maximum of about six messages can be sent out (117/20), which means seven players in the game.

These kinds of ballpark figures explain why games programmers try hard to avoid broadcast models linked to frame rate and why transmitted data is kept as small as possible. Some techniques for reducing data transmission in multiplayer games are discussed in Chapter 32, when I develop a networked version of the Tour3D application.

A network protocol solution is to move from a broadcast model to multicasting. *Multicasting* is a form of subscription-based message distribution: a player sends a single message to a multicast group, where it's automatically distributed to all the other players currently subscribed to that group. The saving is in the number of messages sent out: one instead of n − 1.

A similar saving can be made in a star topology: a player sends a single message to the server, which then sends copies to the other players. This is a software solution, dependent on the server's implementation, which allows for further server-side optimizations of the communication protocols.

Latency

Latency is the amount of time required to transfer data from one place to another (typically from one player's machine to another). In a Massively Multiplayer Online Role-Playing Game (MMORPG), latency exhibits itself as the delays when two players are interacting (e.g., shooting at each other); the goal is to reduce latency as much as possible.

Most latency can be accounted for by the modems involved in the network: typically each one adds 30–40 ms to the transfer time. A client/server system may involve four modems between the sending of a message and its reception by another user: the sender's modem, the modem inbound to the server, the modem outbound from the server, and the receiver's modem result in a total latency of perhaps 160 ms.

Another major contributor, especially over the Internet, are routers, which may easily add hundreds of milliseconds. This is due to their caching of data before forwarding and delays while a router decides where to send a message. Routers may drop data when overloaded, which can introduce penalties in the 400–500 ms range for protocols (like TCP), which detect lost data and resend it.

Another issue is the speed of light because games would certainly benefit if it were faster. A message sent from the East Coast to the West Coast of the United States will take about 20 ms to get there. In general, about 8 ms are added to the travel time for each time zone that a message passes through.

Designers often incorporate tolerances of 250 ms into the communication models used in games. A key observation is that most games don't require complete synchronization between all the players all the time. Synchronization is usually important only for small groups of players (e.g., those in close proximity inside the game world) and then only at certain moments.

This relaxing of the synchronization requirement opens the door to various approaches based on temporarily "guessing" information about other players. For instance, the game running on the user's machine estimates other players' current positions and velocities and corrects them when the correct data arrive over the network.

Another implementation strategy is to decouple general game play from the networking side of the application. A separate thread (or process) waits for incoming data, so the rest of the application can continue unaffected.

Latency is essentially a WAN or Internet issue; applications running over a LAN rarely need to consider latency, which may total less than 10 ms.

Reliability

Increased network reliability may increase latency time. For example, the possibility that a message could be lost while traveling over the network led to the development of the TCP protocol, which deals with data loss by resending. The disadvantage is that the actual arrival time of a message can increase, affecting latency.

A desire to measure reliability has led to more complex checking of data based on cyclic redundancy checks (CRCs), which add further overheads.

An alternative approach is to live with a certain degree of unreliability, reducing overheads as a consequence. Many forms of Internet-based multimedia, such as streaming audio and video, take this view because losing small amounts of data only means a momentary loss in sound or picture quality. The rapid transmission of the data is a more valued attribute.

Protocol

A protocol is a notation for specifying the communication patterns between the components of a networked application. Different protocols support different capabilities, with the choice of protocol depending on many factors, such as the type of data being transmitted, the number of destinations, and the required reliability. Most gaming application uses multiple protocols: one for data, another for control, and perhaps others specialized for particular types of data such as audio or video.

Different protocols exist for different levels of communication, which are defined in the ISO OSI model (see Figure 29-2).

A *protocol suite* is a collection of related protocols for different layers of the OSI model. The most popular is TCP/IP, originally developed by DARPA in the early 1980s. Its wide popularity stems from being implemented on everything from PCs to supercomputers, not being vendor-specific, and its suitability for all kinds of networks, from LANs up to the Internet.

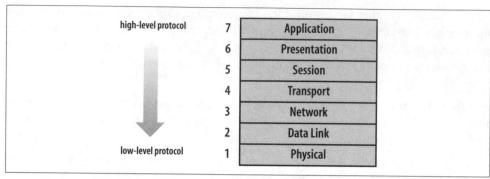

Figure 29-2. The ISO OSI model

This isn't a book about data communications, so I'll only consider TCP/IP within a simplified version of the OSI model, limited to four layers. Communication between two networked systems can be viewed (see Figure 29-3).

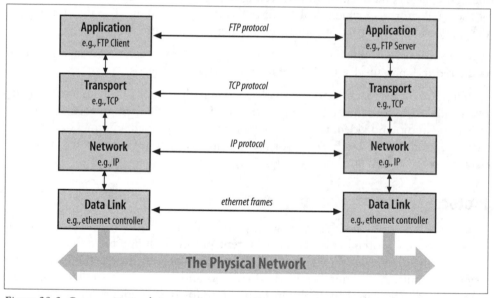

Figure 29-3. Communication between two systems

Figure 29-3 shows that application-level protocols, which include FTP, HTTP (the web protocol), and SMTP (the email protocol), are implemented on top of lower-level protocols (TCP or UDP).

At a particular layer, the data appears to cross directly to the equivalent layer on the other system. In fact, data is passed down through the layers, across the physical network, and back up through the layers of the other system. As each layer is descended, the user's data is wrapped inside more header (and footer) information. The headers (and footers) are removed as the data rises through the layers on the other system.

The data link layer corresponds to the OSI physical and data layers. Frames are delivered between two directly connected machines.

The network layer delivers datagrams between any two machines on the Internet, which may be separated by intervening gateways/routers. Each datagram is routed independently, which means that two datagrams sent from the same source may travel along different paths and may arrive in a different order from the way they were sent. Since a gateway/router has limited memory, it may discard datagrams if too many arrive at once. A node or link in the network may fail, losing packets. For these reasons, the IP protocol makes no guarantees that a datagram will arrive at its destination.

A datagram has size constraints, which often force a single piece of user data to be divided into multiple datagrams. The data arriving at the receiver may, therefore, have missing pieces and parts in the wrong order.

A datagram is sent to an IP address, which represents a machine's address as a 32-bit integer. Programs usually employ IP addresses in dotted-decimal form (e.g., 172.30.0.5) or as a dotted-name (e.g., fivedots.coe.psu.ac.th). Translation of dotted-name form to an IP address is carried out using a combination of local machine configuration information and network naming services such as the Domain Name System (DNS).

The IP protocol is currently in transition from Version 4 to Version 6 (IPv6), which supports 128-bit addresses, a simpler header, multicasting, authentication, and security elements. Java supports IPv4 and IPv6 through its InetAddress class.

The transport layer delivers datagrams between transport endpoints (machine ports) for any two machines on the Internet. An application's location is specified by the IP address of its host, and the number of the port where it is "listening." A port number is a 16-bit integer.

The TCP/IP transport layer protocols are UDP and TCP.

UDP is a connectionless transport service: a user message is split into datagrams and each datagram is sent along an available path to its destination. There is no (expensive) long-term, dedicated link created between the two systems. UDP inherits the drawbacks of the IP protocol: datagrams may arrive in any order, and a datagram has no guarantee of arriving. UDP is often compared to the postal service.

TCP is a connection-oriented transport service. From the user's point of view, a long-term, dedicated link is set up between the sender and receiver, and two-way stream-based communication then becomes possible. For this reason, TCP is often compared to the telephone service.

However, the dedicated link is implemented on top of IP, so packets of information are still being sent with the chance of reordering and loss. Consequently, TCP employs sophisticated internal error-checking to ensure that its component TCP datagrams arrive in the order they were sent and that none will be lost. This overhead may be too severe for gaming applications that value low latency.

UDP and TCP use a socket data structure to represent an endpoint in the communication. For UDP, the socket is something like a mailbox; for TCP socket it is more like a telephone.

Java supports both TCP and UDP. A programmer uses the Socket class for creating a sender's TCP socket and the ServerSocket class for the recipient. Java offers the DatagramSocket for both sides of UDP communication and a DatagramPacket class for creating UDP packets.

The Client/Server Model

The client/server model is the most common networking architecture employed in distributed applications. A server is a program (or collection of cooperating programs) that provides services and/or manages resources on the behalf of other programs, known as its clients. Figure 29-4 shows a typical client/server environment.

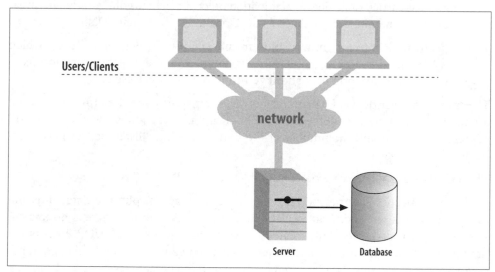

Figure 29-4. A simple client/server

A key advantage of the client/server approach is the ability for the server to control its clients by localizing important processing and data within itself. For example, in online games, decisions about the outcome of a player's actions (e.g., the shooting of a monster) will be made by the server. The alternative is to delegate this to the client's application, which may lead to abuse by hackers.

A central location for client data and processing makes it easier to monitor users, administer them, and charge them for game playing. These are significant benefits for commercial multiplayer gaming.

The server is an arbiter for conflicting client requests. For instance, it's impossible for two clients to update the same data state simultaneously.

Placing state information in one place makes changing it straightforward and avoids inconsistencies arising when updating multiple copies stored on clients.

Concentrating processing on the server side permits the client side to run on a less powerful machine, an important consideration for network applications on PDAs or phones.

Concentrating most of the application in the server makes it is easier to maintain and update, compared to upgrading code spread over a large, possibly nontechnical, user base.

The main disadvantage of a "fat" server is the potential for it to become a bottleneck, overloaded by too many clients, and increasing latency to unacceptable levels. Excessive numbers of clients may overload the server's data storage capacity.

Another significant issue is reliability in that if the server fails, then everyone will be affected. Almost as bad as failure is the (temporary) nonavailability of the server because it's currently dealing with too many users, due to a hacker attack, or it's been taken offline for servicing or upgrades.

These concerns have led to the widespread use of multiple servers, sometimes specialized for different elements of client processing, or acting as duplicates, ready to substitute for a server that fails. Different servers may be in different geographical locations, catering only to clients in those areas, which improves latency times.

Many MMORPGs map areas of their virtual world to different physical servers (e.g., Ultima Online). When clients move across a boundary in the world, they are switched to a different server. This acts as a form of load balancing, though its success depends on the different zones having roughly the same levels of popularity.

High-powered servers are expensive, especially ones with complex database management, transaction processing, security, and reliability capabilities.

A successful application (game) will require an expensive, high-speed Internet connection. A predicted trend is that gaming companies will start to offer their own backbone networks, giving them greater control over bandwidth, latency, and the specification of firewall access. This latter point will make it easier for applications to use multiple protocols (e.g., UDP for data, TCP for commands) without worrying about clients being unable to create the necessary communication links due to firewall restrictions.

The Peer-to-Peer Model

Peer-to-peer (P2P) encourages users to share their resources with others; resources include hard-disk storage, CPU time, and files (audio, video). This is different from today's Web/Internet in which business/government/university servers present information, and the rest of us read it. The difference is illustrated by Figure 29-5.

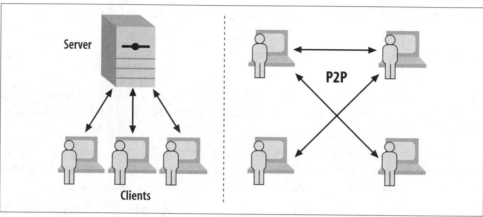

Figure 29-5. Client/server versus P2P

P2P isn't a new idea: the early Internet (at that time, the ARPANET) was designed to be P2P so U.S. universities and government installations could share computing resources.

Many of the killer apps of the 1980s, such as Telnet and email, were client/server-based but their usage patterns were symmetric—i.e., most machines ran clients and servers. Usenet (net news) is a P2P application: it employs a decentralized file-sharing model for distributing news, but an unofficial backbone has developed over time, based around server inequalities in storage capacity, processing speeds, and network connectivity.

Things started to change with the growth of the Web. It's a client/server model like most of the earlier applications, but differences lie in its political and social components. Most users only browse the Web; they don't run their own web servers. This is due to the user's lack of technical knowledge, the difficulty of setting up a server, and because commercial ISPs prohibit server installation. Many ISPs allocate dynamic addresses only to clients, making the running of servers impossible, and impose firewall restrictions that only permit web-page access. Broadband connections, such as cable modems, offer asymmetric bandwidth, which makes the serving of material slow.

The restrictions on users (e.g., firewalls) are recent, triggered by the lack of accountability mechanisms in the IP: the protocol lacks technological barriers to stop users sending spam and attacking machines. Its designers made the fatal assumption that users are responsible. The problem is sometimes called *the Tragedy of the Commons*: a commonly owned resource will be overused until it degrades, due to its users putting self-interest first.

The issue of accountability has led to better support for cryptography in IPv6 and experimental technologies such as micropayments and reputation schemes.

With micropayments, a person wishing to use someone else's resource (e.g., one of their files) must compensate that person in some way. This might be in the form of digital money or another valuable resource. Micropayments have the benefit of solving many forms of hacker attack, such as spam and distributed denial of service (DDoS), since hackers must pay an excessive amount to flood the network with their datagrams.

A reputation scheme typically requires a respected user to verify the reliability of a new user. This idea is well-known in Java, which utilizes encrypted signatures and third-party verifiers to identify trusted JAR files and applets. Some of the technicalities are explored in Appendix B, where I consider how to sign files that are downloaded and installed using Java Web Start.

Many P2P systems are concerned with anonymity to prevent external agencies knowing who is in a P2P group, where files are stored, and who has published what. These aims make accountability and trust harder to support.

Part of the drive behind these P2P features was the fate of Napster, which was closed down because it published music files that it hadn't authored. Napster could be targeted because it was a hybrid of P2P and client/server: a Napster server stored details about who was logged on and the published files. Unfortunately, this is a common situation; most current P2P systems require some server capabilities. For instance, games must validate new players, maintain account information, supply current status information for the game, and notify other users when a player joins or leaves.

Pure P2P has the advantage that there's no central point (no server) whose demise would cause the entire system to come crashing down. This makes P2P resistant to attacks such as DDoS and legal rulings!

The main drawback of pure P2P is paradoxically its lack of a server, which makes it difficult to control and manage the overall application. With no server, how does a new user discover what's available?

The P2P diagram in Figure 29-5 suggests that participants use broadcasting to communicate, but this approach soon consumes all the available bandwidth for reasons outlined earlier. Large-scale P2P applications use IP multicasting with UDP packets, which currently relies on the MBone, a virtual overlay installed on the Internet to facilitate multicasting. A special pseudo-IP address, called a multicast IP address or class D address, is employed, which can be in the range 224.0.0.0 to 239.255.255.255 (though some addresses are reserved).

Multicasting avoids the potential for loops and packet duplication inherent in broadcasting since it creates a tree-based communication pattern between the multicast group members. Java supports IP multicasting with UDP.

JXTA provides core functionality so that developers can build P2P services and applications (see *http://www.jxta.org/*). The core JXTA layer includes protocols and building blocks to enable key mechanisms for P2P networking. These include discovery, transport (e.g., firewall handling and limited security), and the creation of peers and peer groups.

The JXTA specification isn't tied to any particular programming language or platform/device. Its communication model is general enough so that it can be implemented on top of TCP/IP, HTTP, Bluetooth, and many other protocols. Currently JXTA utilizes Java; it was initiated at Sun Microsystems by Bill Joy and Mike Clary. A good site for finding out about P2P is O'Reilly's *http://www.openp2p.com/*.

Client/Server Programming in Java

The four examples in this section have a similar structure: the server maintains a high scores list, and the clients read and add scores to the list. Here are the four variants of this idea:

1. A client and sequential server. The server can process only one client at a time. The TCP/IP protocol is utilized.

2. The same client and the same protocol as (1), but the server is threaded, enabling it to process multiple clients at the same time. Synchronization issues arise because the high score list may be accessed by multiple threads at the same time.

3. The same client and the same protocol as (1) and (2), but Java's NIO is used to implement a multiplexing server without the need of threads.

4. A client and server using UDP. The server exhibits multiplexing due to the self-contained nature of datagram communication.

TCP Client and Sequential Server

The communications network created by the client and server is shown in Figure 29-6.

The server instantiates a ServerSocket object at port 1234 and waits for a connection from a client by calling accept( ). When a connection is established, a new socket is created (some people call this a *rendezvous socket*), which is used for the subsequent communication with the client. Input and output streams are layered on top of the socket, utilizing the bidirectional nature of a TCP link. When the client has finished, the rendezvous socket is closed (terminated), and the server waits for another connection.

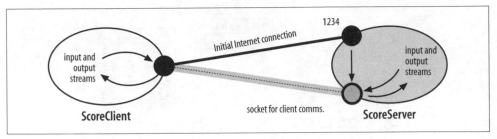

Figure 29-6. Client and sequential server

The client instantiates a Socket object to link to the server at its specified IP address and port. When a connection is obtained, the client layers input and output streams on top of its socket and commences communication.

A great aid to understanding networked applications is to understand the protocol employed between clients and the server. In simple examples (such as the ones in this chapter), that means the message interactions between network entities.

A client can send the following messages, which terminate with a newline character:

get
> The server returns the high score list.

score name & score &
> The server adds the name/score pair to its list.

bye
> The server closes the client's connection.

A client only receives one kind of message from the server, the high scores list, which is sent in response to a get request. The list is sent as a string terminated with a newline character. The string has this format:

    HIGH$$ name1 & score1 & .... nameN & scoreN &

The server stores only 10 names and scores at most, so the string is unlikely to be excessively long.

Class diagrams

The class diagrams for this example are given in Figure 29-7. Only the public methods are shown.

A HighScores object manages the high scores list, with each name/score pair held in a ScoreInfo object.

> The client code (ScoreClient) can be found in the *NetBasics/* directory, while the sequential server (ScoreServer and its support classes) is in *NetBasics/Sequential/*. ScoreClient is used as the client for the sequential, threaded, and multiplexing servers.

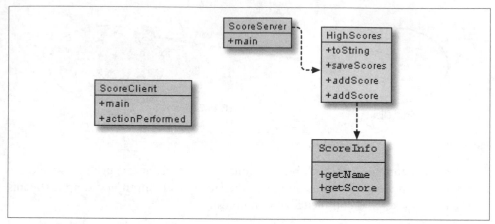

Figure 29-7. Classes for the client and sequential server

The sequential score server

The constructor for the ScoreServer creates the ServerSocket object, then enters a loop that waits for a client connection by calling accept( ). When accept( ) returns, the server processes the client and goes back to waiting for the next connection:

```
public ScoreServer( )
{
  hs = new HighScores( );
  try {
    ServerSocket serverSock = new ServerSocket(PORT);
    Socket clientSock;
    BufferedReader in;     // i/o for the server
    PrintWriter out;

    while (true) {
      System.out.println("Waiting for a client...");
      clientSock = serverSock.accept( );
      System.out.println("Client connection from " +
                 clientSock.getInetAddress( ).getHostAddress( ) );

      // Get I/O streams from the socket
      in  = new BufferedReader(  new InputStreamReader(
                                  clientSock.getInputStream( ) ) );
      out = new PrintWriter( clientSock.getOutputStream( ), true );

      processClient(in, out); // interact with a client

      // Close client connection
      clientSock.close( );
      System.out.println("Client connection closed\n");
      hs.saveScores( );       // backup scores after client finish
    }
  }
  catch(Exception e)
```

```
    { System.out.println(e);  }
  }  // end of ScoreServer()
```

The server-side socket is created with the ServerSocket class:

```
ServerSocket serverSock = new ServerSocket(PORT);
```

The waiting for a connection is done via a call to accept( ):

```
Socket clientSock;
clientSock = serverSock.accept();
```

When accept( ) returns, it instantiates the rendezvous socket, clientSock. clientSock can be used to retrieve client details, such as its IP address and host name.

The input stream is a BufferedReader to allow calls to readLine( ). Since client messages end with a newline, this is a convenient way to read them. The output stream is a PrintWriter, allowing println( ) to be employed. The stream's creation includes a Boolean to switch on auto-flushing, so there's no delay between printing and output to the client:

```
in = new BufferedReader( new InputStreamReader( clientSock.getInputStream() ));
out = new PrintWriter( clientSock.getOutputStream(), true);
```

The client is processed by a call to processClient( ), which contains the application-specific coding. Almost all the rest of ScoreServer is reusable in different sequential servers.

When processClient( ) returns, the communication has finished and the client link can be closed:

```
clientSock.close();
```

The call to saveScores( ) in the HighScores object is a precautionary measure: it saves the high scores list to a file, so data won't be lost if the server crashes.

Most of the code inside the constructor is inside a try-catch block to handle I/O and network exceptions.

Processing a client

processClient( ) deals with message extraction from the input stream, which is complicated by having to deal with link termination.

The connection may close because of a network fault, which is detected by a null being returned by the read, or may be signaled by the client sending a "bye" message. In both cases, the loop in processClient( ) finishes, passing control back to the ScoreServer constructor:

```
private void processClient(BufferedReader in, PrintWriter out)
{
  String line;
  boolean done = false;
  try {
    while (!done) {
```

```
         if((line = in.readLine()) == null)
           done = true;
         else {
           System.out.println("Client msg: " + line);
           if (line.trim().equals("bye"))
             done = true;
           else
             doRequest(line, out);
         }
       }
     }
   catch(IOException e)
   {  System.out.println(e);  }
 }  // end of processClient()
```

The method uses a try-catch block to deal with possible I/O problems.

processClient() does a very common task and is portable across various applications. It requires that the termination message ("bye") can be read using readLine().

doRequest() deals with the remaining two kinds of client message: "get" and "score". Most of the work in doRequest() involves the checking of the input message embedded in the request string. The score processing is carried out by the HighScores object:

```
private void doRequest(String line, PrintWriter out)
{
  if (line.trim().toLowerCase().equals("get")) {
    System.out.println("Processing 'get'");
    out.println( hs.toString() );
  }
  else if ((line.length() >= 6) &&       // "score"
      (line.substring(0,5).toLowerCase().equals("score"))) {
    System.out.println("Processing 'score'");
    hs.addScore( line.substring(5) );    // cut the score keyword
  }
  else
    System.out.println("Ignoring input line");
}
```

It's a good idea to include a default else case to deal with unknown messages. In doRequest(), the server only reports, problems to standard output on the server side. It may be advisable to send a message back to the client.

Maintaining the scores information

The HighScores object maintains an array of ScoreInfo objects, which it initially populates by calling loadScores() to load the *scores.txt* text file from the current directory. saveScores() writes the array's contents back into *scores.txt*.

It's preferable to maintain simple data (such as these name/score pairs) in text form rather than a serialized object. This makes the data easy to examine and edit with ordinary text-processing tools.

The scores client

The ScoreClient class seems complicated because of its GUI interface, shown in Figure 29-8.

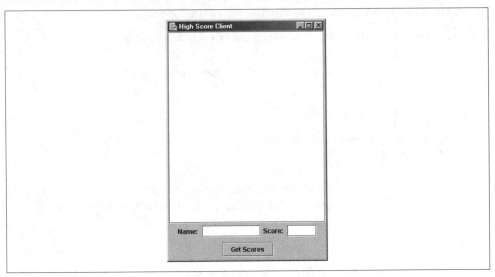

Figure 29-8. A ScoreClient object

The large text area is represented by the jtaMesgs object. Two text fields are used for entering a name and score. Pressing Enter in the score field will trigger a call to actionPerformed( ) in the object, as will pressing the Get Scores button.

ScoreClient calls makeContact( ) to instantiate a Socket object for the server at its specified IP address and port. When the connection is made, input and output streams are layered on top of its socket:

```java
// global constants and variables
private static final int PORT = 1234;       // server details
private static final String HOST = "localhost";

private Socket sock;
private BufferedReader in;       // i/o for the client
private PrintWriter out;


private void makeContact()
{
  try {
    sock = new Socket(HOST, PORT);
    in  = new BufferedReader( new InputStreamReader( sock.getInputStream() ));
    out = new PrintWriter( sock.getOutputStream(), true );
  }
  catch(Exception e)
  {  System.out.println(e);  }
}
```

"localhost" is given as the server's host name since the server is running on the same machine as the client. "localhost" is a loopback address and can be employed even when the machine is disconnected from the Internet, though the TCP/IP must be set up in the OS. On most systems (including Windows), it's possible to type the command ping localhost to check the functioning of the loopback.

actionPerformed( ) differentiates between the two kinds of user input:

```
public void actionPerformed(ActionEvent e)
  /* Either a name/score is to be sent or the "Get Scores"
     button has been pressed. */
  {
    if (e.getSource( ) == jbGetScores)
      sendGet( );
    else if (e.getSource( ) == jtfScore)
      sendScore( );
  }
```

sendGet( ) shows how the client sends a message to the server (in this case a "get" string) and waits for a response (a "HIGH$$..." string), which it displays in the text area:

```
private void sendGet( )
{
// Send "get" command, read response and display it
// Response should be "HIGH$$ n1 & s1 & .... nN & sN & "
  try {
    out.println("get");
    String line = in.readLine( );
    System.out.println(line);
    if ((line.length( ) >= 7) &&      // "HIGH$$ "
       (line.substring(0,6).equals("HIGH$$")))
      showHigh( line.substring(6).trim( ) );
        // remove HIGH$$ keyword and surrounding spaces
    else    // should not happen
      jtaMesgs.append( line + "\n");
  }
  catch(Exception ex)
  { jtaMesgs.append("Problem obtaining high scores\n");
    System.out.println(ex);
  }
}
```

Figure 29-9 shows how the high score list looks in the text area window.

sendGet( ) makes the client wait for the server to reply:

```
out.println("get");
String line = in.readLine( );
```

This means the client will be unable to process further user commands until the server has sent back the high scores information. This is a bad design strategy for more complex client applications. The chat client from Chapter 30 shows how

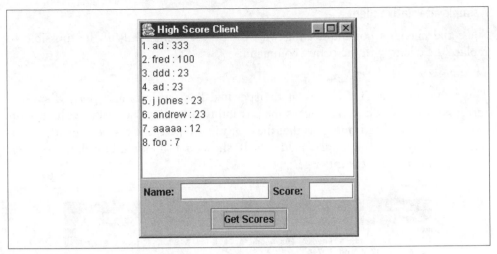

Figure 29-9. High scores output in the client

threads can be employed to separate network interaction from the rest of the application.

The client should send a "bye" message before breaking a connection, and this is achieved by calling closeLink( ) when the client's close box is clicked:

```java
public ScoreClient()
{   super( "High Score Client" );

    initializeGUI();
    makeContact();

    addWindowListener( new WindowAdapter() {
      public void windowClosing(WindowEvent e)
      { closeLink(); }
    });

    setSize(300,450);
    setVisible(true);
} // end of ScoreClient();


private void closeLink()
{ try {
    out.println("bye");      // tell server
    sock.close();
  }
  catch(Exception e)
  { System.out.println( e );  }

  System.exit( 0 );
}
```

A simple alternative client

Since the client is communicating with the server using TCP/IP, it's possible to replace the client with the telnet command:

```
telnet localhost 1234
```

This will initiate a TCP/IP link at the specified host address and port, where the server is listening. The advantage is the possibility of testing the server without writing a client. The disadvantage is that the user must type the messages directly, without the help of a GUI interface. Figure 29-10 shows a Telnet window after the server has responded to a "get" message.

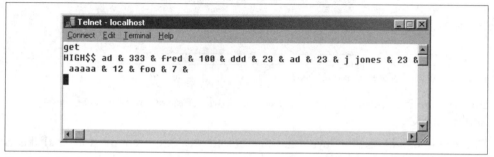

Figure 29-10. A Telnet client

It may be necessary to switch on the Local Echo feature in Telnet's preferences dialog before the user's typing (e.g., the "get" message) is seen on-screen.

TCP Client and Multithreaded Server

The ScoreServer class of the previous example is inadequate for real server-side applications because it can only deal with one client at a time. The ThreadedScoreServer class described in this section solves that problem by creating a thread (a ThreadedScoreHandler object) to process each client who connects. Since a thread interacts with each client, the main server is free to accept multiple connections. Figure 29-11 shows this in diagram form.

The ScoreClient class needn't be changed: a client is unaware that it's talking to a thread.

The HighScores object is referenced by all the threads (indicated by the dotted lines in Figure 29-11), so the scores can be read and changed. The possibility of change means that the data inside HighScores must be protected from concurrent updates by multiple threads and from an update occurring at the same time as the scores are being read. These synchronization problems are quite easily solved, as detailed in the rest of this section.

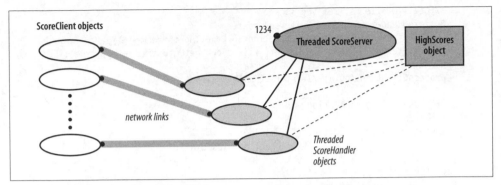

Figure 29-11. Clients and multithreaded server

 The code for the multithreaded server (ThreadedScoreServer and its support classes) is in *NetBasics/Threaded/*. The client code (ScoreClient) can be found in the *NetBasics/* directory.

ThreadedScoreServer is simpler than its sequential counterpart since it no longer processes client requests. It consists only of a constructor that sets up a loop waiting for client contacts, handled by threads:

```
public ThreadedScoreServer( )
{
  hs = new HighScores( );
  try {
    ServerSocket serverSock = new ServerSocket(PORT);
    Socket clientSock;
    String cliAddr;

    while (true) {
      System.out.println("Waiting for a client...");
      clientSock = serverSock.accept( );
      cliAddr = clientSock.getInetAddress( ).getHostAddress( );
      new ThreadedScoreHandler(clientSock, cliAddr, hs).start( );
    }
  }
  catch(Exception e)
  {  System.out.println(e);  }
}  // end of ThreadedScoreServer( )
```

Each thread gets a reference to the client's rendezvous socket and the HighScores object.

ThreadedScoreHandler contains almost identical code to the sequential ScoreServer class; for example, it has processClient( ) and doRequest( ) methods. The main difference is the run( ) method:

```
public void run( )
{
  try {
```

```
              // Get I/O streams from the socket
              BufferedReader in  = new BufferedReader(
                      new InputStreamReader( clientSock.getInputStream() ));
              PrintWriter out = new PrintWriter( clientSock.getOutputStream(), true);

              processClient(in, out); // interact with a client

              // Close client connection
              clientSock.close();
              System.out.println("Client (" + cliAddr +
                                      ") connection closed\n");
            }
          catch(Exception e)
          { System.out.println(e);  }
      }
```

A comparison with the sequential server shows that run( ) contains code like that executed in ScoreServer's constructor after a rendezvous socket is created.

Maintaining scores information

The ThreadedScoreHandler objects call HighScores's toString( ) and addScore( ) methods. toString( ) returns the current scores list as a string, addScore( ) updates the list. The danger of concurrent access to the scores list is easily avoided since the data is maintained in a single object referenced by all the threads. Manipulation only occurs through the toString( ) and addScore( ) methods.

A lock can be placed on the object by making the toString( ) and addScore( ) methods synchronized:

```
      synchronized public String toString()
      { ... }

      synchronized public void addScore(String line)
      { ... }
```

The lock means that only a single thread can be executing inside toString( ) or addScore( ) at any time. Concurrent access is no longer possible. This approach is relatively painless because of my decision to wrap the shared data (the scores list) inside a single shared object. A possible concern may be the impact on response times by prohibiting concurrent access, but toString( ) and addScores( ) are short, simple methods that quickly return after being called.

One advantage of the threaded handler approach isn't illustrated by this example: each handler can store client-specific data locally. For instance, each ThreadedScoreHandler could maintain information about the history of client communication in its session. Since this data is managed by each thread, the main server is relieved of unnecessary complexity.

TCP Client and Multiplexing Server

J2SE 1.4. introduced *nonblocking sockets*, which allow networked applications to communicate without blocking the processes/threads involved. This makes it possible to implement a server that can multiplex (switch) between different clients without the need for threads.

At the heart of this approach is a method called select( ), which may remind the Unix network programmers among you of the select( ) system call. They're closely related, and the coding of a multiplexing server in Java is similar to one written in C on Unix.

An advantage of the multiplexing server technique is the return to a single server without threads. This may be an important gain on a platform with limited resources. A related advantage is the absence of synchronization problems with shared data because there are no threads. The only process is the server.

A disadvantage is that any client-specific state (which had previously been placed in each thread) must be maintained by the server. For instance, if multiple clients are connected to the server, each with a communications history to be maintained, then those histories will have to be held by the server.

Nonblocking sockets mean that method calls that might potentially block forever, such as accept( ) and readLine( ), need to be executed only when data is known to be present or can be wrapped in timeouts. This is particularly useful for avoiding some forms of hacker attack or dealing with users who are too slow.

Figure 29-12 shows the various objects involved in the multiplexing server.

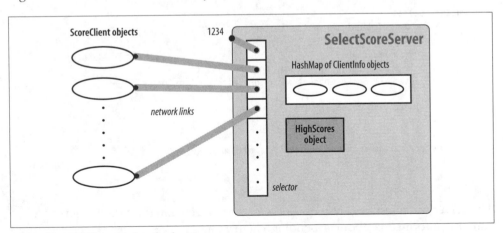

Figure 29-12. Clients and multiplexing server

Selector is the main new class in the nonblocking additions to Java. A Selector object can monitor multiple socket channels and returns a collection of *keys* (client requests) as required. A socket channel is a new type of socket (built using the SocketChannel class).

Each ClientInfo object in the hash map in Figure 29-12 contains details about a client and methods for receiving and sending messages to the client. The principal complexity of ClientInfo is in its handling of nonblocking client input.

The main purpose of the server is to listen to several socket channels at once by using a Selector object. Initially, the server's own socket channel is added to the selector, and subsequent connections by new clients, represented by new socket channels, are also added.

When input arrives from a client, it's read immediately. However, the input may contain only part of a message: there's no waiting for a complete message.

 The code for the multiplexing server (SelectScoreServer and its support classes) is in *NetBasics/NIO/*. The client code (ScoreClient) can be found in the *NetBasics/* directory.

The multiplexing scores server

A pseudocode algorithm for the server is given below:

```
create a SocketChannel for the server;
create a Selector;
register the SocketChannel with the Selector (for accepts);

while(true) {
  wait for keys (client requests) in the Selector;
  for each key in the Selector {
    if (key is Acceptable) {
      create a new SocketChannel for the new client;
      register the SocketChannel with the Selector (for reads);
    }
    else if (key is Readable) {
      extract the client SocketChannel from the key;
      read from the SocketChannel;
      store partial message, or process full message;
    }
  }
}
```

The server waits inside a while loop for keys to be generated by the Selector. A key contains information about a pending client request. A Selector object may store four types of key:

- A request by a new client to connect to the server (an isAcceptable key)
- A request by an existing client to deliver some input (an isReadable key)

- A request by an existing client for the server to send it data (an isWriteable key)
- A request by a server accepting a client connection (an isConnectable key)

The first two request types are used in my multiplexing server. The last type of key is typically employed by a nonblocking client to detect when a connection has been made with a server.

The socket channel for the server is created in the SelectScoreServer( ) constructor:

```
ServerSocketChannel serverChannel = ServerSocketChannel.open();
serverChannel.configureBlocking(false);   // use nonblocking mode

ServerSocket serverSocket = serverChannel.socket();
serverSocket.bind( new InetSocketAddress(PORT_NUMBER) );
```

The nonblocking nature of the socket is achieved by creating a ServerSocketChannel object and then by extracting a ServerSocket.

The server's socket channel has a Selector registered with it to collect connection requests:

```
Selector selector = Selector.open();
serverChannel.register(selector, SelectionKey.OP_ACCEPT);
```

Other possible options to register( ) are OP_READ, OP_WRITE, and OP_CONNECT, corresponding to the different types of keys.

The while loop in the pseudocode can be translated fairly directly into real code:

```
while (true) {
  selector.select();                      // wait for keys
  Iterator it = selector.selectedKeys().iterator();
  SelectionKey key;
  while (it.hasNext()) {                   // look at each key
    key = (SelectionKey) it.next();        // get a key
    it.remove();                           // remove it
    if (key.isAcceptable())        // a new connection?
      newChannel(key, selector);
    else if (key.isReadable())     // data to be read?
      readFromChannel(key);
    else
      System.out.println("Did not process key: " + key);
  }
}
```

Having the server accept a new client

newChannel( ) is called when a new client has requested a connection. The connection is accepted and registered with the selector to make it collect read requests (i.e., notifications that client data have arrived):

```
private void newChannel(SelectionKey key, Selector selector)
{
  try {
```

```
          ServerSocketChannel server = (ServerSocketChannel) key.channel( );
          SocketChannel channel = server.accept( );           // get channel
          channel.configureBlocking (false);          // use nonblocking
          channel.register(selector, SelectionKey.OP_READ);
                                   // register it with selector for reading

          clients.put(channel, new ClientInfo(channel, this) );   // store info
        }
        catch (IOException e)
        {  System.out.println( e ); }
      }
```

The call to accept( ) is nonblocking: it'll raise a NotYetBoundException if there's no
pending connection. The connection is represented by a SocketChannel (a nonblocking version of the Socket class), and this is registered with the Selector to collect its
read requests.

Since a new client has just accepted, a new ClientInfo object is added to the HashMap.
The key for the HashMap entry is the client's channel, which is unique.

Having the server accept a request from an existing client

readFromChannel( ) is called when there's a request by an existing client for the server
to read data. As mentioned earlier, this may not be a complete message, which introduces some problems. It's necessary to store partial messages until they're completed (a complete message ends with a \n). The reading and storage is managed by
the ClientInfo object for the client:

```
      private void readFromChannel(SelectionKey key)
      // process input that is waiting on a channel
      {
        SocketChannel channel = (SocketChannel) key.channel( );
        ClientInfo ci = (ClientInfo) clients.get(channel);
        if (ci == null)
          System.out.println("No client info for channel " + channel);
        else {
          String msg = ci.readMessage( );
          if (msg != null) {
            System.out.println("Read message: " + msg);
            if (msg.trim( ).equals("bye")) {
              ci.closeDown( );
              clients.remove(channel);  // delete ci from hash map
            }
            else
              doRequest(msg, ci);
          }
        }
      } // end of readFromChannel( )
```

readFromChannel( ) extracts the channel reference from the client request and uses it
to look up the associated ClientInfo object in the hash map. The ClientInfo object
deals with the request via a call to readMessage( ), which returns the full message or
null if the message is incomplete.

If the message is "bye", then the server requests that the ClientInfo object closes the connection, and the object is discarded. Otherwise, the message is processed using doRequest( ):

```
private void doRequest(String line, ClientInfo ci)
/*  The input line can be one of:
            "score name & score &"
    or      "get"      */
{
  if (line.trim( ).toLowerCase( ).equals("get")) {
    System.out.println("Processing 'get'");
    ci.sendMessage( hs.toString() );
  }
  else if ((line.length( ) >= 6) &&      // "score "
      (line.substring(0,5).toLowerCase( ).equals("score"))) {
    System.out.println("Processing 'score'");
    hs.addScore( line.substring(5) );    // cut the score keyword
  }
  else
    System.out.println("Ignoring input line");
}
```

The input line can be a "get" or a "score" message. If it's a "get", then the ClientInfo object will be asked to send the high scores list to the client. If the message is a new name/score pair, then the HighScores object will be notified.

Storing client information

ClientInfo has three public methods: readMessage( ), sendMessage( ), and closeDown( ). readMessage( ) reads input from a client's socket channel. sendMessage( ) sends a message along a channel to the client, and closeDown( ) closes the channel.

Data is read from a socket channel into a Buffer object holding bytes. A Buffer object is a fixed-size container for items belonging to a Java base type, such as byte, int, char, double, and Boolean. It works in a similar way to a file: there's a "current position," and after each read or write operation, the current position indicates the next item in the buffer.

There are two important size notions for a buffer: its capacity and its limit. The *capacity* is the maximum number of items the buffer can contain, and the *limit* is a value between 0 and capacity, representing the current buffer size.

Since data sent through a socket channel is stored in a ByteBuffer object (a buffer of bytes), it's necessary to translate the data (decode it) into a String before being tested to see if the data is complete or not. A complete message is a string ending with a \n.

The constructor for ClientInfo initializes the byte buffer and the decoder:

```
// globals
private static final int BUFSIZ = 1024;  // max size of a message

private SocketChannel channel;  // the client's channel
private SelectScoreServer ss;   // the top-level server
```

```
    private ByteBuffer inBuffer;     // for storing input

    private Charset charset;       // for decoding bytes --> string
    private CharsetDecoder decoder;


    public ClientInfo(SocketChannel chan, SelectScoreServer ss)
    {
      channel = chan;
      this.ss = ss;
      inBuffer = ByteBuffer.allocateDirect(BUFSIZ);
      inBuffer.clear();

      charset = Charset.forName("ISO-8859-1");
      decoder = charset.newDecoder();

      showClientDetails();
    }
```

The buffer is a fixed size, 1,024 bytes. The obvious question is whether this is sufficient for message passing. The only long message is the high scores list, which is sent
from the server back to the client, and 1,024 characters (bytes) should be enough.

Reading a message

readMessage( ) is called when the channel contains data:

```
    public String readMessage()
    {
      String inputMsg = null;
      try {
        int numBytesRead = channel.read(inBuffer);
        if (numBytesRead == -1) {     // channel has gone
          channel.close();
          ss.removeChannel(channel); // tell SelectScoreServer
        }
        else
          inputMsg = getMessage(inBuffer);
      }
      catch (IOException e)
      { System.out.println("rm: " + e);
        ss.removeChannel(channel); // tell SelectScoreServer
      }

      return inputMsg;
    }  // end of readMessage()
```

A channel read( ) will not block, returning the number of bytes read (which may be
0). If it returns -1, then something has happened to the input channel; the channel is
closed and the ClientInfo object removed by calling removeChannel( ) in the main
server. read( ) may raise an IOException, which triggers the same removal.

The real work of reading a message is done by getMessage( ):

```
private String getMessage(ByteBuffer buf)
{
  String msg = null;
  int posn = buf.position( );    // current buffer sizes
  int limit = buf.limit( );

  buf.position(0);       // set range of bytes for translation
  buf.limit(posn);
  try {    // translate bytes-->string
    CharBuffer cb = decoder.decode(buf);
    msg = cb.toString( );
  }
  catch(CharacterCodingException cce)
  { System.out.println( cce );  }

  // System.out.println("Current msg: " + msg);
  buf.limit(limit);      // reset buffer to full range of bytes
  buf.position(posn);

  if (msg.endsWith("\n")) {     // I assume '\n' is the last char
    buf.clear( );
    return msg;
  }
  return null;       // since I still only have a partial mesg
} // end of getMessage( )
```

position( ) returns the index position of the next empty spot in the buffer: bytes are stored from position 0 up to posn-1. The current limit for the buffer is stored and then changed to be the current position. This means that when decode( ) is called, only the part of the buffer containing bytes will be considered. After the translation, the resulting string is checked to see if it ends with a \n, in which case the buffer is reset (treated as being empty) and the message returned.

There's a potential problem with this approach: the assumption that the last character in the buffer will be \n. This depends on what data is present in the channel when read( ) is called in readMessage( ). It might be that the channel contains the final bytes of one message and some bytes of the next, as illustrated by Figure 29-13.

The read( ) call in Figure 29-13 will add the bytes for a\nbbb to the byte buffer, placing \n in the midst of the buffer rather than at the end. Consequently, an endsWith( ) test of the extracted string is insufficient:

```
if (msg.endsWith("\n")) {. . .}
```

In my tests, this problem never appeared since read( ) was called quickly, adding each incoming byte to the buffer as soon as it arrived; an \n was always read before the next byte appeared in the channel.

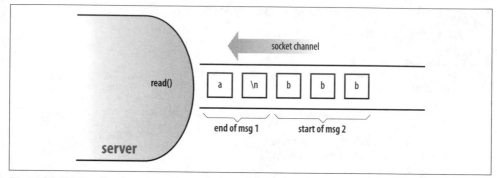

Figure 29-13. Reading bytes in a channel

Sending a message

sendMessage( ) sends a specified message along the channel back to the client:

```
public boolean sendMessage(String msg)
{
  String fullMsg = msg + "\r\n";

  ByteBuffer outBuffer = ByteBuffer.allocateDirect(BUFSIZ);
  outBuffer.clear( );
  outBuffer.put( fullMsg.getBytes( ) );
  outBuffer.flip( );

  boolean msgSent = false;
  try {
    // send the data; don't assume it goes all at once
    while( outBuffer.hasRemaining( ) )
      channel.write(outBuffer);
    msgSent = true;
  }
  catch(IOException e)
  { System.out.println(e);
    ss.removeChannel(channel); // tell SelectScoreServer
  }

  return msgSent;
}  // end of sendMessage( )
```

Two issues are at work here:

- The need to translate the string to bytes in a buffer before transmission
- Dealing with the case that the message requires several writes before it's all placed onto the channel

The buffer is filled with the message. The flip( ) call sets the buffer limit to the current position (i.e., the position just after the end of the message) and then sets the current position back to 0.

The while loop uses hasRemaining( ), which returns true as long as elements remain between the current position and the buffer limit. Each write( ) calls advances the position through the buffer. One write( ) call should be sufficient to place all the bytes onto the channel unless the buffer is large or the channel overloaded.

write( ) may raise an exception, which causes the channel and the ClientInfo object to be discarded.

Waiting to send

There's a potential problem with sendMessage( ), pointed out to me by Marcin Mank. The offending code is in its while loop:

```
while( outBuffer.hasRemaining( ) )
  channel.write(outBuffer);
```

If the channel's output buffer cannot accept any more data, the write( ) call will return 0. outBuffer won't be emptied, and the while loop will keep iterating. This looping will cause sendMessage( ) to wait, which in turn will cause the server to wait in doRequest( ), thereby stopping any other clients from being processed.

Though this is a problem, it's unlikely to occur in this example since the channel is only being written to by a single process. This means that any delays will be brief and probably acceptable.

Implementing a decent solution involves a considerable increase in complexity, so I'll only sketch out what the code might look like.

When sendMessage( ) tries to write outBuffer to the channel and only some (or none) of it is written, the method must request a notification when the write can be completed. The unsent message must be stored until that notification arrives. The ideas are shown in trySendMessage( ):

```
private void trySendMessage( )
{
  int len = outBuffer.hasRemaining( );    // outBuffer must now be global
  try {
    int nBytes = channel.write(outBuffer);
    if (nBytes != len)    // data not all sent
      channel.register(selector, SelectionKey.OP_READ|SelectionKey.OP_WRITE);
          // need a way of referring to server's top-level selector
    else {  // data all sent
      outBuffer.clear( );
      channel.register(selector, SelectionKey.OP_READ);    // remove OP_WRITE
    }
  }
  catch(IOException e)
  { System.out.println(e);
    ss.removeChannel(channel); // tell SelectScoreServer
  }
}
```

The notification technique relies on registering an interest in the OP_WRITE key for that channel. When the channel becomes writeable, the key change will be caught by the while loop in SelectScoreServer, triggering a call to a new finishSend( ) method:

```
// in SelectScoreServer while-loop
else if (key.isWritable( ))      // data can now be written
  finishSend(key);


private void finishSend(SelectionKey key)
// send remaining output
{
  SocketChannel channel = (SocketChannel) key.channel( );
  ClientInfo ci = (ClientInfo) clients.get(channel);
  if (ci == null)
    System.out.println("No client info for channel " + channel);
  else
    ci.trySendMessage( );
} // end of finishSend( )
```

An example of this approach in a complete server can be found in Chapter 12 of *Java Threads* by Scott Oaks and Henry Wong (O'Reilly).

Unfortunately, this coding approach isn't good enough. The server may want to send several messages to the client, so it would have to store each one until the channel becomes writeable. This suggests the need for a buffer list of delayed messages.

 The example in *Java Threads* avoids the messiness of a buffer list by canceling all further sends to the client until the single output buffer has been emptied.

The client

The ScoreClient class from previous examples can stay as the client-side application, unchanged. The advantage is that high-level I/O can be used on the client side instead of byte buffers.

A nonblocking client may be useful for attempting a connection without having to wait for the server to respond. Whether a connection operation is in progress can be checked by calling isConnectionPending( ).

UDP Client and Server

All the previous examples use TCP, but the client and server in this section are recoded to utilize UDP communication. The result is another form of multiplexing server but without the need for nonblocking sockets. The complexity of the code is much less than in the last example.

The downsides of this approach are the usual ones related to UDP: the possibility of packet loss and reordering (these problems didn't occur in my tests, which were run on the same machine) and machines connected by a LAN.

Another disadvantage of using UDP is the need to write a client before the server can be tested. Telnet uses TCP/IP and can't be employed.

Figure 29-14 illustrates the communication between ScoreUDPClient objects and the ScoreUDPServer.

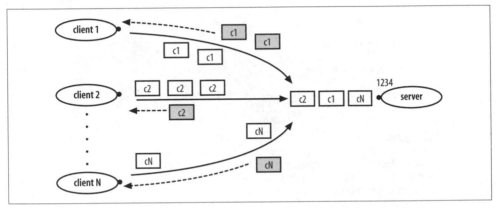

Figure 29-14. UDP clients and server

Since no long-term connection exists between a client and the server, multiple clients could send datagrams at the same time. The server will process them in their order of arrival. A datagram automatically includes the hostname and IP address of its sender, so response messages can be easily sent back to the right client.

 The code for the UDP client and server can be found in the *NetBasics/ udp/* directory.

The UDP-based scores server

The server sets up a DatagramSocket listening at port 1234, enters a loop to wait for a packet, processes it, and then repeats:

```
// globals
private static final int PORT = 1234;
private static final int BUFSIZE = 1024;   // max size of a message

private HighScores hs;
private DatagramSocket serverSock;
```

```
public ScoreUDPServer()
{
  try {  // try to create a socket for the server
    serverSock = new DatagramSocket(PORT);
  }
  catch(SocketException se)
  { System.out.println(se);
    System.exit(1);
  }
  waitForPackets();
}


private void waitForPackets()
{
  DatagramPacket receivePacket;
  byte data[];
  hs = new HighScores();

  try {
    while (true) {
      data = new byte[BUFSIZE];  // set up an empty packet
      receivePacket = new DatagramPacket(data, data.length);
      System.out.println("Waiting for a packet...");
      serverSock.receive( receivePacket );

      processClient(receivePacket);
      hs.saveScores();   // backup scores after each package
    }
  }
  catch(IOException ioe)
  { System.out.println(ioe);  }
} // end of waitForPackets()
```

The data in a packet is written to a byte array of a fixed size. The size of the array should be sufficient for the kinds of messages being delivered.

processClient() extracts the client's address and IP number and converts the byte array into a string:

```
InetAddress clientAddr = receivePacket.getAddress();
int clientPort = receivePacket.getPort();
String clientMesg = new String( receivePacket.getData(), 0,
                        receivePacket.getLength() );
```

These are passed to doRequest(), which deals with the two possible message types: get and score. There's no bye message because no long-term connection needs to be broken. Part of the reason for the simplicity of coding with UDP is the absence of processing related to connection termination (whether intended or due to an error).

A reply is sent by calling sendMessage():

```
private void sendMessage(InetAddress clientAddr, int clientPort, String mesg)
// send message to socket at the specified address and port
```

```
{
  byte mesgData[] = mesg.getBytes( );    // convert to byte[] form
  try {
    DatagramPacket sendPacket =
            new DatagramPacket( mesgData, mesgData.length,
                                      clientAddr, clientPort);
    serverSock.send( sendPacket );
  }
  catch(IOException ioe)
  { System.out.println(ioe);  }
}
```

The UDP-based scores client

The client has the same GUI interface as before (see Figure 29-15), allowing the user
to send commands by clicking on the Get Scores button or by entering name/score
pairs into the text fields.

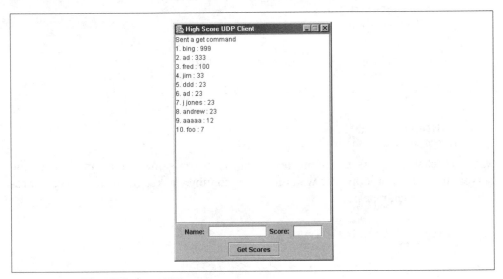

Figure 29-15. The UDP client GUI

The application uses the implicit thread associated with Swing's processing of GUI
events to send commands to the server. Processing of the messages returned by the
server is handled in the application's main execution thread.

The constructor starts the application thread by setting up the client's datagram
socket:

```
// globals
private static final int SERVER_PORT = 1234;      // server details
private static final String SERVER_HOST = "localhost";
private static final int BUFSIZE = 1024;   // max size of a message
```

```
    private DatagramSocket sock;
    private InetAddress serverAddr;

    public ScoreUDPClient( )
    {   super( "High Score UDP Client" );

        initializeGUI( );
        try {    // try to create the client's socket
          sock = new DatagramSocket( );
        }
        catch( SocketException se ) {
          se.printStackTrace( );
          System.exit(1);
        }
        try {  // try to turn the server's name into an internet address
          serverAddr = InetAddress.getByName(SERVER_HOST);
        }
        catch( UnknownHostException uhe) {
          uhe.printStackTrace( );
          System.exit(1);
        }

        setDefaultCloseOperation( JFrame.EXIT_ON_CLOSE );
        setSize(300,450);
        setResizable(false);     // fixed-size display
        setVisible(true);

        waitForPackets( );
    } // end of ScoreUDPClient( );
```

waitForPackets( ) bears a striking resemblance to the same named method in the server. It contains a loop that waits for an incoming packet (from the server), processes it, and then repeats:

```
    private void waitForPackets( )
    { DatagramPacket receivePacket;
      byte data[];
      try {
        while (true) {
          // set up an empty packet
          data = new byte[BUFSIZE];
          receivePacket = new DatagramPacket(data, data.length);

          System.out.println("Waiting for a packet...");
          sock.receive( receivePacket );

          processServer(receivePacket);
        }
      }
      catch(IOException ioe)
      { System.out.println(ioe);  }
    }
```

processServer( ) extracts the address, port number, and message string from the packet, prints the address and port to standard output, and writes the message to the text area.

The GUI thread is triggered by the system calling actionPerformed( ):

```java
public void actionPerformed(ActionEvent e)
{
  if (e.getSource( ) == jbGetScores) {
    sendMessage(serverAddr, SERVER_PORT, "get");
    jtaMesgs.append("Sent a get command\n");
  }
  else if (e.getSource( ) == jtfScore)
    sendScore( );
}
```

An important issue with threads is synchronization of shared data. The DatagramSocket is shared, but the GUI thread only transmits datagrams; the application thread only receives, so conflict is avoided.

The JTextArea component, jtaMesgs, is shared between the threads, as a place to write messages for the user. However, there's little danger of multiple writes occurring at the same time due to the request/response nature of the communication between the client and server: a message from the server only arrives as a response to an earlier request by the client. Synchronization would be more important if the server could deliver messages to the client at any time, as you'll see in the chat systems developed in Chapter 30.

Another reason for the low risk of undue interaction is that the GUI thread only writes short messages into the text area, which are added quickly.

P2P Programming in Java

The simplest form of P2P programming in Java employs *UDP multicasting*, which is datagram packets with a MulticastSocket object. A MulticastSocket requires a multicast IP address (a class D IP address) and a port number. Class D IP addresses fall in the range 224.0.0.0 to 239.255.255.255, though certain addresses are reserved.

A peer wishing to subscribe to a multicast group must create a MulticastSocket representing the group and use joinGroup( ) to begin receiving communication. A peer leaves a group by calling leaveGroup( ) or by terminating.

 Currently, applets aren't allowed to use multicast sockets.

The application described here takes a (welcome) break from accessing/modifying high score lists, which doesn't make for a particularly suitable P2P example. Instead, a MultiTimeServer transmits a packet to a multicast group every second, containing the current time and date. MultiTimeClient objects wait for packets to appear in the group and to print them to standard output. The situation is shown in Figure 29-16.

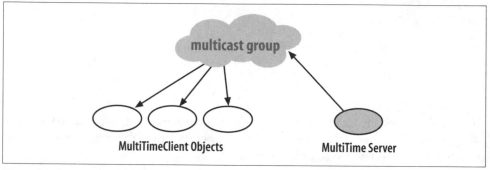

Figure 29-16. UDP multicasting clients and server

The use of the words "client" and "server" are a little misleading since all the objects involved in the group can potentially send and receive messages. It's my choice to restrict the server to sending and the clients to reading.

 The code for the multicasting client and server can be found in the *NetBasics/Multicast/* directory.

The multicasting time server

The MultiTimeServer object creates a multicast socket for a group at IP address 228.5.6.7, port 6789, and enters a loop which sends a packet out every second:

```
public class MultiTimeServer
{
  private static final String MHOST = "228.5.6.7";
  private static final int PORT = 6789;

  public static void main(String args[]) throws Exception
  {
    InetAddress address = InetAddress.getByName(MHOST);
    MulticastSocket msock = new MulticastSocket(PORT);
    msock.joinGroup(address);

    DatagramPacket packet;
    System.out.print("Ticking");
    while(true){
      Thread.sleep(1000);    // one-second delay
```

```
            System.out.print(".");
            String str = (new Date()).toString();
            packet = new DatagramPacket(str.getBytes(), str.length(), address, PORT);
            msock.send(packet);
        }
    }

} // end of MultiTimeServer class
```

The server is started this way:

```
>java MultiTimeServer
Ticking.......
```

The multicasting time client

The client creates a multicast socket for the same group and enters an infinite loop
waiting for packets to appear:

```
public class MultiTimeClient
{
    private static final String MHOST = "228.5.6.7";
    private static final int PORT = 6789;

    public static void main(String args[]) throws IOException
    {
        InetAddress address = InetAddress.getByName(MHOST);
        MulticastSocket msock = new MulticastSocket(PORT);
        msock.joinGroup(address);

        byte[] buf = new byte[1024];
        DatagramPacket packet = new DatagramPacket(buf, buf.length);
        String dateStr;
        while(true){
            msock.receive(packet);
            dateStr = new String( packet.getData() ).trim();
            System.out.println(packet.getAddress() + " : " + dateStr);
        }
    }
}
```

A client's execution is:

```
>java MultiTimeClient
/172.30.3.176 : Mon Jan 24 16:09:48 ICT 2005
/172.30.3.176 : Mon Jan 24 16:09:49 ICT 2005
/172.30.3.176 : Mon Jan 24 16:09:50 ICT 2005
/172.30.3.176 : Mon Jan 24 16:09:51 ICT 2005
/172.30.3.176 : Mon Jan 24 16:09:52 ICT 2005
```

Chapter 30 contains a UDP multicasting version of a chat application.

Firewalls

Firewalls are unfortunately a part of today's networking experience. Most companies, government institutions, universities, and so on, utilize firewalls to block access to the wider Internet: socket creation on all nonstandard ports, and most standard ones, are typically prohibited, and web pages must be retrieved through a proxy that filters (limits) the traffic.

 The firewall-related examples in this section can be found in the *NetBasics/Firewall/* directory.

This situation means that the code described so far may not work because it requires the creation of sockets. The DayPing example given below is a Java application that attempts to contact a "time-of-day" server. The example below uses the server at the National Institute of Standards and Technology in Boulder, Colorado:

```
>java DayPing time-A.timefreq.bldrdoc.gov
time-A.timefreq.bldrdoc.gov is alive at

53394 05-01-24 09:16:12 00 0 0 525.7 UTC(NIST) *
```

DayPing opens a socket to the host at port 13, where the standard time-of-day service is listening. The response is printed out using println() after layering a BufferedReader stream on top of the network link:

```
public class DayPing
{
    public static void main(String args[]) throws IOException
    { if (args.length != 1) {
        System.out.println("usage:  java DayPing <host> ");
        System.exit(0);
      }

      Socket sock = new Socket(args[0],13);   // host and port
      BufferedReader br = new BufferedReader(
            new InputStreamReader( sock.getInputStream() ) );

      System.out.println( args[0] + " is alive at ");
      String line;
      while ( (line = br.readLine()) != null)
        System.out.println(line);
      sock.close();
    }
} // end of DayPing class
```

The desired DayPing output is shown above, but this isn't what's returned to most student machines in my department. For students, this is the result:

```
>java DayPing time-A.timefreq.bldrdoc.gov
  Exception in thread "main"
```

```
java.net.NoRouteToHostException: Operation timed out: no further information
      at java.net.PlainSocketImpl.
          socketConnect (Native Method)
             :  // many lines, which I've edited out
      at DayPing.main(DayPing.java:34)
```

There's a long delay (two to three minutes) before the exception is raised, due to the OS waiting for a possible connection. The exception indicates the presence of a firewall preventing the link.

With TCP client applications such as DayPing, it's possible to check the server with telnet:

```
>telnet time-A.timefreq.bldrdoc.gov 13
```

There's a similar outcome: a delay of a few minutes, followed by an error message saying that the connection couldn't be made.

My university has a policy of disallowing socket creation for hosts outside the local domain, and web pages can be retrieved only by going through a proxy located at cache.psu.ac.th, port 8080. Therefore, there are two choices:

- Use a commercial ISP that does allow socket creation.
- Rewrite the DayPing application to utilize URLs.

The second approach is taken here.

Retrieving a Web Page

The simplest way of obtaining a web page in Java is with a URL object, which retrieves it as a stream of text in a similar way to streams connected to sockets. The GetWebPage application downloads a web page using a URL specified on the command line:

```java
public class GetWebPage
{
  public static void main(String args[]) throws IOException
  { if (args.length != 1) {
      System.out.println("usage:  java GetWebPage <url> ");
      System.exit(0);
    }

    URL url  = new URL(args[0]);

    BufferedReader br = new BufferedReader(
                          new InputStreamReader( url.openStream() ));

    // print first ten lines of contents
    int numLine = 0;
    String line;
    while ( ((line = br.readLine()) != null) && (numLine <= 10) ) {
      System.out.println(line);
      numLine++;
```

```
      }
      if (line != null)
        System.out.println(". . .");

      br.close( );
    }
  } // end of GetWebPage class
```

GetWebPage can access any web page, including one giving the current time in Thailand at *http://www.timeanddate.com/worldclock/city.html?n=28*. However, the command line must include three proxy options (proxySet, proxyHost, and proxyPort) to tell the JVM to employ the university's proxy server. The call and result are:

```
>java -DproxySet=true -DproxyHost=cache.psu.ac.th -DproxyPort=8080 GetWebPage
http://www.timeanddate.com/worldclock/city.html?n=28
<!DOCTYPE HTML PUBLIC "-//W3C//DTD HTML 4.01 Transitional//EN">
<!-- scripts and programs that download content transparent to the user are not
allowed without permision -->
<html>
<head>
<title>Current local time in Bangkok - Thailand</title>
<link rel="stylesheet" type="text/css" href="/common/style.css">
<meta http-equiv="Content-Type" content="text/html; charset=ISO-8859-1">
</head>
<body>

 . . .
 >
```

GetWebPage only displays the first 11 lines of the retrieved web page, which isn't enough to reach the time information on this page.

An alternative to command line settings is to specify the proxy details within the program:

```
Properties props = System.getProperties( );
props.put("proxySet", "true");
props.put("proxyHost", "cache.psu.ac.th");
props.put("proxyPort", "8080");
System.setProperties(props);
```

This should be done before the creation of the URL object.

An important aspect of this coding style is the processing of the text stream arriving from the web server. It's often far from trivial to delve through the mix of HTML tags, JavaScript, and others to find the required piece of information (e.g., that the current time in Bangkok is 4:19 P.M.).

Another problem is that any text analysis code tends to break after awhile as the format of the web page is changed/updated.

Proxy Authorization

Some proxy servers demand a login and password before pages can be downloaded (this is true of one of the high bandwidth lines out of my department).

Supplying these from within a Java application requires the use of a URLConnection object to permit greater control over the URL link:

```
URL url = new URL(args[0]);
URLConnection conn = url.openConnection();
```

The login and password strings must be passed to the proxy server as a single string of the form "login:password" translated into Base64 encoding:

```
Base64Converter bc = new Base64Converter();
String encoding = bc.encode(login + ":" + password );
```

The Base64Converter class was written by David Wallace Croft and is available with documentation from "Java Tip 47," JavaWorld.com, April 6, 2000 (*http://www.javaworld.com/javaworld/javatips/jw-javatip47.html*).

There is also an undocumented BASE64Encoder class in the sun.misc package of J2SE used this way:

```
Base64Encoder bc = new Base64Encoder();
String mesg = login + ":" + password;
String encoding = bc.encode( mesg.getBytes() );
```

The encoded string is sent to the proxy as an authorization request:

```
conn.setRequestProperty("Proxy-Authorization", "Basic " + encoding);
```

GetWebPageP.java contains all of this functionality; it reads the user's password and desired URL from the command line:

```
public class GetWebPageP
{
  private static final String LOGIN = "ad";  // modify this

  public static void main(String args[]) throws IOException
  { if (args.length != 2) {
      System.out.println("usage: java GetWebPageP <password> <url>");
      System.exit(0);
    }

    // set the properties used for proxy support
    Properties props = System.getProperties();
    props.put("proxySet", "true");
    props.put("proxyHost", "cache.psu.ac.th");
    props.put("proxyPort", "8080");
    System.setProperties(props);

    // create a URL and URLConnection
    URL url  = new URL(args[1]);   // URL string
    URLConnection conn = url.openConnection();
```

```
// encode the "login:password" string
Base64Converter bc = new Base64Converter( );
String encoding = bc.encode( LOGIN + ":" + args[0] );

// send the authorization
conn.setRequestProperty("Proxy-Authorization",
                        "Basic " + encoding);

BufferedReader br = new BufferedReader (
          new InputStreamReader ( conn.getInputStream( ) ));

// print first ten lines of contents
int numLine = 0;
String line;
while ( ((line = br.readLine( )) != null) && (numLine <= 10) ) {
  System.out.println(line);
  numLine++;
}
if (line != null)
  System.out.println(". . .");

br.close( );
System.exit(0);
} // end of main( )
} // end of GetWebPageP class
```

A Web-Based Client and Server

These time-of-day examples fit the familiar client/server model in the case when a server exists. However, most applications require new clients and a new server. The question then is how to make the server side of the program act as a web server, deliver web pages, and satisfy the restrictions of the client-side firewall?

Enter the Java 2 Enterprise Edition (J2EE), aimed at the construction of web-based client/server applications: it supports simplified networking, concurrency, transactions, easy access to databases, and much more (*http://java.sun.com/j2ee/*). Aside from Sun's implementation, many companies offer J2EE compatible systems, including Tomcat from the Jakarta Project (*http://jakarta.apache.org/tomcat/*) and JRun from Macromedia (*http://www.macromedia.com/software/jrun*).

J2EE is a complex development environment, centered around servlets, Java Server Pages (JSPs), and Enterprise JavaBeans (EJBs). Servlets are objects specialized for the serving of web content, typically web pages, in response to client requests. JSPs are web pages that may contain embedded Java. EJBs focus on server-side processing, including the connection of server-side applications to other Java functionality, such as the Java Transaction API (JTA), the Java Message Service (JMS), and Java Database Connectivity (JDBC).

Servlets deal with client requests using HTTP, which thankfully only contains a few commands; the two principal ones are the GET and POST methods. A GET method (request) is usually sent by a web browser when it asks for a page from a server. A POST method (request) is more typically associated with the submission of details taken from a web-page form.

A servlet that inherits the HttpServlet class will automatically call its doGet( ) method when a GET request arrives from a client; there's a doPost( ) for processing POST requests.

My web-based client will communicate with a servlet that implements a time-of-day service. The use of HTTP to "bypass" firewall restrictions on client/server communication is called *HTTP Tunneling*.

TimeServlet will be called when the TimeClient application refers to the servlet's URL (i.e., sends a GET request to the web server managing the servlet). The situation is illustrated by Figure 29-17.

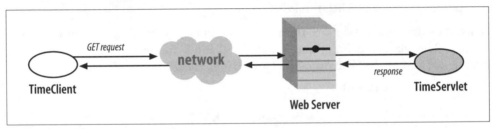

Figure 29-17. Client and servlet configuration

A servlet can output a stream of HTML that is displayed nicely in the client if it's a browser. However, TimeServlet will deliver ordinary text since the client doesn't require extraneous formatting around the result.

An excellent book on servlets and JSPs is *Core Servlets and Java Server Pages* by Marty Hall (Sun Microsystems Press; *http://www.coreservlets.com/*). The complete contents of the first edition can be downloaded from *http://pdf.coreservlets.com/* source code and teaching materials are available for the second edition.

A servlet that serves up time

The doGet( ) method in TimeServlet is called automatically when the servlet's URL is sent to the web server:

```
public class TimeServlet extends HttpServlet
{
    public void doGet( HttpServletRequest request, HttpServletResponse response)
            throws ServletException, IOException
    {
        SimpleDateFormat formatter = new SimpleDateFormat("d M yyyy HH:mm:ss");
        Date today = new Date( );
```

```
            String todayStr = formatter.format(today);
            System.out.println("Today is: " + todayStr);

            PrintWriter output = response.getWriter();
            output.println( todayStr );   // send date & time
            output.close();
        }
    }
```

Various client and request information is made available in the HttpServletRequest object passed to doGet( ), but TimeServlet doesn't need it.

The other argument of doGet( ) is a HttpServletResponse object that permits various forms of output to be delivered to the client. TimeServlet creates an output stream and sends a formatted date and time string.

The time client

The TimeClient application is a variant of the GetWebPage program described earlier except that the servlet's URL is hardwired into it.

Since the client and servlet are running on the same machine, proxy settings aren't needed. The web server is running at port 8100 and stores its servlets in a fixed location referred to by the URL *http://localhost:8100/servlet/*:

```
public class TimeClient
{
    public static void main(String args[]) throws IOException
    {
        URL url = new URL("http://localhost:8100/servlet/TimeServlet");
        BufferedReader br = new BufferedReader(
                new InputStreamReader( url.openStream( ) ));
        String line;
        while ( (line = br.readLine( )) != null )
            System.out.println(line);
        br.close( );
    }
}
Typical output from TimeClient is:
>java TimeClient
24 1 2548 16:27:18

>java TimeClient
24 1 2548 16:27:23
```

The output shows the year to be 2548, which is 2005 in the Buddhist calendar, the system used in Thailand.

An advantage of (simple) servlets is they can be tested from a browser. Figure 29-18 shows the output when *http://localhost:8100/servlet/TimeServlet* is typed into the Opera browser.

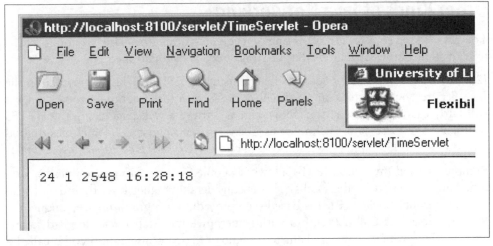

Figure 29-18. A browser as client for TimeServlet

A browser as client for TimeServlet enable clients to use HTTP for communication with the server part of the application (i.e., the clients employ URLs to access the server). This mode of communication is permitted by firewalls, which usually block socket links.

The downside is that HTTP is a request/response protocol—i.e., the client must initiate the communication to receive a reply. It's difficult for the server to send a message to a client without first receiving one from it. This means that a web-based server has trouble broadcasting (multicasting) a message received from one client to all the others, which is a common requirement of multiplayer games and chat applications.

In Chapter 30, I will implement a web-based version of a chat system by having a client periodically query the server to collect messages from the other clients.

Applets as Clients

The default security associated with applets means they can only connect back to their home server. This restriction applies to sockets and to the downloading of web pages. However, the security can be modified with a policy file and by signing the applet. However, most multiplayer games that utilize applets host them on their own servers, so the default security policy is sufficient.

The real problem with applets is the excessive download time required to move the necessary functionality and resources (e.g., images, sounds) to the client side. Commercial games (e.g., Everquest) distribute CDs containing client applications.

Other Kinds of Java Networking

The networking support in Java is one of its greatest strengths. This section is a brief tour of some of the capabilities that I haven't previously mentioned.

J2SE 1.4 added support for secure sockets (using the SSL and TLS protocols) in the Java Secure Socket Extension (JSSE) libraries. Security is a complex topic, but it's still fairly easy to do a common thing such as retrieve a web page using the HTTPS protocol. The Core Java Technologies Tech Tip for August 2004 includes a good introduction to JSSE (*http://java.sun.com/developer/JDCTechTips/2004/tt0817.html*).

Remote Method Invocation (RMI) allows Java objects on separate machines to communicate via remote method calls. This is considerably higher-level than data transmission through sockets. RMI is based on a procedural programming technique, the Remote Procedure Call (RPC), but with some powerful extensions. One is dynamic code loading, which allows a client to download the communication code (called a stub) for accessing a remote method at run time. Code loading from clients can be carried out by a server.

RMI is the basis of a number of expressive networking models, including Jini mentioned below. RMI is integrated with the communications protocol for the Common Object Request Broker Architecture (CORBA), which permits Java objects to interact with objects coded in other languages.

Jini is a service discovery architecture that allows Jini-enabled clients to find and utilize whatever services are available on a network, dynamically adjusting their connections as new services come on-stream and others leave. This is of key importance for mobile devices. The starting point for Jini is *http://www.jini.org/*.

A good book on Java networking is *Java Network Programming* by Elliotte Rusty Harold (O'Reilly).

Network Chat

In the last chapter, I presented an overview of several types of network programming, including client/server, peer-to-peer, and HTTP tunneling. This chapter revisits those topics to see how they can be employed to build networked chat applications. Chat capabilities are found in almost every multiplayer game (e.g., in shared virtual worlds).

The main characteristic of a chat system is its dynamic nature: clients can join or leave at any time, and there's no fixed order to when people can speak. A message sent out by a user should be delivered to all the other clients, preferably labeled with that user's name or ID.

The chat space may be divided into distinct regions or groups, with varying levels of access and communication privacy. The system may allow personal communication between two users, unseen by other people. I'll discuss ways of implementing private messages in the examples.

In this chapter, I'll code the same chat system using three different approaches: client/server, UDP multicasting, and HTTP tunneling to a servlet. Chat messages are broadcast, and a special who message returns a list of the other clients. A client leaves the system by sending a bye message. The multicasting and servlet versions of the application introduce a hi message for joining and support a simple form of private one-to-one communication.

Here are the key technical details of the three systems:

Threaded TCP clients and server
> The server uses threads to communicate with its clients and a shared object to maintain client information. Each client employs a thread to watch for server communications (typically copies of other users' messages).

UDP multicasting clients and a name server
> The clients send messages to each other via UDP multicasting. However, a client wishing to join the chat group must first communicate with a name server, which sends it the group address or rejects the request. A departing client must

notify the name server, so it can maintain a current list of participants. A client wanting a list of other users sends a message to the server, rather than querying the group.

Clients using a servlet as a server

The clients communicate with a chat servlet, sending messages as arguments of the servlet's URL. The servlet maintains client information, which is shared between the multiple threads executing inside the servlet instance. Each client has a separate thread which periodically queries the servlet for any new messages.

 These examples can be found in the *Chat/* subdirectory. The client/ server example is in *Threaded/*, the UDP multicasting version is in *Multicasting/*, and the HTTP tunneling code is in *ChatServlet/*.

Threaded TCP Clients and Server

Figure 30-1 shows the various objects in the threaded chat application.

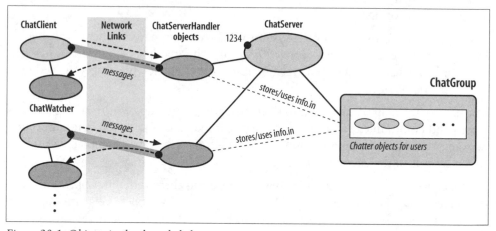

Figure 30-1. Objects in the threaded chat system

Each client is represented by a ChatClient object and a ChatWatcher thread. ChatClient maintains the GUI, processes the user's input, and sends messages to the server over a TCP link. ChatWatcher waits for messages from the server and displays them in ChatClient's GUI text area.

ChatClient can send the following messages:

who

The server returns a string containing a list of the current chat users.

bye

The client sends this message just prior to exiting.

Any message

> Other text strings sent to the server are assumed to be messages and are broadcast to all the current users.

The server can send out two types of message:

`WHO$$ cliAddr1 & port1 & ... cliAddrN & portN &`

> This is sent back to a client in response to a who message. Each client is identified by its address and port number, which are extracted from the TCP link established when a client first connects to the server.

`(cliAddr, port): message`

> This is a broadcast message, originally from the client with the specified address and port number.

Server messages are received by the `ChatWatcher` thread, which is monitoring incoming messages on the `ChatClient`'s TCP link.

`ChatServer` is the top-level server, which spawns a `ChatServerHandler` thread to handle each new client. Since messages are to be transmitted between clients, the `ChatServer` maintains pertinent client information, accessible by all the threads. The shared data is held by a `ChatGroup` object, which offers synchronized methods to control the concurrency issues. A client's details, such as its input stream, are stored in a `Chatter` object.

Figure 30-2 gives the class diagrams for the application, showing the public methods.

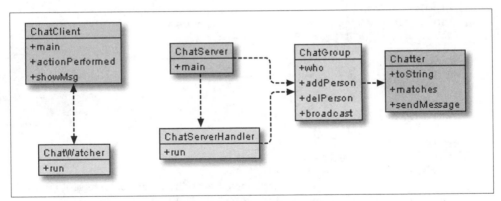

Figure 30-2. Class diagrams for the threaded chat system

The Chat Client

The GUI supported by `ChatClient` is shown in Figure 30-3.

The text area for displaying messages occupies the majority of the window. Outgoing messages are typed in a text field and sent when the user presses enter. A who message is outputted when the Who button is pressed. A bye message is transmitted as a result of the user clicking on the window's Close box.

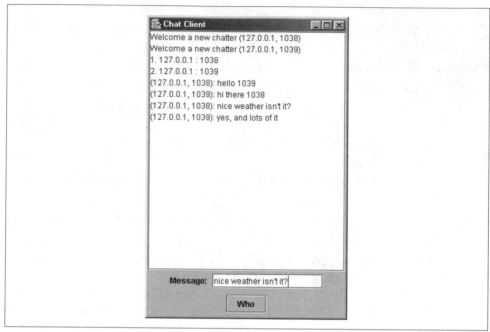

Figure 30-3. The ChatClient GUI

The server is contacted and the ChatWatcher thread is started in makeContact( ):

```
// globals
private static final int PORT = 1234;     // server details
private static final String HOST = "localhost";

private Socket sock;
private PrintWriter out;  // output to the server


private void makeContact()
{
  try {
    sock = new Socket(HOST, PORT);
    BufferedReader in  = new BufferedReader(
                             new InputStreamReader( sock.getInputStream() ));
    out = new PrintWriter( sock.getOutputStream(), true);

    new ChatWatcher(this, in).start();     // watch for server msgs
  }
  catch(Exception e)
  {  System.out.println(e);  }
}
```

The output stream, out, is made global so messages can be sent from various methods in ChatClient. However, server input is only processed by ChatWatcher, so it is declared locally in makeContact( ) before being passed to the thread.

Sending messages is simple; for example, pressing the Who button results in:

```
out.println("who");
```

ChatWatcher is passed a reference to ChatClient, so it can write into the GUI's text area, jtaMesgs. This is done via the method showMsg( ).

Showing a Message and Threads

showMsg( ) adds a message to the end of the jtaMesgs text area and is called by the ChatClient or ChatWatcher object. However, updates to Swing components must be carried out by Swing's event dispatcher thread; otherwise, synchronization problems may arise between Swing and the user threads. The SwingUtilities class contains invokeLater( ), which adds code to the event dispatcher's queue; the code must be packaged as a Runnable object:

```
public void showMsg(final String msg)
{
  Runnable updateMsgsText = new Runnable() {
    public void run()
    { jtaMesgs.append(msg);  // append message to text area
      jtaMesgs.setCaretPosition( jtaMesgs.getText().length() );
              // move insertion point to the end of the text
    }
  };
  SwingUtilities.invokeLater( updateMsgsText );   // add code to queue
} // end of showMsg()
```

Though showMsg( ) can be called concurrently by ChatClient and ChatWatcher, there's no need to synchronize the method; multiple calls to showMsg( ) will cause a series of Runnable objects to be added to the event dispatcher's queue, where they'll be executed in sequential order.

An invokeAndWait( ) method is similar to invokeLater( ) except that it doesn't return until the event dispatcher has executed the Runnable object. Details on these methods, and more background on Swing and threads, can be found at *http://java.sun.com/ products/jfc/tsc/articles/threads/threads1.html*.

My thanks to Rachel Struthers for pointing out the bug in the original version of showMsg( ).

Waiting for Chat Messages

The core of the ChatWatcher class is a while loop inside run( ) that waits for a server message, processes it, and repeats. The two message types are the WHO$$... response and broadcast messages from other clients:

```
while ((line = in.readLine()) != null) {
  if ((line.length() >= 6) &&      // "WHO$$ "
```

```
          (line.substring(0,5).equals("WHO$$")))
        showWho( line.substring(5).trim() );
          // remove WHO$$ keyword and surrounding space
      else  // show immediately
        client.showMsg(line + "\n");
  }
```

showWho( ) reformats the WHO$$... string before displaying it.

The Chat Server

The ChatServer constructor initializes a ChatGroup object to hold client information, and then enters a loop that deals with client connections by creating ChatServerHandler threads:

```
public ChatServer( )
{ cg = new ChatGroup( );
  try {
    ServerSocket serverSock = new ServerSocket(PORT);
    Socket clientSock;
    while (true) {
      System.out.println("Waiting for a client...");
      clientSock = serverSock.accept( );
      new ChatServerHandler(clientSock, cg).start( );
    }
  }
  catch(Exception e)
  { System.out.println(e);  }
}
```

Each handler is given a reference to the ChatGroup object.

The Threaded Chat Handler

The ThreadedChatServerHandler class is similar to the ThreadedScoreHandler class from Chapter 29. The main differences are the calls it makes to the ChatGroup object while processing the client's messages.

The run( ) method sets up the input and output streams to the client and adds (and later removes) a client from the ChatGroup object:

```
public void run( )
{ try {
    // Get I/O streams from the socket
    BufferedReader in  = new BufferedReader(
                          new InputStreamReader( clientSock.getInputStream( ) ));
    PrintWriter out =
      new PrintWriter( clientSock.getOutputStream( ), true);

    cg.addPerson(cliAddr, port, out);  // add client to ChatGroup

    processClient(in, out);              // interact with client
```

```
        // the client has finished when execution reaches here
    cg.delPerson(cliAddr, port);      // remove client details
    clientSock.close();
    System.out.println("Client (" + cliAddr + ", " +
                            port + ") connection closed\n");
  }
  catch(Exception e)
  {  System.out.println(e);  }
}
```

processClient( ) checks for the client's departure by looking for a bye message. Other messages (who and text messages) are passed on to doRequest( ):

```
private void doRequest(String line, PrintWriter out)
{ if (line.trim().toLowerCase().equals("who")) {
    System.out.println("Processing 'who'");
    out.println( cg.who() );
  }
  else  // use ChatGroup object to broadcast the message
    cg.broadcast( "("+cliAddr+", "+port+"): " + line);
}
```

Storing Chat Client Information

ChatGroup handles the addition/removal of client details, the answering of who messages, and the broadcasting of messages to all the clients. The details are stored in an ArrayList of Chatter objects (called chatPeople), one object for each client.

A single ChatGroup object is used by all the ChatServerHandler threads, so methods that manipulate chatPeople must be synchronized. An example of this is the broadcast( ) method, which sends the specified message to all the clients, including back to the sender:

```
synchronized public void broadcast(String msg)
{ Chatter c;
  for(int i=0; i < chatPeople.size(); i++) {
    c = (Chatter) chatPeople.get(i);
    c.sendMessage(msg);
  }
}
```

The Chatter Class

The client details managed by a Chatter object are its address, port, and PrintWriter output stream. The address and port are employed to identify the client (a client has no name). The output stream is used to send messages to the client. For example:

```
private PrintWriter out;    // global

public void sendMessage(String msg)
{  out.println(msg);  }
```

Discussion

Messages can only be broadcast, and there's no capability to send private messages, though that's easily fixed, as you'll see in later examples. The communication protocol is defined by the server, so creating a new message format is simple:

```
message / toName
```

The implementation would require that clients be named; then `ChatServerHandler` could examine the `toName` part of the message and route the message only to that client. The delivery would use a new method in `ChatGroup` (e.g., `void sendPrivate(String message, String toName)`) to call the `sendMessage()` method of the `Chatter` object for `toName`.

Other communication patterns (e.g., periodic announcements linked to the current time) are straightforward to implement by extending the protocols supported by `ChatServer`. This illustrates one of the advantages of localizing communication management in the server.

Central control has its drawbacks as well, namely that if `ChatServer` fails, then the entire system fails. However, the nonfunctioning of a single `ChatServerHandler` thread doesn't affect the others. A likely scenario is one thread being made to wait indefinitely by a client who doesn't communicate with it.

UDP Multicasting Clients and a Name Server

Figure 30-4 shows the various objects in the multicasting chat application.

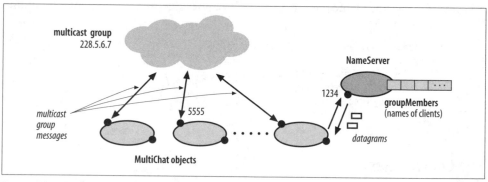

Figure 30-4. Multicasting chat system

Each user is represented by a `MultiChat` object that can send and receive messages from the multicast group. However, this isn't a pure peer-to-peer example since a client must first log in to the `NameServer` object and receive the address of the group. Upon leaving the group, the client must log out from the server. Each client has a name that is checked by `NameServer` for uniqueness. If the name is being used by a group member, then `NameServer` rejects the request to log in.

As a side effect of storing user names, NameServer can process who messages. Instead of a client multicasting a who message to all the other group members and receiving multiple replies, a single who message is directed to the NameServer followed by a single response. This approach significantly reduces the number of messages circulating in the system.

As discussed in the context of the threaded chat server, the main drawback of using NameServer is that it represents a single point of failure. However, NameServer's disappearance only prevents new clients from joining the group. Communication between existing members can continue. The other consequence of NameServer's demise is that who messages will no longer be answered.

NameServer must be able to handle multiple concurrent accesses from clients (to log in, log out, or request who information). The server uses UDP as its communication protocol, permitting it to multiplex easily between the various requests (since each request is a datagram).

The messages that a client can send to NameServer are:

hi <client name>
> This is the login message, which results in NameServer sending the client the multicast address (as a string) or in a no message.

bye <client name>
> This is the logout message, which allows NameServer to discard the client's name from its group members list.

who
> This is the server, which returns the names of all the current group members.

A client can send messages to the group for transmission to the other members. The message format is:

    (<client name>): <message> [/ <toClientName>]

The client's name is prepended to the front of the message. The square brackets mean the message may have an optional / extension, which makes the message visible only to that particular client. For example:

    Andrew: come in for dinner / John

is the message "come in for dinner" sent from Andrew to John. Whereas:

    Andrew: has anyone seen John's football?

broadcasts the message "has anyone seen John's football?" from Andrew to everyone (including himself).

The class diagrams for the application are given in Figure 30-5 but are uninformative. Almost no public methods are required since communication is datagram-based.

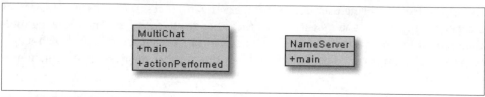

Figure 30-5. Class diagrams for the multicasting chat system

The Name Server

The NameServer class is similar to the top-level to the UDP-based server, ScoreUDPServer, in Chapter 29. It creates a DatagramSocket for receiving client packets and then enters a loop waiting for them to arrive. The client's address, port, and the text of the message are extracted from an arriving packet and from the information passed to a processClient( ) method.

processClient( ) employs a four-way branch to handle the various kinds of message (hi, bye, who) along with a default catch-all branch:

```
// globals
private static final String GROUP_HOST = "228.5.6.7";
    // the multicast group address sent to new members

private ArrayList groupMembers;
  // holds the names of the current members of the multicast group


private void processClient(String msg, InetAddress addr, int port)
{
  if (msg.startsWith("hi")) {
    String name = msg.substring(2).trim( );
    if (name != null && isUniqueName(name)) {
        groupMembers.add(name);
        sendMessage(GROUP_HOST, addr, port); // send multicast addr
    }
    else
      sendMessage("no", addr, port);
  }
  else if (msg.startsWith("bye")) {
    String name = msg.substring(3).trim( );
    if (name != null)
        removeName(name);  // removes name from list
  }
  else if (msg.equals("who"))
    sendMessage( listNames( ), addr, port);
  else
    System.out.println("Do not understand the message");

} // end of processClient( )
```

The client's name is added to an ArrayList called groupMembers if it isn't present in the list. A bye message removes the name. A who message triggers a call to listNames( ), which builds a string of all the groupMembers names.

sendMessage( ) creates a datagram that's sent back to the client's address and port:

```
private void sendMessage(String msg, InetAddress addr, int port)
{
  try {
    DatagramPacket sendPacket =
        new DatagramPacket( msg.getBytes( ), msg.length( ), addr, port);
    serverSock.send( sendPacket );
  }
  catch(IOException ioe)
  { System.out.println(ioe);  }
}
```

Improving Client Login and Logout

The simplicity of processClient( ) in NameServer shows that the login and logout mechanisms could be improved. There's no password associated with the name used in hi, so a client can use any name to log in. A bye message can come from anywhere, so it's possible for any client to log out another client. In any case, the removal of a client from the NameServer doesn't force a client to leave the multicast group.

The introduction of a password, together with encryption of the message inside the datagram would solve many of these problems. The remaining concern is that the server cannot force a client to leave the multicast group. The protocol is supported at the IP level, so beyond the reach of the Java MuticastSocket API. Indeed, the server has no control over the group at all, aside from deciding who will be given the multicast group address. This is hardly effective since the address can be shared between clients once one user has it. This lack of control is a crucial difference between the client/server approach and peer-to-peer.

Multicast Chatting

A MultiChat object is capable of two forms of network communication: it can send ordinary UDP datagrams to the NameServer (and receive replies) and can post datagrams to the multicast group (and receive messages from the group).

A MultiChat object is invoked with the client name supplied on the command line:

```
$ java MultiChat andy
```

Its GUI is similar to the one for the threaded chat client, as shown in Figure 30-6.

One obvious difference is that messages are now prefixed with the client's name rather than an address and port.

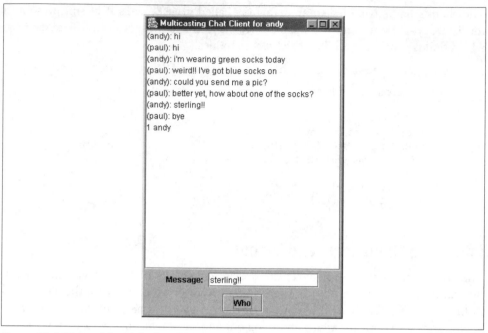

Figure 30-6. The multicasting chat client

The MultiChat constructor creates a DatagramSocket for the NameServer and sends it a hi <name> message requesting the multicast group's address. If the address is sent back, the group will be joined and a hi message sent to it (the message could be anything):

```
public MultiChat(String nm)
{
    super( "Multicasting Chat Client for " + nm);
    userName = nm;
    initializeGUI( );

    /* Attempt to register name and get multicast group
       address from the NameServer */
    makeClientSock( );
    sendServerMessage("hi " + userName);  // say "hi" to NameServer
    checkHiResponse( );

    // Connect to the multicast group; say hi to everyone
    joinChatGroup( );
    sendPacket("hi");

    addWindowListener( new WindowAdapter( ) {
      public void windowClosing(WindowEvent e)
      { sayBye( ); }    // say bye at termination time
    });

    setSize(300,450);
    show( );
```

```
    waitForPackets();
  } // end of MultiChat();
```

Having the client talk to the name server

makeClientSock() creates a DatagramSocket for sending and receiving communication from the NameServer. However, it's given a timeout of five seconds:

```
clientSock = new DatagramSocket();
clientSock.setSoTimeout(5000);
```

A timeout is useful when the client is waiting for a datagram inside receive(). This occurs after a hi message has been sent and after who queries. If the server has died, the timeout will limit the wait to five seconds before a SocketTimeoutException is raised.

The drawback is deciding on a reasonable timeout value. For instance, five seconds would probably be too short if the link was across the internet, through slow modems. This is why most programmers prefer to put blocking calls into separate threads so they can wait as long as they like. An alternative for TCP is to use non-blocking sockets, as illustrated in Chapter 29.

Messages are sent to the server from sendServerMessage() by creating a datagram and sending it through clientSock. Messages coming from the server are read by readServerMessage(). Its clientSock.receive() call is wrapped in a try-catch block in case of a timeout (or other network problems).

A call is made to readServerMessage() immediately after a message is sent to the server. There's no attempt to use a separate thread for server processing. For example, a who message is followed by a readServerMessage() call:

```
sendServerMessage("who");
String whoResponse = readServerMessage();
```

Having the client talk to the multicast group

The multicast group address string is extracted from the hi response and used by joinChatGroup() to create the multicast socket. A code fragment that does this is:

```
groupAddr = InetAddress.getByName(hiResponse);

groupSock = new MulticastSocket(GROUP_PORT);  // port 5555
groupSock.joinGroup(groupAddr);
```

sendPacket() is used to send a message to the group and adds the (userName): prefix prior to delivery:

```
private void sendPacket(String msg)
{ String labelledMsg = "(" + userName + "): " + msg;
  try {
    DatagramPacket sendPacket =
        new DatagramPacket(labelledMsg.getBytes(),
                      labelledMsg.length(), groupAddr, GROUP_PORT);
```

```
      groupSock.send(sendPacket);
    }
    catch(IOException ioe)
    {  System.out.println(ioe);  }
  }
```

Text messages are sent to the group when the user hits Enter in the messages text field. actionPerformed( ) calls sendMessage( ):

```
public void actionPerformed(ActionEvent e)
{ if (e.getSource( ) == jbWho)
    doWho( );
  else if (e.getSource( ) == jtfMsg)
    sendMessage( );
}
```

sendMessage( ) extracts the string from the text field, checks it for validity, and passes it to sendPacket( ). All of this is done inside the GUI thread of the MultiChat application.

Hearing from the multicast group

Multicast messages may arrive at any time, so must be handled in a separate thread. Instead of creating a new Thread object, MultiChat uses the application thread by entering an infinite loop inside waitForPackets( ):

```
private void waitForPackets( )
{ DatagramPacket packet;
  byte data[];

  try {
    while (true) {
      data = new byte[PACKET_SIZE];     // set up an empty packet
      packet = new DatagramPacket(data, data.length);
      groupSock.receive(packet);        // wait for a packet
      processPacket(packet);
    }
  }
  catch(IOException ioe)
  {  System.out.println(ioe);  }
}
```

This is the same approach as in the ScoreUDPClient in Chapter 29.

processPacket( ) extracts the text from the incoming packet and displays it (if it's visible to this client):

```
private void processPacket(DatagramPacket dp)
{ String msg = new String( dp.getData( ), 0, dp.getLength( ) );
  if (isVisibleMsg(msg, userName))
    showMsg(msg + "\n");
}
```

A message is visible if it has no / <name> part if / <name> contains the client's name, or if the message is originally from the client. This latter condition can be checked by looking at the start of the message that has the sender's name in brackets.

How Invisible Are Invisible Messages?

A message won't appear in a client's text display area if it has a / name extension that refers to a different client. Is this sufficient for private communication between two users? Unfortunately, this is not sufficient since the message is still being multicast to every client. This means that a hacker could modify the MultiChat code to display everything that arrives. Privacy requires that the messages be encrypted.

The other misleading thing about private communication is that it appears to be point-to-point between users and seemingly more efficient than multicasting. Unfortunately, this is false. True point-to-point communication would require another communication link, perhaps utilizing the DatagramSockets utilized for client/server interaction.

Ways to Implement who

MultiChat handles a who message by querying the server for a list of names. Another approach would be to multicast the message to all the clients to gather responses. The main benefit would be communication without relying on the server, which can fail or otherwise stop responding.

I didn't use multicasting to process a who message because of the large number of messages it would add to the system. With multicasting, the client's who query would be sent to n clients. Each client would send a reply, multicasting to every client, not just the one interested in the answer. This would mean a total of $n \times n$ messages circulating through the group. The grand total for a single who query is $n + n^2$. By using the server, I replaced this large number with two messages: the request sent to NameServer and its reply. Alternatives to multicasting should always be explored since bandwidth is such a crucial commodity.

Clients Using a Servlet as a Server

Figure 30-7 shows the various objects in the servlet-based chat application.

Each client is represented by two objects: a URLChat object manages the GUI and translates user input into messages for the web server. The URLChatWatcher thread periodically queries the server for new messages sent by the other users.

The communication is implemented by sending the server a GET request for the ChatServlet object, with message details added as arguments to the URL. A client is identified by a name and a cookie. The cookie is presented to users when they send a

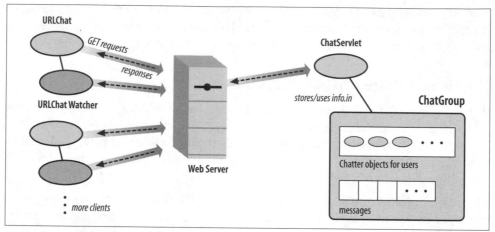

Figure 30-7. The servlet-based chat system

hi message to the servlet upon joining the chat system. Most messages require the name and cookie information, which verify the identity of the message sender.

The servlet maintains a synchronized ChatGroup object, which bears many similarities to the ChatGroup object used in the threaded chat application. Client information is held in Chatter objects, while client messages are stored in a messages ArrayList.

A key difference between ChatServlet and the server in the first chat example is that ChatServlet cannot initiate communication with its clients. It must wait for a URLChatWatcher thread to ask for messages before it can send them out.

URLChat transmits its messages as arguments attached to the URL *http://localhost:8100/servlet/ChatServlet*. The notation for an argument in a GET request is arg-name=arg-value, with multiple argument name/value pairs separated by &. The argument pairs follow a ? after the URL.

The four possible message types are:

ChatServlet?cmd=hi&name=??
> This is a hi message, used by a client to ask for chat group membership. The name parameter value (represented by ??) holds the client's name. The servlet returns a cookie containing a user ID (uid) or rejects the client.

ChatServlet?cmd=bye&name=?? *and* uid *cookie*
> This is a bye message, which signals the client's departure. The cookie is included in the header part of the GET message, not as a URL argument.

ChatServlet?cmd=who
> The who message requires no client name or cookie parameters. The servlet returns the names of the clients currently using the application.

ChatServlet?cmd=msg&name=??&msg=?? *and* uid *cookie*
> This message sends chat text to the servlet as the msg parameter value. The string is added to the servlet's messages list if the client name and uid are correct.

The chat message format is the same as in the multicasting example: if the text has a / toName extension, then it will be intended only for the client with that name.

URLChatWatcher periodically sends a read message:

ChatServlet?cmd=read&name=?? *and* uid *cookie*
>This retrieves all the *visible* chat messages stored by the servlet since the last read. Visible messages are intended for everyone (the default) or have a / toName extension which matches this client's name.

The cookie acts as an additional form of identification, paired with the client's name. However, cookies are not passwords, being passed in plain text form in the headers of the messages. To act as a password, it would be necessary to add encryption to the interaction, possibly by using HTTPS rather than HTTP.

Figure 30-8 gives the class diagrams for the application, showing the public methods.

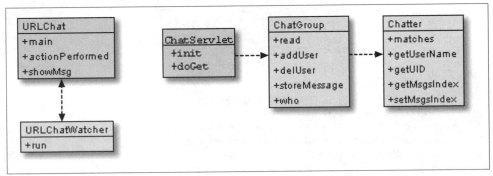

Figure 30-8. Class diagrams for the servlet-based chat system

The URL-Based Chat Client

Figure 30-9 shows the GUI for URLChat, which is identical to the earlier examples. A hi message is generated when the client is first invoked, a bye message is sent when the user clicks on the window's close box, a who message is transmitted when the Who button is pressed, and the entering of a string in the text field results in a msg message.

The constructor carries out several tasks—it creates the GUI, sets timeout properties, sends a hi message, links the bye output to the close box, and invokes a URLChatWatcher:

```
// globals
private String userName;  // for this client
private String cookieStr = null;

public URLChat(String nm)
{  super( "URL Chat Client for "+ nm);
   userName = nm;
   initializeGUI();
```

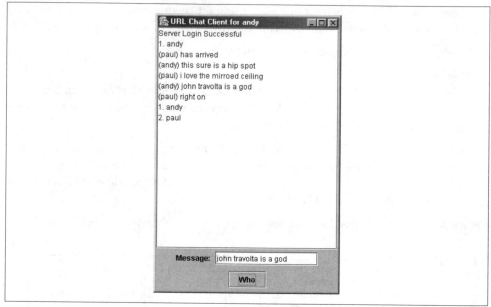

Figure 30-9. The URLChat GUI

```
// set the properties used for URL timeouts (in ms)
Properties props = System.getProperties();
props.put("sun.net.client.defaultConnectTimeout", "2000");
props.put("sun.net.client.defaultReadTimeout", "2000");
System.setProperties(props);

sayHi();

addWindowListener( new WindowAdapter() {
  public void windowClosing(WindowEvent e)
  { sayBye(); }
});

setSize(300,450);
show();

  new URLChatWatcher(this, userName, cookieStr).start();
} // end of URLChat();
```

A client utilizes URL GET requests to communicate with the servlet. If the server is down or the servlet is unavailable, then the client will have to wait for the URL request to timeout. This often amounts to several minutes delay before an exception is raised. Fortunately, J2SE 1.4 introduced two properties for adjusting the default connection timeout and the reading timeout (how long to wait when the reading of a web page is delayed). These are associated with every URLConnection object created in the application. The main problem with timeouts, as always, is deciding on a reasonable value that takes network latency into account.

Another approach is to wrap each connection in a thread using `Thread.join()` as a timeout mechanism. This has the advantage that different timeout values can be assigned to different URLs.

`sayHi()` illustrates how a GET request is constructed using a URL object. The response from the servlet may include a Set-Cookie header: this is the usual way that a cookie is sent to a browser. Set-Cookie isn't a part of the HTTP standard but is used by all web servers and browsers. The need to read the response page's headers requires a `URLConnection` object.

The returned page is plain text consisting of a single line containing "ok" or "no":

```java
private void sayHi()
{
  try {
    URL url  = new URL(SERVER + "?cmd=hi&name=" +
                         URLEncoder.encode(userName, "UTF-8") );

    URLConnection conn = url.openConnection();
    cookieStr = conn.getHeaderField("Set-Cookie");  // get cookie

    System.out.println("Received cookie: " + cookieStr);
    if (cookieStr != null) {
      int index = cookieStr.indexOf(";");
      if (index != -1)
        cookieStr = cookieStr.substring(0, index);  //remove extras
    }

    BufferedReader br = new BufferedReader(
                        new InputStreamReader( conn.getInputStream() ));
    String response = br.readLine().trim();
    br.close();

    if (response.equals("ok") && (cookieStr != null))
      showMsg("Server Login Successful\n");
    else {
      System.out.println("Server Rejected Login");
      System.exit(0);
    }
  }
  catch(Exception e)
  { System.out.println(e);
    System.exit(0);
  }
}  // end of sayHi()
```

The client name must be URL-encoded prior to transmission. Essentially, this replaces any spaces in the string by +s and alters certain other characters to a hexadecimal format.

The value of a Set-Cookie header is a string containing the cookie value separated from various other things by a ; (these may include a comment, path and domain qualifiers, a maximum age, and a version number). This additional information isn't required, so sayHi( ) strips it away before storing the string in the cookieStr global. In fact, the servlet creates a cookie holding only a value, so the editing code is not really necessary in this example.

The client will terminate if the response to the hi message is "no," or the cookie string is not initialized. All further communication with the servlet (aside from who messages) requires the cookie value.

If a servlet (or its web server) is unavailable, then the URL request will timeout after two seconds (due to the timeout properties set in the constructor), and raise an exception. This allows a client to respond to the server's absence by exiting.

sayHi( ) uses showMsg( ) to write into the GUI's text area, which is implemented in the same way as in the threaded client that I discussed first. The updates to the text area are performed by Swing's event dispatching thread.

Talking to the servlet

URLChat employs sendURLMessage( ) to send a chat message to the servlet. It's quite similar to sayHi( ) except that it adds the cookie value to the GET request by including a Cookie header in the output.

The response page returned by the servlet is one line containing "ok" or "no":

```
private void sendURLMessage(String msg)
{
  try {
    URL url  = new URL(SERVER + "?cmd=msg&name=" +
            URLEncoder.encode(userName, "UTF-8") +
                "&msg=" + URLEncoder.encode(msg, "UTF-8") );
    URLConnection conn = url.openConnection( );

    conn.setRequestProperty("Cookie", cookieStr); // add cookie

    BufferedReader br = new BufferedReader(
            new InputStreamReader( conn.getInputStream( ) ));
    String response = br.readLine( ).trim( );
    br.close( );

    if (!response.equals("ok"))
      showMsg("Message Send Rejected\n");
    else // display message immediately
      showMsg("(" + userName + ") " + msg + "\n");
  }
  catch(Exception e)
  { showMsg("Servlet Error. Did not send: " + msg + "\n");
    System.out.println(e);
  }
}  // end of sendURLMessage( )
```

A small but significant part of sendURLMessage( ) is the call to showMsg( ) to display the output message if the servlet's response was "ok." This means the message appears in the client's text area almost as soon as it is typed.

The alternative would be to wait until it was retrieved, together with the other recent messages, by URLChatWatcher. The drawback of this approach is the delay before the user sees a visual conformation that their message has been sent. This delay depends on the frequency of URLChatWatcher's requests to the servlet (currently every two seconds). A message echoing delay like this gives an impression of execution slowness and communication latency, which is best avoided.

The drawback of the current design (immediate echoing of the output message) is that the user's contribution to a conversation may not appear on screen in the order that the conversation is recorded in the servlet.

Polling for Chat Messages

URLChatWatcher starts an infinite loop that sleeps for a while (two seconds) and then sends a read request for new chat messages. The answer is processed and displayed in the client's text area, and the watcher repeats:

```
public void run( )
{ URL url;
  URLConnection conn;
  BufferedReader br;
  String line, response;
  StringBuffer resp;

  try {
    String readRequest = SERVER + "?cmd=read&name=" +
                              URLEncoder.encode(userName, "UTF-8") ;
    while(true) {
      Thread.sleep(SLEEP_TIME);  // sleep for 2 secs

      url  = new URL(readRequest);   // send a "read" message
      conn = url.openConnection( );

      // Set the cookie value to send
      conn.setRequestProperty("Cookie", cookieStr);

      br = new BufferedReader( new InputStreamReader( conn.getInputStream( ) ));
      resp = new StringBuffer( );    // build up the response
      while ((line = br.readLine( )) != null) {
        if (!fromClient(line))   // if not from client
          resp.append(line+"\n");
      }
      br.close( );

      response = resp.toString( );
      if ((response != null) && !response.equals("\n"))
        client.showMsg(response);    // show the response
```

```
      }
    }
    catch(Exception e)
    { client.showMsg("Servlet Error: watching terminated\n");
      System.out.println(e);
    }
  } // end of run( )
```

The try-catch block allows the watcher to respond to the server's absence by issuing an error message before terminating.

The response page may contain multiple lines of text, one line for each chat message. The watcher filters out chat messages originating from its client since these will have been printed when they were sent out. A drawback of this filtering is that when a client joins the chat system again in the future, messages stored from a prior visit won't be shown in the display text area. This can be remedied by making the fromClient( ) test a little more complicated than the existing code:

```
private boolean fromClient(String line)
{ if (line.startsWith("("+userName))
    return true;
  return false;
}
```

The Chat Servlet

The initialization phase of a ChatServlet object creates a new ChatGroup object for holding client details. Its doGet( ) method tests the cmd parameter of GET requests to decide what message is being received:

```
// globals
private ChatGroup cg;    // for storing client information

public void init( ) throws ServletException
{  cg = new ChatGroup( );  }


public void doGet( HttpServletRequest request, HttpServletResponse response)
                    throws ServletException, IOException
// look at cmd parameter to decide which message the client sent
{
  String command = request.getParameter("cmd");
  System.out.println("Command: " + command);

  if (command.equals("hi"))
    processHi(request, response);
  else if (command.equals("bye"))
    processBye(request, response);
  else if (command.equals("who"))
    processWho(response);
  else if (command.equals("msg"))
```

```
      processMsg(request, response);
    else if (command.equals("read"))
      processRead(request, response);
    else
      System.out.println("Did not understand command: " + command);
  } // end of doGet()
```

An understanding of this code requires a knowledge of the servlet lifecycle. A web server will typically create a single servlet instance, resulting in init( ) being called once. However, each GET request will usually be processed by spawning a separate thread which executes doGet( ) for itself. This is similar to the execution pattern employed by the threaded server in the first chat example.

The consequence is that data which may be manipulated by multiple doGet( ) threads must be synchronized. The simplest solution is to place this data in an object that is only accessible by synchronized methods. Consequently, the single ChatGroup object (created in init( )) holds client details and the list of chat messages.

Dealing with a new client

processHi( ) handles a message with the format ChatServlet?cmd=hi&name=??. The name parameter must be extracted and tested, and a cookie must be created for the client's new user ID. The cookie is sent back as a header, and the response page is a single line containing "ok," or "no" if something is wrong:

```
private void processHi(HttpServletRequest request, HttpServletResponse response)
                        throws IOException
{
  int uid = -1;  // default for failure
  String userName = request.getParameter("name");

  if (userName != null)
    uid = cg.addUser(userName);  // attempt to add to group

  if (uid != -1) {  // the request has been accepted
    Cookie c = new Cookie("uid", ""+uid);
    response.addCookie(c);
  }

  PrintWriter output = response.getWriter();
  if (uid != -1)
    output.println("ok");
  else
    output.println("no");  // request was rejected
  output.close();
} // end of processHi()
```

The cookie is created using the Cookie class and is added to the headers of the response with the addCookie( ) method. The actual cookie header has this format:

```
Set-Cookie: uid= <some number>
```

The uid number is generated when ChatGroup creates a Chatter object for the new client. It may have any value between 0 and 1024. If the value is –1, then the membership request will be rejected because the client's name is being used by another person.

Processing client messages

processMsg( ) is typically of the other processing methods in ChatServlet. It handles a message with the format ChatServlet?cmd=msg&name=??&msg=?? and a uid cookie in the header.

It attempts to add the chat message to the messages list maintained by ChatGroup:

```
private void processMsg(HttpServletRequest request,
                        HttpServletResponse response)
                                          throws IOException
{ boolean isStored = false;    // default for failure
  String userName = request.getParameter("name");
  String msg = request.getParameter("msg");

  System.out.println("msg: " + msg);

  if ((userName != null) && (msg != null)) {
    int uid = getUidFromCookie(request);
    isStored = cg.storeMessage(userName,uid,msg); //add msg to list
  }

  PrintWriter output = response.getWriter();
  if (isStored)
    output.println("ok");
  else
    output.println("no");    // something wrong
  output.close();
} // end of processBye()
```

Processing is aborted if the name or chat message is missing. The call to getUidFromCookie( ) will return a number (which may be –1, signifying an error). The ChatGroup object is then given the task of storing the chat message, which it only does if the name/uid pair match an existing client. The resulting isStored value is employed to decide on the response page sent back to the client.

getUidFromCookie( ) must deal with the possibility of multiple cookies in the request, so has to search for the one with the uid name. A missing uid cookie, or one with a nonnumerical value, causes a –1 to be returned:

```
private int getUidFromCookie(HttpServletRequest request)
{
  Cookie[] cookies = request.getCookies();
  Cookie c;
  for(int i=0; i < cookies.length; i++) {
    c = cookies[i];
    if (c.getName().equals("uid")) {
```

```
        try {
          return Integer.parseInt( c.getValue( ) );
        }
        catch (Exception ex){
          System.out.println(ex);
          return -1;
        }
      }
    }
    return -1;
  } // end of getUidFromCookie( )
```

The getCookies( ) method returns an array of Cookie objects, which can be examined with getName( ) and getValue( ).

Storing Chat Group Information

ChatGroup maintains two ArrayLists: chatUsers and messages. chatUsers is an ArrayList of Chatter objects; each Chatter object stores a client's name, uid, and the number of messages read by its CharURLWatcher thread. messages is an ArrayList of strings (one for each chat message).

All the public methods are synchronized since many doGet( ) threads may be competing to access the ChatGroup object simultaneously.

The messages ArrayList solves the problem of storing chat messages. The drawback is the list will grow long as the volume of communication increases. However, the messages list is cleared when no users are in the chat group.

Another possible optimization, which isn't utilized in this code, is to delete messages which have been read by all the current users. This would keep the list small since each client's URLChatWatcher reads the list every few seconds. The drawback is the extra complexity of adjusting the list and the Chatter objects' references to it.

A possible advantage of maintaining a lengthy messages list is that new members get to see earlier conversations when they join the system. The list is sent to a new client when its watcher thread sends its first read message.

Another approach might be to archive older messages in a text file. This could be accessed when required without being a constant part of the messages list. It could be employed as a backup mechanism in case of server failure.

Adding a new client to the group

addUser( ) adds a new client to the ChatGroup if his or her name is unique. A uid for the user is returned:

```
// globals
private ArrayList chatUsers;
private ArrayList messages;
private int numUsers;
```

```
synchronized public int addUser(String name)
// adds a user, returns uid if okay, -1 otherwise
{
  if (numUsers == 0)    // no one logged in
    messages.clear();

  if (isUniqueName(name)) {
    Chatter c = new Chatter(name);
    chatUsers.add(c);
    messages.add("(" + name + ") has arrived");
    numUsers++;
    return c.getUID();
  }
  return -1;
}
```

Reading client messages

One of the more complicated methods in ChatGroup is read( ), which is called when a watcher thread requires new messages:

```
synchronized public String read(String name, int uid)
{
  StringBuffer msgs = new StringBuffer();
  Chatter c = findUser(name, uid);

  if (c != null) {
    int msgsIndex = c.getMsgsIndex();  // where read to last time
    String msg;
    for(int i=msgsIndex; i < messages.size(); i++) {
      msg = (String) messages.get(i);
      if (isVisibleMsg(msg, name))
        msgs.append( msg + "\n" );
    }
    c.setMsgsIndex( messages.size());  //update client's read index
  }
  return msgs.toString();
}
```

The method begins by calling findUser( ) to retrieve the Chatter object for the given name and uid, which may return null if there isn't a match.

Since the messages list retains all the chat messages, it's necessary for each Chatter object to record the number of messages read. This is retrieved with a call to getMsgsIndex( ) and updated with setMsgsIndex( ). This number corresponds to an index into the messages list, and can be used to initialize the for loop that collects the chat messages.

If the messages list was periodically purged of messages that had been read by all the current users, then it would be necessary to adjust the index number stored in each Chatter object.

Only visible messages are returned—i.e., those without a / toName extension, or an extension, which names the client.

The Chatter Class

Each Chatter object stores the client's name, the uid, and the current number of messages read from the chat messages list.

The uid is generated in a trivial manner by generating a random number between 0 and ID_MAX (1024). The choice of ID_MAX has no significance:

```
uid = (int) Math.round( Math.random( )* ID_MAX);
```

CHAPTER 31

A Networked Two-Person Game

Chapter 30 described three versions of a chat system, built using a threaded client/server model, UDP multicasting, and HTTP tunneling with servlets. Chatting utilizes a multi-player game model which allows players to join and leave at any time and doesn't impose an ordering on when the users interact.

This chapter focuses on the more complex networked two-person game model (two-person games include chess, battleships, and tic-tac-toe). The complexity is due to the stricter gaming conditions: two players must be present, and they must take turns. Two-person games can be generalized to n-person contests, which only start when n people are present, who each take turns to play. Most board games have this kind of structure.

The additional rules complicate the three phases of a game: initialization, game play, and termination. The game only starts when there are two players, which means that one player may have to wait, and late arrivals after two players have been found must be sent away or invited to create a new game. During the game, a player who moves out of turn may be penalized or ignored until the other player has moved. A game can terminate in several ways: one of the players may win (or lose), a player may give up, or the game can stop when one of the client network links breaks.

This complexity motivates the strategy used in this chapter: first, a standalone version of the game is designed, built, and debugged, and only then is the networked version considered. This allows issues such as game logic, 3D modeling, and GUI design to be addressed without the headaches of networking.

Once the network phase is entered, utilizing design tools is useful before sitting down to hack. I use three diagramming tools here: informal network protocol diagrams, UML activity, and sequence diagrams. The protocol diagrams highlight the network interactions between the clients, focusing on the three game phases (initialization, game play, and termination). The activity and sequence diagrams allow me to trace turn-taking easily from one player, through the server, to the other player.

The implementation employs a threaded client/server model: each client has a thread to send messages to the server (e.g., details of the player's turn) and another to receive data from the server (e.g., information about the other player). The server is threaded as well: one thread for each client. These networking elements are similar to those used in the threaded client/server chat system in Chapter 30, allowing me to reuse a lot of the code.

The clients are *fat* in the sense that they do most of the game processing; the server is little more than a message forwarder. An important advantage of the fat client approach is that most of the GUI and game play code developed in the standalone version of the game can be carried over to the client in the networked version without modification.

This chapter utilizes the perennial favorite of two-person gaming, tic-tac-toe, but with a Java 3D makeover to display the board and player counters as 3D objects. I'll assume you know Java 3D.

The standalone FourByFour tic-tac-toe game is shown in Figure 31-1 (the network version looks similar and is shown in Figure 31-11). Player 1's markers are red spheres; player 2 has blue cubes. The aim is to create a line of four markers, all of the same type, along the x-, y-, or z-axes, or the diagonals across the XY, XZ, or YZ planes or from corner to corner.

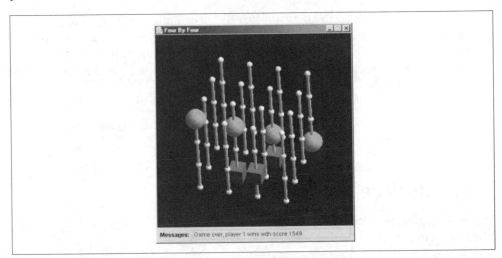

Figure 31-1. FourByFour in action

The nonnetworked FourByFour game described in the first part of this chapter is a simplified version of a game available in the Java 3D distribution. The main elements are:

Parallel projection
> The poles and markers at the back of the scene are the same size as the ones at the front. Up to now, all my examples have used Java 3D's default perspective projection.

Marker caching
> Red and blue markers are created for all the possible game positions (64 total) at game startup time and are made invisible. When a marker is needed in a certain position, the relevant one only has to be made visible, which is a fast operation for Java 3D. The alternative is to create the required marker dynamically at runtime and attach it to the scene graph, which is much slower. The disadvantage is that the markers take time to be built, and many will never be used but the overhead is small.

> The markers are hidden by using Java 3D Switch nodes.

Marker labels
> Any Java 3D scene graph object can be assigned a user data reference, which can point to an arbitrary object. This allows scene graph nodes to store user-specific data. I employ this feature to label the game markers, which identifies them to the rest of the program.

User interaction
> Java 3D picking is used to allow a player to select a position by clicking with the mouse, and to rotate the game board via mouse dragging. In the networked version, the Java 3D Canvas3D class is extended to support overlaying (see Figure 31-11). This allows the program to write messages onto the screen without the overhead of creating 3D data structures.

 The standalone version of the game is in the directory *FourByFour/*; the networked version is in *NetFourByFour/*.

The Standalone Tic-Tac-Toe Game

Figure 31-2 gives the class diagrams for the standalone tic-tac-toe game, FourByFour. The class names and public methods are shown.

The FourByFour class is a Java 3D JFrame, which contains a GUI made up of a WrapFourByFour object for the 3D canvas and a text field for messages. The public showMessage( ) method allows objects to write into that field.

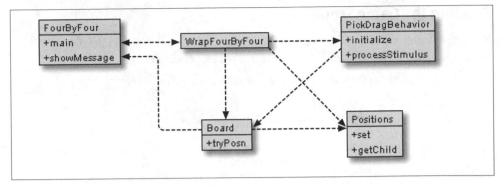

Figure 31-2. Class diagrams for FourByFour

WrapFourByFour constructs the scene: the lights, background, the parallel projection, and 16 poles, but leaves the initialization of the markers to a Positions object. WrapFourByFour creates a PickDragBehavior object to handle mouse picking and dragging.

The Board object contains the game logic, with data structures representing the current state of the board and methods for making a move and reporting a winner.

 The FourByFour application can be found in the *FourByFour/* directory.

The Origins of the Game

A tic-tac-toe game, FourByFour, has been part of the Java 3D distribution for many years. It has a more extensive GUI than the version described in this chapter, supporting repeated games, varying skill levels, and listing the high scores. A crucial difference is that the demo pits the machine against a single player, rather than player versus player. This requires a much more complicated Board class, weighing in at 2,300 lines (compared to 300 in my version of Board). It's possible to change the machine's skill level (from dumb to expert), which makes Board carry out increasingly comprehensive analyses of the player's moves and the current game state. The original Board renders the game to a 2D window in addition to a 3D canvas.

The original FourByFour demo utilizes its own versions of the Box and Cylinder utilities and builds its GUI with AWT. My version uses the Java 3D shape utility classes and Swing. The demo employs its own ID class to number the marker shapes; my code uses the userData field of the Java 3D Shape3D class.

Building the Game Scene

My WrapFourByFour class uses the same coding style as earlier 3D examples in that it creates the 3D canvas and adds the scene in createSceneGraph( ):

```
private void createSceneGraph(Canvas3D canvas3D, FourByFour fbf)
{
  sceneBG = new BranchGroup( );
  bounds = new BoundingSphere(new Point3d(0,0,0), BOUNDSIZE);

  // Create the transform group which moves the game
  TransformGroup gameTG = new TransformGroup( );
  gameTG.setCapability(TransformGroup.ALLOW_TRANSFORM_READ);
  gameTG.setCapability(TransformGroup.ALLOW_TRANSFORM_WRITE);
  sceneBG.addChild(gameTG);

  lightScene( );          // add the lights
  addBackground( );       // add the background

  gameTG.addChild( makePoles( ) );        // add poles

  // posns holds the spheres/boxes which mark a player's turn.
  // Initially posns displays a series of small white spheres.
  Positions posns = new Positions( );

  // board tracks the players' moves on the game board
  Board board = new Board(posns, fbf);

  gameTG.addChild( posns.getChild( ) );  // add markers

  mouseControls(canvas3D, board, gameTG);

  sceneBG.compile( );   // fix the scene
}
```

A TransformGroup, gameTG, is added below the scene's BranchGroup; it's used by the PickDragBehavior object to rotate the game when the mouse is dragged. Consequently, all the visible game objects (e.g., poles, markers) are linked to gameTG; static entities (e.g., the lights, background) are connected to sceneBG.

makePoles( ) creates the 16 poles where the game markers appear. The initial positions of the poles are shown in Figure 31-3.

The first pole (the leftmost pole of the first row) is centered at (−30,0,30) and has length 60 units. The other three poles in the row are spaced at 20-unit intervals to the right, and the next row begins, 20 units along the z-axis. There's no particular significance to these dimensions, aside from making the various parts of the game easier to see:

```
private BranchGroup makePoles( )
{
  Color3f grey = new Color3f(0.25f, 0.25f, 0.25f);
  Color3f black = new Color3f(0.0f, 0.0f, 0.0f);
```

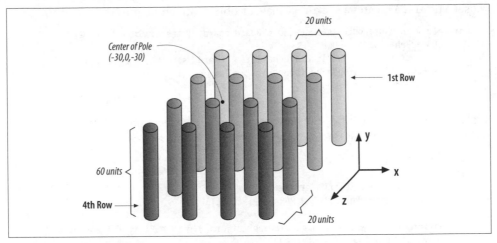

Figure 31-3. The game poles

```
Color3f diffuseWhite = new Color3f(0.7f, 0.7f, 0.7f);
Color3f specularWhite = new Color3f(0.9f, 0.9f, 0.9f);

// Create the pole appearance
Material poleMaterial =
    new Material(grey, black, diffuseWhite,specularWhite,110.f);
poleMaterial.setLightingEnable(true);
Appearance poleApp = new Appearance();
poleApp.setMaterial(poleMaterial);

BranchGroup bg = new BranchGroup();
float x = -30.0f;
float z = -30.0f;

for(int i=0; i<4; i++) {
  for(int j=0; j<4; j++) {
    Transform3D t3d = new Transform3D();
    t3d.set( new Vector3f(x, 0.0f, z) );
    TransformGroup tg = new TransformGroup(t3d);
    Cylinder cyl = new Cylinder(1.0f, 60.0f, poleApp);
    cyl.setPickable(false);  // user cannot select the poles
    tg.addChild( cyl );
    bg.addChild(tg);
    x += 20.0f;
  }
  x = -30.0f;
  z += 20.0f;
}
return bg;
} // end of makePoles()
```

A pole is represented by a `Cylinder`, below a `TransformGroup` which positions it. The poles (and transforms) are grouped under a `BranchGroup`. The cylinders are made unpickable, which simplifies the picking task in `PickDragBehavior`.

mouseControls( ) creates a PickDragBehavior object, attaching it to the scene:

```
private void mouseControls(Canvas3D c,Board board, TransformGroup gameTG)
{ PickDragBehavior mouseBeh =
                    new PickDragBehavior(c, board, sceneBG, gameTG);
  mouseBeh.setSchedulingBounds(bounds);
  sceneBG.addChild(mouseBeh);
}
```

initUserPosition( ) modifies the view to use parallel projection and moves the view-point along the +z axis so the entire game board is visible and centered in the canvas:

```
private void initUserPosition( )
{
  View view = su.getViewer( ).getView( );
  view.setProjectionPolicy(View.PARALLEL_PROJECTION);

  TransformGroup steerTG = su.getViewingPlatform( ).getViewPlatformTransform( );
  Transform3D t3d = new Transform3D( );
  t3d.set(65.0f, new Vector3f(0.0f, 0.0f, 400.0f));
  steerTG.setTransform(t3d);
}
```

Building the Game Markers

The Positions object creates three sets of markers: 64 small white balls, 64 larger red balls, and 64 blue cubes. The white balls are visible, the other shapes are invisible when the game starts. When a player makes a move, the selected white ball is replaced by a red one (if it was player 1's turn) or a blue cube (for player 2).

This functionality is achieved by creating three Java 3D Switch nodes, one for each set of markers, linked to the scene with a Group node, as shown in Figure 31-4.

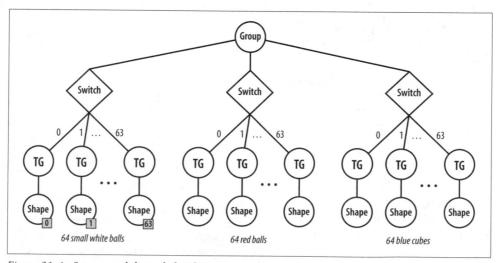

Figure 31-4. Scene graph branch for the game markers

Each Shape3D is positioned with a TransformGroup and allocated a bit in a Java 3D BitSet object corresponding to its position in the game (positions are numbered 0 to 63). The BitSet is used as a mask in the Switch node to specify what shapes are visible or invisible.

The three Switch branches are created with calls to makeWhiteSpheres( ), makeRedSpheres( ), and makeBlueCubes( ), which are functionally similar. The code for makeWhiteSpheres( ) is:

```
private void makeWhiteSpheres( )
{
  // Create the switch nodes
  posSwitch = new Switch(Switch.CHILD_MASK);
  // Set the capability bits
  posSwitch.setCapability(Switch.ALLOW_SWITCH_READ);
  posSwitch.setCapability(Switch.ALLOW_SWITCH_WRITE);
  posMask = new BitSet( );    // create the bit mask

  Sphere posSphere;
  for (int i=0; i<NUM_SPOTS; i++) {
    Transform3D t3d = new Transform3D( );
    t3d.set( points[i] );     // set position
    TransformGroup tg = new TransformGroup(t3d);
    posSphere = new Sphere(2.0f, whiteApp);
    Shape3D shape = posSphere.getShape( );
    shape.setUserData( new Integer(i) );
              // add board position ID to each shape
    tg.addChild( posSphere );
    posSwitch.addChild(tg);
    posMask.set(i);    // make visible
  }
  // Set the positions mask
  posSwitch.setChildMask(posMask);

  group.addChild( posSwitch );
} // end of makeWhiteSpheres( )
```

All the game marker Shape3D objects are pickable by default, which means that the PickDragBehavior object can select them.

An important feature of makeWhiteSpheres( ) is that each ball is assigned user data (i.e., an Integer object holding its position index). makeRedSpheres( ) and makeBlueCubes( ) don't set user data for their markers.

 This difference is denoted by little numbered boxes in Figure 31-4.

The integer field for a selected white ball is read by PickDragBehavior to determine its position. There's no need for integer fields in the red balls or blue cubes since they occupy positions on the board.

Another difference between makeWhiteSpheres( ) and the other two methods is that the white balls are all set to be visible initially, and the red balls and blue cubes are invisible. This is changed during the course of the game by calls to set( ):

```
public void set(int pos, int player)
// called by Board to update the 3D scene
{
  // turn off the white marker for the given position
  posMask.clear(pos);
  posSwitch.setChildMask(posMask);

  // turn on one of the player markers
  if (player == PLAYER1) {
    player1Mask.set(pos);
    player1Switch.setChildMask(player1Mask);   // red for p1
  }
  else if (player == PLAYER2) {
    player2Mask.set(pos);
    player2Switch.setChildMask(player2Mask);   // blue for p2
  }
  else  // should not happen
    System.out.println("Illegal player value: " + player);
}
```

The pos argument is the position index (a number between 0 and 63), extracted from the user data field of the selected white marker. The player value represents the first or second player.

The main design choice in the Positions class is to create all the possible markers at scene creation time. This makes the scene's initialization a little slower, but the rendering speed for displaying a player's marker is improved because Shape3D nodes don't need to be attached or detached from the scene graph at runtime.

The position indexes for the markers (0–63) are tied to locations in space by the initLocations( ) method, which creates a points[] array of markers' coordinates. The positions correspond to the indexes of points[]:

```
private void initLocations()
{ points = new Vector3f[NUM_SPOTS];
  int count = 0;
  for (int z=-30; z<40; z+=20)
    for (int y=-30; y<40; y+=20)
      for (int x=-30; x<40; x+=20) {
        points[count] = new Vector3f((float)x, (float)y, (float)z);
        count++;
      }
}
```

points[] is used to initialize the TransformGroups for the markers, positioning them in space.

The coordinates were chosen so the markers appear embedded in the poles. Figure 31-5 shows the first row of poles (the back row in Figure 31-3) and its 16 markers, which have position indexes 0–15.

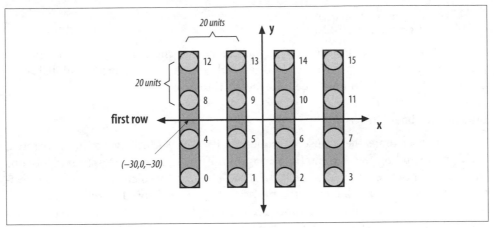

Figure 31-5. Marker positions in the first row of poles

Picking and Dragging

The PickDragBehavior object allows the user to click on a white marker to signal that the next move should be in that position, and to utilize mouse dragging to rotate the scene. The object monitors mouse drags, presses, and releases. A mouse release is employed as a way of detecting that a new mouse drag may start during the next user interaction.

processStimulus( ) responds to the three mouse operations:

```
public void processStimulus(Enumeration criteria)
{
  WakeupCriterion wakeup;
  AWTEvent[] event;
  int id;
  int xPos, yPos;
  while (criteria.hasMoreElements()) {
    wakeup = (WakeupCriterion) criteria.nextElement();
    if (wakeup instanceof WakeupOnAWTEvent) {
      event = ((WakeupOnAWTEvent)wakeup).getAWTEvent();
      for (int i=0; i<event.length; i++) {
        xPos = ((MouseEvent)event[i]).getX();
        yPos = ((MouseEvent)event[i]).getY();
        id = event[i].getID();
        if (id == MouseEvent.MOUSE_DRAGGED)
          processDrag(xPos, yPos);
        else if (id == MouseEvent.MOUSE_PRESSED)
          processPress(xPos, yPos);
```

```
          else if (id == MouseEvent.MOUSE_RELEASED)
            isStartDrag = true;    // a new drag may start next time
        }
      }
    }
    wakeupOn (mouseCriterion);
  } // end of processStimulus()
```

processDrag() handles mouse dragging and is passed the current (x, y) position of the cursor on screen. processPress() deals with a mouse press, and the global Boolean isStartDrag is set to true when the mouse is released.

Dragging the board

When the user drags the mouse, a sequence of MOUSE_DRAGGED events are generated, each one including the current (x, y) position of the cursor. processDrag() obtains the movement covered by a single MOUSE_DRAGGED event by calculating the offset relative to the (x, y) coordinate from the previous drag event (stored in xPrev and yPrev). The x and y components of the move are converted into x- and y-axis rotations and are applied to the TransformGroup for the board.

However, this approach only works after the first event, so the second event (and subsequent ones) have a previous coordinate to consider. The first event in a drag sequence is distinguished by the isStartDrag Boolean:

```
    private void processDrag(int xPos, int yPos)
    {
      if (isStartDrag)
        isStartDrag = false;
      else {  // not the start of a drag, so can calculate offset
        int dx = xPos - xPrev;           // get dists dragged
        int dy = yPos - yPrev;
        transformX.rotX( dy * YFACTOR );    // convert to rotations
        transformY.rotY( dx * XFACTOR );
        modelTrans.mul(transformX, modelTrans);
        modelTrans.mul(transformY, modelTrans);
                      // add to existing x- and y- rotations
        boardTG.setTransform(modelTrans);
      }
      xPrev = xPos;      // save locs so can work out drag next time
      yPrev = yPos;
    }
```

modelTrans is a global Transform3D object that stores the ongoing, total rotational effect on the board. transformX and transformY are globals. boardTG is the TransformGroup for the board, passed in from WrapFourByFour when the PickDragBehavior object is created.

Picking a marker

processPress() sends a pick ray along the z-axis into the world, starting from the current mouse press position. The closest intersecting node is retrieved and if it's a

Shape3D containing a position index, then that position will be used as the player's desired move.

One problem is translating the (x, y) position supplied by the MOUSE_PRESSED event into world coordinates. This is done in two stages: The screen coordinate is mapped to the canvas' image plate and then to world coordinates.

The picking code is simplified by the judicious use of setPickable(false) when the scene is set up. The poles are made unpickable when created in makePoles() in WrapFourByFour, which means that only the markers can be selected:

```
// global
private final static Vector3d IN_VEC = new Vector3d(0.f,0.f,-1.f);
        // direction for picking -- into the scene

private Point3d mousePos;
private Transform3D imWorldT3d;
private PickRay pickRay = new PickRay();
private SceneGraphPath nodePath;


private void processPress(int xPos, int yPos)
{
  canvas3D.getPixelLocationInImagePlate(xPos, yPos, mousePos);
              // get the mouse position on the image plate
  canvas3D.getImagePlateToVworld(imWorldT3d);
              // get image plate --> world transform
  imWorldT3d.transform(mousePos);    // convert to world coords

  pickRay.set(mousePos, IN_VEC);
            // ray starts at mouse pos, and goes straight in

  nodePath = bg.pickClosest(pickRay);
          // get first node along pickray (and its path)
  if (nodePath != null)
    selectedPosn(nodePath);
}
```

The image plate to world coordinates transform is obtained from the canvas and applied to mousePos, which changes it in place. A ray is sent into the scene starting from that position, and the closest SceneGraphPath object is retrieved. This should be a branch ending in a game marker or null (i.e., the user clicked on a pole or the background).

selectedPosn() gets the terminal node of the path and checks that it's a Shape3D containing user data (only the white markers hold data, which is their position index):

```
private void selectedPosn(SceneGraphPath np)
{ Node node = np.getObject();        // get terminal node of path
  if (node instanceof Shape3D) {     // check for shape3D
    Integer posID = (Integer) node.getUserData();  //get posn index
```

```
        if (posID != null)
          board.tryPosn( posID.intValue( ) );
    }
  }
```

The position index (as an int) is passed to the Board object where the game logic is located.

If a red or blue marker was selected, the lack of user data will stop any further processing since it's not possible for a player to make a move in a spot which has been used.

Picking comparisons

This is the third example of Java 3D picking in this book, and it's worth comparing the three approaches:

- In Chapter 23, picking was used to select a point in the scene, and a gun rotated and shot at it. The picking was coded using a subclass of PickMouseBehavior, and details about the intersection coordinate were required.

- In Chapter 26, a ray was shot straight down from the users' position in a landscape to get the floor height of the spot where they were standing. The picking was implemented with PickTool, and an intersection coordinate was necessary.

- The picking employed here in processPress( ) doesn't use any of the picking utilities (i.e., PickMouseBehavior, PickTool) and only requires the shape that is first touched by the ray. Consequently, the task is simple enough to code directly, though the conversion from screen to world coordinates is somewhat tricky.

The Game Representation

The Board object initializes two arrays when it's first created: winLines[][] and posToLines[][].

winLines[][] lists all the possible winning lines in the game, in terms of the four positions that make up a line. For example, referring to Figure 31-5, {0,1,2,3}, {3,6,9,12}, and {0,4,8,12} are winning lines; the game has a total of 76 winning lines. For each line, winLines[][] records the number of positions occupied by a player. If the total reaches four for a particular line, then the player has completed the line and won.

posToLines[] specifies all the lines that utilize a given position. Thus, when a player selects a given position, all of those lines can be updated simultaneously.

Processing a selected position

The main entry point into Board is tryPosn( ), called by PickDragBehavior to pass the player's selected position into the Board object for processing:

```
public void tryPosn(int pos)
{
  if (gameOver)    // don't process position when game is over
    return;

  positions.set(pos, player);  // change the 3D marker shown at pos
  playMove(pos);               // play the move on the board

  // switch players, if the game isn't over
  if (!gameOver) {
    player = ((player == PLAYER1) ? PLAYER2 : PLAYER1 );
    if (player == PLAYER1)
      fbf.showMessage("Player 1's turn (red spheres)");
    else
      fbf.showMessage("Player 2's turn (blue cubes)");
  }
} // end of tryPosn( )
```

Board uses a global Boolean, gameOver, to record when the game has ended. The test of gameOver at the start of tryPosn( ) means that selecting a marker will have no effect once the game is finished.

The player's marker is made visible by a call to set( ) in the Positions object, and playMove( ) updates winLines[][]. After the move, the current player is switched; the player variable holds the current player's ID. However, the move may have been a winning one, so gameOver is checked before the switch. The calls to showMessage( ) cause the text field in the GUI to be updated.

Storing the selected position

playMove( ) uses the supplied position index to modify the various lines in which it appears. If the number of used positions in any of those lines reaches four, then the player will have won, and reportWinner( ) will be called:

```
private void playMove(int pos)
{
  nmoves++;                     // update the number of moves

  // get number of lines that this position is involved in
  int numWinLines = posToLines[pos][0];

  /* Go through each line associated with this position
     and update its status. If I have a winner, stop game. */
```

```
      int line;
      for (int j=0; j<numWinLines; j++) {
        line = posToLines[pos][j+1];
        if (winLines[line][1] != player &&
            winLines[line][1] != UNOCCUPIED)
          winLines[line][0] = -1;
          /* The other player has already made a move in this line
             so this line is now useless to both players. */
        else {
          winLines[line][1] = player;  //this line belongs to player
          winLines[line][0]++;         // one more posn used in line
          if (winLines[line][0] == 4) {  // all positions used,
            gameOver = true;             // so this player has won
            reportWinner();
          }
        }
      }
    } // end of playMove()
```

The winLines[x][1] field for line x states whether a player has made a move in that line. If a player selects a position in a line being used by another player, then the line becomes useless, which is signaled by setting winLines[x][0] == -1.

Reporting a winner

reportWinner() does some numerical "hand-waving" to obtain a score, based on the running time of the game and the number of moves made. The score is reported in the text field of the GUI:

```
    private void reportWinner()
    {
      long end_time = System.currentTimeMillis();
      long time = (end_time - startTime)/1000;

      int score = (NUM_SPOTS + 2 - nmoves)*111 - (int) Math.min(time*1000, 5000);

      if (player == PLAYER1)
        fbf.showMessage("Game over, player 1 wins with score "+score);
      else    // PLAYER2
        fbf.showMessage("Game over, player 2 wins with score "+score);
    } // end of reportWinner()
```

The Networked Tic-Tac-Toe Game

NetFourByFour is based on the FourByFour game, retaining most of its game logic, 3D modeling, and GUI interface, and it adds a threaded client/server communications layer.

This development sequence is deliberate, as it allows most of the game-specific and user interface issues to be addressed before networking complexity is introduced.

Figure 31-6 shows the main functional components of NetFourByFour.

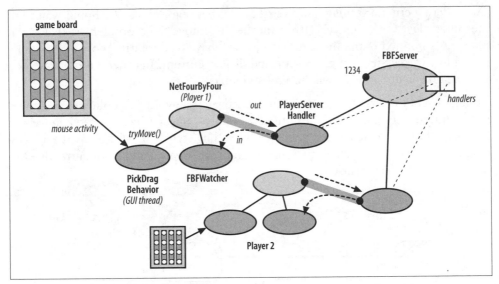

Figure 31-6. NetFourByFour clients and server

The top-level server, FBFServer, creates two PlayServerHandler threads to manage communication between the players. The server and its threads are thin in that they carry out little processing and act mainly as a switchboard for messages passing between the players.

An advantage of this approach is that most of the client's functionality can be borrowed from the standalone FourByFour, and the server side is kept simple. Processing is carried out locally in the client, whereas server-side processing would introduce networking delays between the user's selection and the resulting changes in the game window. A drawback is the need to duplicate processing across the clients.

Each NetFourByFour client utilizes the Java 3D GUI thread (where PickDragBehavior executes), the application thread for game processing, and an FBFWatcher thread to handle messages coming from the server. This threaded model was last seen in the chat application of Chapter 30, but there are some differences in building two-person networked games.

One change is the restriction on the number of participants: A chat system allows any number of users, who may join and leave at any time. A two-person game can begin only when both players are present and stops if one of them leaves. There cannot be more than two players, and I prohibit the mid-game change of players (i.e., substitutes aren't allowed).

Another complication is the need to impose an order on the game play: first player 1, then player 2, then back to player 1, and so on. A chat system doesn't enforce any sequencing on its users.

The ordering criteria seems to suggest that a player (e.g., player 2) should wait until the other player (e.g., player 1) has finished his move. The problem is that when player 2 is notified of the finished move, it will have to duplicate most of player 1's processing to keep its own game state and display current. In other words, player 2's waiting time before its turn will be almost doubled.

Though latency is less of an issue in turn-based games, avoid a doubling in wait time. One solution is for player 2 to be notified as soon as player 1 has selected a move and before it's been executed and rendered. This coding style is illustrated by the activity diagram in Figure 31-7, where the game engines for player 1 and 2 concurrently evaluate player 1's selected move.

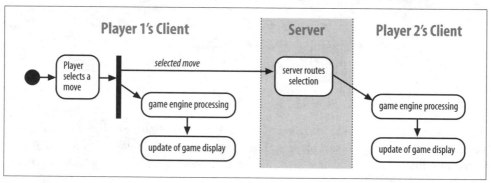

Figure 31-7. Concurrent processing of player 1's move

Issues need to be considered with this technique. One is whether the selection will result in too much overhead in the server and second player's client software. This is especially true if the move is rejected by player 1's game engine, which makes the overhead of the network communication and processing by player 2 superfluous. For this reason, do some preliminary, fast testing of the selection before sending it over the network.

Another concern is whether the two game engines will stay synchronized with each other. For example, the processing of player 1's move by player 2's game engine may be much quicker than in player 1's client. Consequently, player 2 may send his turn to player 1 before player 1 has finished the processing of his own move. Player 1's client must be prepared to handle "early" move messages. Of course, early moves may arrive at player 2 from player 1.

This is one reason why it's useful to have a separate "watcher" thread as part of the client. Another reason is to handle server messages, such as the announcement that the other player has disconnected, which may arrive at any time.

Two-Person Communication Protocols

A good starting point for changing a two-person game into a networked application is to consider the communication protocols (e.g., the sequences of messages) required during the various stages of the game. It's useful to consider three stages: initialization, termination, and game play:

Initialization

> In a two-person game, initialization is problematic due to the need to have two participants before the game can start and to restrict more than two players from joining.

Termination

> This stage is entered when a player decides to stop participating in the game, which may be due to many reasons. When a player leaves the game, the other player must be notified.

Game play

> This stage is usually the simplest to specify since it often involves the transmission of a move from one player to another.

In the following diagrams, I usually only consider the cases when player 1 starts the communication (e.g., when player 1 sends a new move to player 2). However, the communication patterns apply equally to the cases when player 2 initiates matters.

Initialization

The initialization stage in NetFourByFour uses the protocol shown in Figure 31-8.

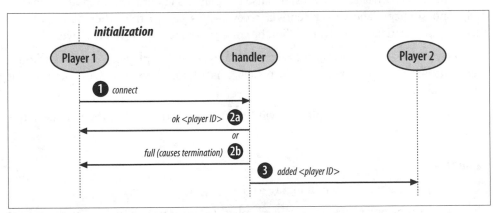

Figure 31-8. Initialization stage protocol in NetFourByFour

The connect message is implicit in the connection created when player 1's client opens a socket link to the server. The handler can send back an ok message containing an assigned ID or can reject the link with a full reply. If the connection was accepted, then an added message would be sent to the other player (if there is one).

The game will commence when the player ID value is 2 in the ok and added messages, meaning that two players are ready to compete.

Termination

The termination stage uses the protocol given in Figure 31-9.

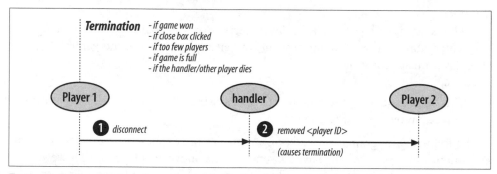

Figure 31-9. Termination stage protocol in NetFourByFour

The five conditions that cause a player to leave the game are listed at the top of Figure 31-9. The player sends a disconnect message and breaks its link with the server. In NetFourByFour, this doesn't cause the player's client to exit (though that is a design possibility). The server sends a removed message to the other player (if one exists), which causes it to break its link because there are now too few players.

The server will send a removed message if its socket link to player 1 closes without a preceding disconnect warning. This behavior is required to deal with network or machine failure.

If the handler dies, then the players will detect it by noticing that their socket links have closed prematurely.

Game play

The game play stage is shown in Figure 31-10.

The three conditions necessary for game play to continue are shown at the top of Figure 31-10. The selected move is sent as a try message via the server and arrives as an otherTurn message. The otherTurn message may arrive at the player while the previous move is still being processed for reasons described above. If player 2 has suddenly departed, perhaps due to a network failure, then the server may send a tooFewPlayers message back to player 1.

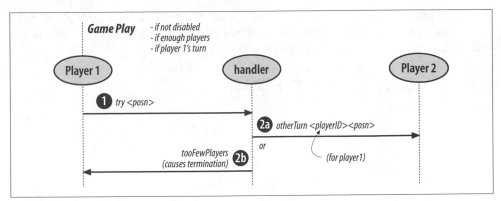

Figure 31-10. Game play stage protocol in NetFourByFour

Playing the Game

Figure 31-11 shows two NetFourByFour players in fierce competition. It looks like player 1 is about to win.

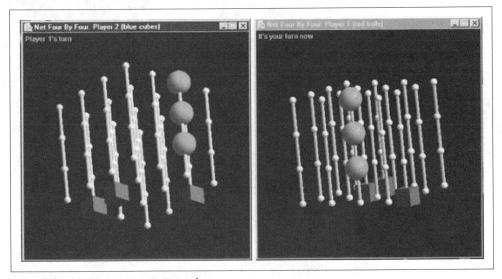

Figure 31-11. Two NetFourByFour players

The players have rotated their game boards in different ways, but the markers are in the same positions in both windows.

The GUI in NetFourByFour is changed from the FourByFour game: the message text field has been replaced by a message string which appears as an overlay at the top-left corner of the Canvas3D window. This functionality is achieved by subclassing the Canvas3D class to implement the mixed-mode rendering method postSwap( ), resulting in the OverlayCanvas class.

The class diagrams for the NetFourByFour client are given in Figure 31-12, and the server side classes appear in Figure 31-13. Only public methods are listed, and methods which are synchronized are prefixed with an S.

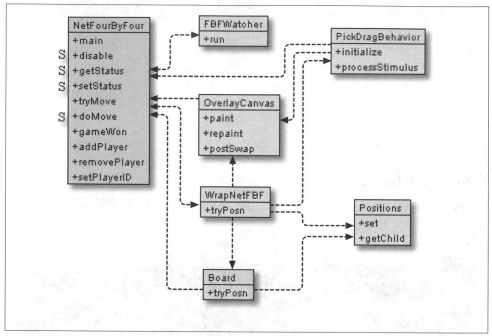

Figure 31-12. Class diagrams for the NetFourByFour client

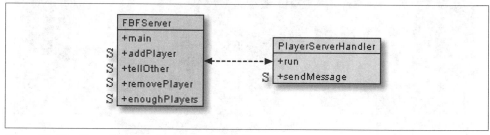

Figure 31-13. Class diagrams for the NetFourByFour server

FBFServer is the top-level class on the server-side.

As with previous networked examples, the connections between the client and server are unclear since the links are in terms of messages passing rather than method calls.

All the code (i.e., the NetFourByFour client and the FBFServer server) can be found in the *NetFourByFour/* directory.

The Top-Level Server

As indicated in Figure 31-6, the FBFServer class manages a small amount of shared data used by its two handlers: an array of PlayServerHandler references and the current number of players.

```
private PlayerServerHandler[] handlers;    // handlers for players
private int numPlayers;
```

The references allow a message to be sent to a handler by calling its sendMessage( ) method:

```
synchronized public void tellOther(int playerID, String msg)
// send mesg to the other player
{ int otherID = ((playerID == PLAYER1) ? PLAYER2 : PLAYER1 );
  if (handlers[otherID-1] != null)       // index is ID-1
    handlers[otherID-1].sendMessage(msg);
}
```

tellOther( ) is called from the handler for one player to send a message to the other player.

The numPlayers global is modified as a side effect of adding and removing a player, and it is used to decide if enough players exist to start a game:

```
synchronized public boolean enoughPlayers( )
{ return (numPlayers == MAX_PLAYERS); }
```

The Player Handlers

The PlayServerHandler thread for a client deals with the various handler messages defined in the initialization, termination, and game play stages shown in Figures 31-8, 31-9, and 31-10.

When the thread is first created, it's passed the socket link to the client, and I/O streams are layered on top of it:

```
// globals
private FBFServer server;
private Socket clientSock;
private BufferedReader in;
private PrintWriter out;

private int playerID;      // player id assigned by FBFServer


public PlayerServerHandler(Socket s, FBFServer serv)
{
  clientSock = s;
  server = serv;
  System.out.println("Player connection request");
  try {
    in  = new BufferedReader( new InputStreamReader(
                           clientSock.getInputStream( ) ) );
```

```
      out = new PrintWriter( clientSock.getOutputStream( ), true );
    }
    catch(Exception e)
    {  System.out.println(e);  }
  }
```

run( ) starts by carrying out the messages specified in the initialization stage of the
network communication. It calls addPlayer( ) in the server to add the new player.
This may fail if there are two players and a full message is sent back to the client. If
the joining is successful, then an ok message will be sent to the new player and an
added message to the other player (if one exists):

```
public void run( )
{
  playerID = server.addPlayer(this);
  if (playerID != -1) {    // -1 means player was rejected
    sendMessage("ok " + playerID); // tell player his/her ID
    server.tellOther(playerID, "added " + playerID);

    processPlayerInput( );

    server.removePlayer(playerID);   // goodbye
    server.tellOther(playerID, "removed " +
                              playerID); // tell others
  }
  else    // game is full
    sendMessage("full");

  try {     // close socket from player
    clientSock.close( );
    System.out.println("Player "+playerID+" connection closed\n");
  }
  catch(Exception e)
  {  System.out.println(e);  }
}
```

When processPlayer( ) returns, it means that the player has broken the network
link, so the server must be updated and the other player notified with a removed message. Thus, run( ) finishes by carrying out the termination stage.

processPlayer( ) monitors the input stream for its closure of a disconnect message.
Otherwise, messages are sent to doRequest( ), which deals with the game play stage
of the communication:

```
private void doRequest(String line)
{
  if (line.startsWith("try")) {
    try {
      int posn = Integer.parseInt( line.substring(4).trim( ) );

      if (server.enoughPlayers( ))
        server.tellOther(playerID, "otherTurn " + playerID +
                      " " + posn);  // pass turn to others
```

```
      else
        sendMessage("tooFewPlayers");
    }
    catch(NumberFormatException e)
    { System.out.println(e); }
  }
}
```

A try message is sent to the other player as an otherTurn message.

sendMessage() writes a string onto the PrintWriter stream going to the player. However, the method must be synchronized since it's possible that the handler and top-level server may call it at the same time:

```
synchronized public void sendMessage(String msg)
{ try {
    out.println(msg);
  }
  catch(Exception e)
  {  System.out.println("Handler for player "+playerID+"\n"+e); }
}
```

Comparing NetFourByFour and FourByFour

Many classes in NetFourByFour are similar to those in FourByFour; this is a consequence of keeping the game logic on the client side.

The Positions class, which manages the on-screen markers is unchanged from FourByFour. PickDragBehavior still handles user picking and dragging, but reports a selected position to NetFourByFour rather than to Board. The game data structures in Board are as before, but the tryMove() method for processing a move and the reportWinner() are different. WrapNetFourByFour is similar to WrapFourByFour but utilizes the OverlayCanvas class rather than Canvas3D.

The NetFourByFour class is changed since the networking code for the client side is located there. FBFWatcher is used to monitor messages coming from the server, so it is new.

Game Initialization in the Client

The network initialization done in NetFourByFour consists of opening a connection to the server and creating a FBFWatcher thread to wait for a response:

```
// globals in NetFourByFour
private Socket sock;
private PrintWriter out;


private void makeContact()    // in NetFourByFour
{
  try {
```

```
    sock = new Socket(HOST, PORT);
    BufferedReader in  = new BufferedReader(
                           new InputStreamReader( sock.getInputStream( ) ));
    out = new PrintWriter( sock.getOutputStream( ), true );

    new FBFWatcher(this, in).start( );  // start watching server
  }
  catch(Exception e)
  { System.out.println("Cannot contact the NetFourByFour Server");
    System.exit(0);
  }
} // end of makeContact( )
```

A consideration of Figure 31-8 shows that an ok or full message may be delivered from the server. These responses, and the other possible client-directed messages, are caught by FBFWatcher in its run( ) method:

```
public class FBFWatcher extends Thread
{
  private NetFourByFour fbf;      // ref back to client
  private BufferedReader in;

  public FBFWatcher(NetFourByFour fbf, BufferedReader i)
  {  this.fbf = fbf;
     in = i;
  }

  public void run( )
  { String line;
    try {
      while ((line = in.readLine( )) != null) {
        if (line.startsWith("ok"))
          extractID(line.substring(3));
        else if (line.startsWith("full"))
          fbf.disable("full game");
        else if (line.startsWith("tooFewPlayers"))
          fbf.disable("other player has left");
        else if (line.startsWith("otherTurn"))
          extractOther(line.substring(10));
        else if (line.startsWith("added"))      // don't use ID
          fbf.addPlayer( );            // client adds other player
        else if (line.startsWith("removed"))  // don't use ID
          fbf.removePlayer( );       // client removes other player
        else   // anything else
          System.out.println("ERR: " + line + "\n");
      }
    }
    catch(Exception e) // socket closure will end while
    {  fbf.disable("server link lost");  }   // end game as well
  } // end of run( )

  // other methods...
} // end of FBFWatcher class
```

The messages considered inside run( ) match the communications that a player may receive, as given in Figures 31-8, 31-9, and 31-10.

An ok message causes extractID( ) to extract the player ID and call NetFourByFour's setPlayerID( ) method. This binds the playerID value used throughout the client's execution.

A full message triggers a call to NetFourByFour's disable( ) method. This is called from various places to initiate the client's departure from the game.

The handler for the player sends an added message to the FBFWatcher of the other player, leading to a call of it's NetFourByFour addPlayer( ) method. This increments the client's numPlayers counter, which permits game play to commence when equal to 2.

Game Termination in the Client

Figure 31-9 lists five ways in which game play may stop:

- The player won.
- The close box was clicked.
- There are too few players to continue (i.e., the other player has departed).
- The game has enough participants.
- The handler or other player dies.

Each case is considered in the following sections.

The player has won

The Board object detects whether a game has been won in the same way as the FourByFour version and then calls reportWinner( ):

```
private void reportWinner(int playerID)  // in Board
{
  long end_time = System.currentTimeMillis( );
  long time = (end_time - startTime)/1000;

  int score = (NUM_SPOTS + 2 - nmoves)*111 - int) Math.min(time*1000, 5000);

  fbf.gameWon(playerID, score);
}
```

reportWinner( ) has two changes: it's passed the player ID of the winner, and it calls gameWon( ) in NetFourByFour rather than write to a text field. gameWon( ) checks the player ID against the client's own ID and passes a suitable string to disable( ):

```
public void gameWon(int pid, int score)  // in NetFourByFour
{
  if (pid == playerID)    // this client has won
    disable("You've won with score " + score);
```

```
    else
        disable("Player " + pid + " has won with score " + score);
}
```

disable( ) is the core method for terminating game play for the client. It sends a disconnect message to the server (see Figure 31-9), sets a global Boolean isDisabled to true, and updates the status string:

```
synchronized public void disable(String msg)   // in NetFourByFour
{ if (!isDisabled) {      // client can only be disabled once
    try {
      isDisabled = true;
      out.println("disconnect");   // tell server
      sock.close( );
      setStatus("Game Over: " + msg);
      // System.out.println("Disabled: " + msg);
    }
    catch(Exception e)
    {  System.out.println( e );  }
  }
}
```

disable( ) may be called from the client's close box, FBFWatcher, or from Board (via gameWon( )), so it must be synchronized. The isDisabled flag means the client can only be disabled once. Disabling breaks the network connection and makes it so further selections have no effect on the board. However, the application is left running, and the player can rotate the game board.

The close box was clicked

The constructor for NetFourByFour sets up a call to disable( ) and exit( ) in a window listener:

```
addWindowListener( new WindowAdapter( ) {
  public void windowClosing(WindowEvent e)
  { disable("exiting");
    System.exit( 0 );
  }
});
```

Too few players, and the game is full

If FBFWatcher receives a tooFewPlayers or a full message from its handler, it will call disable( ):

```
public void run( )    // in FBFWatcher
{ String line;
  try {
    while ((line = in.readLine( )) != null) {
      if (line.startsWith("ok"))
        extractID(line.substring(3));
      else if (line.startsWith("full"))
        fbf.disable("full game");
```

```
        else if (line.startsWith("tooFewPlayers"))
          fbf.disable("other player has left");
        : // other message else-if-tests
      }
    }
    catch(Exception e)
    {// exception handling... }
  } // end of run( )
```

The handler or other player has died

If the other player's client suddenly terminates, then its server-side handler will detect the closure of its socket and will send a removed message to the other player:

```
public void run( )      // in FBFWatcher
{ String line;
  try {
    while ((line = in.readLine( )) != null) {
      if (line.startsWith("ok"))
        extractID(line.substring(3));

      // other message else-if-tests, and then...
      else if (line.startsWith("removed"))  // don't use ID
        fbf.removePlayer( );      // client removes other player
      // other message else-if-tests
    }
  }
  catch(Exception e)      // socket closure will end while
  {  fbf.disable("server link lost");  }  // end game as well

} // end of run( )
```

FBFWatcher will see the removed message and call removePlayer( ) in NetFourByFour. This will decrement its number of players counter which prevents any further selected moves from being carried out.

If the server dies then FBFWatcher will raise an exception when it reads from the socket. This triggers a call to disable( ) which ends the game.

Game Play in the Client

Figure 31-7 presents an overview of typical game play using an activity diagram. Player 1 selects a move that is processed locally while being sent via the server to the other player to be processed.

A closer examination of this turn-taking operation is complex because it involves the clients and the server. I'll break it into three parts, corresponding to the swimlanes in the activity diagram. Each part will be expanded into its own UML sequence diagram, which allows more detail to be exposed.

Perhaps the most important point in this section is the usefulness of UML activity diagrams and sequence diagrams for designing and documenting network code. A networked application utilizes data and methods distributed across many distinct pieces of software, linked by complex, low-level message passing mechanisms. Abstraction tools are essential.

Player 1's client

The sequence diagram for the left side of Figure 31-7 (player 1's client) is shown in Figure 31-14.

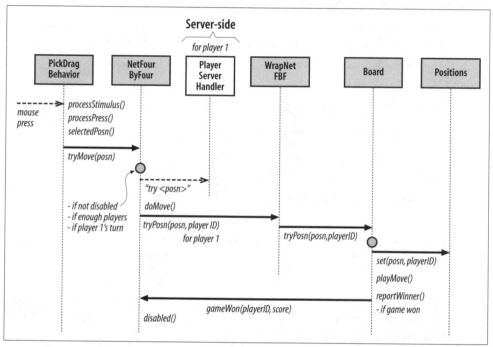

Figure 31-14. Sequence diagram for player 1's client

The mouse press is dealt with by PickDragBehavior in a similar way to FourByFour, except that tryMove() is called in NetFourByFour and passed the selected position index.

tryMove() carries out simple tests before sending a message off to the server and calling doMove() to execute the game logic:

```
public void tryMove(int posn)  // in NetFourByFour
{
  if (!isDisabled) {
    if (numPlayers < MAX_PLAYERS)
      setStatus("Waiting for player " + otherPlayer(playerID) );
    else if (playerID != currPlayer)
      setStatus("Sorry, it is Player " + currPlayer + "'s turn");
    else if (numPlayers == MAX_PLAYERS) {
      out.println( "try " + posn );   // tell the server
```

```
      doMove(posn, playerID);        // do it, don't wait for response
    }
    else
      System.out.println("Error on processing position");
  }
} // end of tryMove()
```

tryPosn( ) in Board is simpler than the version in FourByFour:

```
public void tryPosn(int pos, int playerID)  // in Board
{ positions.set(pos, playerID);  // change 3D marker shown at pos
  playMove(pos, playerID);        // play the move on the board
}
```

A gameOver Boolean is no longer utilized, the isDisabled Boolean has taken its place back in NetFourByFour. tryPosn( ) no longer changes the player ID since a client is dedicated to a single player.

The playerID input argument of tryPosn( ) is a new requirement since this code may be called to process moves by either of the two players.

set( ) in Positions is unchanged from FourByFour, and playMove( ) utilizes the same game logic to update the game and test for a winning move. reportWinner( ) is a little altered, as explained when considering the termination cases.

Server-side processing

The sequence diagram on the server side (Figure 31-15) shows how a try message from player 1 is passed to player 2 as an otherTurn message.

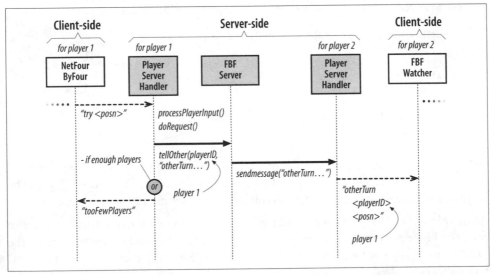

Figure 31-15. Sequence diagram for the server

I considered the coding behind these diagrams when I looked at the server-side classes.

The diagram shows that the otherTurn message is received by the FBFWatcher of player 2:

```
public void run( )    // in FBFWatcher
{ String line;
  try {
    while ((line = in.readLine( )) != null) {
      if (line.startsWith("ok"))
        extractID(line.substring(3));
      :  // other message else-if-tests, and then...
      else if (line.startsWith("otherTurn"))
        extractOther(line.substring(10));
      :  // other message else-if-tests
    }
  }
  catch(Exception e)
  { // exception handling... }
} // end of run( )
```

Player 2's client

The sequence diagram for the righthand side of Figure 31-7 (player 2's client) is shown in Figure 31-16.

The call to extractOther( ) in FBFWatcher extracts the player's ID and the position index from the otherTurn message. It then calls doMove( ) in NetFourByFour:

```
synchronized public void doMove(int posn,int pid) //in NetFourByFour
{
  wrapFBF.tryPosn(posn, pid);    // and so to Board
  if (!isDisabled) {
    currPlayer = otherPlayer( currPlayer );  // player's turn over
    if (currPlayer == playerID)  // this player's turn now
      setStatus("It's your turn now");
    else    // the other player's turn
      setStatus("Player " + currPlayer + "'s turn");
  }
}
```

doMove( ) and the methods it calls (e.g., tryPosn( ) in WrapNetFBF and Board) are used by the client to execute its moves and to execute the moves of the other player. The methods all take the player ID as an argument, so the owner of the move is clear.

As mentioned before, the client could still be processing its move when a request to process the opponent's move comes in. This situation is handled by the use of the synchronized keyword with doMove( ): a new call to doMove( ) must wait until the current call has finished.

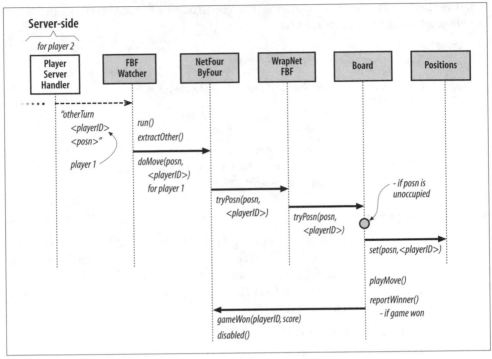

Figure 31-16. Sequence diagram for player 2's client

Writing on the Canvas

OverlayCanvas is a subclass of Canvas3D which draws a status string onto the canvas in its top-left corner (see Figure 31-11). The display is implemented as an overlay, meaning that the string is not part of the 3D scene; instead, it's resting on "top" of the canvas. This technique utilizes Java 3D's mixed mode rendering, which gives the programmer access to Java 3D's rendering loop at different stages in its execution.

The client makes regular calls to setStatus() in NetFourByFour to update a global status string:

```
synchronized public void setStatus(String msg) //in NetFourByFour
{  status = msg;  }
```

This string is periodically accessed from the OverlayCanvas object by calling getStatus():

```
synchronized public String getStatus()  // in NetFourByFour
{  return status; }
```

The get and set methods are synchronized—the calls from OverlayCanvas may come at any time and should not access the string while it's being updated.

The OverlayCanvas object is created in the constructor of WrapNetFBF, in the usual way that a Canvas3D object is created:

```
GraphicsConfiguration config =
        SimpleUniverse.getPreferredConfiguration();

OverlayCanvas canvas3D = new OverlayCanvas(config, fbf);
add("Center", canvas3D);
canvas3D.setFocusable(true);      // give focus to the canvas
canvas3D.requestFocus();
```

The only visible difference is the passing of a reference to the NetFourByFour object into the OverlayCanvas constructor (the fbf variable). This is used by OverlayCanvas to call the getStatus() method in NetFourByFour.

Mixed mode rendering

Canvas3D provides four methods for accessing Java 3D's rendering loop: preRender(), postRender(), postSwap(), and renderField(). By default, these methods have empty implementations and are called automatically at various stages in each cycle of the rendering loop. I can utilize them by subclassing Canvas3D and by providing implementations for the required methods.

Here are the four methods in more detail:

preRender()
> Called after the canvas has been cleared and before any rendering is carried out at the start of the current rendering cycle.

postRender()
> Called after all the rendering is completing but before the buffer swap. This means the current rendering has not yet been placed on screen.

postSwap()
> Called after the current rendering is on the screen (i.e., after the buffer has been swapped out to the frame) at the end of the rendering cycle.

renderField()
> Useful in stereo rendering. It's called after the left eye's visible objects are rendered and again after the right eye's visible objects are rendered.

Drawing on the overlay canvas

postSwap() is used to draw the updated status string on screen:

```
// globals
private final static int XPOS = 5;
private final static int YPOS = 15;
private final static Font MSGFONT = new Font( "SansSerif", Font.BOLD, 12);
```

```
private NetFourByFour fbf;
private String status;


public void postSwap()
{
  Graphics2D g = (Graphics2D) getGraphics();
  g.setColor(Color.red);
  g.setFont( MSGFONT );

  if ((status = fbf.getStatus()) != null)  // it has a value
    g.drawString(status, XPOS, YPOS);

  // this call is made to compensate for the javaw repaint bug,
  Toolkit.getDefaultToolkit().sync();
} // end of postSwap()
```

The call to getStatus() in NetFourByFour may return null at the start of the client's execution if the canvas is rendered before status gets a value.

The repaint() and paint() methods are overridden:

```
public void repaint()
// Overriding repaint() makes the worst flickering disappear
{ Graphics2D g = (Graphics2D) getGraphics();
  paint(g);
}

public void paint(Graphics g)
// paint() is overridden to compensate for the javaw repaint bug
{ super.paint(g);
  Toolkit.getDefaultToolkit().sync();
}
```

repaint() is overridden to stop the canvas from being cleared before being repainted, which otherwise causes a nasty flicker.

The calls to sync() in postSwap() and paint() are bug fixes to avoid painting problems when using javaw to execute Java 3D mixed-mode applications.

CHAPTER 32

A Networked Virtual Environment

This chapter utilizes the threaded client/server model, which first appeared in the multiplayer chat system in Chapter 30 and now appears in the service of a networked virtual environment (NVE).

When clients connect to the server, they appear as a 3D sprite in a shared world filled with sprites representing other users. The scenery is the familiar checkerboard seen in many of the earlier Java 3D examples, along with a castle and some red poles. Users can move their sprites around the world but cannot pass through the poles.

Figure 32-1 shows the NetTour3D application being run by two clients. Each window is the clients' view of the shared world, represented by a third-person camera that follows the clients' sprite as it moves. All the visitors use the same robot image, but each user's name floats above their robot.

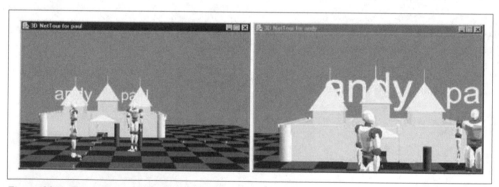

Figure 32-1. Two visitors to the NetTour3D world

Key features demonstrated include:

Local and distributed sprites
>   Each user is represented by two kinds of sprites: a *local* sprite on the users' machine, and distributed sprites present on every other machine. When users moves their local sprites, the distributed sprites are updated as well via messages

sent from the client, through the server, and finally to the other clients. The local and distributed sprites are subclasses of a `Sprite3D` class, so they share a great deal of functionality.

Fast local updates

Local sprites are updated directly by the client, rather than by transmitting a message to the server and waiting for it to be echoed back. This removes latency delays for local sprite updates. The sprite's changes are transmitted to the server but only for delivery to the other clients

Fat clients, thin server

A copy of the world is directly created by every client, rather than transmitted to the client from the server. This reduces the data flow sent over the network at the expense of duplicating information about the world on every client.

 Each client is essentially a version of the Tour3D application described in Chapter 18, with additional networking code lifted from the threaded client/server chat application in Chapter 30. Read those chapters before reading this one.

Since the clients do most of the work, the server is demoted to little more than a mail boy, routing messages between its high-powered clients.

Activity diagram design

As in the last chapter, considerable use if made of activity diagrams to specify client activity (joining the world, moving about, leaving) and to depict the communication between the clients via the server

A simplification in the application is that sprites cannot communicate with each other. However, adding a multiplayer chat component to NetTour3D would be easy. NetTour3D is a simple NVE, so I'll begin by describing NVEs. Information on NVEs coded in Java and Java 3D are given at the end of the chapter.

Background on NVEs

Technically speaking, an NVE is a computer-based artificial world of 3D spaces, visited by geographically dispersed users who interact and collaborate with each other and with objects/entities local to the world. The world's 3D spaces and their objects may be maintained/hosted by numerous computers spread around the network. In other words, it's an online place to hang out, to be seen, and to fight to the death with swords and laser cannons.

The NVE is a descendant of the Multiple-User Dungeons (MUDs), text-based role-playing adventure games that achieved enormous popularity from the mid-1970s onward. In the 1990s, MUDs object oriented (MOOs) started to use object-oriented programming techniques to implement their worlds, 2D and 3D chat environments appeared, and the first multiplayer games were released.

The current in-vogue gaming acronyms are MMORPG (Massively Multiplayer Online Role-Playing Game), MMOG, and MMO (both standing for Massive Multiplayer Online Game), typified by EverQuest, Asheron's Call, Ultima Online, and a growing list of others. Some sites maintain lists, news, FAQs, and reviews:

- MPOGD.com. The Multiplayer Online Games Directory (*http://www.mpogd.com/*).
- OMGN.com. The Online Multiplayer Gaming Network (*http://www.omgn.com/*).
- MMORPG.com (*http://www.mmorpg.com/*).

Aside from the game-playing potential for NVEs, they're the subject of much academic research. In the 1990s, DARPA's SIMNET project developed the Distributed Interactive Simulation (DIS) protocol for modeling real-world scenarios (usually military-related but also complex, distributed applications such as Air Traffic Control systems). DIS has greatly influenced the communication protocols utilized in NVEs and the utilization of real-time within the worlds.

A follow-up to DIS is the High Level Architecture (HLA), focusing on support for simulations composed from multiple distributed components (see *https://www.dmso.mil/ public/transition/hla/*). The HLA offers federation rules to govern the interactions between components, and numerous management tools, called Run-Time Infrastructure (RTI) services. These include time management (e.g., federated clocks), data distribution management (e.g., to filter user messages), and object ownership tools.

Another source of ideas comes from Collaborative Virtual Environments (CVEs), which emphasize human interaction in collaborative working frameworks when the users are at different physical locations.

The Elements of an NVE

The most immediately noticeable elements of an NVE are spaces, users, objects, and views. Less evident are the notions of consistency, real-time, dead reckoning, security, and scalability.

 NVEs are network applications, so they must deal with the network challenges described in Chapter 29: latency, bandwidth, reliability, protocol, and topology.

Spaces

The 3D spaces in an NVE define the world's topology. A space may be a large common area (a landscape, playground, street), a smaller private space for select groups (e.g., a conference room, gym, hall), or a place for individual interactions (an office, a kitchen). Spaces may be unchanging, or privileged users may be able to reconfigure them, delete them, or create new ones. Each space has a set of attributes, privileges, and/or security features (e.g., passwords) that govern who can use it and in what ways.

The largest granularity of spaces are often known as *zones* and play an important role in the underlying implementation of the NVE. In Ultima Online and EverQuest, zones are supported by different servers, so a user who moves between zones will move between servers. This approach lends itself to load balancing, though a popular zone will still cause overloading. In Asheron's Call, *portal storming* is a mechanism for "teleporting" users away from a high-traffic zone to a randomly selected destination. Zones make message filtering easier since users only need to receive information related to their current zone.

Zones may be duplicated to deal with the popularity of a particular space (e.g., the chat area, the dragon's lair), with duplicates known as shards. Duplication may make the overall system more fault-tolerant since users can be moved from a failed shard to another copy. A drawback is that friends may believe themselves to be in the same game space, but they won't meet since they're located in different shards of that space.

Users

Users in an NVE are visually represented by *avatars*, created by users when they first join the world. At the implementation level, a user may be denoted by two kinds of avatar—a *local avatar* present on the player's own machine, and a *ghost avatar* employed on all the other machines connected to the world. The avatars look the same on the screen; the differences lie at the communication layer. A local avatar may be controlled directly by the user without the overhead of the communication passing through a server first. A ghost avatar will require its state and behavior updates to be delivered over the network, which introduces the issue of latency.

NVEs frequently distinguish between different groups of users (e.g., novices, gurus, farmers) with corresponding differences in their abilities to affect spaces, objects, and other users. Differing abilities lead to users forming groups to collaborate on common tasks. A task may be a CVE-style activity such as report writing, or a gaming-style objective such as treasure seeking. Collaboration usually requires a richer communications protocol to support forms of interaction such as negotiation, brokering, bargaining, contracts, task division, and result combination.

Objects

Objects in a space can be classified in various ways. Some objects may never change, such as buildings, signposts, and street fittings, and others may be mobile but still passive (e.g., coins, maps). Movement in the world may require a corresponding implementation level movement of the object's representation between machines. Objects may react when a user "triggers" them—for example, a door opening when a user touches it. A dynamic object will have its own behavior, often AI-based, allowing richer interactions with users, which may be initiated by the object.

Objects are one of the ways that users communicate. This is done by giving objects to each other, by making copies for others, or by dividing a single object into smaller pieces.

Views

Views govern how a client sees a space, objects, or other users. Most multiplayer games are first-person-oriented, so the player sees little of his own avatar. However, each user will be able to employ several views into the space, which can be dynamically adjusted. Views may be abstractions, as with maps showing player activities or a list of objects currently being carried by the player.

Interest management permits a player to subscribe and unsubscribe to the reception of messages concerning other users, objects, or spaces. For example, when a user changes position, all the subscribed players will be notified. IP multicasting is often utilized to implement this mechanism, though the large number of users and objects in a world may mean that the number of available multicast groups is exhausted. Zone-based notification schemes are more viable due to the relatively small number of zones in a world. Only users currently in the zone will receive updates when something changes in that zone.

Consistency

Consistency states that all users should see the same sequence of events in the same order. For instance, if user X walks through a door and user Y shoots a gun, then X, Y, and all the other users in the vicinity should see that same sequence. The problem is that the events may have occurred on geographically separated machines and that event details must be sent between the player's machines by message passing. The presentation of these events to every user in the same order implies that they can be temporally ordered. This means timestamping the events on different machines with clocks that are synchronized.

Fortunately, not all users require the same level of consistency. In the above example, only users close to X and Y require complete consistency. Other users will receive the events, but their ordering may not be so critical.

Real-time

Real-time requirements mean that when an event occurs at time t for one user, other users should see that event at time t as well. This assumes a globally consistent logical clock, usually implemented using synchronized local clocks on each machine.

Real-time requires assumptions about typical network latency and reliability. For example, bucket synchronization relies on the setting of a suitable playback delay, derived from the network latency. If the latency increases above 100 ms, as it will over larger networks, the delay will need to be increased. This will further retard event processing, including events initiated by users on their own machine. The increased delay will degrade the application's apparent response time and will become unacceptable to the user.

Another aspect of the problem is the likelihood of packet loss when utilizing UDP transmission. Moving to TCP is often ruled out since its guaranteed delivery can affect latency time severely.

Dead reckoning

A popular solution to the problems with real-time support is to combine UDP, timestamping, and related algorithms with dead reckoning (also known as predictive modeling). The basic idea is that each client runs simulations of the other clients in the NVE. When it comes time to update the global state on the machine, any missing data from other clients will be replaced by extrapolations taken from the simulations of those clients. Therefore, delays caused by latency and lost data are hidden.

The client may run a simulation of itself and regularly compare its actual state with the one generated by the simulation. When the differences between them become too great, it can send a state update message to its peers and ask them to correct their details for the client. Consequently, state messages will probably need to be sent out less often, reducing network congestion.

Dead reckoning was first introduced in DARPA's SIMNET project and was mostly concerned with updating the position of entities. For instance, the current position of an object (e.g., a tank) could be extrapolated by using its last known position and velocity or by using position, velocity, and acceleration information.

Other dead reckoning algorithms take the orientation of the entity (i.e., its roll, pitch, heading) into account, and handle moving subparts. A recent DARPA initiative, the Advanced Distributed Simulation (ADS) architecture, introduced predictive contracts, which encourage extrapolations using non-physics-based equations and a wider range of object attributes. The drawback with mathematical complex algorithms is the increased cost of their calculation.

A fundamental problem with dead reckoning is its assumption that an entity's state change (e.g., its movement) is predictable. This is often false for user avatars in an NVE. Another issue is deciding when a simulated state and actual state are sufficiently different to warrant the sending of update messages. If the difference threshold is too large, then the client's ghost avatar may undergo a noticeable change in position (or other attribute) when the update message is processed. If the threshold is too small, then unnecessary messages will be sent out contributing to network congestion.

The means by which a simulated state is changed to the correct value is called *convergence*. The simplest technique is to change the state in a single step, causing the avatar to jump, jitter, or snap to a new state. Other approaches rest on the idea of gradually interpolating between the simulated state and new one.

Security

NVE security takes many forms. Within the world, security determines how users behave with each other and how they interact with spaces and objects. Active objects must be monitored since they have their own behavior and may be able to move between client and server machines.

Security is usually distributed. Typically, there's a connection manager that new users must deal with before they enter the world. Internal world security is handled by the servers responsible for each zone, and/or by the client software. The drawback with delegating security to the client is the possibility that it may be circumvented by hackers.

Scalability

NVE scalability is a complex problem since an increase in world size often makes implementations based upon a single server inadequate. The typical solution used by pay-for-play models, such as EverQuest and Ultima Online, is to use multiple servers, each managing a zone, and to use a connection manager to supervise user admission.

The zoning metaphor allows issues like consistency management, message volumes, and sharing to be kept under control. Zones may be duplicated across several servers to improve load balancing, dissuade some forms of hacker attack, and act as backups if a server fails. Multiple servers can be geographically dispersed to help reduce latency since international packets transfer times can easily extend beyond 200 ms. Systems may utilize peer-to-peer communication for aspects of the game that don't need monitoring (e.g., chatting).

An Overview of NetTour3D

Figure 32-2 shows the main objects involved in a NetTour3D world.

The application uses a threaded client/server model, much like the threaded chat application in Chapter 30.

The NetTour3D application is the client. It creates a WrapNetTour3D object to build the world and to handle communication with the TourServer server. The world consists of a checkerboard, background, lighting, and scenery loaded from a tour file with the help of a PropManager object (first used in Chapter 16). No 3D objects or images need to be transferred over the network; all the necessary 3D models are present on the client.

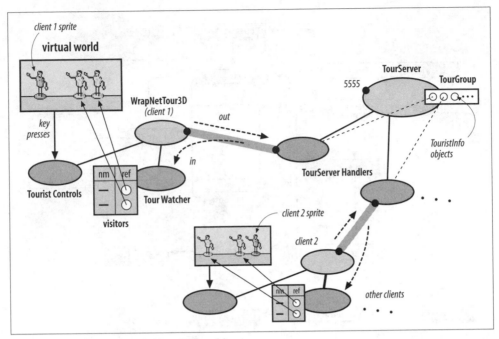

Figure 32-2. Objects in a NetTour3D world

`WrapNetTour3D` starts a `TouristControls` object to monitor the client's key presses, which move the client's local sprite (the ones colored blue in Figure 32-1) or adjust the third-person camera. `TouristControls` is unchanged from the `Tour3D` example in Chapter 18. `WrapNetTour3D` sends messages to the server, and the monitoring of messages coming from the server is delegated to a `TourWatcher` object. Most of these messages will be related to the creation and movement of distributed sprites (the sprites representing other clients, colored orange in Figure 32-1). `TourWatcher` manages these sprites and updates them in response to the server's messages.

`TourServer` creates a `TourServerHandler` thread for each client who connects to it and stores information about the connections in a shared `TourGroup` object in an ArrayList of `TouristInfo` objects. The main task of the server is to accept a message from one client and broadcast it to the others.

Class Diagrams for NetTour3D

Figure 32-3 shows class diagrams for the `NetTour3D` client application and the `TourServer` server. Only the class names are shown. Most of the classes in Figure 32-3 have been summarized.

`CheckerFloor` and `ColouredTiles` create the checkerboard floor. `PropManager` loads the scenery, and `Obstacles` sets up the obstacles specified in a tour file.

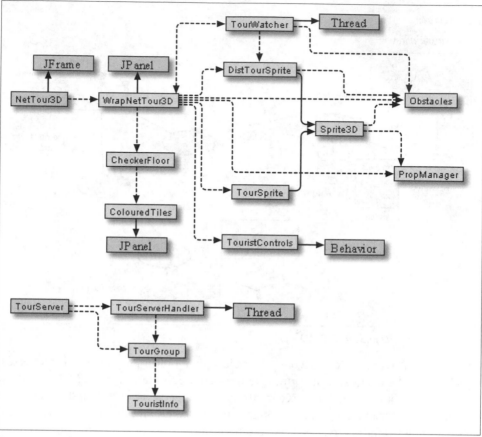

Figure 32-3. Class diagrams for NetTour3D and TourServer

 All the code for this example (the NetTour3D client and TourServer server) is in the *NetTour3D/* directory.

NetTour3D as a Simple NVE

The key elements that make up a fully featured NVE are spaces, users, objects, views, and the notions of consistency, real-time, dead reckoning, security, and scalability. How does NetTour3D measure up against these?

NetTour3D utilizes only one space (the checkerboard), and users all have the same appearance (but different names). The local and ghost avatars idea is present, called local and distributed sprites in this chapter. TourSprite manages the local sprite, and DistTourSprite manages a distributed sprite. The only view is a third-person camera. Objects in the form of scenery and obstacles can be easily added to the world, but they are static (not mobile, reactive, or intelligent). There is no way for NetTour3D users to interact. None of the NVE ideas of consistency, real-time, dead reckoning, security, and scalability are addressed here.

A TCP/IP client/server communication model is employed in NetTour3D, whereas a more realistic approach would include UDP multicasting and peer-to-peer elements and deploy some kind of connection manager.

Scene Creation on the Client

createSceneGraph( ) starts the main tasks of WrapNetTour3D: the 3D scene is created, contact is made with the server, and a local sprite is initialized:

```
void createSceneGraph(String userName, String tourFnm,
                                        double xPosn, double zPosn)
{ sceneBG = new BranchGroup( );
  bounds = new BoundingSphere(new Point3d(0,0,0), BOUNDSIZE);

  // allow clients to be added/removed from the world at run time
  sceneBG.setCapability(Group.ALLOW_CHILDREN_READ);
  sceneBG.setCapability(Group.ALLOW_CHILDREN_WRITE);
  sceneBG.setCapability(Group.ALLOW_CHILDREN_EXTEND);

  lightScene( );        // add the lights
  addBackground( );     // add the sky
  sceneBG.addChild( new CheckerFloor( ).getBG( ) );  // add the floor

  makeScenery(tourFnm);      // add scenery and obstacles

  makeContact( ); // contact server (after Obstacles object created)

  addTourist(userName, xPosn, zPosn);
                  // add the user-controlled 3D sprite
  sceneBG.compile( );   // fix the scene
}
```

Capability bits are set to allow distributed sprites to be added to and removed from the scene at runtime.

makeContact( ) sets up an input and output stream to the server and passes the input stream to TourWatcher to monitor. TourWatcher creates distributed sprites when requested by the server, and so must know about the obstacles present in the world:

```
private void makeContact( )
{ try {
    sock = new Socket(HOST, PORT);
    in  = new BufferedReader( new InputStreamReader( sock.getInputStream( ) ));
    out = new PrintWriter( sock.getOutputStream( ), true);

    new TourWatcher(this, in, obs).start( );   // watch server msgs
  }
  catch(Exception e)
```

```
        {  System.out.println("No contact with server");
           System.exit(0);
        }
   }
}
```

addTourist( ) creates a TourSprite object and connects a TouristControls object to it
so key presses can make it move and rotate:

```
    private void addTourist(String userName,double xPosn,double zPosn)
    {
       bob = new TourSprite(userName, "Coolrobo.3ds", obs, xPosn, zPosn, out);
       sceneBG.addChild( bob.getBG( ) ); // local sprite

       ViewingPlatform vp = su.getViewingPlatform( );
       TransformGroup viewerTG = vp.getViewPlatformTransform( );

       TouristControls tcs = new TouristControls(bob, viewerTG);
       tcs.setSchedulingBounds( bounds ); // sprite's controls

       sceneBG.addChild( tcs );
    }
```

The TourSprite object is passed a reference to the output stream going to the server.
The object can then notify the server of its creation, and when it moves or rotates.
The server will tell the other clients, which can affect the distributed sprite represent-
ing the user.

Defining Sprites

Sprite3D is the superclass for the local sprite class, TourSprite, and the distributed
sprite class, DistTourSprite. Figure 32-4 shows the class hierarchy and all its public
methods.

TourSprite and DistTourSprite offer a simplified interface for Sprite3D, setting the
sprite's rate of movement and rotation increment. TourSprite contains networking
code to send its details to the server.

The version of Sprite3D in NetTour3D is similar to the one in Tour3D. The main differences are in the subgraph created for a sprite, which looks like Figure 32-5.

The subgraph has a BranchGroup node at its top (objectBG), with capabilities set to
make the branch detachable. This permits the sprite to be removed from the scene
when the sprite's client leaves the world.

The other change is the addition of an OrientedShape3D shape holding the client's
name and being set to rotate around the y-axis to follow the client's viewpoint. The
shape is added to the TransformGroup above the Switch node, which means that the
sprite's name will remain on the screen if it is made inactive (invisible). The idea is
that the sprite is unavailable but still present in the world.

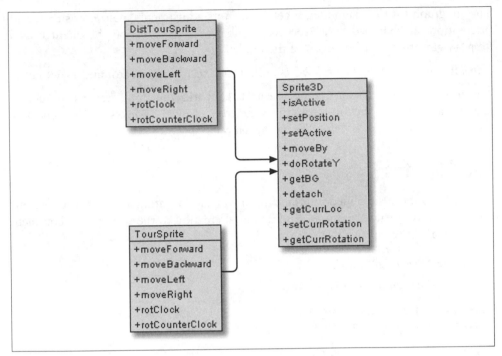

Figure 32-4. The sprite classes

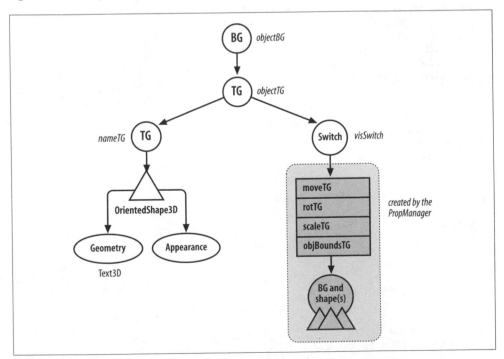

Figure 32-5. The subgraph for the Sprite3D sprite

The subgraph for the 3D model, together with its adjustments in size, position, and orientation, are handled by a PropManager object. Each sprite on the client uses a PropManager object to load a copy of the model.

The subgraph shown in Figure 32-5 is built in Sprite3D's constructor and makeName( ).

The movement and rotation code in Sprite3D works the same way as in Tour3D: changes are made to the top-level TransformGroup, objectTG. Moves are first checked with the Obstacles object before being carried out.

Local Sprites

TourSprite offers a simplified interface for moving and rotating a local sprite. It communicates movements, rotations, and its initial creation to the server. The complete class appears in Example 32-1.

Example 32-1. The TourSprite class

```
public class TourSprite extends Sprite3D
{
  private final static double MOVERATE = 0.3;
  private final static double ROTATE_AMT = Math.PI / 16.0;

  PrintWriter out;     // for sending commands to the server

  public TourSprite(String userName, String fnm, Obstacles obs,
                  double xPosn, double zPosn, PrintWriter o)
  { super(userName, fnm, obs);
    setPosition(xPosn, zPosn);
    out = o;
    out.println("create " + userName + " " + xPosn + " " + zPosn);
  }

  // moves
  public boolean moveForward( )
  { out.println("forward");
    return moveBy(0.0, MOVERATE);
  }

  public boolean moveBackward( )
  { out.println("back");
    return moveBy(0.0, -MOVERATE);
  }

  public boolean moveLeft( )
  { out.println("left");
    return moveBy(-MOVERATE,0.0);
  }

  public boolean moveRight( )
  { out.println("right");
```

Example 32-1. The TourSprite class (continued)

```
    return moveBy(MOVERATE,0.0);
}

// rotations in Y-axis only
public void rotClock()
{ out.println("rotClock");
  doRotateY(-ROTATE_AMT); // clockwise
}

public void rotCounterClock()
{ out.println("rotCClock");
  doRotateY(ROTATE_AMT);  // counter-clockwise
}

} // end of TourSprite
```

Creating a Local Sprite

WrapNetTour3D creates a local sprite by invoking a TourSprite object and adding it to the scene graph. As part of TourSprite's construction, a create n x z message is sent to the server; n is its client's name, and (x, z) is its position on the XZ plane.

The pattern of communication following on from the sending of the "create" message is shown by the activity diagram in Figure 32-6.

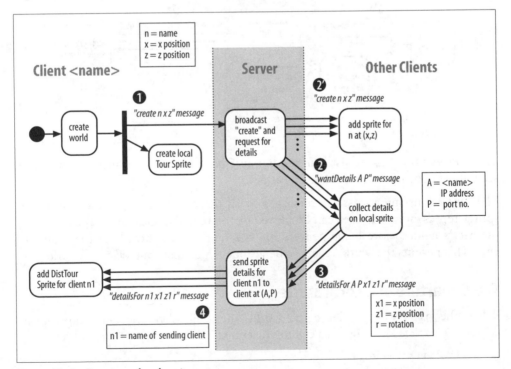

Figure 32-6. Creating a local sprite

The create message must be broadcast by the server to all the other current clients, as represented by the message labeled 2´ in Figure 32-6. The new client must populate its copy of the world with distributed sprites representing the other users. This task is started by the server sending a wantDetails message to all the other clients (message 2), which triggers a series of detailsFor replies (message 3) passed back to the new client as messages of type 4.

The reception of the "create" and "wantDetails" messages in the other clients are handled by their TourWatcher threads and TourWatcher in the new client deals with the "detailsFor" replies. Each "detailsFor" message causes a distributed sprite (an object of the DistTourSprite class) to be added to the client's world.

Moving and Rotating a Local Sprite

Each movement and rotation of the local sprite has the side effect of sending a message to the server, as illustrated by the activity diagram in Figure 32-7.

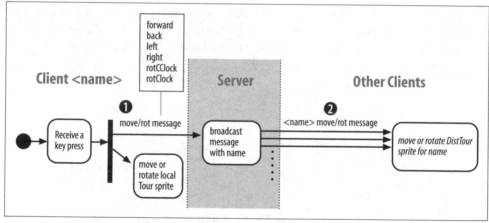

Figure 32-7. Moving/rotating a local sprite

The various messages are listed in the box in Figure 32-7; their transmission can be seen in the code for TourSprite given earlier.

The server must broadcast the messages to all the other clients so the distributed sprites representing the user can be moved or rotated. The message is prefixed with the user's name before being delivered to the TourWatcher threads of the other clients. This permits the TourWatchers to determine which distributed sprite to affect.

The Departure of a Local Sprite

When the users want to leave the world, they will click the close box of the NetTour3D JFrame. This triggers a call to closeLink( ) in the WrapNetTour3D object:

```
public void closeLink( )
{ try {
```

```
    out.println("bye");    // say bye to server
    sock.close( );
  }
  catch(Exception e)
  { System.out.println("Link terminated"); }

  System.exit( 0 );
}
```

The "bye" message causes the server to notify all the other clients of the user's departure, as shown by the activity diagram in Figure 32-8.

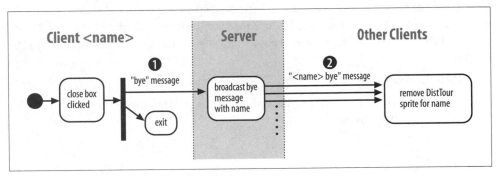

Figure 32-8. The departure of a local sprite

The TourWatcher threads for each of the clients receives a bye message and uses the name prefix to decide which of the distributed sprites should be detached from the scene graph.

Watching the Server

A TourWatcher thread monitors the server's output, waiting for messages. The message types are listed below with a brief description of what the TourWatcher does in response:

create n x z
> Create a distributed sprite in the local world with name n at position (x, 0, z). By default, the sprite will face forward along the positive z-axis.

wantDetails A P
> The client at IP address A and port P is requesting information about the local sprite on this machine. Gather the data and send the data back in a "detailsFor" message.

detailsFor n1 x1 z1 r
> Create a distributed sprite with the name n1 at location (x1,0,z1), rotated r radians away from the positive z-axis.

n *<move or rotation command>*

> *<command>* can be one of forward, back, left, right, rotCClock, or rotClock. The distributed sprite with name n is moved or rotated. rotCClock is a counter-clockwise rotation, and rotClock is clockwise.

n bye

> A client has left the world, so the distributed sprite with name n is detached (deleted).

The activities using these messages are shown in Figures 32-6, 32-7, and 32-8.

Almost all the messages are related to distributed sprites in the local world: creation, movement, rotation, and deletion. Therefore, these tasks are handled by TourWatcher, which maintains its sprites in a HashMap, mapping sprite names to DistTourSprite objects:

```
private HashMap visitors;    // stores (name, sprite object) pairs
```

The run( ) method in TourWatcher accepts a message from the server and tests the first word in the message to decide what to do:

```
public void run( )
{ String line;
  try {
    while ((line = in.readLine( )) != null) {
      if (line.startsWith("create"))
        createVisitor( line.trim( ) );
      else if (line.startsWith("wantDetails"))
        sendDetails( line.trim( ) );
      else if (line.startsWith("detailsFor"))
        receiveDetails( line.trim( ) );
      else
        doCommand( line.trim( ) );
    }
  }
  catch(Exception e) // socket closure causes termination of while
  { System.out.println("Link to Server Lost");
    System.exit( 0 );
  }
}
```

Creating a Distributed Sprite

A distributed sprite is made in response to a create n x z message by creating a DistTourSprite object with name n at location (x, 0, z) oriented along the positive z-axis. The name and sprite object are stored in the visitors HashMap for future reference.

```
private void createVisitor(String line)
{
  StringTokenizer st = new StringTokenizer(line);
```

```
    st.nextToken();    // skip "create" word
    String userName = st.nextToken();
    double xPosn = Double.parseDouble( st.nextToken() );
    double zPosn = Double.parseDouble( st.nextToken() );

    if (visitors.containsKey(userName))
      System.out.println("Duplicate name -- ignoring it");
    else {
      DistTourSprite dtSprite =
              w3d.addVisitor(userName, xPosn, zPosn, 0);
      visitors.put( userName, dtSprite);
    }
  }
```

A potential problem is if the proposed name has been used for another sprite. TourWatcher only prints an error message to standard output; it would be better if a message was sent back to the originating client.

The Distributed Sprites Class

DistTourSprite is a simplified version of TourSprite: its sprite movement and rotation interface is the same as TourSprite's, but DistTourSprite doesn't send messages to the server. The complete class appears in Example 32-2.

Example 32-2. The DistTourSprite class

```
public class DistTourSprite extends Sprite3D
{
  private final static double MOVERATE = 0.3;
  private final static double ROTATE_AMT = Math.PI / 16.0;

  public DistTourSprite(String userName, String fnm, Obstacles obs,
                    double xPosn, double zPosn)
  { super(userName, fnm, obs);
    setPosition(xPosn, zPosn);
  }

  // moves
  public boolean moveForward()
  { return moveBy(0.0, MOVERATE); }

  public boolean moveBackward()
  { return moveBy(0.0, -MOVERATE); }

  public boolean moveLeft()
  { return moveBy(-MOVERATE,0.0); }

  public boolean moveRight()
  { return moveBy(MOVERATE,0.0); }

  // rotations in Y-axis only
  public void rotClock()
  { doRotateY(-ROTATE_AMT); }    // clockwise
```

Example 32-2. The DistTourSprite class (continued)

```
public void rotCounterClock()
{ doRotateY(ROTATE_AMT); }   // counter-clockwise

} // end of DistTourSprite class
```

Moving and Rotating a Distributed Sprite

doCommand() in TourWatcher distinguishes between the various move and rotation messages and detects bye:

```
private void doCommand(String line)
{
  StringTokenizer st = new StringTokenizer(line);
  String userName = st.nextToken();
  String command = st.nextToken();

  DistTourSprite dtSprite =
              (DistTourSprite) visitors.get(userName);
  if (dtSprite == null)
    System.out.println(userName + " is not here");
  else {
    if (command.equals("forward"))
      dtSprite.moveForward();
    else if (command.equals("back"))
      dtSprite.moveBackward();
    else if (command.equals("left"))
      dtSprite.moveLeft();
    else if (command.equals("right"))
      dtSprite.moveRight();
    else if (command.equals("rotCClock"))
      dtSprite.rotCounterClock();
    else if (command.equals("rotClock"))
      dtSprite.rotClock();
    else if (command.equals("bye")) {
      System.out.println("Removing info on " + userName);
      dtSprite.detach();
      visitors.remove(userName);
    }
    else
      System.out.println("Do not recognise the command");
  }
}  // end of doCommand()
```

All of the commands start with the sprite's name, which is used to look up the DistTourSprite object in the visitors HashMap. If the object cannot be found then TourWatcher notifies only the local machine; it should probably send an error message back to the original client.

The various moves and rotations are mapped to calls to methods in the DistTourSprite object. The bye message causes the sprite to be detached from the local world's scene graph and removed from the HashMap.

Responding to Sprite Detail Requests

Figure 32-6 shows that a wantDetails A P message causes TourWatcher to collect information about the sprite local to this machine. The details are sent back as a detailsFor A P x1 z1 r message to the client at IP address A and port P. The information states that the sprite is currently positioned at (x1, 0, z1) and rotated r radians away from the positive z-axis.

TourWatcher doesn't manage the local sprite, so passes the wantDetails request to the WrapNetTour3D object for processing:

```
private void sendDetails(String line)
{ StringTokenizer st = new StringTokenizer(line);
  st.nextToken(); // skip 'wantDetails' word
  String cliAddr = st.nextToken();
  String strPort = st.nextToken();    // don't parse

  w3d.sendDetails(cliAddr, strPort);
}
```

sendDetails() in WrapNetTour3D accesses the local sprite (referred to as bob) and constructs the necessary reply:

```
public void sendDetails(String cliAddr, String strPort)
{ Point3d currLoc = bob.getCurrLoc();
  double currRotation = bob.getCurrRotation();
  String msg = new String("detailsFor " + cliAddr + " " +
              strPort + " " +
              df.format(currLoc.x) + " " +
              df.format(currLoc.z) + " " +
              df.format(currRotation) );
  out.println(msg);
}
```

The (x, z) location is formatted to four decimal places to reduce the length of the string sent over the network.

Receiving Other Client's Sprite Details

Figure 32-6 shows that when a user joins the world, it will be sent detailsFor messages by the existing clients. Each of these messages is received by TourWatcher, and leads to the creation of a distributed sprite.

TourWatcher's receiveDetails() method pulls apart a detailsFor n1 x1 z1 r message and creates a DistTourSprite with name n1 at (x1, 0, z1) and rotation r:

```
private void receiveDetails(String line)
{
  StringTokenizer st = new StringTokenizer(line);

  st.nextToken(); // skip 'detailsFor' word
  String userName = st.nextToken();
  double xPosn = Double.parseDouble( st.nextToken() );
```

```
double zPosn = Double.parseDouble( st.nextToken( ) );
double rotRadians = Double.parseDouble( st.nextToken( ) );

if (visitors.containsKey(userName))
  System.out.println("Duplicate name -- ignoring it");
else {
  DistTourSprite dtSprite =
          w3d.addVisitor(userName, xPosn, zPosn, rotRadians);
  visitors.put( userName, dtSprite);
  }
}
```

The new sprite must be added to the local world's scene graph, so it is created in WrapNetTour3D by addVisitor( ):

```
public DistTourSprite addVisitor(String userName,
                      double xPosn, double zPosn, double rotRadians)
{
  DistTourSprite dtSprite =
              new DistTourSprite(userName,"Coolrobo.3ds", obs, xPosn, zPosn);
  if (rotRadians != 0)
    dtSprite.setCurrRotation(rotRadians);

  BranchGroup sBG = dtSprite.getBG( );
  sBG.compile( );      // generally a good idea
  try {
    Thread.sleep(200);      // delay a little, so world is finished
  }
  catch(InterruptedException e) {}
  sceneBG.addChild( sBG );

  if (!sBG.isLive( ))     // just in case, but problem seems solved
    System.out.println("Visitor Sprite is NOT live");
  else
    System.out.println("Visitor Sprite is now live");

  return dtSprite;
}
```

Two important elements of this code are that the sub-branch for the distributed sprite is compiled, and the method delays for 200 ms before adding it to the scene. Without these extras, the new BranchGroup, sBG, sometimes fails to become live, which means that it subsequently cannot be manipulated (e.g., its TransformGroup cannot be adjusted to move or rotate the sprite).

The problem appears to be due to the threaded nature of the client: WrapNetTour3D may be building the world's scene graph at the same time that TourWatcher is receiving detailsFor messages, so it is adding new branches to the same graph. It is (just about) possible that addVisitor( ) is called before the scene graph has been compiled (and made live) in createSceneGraph( ). This means Java 3D will be asked to add a branch (sBG) to a node (sceneBG) which is not yet live, causing the attachment to fail.

My solution is to delay the attachment by 200 ms, which solves the problem, at least in the many tests I've carried out.

Another thread-related problem of this type is when multiple threads attempt to add branches to the same live node simultaneously. This may cause one or more of the attachments to fail to become live. The solution is to add the synchronization code to the method doing the attachment, preventing multiple threads from executing it concurrently. Fortunately, this problem doesn't arise in NetTour3D since new branches are only added to a client by a single TourWatcher thread.

Server Activities

The processing done by the server is illustrated in Figures 32-6, 32-7, and 32-8, and is of two types:

- A message arrives and is broadcast to all the other clients.
- A detailsFor message arrives for a specified client and is routed to that client. This is a client-to-client message.

Broadcasting

The most complex broadcasting is triggered by the arrival of a create message at the server.

Figure 32-6 shows how create fits into the overall activity of creating a new sprite. Figure 32-9 expands the "broadcast create and request for details" box in the server swimlane in Figure 32-6.

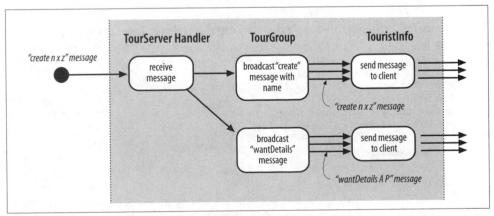

Figure 32-9. Server activities for a create message

TourServerHandler is principally concerned with differentiating between the messages it receives. TourGroup handles the two modes of client communication: broadcasting or client-to-client. TourGroup maintains an ArrayList of TouristInfo objects, which contain the output streams going to the clients.

When a create n x z message arrives at the TourServerHandler, it's passed to doRequest( ), which decides how to process it (by calling sendCreate( )):

```
private void doRequest(String line, PrintWriter out)
{
  if (line.startsWith("create"))
    sendCreate(line);
  else if (line.startsWith("detailsFor"))
    sendDetails(line);
  else  // use TourGroup object to broadcast the message
    tg.broadcast(cliAddr, port, userName + " " + line);
}
```

sendCreate( ) extracts the sprite's name from the message and stores it for later use. It then uses the TourGroup object to broadcast wantDetails and create messages to the other clients:

```
private void sendCreate(String line)
{
  StringTokenizer st = new StringTokenizer(line);
  st.nextToken( ); // skip 'create' word
  userName = st.nextToken( );        // userName is a global
  String xPosn = st.nextToken( );    // don't parse
  String zPosn = st.nextToken( );    // don't parse

  // request details from other clients
  tg.broadcast(cliAddr, port, "wantDetails " + cliAddr + " " + port);

  // tell other clients about the new one
  tg.broadcast(cliAddr,port,"create "+userName +" "+xPosn+" "+zPosn);
}
```

The broadcast( ) method in TourGroup iterates through its TouristInfo objects and sends the message to all of them, except the client that transmitted the message originally:

```
synchronized public void broadcast(String cliAddr, int port, String msg)
{ TouristInfo c;
  for(int i=0; i < tourPeople.size( ); i++) {
    c = (TouristInfo) tourPeople.get(i);
    if (!c.matches(cliAddr, port))
      c.sendMessage(msg);
  }
}
```

All the methods in TourGroup are synchronized since the same TourGroup object is shared between all the TourServerHandler threads. The synchronization prevents a TouristInfo object being affected by more than one thread at a time.

`sendMessage( )` in `TouristInfo` places the message on the output stream going to its client:

```
public void sendMessage(String msg)
{  out.println(msg);  }
```

Client-to-Client Message Passing

Client-to-client message passing is only used to deliver a `detailsFor` message to a client. Figure 32-6 shows how `detailsFor` fits into the overall activity of creating a new sprite. Figure 32-10 expands the "send sprite details for client n1 to client at (A, P)" box in the server swimlane in Figure 32-6.

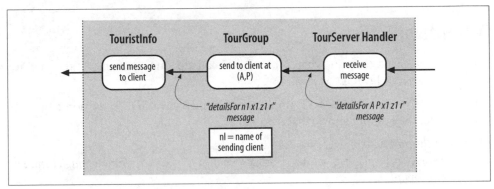

Figure 32-10. Server activities for a detailsFor message

The `TourServerHandler` processes the message in `doRequest( )`, as shown in the previous section, and calls `sendDetails( )`:

```
private void sendDetails(String line)
{
  StringTokenizer st = new StringTokenizer(line);

  st.nextToken( ); // skip 'detailsFor' word
  String toAddr = st.nextToken( );
  int toPort = Integer.parseInt( st.nextToken( ) );
  String xPosn = st.nextToken( );          // don't parse
  String zPosn = st.nextToken( );          // don't parse
  String rotRadians = st.nextToken( );  // don't parse

  tg.sendTo(toAddr, toPort,  "detailsFor " + userName + " " +
              xPosn + " " + zPosn +  " " + rotRadians);
}
```

`sendDetails( )` passes the message to `TourGroup`'s `sendTo( )` method. However, the client's IP address and port number are extracted first to "aim" the message at the correct recipient. The name of the sprite (`userName`) is added to the message, obtained from a global in `TourServerHandler`.

TourGroup's sendTo( ) cycles through its ArrayList of TouristInfo objects until it finds the right client and sends the message:

```
synchronized public void sendTo(String cliAddr,int port,String msg)
{
  TouristInfo c;
  for(int i=0; i < tourPeople.size( ); i++) {
    c = (TouristInfo) tourPeople.get(i);
    if (c.matches(cliAddr, port)) {
      c.sendMessage(msg);
      break;
    }
  }
}
```

Other Java NVEs

NetTour3D is only a taste of what a Java NVE can do; more extensive systems are available, coded in Java 3D or Java.

Three excellent commercial NVE applications utilize Java 3D. They don't provide source code, they do but show what's possible.

Magicosm (http://www.magicosm.net/)
> A fantasy role-playing game. For screenshots, see *http://www.magicosm.net/ screenshots.php.*

Pernica (http://www.starfireresearch.com/pernica/pernica.html)
> A fantasy role-playing game. For screenshots, see *http://www.starfireresearch. com/pernica/graphics.html.*

City of Nights BBS (http://citynight.com/vc)
> A long-running chat service with a 3D interface.

For Java 3D source code for NVE construction, see:

eXtensible MUD (xmud) (http://xmud.sourceforge.net/index.html)
> Handles avatar animation, terrain following, collision detection, and the creation of new objects for the world. The client/server network communication is sockets-based but uses object serialization. The server employs MySQL for data storage. There's a security manager for client authentication The screenshots look similar to the commercial products already mentioned. (See *http://xmud.sourceforge.net/ screenshots.html.*)

The Salamander Project (http://www.kitfox.com/salamander/)
> Salamander was started by Mark McKay in February 2004 to create a 3D MMORPG game engine. Development is on hold at the moment, but 2D and 3D utilities are available, along with a network "lobby" that could be used as a server for networked games.

ChickenBall (http://www.networkedworlds.com/chickenball.html)

A 3D networked football game by Carlos D. Correa, developed to test techniques such as dead-reckoning, distributed consistency, and latecomer handling.

Java 3D Community MMORPG Project (http://starfireresearch.com/services/java3d/mmorpg/mmorpg.html)

A project hosted at Starfire Research, the creators of Pernica. Unfortunately, it's development seems to be on hold, but there's some code available, written by David Yazel and Kevin Dulig.

Tag3D (http://www.croftsoft.com/portfolio/tag3d/)

A prototype multiplayer online virtual reality using Java 3D and RMI, dating from 1999. Written by David Wallace Croft.

Sites with Java source code, but not Java 3D, are:

WolfMUD (http://www.wolfmud.org/)

Supports multiplayer, networked adventure games, including a GUI-based world builder consisting of zones with objects. Unlike a large number of MUD development sites, this one is actively supported and even has good online documentation.

DimensioneX (http://www.dimensionex.net/en/default.htm)

For developing browser-based, graphical multiplayer games. DimensioneX runs on any Java-enabled web server (e.g., Tomcat).

The Mars Simulation Project (http://mars-sim.sourceforge.net/)

The aim is human settlement on Mars, represented by a multi-agent simulation. The emphasis is on setting various parameters to encourage the society to grow and develop.

XiStrat (http://xistrat.sourceforge.net)

XiStrat (Extended Strategy) supports the implementation of turn-based, networked multiplayer, noncooperative, zero-sum, strategy board games (e.g., chess, Go, Reversi), visualized on 3D polyhedra.

Millport (http://millport.sourceforge.net/)

A MUD with a graphical interface.

MiMaze (http://www-sop.inria.fr/rodeo/MiMaze/)

MiMaze3D is a 3D maze game utilizing Java and VRML. It is totally distributed, using RTP/UDP/IP multicast communication between the players. MiMaze utilizes the bucket synchronization algorithm and dead-reckoning for its real-time and consistency requirements.

The Sun Game Server

Sun's Game Technology Group is working on a Sun Game Server, scheduled for early access release sometime in 2005. Some technical details can be found in a white paper at *https://games.dev.java.net/docs/simserverwp052604.pdf*.

The server has three layers: communications, simulation logic, and an object store. The object store is an abstraction hiding an efficient, fault-tolerant, transactional database for storing objects. Objects represent almost everything in the game, which permits the simulation logic (the game code) to be written in terms of method calls, message passing, and event handling. This has the side effect of allowing programmers to code in a single-threaded model. The server has no zones, regions, or shards; user grouping is dynamic and controlled by servers in the communications layer. The aim is to distribute the workload based on player activity rather than by artificial zone divisions.

Installation Using install4j

This appendix describes install4j (*http://www.ej-technologies.com/products/install4j/overview.html*), a cross-platform tool for creating native installers for Java applications. install4j supports Windows, Unix, Linux, and the Mac OS, though I'll only be creating installers for Windows. This is mainly to keep things simple and because I only have regular access to Windows machines. Any kind souls who have written example install4j installers for other platforms should contact me, and I'll include a link to their work in a future version of this book.

I'll develop installers for two examples from the book: BugRunner and Checkers3D. BugRunner comes from Chapter 11 and uses the standard parts of J2SE *and* the J3DTimer class from Java 3D. Checkers3D, from Chapter 15, was my first Java 3D example.

install4j can create an installer that includes a JRE as part of the EXE file or downloaded automatically from install4j's web site when the installer first runs. However, I'll assume that Java is installed. Creating an installer is tricky for an application that requires parts of Java 3D, an extension that isn't included with J2SE or JRE. That's a large part of the reason for choosing the version of BugRunner that uses J3DTimer.

The installers will be built with an evaluation copy of install4j Enterprise Edition v.2.0.7. It's fully functional but adds several "this is not a registered copy" messages to the installation sequence.

install4j Versus JWS

Before starting, it's worthwhile to compare install4j and Java Web Start (JWS), the subject of Appendix B. install4j creates a standalone installer for an application, which can be delivered to the user on a CD or downloaded via a web page link. A great advantage is the familiarity of the installation concept: double-click on the EXE file, press a few Yes buttons, and the application appears as a menu item and a desktop icon. The fact that the executable is coded in Java becomes irrelevant.

JWS is a network solution, which offers better protection from potentially renegade downloads, and supports application updates. JWS is typically utilized via the JWS client that comes as part of the J2SE installation. The reliance on a network model seems restrictive, especially when applications are large. The possibility of being queried about security levels and updates is off-putting to novice computer users.

The Java 3D Components

To get BugRunner and Checkers3D to compile and run, you'll need to include relevant bits from Java 3D. On Windows, the OpenGL version of Java 3D consists of four JAR files and three DLLs. The JAR files are *j3dcore.jar*, *j3daudio.jar*, *vecmath.jar*, and *j3dutils.jar* in *<JRE_DIR>\lib\ext*. The DLLs are *J3D.dll*, *j3daudio.dll*, and *J3DUtils.dll* in *<JRE_DIR>\bin*. *<JRE_DIR>* is the directory holding the JRE, typically something like *C:\Program Files\Java\j2re1.4.2_02*. If the Java 3D development kit is installed, the files will be found below the J2SE home directory, which is usually something like *C:\j2sdk1.4.2_02* or *C:\Program Files\Java\jdk1.5.0*.

The OS level libraries will vary if the DirectX version of Java 3D is used or if the platform is Linux or the MacOS. The easiest way of finding out Java 3D's composition on your machine is to look through the Java 3D *readme* file, which is added to the J2SE home directory at installation time.

Java 3D Components for BugRunner

The BugRunner application uses only the J3DTimer, so which of the JAR and DLL files are required? The J3DTimer class is part of the com.sun.j3d.utils.timer package, which is stored in *j3dutils.jar* (confirm this by looking inside the JAR with a tool such as WinZip), as shown in Figure A-1.

The J3DTimer class (and its inner class) account for about 1 KB out of the 1.2-MB JAR.

A look at the decompiled J3DTimer class, using software such as the DJ Java decompiler (*http://members.fortunecity.com/neshkov/dj.html*), shows that a small amount of Java code calls *J3DUtils.dll* to do all the work (see Figure A-2).

For example, the Java method getValue( ) calls the *J3DUtils.dll* function getNativeTimer( ).

An alternative to decompiling the .*class* file is to download the original source, which is available from the Java 3D web site.

J3DUtils.dll can be examined with HT Editor, a file editor/viewer/analyzer for Windows executables, available from *http://hte.sourceforge.net/* (shown in Figure A-3).

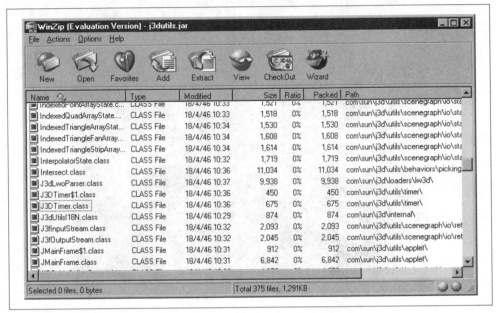

Figure A-1. A WinZip view of j3dutils.jar

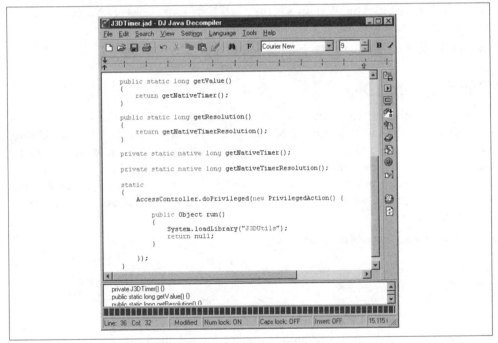

Figure A-2. The DJ Java decompiler view of J3DTimer

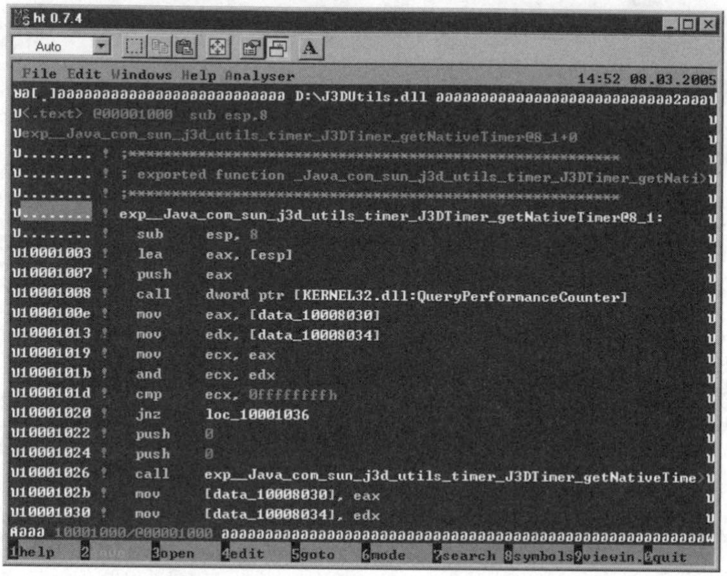

Figure A-3. The HT editor view of J3DUtils.dll

getNativeTimer() uses the Windows *kernel32.dll* functions QueryPerformanceCounter() and QueryPerformanceFrequency().

In summary, the calls to J3DTimer require *j3dutils.jar* and *J3DUtils.dll*.

j3dutils.jar on a Diet

It may be worthwhile to separate the timer code from *j3dutils.jar* and put it into its own JAR, thereby saving about 1.2 MB of space. The technique involves un-JARing *j3dutils.jar* using WinZip or similar compression software. The result is two folders: *com/* and *meta-inf/*. *com/* holds the various classes in j3dutils, which can be deleted, aside from the two timer classes in *com/sun/j3d/utils/timer/*. *meta-inf/* holds a manifest file, *Manifest.mf*, which should be pulled out of the directory and used in the re-JARing process:

```
jar cvmf Manifest.mf j3dutils.jar com
```

The size of the slimmed down *j3dutils.jar* is 2 KB, which is quite a difference.

The real drawback with this technique may be a legal one since a Sun-created JAR is being dismembered. Java 3D is open source with some provisos, which may make it okay to release modifications; license information can be found at *https://*

---

java3d.dev.java.net/. In the rest of this appendix, I'll use the full version of *j3dutils. jar* to play it safe.

The BugRunner Application

The BugRunner code is unchanged from Chapter 11, aside from the addition of one new method in the BugRunner class, which is explained in the next section.

Preparing the JARs

I'm assuming that the target machine for the installation doesn't have Java 3D installed, so the test machine where I develop the installation shouldn't have it either. Instead, *j3dutils.jar* and *J3DUtils.dll* are placed in the *BugRunner/* directory (as shown in Figure A-4).

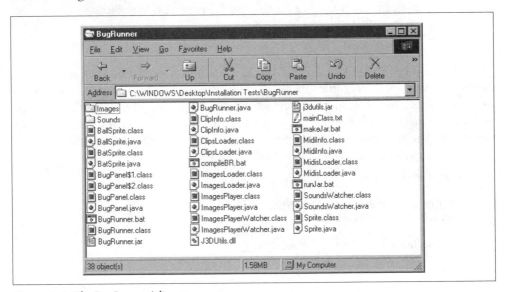

Figure A-4. The BugRunner/ directory

Since Java 3D isn't installed in a standard location checked by javac and java, the calls to the compiler and JVM must include additional classpath information. The *compileBR.bat* batch file in *BugRunner/* contains this line:

```
javac -classpath "%CLASSPATH%;j3dutils.jar" *.java
```

The *BugRunner.bat* batch file contains a similar line:

```
java -cp "%CLASSPATH%;j3dutils.jar" BugRunner
```

There's no need to mention *J3DUtils.dll*, which will be found by the JAR as long as it's in the same directory.

Once the program has been tested, the classes and all other application resources must be packaged up as JARs prior to being passed to install4j. The BugRunner application consists of various classes and the two subdirectories, *Images/* and *Sounds/*. These should be thrown together into a single *BugRunner.jar* file, along with any DLLs. The *makeJar.bat* batch file contains the following line:

```
jar cvmf mainClass.txt BugRunner.jar *.class *.dll Images Sounds
```

The manifest details in *mainClass.txt* are as follows:

```
Main-Class: BugRunner
Class-Path: j3dutils.jar
```

The manifest specifies the class location of the application's main( ) method and adds *j3dutils.jar* to the classpath used when *BugRunner.jar* is executed. For this example, the application assumes this JAR in the same directory as *BugRunner.jar*.

 Since you're controlling the installation process, this isn't that big of a requirement and not a limitation.

The DLL is stored in the JAR because the installation is easier if install4j only has to deal with JARs. However, after the installation EXE file has been downloaded to the user's machine, the DLL must be removed from *BugRunner.jar* and written to the new *BugRunner/* directory. This copying from the JAR to the local directory is carried out by the BugRunner class, which is the new method I mentioned earlier. main( ) in BugRunner calls an installDLL( ) method:

```
public static void main(String args[])
{
  // DLLs used by Java 3D J3DTimer extension
  installDLL("J3DUtils.dll");

  long period = (long) 1000.0/DEFAULT_FPS;
  new BugRunner(period*1000000L);    // ms --> nanosecs
}


private static void installDLL(String dllFnm)
/* Installation of the DLL to the local directory
   from the JAR file containing BugRunner. */
{
  File f = new File(dllFnm);
  if (f.exists())
    System.out.println(dllFnm + " already installed");
  else {
    System.out.println("Installing " + dllFnm);
    // access the DLL inside this JAR
    InputStream in = ClassLoader.getSystemResourceAsStream(dllFnm);
```

```
      if (in == null) {
        System.out.println(dllFnm + " not found");
        System.exit(1);
      }
      try {    // write the DLL to a file
        FileOutputStream out = new FileOutputStream(dllFnm);

        // allocate a buffer for reading entry data.
        byte[] buffer = new byte[1024];
        int bytesRead;
        while ((bytesRead = in.read(buffer)) != -1)
          out.write(buffer, 0, bytesRead);

        in.close();
        out.flush();
        out.close();
      }
      catch (IOException e)
      { System.out.println("Problems installing " + dllFnm); }
    }
  }  // end of installDLL()
```

installDLL() will be called every time that BugRunner is executed, so installDLL() first
checks whether the DLL is present in the local directory. If not, it's installed by being
written out to a file. The stream from the DLL file inside the JAR is created with:

```
    InputStream in = ClassLoader.getSystemResourceAsStream(dllFnm);
```

This works since the DLL is in the same JAR as BugRunner, so the class loader for
BugRunner can find it. Figure A-5 illustrates the technique.

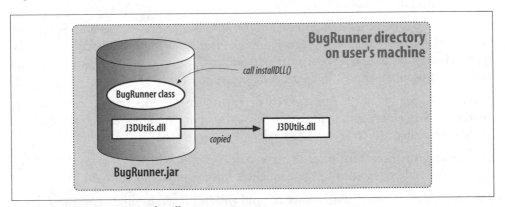

Figure A-5. Installing a DLL locally

The result is that the BugRunner application installed on the user's machine will consist of two JARs, *BugRunner.jar* and *j3dutils.jar*. After the first execution of BugRunner,
these two JARs will be joined by *J3DUtils.dll*.

Testing

The best testing approach is to move the two JARs to a different machine, specifically one that doesn't have Java 3D installed (but J2SE or JRE must be present). Double-click on *BugRunner.jar*, and the game should begin. The *J3DUtils.dll* will magically appear in the same directory. Alternatively, the application can be tested with this command:

```
java -jar BugRunner.jar
```

Executing this in a command window will allow standard output and error messages to be seen on the screen, which can be useful for testing and debugging.

You could stop at this point since the game is nicely wrapped up inside two JARs. However, an installer will allow a professional veneer to be added, including installation screens, splash windows, desktop and menu icons, and an uninstaller. These are essential elements for most users.

Creating the BugRunner Installer

This is not a book about install4j, so I'll only consider the more important points in creating the BugRunner installer. install4j has an extensive help facility and links to a tutorial at its web site at *http://www.ej-technologies.com/products/install4j/tutorials. html*. Another good way of understanding things is to browse through the various screens of the BugRunner installation script, bugRun.install4j. The screenshots are taken from install4j v.2.0.7; the latest release has modified some of the configuration screens and added lots of new features.

A crucial step is to define the *distribution tree*, the placement of files and directories in the *BugRunner/* directory created on the user's machine at install time. My approach is to include an *Executables/* subdirectory to hold the two JAR files. This directory structure is shown in Figure A-6.

A quick examination of Figure A-6 will reveal three JARs inside *Executables/*: *BugRunner.jar*, *j3dutils.jar*, and *custom.jar*. *custom.jar* contains Java code deployed by the uninstaller, which is explained below.

BugRunner.jar is not called directly but via an EXE file, which is set up on the Configure executable screen during the Launchers stage (shown in Figure A-7).

The executable's name is *BugRunner.exe* and will be placed in the *Executables/* directory along with the JARs. It's important to set the working directory to be ".", so the JAR will search for resources in the correct place.

 Under the Advanced Options button, redirecting stdout and stderr into log files is possible and a good idea for testing and debugging.

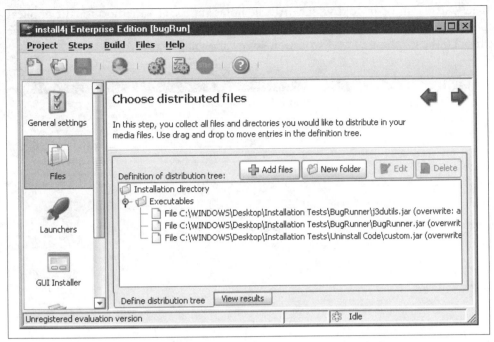

Figure A-6. Distribution tree for the BugRunner installer

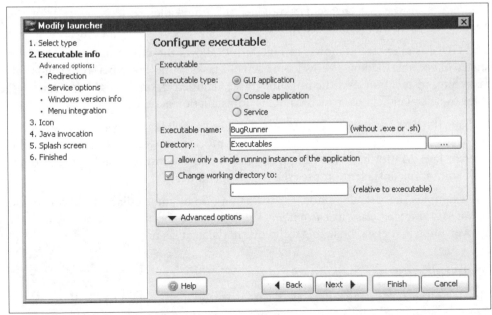

Figure A-7. Configuring the BugRunner executable

The EXE file must be told which JAR file holds the main( ) method for the application and which JARs are involved in the application's execution. This is done through the Configure Java Invocation screen shown in Figure A-8.

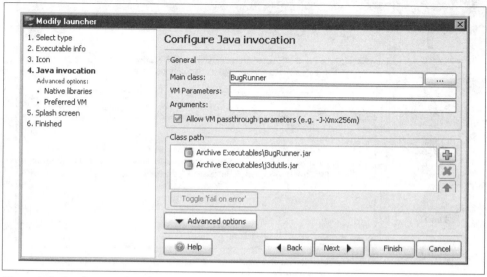

Figure A-8. Configuring the Java invocation

Figure A-8 shows that *custom.jar* (holding the uninstaller code) isn't part of the application since it isn't included in the Class path list.

The GUI Installer stage (shown in Figure A-9) allows the customization of various stages of the installation: the welcome screen, tasks to be done before installation, tasks after installation, and the finishing phase. The screen on the right of Figure A-9 is for the installer actions, which contains uninstallation actions.

Perhaps the best advantage of using install4j is its close links to Java, most evident in the way the installation (and uninstallation) process can be customized. install4j offers a Java API for implementing many tasks, and the install4j distribution comes with an example installer that uses the API's capabilities.

For example, the default action carried out prior to uninstallation is to call the DLLUninstallAction class in *custom.jar*, so application-specific tasks can be defined by overriding that class. I use this technique in the next section.

Uninstallation

The default install4j uninstaller will delete the JARs that it added to the *Executables/* directory along with all the other files and directories it created at installation time. However, the installer didn't add *J3DUtils.dll* to *Executables/*; that task was carried out by the BugRunner class when it first ran.

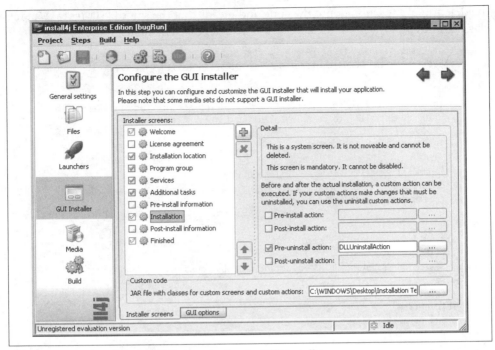

Figure A-9. The installer/uninstaller actions for the GUI installer

install4j knows nothing about *J3DUtils.dll*, so it won't delete it or the subdirectory that holds it. The outcome is that a basic BugRunner uninstaller won't remove the *BugRunner/Executables/* directory or the *J3DUtils.dll* file inside it. To get around this, you need to define a pre-uninstall operation that removes the DLL, so the main uninstaller can delete everything else.

custom.jar contains the DLLUninstallAction class, which extends install4j's UninstallAction class. UninstallAction offers two abstract methods for custom behavior:

```
public abstract boolean performAction(Context context, ProgressInterface pi);
public abstract int getPercentOfTotalInstallation();
```

The uninstallation task (in this case, deleting the DLL) should be placed inside performAction( ). User messages can be sent to the uninstallation screen via the ProgressInterface object. performAction( ) should return true if the task is successful or false to abort the uninstallation process. getPercentOfTotalInstallation( ) gets the amount of the progress slider assigned to the task, returning a number between 0 and 100.

My implementation of performAction( ) obtains a list of the DLLs in the *Executables/* directory and then deletes each one. This approach is more flexible than hardwiring the deletion of *J3DUtils.dll* into the code and means that the same DLLUninstallAction class can be employed with the Checkers3D installer discussed later:

```
private static final String PATH = "../Executables";
// location of the DLLs relative to <PROG_DIR>/.install4j


public boolean performAction(Context context, ProgressInterface progReport)
// called by install4j to do uninstallation tasks
{
  File delDir = new File(PATH);

  FilenameFilter dllFilter = new FilenameFilter() {
    public boolean accept(File dir, String name)
    { return name.endsWith("dll");  }
  };

  String[] fNms = delDir.list(dllFilter);  // list of dll filenames
  if (fNms.length == 0)
    System.out.println("Uninstallation: No DLLs found");
  else
    deleteDLLs(fNms, progReport);
  return true;
 // end of performAction( )
}
```

The tricky aspect of the code is the use of the PATH variable. The uninstaller is executed in the *.install4j/* directory, which is at the same level as *Executables/*. Both of these are located in the *BugRunner/* directory installed on the user's machine (see Figure A-10).

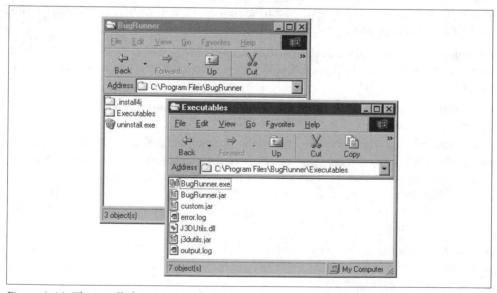

Figure A-10. The installed BugRunner directories

The PATH string redirects the File object to refer to *Executables/*. A list of filenames ending in ".dll" is collected by using a FileFilter anonymous class, and the list is passed to deleteDLLs( ):

```
private void deleteDLLs(String[] fNms,ProgressInterface progReport)
// delete each DLL file, and report the progress
{
  progReport.setStatusMessage("Deleting installed DLLs");

  int numFiles = fNms.length;
  String msg;
  for (int i=0; i < numFiles; i++) {
    msg = new String("" + (i+1) + "/" + numFiles + ": " + fNms[i] + "... ");
    deleteFile(fNms[i], progReport, msg);
    progReport.setPercentCompleted( ((i+1)*100)/numFiles );
    try {
      Thread.sleep(500);    // 0.5 sec to see something
    }
    catch (InterruptedException e) {}
  }
}
```

deleteDLLs( ) loops through the filenames, calling deleteFile( ) for each. The ProgressInterface object informs the user of the progress of these deletions.

deleteFile( ) creates a File object for the named file and then calls File.delete( ).

The DLLUninstallAction class must be compiled with the install4j API classes added to the classpath:

```
javac -classpath "%CLASSPATH%;d:\install4j\resource\i4jruntime.jar"
                                        DLLUninstallAction.java
```

The creation of the JAR file is standard:

```
jar cvf custom.jar *.class
```

The BugRunner Installer

The resulting installer, called *BR_1.0.exe*, takes a few seconds to generate and is about 1.4 MB.

The size will drop to 950 KB if the timer-specific version of *j3dutils.jar* is employed.

A version bundled with JRE 1.4.2 comes in at 12 MB.

The Checkers3D Application

The Checkers3D code is unchanged from the example in Chapter 15, aside from the addition of the installDLL( ) method in the Checkers3D class.

Preparing the JARs

As with Checkers3D, I'm assuming that the target machine for the installation doesn't have Java 3D installed, so the test machine where I develop the installation shouldn't have it either. Instead, all of its JARs and DLLs (seven files) are copied to the *Checkers3D/* directory (see Figure A-11).

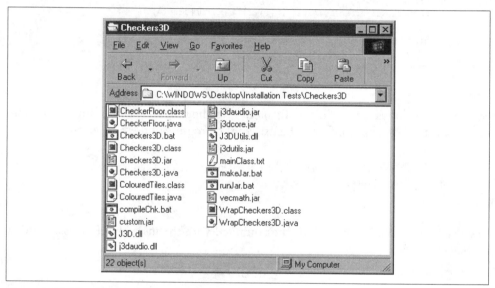

Figure A-11. The Checkers3D/ application directory

Since Java 3D isn't installed in the standard location, the calls to the compiler and JVM must include additional classpath information:

```
javac -classpath "%CLASSPATH%;vecmath.jar;j3daudio.jar;
                                    j3dcore.jar;j3dutils.jar" *.java
java -cp "%CLASSPATH%;vecmath.jar;j3daudio.jar;
                                    j3dcore.jar;j3dutils.jar" Checkers3D
```

There's no need to mention the three DLLs (*J3D.dll*, *j3daudio.dll*, and *J3DUtils.dll*), which will be found by the JARs as long as they're in the same directory.

The Checkers3D classes should be collected into a single *Checkers3D.jar* file, along with all the required DLLs:

```
jar cvmf mainClass.txt Checkers3D.jar *.class *.dll
```

The manifest information in *mainClass.txt* is:

```
Main-Class: Checkers3D
Class-Path: vecmath.jar j3daudio.jar j3dcore.jar j3dutils.jar
```

The manifest specifies the class location of main( ) and adds the Java 3D JARs to the classpath used by *Checkers3D.jar*.

Changes to Checkers3D.java

Checkers3D contains the same installDLL( ) method as found in BugRunner but calls it three times:

```
public static void main(String[] args)
{
  // DLLs used by Java 3D extensions
  installDLL("J3D.dll");
  installDLL("j3daudio.dll");
  installDLL("J3DUtils.dll");
  new Checkers3D( );
}
```

The Checkers3D application installed on the user's machine will consist of five JARs: *Checkers3D.jar*, *j3dcore.jar*, *j3daudio.jar*, *vecmath.jar*, and *j3dutils.jar*. After the first execution, they'll be joined by the three DLLs: *J3D.dll*, *j3daudio.dll*, and *J3DUtils.dll*.

Creating the Checkers3D Installer

The distribution tree for the installer has the same shape as the one for BugRunner: an *Executables/* subdirectory holds the JARs. The directory structure is shown in Figure A-12.

The five JARs required by the application are there, as well as *custom.jar* for uninstallation. It's the same one as used in BugRunner, and no changes are necessary.

Most of the other installer configuration tasks are similar to those carried out for BugRunner, such as configuring the executable and Java invocation and the definition of the pre-uninstall action using the DLLUninstallAction class in *custom.jar*.

The Checkers3D Installer

The resulting installer, called *C3D_1.0.exe*, takes around 8 seconds to generate and is about 3.6 MB. A version bundled with JRE 1.4.2 comes in at 14.3 MB.

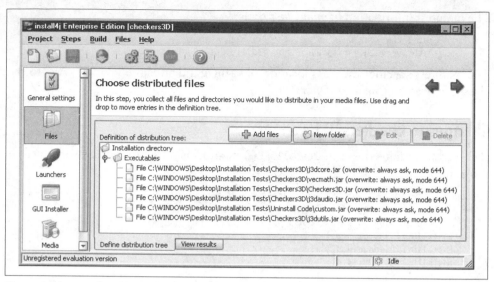

Figure A-12. Distribution tree for the Checkers3D installer

Installation Using Java Web Start

Java Web Start (JWS) is a web-enabled installer for Java applications (*http://java.sun. com/products/javawebstart/*). Typically, the user points a browser at a page containing a link to a deployment file; the retrieval of that file triggers the execution of JWS on the client, which takes over from the browser.

This assumes that JWS is present on the target machine.

JWS uses the information in the deployment file to download the various JAR files making up the application, together with installation icons, a splash screen, and other details. The application is stored in a local cache and executed inside a JVM sandbox. Subsequent executions of the application utilize the cached copy unless the original has been modified, in which case the changed JARs are downloaded again.

This appendix shows how the BugRunner and Checkers3D applications in Chapters 11 and 15 can be deployed with JWS. BugRunner is the beginnings of a 2D arcade-style game but uses the Java 3D timer. Checkers3D is a basic Java 3D application that displays a blue sphere floating above a checkerboard surface.

Both applications require native libraries, and I'll cover how JWS installers suitable for Windows can be created. However, JWS is a cross-platform tool, so I'll briefly examine the issues in making BugRunner and Checkers3D work on the Linux and Mac operating systems.

Deployment links are usually placed in a *JWS portal page*, a page using JavaScript and VBScript to detect whether the intended client platform possesses JWS. If JWS isn't found, then it needs to be downloaded before the application installation can begin. I'll use a portal page for accessing BugRunner and Checkers3D, located at *http:// fivedots.coe.psu.ac.th/~ad/jws/*.

JWS uses digital signing and certificates to secure applications, so I'll finish by looking at how to use third-party certificates.

JWS Benefits

JWS works the same way across multiple platforms unlike the downloading and execution of applets, which is plagued by irritating variations between browsers. The headaches caused by browsers' nonstandard programming frameworks (such as JavaScript and HTML variants on different platforms and browsers) are one reason for the decline in popularity of complex applets and the growth in thin clients linked to J2EE-built servers.

Client-side caching avoids an essential problem familiar from applets, which is the need to download an applet every time it's used. That's a waste of bandwidth if the applet hasn't changed and further discourages the development of large applets. JWS suffers from network overheads during the first download, but the copy of the application in the local cache is used after that until changes are detected in the original. This cached copy means network failure doesn't stop the application from executing unless it requires network access for specific tasks. By comparison, an applet is out of reach when the network is down.

JWS only retrieves Java software packaged as JARs. However, the JARs may contain native libraries for different operating systems and platforms, a feature you'll need to utilize the Java 3D libraries. My examples concentrate on Java applications retrieved by JWS, but applets can be downloaded as well.

JWS prevents hacker attacks by executing the installed code inside a sandbox, stopping antisocial behavior such as hard disk wiping or spamming from your machine. Sometimes the security restrictions can be too harsh, and JWS offers two ways of relaxing them: the Java Network Launching Protocol (JNLP) API supports controlled ways to interact with the OS, such as reading and writing files and accessing the clipboard; the second way is to sign software digitally, permitting its security level to be reduced. I'll detail this latter approach, which is mandatory if a program uses native libraries.

Since the downloaded application is running free of the browser, there's complete freedom over the kinds of user interaction and GUI elements that can be employed.

JWS Downsides

Using JWS has downsides. One is the need to have JWS present on the client machine before the application is downloaded. For existing Java users, this isn't a problem since JWS is installed as part of J2SE or JRE. But what about game players who don't have any desire to join the Java faithful? The answer is somewhat messy since it requires the web page containing the deployment link to detect whether the client machine has JWS installed. If it hasn't, then a JRE must be downloaded before the application. Unfortunately, the standardization problems with browsers complicate this detection work.

Another problem with JWS is version skew. There have been several versions of JWS: JWS 1.0 shipped with JRE 1.4, JWS 1.2 was included with JRE 1.4.1, and JWS 1.4.2 arrived with JRE 1.4.2. J2SE/JRE 5.0 comes with a considerably revamped JWS 5.0, which replaces the application manager with a control panel and a cache viewer. The earlier versions of JWS (before 1.4.2) have problems correctly setting up proxy network settings and placing the cache in an accessible location on multiuser machines.

JWS cannot be (legally) modified or reconfigured prior to its installation. For example, you cannot distribute a version of JWS that never places an application icon in the menu list or always pops up a console window to display output. The location of the cache cannot be preset, and there's no way to create an uninstallation menu item. Many of these things can be changed, but only after JWS is present on the client machine, which means these actions must be carried out by the user rather than the developer or deployer. These tasks may be beyond the ability of novices. To be fair, the deployment file does allow some installation elements to be configured, including what is displayed during the retrieval process.

The automatic updating of an application requires that JWS checks the home server for changes every time the program is run, which causes a (small) delay. Normally, an entire JAR will be downloaded, even if only one line of it has changed. The solution to this problem is jardiff, which specifies the changes necessary to update a JAR to its current version. jardiffs are much smaller than JARs since they only need to store modifications. However, jardiffs require specialized server settings before they can be utilized.

JWS deployment files need the JNLP MIME type to be set up in their host server. For example, the mime.types file in Apache must include this line:

```
application/x-java-jnlp-file   JNLP
```

The problem is that the application developer may not have access to the server to do this. However, this is not much of an issue as most current web servers come preconfigured with the JNLP MIME type.

Though JWS is aimed at web-based downloads, it's possible to a supply a link to a local deployment file (using the *file://<path>* notation). However, the file must contain a reference to its current location, which will often be unknown to the developer at build time. For instance, at installation time, the file may be stored on a CD created by a third party, and it may be mounted on a drive with a name that could be almost anything. There are add-on JWS tools for building CD installers, including Clio (*http://www.vamphq.com/clio.html*) and Jess (*http://www.vamphq.com/jess.html*).

Clio adds a built-in web server to the CD, and Jess writes the application directly to the JWS cache. JWS 5.0 offers improved support for CD-based installation.

The JNLP Deployment File

A deployment file is written in XML and has a *.jnlp* extension. The file format is defined by the JNLP and API specifications (JSR-56) available from *http://java.sun.com/products/javawebstart/download-spec.html*. A subset is described in the developers guide in the J2SE documentation (see *<JAVA_HOME>/docs/guide/jws/developersguide/contents.html*).

Most JNLP files have a structure similar to Example B-1.

Example B-1. Structure of JNLP deployment file

```
<?xml version="1.0" encoding="UTF-8"?>
<jnlp spec="1.0+"
  codebase="http://www.foo.com/loc/"
  href="appl.jnlp" >

  <information> ... </information>

  <security> ... </security>

  <resources> ... </resources>

  <application-desc> ... </application-desc>
</jnlp>
```

The codebase attribute gives the base URL where this file and the other application components are stored. A file:// location may be used instead if the software is to be loaded locally. The href attribute gives the URL reference for this JNLP file, which can be relative to the codebase (as in Example B-1) or can be an absolute address. The information tag contains textual information about the application, utilized by JWS at retrieval and execution time. For example, references to icons and a splash screen image are placed in this element.

The security tag is optional. If present, it defines the level of increased access given to the application. Two values are possible: <all-permissions/> or the slightly less powerful <j2ee-application-client-permissions/>. They require that the application's JARs be digitally signed. The resources tag lists the JARs comprising the program. The application-desc tag states how the program is to be executed along with optional input arguments.

Steps in Developing a JWS Application

The following seven steps outline the development process for a JWS installer. They'll be explained in greater detail as the BugRunner and Checkers3D applications are converted into JWS applications:

1. Write and test the application on a standalone machine, packaging it (and all its resources) as JAR files.

2. Modify the application code to make it suitable for deployment. The necessary changes will be minimal unless native libraries are used. In that case, each library must be wrapped up inside a JAR and loaded by the application's main() method via System.loadLibrary().

3. Create a new public/private keypair for signing the application and its component JARs. At this stage, a third-party certificate may be obtained from a certificate authority (CA). I'll delay talking about this until near the end of the appendix.

4. Sign everything with the private key: the application JAR, the extension JARs, and any native library JARs.

5. Create a deployment file (a JNLP file) using a file:// codebase so the installation can be tested locally. This stage requires the creation of application icons and a splash screen image, used by JWS.

6. Change the deployment file to use the host server's URL and place everything on that server. The deployment file will usually be accessed through a JWS portal page.

7. Test the installer on various client platforms, OSs, and browsers.

 Some of these test clients shouldn't possess JWS.

A JWS Installer for BugRunner

BugRunner is a basic 2D arcade game (see Chapter 11. I'll work with the version that uses the J3DTimer class, which means the deployment file must install the relevant Java 3D library. I can't assume it's present on the user's machine.

Write the Application

The installer version of the application shouldn't rely on nonstandard extensions or native libraries being present on the client machine. However, BugRunner uses the Java 3D timer, which is part of the Java 3D extension. The OpenGL Windows version of Java 3D is implemented across seven files:

j3daudio.jar
j3dcore.jar
j3dutils.jar
vecmath.jar
    JAR files

J3D.dll
j3daudio.dll
J3DUtils.dll
    Native libraries

 The native libraries will vary across different platforms, and the JAR versions may also vary.

Only *j3dutils.jar* and *J3DUtils.dll* are needed for the timer functionality as explained in Appendix A. They should be placed in the *BugRunner/* directory to be locally accessible to the application. Java 3D should not be installed on your test machine.

Figure B-1 shows the *BugRunner/* directory prior to compilation. It contains all the Java files (unchanged from Chapter 11), *j3dutils.jar*, and *J3DUtils.dll*. The batch files are optional but reduce the tedium of typing long command lines.

Since Java 3D isn't installed in a standard location checked by javac and java, the calls to the compiler and JVM must include additional classpath information. The *compileBR.bat* batch file contains this line:

```
javac -classpath "%CLASSPATH%;j3dutils.jar" *.java
```

The *BugRunner.bat* batch file has this:

```
java -cp "%CLASSPATH%;j3dutils.jar" BugRunner
```

There's no need to mention *J3DUtils.dll*, which will be found by the JAR as long as it's in the local directory.

Once the program has been fully debugged, it should be packaged as a JAR. The BugRunner application consists of various classes, and the subdirectories *Images/* and *Sounds/*. These should be thrown together into a single *BugRunner.jar* file. The *makeJar.bat* batch file contains the line:

```
jar cvmf mainClass.txt BugRunner.jar *.class Images Sounds
```

Figure B-1. The BugRunner/ directory

The manifest details in *mainClass.txt* are:

```
Main-Class: BugRunner
Class-Path: j3dutils.jar
```

The manifest specifies the class location of main( ) and adds *j3dutils.jar* to the class-path used when *BugRunner.jar* is executed. This setup assumes that it's in the same directory as *BugRunner.jar*.

 The required DLLs (only *J3DUtils.dll* in this case) aren't added to *BugRunner.jar*.

The application now consists of three files: *BugRunner.jar*, *j3dutils.jar*, and *J3DUtils.dll*. These should be moved to a different directory on a different machine and tested again. Double-clicking on *BugRunner.jar* should start it running. Alternatively, type:

```
java -jar BugRunner.jar
```

Modify the Application for Deployment

Since the native library *J3DUtils.dll* is utilized by BugRunner, two tasks must be carried out. The DLL must be placed inside its own JAR:

```
jar cvf J3DUtilsDLL.jar J3DUtils.dll
```

There's no need for additional manifest information.

The main( ) method of BugRunner, in *BugRunner.java*, must be modified to call System.loadLibrary( ) for each DLL:

```
public static void main(String args[])
{
  // DLL used by Java 3D J3DTimer extension
  String os = System.getProperty("os.name");
  if (os.startsWith("Windows")) {
    System.out.println("Loading '" + os + "' native libraries...");
    System.out.print("  J3DUtils.dll... ");
    System.loadLibrary("J3DUtils");  // drop ".dll"
    System.out.println("OK");
  }
  else {
    System.out.println("Sorry, OS '" + os + "' not supported.");
    System.exit(1);
  }

  long period = (long) 1000.0/DEFAULT_FPS;
  new BugRunner(period*1000000L);     // ms --> nanosecs
}
```

If several libraries are loaded, the load order will matter if dependencies exist between them.

The checking of the os.name property string gives the program a chance to report an error if the application is started by an OS that doesn't support the library. This coding style also allows the application to load different libraries depending on the OS name. For instance:

```
String os = System.getProperty("os.name");
System.out.println("Loading " + os + " native libraries...");
if (os.startsWith("Windows")) {
  System.loadLibrary("J3DUtils");  // drop ".dll"
      :  // other libraries loaded
}
else if (os.startsWith("Linux")) {
  System.loadLibrary("J3DUtils"); // drop "lib" prefix & ".so"
      :
}
else if (os.startsWith("Mac")) {
  System.loadLibrary("J3DUtils"); // drop ".jnilib"
      :
```

```
  }
  else {
    System.out.println("Sorry, OS '" + os + "' not supported.");
    System.exit(1);
  }
```

 A longer example of this kind can be found in "Marc's Web Start Kamasutra," a JWS and JNLP forum thread at *http://forum.java.sun.com/
thread.jsp?forum=38&thread=166873*.

A lengthy list of the possible os.name values is presented in *http://
www.vamphq.com/os.html*.

These changes to *BugRunner.java* mean it must be recompiled and re-JARed:

```
javac -classpath "%CLASSPATH%;j3dutils.jar" *.java
jar cvmf mainClass.txt BugRunner.jar *.class Images Sounds
```

Create a Public/Private Keypair for Signing the Application

The digital signing of a JAR requires two of Java's security tools: keytool and
jarsigner. They're described in the security tools section of the J2SE documentation
in *<JAVA HOME>/docs/tooldocs/tools.html#security*.

keytool generates and manages keypairs, collected together in a keystore. Each keypair is made up of a public key and private key, and an associated public-key certificate. A simplified diagram showing a typical keypair is shown in Figure B-2.

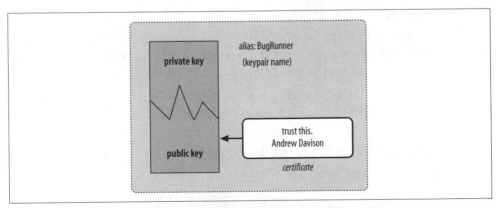

Figure B-2. The elements of a keypair

The two keys can be used to encrypt documents. Something encrypted with a private key can only be decrypted with the corresponding public key; if the encryption
uses the public key, then only the private key can unlock it. The intention is that the
public key is widely distributed, but users keep their private key secret. Determining
the private key from examining the public key is impossible.

A message sent to users can be encrypted with the public key, so only they can read it by applying their private key. A message from users to another person can be encrypted with the private key. The fact that the user's public key can decrypt the message means that it must have come from that user. The private key is being used as a digital signature.

One of the problems with the public/private keys approach is how to distribute a public key safely. For instance, if I receive an email from "Stan Lee" giving me his public key, how do I know that it is from the famous Atlas/Timely editor? This is where the public-key certificate comes into play.

A certificate is a digitally signed statement from a third party, perhaps my respected friend "Alan Moore," that is "Stan Lee's public key." Of course, the question of authenticity still applies, but now to the "Alan Moore" signature, which can be combated by signing it with the certificate of yet another person. This process leads to a chain of certificates, ending with a certificate that can be proved genuine in some unforgeable way (for example, by visiting the person and asking them).

Whenever keytool generates a new keypair it adds a self-signed certificate to the public key. In effect, all my public keys contain certificates signed by me saying they're genuine. This is useless in a real situation, but it's sufficient for these demos. You'll see that JWS issues a dire warning when it sees a self-signed certificate but will let it pass if the client gives the okay. I'll discuss how to obtain better certificates later in this appendix.

A new keypair is written to the keystore called MyKeyStore by typing the following:

```
keytool -genkey -keystore MyKeyStore -alias BugRunner
```

The user is prompted for the keystore password, a lengthy list of personal information, and a password for the new keypair (see Figure B-3). The keypair's alias (name) is BugRunner in this example, though any name could be used.

Better passwords should be thought up than those used in my examples; a good password uses letters, numbers, and punctuation symbols, and should be at least eight characters long.

The keystore's contents can be examined with this command:

```
keytool -list -keystore MyKeyStore
```

Sign Everything with the Private Key

You're ready to use the jarsigner tool to start signing the JARs in the BugRunner application. Figure B-4 presents a simple diagram of what jarsigner does to a JAR.

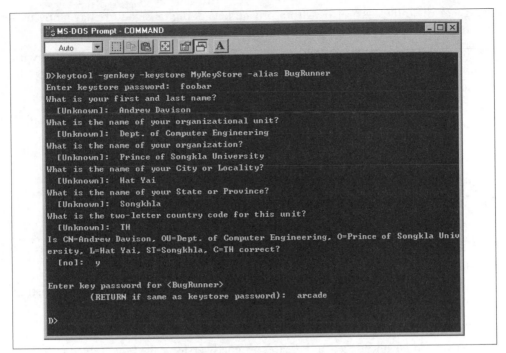

Figure B-3. Generate a new keypair

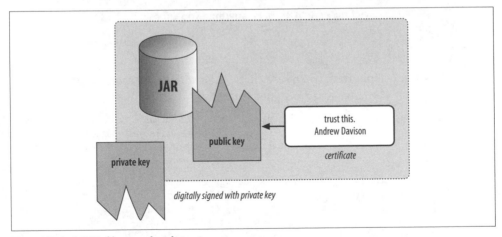

Figure B-4. A JAR file signed with jarsigner

jarsigner digitally signs a JAR with a private key. A digital signature has many useful characteristics:

- Its authenticity can be checked by seeing if it matches the public key stored with the JAR. This relies on the public key being trusted, which depends on the certificates attached to it.
- The digital signature cannot be forged since the private key is only known to the sender of the JAR.
- Unlike a real signature, the digital signature is partly derived from the data it's attached to (i.e., the JAR file). This means that it cannot be removed from its original JAR, stuck on a different one, and still be authenticated successfully.

The actual mechanics of creating a signed JAR are simple:

```
jarsigner -keystore MyKeyStore foo.jar BugRunner
```

This signs *foo.jar* using the BugRunner keypair stored in MyKeyStore. jarsigner will prompt the user for the keystore and keypair passwords.

A variant of this is to create a new signed JAR file rather than modify the existing one:

```
jarsigner -keystore MyKeyStore -signedjar foo_signed.jar  foo.jar BugRunner
```

This leaves *foo.jar* unchanged and creates a signed version called *foo_signed.jar*.

 The name of the new JAR can be anything you choose.

For the BugRunner application, there are three JARs: *BugRunner.jar*, *j3dutils.jar*, and *J3DUtilsDLL.jar*. The latter two are signed this way:

```
jarsigner -keystore MyKeyStore -signedjar j3dutils_signed.jar
                                          j3dutils.jar  BugRunner
jarsigner -keystore MyKeyStore J3DUtilsDLL.jar BugRunner
```

 The creation of a new JAR for the signed version of *j3dutils.jar* is to avoid any confusion with the original JAR created by Sun.

This process means yet another reJARing of BugRunner since the manifest information in *mainClass.txt* must be changed to reference the signed filenames:

```
Main-Class: BugRunner
Class-Path: j3dutils_signed.jar
```

The jar command in *makeJar.bat* is unchanged:

```
jar cvmf mainClass.txt BugRunner.jar *.class Images Sounds
```

After *BugRunner.jar* is regenerated and then it's signed:

```
jarsigner -keystore MyKeyStore BugRunner.jar BugRunner
```

Create a Deployment File

The deployment file for the BugRunner application, *BugRunner.jnlp*, is shown in Example B-2.

Example B-2. JNLP deployment file for BugRunner

```xml
<?xml version="1.0" encoding="utf-8"?>
<jnlp spec="1.0+"
  <!-- codebase="http://fivedots.coe.psu.ac.th/~ad/jws/BugRunner/"-->
  codebase="file:///D:/Teaching/Java Games/Code/JWS/BugRunner/"
  href="BugRunner.jnlp"
  >

  <information>
    <title>BugRunner</title>
    <vendor>Andrew Davison</vendor>
    <homepage href="http://fivedots.coe.pcu.ac.th/~ad/jg"/>
    <description>BugRunner</description>
    <description kind="short">BugRunner: a 2D arcade-style game,
                         using the J3DTimer class</description>
    <icon href="bug32.gif"/>
    <icon kind="splash" href="BRBanner.gif"/>
    <offline-allowed/>
  </information>

  <security>
    <all-permissions/>
  </security>

  <resources os="Windows">
    <j2se version="1.4+"/>
    <jar href="BugRunner.jar" main="true"/>
    <jar href="j3dutils_signed.jar"/>
    <nativelib href="J3DUtilsDLL.jar"/>
  </resources>

  <application-desc main-class="BugRunner"/>
</jnlp>
```

The URL codebase value is commented out at this stage; instead, use a path to the local development directory.

The information tag contains two forms of textual description: a one-line message and a longer paragraph (confusingly labeled with the attribute value short). The icon and splash screen images are named; they should be located in the BugRunner directory. The icon is the default size of 32×32 pixels, but other sizes are possible and several icons with different resolutions can be supplied. GIF or JPEG images can be used. Unfortunately, transparent GIF are rendered with black backgrounds, at least on Windows.

The offline-allowed tag states that the application can run when JWS detects that the network is unavailable. all-permissions security is used, which requires that all the JARs named in the resources section are signed. The resources will be downloaded only if the client-side OS matches the os attribute. There's also an optional arch attribute to further constrain the installation.

For example, the following is able to retrieve any one of five different versions of j3daudio.jar depending on the OS and architecture:

```
<resources os="Windows">
  <jar href="jars/j3d/windows/j3daudio.jar"/>
</resources>

<resources os="Linux" arch="x86">      <!-- Linux IBM -->
  <jar href="jars/j3d/linux/i386/j3daudio.jar"/>
</resources>

<resources os="Linux" arch="i386">      <!-- Linux Sun -->
  <jar href="jars/j3d/linux/i386/j3daudio.jar"/>
</resources>

<resources os="Solaris" arch="sparc">
  <jar href="jars/j3d/solaris/j3daudio.jar"/>
</resources>

<resources os="Mac OS X" arch="ppc">
  <jar href="jars/j3d/osx/j3daudio.jar"/>
</resources>
```

The *jars/* directory should be in the same directory as the deployment file.

It may seem rather silly to have five different JARs when their contents should be identical because they're coded in Java. In practice, however, this approach avoids incompatibles that may have crept into the different versions.

More details on how the Java 3D libraries can be divided into multiple resource tags are given in the "Marc's Web Start Kamasutra" forum thread (*http://forum.java.sun.com/thread.jsp?forum=38&thread=166873*).

The j2se version tag in *BugRunner.jnlp* specifies that any version of J2SE or JRE from 1.4.0 on can execute the application. JWS will abort if it detects an earlier version when it starts the program. It's possible to specify initial settings for the JRE when it starts and to trigger an automatic download of a JRE if the client's version is incompatible. The following tags illustrate these features:

```
<j2se version="1.4.2" initial-heap-size="64m"/>
<j2se version="1.4.2-beta" href="http://java.sun.com/products/autodl/j2se"/>
```

BugRunner.jnlp specifies that three JARs should be retrieved:

```
<jar href="BugRunner.jar" main="true"/>
<jar href="j3dutils_signed.jar"/>
<nativelib href="J3DUtilsDLL.jar"/>
```

BugRunner.jar contains the application's main( ) method and *J3DUtilsDLL.jar* holds the native library. The JARs must be in the same directory as the JNLP file and must be signed.

The resources tag is considerably more versatile than this example shows. For instance, it's possible to request that resources be downloaded lazily. This may mean that a resource is only retrieved when the application requires it at runtime (but JWS may choose to download it at installation time):

```
<jar href="sound.jar" download="lazy"/>
```

Resources may be grouped together into parts and subdivided into extensions. Each extension is in its own deployment file.

Property name/value pairs, which can be accessed in code with System.getProperty( ) and System.getProperties( ) calls may appear inside the resources section. For example:

```
<property name="key" value="overwritten"/>
```

The application-desc tag states how the application is to be called and may include argument tags:

```
<application-desc main-class="Foo">
  <argument>arg1</argument>
  <argument>arg2</argument>
</application-desc>
```

The development guide in the J2SE documentation explains many of these tags (*<JAVA_HOME>/docs/guide/jws/developersguide/contents.html*). An extensive JNLP tag reference page is located at *http://lopica.sourceforge.net/ref.html*.

Deployment testing

Deployment testing should be carried out by moving the relevant files to a different directory on a different machine. For BugRunner, there are six files:

BugRunner.jnlp
>   The deployment file

bug32.gif
BRBanner.gif
>   The installer icon and splash

BugRunner.jar
j3dutils_signed.jar
J3DUtilsDLL.jar
>   The resource JARs

The chosen directory must match the one used in the codebase attribute at the start of the deployment file.

Double-clicking on *BugRunner.jnlp* should initiate JWS and the installation process, which is shown in Figure B-5.

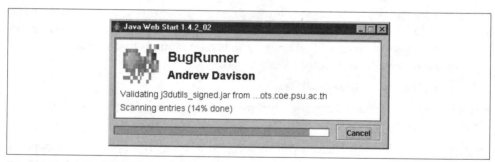

Figure B-5. BugRunner installation

The dialog box in Figure B-6 appears at the point when the application should start executing.

Since BugRunner has requested <all-permissions/> access and the digital signature uses a self-signed public-key certificate, then JWS reports that "it is highly recommended not to install and run this code." This sort of message is deeply worrying to novice users. It can only be removed if you replace the self-signed certificate by a third-party certificate as outlined at the end of this appendix.

Clicking on Details will show information obtained from the certificate, or chain of certificates, attached to the JAR. Clicking on Exit will stop JWS without executing

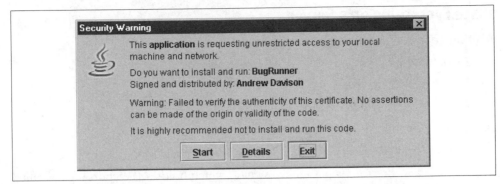

Figure B-6. Execute at your peril

the application. Start will start the application and, depending on how JWS is configured, add a BugRunner item to the Windows Start menu and a BugRunner icon to the
desktop.

For more details about the application and how to configure JWS the application
manager should be started. Figure B-7 shows the manager for JWS 1.4.2.

Figure B-7. The JWS 1.4.2. application manager

 This manager has been pensioned off in Version 5.0, replaced by a
control panel and a cache manager.

Place Everything on a Server

It's time to move the following six BugRunner files to a server:

- *BugRunner.jnlp*
- *bug32.gif* and *BRBanner.gif*
- *BugRunner.jar*, *j3dutils_signed.jar*, and *J3DUtilsDLL.jar*

BugRunner.jnlp must be modified to have its codebase use the server's URL:

```
codebase="http://fivedots.coe.psu.ac.th/~ad/jws/BugRunner/"
```

The *BugRunner/* directory is placed below *jws/*, which holds a JWS portal page called *index.html*. The directory structure is shown in Figure B-8.

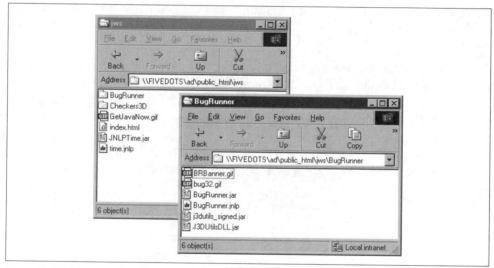

Figure B-8. The server directories used for JWS

The portal page (loaded from *http://fivedots.coe.psu.ac.th/~ad/jws/*) appears as shown in Figure B-9.

Clicking on the BugRunner link will cause the application to be downloaded, with JWS showing the same dialogs as in Figures B-5 and B-6.

Before starting this phase of the testing, any previous client-side installation of BugRunner should be removed via the JWS application manager.

A JWS Installer for Checkers3D

I'll go through the six installer development steps again, this time for the Checkers3D application. Checkers3D was the first Java 3D example considered in Chapter 15.

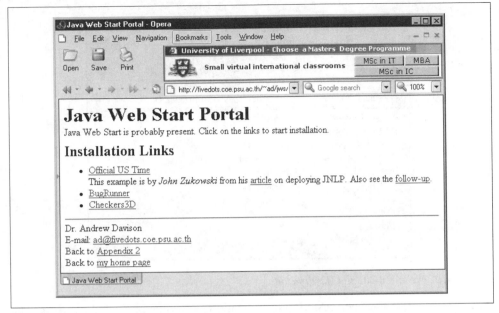

Figure B-9. The JWS portal page

Write the Application

Checkers3D uses the OpenGL Windows version of Java 3D, and so requires:

j3daudio.jar
j3dcore.jar
j3dutils.jar
vecmath.jar
    JAR files

J3D.dll
j3daudio.dll
J3DUtils.dll
    Native libraries

They must be copied into the *Checkers3D/* directory, resulting in Figure B-10.

The *compileChk.bat* batch file contains this line:

```
javac -classpath "%CLASSPATH%;vecmath.jar;j3daudio.jar;
                  j3dcore.jar;j3dutils.jar" *.java
```

The *Checkers3D.bat* batch file has this:

```
java -cp "%CLASSPATH%;vecmath.jar;j3daudio.jar;
          j3dcore.jar;j3dutils.jar" Checkers3D
```

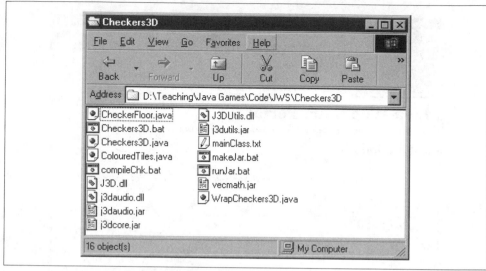

Figure B-10. The initial Checker3D/ directory

Once the program has been tested, the application should be packaged as a JAR. The *makeJar.bat* batch file has this line to handle that:

```
jar cvmf mainClass.txt Checkers3D.jar *.class
```

The manifest details in *mainClass.txt* are:

```
Main-Class: Checkers3D
Class-Path: vecmath.jar j3daudio.jar j3dcore.jar j3dutils.jar
```

The application now consists of eight files:

- The application JAR file: *Checkers3D.jar*
- Four Java 3D JAR files: *j3daudio.jar*, *j3dcore.jar*, *j3dutils.jar*, and *vecmath.jar*
- Three native libraries: *J3D.dll*, *j3daudio.dll*, and *J3DUtils.dll*
- And a partridge in a pear tree (no, I'm joking about that one).

These should be moved to a different directory on a different machine and tested. Double-clicking on *Checkers3D.jar* should start the application.

Modify the Application for Deployment

The three DLLs must be placed inside their own JARs:

```
jar cvf J3DDLL.jar J3D.dll
jar cvf j3daudioDLL.jar j3daudio.dll
jar cvf J3DUtilsDLL.jar J3DUtils.dll
```

The main( ) method of Checkers3D must be modified to call System.loadLibrary( ) for the three DLLs:

```
public static void main(String[] args)
{
```

```
      // DLLs used by Java 3D extension
      String os = System.getProperty("os.name");
      if (os.startsWith("Windows")) {
        System.out.println("Loading '" + os + "' native libraries...");
        System.out.print("  J3D.dll... ");
        System.loadLibrary("J3D");  // drop ".dll"
        System.out.println("OK");

        System.out.print("  j3daudio.dll... ");
        System.loadLibrary("j3daudio");
        System.out.println("OK");

        System.out.print("  J3DUtils.dll... ");
        System.loadLibrary("J3DUtils");
        System.out.println("OK");
      }
      else {
        System.out.println("Sorry, OS '" + os + "' not supported.");
        System.exit(1);
      }

      new Checkers3D( );
    } // end of main( )
```

Create a Public/Private Keypair for Signing the Application

A new keypair is generated in the keystore:

```
keytool -genkey -keystore MyKeyStore -alias Checkers3D
```

Sign Everything with the Private Key

For the Checkers3D application, there are (now) eight JAR files:

Checkers3D.jar
> The application JAR file

j3daudio.jar
j3dcore.jar
j3dutils.jar
vecmath.jar
> Four JAVA 3D JAR files

J3DDLL.jar
j3daudioDLL.jar
J3DUtilsDLL.jar
> Three native-library JARs

The Sun JAR files are copied and signed with these commands:

```
jarsigner -keystore MyKeyStore -signedjar j3daudio_signed.jar
                                       j3daudio.jar  Checkers3D
```

```
jarsigner -keystore MyKeyStore -signedjar j3dcore_signed.jar
                                          j3dcore.jar Checkers3D
jarsigner -keystore MyKeyStore -signedjar j3dutils_signed.jar
                                          j3dutils.jar Checkers3D
jarsigner -keystore MyKeyStore -signedjar vecmath_signed.jar
                                          vecmath.jar Checkers3D
```

The DLL JAR files are signed in place:

```
jarsigner -keystore MyKeyStore J3DDLL.jar Checkers3D
jarsigner -keystore MyKeyStore j3daudioDLL.jar Checkers3D
jarsigner -keystore MyKeyStore J3DUtilsDLL.jar Checkers3D
```

The manifest information in *mainClass.txt* is changed to reference these signed files:

```
Main-Class: Checkers3D
Class-Path: vecmath_signed.jar j3daudio_signed.jar
                       j3dcore_signed.jar j3dutils_signed.jar
```

Finally, after *Checkers3D.jar* is regenerated, it is signed:

```
jarsigner -keystore MyKeyStore Checkers3D.jar Checkers3D
```

Create a Deployment File

The deployment file for the Checkers3D application, *Checkers3D.jnlp*, is shown in Example B-3.

Example B-3. Deployment file for Checkers3D

```
<?xml version="1.0" encoding="utf-8"?>
<!-- Checkers3D Deployment -->

<jnlp spec="1.0+"
  codebase="file:///D:/Teaching/Java Games/Code/JWS/Checkers3D/"
  href="Checkers3D.jnlp"
  >

  <information>
    <title>Checkers3D</title>
    <vendor>Andrew Davison</vendor>
    <homepage href="http://fivedots.coe.pcu.ac.th/~ad/jg"/>
    <description>Checkers3D</description>
    <description kind="short">Checkers3D: a simple java 3D example
        showing a blue sphere above a checkboard.</description>
    <icon href="chess32.gif"/>
    <icon kind="splash" href="startBanner.gif"/>
    <offline-allowed/>
  </information>

  <security>
    <all-permissions/>
  </security>
```

Example B-3. Deployment file for Checkers3D (continued)

```
<resources os="Windows">
  <j2se version="1.4+"/>
  <jar href="Checkers3D.jar" main="true"/>

  <jar href="j3daudio_signed.jar"/>
  <jar href="j3dcore_signed.jar"/>
  <jar href="j3dutils_signed.jar"/>
  <jar href="vecmath_signed.jar"/>

  <nativelib href="J3DDLL.jar"/>
  <nativelib href="j3daudioDLL.jar"/>
  <nativelib href="J3DUtilsDLL.jar"/>
</resources>

<application-desc main-class="Checkers3D"/>
</jnlp>
```

At this stage, codebase is pointing to a local directory. The icons and splash screen images, *chess32.gif* and *startBanner.gif*, must be placed in the *Checkers3D/* directory. The resources section lists eight JAR files.

Double-clicking on *Checkers3D.jnlp* should initiate JWS and the installation process, as shown in Figure B-11.

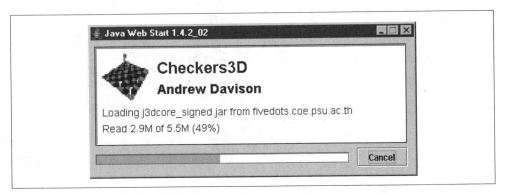

Figure B-11. Checkers3D installation

The dialog box in Figure B-12 appears at the point when the application should start executing.

Checkers3D suffers from the "highly recommended not to install and run this code" message since it uses a self-signed certificate just like BugRunner.

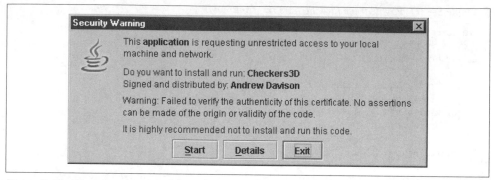

Figure B-12. Execute at your peril (again)

Place Everything on a Server

Now move the folowing 11 Checkers3D files to your server:

- *Checkers3D.jnlp*
- *Checkers3D.jar*
- *j3daudio.jar, j3dcore.jar, j3dutils.jar*, and *vecmath.jar*
- *J3DDLL.jar, j3daudioDLL.jar*, and *J3DUtilsDLL.jar*
- *chess32.gif* and *startBanner.gif*

Checkers3D.jnlp must be modified to have its codebase use the server's URL:

```
codebase="http://fivedots.coe.psu.ac.th/~ad/jws/Checkers3D/"
```

The *Checkers3D/* directory is placed below *jws/* on the server, as shown in Figure B-13.

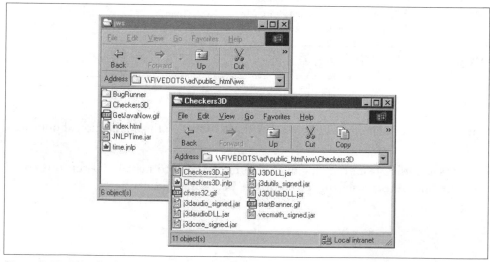

Figure B-13. The Checkers3D directory on the server

Clicking on the Checkers3D link on the JWS portal page (see Figure B-13) will cause it to be downloaded, with JWS showing the same dialogs as in Figures B-11 and B-12.

Before starting this phase, any previous installation of Checkers3D should be removed via the JWS application manager.

Another Way to Install Checkers3D

The Checkers3D example works on the principle of including the Java 3D libraries as part of the application. An alternative approach is available at *https://j3d-webstart. dev.java.net*: making the Java 3D binaries accessible through their own JNLP deployment file.

This means that the deployment file for an application—such as Checkers3D—can specify that Java 3D be downloaded at runtime if it's not available on the client's machine. The size of the Checkers3D-specific part of installation will be substantially reduced since the Java 3D elements are separated.

A sample JNLP file that uses this approach can be found at *https://j3d-webstart.dev. java.net/example.html*. The relevant line employs a resource extension:

```
<resources>
  <j2se version="1.4+"/>
  <jar href="MyExample.jar" main="true"/>

  <extension href="https://j3d-webstart.dev.java.net/release/java3d-1.3-latest.jnlp"/
>
  </resources>
```

The Java 3D binaries will be retrieved from *https://j3d-webstart.dev.java.net/release/* using *java3d-1.3 –latest.jnlp*.

There are two simple JWS-enabled Java 3D applications in *https://j3d-webstart.dev. java.net/prototype/test/*. There's a thread discussing this work at the Java Desktop forum on Java 3D, *http://www.javadesktop.org/forums/thread.jspa?threadID=4563*.

The idea of using JNLP resource extensions to include the Java 3D libraries as a separate deployment is also utilized in the FlyingGuns game/simulation (*http:// www.flyingguns.com*). The direct link to its top-level deployment file is *http://www. hardcode.de/fg/webstart/flyingguns.jnlp*. The extension part of the JNLP file is:

```
<resources>
  <j2se version="1.4+" initial-heap-size="128m" max-heap-size="256m"/>
  <jar href="StarFireExt.jar"/>
  <jar href="flyingguns_core_client.jar"  main="true"/>
        :  // other application JARS

  <extension name="Java3D"
            href="http://www.hardcode.de/java3dext/java3dext.jnlp"/>
        :  // other tags
  </resources>
```

The JWS Portal Page

The portal page (shown in Figure B-9) contains a mix of JavaScript and VBScript, which attempts to detect if JWS is present on the client machine. If it isn't, then the user will be given the option of downloading a JRE. The task is considerably complicated by the many variations between browsers, operating systems, and platforms. Example B-4 is a simplified version of the page.

Example B-4. Simple version of JNLP portal page

```
<HTML>
<HEAD><TITLE>Java Web Start Portal</TITLE>
<script language="JavaScript" type="text/javascript">

  // check in various ways if JWS is installed;
  // decide if the browser is IE on Windows

  function insertLink(url, name) {...}
  // add a link to the named URL if JWS is present

  function installInfo() {...}
  // report whether JWS has been found

  function nativeReport() {...}
  // warn about the use of Windows DLLs by BugRunner and Checkers3D</script>

<script language="VBScript">
  // check for various JWS objects in the Windows registry
</script>

</HEAD>
<BODY><H1>Java Web Start Portal</H1>

<script language="JavaScript" type="text/javascript">
  installInfo();
  nativeReport();
</script>

<h2>Installation Links</h2>
<P><ul>
  <li><script language="JavaScript" type="text/javascript">
    insertLink("time.jnlp", "Official US Time");
  </script>

  <li><script language="JavaScript" type="text/javascript">
    insertLink("BugRunner/BugRunner.jnlp", "BugRunner");
  </script>

  <li><script language="JavaScript" type="text/javascript">
    insertLink("Checkers3D/Checkers3D.jnlp", "Checkers3D");
  </script>
</ul></P></BODY>
</HTML>
```

The JavaScript part of the page sets a flag, javawsInstalled, to the value of 1 if it thinks that JWS is installed. It determines if Windows and Internet Explorer are being used. Three functions are defined—insertLink( ), installInfo( ), and nativeReport( )—which are called in the body of the page. If the client's browser is Internet Explorer on Windows, then some VBScript code has a go at setting javawsInstalled.

Setting javawsInstalled in JavaScript

There are four tests attempted:

1. Check if the JNLP or applet MIME type is set in the browser:

```
if (navigator.mimeTypes && navigator.mimeTypes.length) {
  if (navigator.mimeTypes['application/x-java-jnlp-file'])
    javawsInstalled = 1;
  if (navigator.mimeTypes['application/x-java-applet'])
    javawsInstalled = 1;
}
```

2. Check if Java is enabled on non-Windows operating systems:

```
if (!isWin && navigator.javaEnabled())
  javawsInstalled = 1;
```

3. Check for the presence of LiveConnect, an indicator of JWS's presence:

```
if (window.java != null)
  javawsinstalled = 1;
```

4. Check for the Java plug-in:

```
var numPlugs=navigator.plugins.length;
if (numPlugs) {
  for (var i=0; i < numPlugs; i++) {
    var plugNm = navigator.plugins[i].name.toLowerCase();
    if (plugNm.indexOf('java plug-in') != -1) {
      javawsinstalled = 1;
      break;
    }
  }
}
```

None of these approaches is guaranteed to work on every platform, OS, or browser. For example, the JNLP MIME type must be set by an Opera user manually; otherwise, it's not detected even on a machine with JWS. Only Mozilla-based browsers and Opera support LiveConnect. A javaEnabled( ) call will always return true on a Windows machine because it detects the less-than-useful Microsoft JVM. Several browsers don't store plug-in information, and even if the Java plug-in is found, it may not be the JVM utilized by the browser.

The JavaScript Functions

`installInfo( )` prints a link to one of Sun's download pages for JREs if `javawsInstalled` is 0. The section in the JWS developers guide called "Creating the Web Page that Launches the Application" (*<JAVA_HOME>/docs/guide/jws/developersguide/launch.html*) gives an example of the auto-installation of a JRE for Windows from a portal page. I haven't used this approach since it seems better to leave the download choice up to the user.

`nativeReport( )` prints a warning if the client OS isn't Windows since `BugRunner` and `Checkers3D` rely on DLLs. `insertLink( )` adds a JNLP link to the page only if `javawsInstalled` is 1.

The VBScript Code

The VBScript code is a long multi-way branch that checks the Windows registry for different versions of the JWS. Here's a typical test:

```
If (IsObject(CreateObject("JavaWebStart.isInstalled.1.4.2"))) Then
    javawsInstalled = 1
```

The numerous JWS versions necessitate several branches. The developers guide—up to Version 1.4.2—refers to `JavaWebStart.isInstalled.1`, `JavaWebStart.isInstalled.2`, and `JavaWebStart.isInstalled.3`, which in all likelihood never existed.

There are tests for the JWS-related MIME types, *application/x-java-jnlp-file* and *application/x-java-applet*.

More Information on Portal Pages

The portal page example in the developers guide for Version 5.0 uses a similar approach to the code here; the main difference is the auto-installation of a Windows JRE.

Crucial to portal page code is the ability to detect the browser and OS accurately. A good discussion of these problems can be found at the QuirksMode JavaScript site, *http://www.quirksmode.org/index.html?/js/detect.html*. A more rigorous way of determining the browser's JRE is to load an applet that interrogates the JVM's `java.version` property. This approach is described in the Java Plug-in forum thread "How to Detect a Java Plugin from JavaScript" (*http://forum.java.sun.com/thread.jsp?thread=168544&forum=30&message=527124*). Two online example of this approach, containing many other good Java detection techniques as well, are at *http://members.toast.net/4pf/javasniff.html* and *http://cvs.sdsc.edu/cgi-bin/cvsweb.cgi/mbt/mbt/apps/Explorer/Detect.js?rev=1.2*.

Third-Party Certificates

Figures B-6 and B-12 show the problem with using self-signed certificates in an application: JWS issues a scary message. The solution is to replace the certificate by one generated by a trusted third party: a CA. Popular CAs include Verisign (*http://www.verisign.com/*), Thawte (*http://www.thawte.com/*), and Entrust (*http:// www.entrust.com*). These companies charge money for their services, but a free alternative is CACert.org (*https://www.cacert.org/*).

Beefing up the certificate for a keypair consists of the following steps:

1. Extract a Certificate Signing Request (CSR) from the keypair.

2. Send the CSR to the CA, requesting a certificate.

3. After checking the returned certificate, import it into the keystore, replacing the keypair's self-signed certificate.

4. Start signing JARs with the keypair.

Extract a CSR

Generate a CSR with the -certreq option to keytool:

```
keytool -certreq -keystore MyKeyStore -alias BugRunner -file BugRunner.csr
```

This generates a CSR for the BugRunner keypair, stored in *BugRunner.csr*, a text file of this form:

```
-----BEGIN NEW CERTIFICATE REQUEST-----
MIICoDCCAl4C..... // many more lines
.....
-----END NEW CERTIFICATE REQUEST-----
```

Request a Certificate

The CSR is sent to the CA, usually by pasting its text into a web form accessed via a secure link (a https URL). At CACert.org, this step requires some preliminary work. The users must first join the free CACert.org and send in details about the web domain that they control. This information is checked with the site's web administrator by email. Only then can CSRs be submitted. The certificate generated in response to a CSR is called a server certificate by CACert.org.

Import the Certificate into the Keystore

The server certificate is received in an ordinary email and should be examined before being added to the keystore:

```
keytool -printcert -file certfile.cer
```

Assume that the text message is stored in *certfile.cer*. If the *.cer* extension is used, then many browsers will be able to open and interpret the file's certificate contents. The text should look like this:

```
-----BEGIN CERTIFICATE-----
MIICxDCCAio.... // many more lines
....
-----END CERTIFICATE-----
```

Though people often talk about a server certificate, the data may actually consist of a chain of certificates, rather than just one.

Once the user is happy that the details match those supplied in the original CSR, the server certificate can be imported into the keystore. In this case, it replaces the self-signed certificate for the BugRunner keypair:

```
keytool -import -trustcacerts -keystore MyKeyStore
                    -alias BugRunner -file certfile.cer
```

The server certificate is automatically verified; in a chain, the current certificate is trusted because of the certificate at the next level up. This continues until the certificate for the CA is reached. This may be a trusted (or root) certificate, stored in JWS's cacerts keystore. cacerts comes pre-built with Verisign, Thawte, and Entrust trusted certificates but doesn't have any from CACert.org.

CACert.org offers a root certificate for download, which can be added to cacerts (if you have write permissions). Alternatively, it can be placed in the local MyKeyStore keystore as a trusted certificate:

```
keytool -import -alias cacertOrg -keystore MyKeyStore  -file caRoot.cer
```

Here, I'm assuming that the root certificate is stored in *caRoot.cer* and is saved under the name (alias) cacertOrg. Since no keypair exists for cacertOrg, keytool assumes it's a trusted certificate. This can be verified by listing the contents of the keystore:

```
keytool -list -keystore MyKeyStore
```

The root certificate should be imported before the server certificate, or the server certificate's authentication process will end with the warning "Failed to establish chain from reply."

An alternative is to "glue" the root and server certificates together as a single entity and then import the result into the keystore as a replacement for the self-signed certificate. This process is described by Chris W. Johnson at *http://gargravarr.cc.utexas.edu/chrisj/misc/java-cert-parsing.html*.

Sign JARs with the Keypair

Signing can now commence with the third-party-certified BugRunner keypair:

```
jarsigner -keystore MyKeyStore foo.jar BugRunner
```

More Information

If you've installed the J2SE documentation, then there's a lot of JWS information available locally in *<JAVA_HOME>/docs/guide/jws/index.html*, including the developers guide. In J2SE 5.0, several JWS examples are in the distribution (in the *sample/* directory). In earlier JWS versions, the code was scattered throughout the developers guide. The JWS home page at Sun (*http://java.sun.com/products/javawebstart/*) contains links to an official FAQ, technical articles, and installer demos.

In J2SE/JRE 1.4.2. or earlier, the JWS materials didn't contain the developers pack, which includes the complete JWS specification, JNLP API documentation, jardiff tool, and additional libraries. These have been folded into the main JWS release since 5.0. The pack is also available from *http://java.sun.com/products/javawebstart/download-jnlp.html*. The JWSt and JNLP developers forum is an active place (*http://forum.java.sun.com/forum.jsp?forum=38*).

The best unofficial JWS site is *http://lopica.sourceforge.net/* with a lengthy FAQs page, useful reference sections, and links. However, it hasn't been updated in some time, and a lot of the FAQs page is about earlier versions of JWS.

The installer examples from Sun are at *http://java.sun.com/products/javawebstart/demos.html*. Another great source is Up2Go.Net (*http://www.up2go.net*), with installer categories including multimedia, communications, and over 40 games. Many of the games at the Java Games Factory can be downloaded using JWS, so their installers can be examined (*http://grexengine.com/sections/externalgames/*).

JWS and Java 3D

The ongoing work on making Java 3D available via JWS is based at *https://j3d-webstart.dev.java.net*.

The problems that arise when utilizing native libraries in standalone applications, JWS installers, and applets are discussed in the paper "Transparent Java Standard Extensions with Native Libraries on Multiple Platforms," available online at *http://atlas.dsv.su.se/~pierre/a/papers/nativelibs.pdf*. This paper is of particular interest since it uses Java 3D as its example extension with native libraries. The code is available from *http://www.dsv.su.se/~adapt/im/t_nativelibs/* with an explanation in Swedish (*http://www.almac.co.uk/chef/chef/chef.html*).

JWS and Other Libraries

Developers using JWS with other native libraries have come across similar problems to those with JWS and Java 3D.

Xith3D is a scene graph–based 3D programming API similar to Java 3D. However, Xith3D runs on top of JOGL, a set of Java bindings for OpenGL. William Denniss has a detailed example of how to use JWS to install Xith3D at *http://www.xith.org/tutes/GettingStarted/html/deploying_xith3d_games_with.html*.

A brief introduction to JWS by Kevin Glass, for a space game using JOGL, is at *http://www.cokeandcode.com/info/webstart-howto.html*.

Index

We'd like to hear your suggestions for improving our indexes. Send email to *index@oreilly.com*.

J

About the Author

Andrew Davison is a lecturer in the department of computer engineering at Prince of Songkla University in Hat Yai, Thailand. He has lived in the "Land of Smiles" for over 10 years and would recommend it to anyone with a love of Asia. Prior to that, he was a lecturer in the department of computer science at the University of Melbourne ("the World's Most Livable City"). He received his Ph.D. from Imperial College in London ("When a man is tired of London, he is tired of life").

Andrew's abiding interest is his family: wife Supatra and son John. They are the joy and meaning of everything he does.

When not slumped in front of a computer or shouting at students, Andrew is fond of reading to John, and now knows more than he should about the Lorax, Angelina Ballerina, and Flat Stanley.

Colophon

Our look is the result of reader comments, our own experimentation, and feedback from distribution channels. Distinctive covers complement our distinctive approach to technical topics, breathing personality and life into potentially dry subjects.

The animal on the cover of *Killer Game Programming in Java* is a jungle cat (*Felis chaus*), a solitary felid known for its marvelous adaptability. Also known in some places as the swamp or reed cat, the jungle cat is found across a wide geographic area, ranging from Egypt to the Middle East to parts of Southern Asia and Western China. The name jungle cat, however, is a misnomer because, while this animal is often found in open grasslands, marshes, swamps, and tropical deciduous and evergreen forests, it is never found in dense tropical rain forests. The jungle cat varies in weight across its range. Cats living in Central Asia weigh up to 36 pounds, about 5 or 6 pounds more than those from Thailand and other neighboring areas.

Jungle cats can be distinguished from other wild cat species by their long legs and uniform coat color, which ranges from sandy yellow to reddish brown. In ancient Egypt, these cats were held in high esteem for their stealth and agility. Etchings found on the walls of ancient temples depict jungle cats hunting beside humans. Their mummified remains can also be found in tombs of the period.

The jungle cat's long survival as a species is attributed in part to its great resourcefulness. These cats often inhabit the disused burrows of other animals, and in India, they are sometimes known to take up residence in abandoned buildings on the outskirts of human settlements, hunting in nearby crop fields for small rodents. They are mostly crepuscular in their hunting habits (active at twilight), but are known to be more active during daylight hours in some regions. Their prey includes rodents, small mammals, birds, reptiles, insects, and occasionally wild pigs, chital deer, and fish. Keen hearing, a contribution from the cat's large ears, help it locate prey in areas of dense vegetation. It can jump 13 feet to swipe a desert quail from the air, dive into water to capture fish, and even climb trees to hunt when necessary. The jungle cat, some say, can make it anywhere.

Matt Hutchinson was the production editor for *Killer Game Programming in Java*. GEX, Inc. provided production services. Adam Witwer, Jamie Peppard, and Claire Cloutier provided quality control.

Emma Colby designed the cover of this book, based on a series design by Edie Freedman. The cover image is a 19th-century engraving from *Royal Natural History*. Karen Montgomery produced the cover layout with Adobe InDesign CS using Adobe's ITC Garamond font.

David Futato designed the interior layout. This book was converted by Keith Fahlgren to FrameMaker 5.5.6 with a format conversion tool created by Erik Ray, Jason McIntosh, Neil Walls, and Mike Sierra that uses Perl and XML technologies. The text font is Linotype Birka; the heading font is Adobe Myriad Condensed; and the code font is LucasFont's TheSans Mono Condensed. The illustrations that appear in the book were produced by Chris Reilley using Macromedia FreeHand MX and Adobe Photoshop CS. The tip and warning icons were drawn by Christopher Bing. This colophon was written by Lydia Onofrei.

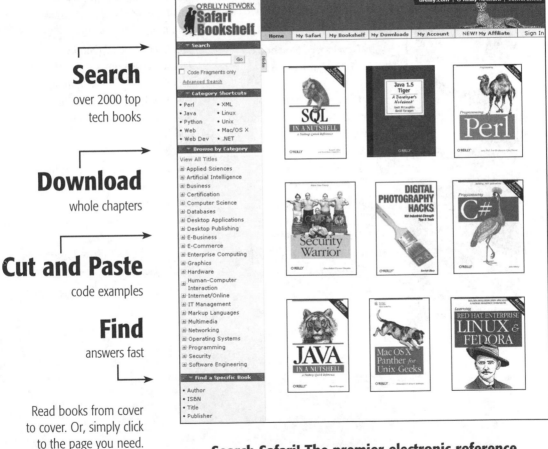

Related Titles Available from O'Reilly

Java

Ant: The Definitive Guide

Better, Faster, Lighter Java

Eclipse

Eclipse Cookbook

Enterprise JavaBeans,
4th Edition

Hardcore Java

Head First Java

Head First Servlets & JSP

Head First EJB

Hibernate:
A Developer's Notebook

J2EE Design Patterns

Java 1.5 Tiger:
A Developer's Notebook

Java & XML Data Binding

Java & XML

Java Cookbook, 2nd Edition

Java Data Objects

Java Database Best Practices

Java Enterprise Best Practices

Java Enterprise in a Nutshell,
2nd Edition

Java Examples in a Nutshell,
3rd Edition

Java Extreme Programming
Cookbook

Java in a Nutshell, 4th Edition

Java Management Extensions

Java Message Service

Java Network Programming,
2nd Edition

Java NIO

Java Performance Tuning,
2nd Edition

Java RMI

Java Security, 2nd Edition

JavaServer Faces

Java ServerPages, 2nd Edition

Java Servlet & JSP Cookbook

Java Servlet Programming,
2nd Edition

Java Swing, 2nd Edition

Java Web Services in a Nutshell

Learning Java, 2nd Edition

Mac OS X for Java Geeks

Programming Jakarta Struts
2nd Edition

Tomcat: The Definitive Guide

WebLogic:
The Definitive Guide

O'REILLY®

Our books are available at most retail and online bookstores.
To order direct: 1-800-998-9938 • order@oreilly.com • www.oreilly.com
Online editions of most O'Reilly titles are available by subscription at safari.oreilly.com

Keep in touch with O'Reilly

1. Download examples from our books

To find example files for a book, go to:

www.oreilly.com/catalog

select the book, and follow the "Examples" link.

2. Register your O'Reilly books

Register your book at *register.oreilly.com*

Why register your books?
Once you've registered your O'Reilly books you can:

* Win O'Reilly books, T-shirts or discount coupons in our monthly drawing.
* Get special offers available only to registered O'Reilly customers.
* Get catalogs announcing new books (US and UK only).
* Get email notification of new editions of the O'Reilly books you own.

3. Join our email lists

Sign up to get topic-specific email announcements of new books and conferences, special offers, and O'Reilly Network technology newsletters at:

elists.oreilly.com

It's easy to customize your free elists subscription so you'll get exactly the O'Reilly news you want.

4. Get the latest news, tips, and tools

www.oreilly.com

* "Top 100 Sites on the Web"—PC Magazine
* CIO Magazine's Web Business 50 Awards

Our web site contains a library of comprehensive product information (including book excerpts and tables of contents), downloadable software, background articles, interviews with technology leaders, links to relevant sites, book cover art, and more.

5. Work for O'Reilly

Check out our web site for current employment opportunities:

jobs.oreilly.com

6. Contact us

O'Reilly & Associates
1005 Gravenstein Hwy North
Sebastopol, CA 95472 USA

TEL: 707-827-7000 or 800-998-9938
(6am to 5pm PST)

FAX: 707-829-0104

order@oreilly.com
For answers to problems regarding your order or our products. To place a book order online, visit:

www.oreilly.com/order_new

catalog@oreilly.com
To request a copy of our latest catalog.

booktech@oreilly.com
For book content technical questions or corrections.

corporate@oreilly.com
For educational, library, government, and corporate sales.

proposals@oreilly.com
To submit new book proposals to our editors and product managers.

international@oreilly.com
For information about our international distributors or translation queries. For a list of our distributors outside of North America check out:

international.oreilly.com/distributors.html

adoption@oreilly.com
For information about academic use of O'Reilly books, visit:

academic.oreilly.com

O'REILLY®

Our books are available at most retail and online bookstores.
To order direct: 1-800-998-9938 • *order@oreilly.com* • *www.oreilly.com*
Online editions of most O'Reilly titles are available by subscription at *safari.oreilly.com*